# THE CAMBRIDGE HISTORY OF SOUTHEAST ASIA

## VOLUME ONE

From early times to c. 1500

# THE CAMBRIDGE HISTORY OF SOUTHEAST ASIA

**Volume One**
**From early times to c. 1500**

1 The Writing of Southeast Asian History (J. D. Legge)
2 Southeast Asia before History (Peter Bellwood)
3 The Early Kingdoms (Keith W. Taylor)
4 Economic History of Early Southeast Asia (Kenneth R. Hall)
5 Religion and Popular Beliefs of Southeast Asia before c. 1500 (J. G. de Casparis and I. W. Mabbett)

**Volume Two**
**From c. 1500 to c. 1800**

1 Interactions with the Outside World and Adaptation in Southeast Asian Society, 1500–1800 (Leonard Y. Andaya)
2 Political Development between the Sixteenth and Eighteenth Centuries (Barbara Watson Andaya)
3 Economic and Social Change, c. 1400–1800 (Anthony Reid)
4 Religious Developments in Southeast Asia, c. 1500–1800 (Barbara Watson Andaya and Yoneo Ishii)
5 The Age of Transition: The Mid-eighteenth to the Early Nineteenth Centuries (J. Kathirithamby-Wells)

**Volume Three**
**From c. 1800 to the 1930s**

1 The Establishment of the Colonial Régimes (Nicholas Tarling)
2 Political Structures in the Nineteenth and Early Twentieth Centuries (Carl A. Trocki)
3 International Commerce, the State and Society: Economic and Social Change (Robert E. Elson)
4 Religion and Anti-colonial Movements (Reynaldo Ileto)
5 Nationalism and Modernist Reform (Paul Kratoska and Ben Batson)

**Volume Four**
**From World War II to the present**

1 Southeast Asia in War and Peace: The End of European Colonial Empires (A. J. Stockwell)
2 The Political Structures of the Independent States (Yong Mun Cheong)
3 Economic and Social Change (Norman G. Owen)
4 Religious Change in Contemporary Southeast Asia (Paul Stange)
5 Regionalism and Nationalism (C. M. Turnbull)
Bibliographies (Paul Kratoska)

# The Cambridge History of Southeast Asia

## VOLUME ONE

From early times to c. 1500

edited by
NICHOLAS TARLING

CAMBRIDGE
UNIVERSITY PRESS

PUBLISHED BY THE PRESS SYNDICATE OF THE UNIVERSITY OF CAMBRIDGE
The Pitt Building, Trumpington Street, Cambridge, United Kingdom

CAMBRIDGE UNIVERSITY PRESS
The Edinburgh Building, Cambridge CB2 2RU, UK www.cup.cam.ac.uk
40 West 20th Street, New York, NY 10011–4211, USA www.cup.org
10 Stamford Road, Oakleigh, Melbourne 3166, Australia
Ruiz de Alarcón 13, 28014, Madrid, Spain



*The Cambridge History of Southeast Asia* was first published in hardback
in two volumes in 1992, reprinted 1994
Volume One ISBN 0 521 35505 2 (hardback)
Volume Two ISBN 0 521 35506 0 (hardback)

*The Cambridge History of Southeast Asia* is first published in paperback
in four volumes in 1999
Volume One Part One: From early times to c. 1500
ISBN 0 521 66369 5 (paperback)
Volume One Part Two: From c. 1500 to c. 1800
ISBN 0 521 66370 9 (paperback)
These two volumes contain the contents of 0 521 35505 2 (hardback),
with additional supplementary material
Volume Two Part One: From c. 1800 to the 1930s
ISBN 0 521 66371 7 (paperback)
Volume Two Part Two: From World War II to the present
ISBN 0 521 66372 5 (paperback)
These two volumes contain the contents of 0 521 35506 0 (hardback),
with additional supplementary material

The set of four paperbacks, containing the complete contents of *The Cambridge History of Southeast Asia*, ISBN 0 521 77864 6 (paperback).

*Typeface* Palatino 10/11 pt. *System* Penta [MT]

*A catalogue record for this book is available from the British Library*

*National Library of Australia Cataloguing in Publication data*
The Cambridge history of Southeast Asia.
Bibliography.
Includes index.
ISBN 0 521 66369 5 (Volume One Part One).
ISBN 0 521 66370 9 (Volume One Part Two).
ISBN 0 521 66371 7 (Volume Two Part One).
ISBN 0 521 66372 5 (Volume Two Part Two).
ISBN 0 521 77864 6 (set).
1. Asia, Southeastern – History. I. Tarling, Nicholas.
959

ISBN 0 521 66369 5 paperback

**Transferred to digital printing 2004**

# CONTENTS

# MAPS

# NOTE ON SPELLING

The spelling of proper names and terms has caused editor and contributors considerable problems. Even a certain arbitrariness may have not produced consistency across a range of contributions, and that arbitrariness contained its own inconsistencies. In general we have aimed to spell place-names and terms in the way currently most accepted in the country, society or literature concerned. We have not used diacritics for modern Southeast Asian languages, but have used them for Sanskrit and Ancient Javanese. We have used pinyin transliterations except for some names which are well known in English in the Wade–Giles transliteration.

# NOTE ON GENDER IN SOUTHEAST ASIAN LANGUAGES

Southeast Asian languages do not distinguish the sexes in general. Many references to individuals or groups of people in ancient indigenous sources leave it unclear whether women are meant or included. For example, we usually do not know whether a certain function is occupied by a male or a female. Even words borrowed from Sanskrit (which has genders corresponding to sex) are sometimes applied without observing this correspondence: Queen Tribhuwanā (sic) or Tribhuwanottungadewī is called *mahārāja* (a masculine word). These languages do not distinguish between brothers and sisters, but they do between younger and older siblings.

There also seems to have been little discrimination between sexes as far as functions are concerned. There were not only queens reigning in their own right in ancient Java, but also 'prime ministers', such as Airlangga's Mahārastrī *i* Hino with a name ending in '-Dewī'. As to Kĕrtanagara's four daughters, it seems that this king had no sons—at least they are never mentioned. Therefore what the sources tell us about the daughters provides no evidence of matrilineal descent. Apparently, both lineages were equally important. In some ways ancient Indonesian society was less 'sexist' than our own still is.

# ABBREVIATIONS

| | |
|---|---|
| AP | *Asian Perspectives*, Honolulu. |
| BEFEO | *Bulletin de l'École Française d'Extrême-Orient*, Paris. |
| BIPPA | *Bulletin of the Indo-Pacific Prehistory Association*, Canberra. |
| BKI | *Bijdragen van het Koninklijk Instituut voor de Taal-, Land- en Volkenkunde*, 's-Gravenhage. |
| BSOAS | *Bulletin of the School of Oriental and African Studies*, London. |
| FMJ | *Federation Museums Journal*, Kuala Lumpur. |
| JAS | *Journal of Asian Studies*, Ann Arbor. |
| JBRS | *Journal of the Burma Research Society*, Rangoon. |
| JMBRAS | *Journal of the Malay/Malaysian Branch of the Royal Asiatic Society*, Singapore/Kuala Lumpur. |
| JRAS | *Journal of the Royal Asiatic Society*, London. |
| JSEAH | *Journal of Southeast Asian History*, Singapore. |
| JSEAS | *Journal of Southeast Asian Studies*, Singapore. |
| JSS | *Journal of the Siam Society*, Bangkok. |
| MAS | *Modern Asian Studies*, Cambridge, UK. |
| MQRSEA | *Modern Quaternary Research in Southeast Asia*, Rotterdam. |
| TBG | *Tijdschrift van het Bataviaasch Genootschap van Kunsten et Wetenschappen*, Batavia/Jakarta. |
| VKI | *Verhandelingen van het Koninklijk Instituut voor de Taal-, Land- en Volkenkunde*, 's-Gravenhage. |

# PREFACE TO THE ORIGINAL EDITION

Two ideas came together in the project for a Cambridge History of Southeast Asia. One was the concept of the Cambridge Histories themselves. The other was the possibility of a new approach to the history of Southeast Asia.

In the English-speaking and English-reading world the Cambridge Histories have, since the beginning of the century, set high standards in collaborative scholarship and provided a model for multi-volume works of history. The original *Cambridge Modern History* appeared in sixteen volumes between 1902 and 1912, and was followed by the *Cambridge Ancient History*, the *Cambridge Medieval History*, the *Cambridge History of India* and others.

A new generation of projects continues and builds on this foundation. Recently completed are the Cambridge Histories of Africa, Latin America and the Pacific Islanders. Cambridge Histories of China and of Japan are in progress, as well as the New Cambridge History of India. Though the pattern and the size have varied, the essential feature, multi-authorship, has remained.

The initial focus was European, but albeit in an approach that initially savoured rather of the old Cambridge Tripos course 'The Expansion of Europe', it moved more out of the European sphere than the often brilliant one-author Oxford histories. But it left a gap which that course did not leave, the history of Southeast Asia.

Southeast Asia has long been seen as a whole, though other terms have been used for it. The title Southeast Asia, becoming current during World War II, has been accepted as recognizing the unity of the region, while not prejudging the nature of that unity. Yet scholarly research and writing have shown that it is no mere geographical expression.

There have indeed been several previous histories of Southeast Asia. Most of them have been the work of one author. The great work of the late D. G. E. Hall dates back to 1955, but it has gone through several editions since. Others include B. Harrison, *South-east Asia, A Short History*, London, 1954; Nicholas Tarling, *A Concise History of Southeast Asia*, 1966; and D. J. Steinberg, et al., *In Search of Southeast Asia*, 1971. The authors of these works faced difficult tasks, as a result of the linguistic diversity of the area; the extent of the secondary material; and the lacunae within it.

Given its diversity, Southeast Asia seemed to lend itself to the Cambridge approach. A magisterial single-volume history existed; others had also made the attempt. A single volume by several authors working together had also been successful. But a more substantial history by a larger number of authors had not been attempted.

The past generation has seen a great expansion of writing, but Southeast Asia's historiography is still immature in the sense that some aspects have been relatively well cultivated, and others not. The historical literature on the area has become more substantial and more sophisticated, but much of it deals with particular countries or cultures, and many gaps remain. A range of experts might help to bring it all together and thus both lay the foundation and point the way for further research effort.

The Cambridge approach offered a warning as well as an invitation. There were practical obstacles in the way of histories on the scale of the original European histories. They got out of hand or were never finished. A summation that was also to lead other scholars forward must be published within a reasonable time-span. It must not be too voluminous; it must not involve too many people.

Practical indications of this nature, however, coincided with historiographical considerations. There were some good histories of Southeast Asia; there were also some good histories of particular countries; but there was, perhaps, no history that set out from a regional basis and took a regional approach. This seemed worthwhile in itself, as well as establishing a coherence and a format for the volumes.

In almost every case—even when chapters are the work of more than one person—authors have been taken out of their particular area of expertise. They were ready to take risks, knowing that, whatever care they took, they might be faulted by experts, but recognizing the value all the same in attempting to give an overview. Generally contributors felt that the challenge of the regional approach was worth the hazardous departure from research moorings.

Authors invited to contribute recognized that they would often find themselves extended beyond the span of the published work which has made them well known. The new history did, however, give them a chance—perhaps already enjoyed in many cases in their teaching—to extend into other parts of the region and to adopt a comparative, regional approach. The publishers sought a history that stimulated rather than presented the last word. Authors were the more ready to rely where necessary on published or secondary works, and readers will not expect equally authoritative treatment of the whole area, even if the sources permitted it.

At the same time, the editor and the contributors have had, like any historians, to cope with problems of periodization. That is, of course, always contentious, but particularly so if it seems to result from or to point to a particular emphasis. In the case of Southeast Asia the most likely temptation is to adopt a chronology that overdoes the impact of outside forces, in particular the Europeans. The structure of this history is not free from that criticism, but the contributors have sought, where appropriate, to challenge rather than meekly to accept its implications.

A similar risk is attached to the division of the material into chapters. The scope of a work such as this makes that all the more difficult but all the more necessary. Sometimes the divisions appear to cut across what ought to be seen as a whole, and sometimes repetition may result. That has been allowed when it seemed necessary. But it may still be possible to pursue certain themes through the book and not to read it merely in chronological sequence. Within the four major chronological divisions, chapters are in general organized in a similar order. The work may thus in a sense be read laterally as well as horizontally.

Some topics, including treatment of the arts, literature and music, have been virtually excluded. The focus of the work is on economic, social, religious, and political history. But it will still be difficult to pursue the history of a particular people or country. The work does not indeed promise to offer this; though it offers guidance to those who wish to do this in its apparatus, the footnotes and bibliographic essay to each chapter, the historiographical survey, the list of bibliographies, and the index.

The regional approach has tested the authors, but it has also emphasized the deficiencies of the sources available. Much work has still to be done; much of the earlier life of Southeast Asia remains outside our reach. Each author found a different problem: too much material in one respect, too little in another.

The contributors come from Europe, Japan, Hong Kong, Southeast Asia, Australia and New Zealand, the USA. They have received help from other scholars, acknowledged in the notes to their chapters. The whole project benefited from a meeting of the contributors, held in Singapore with aid from the Sasakawa Foundation. In particular they received comment on their drafts from a number of Southeast Asian scholars at that conference, brought there with the aid of the Toyota Foundation. The editor expresses his grateful thanks to them, Dr Cheah Boon Kheng, Dr Abu Talib Ahmad, Professor Khoo Kay Kim, Dr Taufik Abdullah, and Dr Sombat Chantornvong, to Dr Kathirithamby-Wells, who became a formal contributor, and to Professor Wang Gungwu, who also attended. Other scholars have been of assistance to particular authors, such as Victor Lieberman, Ann Kumar, A. H. Johns, Taufik Abdullah, and Adrian Vickers.

Those to be thanked, indeed, are too numerous to mention. But the editor must record the encouragement, aid and support of Dr Robin Derricourt of the Cambridge University Press, and of his colleagues, Leonard and Barbara Andaya.

Nicholas Tarling 1992

# PREFACE TO THE PAPERBACK EDITION

This work was originally published in 1992 in two hardbound volumes. The paperback edition is a reprint in four volumes with minor revisions. While the work in its two-volume format has been quite widely welcomed, it is hoped that the new format will make it more accessible, and in particular bring it more readily within the reach of those who teach and are taught about the region, as well as those who are simply curious about it. The four paperbacks may stand on their own, though it is also the case that the whole is more than the sum of the parts.

The present volume contains an essay on the historiography of Southeast Asia and Part 1 of the original Volume 1, 'From Prehistory to c. 1500 CE'. The next volume contains Part 2 of the original Volume 1, covering the years c. 1500 to c. 1800. The third paperback covers the region from c. 1800 to the 1930s, and the fourth the period from the World War II to the late 1980s. While all the chapters have a bibliographic essay, the list of bibliographies will be found at the conclusion of Volume 4.

Each of the paperback volumes has a new preface. That, though short, is intended to fulfil two purposes: to point to the relationships with the other volumes; and to comment on some of the research into and thinking about the subject undertaken since the original contributions were completed in 1990–91. Some of that has been generated by the challenges the region's past offers the historian and the historian's techniques. Some of it has been generated by a growing public interest in the region, the nature of which also affects the historian's approach.

At the beginning of the decade the region seemed to be enjoying an extraordinary economic boom, and at the end to be suffering a collapse, the remedy for which seemed even more uncertain than the reasons. A history may at least offer a longer-term perspective on these changes, their origins and effects. The same comment applies, second, in respect of the current relationship between China and Southeast Asia. China's growing economic importance and its increasing power invite the attention of both historians and their readers to the earlier relationships. A third context comprises the so-called globalization of the closing years of the twentieth century and its as yet ambiguous challenge to the nation-state. That may result both in renewed assertions of the century's nationalism, but also, perhaps, in assertions of differing kinds of identity, ethnic or otherwise, with a larger or a more local focus.

Once more the historian will be engaged, more or less willingly; and once more the reader will look to the historian. Arguably, indeed, the significance of the historical approach will increase. If, in one sense, the historian's inspiration has always been dual—both to respond to the interests of the present and to offer a better understanding of the past—the historian's task has also been two-fold. It is concerned with uncovering what are called facts, but also with eliciting trends or processes. Yet, as Stephen J. Gould puts it, in history 'events occur but once in detailed glory' ('Evolution and the Triumph of Homology, or Why History Matters', *American Scientist* 70, January–February 1986, p. 64). The discipline is in some sense specially suited to a world where once ruling ideologies have been challenged or overthrown, and not as yet replaced by credible new visions, try as the protagonists of the 'market' may.

An array of 'new conceptual tools' is available, to use Ruth McVey's phrase, whose 'very names—post-modernism, post-structuralism, post-Marxism—betray the ideological exhaustion of our time' ('Change and Continuity in Southeast Asian Studies', *Journal of Southeast Asian Studies* 26, 1, March 1995, p. 9). For many historians the tools were not so new: they were burnished remodellings of the old, which, misused, could injure the user. Historians could readily accept Dominick LaCapra's view that the past has its voices which must be respected, 'especially when they resist or qualify the interpretations we would like to place on them' (quoted by L. Kramer in Lynn Hunt, ed., *The New Cultural History* University of California Press, 1989, p. 103). Historians might less readily take the further step that Hayden White took, when he suggested that it was possible to 'imagine not only one or two but any number of alternative stories of . . . any culturally significant event, all equally plausible and equally authoritative by virtue of their conformity to generally accepted rules of historical construction' (quoted in P. Nozick, *That Noble Dream. The 'Objectivity Question' and the American Historical Profession* Cambridge University Press, 1988, p. 602). Gertrude Himmelfarb argued by contrast that the discipline of history was in a sense designed 'to forestall the absolutistic relativism of post-modernism'. Aware of the deficiencies of the historian and the historical record, 'of the ambiguous relationship of past and present', the historical profession created the checks and controls associated with 'critical history'. The aim was to encourage 'a maximum exertion of objectivity' (in *Times Literary Supplement* 16 October 1992).

McVey suggests that the tools 'may help the researcher to go beyond the terms of the established framework. . . . It is in periods of intellectual uncertainty and unease, of a lack of orientation, that scholarship is likely to be most creative' (p. 9). Those who study have indeed been affected by the intellectual currents of the 1990s. Though McVey had in mind a challenge to what she saw as the 'regnant paradigm' in the study of Southeast Asia—the emergence of the nation-states and their progress to modernity—the 1990s has also seen a renewed questioning of the concept of Southeast Asia as a region.

That did not begin with the impact of deconstruction. Philosophers warned about reification, Waddell observed in 1972. 'Words like "Southeast Asia" and "unicorn" enable us to discuss topics about which we would not otherwise be able to hold a conversation, but we should be wary of attributing any more solidity to these concepts than the facts will allow' (J. R. E. Waddell, *An Introduction to Southeast Asian Politics* Sydney: Wiley, 1972, p. 3). In an article published in 1984, Donald K. Emmerson quoted this alongside Shakespeare's *Romeo and Juliet*: 'What's in a name? That which we call a rose by any other name would smell as sweet'. 'Some names', wrote Emmerson, 'like "rose", acknowledge what exists. Others, like "unicorn", create what otherwise would not exist. In between lie names that simultaneously describe and invent reality. "Southeast Asia" is one of these' ('"Southeast Asia": What's in a Name?', *Journal of Southeast Asian Studies* 15, 1, March 1984, p. 1).

The description, as Emmerson says, was rarely used in the imperial phase, and the sense of it as a region was more common among Germans and Austrians, who did not possess colonies in the region, than among those Europeans who did. In the 1930s it became somewhat more common, but it was the war that gave it currency and literally put it on the map. Its dimensions remained, however, uncertain, and, though scholars more or less reached a consensus on them, the public, at least outside the region, even now perhaps shares no such certainty. '"Southeast Asia" turned out to be an aggregate of nations—individually distinct and collectively a battleground in, first, the Pacific War, then the Cold War, including two Indo-China Wars, and finally, in Cambodia, a Sino-Soviet "proxy war"'. Creating 'a need to talk about the region', Emmerson suggests, international conflicts ironically 'underwrote the popularity of the name in the very act of undermining its empirical prospects' (p. 10).

He pointed, however, to the neutrality of the term. 'Unlike the "Near" and "Far East", the name does not betray the location of an outside namer. Because it is not a reminder of dependence, the term is easier for the region's inhabitants to use.' It did not have the imperialist overtones of 'Orientalism' (p. 17). But how meaningful was it? Was it yet a rose or still a unicorn?

Some historians sought to make a virtue of necessity. The present editor's own *A Concise History of Southeast Asia* (New York: Praeger, 1966)—also published in Australia under a title later used by D. R. SarDesai, *Southeast Asia Past and Present*—suggested that the region had 'a unity in its very diversity' (p. xii). Later scholarship gave the regional approach a more positive connotation. Perhaps the most obvious example is the masterly work of one of our contributors, the appearance of which straddled the publication of *The Cambridge History of Southeast Asia*. For Anthony Reid, Southeast Asia was a region in the sense that the Mediterranean was for Fernand Braudel, and it possessed at a deeper level a unity which event-oriented historiography tended to conceal. It was thus possible to go beyond the study of diversity, even beyond a comparative approach. In his *Southeast Asia in the Age of Commerce* (New Haven: Yale University Press, 1988, 1993), Reid suggested 'that treating Southeast Asia as a whole makes it possible to describe a number of areas of life which would otherwise remain in the shadows'. For each cultural area sources for his period, the fifteenth, sixteenth and seventeenth centuries, are fragmentary; but studying them together offers 'a coherent picture . . . of the life-styles of the region as a whole' (vol. 1, Preface, p. xiv). The process put 'Southeast Asians' on the stage, though none of the actors would then have so recognised themselves.

If historians were enhancing the reality of Southeast Asia, so, too, were some of the contemporary political processes. Nation-states were more than ever the dominant political entities, but their leaders saw a need, if only to preserve those entities, to collaborate and build a sense of region. The main focus of their endeavour was ASEAN. In the course of the 1990s it came to encompass almost the whole region.

Yet neither the example of historians outside Southeast Asia, nor this somewhat ambivalent political regionalism, induced historians within Southeast Asia to engage in writing the history of Southeast Asia as distinct from the history of countries within Southeast Asia. 'My aim', Emmerson wrote, 'is . . . to help indigenous scholars increase understanding and reduce mistrust by getting out from under the imprint of the nation–state—for example, through collaborative research on Southeast Asian topics that are nonpolitical, crosscultural, and sub- or supra-national.' The question, he added, was 'not whether regional unity is a fiction. The question is how to make the fiction useful enough to become true' (p. 21). Apparently it did not become true enough to be useful.

Hong Lysa has argued that 'indigenous scholars have no need to justify their national focus, and in fact have a compelling sense of mission in pursuing their work, which often simply cannot be divorced from their responsibility as members of that society' (Hong Lysa in Mohammed Talib and Tim Huxley, eds, *An Introduction to Southeast Asian Studies* London and New York: Tauris, 1996, p. 66). That comment could be supported by the case of Thailand, where the breakdown of the military regime led to the recovery and development of alternative views of the past. It was also relevant to the Philippines, where the school of historians associated with Zeus Salazar criticised those more concerned to sustain 'a discourse that defensively reckons with the view of the foreigner', rather than 'inquiring into the internal dynamics of Philippine society as it evolved over the centuries' (F. Llanes in Putu Davies, ed., *Constructing a National Past* Bandar Sri Begawan: Universiti Brunei Darussalam, 1996, p. 315).

Such a nationalist emphasis, Hong added, was 'not permanent'. The region, once one of 'revolt', then part of the exploited Third World, was being redefined as one of economic growth and political stability. 'Southeast Asians may well find impetus, and indeed sponsorship, to master a second Southeast Asian language and to research the history of their neighbours' (p. 66). The undermining of economic prosperity in the closing years of the 1990s, together with the threats to stability, again put this prospect in question. Amid many other uncertainties, the stance of the region's historians is still to be determined.

At the same time, historians outside Southeast Asia at once wondered whether they had begun to over-emphasize the commonalities in the experience of its peoples, and to cut that experience off from the experience of peoples in other regions of the world. The first might underplay the particularities of the societies and polities within the region. The second might reduce the chances of understanding them more fully through a wider range of comparisons. The leading figure in this thinking has been Vic Lieberman, who has been particularly concerned that the history of mainland Southeast Asia in the early modern period has been skewed as a result.

His work has even broader implications. He asks himself whether it is not partly driven 'by a desire to compensate for Southeast Asia's obscurity' ('Transcending East–West Dichotomies . . .', *Modern Asian Studies* 31, 3, 1997, p. 537). Certainly it has rarely featured in the works on historiography currently used in universities, suggesting that, so far as their colleagues are concerned, historians of Southeast Asia tend to be quartered off like foreign traders in the early modern cities of the region. Only a few works have made a wide impact: those of Ben Anderson (on nationalism), James Scott (on the 'moral economy' of the peasant), Clifford Geertz (on the 'theatre state'), for example. The work of many others—applying, even anticipating, deconstructionism, or pursuing 'history from below'—has received little general recognition. Yet what they have done could amplify the historiographical debate, and enrich the historiography of all the countries concerned.

Lieberman's work is perhaps yet more significant in its response to the world of the 1990s, marked by the end of the Cold War, the increased urge to globalization, the loss of old Western certainties. The opportunity should be taken to transcend, rather than reinforce, the East–West dichotomies that have so long marked the history of Asia through a focus on what he calls 'Eurasian' history.

It is in this context that *The Cambridge History of Southeast Asia* is reprinted. It sought to emphasize the regional rather than the national, and partly for that reason, perhaps, most of the contributors came from scholars outside the region. They were convinced of the advantages of attempting a regional approach, though also thoroughly aware of the risks to themselves and their topics. One object was indeed to diminish the 'obscurity' of Southeast Asia. Rather less, perhaps, than Emmerson, if at all, did they seek to turn a unicorn into a rose, though recognizing that their words were also deeds. If what they wrote and did aroused controversy, they were ready to welcome it, and if others made up for their shortcomings, or filled gaps that they left, so much the better. This reprint emerges in a more tumultuous region and amid new historiographical controversies. It may still form a useful stepping-out point.

If the kind of regional approach the work adopts has been contested, so also have its chronological divisions. '(P)eriods', Anthony Reid wrote, 'are modes of dealing with specific questions and must change with the questions' (*Southeast Asia in the Age of Commerce* vol. 2, p. xiv). That offers little guidance, though some caution, in respect of a general work. The contributors to *The Cambridge History of Southeast Asia* were indeed not entirely happy with the divisions that were adopted for each part, and that now form the divisions between the volumes. Those divisions are indeed somewhat indeterminate as a result.

The division at c. 1500 CE implied, though it did not specifically assert, that the advent of the Europeans was a more significant event than many are now prepared to consider it. More important perhaps was the expansion of commerce in the fifteenth century, in which China played a major role. Adopting even that date may run the risk of over-emphasizing the external factors in the history of the region, and down-playing its own initiatives and capacities to innovate. Lieberman, for example, is convinced 'that the heavy emphasis on maritime influences to explain local change tends to be reductionist and exaggerated, at least for the mainland' ('Local Integration and Eurasian Analogies: Structuring Southeast Asian History', *Modern Asia Studies* 27, 3, 1993, p. 478). Divisions of some kind are unavoidable, particularly in structuring a large project. The reader must accept them, but also the health warning that goes along with them.

Over the other divisions we also argued. That between what are Volumes 2 and 3 of the paperback edition took some account of the revisionary view of the eighteenth century, again associated with Lieberman's work, but well argued in our volume by Jeya Kathirithamby-Wells. The division between Volumes 3 and 4 we also subjected to criticism. Did it over-emphasize the impact of the Japanese? Did it obscure continuities within Southeast Asia? Whether the crisis of the 1990s marks another division, or should suggest another kind of division of the past, remains to be seen.

Nicholas Tarling 1999

CHAPTER

1

# THE WRITING OF SOUTHEAST ASIAN HISTORY

The writing of Southeast Asian history, as distinct from the history of its several parts, is a comparatively recent development. The first major history of the region as a whole, D. G. E. Hall's *A History of South-East Asia*, appeared only in 1955.[1] Hall's work, though describing itself as 'a bare outline, perilously compressed and oversimplified in many parts',[2] was a massive achievement, basing itself on the detailed work of other scholars and reflecting a knowledge of the critical issues of debate amongst them. Apart from urging that Southeast Asia be studied as an area 'worthy of consideration in its own right' and not as an appendage of India, China or the West, it offered no new conceptual or methodological approaches of its own. But in bringing together the fruits of existing scholarship it provided a kind of stocktaking of the state of that scholarship.

Since then the suitability of the region as a whole as an object of study has been more readily accepted. Cornell University had already established, in 1950, its Southeast Asia Program, and a number of other institutions in various countries followed suit. And, increasingly, comparative works focused on the region as a whole. Charles Fisher's social, economic and political geography (London, 1964) was entitled simply *South-east Asia*, and other works with a similar ambit followed: John F. Cady's *Southeast Asia: its Historical Development* (New York, 1964) and his *Post-War Southeast Asia* (Athens, Ohio, 1974) and Nicholas Tarling's *South-east Asia: Past and Present* (Melbourne, 1966) are but a few examples. The very perception of Southeast Asia is, of course, a modern and external perception. Southeast Asians themselves, though aware of local, ethnic and cultural identities, did not, until very recently, perceive a Southeast Asian identity. And the external perception was, of necessity, somewhat contrived. The preface to *Governments and Politics of Southeast Asia*, edited by George McT. Kahin in 1959, still hesitated to see Southeast Asia as a significant unity. 'Southeast Asia is not an area of great political homogeneity. Politically as well as culturally its component states are more

[1] 2nd edn, 1964; 3rd edn, 1968; 4th edn, 1981. Brian Harrison's useful *South-East Asia: A Short History*, London, 1954, had appeared in the preceding year, but it was directed to the general reader and not to the specialist (Preface, v).

[2] Hall, *History*, Preface to the First Edition, v.

varied than those of Europe.'[3] And as late as 1971 six authors attempting an integrated and thematic history of the region entitled their work *In Search of Southeast Asia*.[4]

Hall's work, coming ten years after the end of World War II, constituted a watershed, embodying the changes in the direction of scholarship that had begun to make themselves felt after the war, and setting the stage for the expansion of Southeast Asian studies which followed. However, it was, of course, the war itself which changed the whole setting within which the region was studied, and it will be convenient, for the purposes of this chapter, to take that as a main dividing line in the development of the writing of Southeast Asian history.

Two further points must be made at the outset. First, in surveying writings about Southeast Asia's past, certain limits have been set. Attention will be confined to works that may be described as belonging to a modern, international tradition of historical enquiry. It would have been possible, in a chapter of this kind, to examine the different types of indigenous writing which contain views about, or presentations of, the past: *babads*, *hikayats*, chronicles of various kinds, literary works and inscriptions. One might have viewed these not merely as sources to be subjected to the critical scrutiny of modern historians, and examined for the light they might throw on past cultural configurations, but as historical writings in their own right, to be approached in their own terms and considered for their assumptions about the nature of the historical process. On the other hand it can be argued that—with the exception of Vietnam, whose dynastic historians did attempt to preserve a record of events—there was no genuinely historical tradition in Southeast Asia. For the most part the function of indigenous chronicles, even when they purported to deal with the course of events—the rise and fall of dynasties, battles, victories and defeats—was not to record a factual past but to perform other, largely moral, functions: to legitimize, to glorify, to assert unity or to express a perceived moral order of society. They might sometimes create a different past in the interests of the present, devising, for example, an appropriate lineage for a usurper. They might serve as part of the regalia of a ruler.[5] There are possible exceptions. One student of Javanese history draws a distinction between 'historical' and 'mythical' Javanese texts and takes the view that, where texts do purport to describe actual events, they are 'often more accurate than a survey of the secondary literature on

3 Ithaca, 1959, Preface, v.

4 David Joel Steinberg, David K. Wyatt, John R. W. Smail, Alexander Woodside, William R. Roff and David P. Chandler, ed. Steinberg, New York, 1971; 2nd edn, with additional author, R. H. Taylor, Honolulu, 1988.

5 These issues were discussed at a seminar held in Canberra in 1976 at which an attempt was made to consider indigenous writings in their own terms. See Anthony Reid and David Marr eds, *Perceptions of the Past in Southeast Asia*, Kuala Lumpur, 1979. Contributors were of the view that these works could not be described as historical. As examples, see the essays of Charnvit Kasetsiri who contrasted religious and dynastic histories in Thailand with modern analytical history; Michael Vickery who argued that, in Cambodia, a recorded antiquity was necessary to validate kingship; and O. W. Wolters, who suggested that the function of eleventh-century Vietnamese texts was to assert the equality of Vietnamese and Chinese empires.

Javanese historiography might suggest'.[6] And it is possible, of course, to draw too sharp a contrast between the ritualistic function of texts and the purposes of the so-called 'scientific' historians. Scientific history, too, may justify or legitimize a later state of affairs and create a past to serve the needs of the present. The difference, reflecting a difference of intention, is that it can be called to account and criticized in terms of evidence and argument. It is, after all, perhaps a difference of degree. However, for the purposes of the present chapter it has been decided to regard traditional writings as amongst the sources for the study of Southeast Asia rather than as contributions to that study in their own right, and to confine attention to works based on a critical consideration of surviving sources and belonging to a modern scholarly tradition.

Second, it is not intended to offer here an exhaustive bibliographical survey. In the space available it is possible to refer to only a small minority of the significant works dealing with Southeast Asian history. What is proposed is rather an essay which will seek to identify the main characteristics of historical writing and to notice the principal shifts of focus, emphasis and modes of interpretation. Reference will be made to individual works merely by way of example.

## SOUTHEAST ASIAN STUDIES BEFORE WORLD WAR II

Before World War II the study of Southeast Asian history may be divided into two broad categories. There was first of all a concern with early history, with an attempt, in effect, to piece together from archaeological, epigraphical and literary sources, the outlines of a previously unexamined chronology. Second, attention was given to the activities of the European powers from the sixteenth century on, to the gradual creation of commercial and territorial empires in Southeast Asia and to the colonial policies pursued therein.

The first type of enquiry was severely constrained by the nature of the available evidence. It is only from about the fifth century CE that evidence exists to support some kind of genuinely historical perception of Southeast Asia. There are material remains deriving from before that period that allow tentative conclusions to be drawn about the indigenous prehistoric cultures of the region. Little can be known about original migrations. Stone tools, both chipped and polished, and bone artefacts give some evidence of palaeolithic and neolithic periods. There are tentative conclusions about the development of agriculture and about whether it was an indigenous development or was introduced from outside. The bronze drums discovered in the north Vietnamese village of Dong-son testify to the existence of a metal-working culture in about the fourth century BC. Megaliths and burial places provide evidence of a different kind. But the character and

[6] M. C. Ricklefs, *Jogjakarta under Sultan Mangkubumi, 1749–1792*, London, 1974, xix. A similar view is implied by Victor Lieberman whose study of Burma from the sixteenth to the eighteenth century draws heavily on indigenous sources: *Burmese Administrative Cycles: Anarchy and Conquest, c. 1580–1760*, Princeton, 1984, 6 and 271ff.

the scarcity of such remains meant that their interpretation required considerable speculation.

Even for the period where written sources and architectural monuments exist, there is considerable obscurity. According to de Casparis, the earliest known written materials in Southeast Asia are inscriptions on seals and other objects, discovered in south Vietnam and dated as belonging to between the second and fifth centuries CE[7] and the Vo-canh (Vietnam) inscription dated as third century. From about the fifth century epigraphical evidence becomes more plentiful, both on the mainland and in the archipelago, and this provides evidence of polities of substance. It is accompanied by monumental remains such as the ninth-century Buddhist stupa, the Borobodur, and the tenth-century Śaivite Lara Jonggrang complex at Prambanan in central Java, the splendours of Angkor from the ninth to the thirteenth century and of Pagan from the eleventh to the thirteenth century.[8] The evidence of organized power is there, but not a detailed political history of the kingdoms which created these monuments. On the basis of evidence of this kind, scholars have been free to debate such issues as, for example, the exact nature of early trading patterns or questions of political authority such as the Śailendra problem—the apparent simultaneous presence in central Java of both a Śaivite kingdom of the Sanjaya house and a Buddhist kingdom under the Śailendra dynasty (later to be rulers of Śrīvijaya in south Sumatra) in the eighth and ninth centuries—without a conclusive result.[9] Chronicles and other literary works have survived from about the fourteenth century.[10] In Java the more extended texts such as the *Pararaton*, the *Nāgarakĕrtāgama* and the *Babad Tanah Jawi* appear to contain details of political history. These works have survived only because they have been copied and recopied and, in their present form, they are therefore not documents of the period in which they were first written. In any case, for the reasons already suggested, they cannot be taken as reliable sources for the events they purport to describe.

For the second type of pre-war enquiry into the history of Southeast Asia, sources are much more abundant. Whereas students of early history had, perforce, to make what they could of very fragmentary evidence, students of the later period were able to draw on extensive sources provided by the writings of European observers and, in due course, by the colonial archives of the Western powers—Portuguese, Spanish, Dutch, French, British and American. To a European eye these appeared to provide sure ground for historical knowledge, though, as will become apparent, they have always presented their own problems of interpretation and perspective.

The two categories of enquiry shared certain features. The first of these has already been noticed: the almost universal tendency of historians to

[7] *Indonesian Paleography*, Leiden, 1975, 12.

[8] For Pagan see G. H. Luce, *Old Burma—Early Pagan*, 3 vols, New York, 1969–70.

[9] For a consideration of that debate and a suggested solution to the problem see J. G. de Casparis, *Inscripties uit de Çailendratijd*, I: *Prasasti Indonesia*, Bandung, 1950, and II: *Selected Inscriptions from the Seventh to the Ninth Century A.D. Prasasti Indonesia*, Bandung, 1956.

[10] de Casparis, *Indonesian Paleography*, 53.

focus on the constituent parts of Southeast Asia rather than to develop a perception of the region as a whole as a suitable object of study. This was perhaps inescapable where it was a matter of studying the activities of the imperial powers in the area. The very names, British Malaya, Netherlands India, French Indochina, indicated the territorial constraints of Western students of Southeast Asia.[11] Much of their work was concerned either with the broad goals of imperial policies or with administrative structures and methods, and such studies concentrated naturally on particular colonial dependencies. But the students of early history, too, focused for the most part on the past of the potential nations of the future, nations defined sometimes by the accidents of colonial rule, rather than on what might be described as 'natural' ethnic, linguistic or cultural entities cutting across the artificially established political boundaries. This represented, of course, the hindsight of nineteenth- and twentieth-century authors, though it is true that, by the eighteenth century, outside observers were bringing European notions of 'country' and 'state' and were imposing their own perceptions of the main political divisions of Southeast Asia. As examples taken almost at random may be cited the epigraphical work of G. H. Luce and Pe Maung Tin in Burma,[12] Georges Cœdès in Thailand and Cambodia,[13] and Cœdès, G. Ferrand, K. A. Nilakanta Sastri, F. D. K. Bosch and others in Indonesia.[14] In the field of archaeological studies and art history were Paul Mus' study of the Borobodur, the archaeological description of the same monument prepared by N. J. Krom while head of the archaeological service of Netherlands India, Bernet Kempers' work on Hindu-Javanese art, Stutterheim on Balinese art, Le May's history of Buddhist art in Siam, and Parmentier on Khmer art.[15] Textual and philological studies, too, followed the same pattern of local concentration, necessarily so in this type of enquiry because of the linguistic specialization required.[16]

[11] The literature is extensive. As examples one might cite J. L. Christian, *Modern Burma*, Berkeley, 1942; P. Le Boulanger, *Histoire de Laos Française*, Paris, 1931; A. Leclère, *Histoire du Cambodge*, Paris, 1914; G. Maspero, ed., *Un Empire Colonial Français: L'Indochine*, Paris, 1929–30; C. B. Maybon, *Histoire Moderne du Pays d'Annam*, Paris, 1920; V. Thompson, *French Indochina*, London, 1937; J. S. Furnivall, *Netherlands India*, Cambridge, UK, 1939; Clive Day, *The Dutch in Java*, New York, 1904; E. S. de Klerck, *History of the Netherlands East Indies*, Rotterdam, 1938; F. W. Stapel, ed., *Geschiedenis van Nederlandsch-Indië*, Amsterdam, 1939; L. A. Mills, *British Malaya 1824–1867*, Singapore, 1925.

[12] *Inscriptions of Burma*, published in the form of rubbings, 1933–9.

[13] *Reçueil des Inscriptions du Siam*, Bangkok, 1924–9; *Inscriptions de Sukhodaya*, Bangkok, 1924; and *Inscriptions du Cambodge*, Hanoi, 1937–51.

[14] Cœdès, 'Le Royaume de Çrivijaya', BEFEO, 18 (1918), and 'Les inscriptions malaises de Çrivijaya', BEFEO, 30 (1930); Ferrand, 'L'Empire Sumatranais de Çrivijaya', *Journal Asiatique*, 11th series, 20 (1922), and 'Quatre textes épigraphiques malayo-sanskrits de Sumatra et de Banka', *Journal Asiatique*, 221 (1932); Sastri, 'Sri Vijaya', BEFEO, 40 (1940), and 'Takuapa and its Tamil Inscription', JMBRAS, 22 (1949); Bosch, 'De Inscriptie van Keloerak', *Tijdschrift van het Bataviaasch Genootschap*, 48 (1928).

[15] Mus, 'The Barabadur: Les origines du stupa et la transmigration', BEFEO, 32 (1923); Krom, *Barabadur: Archaeological Description*, The Hague, 1927; Kempers, *The Bronzes at Nalanda and Hindu-Javanese Art*, Leiden, 1930; W. F. Stutterheim, *Indian Influences on Old Balinese Art*, London, 1935, and other works; R. S. Le May, *A Concise History of Buddhist Art in Siam*, Cambridge, 1938; H. Parmentier, *L'Art Khmer Primitif*, Paris, 1927, and *L'Art Khmer Classique*, Paris, 1930.

[16] Editions and translations of major texts include, for Indonesia, J. J. Meinsma's Javanese edition of the *Babad Tanah Jawi* (1874), H. Kern's Dutch translation of the *Nāgarakĕrtāgama*

The same division of labour was apparent in works of synthesis, drawing together the detailed findings of scholarship. An example was the publication in 1926 of the first edition of N. J. Krom's monumental *Hindoe-Javaansche Geschiedenis* (Hindu-Javanese History) which represented a milestone in the study of early Javanese history. Based on the archaeological, epigraphical and textual work of earlier scholars as well as of Krom himself, it addressed questions that had been the subject of debate and aimed to present, in detail, what he believed to be the established record of that particular society. His methods and findings were later to be the subject of systematic criticism, specifically by C. C. Berg. For the time being, however, his work represented an important examination of earlier scholarship and the presentation of what was thought to be known about the history of Java.

There were important exceptions to the country-by-country study of the region. The publication of the first edition of Georges Cœdès' work, *Les États Hindouisés d'Indochine et d'Indonésie* in 1944[17] represented a culmination of his pre-war work and dealt in terms of cultures and political organization over a wider geographical area. Using the concept of 'Hinduization', he developed a broad analysis of Southeast Asian societies and polities and the ideas which supported them. The picture was one of inland kingdoms based on intensive wet-rice cultivation; they were hierarchical in character and sustained by ideas of cosmic order and of rulers embodying that order. But for the most part specialist historians focused on the past of what were to become the individual states of post-war Southeast Asia, and general historians, concerned not with the reading of a particular text or the interpretation of a particular inscription, still devoted themselves to the histories of the political entities created by the colonial era: G. H. Harvey's *History of Burma from the Earliest Times to the Beginning of the British Conquest* (London, 1925), W. A. R. Wood's *History of Siam* (London, 1926), H. G. Quaritch Wales' *Ancient Siamese Government and Administration* (London, 1934), E. d'Aymonier's *Le Cambodge* (Paris, 1900–4), C. B. Maybon's *Histoire Moderne du Pays d'Annam* (Paris, 1920), Richard Winstedt's *History of Malaya* (Singapore, 1935).

A second characteristic of most pre-war studies, whether of the earlier or the later periods of Southeast Asian history, was the tendency of scholars to see that history as shaped by influences external to the region rather than as the product of an internal dynamic. This was partly a consequence of the prior training of many scholars in either Indology or Sinology, which tended to lead them to see Southeast Asia from one or other of those perspectives; but it was perhaps more a consequence of the nature of the available sources. The presence, after about the fifth century CE, of the more extensive archaeological, epigraphical and architectural evidence

(1919), Krom's edition of the *Parataton* (1920), and Olthof's translation of the *Babad Tanah Jawi* (1941); for Malaya, Winstedt's edition of the *Sejarah Melayu* (1938); for Burma, the translation by Pe Maung Tin and G. H. Luce of *The Glass Palace Chronicle* (1923); for Thailand, the translation of the *Annales du Siam* by C. Notton (1926–39).

17 Published under the title *Histoire ancienne des états hindouisés d'Extrême-Orient*. See Notes on the 2nd and 3rd Editions in the translation edited by Walter F. Vella, *The Indianized States of Southeast Asia*, Honolulu, 1968.

to which reference has already been made corresponds with the period when the cultural influence of India is so obviously apparent in the language and paleography of inscriptions, in the general style and the decorative detail of architectural remains, in the religious ideas of Hinduism and Buddhism and in other artistic forms such as the borrowing of the Sanskrit epics, the *Rāmāyaṇa* and *Mahābhārata*. So extensive were the signs of that influence that many saw it as the result of Indian emigration to, and colonization of, parts of Southeast Asia or of actual conquest, and wrote of Southeast Asia as 'Further India' or 'Greater India'.[18]

The character of this influence, and the way in which it was transmitted, formed a major subject of debate amongst pre-war students of Southeast Asia. A number of Indian scholars, R. C. Majumdar for example, advanced variants of the trade, colonization or conquest theories, even though Indian sources did not provide evidence of a colonizing process in Southeast Asia. And some European scholars argued in similar vein. C. C. Berg argued that Indianization was the result of conquest and settlement by Indian warriors, and N. J. Krom, in his *Hindu-Javanese History*, saw it as the result of the expansion of Indian trade and consequent settlement and intermarriage.[19] A contrary view, which emphasized indigenous impetus, was argued in different forms by other scholars. To take three examples, significant contributions of quite distinct kinds were published by Paul Mus in 1933, J. C. van Leur in 1934 and F. D. K. Bosch in 1946.

Mus, who had received his initial education in Indochina, and who was subsequently employed by the École Française d'Extrême-Orient in Hanoi, argued, with particular reference to earth cults in Champa, the existence of a common, primordial substratum of belief and culture in both Indian and Southeast Asian societies. Thus, when Hinduism and Buddhism became, as it were, available, there was a local basis in Southeast Asia for the acceptance of these beliefs and for their absorption into a local totality of belief.[20]

In 1934 van Leur, subsequently an official of the Netherlands Indies government (he was killed in the Battle of the Java Sea in 1942) published his doctoral thesis for the University of Leiden which applied new theoretical concepts to the study of Southeast Asian trade and which challenged the way in which scholars had approached the study of the region.[21] He insisted that Indian influence in Southeast Asia, and subsequently that of Islam, powerful though they may have been, were nevertheless comparatively superficial when seen in the context of the societies they were affecting—'a thin and flaking glaze' under which the

[18] e.g., R. C. Majumdar, *Ancient Indian Colonies in the Far East*, I, Lahore, 1927, II, Dacca, 1937–8.

[19] Berg, *Hoofdlijnen der Javaansche Literatuur-Geschiedenis*, Groningen, 1929; N. J. Krom, *Hindoe-Javaansche Geschiedenis*, The Hague, 1926.

[20] P. Mus, 'Cultes indiens et indigènes au Champa', BEFEO, 33 (1933), published as *L'Inde vu de l'Est: Cultes indiens et indigènes au Champa*, Hanoi, 1934; trans. I. W. Mabbett, and edited by Mabbett and D. P. Chandler as *India Seen From the East*, Monash Papers on Southeast Asia, no. 3, Clayton, 1975.

[21] Van Leur's thesis was published in 1934 under the title *Eenige beschouwingen betreffende den ouden Aziatischen handel* (Some Observations concerning Early Asian Trade). An English translation, 'On Early Asian Trade', was published, together with some of his other writings, in 1955 in a volume entitled *Indonesian Trade and Society*, The Hague and Bandung.

main form of an older indigenous culture continued to exist.[22] Van Leur rejected, first of all, hypotheses of Indian colonization and of cultural influence carried by trade, and advanced instead the idea of a deliberate Southeast Asian borrowing of ideas, artistic styles and modes of political organization as local polities of substance emerged. His view was based on arguments about the particular aspects of Indian culture that found a ready home in Southeast Asia and about the nature of early Asian trade which, according to some scholars, had been the bearer of that culture. In brief, he characterized Southeast Asian trade as a pre-capitalist, peddling trade which, by its nature, could not have been the means of transmitting those elements of Indian culture that were absorbed into the local scene. These were aspects of high culture—art, literature, ideas of power, sovereignty and kingship—and must therefore have been brought by brahmins, not by petty traders. Indian influence was a court matter and the process, in consequence, could only have been one of deliberate borrowing by Southeast Asian rulers seeking ideas, rituals and organization, not an example of general cultural diffusion. Second, the view that foreign influences did not transform indigenous culture but were a thin and flaking glaze imposed on it, followed from the idea of local initiative. The form of van Leur's analysis became the subject of renewed discussion after the publication of an English translation of his thesis in 1955.

F. D. K. Bosch's argument, advanced in a lecture at Leiden in 1946 which brought together the fruits of his pre-war work,[23] supported van Leur's general view. But whereas van Leur based his case to a considerable extent upon a conceptual analysis of Southeast Asian trade, Bosch had an eye to specific evidence. This included the absence of references to Indian conquest in any inscriptions; the character of linguistic borrowings; and the fact that signs of Indian influence were strongest in inland kingdoms, not coastal ones, as might have been expected if culture had been carried by commerce.

In spite of the growing conviction carried by these arguments, the idea of Greater India had considerable staying power and was reaffirmed in the synthesizing work of Cœdès in 1944 (his term was 'l'Inde extérieure'). His ideas about how Indian influence was conveyed were, however, not so very different from those of van Leur. He saw Indian influence as manifested not through conquest or colonization, but initially through trade; this laid the foundations for the subsequent transmission of the higher culture associated with the development of indigenous kingdoms able and ready to receive, or to take an initiative in acquiring, Indian conceptions of royalty, the sacred language of Sanskrit and the prescriptions of Hinduism.

The debate had many dimensions: the mechanics of transmission with which we have been concerned, the peculiar blend of Buddhism and Hinduism to be found in Southeast Asia, the question of passive acceptance as against active borrowing, of borrowed forms and local genius,[24]

[22] *Indonesian Trade and Society*, 95.

[23] Subsequently published as 'The Problem of the Hindu Colonization of Indonesia' in his *Selected Studies in Indian Archaeology*, The Hague, 1961.

[24] A notion later used by H. G. Quaritch Wales in his *The Making of Greater India*, London, 1951.

and these themes continued to be the subject of later argument. So did the more general issue: that of the 'autonomy' of Southeast Asian history. How is one, in the light of the available evidence, to judge the shaping forces of Southeast Asian culture? Is it indeed a matter of evidence? Or is it perhaps a matter of choice of perspective and framework and point of view? Do contending analyses contradict each other or do they present complementary points of view? In the post-war period, a new generation of scholars were to be less concerned with the details of the evidence than were their predecessors of the 1920s and 1930s, and more with the ways in which the process might be described.

The Indianization debate was so extensive because of the inconclusive nature of the evidence. China's impact on Southeast Asia was less a matter of controversy, perhaps because the record is established more clearly. That influence was felt directly through almost a thousand years of Chinese rule in Vietnam, but it had its effect beyond that. Chinese trade was carried on throughout the region as a whole, and Chinese political dealings with Southeast Asian kingdoms extended as far afield as the Indonesian archipelago. The fact that Chinese sources provide evidence of trading relations and of the receipt by China of tribute missions again means that a good deal of early Southeast Asian history is seen through Chinese eyes.

The penetration of Islam into the Malay peninsula and the archipelago from perhaps about the ninth century provided a further powerful external influence. Controversies about the coming of Islam, however, belong rather to the post-war period of Southeast Asian historiography.

For the period after 1500 the use of European sources has perhaps had an even more dramatic effect on the perspectives of historians. With the establishment of European trade monopolies and of an Asia-wide commercial network, followed by the acquisition of territory and the formation of directly ruled colonial dependencies, it seemed that Southeast Asian history had lost its autonomy. And colonial history, almost by its nature, was necessarily Eurocentric. Even if an attempt were made to read European sources 'against the grain' in an effort to recapture a Southeast Asian perspective, the issues they presented and the categories they used were inevitably those of the invader and not necessarily appropriate to the experiences of the region. Van Leur's analysis was relevant here, too, and one can hardly avoid quoting his famous remark, made with reference to Indonesian history, that 'with the arrival of ships from western Europe, the point of view is turned a hundred and eighty degrees and from then on the Indies are observed from the deck of the ship, the ramparts of the fortress, the high gallery of the trading house'.[25] In that sentence he caught the prevailing tendency of existing Southeast Asian historiography to interpret events after 1500 in terms of Western challenge and Southeast Asian response, and to imply his own contrary view that, at least until the nineteenth century, Europeans in Southeast Asia were fitting into Southeast Asia's existing political and economic patterns rather than making them over.

[25] Van Leur, *Indonesian Trade and Society*, 261.

It was characteristic of the pre-war study of Southeast Asia, then, to focus on the parts rather than the whole, and to see events as being shaped by external influences. A third feature of the pre-war study of Southeast Asia, both of the earlier and later periods, is that it was almost entirely the work of outside observers, European, Middle Eastern and Asian. In the nineteenth and twentieth centuries a number of indigenous Southeast Asian scholars emerged, but such individuals as R. Ng. Perbatjaraka and Hoesein Djajadiningrat in Netherlands India, U Tin in Burma, Tran Van Giap in Vietnam, and Prince Damrong in Thailand were themselves the products of Western education and were scholars in a modern international tradition.

Western students of Southeast Asia in the late nineteenth century were, of course, the latest in a long line of foreign observers of the region. Some of the earliest available information about Southeast Asia is in the form, not of local archaeological or epigraphic remains, but of written reports of travellers from elsewhere, whose accounts have served as sources for the later study of the trading patterns and the cultures of the area. Such accounts included those of the seventh-century Chinese traveller, I Ching (I Tsing), who is one of the sources for the existence of the kingdom of Śrīvijaya;[26] Marco Polo, who visited parts of Southeast Asia while at the Chinese imperial court and who returned to Europe by way of the Indonesian archipelago and the Malay peninsula in the late thirteenth century; Arab travellers such as Ibn Batuta in the early fourteenth century;[27] Pigafetta who accompanied Magellan;[28] the Portuguese, Tomé Pires, in the early sixteenth century;[29] John Jourdain, who visited India and the archipelago between 1608 and 1617;[30] and many others.

From the beginning of the sixteenth century, with the establishment of the Portuguese at Melaka (Malacca) and, later in the century, of the Spaniards at Manila, the period of European empire had begun—the 'Age of Vasco da Gama' as the Indian historian, K. M. Panikkar, has called it[31]—and reflective accounts of the societies and cultures they encountered become more abundant. A wide range of observers, such as Portuguese or Spanish missionaries, or those employed in the service of one or other of the European powers or engaged, sometimes, in the conduct of an official mission, produced significant works of reportage. Examples may be given almost at random. The Jesuit missionary, Alexander of Rhodes, published a history of Tonkin in 1651. Michael Symes, who represented the govern-

[26] See J. Takakusu, *A Record of the Buddhist Religion as practised in India and the Malay Archipelago, 671–695 by I Tsing*, Oxford, 1896. See also W. P. Groeneveldt, 'Notes on the Malay Archipelago and Malacca, compiled from Chinese sources', *Verhandelingen v. h. Bataviaasch Genootschap*, 39 (1876).

[27] See S. Lee, trans., *The Travels of Ibn Batuta in Asia and Africa, 1324–25*, London, 1829. See also G. Ferrand, *Relations de Voyages et Textes Géographiques Arabes, Persans et Turcs relatives à l'Extrême-Orient du VIII au XVIII siècles*, Paris, 1913–14.

[28] Lord Stanley of Alderley, trans., *The First Voyage Round the World by Magellan*, translated from the account of Pigafetta and other contemporary writers, Hakluyt Society, First series, no. 52, 1874.

[29] See A. Cortesão, ed. and trans., *The Suma Oriental of Tomé Pires*, London, 1944.

[30] William Foster, ed., The *Journal of John Jourdain, 1608–1617*, Hakluyt Society, Second Series, vol. XVI, Cambridge, UK, 1905.

[31] *Asia and Western Dominance*, London, 1953.

ment of India in two missions to Burma in 1795 and 1802 gave one of the first full accounts of the history, political system and society of that country in the published account of his first mission, *An Embassy to the Kingdom of Ava sent by the Governor-General of India in 1795*.[32] Thomas Stamford Raffles used his period as Lieutenant-Governor in Java between 1811 and 1816 to collect material for his *History of Java*.[33]

From the eighteenth century many European observers of Asia combined a philosophical interest in the exotic with a scientific temper. Asian and Pacific societies provided material for reflection on the nature of social evolution, perceived, sometimes, within the framework of contemporary romanticism. This coincided with the more general development of scientific enquiry and the establishment of divisions between emerging disciplines. Just as, in the observation of the natural world, botany, geology and geography began to establish themselves as distinct lines of enquiry, so one could perceive, in the study of other societies, the laying of the foundations of what were to become sociology and anthropology. In the nineteenth century such observations multiplied. Sir Arthur Phayre, who led a mission from the government of India in 1855 and subsequently became Chief Commissioner of British Burma, wrote the *History of Burma* (London, 1883), the first such work in English. Henry Yule, secretary to the 1855 mission, prepared the report of the mission and published Phayre's journal.[34] Francis Garnier's *Voyage d'Exploration en Indo-Chine* was an account of a journey up the Mekong under the command of Doudart de Lagrée, but it included what might be called philosophical observations on the customs observed and a vision of the Mekong as a way of entry to China.[35] Auguste Pavie, whose two missions to Luang Prabang between 1887 and 1892 helped to resist Siamese claims to part of Laos and to expand French control in Indochina, produced a massive account of his work.[36] These are but a few examples.

With the territorial expansion of the European powers and the rounding out of their colonial empires in the course of the late nineteenth and early twentieth centuries, a new class of colonial administrators emerged, many of whom engaged in the study of the societies in which they worked. For some this was an amateur interest, and the tradition of the scholarly amateur observer became a strong one. Many developed a high degree of professionalism and, as scholar administrators, they pioneered the archaeological, linguistic and historical study of Southeast Asia. Winstedt, Swettenham, Braddell and Wilkinson in Malaya, and Furnivall in Burma were distinguished examples. In the Netherlands Indies there emerged, at the end of the nineteenth century, a direct official interest in the study and

32 London, 1800. For documents relating to his second mission, and for a defence of Symes' role, see D. G. E. Hall, ed., *Michael Symes: Journal of his Second Embassy to the Court of Ava in 1802*, London, 1955.

33 London, 1817; published in facsimile by Oxford University Press, Kuala Lumpur, 1965.

34 Hugh Tinker, ed., facsimile edn of Sir Henry Yule, *Narrative of the Mission to the Court of Ava in 1855*, Kuala Lumpur, 1968.

35 *Voyage d'Exploration en Indo-Chine effectué pendant les années 1866, 1867 et 1868*, Paris, 1873, and the unofficial posthumous account published by Garnier's brother Leon, 1885. See also M. E. Osborne, *River Road to China: The Mekong River Expedition, 1866–73*, New York, 1975.

36 *Mission Pavie*, Paris, 1898–1904.

preservation of antiquities, and scholars with a background in philology, Sanskrit and Indology were appointed to appropriate positions. Brandes was Government Philologist, Krom was President of the Archaeological Commission established in 1901 and, from 1913, head of the Archaeological Service which replaced it. Snouck Hurgronje was adviser to the government on Islamic affairs. But the amateur tradition was represented there also, for example, in G. P. Rouffaer whose extensive work earned a major tribute from Krom.[37] And after the introduction of the requirement that recruits to the colonial service receive an appropriate linguistic and cultural training, many officials had a more thorough preparation for extending that kind of interest in the field. There were significant differences in the kind of Indological training provided. The University of Leiden placed its emphasis on language, literature and sociology, while Utrecht was more interested in legal studies and in the nature, in particular, of customary law in Indonesian societies. These different emphases had certain policy implications. In practice the former emphasis became associated with reforming tendencies within the bureaucracy. There was a Leiden influence in the so-called Ethical Policy of 1900 which emphasized the responsibility of the metropolitan government to promote the welfare of its colonial subjects and which believed, too optimistically, in the possibility of effecting modernization and desirable social change by benign government action. The Utrecht approach, by contrast, tended to emphasize the social inertia of traditional social orders, the damage that could follow contact with the West, and the importance of shielding vulnerable societies from the worst effects of change.

Professional and amateur interests were supported by the growth of learned societies and their establishment of scholarly journals. In 1851 the Koninklijk Instituut voor Taal-, Land- en Volkenkunde van Nederlandsch-Indië (Royal Institute for Linguistics, Geography and Culture of the Netherlands Indies) was established at The Hague and its journal, the *Bijdragen* was, as it continues to be, a forum for the publication of scholarly work and debate. In the Indies the Batavia Genootschap van Kunsten en Wetenschappen (Batavian Society for Arts and Sciences), founded in 1788, provided a centre for scholars, officials and others with an interest in, amongst other things, the history and cultures of the Indies. Its *Verhandelingen* was launched in 1779 and its *Tijdschrift* in 1853. A similar highly significant role was played by a local organization in the Straits Settlements. In 1877 a Straits Asiatic Society was formed and within months it had arranged its affiliation with the Royal Asiatic Society (founded in 1826) and become the Straits Branch of the Royal Asiatic Society. In 1923 it was converted to the Malayan Branch and, in due course, after the formation of Malaysia, it became the Malaysian Branch (1964). Its distinguished journal went through similar metamorphoses.[38] The Burma Research Society and its journal (*Journal of the Burma Research Society*, 1911), the bulletin of the London School of Oriental Studies, later the School of Oriental and African

[37] 'Herdenking van Dr G. P. Rouffaer', BKI, 84 (1928).

[38] See the centenary volume of the Malaysian Branch of the Royal Asiatic Society, Reprint Series, no. 4, 1977.

Studies (1917), and the Siam Society and its journal (*Journal of the Siam Society*, 1904) provided further support for scholarly study and publication. Comparable roles were performed for French scholarship by the Societé Asiatique in Paris and the École Française d'Extrême-Orient in Indochina and their respective journals, *Journal Asiatique* (1822) and the *Bulletin de l'École Française d'Extrême-Orient* (1901).

The picture of Southeast Asia that had emerged from the work of these individuals, organizations and societies before World War II was clear enough in its main outlines, though highly debatable in its details. It was a picture of ethnic and cultural diversity, but some common patterns were also perceived. A broad distinction was made between societies based on intensive wet-rice cultivation, to be found in river valleys and on volcanic plains, and those in upland areas engaged in shifting slash-and-burn methods of agriculture. These societies participated to varying degrees in an extensive international trade, extending round the coasts of Asia from China to the Middle East. The picture was one of pockets of dense population where the economy allowed it, and of complex civilizations centred, in the so-called Indianized areas, on royal cities rather than on a perception of firm territorial boundaries. Indeed for the pre-colonial period it was seen as more appropriate to think of political centres rather than of states or kingdoms. Capitals were centres of the realm, reflective of a cosmic order, and shifted as dynasties rose and fell. Visible also were the influences of foreign religions—Hinduism, Buddhism, Theravāda and Mahāyāna, Confucianism, Islam and Christianity. Efforts were made to impose some sort of order on this diversity by classifying it in terms of dominant religious traditions—Confucian Southeast Asia (Vietnam), Theravāda Buddhist Southeast Asia (Burma, Thailand, Cambodiá), Muslim Southeast Asia (Malaya and Indonesia), Christian Southeast Asia (the Philippines)—rather than in ethnic terms, such as Thai, Burman, Mon, Malay, Khmer, etc., or in terms of patterns or dominant cultures as shaped by outside influences, such as Sinicized Southeast Asia, Hispanized Southeast Asia, Indianized Southeast Asia. The main difference between these attempts to group defining characteristics is that a cultural classification might see Indonesia as part of Indianized Southeast Asia, and link it with the Buddhist countries rather than with Malaya as part of Islamic Southeast Asia. For Cœdès, for instance, the features of Indonesia which justified such a linking were far more important than were religious links. As he said in the concluding sentence of *Les États Hindouisés*, it is 'the imprint of the Indian genius which gives the countries studied in this volume a family likeness and produces a clear contrast between these countries and the lands that have been civilized by China'.[39] And the whole is ultimately subjected to, and transformed by, the power of expanding Europe.

These perceptions were reflected in the conventional periodizations of Southeast Asian history: prehistory, Indian influence from, say, the fifth century CE to the thirteenth century, followed in the Malay peninsula and the Indonesian archipelago by the penetration of Islam and, in due course,

[39] Cœdès, ed. Vella, *Indianized States*, 256.

by the impact of Europe from the sixteenth century. In the works of colonial historians the effects of European empire were seen as so profound, at least by the end of the nineteenth century and the beginning of the twentieth—restructuring the economies of Southeast Asia, stimulating enormous social changes, establishing modern political systems, and bringing order and unity to the individual parts of the region—that they constituted a fundamental break in the continuity of Southeast Asian history.

It was a neat picture and, no doubt, it had its patronizing elements. The scholar administrators of the late nineteenth and early twentieth centuries belonged to a broad orientalist tradition which tended to see other cultures as objects of study—and perhaps as inferior objects. Some, who became deeply attached to the societies in which they worked, were attracted by the romanticism of the exotic. Others displayed a paternalistic conviction that their duty was to achieve the uplift of those they had come to rule. Even when scholarly study was based on respect for the local society rather than on a sense of superiority, there was likely to be an unquestioned assumption that the ultimate and inevitable outcome would be the transformation of that society by Western civilization. (There was, perhaps, a more open-minded acceptance of the patterns and values of other cultures on the part of eighteenth-century observers than on the part of their successors who belonged to the high imperialism of the late nineteenth century.)

This general outlook, and, in particular, a periodization leading up to the imperial present, served the interests of empire, and, in spite of the emergence of nationalist movements in some colonial dependencies, there seemed no reason why the processes set in motion by European rule should not continue indefinitely. Different powers had different views about the ultimate goals to be pursued in colonial policy. Self-government was at least the professed goal of Britain in Malaya and Burma, though, in the former case at least, it was not seen as likely to be an early outcome. In the Philippines the United States, having succeeded Spain after the war of 1898, did envisage a specific transition to independence. In the Indies the Dutch spoke of a planned development of Indies society and, again in an indefinite future, a degree of autonomy for the colony within an as yet undefined relationship with the Netherlands. The future 'East Indian Society' would have a place for a permanent European component. The French, pursuing their 'mission civilisatrice' (civilizing mission), looked to self-government of a different kind: the incorporation of the dependencies, in due course, within the framework of metropolitan France. Colonial nationalism did not appear to be inconsistent with these various perspectives for it, too, was part of the progressive forces perceived by colonial historians. Its élite leadership was itself a product of the modernizing process that imperialism had set in motion.

The basis of this way of looking at Southeast Asia was effectively destroyed between 1942 and 1945, and scholars after the war came to the study of the region in an entirely different setting from that of the past. They had different expectations, different preoccupations and found different answers to different questions. And they were present in much greater numbers than before.

## SOUTHEAST ASIAN STUDIES SINCE WORLD WAR II

The tremendous expansion of Southeast Asian studies in the post-war years was hardly a surprising phenomenon. The Japanese occupation of most of the region had swept away the apparatus of colonial rule, and rendered impossible its simple restoration when the war was over. The struggles of new nations for independence, the attainment of that independence in the first instance by the Philippines, Burma and Indonesia and in due course by Malaya, the intensification of nationalist struggle in the French dependencies of Indochina, and changes in the surrounding areas of Asia—the establishment of India and Pakistan and, in 1949, the victory of the Chinese Communist Party—combined to evoke a concentrated study of the region in the West and to transform what it was that was being studied. The same developments stimulated the study of their history by the new nations of Southeast Asia themselves.

A mixture of imperatives was present. The emerging republics of the region required, as part of the creation of their identity, new perceptions of their past, perceptions going back beyond the intrusion of the Western powers and finding earlier roots in older pattens of culture and polity. For observers from outside Southeast Asia there were issues of policy which made a focus on the region not just a matter of scholarly investigation but a matter of practical urgency, arising from the changed distribution of power in the area. For the major powers these included what might be called Cold War issues. Southeast Asia was perceived in a global context. Political affiliations and questions of economic development, modernization and growth interlocked as the powers adjusted to the turbulence of what had appeared, in the past, to be a stable area, firmly under the benevolent rule of Western Europe and America. The Korean War and, in due course, the long-drawn-out trauma of Vietnam, accentuated the concern of Western students of Asia. The result was a massive expansion—one might almost say an explosion—of Asian studies in general, and Southeast Asian studies in particular, in the Western world.

The effect was apparent both in the expansion of institutional arrangements for the study of Asia and in changes in approach and in methods of study. In some cases these took the form of 'area studies' in which the methods of a variety of social sciences—sociology, anthropology, political science, economics—together with history, literature and philosophy, were brought together for the study of a defined area. In other cases the disciplines were preserved as providing distinctive methods of understanding. With differing emphases and styles of organization, a variety of programmes was developed in America, Canada, Britain, the Netherlands, and the Soviet Union; in Australia and New Zealand, which felt themselves to be in an exposed position on the edge of the region; and also in new or expanding universities in the countries of Southeast Asia itself.

Space does not allow a full catalogue, but some examples should be mentioned. In the West the United States was the powerhouse of the expansion and change of direction. Cornell University's Southeast Asia Program co-ordinated the study of the region at undergraduate and graduate levels, and its Modern Indonesia Project, supported by Rockefeller funds, launched a sustained research and publications programme. On a more modest scale Yale also developed a Southeast Asian emphasis and other universities, amongst them Berkeley, Michigan, Northern Illinois, Ohio, Washington, Wisconsin, followed suit. In Canada, the Department of Asian Studies in the University of British Columbia cast its net more widely and placed most emphasis on China and Japan, but Southeast Asia was included also. In Britain the London School of Oriental and African Studies (originally founded in 1917 as the School of Oriental Studies) expanded its activities; and after a committee of enquiry, appointed by the University Grants Committee, and chaired by Sir William Hayter, several new institutional initiatives were taken in order to strengthen Asian studies and to shift the emphasis from a traditional orientalist approach, concentrating on classical literature and philosophy, to a study of modern problems. St Antony's College, a new Oxford foundation, gave a special place to the graduate study of Asia. The University of Sussex established a School of African and Asian Studies, and its Institute of Development Studies (1966) gave some attention to Asia. For Southeast Asia the Centre of South-East Asian Studies at Hull and, later, the Board of Southeast Asian Studies at Kent were examples. In Australia, the establishment of the Research School of Pacific Studies, and later the Faculty of Asian Studies, at the Australian National University, of departments of Indonesian Studies at the Universities of Sydney and Melbourne, of the Centre of Southeast Asian Studies at Monash and the School of Modern Asian Studies at Griffith, and the placing of similar emphases at the University of Western Australia and at Flinders, reflected the same kind of interest.

At the same time Asian countries expanded the Southeast Asian emphases of existing universities—in the Ateneo de Manila, in Chulalongkorn and Thammasat University in Bangkok, for example—and founded new universities—Gadjah Mada University in Yogyakarta, the University of Malaya in Kuala Lumpur, the University of Singapore and others. In all of these, local circumstances and national interest dictated the placing of a Southeast Asian emphasis in undergraduate offerings and graduate programmes in the humanities and social sciences. The history of individual nations rather than of the region as a whole normally formed the main focus, but this was not always the case. The foundation in Singapore in 1968 of an Institute of Southeast Asian Studies represented an attempt to break the pattern. Set up by the government of Singapore as a research body, the institute had, amongst its other goals, the idea of giving fellowships to Southeast Asian scholars to enable them to study countries other than their own. In Japan a Southeast Asian focus was developed in, amongst other places, Waseda University in Tokyo and in Kyoto's Centre of Southeast Asian Studies, founded in 1963.

The institutional expansion was accompanied by the rejuvenation of old scholarly societies, the formation of new ones and the development of new avenues of publication. Earlier associations and their journals remained—the Koninklijk Instituut and its *Bijdragen*, the École Française and its bulletin, the Siam Society and the Malayan branch of the Royal Asiatic Society and their journals. Others changed their character. In America the Far Eastern Association transformed itself into the Association for Asian Studies in 1956, and its journal, the *Far Eastern Quarterly*, which had been launched in 1941, became the *Journal of Asian Studies*. This change meant both a shift from a Eurocentric perception of the 'Far East' and a widening of geographical scope to include the whole of Asia. In the Netherlands the journal *Indonesië*, launched in 1947 by the van Hoeve publishing house, was an important new organ of analysis, though it was to last for only ten years. The first issue of *Indonesia*, published by the Cornell Modern Indonesia Project in 1966, noted that Indonesian specialists had tended to confine themselves too narrowly within their respective disciplines, and aimed to publish articles covering a wide range of subject matter and methods of approach. It has continued to offer an avenue for innovative and provocative work, designed to 'stir discussion and criticism'. In Singapore the *Journal of Southeast Asian History* was launched in 1960. In 1969 it decided to widen its scope and changed its name to the *Journal of Southeast Asian Studies*. *Archipel*, published from 1977 under the patronage of the École Pratique dés Hautes-Études in Paris, provided a forum for the study of island Southeast Asia. And a variety of publication series also served the growing market: the Cornell Southeast Asia Program's Data Paper series, the Interim Report Series and the Monograph Series of the same university's Modern Indonesia Project, Yale's Monograph Series, Ohio's Centre for International Studies Series, the Monograph Series of Monash University, the Southeast Asia Publications Series of the Asian Studies Association of Australia, and many others.

While it would be true to say that the greater part of the new effort was directed to the study of the contemporary scene, the study of Southeast Asia's past also had its place in the radically altered environment.

Between 1956 and 1958 a series of seminars was held at the London School of Oriental and African Studies to survey the current state of historical writing about Southeast Asia. The seminars attempted an evaluation of what had been done in the pre-war years and in the first dozen years after the war, noticed some of the changes that were taking place, and posed questions for the future. Attention was drawn to a variety of special problems facing historians of Southeast Asia: the paucity and difficulty of the sources for the early history of the region; the multiplicity of indigenous languages, classical and vernacular, and of European languages also; the tendency of earlier scholars to concentrate on parts of the region without being fully aware of what was going on in other parts; and changes in perspective as new nations came into being.

It is interesting, thirty and more years later, to look back at the papers resulting from these seminars.[40] It would be fair to judge the outlook of the participants as compounded of a mixture of humility and confidence. They

[40] D. G. E. Hall, ed., *Historians of South-East Asia*, London, 1961.

were humble in the face of the sheer difficulty of the task, and were aware of the danger of bias of various kinds, whether arising from the Eurocentric perspectives of European historians in the past or from the Southeast Asian perspectives of new nationalist historians. But bias was seen in comparatively simple terms, as something that, with care and goodwill, could be corrected or avoided. Hence the ground for confidence. Was it possible, asked the editor of the collected papers, 'to write a real history of South-East Asia before the coming of the European?' (p. 7). The expectation appeared to be that it was possible. The problem here, however, was one of sources and whether they were such as to enable satisfactory knowledge to be achieved: a knowledge comparable, say, to that available for Greece and Rome. What was not questioned, but would certainly be questioned by historians of a later generation, was the very notion of a 'real history', a notion reminiscent of the confidence of Acton introducing the first *Cambridge Modern History*. In the same vein D. G. E. Hall, as convenor of the seminars, referred to a 'new enlightenment' in the approach of Western scholars to the study of the history of the region, revealed in a readiness to see Southeast Asia from a Southeast Asian centre rather than from outside, and in the search for an appropriate nomenclature and for 'a periodization free from colonial implications' (p. 9). Hall referred also to the idea of scientific enquiry by which the 'real' history would be achieved. Indeed Southeast Asia's awareness of its own past and its 'first real notions of history' were largely the product of its contact with the scientific tradition of the West (p. 2). The historians who gathered in London at that time, though cautious about the problems of dealing with Southeast Asia's past, were certainly not plagued to any great extent by fundamental doubts about their craft.

Against that background one might judge post-war historical scholarship, as it continued after the date of the London seminar, as revealing, at first, a considerable confidence in the historical enterprise—a confidence very much in line with that of the historians' social-science colleagues in their onslaught on the problems of the modern world—but with a growing awareness of the sheer difficulty of securing any genuine understanding of other cultures and other times. Such an attitude was not confined to the study of Southeast Asian history. It is possible to detect, in the profession of history in general in the latter part of the twentieth century, a sense of uncertainty and a recognition of the precarious nature of historical knowledge: a reflection, no doubt, of the scepticism of the age.

The initial mood of historians of Southeast Asia in the post-war years was certainly one of confidence, a confidence which must be seen against the background of the expansion of Southeast Asian studies in general to which reference has been made. That expansion, it was noted, involved changes in method as well as in focus. Since much of the motivation came from urgent issues of policy, a great deal of the effort was concentrated at first on the study of current political and economic issues: questions of political trends and political stability, the nature of emerging political systems, the conflict of ideologies, questions of economic development and distribution. To a great extent the methods used were, in consequence, those of the social sciences: economics, political science, sociology and anthropology. These were the disciplinary approaches that were regarded as likely to provide an understanding of the modern Southeast Asian world.

The same general outlook was to be found amongst historians. In the post-war period they were affected both by the methodological themes of their social-science colleagues and by the concern with the immediate problems of the post-war scene. On the methodological front they learned more and more to draw on the methods and the findings of neighbouring disciplines. In a seminal article of the early 1960s, H. J. Benda argued vigorously that historians must be social scientists as well, and should address themselves to the structure of Southeast Asian history as distinct from 'the mere charting of dynastic cycles or the chronicling of wars, as ends in themselves'.[41] He sought to establish a periodization based not merely on political developments but on major structural changes in the social, economic and political relationships of the region. In similar vein, W. F. Wertheim called on historians to apply the techniques of sociology in studying Southeast Asian history.[42] And J. H. Romein urged historians of Southeast Asia to adopt a comparative approach as a means of developing a more systematically scientific method and of coming to grips with such processes as nationalism, revolution and social change in Asian societies.[43] The fact that the countries of Southeast Asia had shared a broadly common experience of Western imperialism over the previous couple of centuries was, in itself, a stimulus to the development of comparative enquiries. It must be conceded that, in spite of a growing disposition to see Southeast Asia as a region, much of the post-war work in history and the social sciences continued to be directed to individual countries rather than to the region as a whole. However, most scholars were aware of comparative considerations even when focusing on one area, and that awareness did give substance to the idea of Southeast Asian history.

The emphasis on the need for historians to draw upon the techniques of neighbouring disciplines went, naturally enough, with a focus on recent history. Such a focus was, indeed, characteristic of a general approach to Southeast Asian history at least in the first two decades of the post-war period. Historians shared the general concern with the major political and international issues of the day and it was not unusual for them to direct their enquiries to the immediate background of the contemporary scene, to the point where the boundaries between disciplines, especially those between politics and history, tended to become blurred.[44] The work of

[41] 'The Structure of Southeast Asian History: Some Preliminary Observations', in JSEAH, 3 (1962), reprinted in *Continuity and Change in Southeast Asia: Collected Journal Articles of Harry J. Benda*, Yale University Southeast Asian Studies Monograph Series, No. 18, New Haven, 1972.

[42] 'The Sociological Approach', in Soedjatmoko, Mohammad Ali, G. J. Resink and G. McT. Kahin eds, *An Introduction to Indonesian Historiography*, Ithaca, 1965, 340ff.

[43] 'The Significance of the Comparative Approach in Southeast Asian Historiography', ibid., 380ff.

[44] For a discussion of these issues J. D. Legge, 'Southeast Asian History and the Social Sciences', in C. D. Cowan and O. W. Wolters, eds, *Southeast Asian History and Historiography: Essays Presented to D. G. E. Hall*, Ithaca and London, 1976.

George McT. Kahin, a political scientist with historical training, provided an example of a dominant style. Kahin carried out fieldwork in Indonesia in 1948 and 1949, formed close links with leading figures of the young republic, and was a first-hand observer of events as they unfolded during the closing months of the struggle for independence. This privileged position gave a sharpness and an immediacy to his study of the Revolution, but he added depth and analytical coherence by placing it in an historical context of Dutch rule, the rise of a nationalist movement and the impact of the Japanese Occupation.[45]

This became a familiar pattern. John F. Cady's *A History of Modern Burma* (Ithaca, 1958) devoted over half of its length to pre-war history. F. N. Trager's *Burma from Kingdom to Republic* (London, 1966) was subtitled 'a historical and political analysis', and dealt with British rule as the background to independence. The Cornell tradition of linking politics and history received further expression in a major textbook, *Government and Politics of Southeast Asia*, the seven authors of which wrote to a prescribed pattern in which a substantial historical chapter preceded an examination of the contemporary setting and the political processes of the individual countries of Southeast Asia.[46]

Given this style, it was sometimes difficult not only to distinguish historical writing from that of political scientists (such works, for example as J. H. Brimmell's examination of Southeast Asian communism or Ellen J. Hammer's account of the initial stages of the Indochina conflict),[47] but to distinguish either from the enormous body of works of serious reportage of, and comment on, the contemporary scene. One might mention, as distinguished examples of the latter, Bernard Fall's *Street Without Joy: Indochina at War, 1946–1954* (Harrisburg, 1961) or, from a decade later, Frances FitzGerald's *Fire in the Lake: The Vietnamese and the Americans in Vietnam* (Boston, 1972). Some of the writings on the borders of history, politics and the other social sciences were more concerned than others to develop, self-consciously, a conceptual analytical framework and this served to mark them off from narrative accounts. Herbert Feith, a political scientist, placed his political history of the first ten years of the Republic of Indonesia within a framework of contrasting leadership styles—solidarity-makers and administrators—and contrasting political cultures—Javanese aristocratic and Islamic entrepreneurial—as a means of explaining the instability of successive governments during the 1950s.[48] A specifically sociological approach was adopted by G. W. Skinner in his history of Chinese society in Thailand.[49] And other conceptual tools lay to hand: Fred Riggs' distinction between 'diffused', 'prismatic' and 'diffracted' societies;[50] Lucian Pye's exploration of personality traits in shaping leadership modes in transitional societies;[51] Karl Deutsch's attempt to define the

[45] *Nationalism and Revolution in Indonesia*, Ithaca, 1952.
[46] George McT. Kahin, ed., Ithaca, 1959.
[47] Brimmell, *Communism in South-East Asia*, London, 1959; Hammer, *The Struggle for Indochina, 1940–1955*, Stanford, 1955.
[48] *The Decline of Constitutional Democracy in Indonesia*, Ithaca, 1962.
[49] *Chinese Society in Thailand: an Analytical History*, Ithaca, 1957.
[50] *Administration and Developing Countries: The Theory of Prismatic Society*, Boston, 1964.
[51] *Politics, Personality and Nation Building: Burma's Search for Identity*, New Haven, 1962.

essential characteristics of nationalism;[52] John Kautsky's consideration of class formation;[53] and Clifford Geertz's notions of primordial loyalties, cultural 'streams' and agricultural involution.[54]

Not all historians were concerned with the contemporary scene and its immediate background, though most of those who directed their enquiries to earlier periods still tended to remain within the period of European contact with Southeast Asia. Walter Vella, A. L. Moffat and David Wyatt explored the successive reigns of Rama III, Mongkut and Chulalongkorn.[55] An historian, M. A. P. Meilink-Roelofsz, and an economic historian, Kristof Glamann, brought different tools to the study of trade in the Indonesian archipelago.[56] Wong Lin Ken surveyed the development of the Malayan tin industry and later R. E. Elson subjected the cultivation system in nineteenth-century Java to a new and close scrutiny.[57] Imperial history, in the sense of a focus on the motives and policies of the metropolitan powers, continued to be studied in the post-war period, especially the history of Britain in Malaya. Nicholas Tarling examined the circumstances surrounding the British interest in the Malay world in the late eighteenth and early nineteenth centuries.[58] Mary Turnbull traced the evolution of British policy in the Straits Settlements.[59] C. N. Parkinson and C. D. Cowan considered, from different angles, the reasons lying behind the British 'forward movement' in Malaya.[60] And a number of studies were devoted to the methods and character of British administration and to the economic history of the peninsula.[61]

Increasingly, historians writing of the nineteenth and early twentieth centuries were as ready to draw on the methods and conceptual schemes of neighbouring social sciences as were their colleagues who focused on more recent developments. Edgar Wickberg brought the skills of an

52 *Nationalism and Social Communication*, New York, 1953.

53 *Political Change in Underdeveloped Countries: Nationalism and Communism*, New York, 1963.

54 *The Religion of Java*, Glencoe, 1962; *Agricultural Involution*, Berkeley, 1963; *Peddlers and Princes: Social Change and Modernization in Two Indonesian Towns*, Chicago, 1963; and *The Social History of an Indonesian Town*, Cambridge, Mass., 1965.

55 e.g., Vella, *Siam Under Rama III*, New York, 1957; Moffat, *Mongkut, the King of Siam*, Ithaca, 1961; Wyatt, *The Politics of Reform in Thailand: Education in the Reign of King Chulalongkorn*, New Haven, 1969.

56 Meilink-Roelofsz, *Asian Trade and European Influence in the Indonesian Archipelago between 1500 and about 1630*, The Hague, 1962; Glamann, *Dutch–Asiatic Trade, 1620–1740*, Copenhagen and The Hague, 1958. C. R. Boxer's two volumes, *The Dutch Seaborne Empire, 1600–1800*, London, 1965, and *The Portuguese Seaborne Empire, 1415–1825*, London, 1969, though magisterial works of maritime history, were more conventional in approach and style.

57 Wong Lin Ken, *The Malayan Tin Industry to 1914*, Tucson, 1965; Elson, *Javanese Peasants and the Colonial Sugar Industry: Impact and Change in an East Java Residency, 1830–1940*, Singapore, 1984.

58 *British Policy in the Malay Peninsula and the Archipelago, 1824–1871*, Singapore, 1957; *Anglo-Dutch Rivalry in the Malay World, 1780–1824*, St Lucia, Qld, and Cambridge, UK, 1962; and *Piracy and Politics in the Malay World*, Melbourne and Singapore, 1963.

59 *The Straits Settlements, 1826–67: Indian Presidency to Crown Colony*, London, 1972.

60 Parkinson, *British Intervention in Malaya, 1867–77*, Singapore, 1960; Cowan, *Nineteenth-Century Malaya: The Origins of British Political Control*, London, 1961.

61 E. Sadka, *The Protected Malay States, 1874–1895*, Kuala Lumpur, 1968; Eunice Thio, *British Policy in the Malay Peninsula, 1880–1910*, Singapore, 1969; Khoo Kay Kim, *The Western Malay States, 1850–1873*, Kuala Lumpur, 1972; G. C. Allen and Audrey Donnithorne, *Western Enterprise in Indonesia and Malaya*, London, 1957; J. Norman Parmer, *Colonial Labor Policy and Administration: A History of Labor in the Rubber Plantation Industry in Malaya*, New York, 1960.

economic and social historian to his study of the Chinese community in the Philippines in the last fifty years of Spanish rule, observing its internal structure and consciousness and its relations with the surrounding society in a period of rapid economic and social change.[62] Daniel Doeppers' study of Manila between 1900 and the outbreak of World War II—a study in social mobility—focused on the city as 'a set of employment structures and as a stratified society', and buttressed its findings by close statistical analysis.[63] The Indonesian historian, Sartono Kartodirdjo, endeavoured to construct a taxonomy to distinguish between various categories of peasant unrest in Java.[64] In an exercise in economic geography, Michael Adas sought to provide a new framework of analysis of British rule in Burma by focusing on the 'Burma Delta'. This enabled him to develop Furnivall's notion of a plural society and, by using a demographic approach based on information drawn from the settlement reports of the Revenue Department, to integrate the role of the peasantry with that of traditional rulers, British administrators and a nationalist élite from the mid-nineteenth century.[65] Many other examples could be cited. The contributors to the book edited by A. W. McCoy and E. de Jesus, *Philippines Social History: Global Trade and Local Transformations* (Quezon City and Sydney, 1982), took as their starting point the intensive work done on Philippines regional history over the previous two decades, and brought the techniques of economic history and sociology to their assessment of late colonial Philippines society. In Thailand, Jit Poumisak offered a class interpretation of what he saw as Thai feudalism.[66] And following the students' uprising of 1973 a new emphasis could be seen in Thai historical studies, an emphasis on socio-economic history led by such scholars as Chattip Nartsupha, Chai-anan Samudavanija and Nidhi Aeusrivongse, and directed, in different ways, to the study of the structure of pre-capitalist society and culture.[67]

The post-war concentration on the nineteenth and twentieth centuries, taking place as it did within the context of a greatly expanded Asian studies 'industry', tended to overshadow the study of earlier periods, but did not entirely eclipse it. Early history continued to command the attention of distinguished scholars. Wang Gungwu's examination of early Chinese trading patterns in Southeast Asia, O. W. Wolters' study of early Indonesian commerce and of political rhythms in the Malay world in the fourteenth and fifteenth centuries, the epigraphic work of J. G. de Casparis, and Paul Wheatley's construction of the historical geography of the Malay peninsula before 1500, may be given as examples.[68] More

[62] *The Chinese in Philippine Life, 1850–1898*, New Haven and London, 1965.

[63] *Manila, 1900–1914: Social Change in a Late Colonial Metropolis*, New Haven, 1984.

[64] *Protest Movements in Rural Java*, Singapore, 1973.

[65] *The Burma Delta: Economic Development and Social Change on an Asian Rice Frontier, 1852–1941*, Madison, 1974.

[66] *The Real Face of Thai Feudalism Today*, 1957, trans. Craig J. Reynolds in *Thai Radical Discourse: The Real Face of Thai Feudalism Today*, Ithaca, 1987.

[67] Craig J. Reynolds, 'Marxism in Thai Historical Studies', JAS, 43, 1 (1983).

[68] Wang Gungwu, 'The Nanhai Trade: A Study of the Early History of Chinese Trade in the South China Sea', JMBRAS, 31 (1958); Wolters, *Early Indonesian Commerce: A Study in the Origins of Srivijaya*, Ithaca, 1967, and *The Fall of Srivijaya in Malay History*, London, 1970; de Casparis, *Prasasti Indonesia*; Wheatley, *The Golden Khersonese*, Kuala Lumpur, 1961.

recently, the early history of the region has attracted a growing number of younger scholars, such as Michael Aung-Thwin (Pagan), Pierre-Yves Manguin (Śrīvijaya), Nidhi Aeusrivongse (Angkor), and K. W. Taylor and J. K. Whitmore (ninth- and tenth-century Vietnam).[69] Many of the recent advances made in the study of early history have been, in effect, archaeological in character.[70] Archaeological enquiry using modern techniques has also begun to transform views about the prehistory of the region. The archaeological services of the individual republics of Southeast Asia have played an increasingly significant part in these enquiries and have contributed to a rethinking of the conclusions of pre-war studies and to a clearer perception of cultural development taking place over some thousands of years and predating influences from outside the region.[71]

## MAJOR THEMES IN POST-WAR STUDIES

Against the background of these general remarks about the methods of approach and the focus of historical writing after World War II, some of the main themes that attracted the attention of historians may be indicated.

One of the most important of these took up the thread of the pre-war debates about the nature and significance of external influences, Indian, Islamic and European, on Southeast Asian societies. The publication, in 1955, of the English translation of van Leur's doctoral thesis and other writings under the general title, *Indonesian Trade and Society: Essays in Asian Social and Economic History* (The Hague and Bandung, 1955), captured the attention of historians. It revived the earlier debate but carried it in a somewhat different direction. Whereas the pre-war argument had focused largely on the processes of 'Indianization' and the extent to which it shaped, or was shaped by, local cultures, the new debate was conducted to a considerable degree at a more general and conceptual level. It was concerned with the notion of the 'autonomy' of Southeast Asian history.

The Indianization question as such was not, of course, ignored. A

69 See articles by Michael Aung-Thwin, Nidhi Aeusrivongse, K. W. Taylor and J. K. Whitmore in Whitmore and K. R. Hall, eds, *Explorations in Early Southeast Asian History: The Origins of Southeast Asian Statecraft*, Ann Arbor, 1976; Pierre-Yves Manguin, 'Études Sumatranaises: I. Palembang et Sriwijaya: anciennes hypothèses, recherches nouvelles', BEFEO, 76 (1987); K. W. Taylor, *The Birth of Vietnam*, Berkeley, 1983; and articles by a number of scholars in David Marr and A. C. Milner, eds, *Southeast Asia in the 9th to 14th Centuries*, Singapore and Canberra, 1986.

70 See, e.g. Alastair Lamb, 'Takuapa: The Probable Site of a Pre-Malaccan Entrepôt in the Malay Peninsula' in J. Bastin and R. Roolvink eds, *Malayan and Indonesian Studies: Essays Presented to Sir Richard Winstedt*, Oxford, 1964; E. Edwards McKinnon, 'Kota Cina: Its Context and Meaning in the Trade of Southeast Asia in the Twelfth to Fourteenth Centuries', Ph.D. thesis, Cornell University, 1984, and McKinnon and A. C. Milner, 'A Letter from Sumatra: A visit to some early Sumatran historical sites', *Indonesia Circle*, 18 (1978); C. C. Macknight, *The Voyage to Marege*, Melbourne, 1976; J. N. Miksic, 'From Seri Vijaya to Melaka: Batu Tagak in Historical and Cultural Context', JMBRAS, 60, 2 (1987).

71 For an account of post-war archaeological findings see R. B. Smith and W. Watson eds, *Early South East Asia: Essays in Archeology, History and Historical Geography*, London and New York, 1979. See also Peter Bellwood, *Man's Conquest of the Pacific: The Prehistory of Southeast Asia and Oceania*, New York, 1979, and *Prehistory of the Indo-Malaysian Archipelago*, Sydney, 1985.

number of new contributions were made, notably by H. G. Quaritch Wales, Alastair Lamb, O. W. Wolters, I. W. Mabbett and others. Wolters, in his seminal work *Early Indonesian Commerce*, threw light on the nature of trade in the archipelago before the seventh century CE. He took as his point of departure Cœdès' rediscovery of Śrīvijaya.[72] Exactly where Śrīvijaya was based and what sort of a kingdom it was remained obscure, but Wolters attempted, through his notion of the 'favoured coast' of Sumatra, to show why the emergence of a maritime power in south Sumatra in the seventh century made sense. Though he was concerned only obliquely with the process of Indianization, it was an important part of his argument that 'the expansion of trade at that time was an indigenous and not an Indian achievement'.[73]

Wolters confronted the Indianization question more directly in a consideration of the processes by which Hindu influences were received in Cambodia. In an article of 1979 he substituted the notion of 'prowess' for that of descent and dynasty as a means of understanding political authority in seventh-century Cambodia, and proceeded to argue that prowess was able to make use of Hindu notions of authority. In this and other ways the Khmers were able to construe Hinduism in terms familiar to them within their own culture and to 'empathize' with it on the basis of an experience that was 'as much Khmer as "Hindu"'.[74] Elsewhere he introduced the idea of 'localization' to characterize the way in which external influences might be absorbed into the local scene and restated in a local idiom to the point where a local–external antithesis becomes irrelevant.[75]

The arguments about Indianization and the nature of the relevant evidence were brought together and surveyed convincingly by Mabbett, who argued that different categories had been confused by earlier participants in the argument.[76] Mabbett's contribution was to clarify the issues by sorting out the separate and distinct questions which are involved. These questions relate to the evolving patterns of Southeast Asian agriculture; the date at which wet-rice cultivation might have begun; the kind of political order which might have preceded the emergence of centralized kingdoms like Angkor; and the kind of interaction which might have developed between local custom and Sanskrit lore, not only in Southeast Asia but in India itself. Pointing out that the evidence was inconclusive, Mabbett proposed a distinction between arguments about the process by which Indian influence spread and those about the extent to which it could be said to have dominated local cultures, and he then proceeded to dissolve both types. After surveying the evidence presented by a wide range of scholars,[77] he pointed out that in fact no evidence exists about

72 Cœdès, 'Le Royaume de Çrivijaya'.

73 *Early Indonesian Commerce*, 247. Further discussion of the location of Śrīvijaya can be found in Bennet Bronson, 'The Archaeology of Sumatra and the Problem of Srivijaya', in Smith and Watson, eds, *Early Southeast Asia*, 406–26, and in Manguin, Études Sumatranaises'.

74 'Khmer "Hinduism" in the Seventh Century', Smith and Watson, 427.

75 *History, Culture and Region in Southeast Asian Perspectives*, Singapore, 1984.

76 'The "Indianization" of Southeast Asia': I. Reflections on the Prehistoric Sources; II. Reflections on the Historical Sources, JSEAH, 8, 1 and 2 (1977).

77 Amongst others, H. G. Quaritch Wales, H. A. Lamb, Paul Wheatley, W. G. Solheim II, R. D. Hill, L. Malleret, K. A. N. Sastri, K. C. Chang, B. Bronson.

process. All we have is evidence in Chinese, epigraphic and archaeological sources, of Southeast Asian polities already showing signs of Indian influence. And with regard to the second type of question he concluded that to oppose Indian imperialism and local autonomy is to present a false dichotomy, given the complexity of local patterns; the fact that in any case there was not a single, homogeneous 'India'; and that, in India itself, 'Sanskritization' was uneven and patchy.

While the search for evidence of process and character, and the analysis and discussion of that evidence, continued, the main interest of modern historians was captured by other aspects of van Leur's writings.

There were two features of his overall argument which were of particular interest in the late 1950s and early 1960s. First of all was the method by which he argued his case. The greater part of the pre-war discussion was concerned with the interpretation of particular items of evidence of an Indian presence, or the lack of items of evidence of conquest and settlement and, as we have seen, those who saw Indianization as a positive shaping process regarded India-based commerce as an important element in the transmission of that influence. Van Leur, by contrast, developed his conclusions not by examining existing evidence in detail, or by presenting new evidence, but on the basis of definitions of different types of trade. His thesis, indeed, was essentially a methodological discussion. At the centre of his argument was a definition of capitalism, not in terms of accumulation, investment and profit, but, more narrowly, as 'modern capitalism'—in terms of mass production based on a free market, a financial system involving stock market exchange, and a free market for sales—none of which, of course, applied to early Asian commercial activity.[78] Asian trade, he pointed out, was based on handicraft industry and was financed not by a capitalist class but by rulers or aristocrats, investing in individual voyages. From this conceptual framework followed the further concept: that of a peddling trade. Though trade was carried out over vast distances its actual conduct was in the hands of small traders—pedlars—who carried the goods, exchanged them, and formed foreign enclaves in the port cities of Southeast Asia.

The final conclusion formed part of the same conceptual rearrangement. It was a logical step to his view that commerce could not have been central to the transmission of high cultural forms; that the influence was therefore likely to have been the result of borrowings of those features of Indian culture which were of use in the emerging kingdoms of the region; and that India was therefore not imposing itself on indigenous cultures.[79] Southeast Asia becomes, not a passive recipient of external influences, but the active agent in the process. The conceptual device reversed, at one stroke, the framework within which the question was discussed.

The second feature of the post-war debate followed closely from this method of analysis. By changing sharply the terms of the debate, van Leur directed attention away from details of evidence and towards the more general notion of autonomy. If Indian influence were to be seen as

[78] *Indonesian Trade and Society*, 17.
[79] ibid., 103.

borrowed or absorbed, it allowed continuing independence and authority to local cultures which might otherwise be seen as subject to, or conquered by, external pressures.

If this argument could be applied to Indian influence and to the coming of Islam, might it not also be applied to the period of European penetration into the region? This question, which was especially the subject of discussion for a decade after 1955, had obvious value implications. A view of Southeast Asia as continuously 'in charge' of its own history appealed alike to nations concerned with the consolidation of their newly acquired independence and to outside observers who wished to think in terms of the autonomy of the region as an object of study.

Van Leur himself argued that European influence had indeed been overemphasized by earlier historians. He did so by using much the same conceptual tools as had supported his discussion of indigenous and selective borrowings of Indian culture. The Dutch East India Company in the seventeenth and eighteenth centuries was not unlike a merchant prince financing successive voyages, and its employees in the Indies were performing functions similar to those of the pedlars. To that extent it fitted the existing patterns of trade of the archipelago. Even as its power expanded and it was able to impose its own monopoly over the area, and acquired territorial footholds, it was still far short of being a sovereign ruler. Its relations with indigenous authorities, van Leur argued, were more like international relations than relations between ruler and subjects, a point later developed in detail by G. J. Resink.[80] At the very most it might be regarded as a paramount power, stronger than other individual polities but not entirely different from them in kind.

While van Leur's criticism of historians who looked at Southeast Asia through European eyes was readily accepted, and the idea of an Asia-centric history became a goal to be achieved by a sensitive approach to local cultures, his argument that the coming of the European made almost no difference, at least until the late eighteenth century, would seem an overstatement. The Dutch East India Company, to take the example that van Leur focused on, was an organization very different in size, in the scope of its operations and in power, from the pedlars whom he saw as the bearers of trade in the past. It was able to enforce its control over trade and, in due course, to acquire territorial influence as well. There is certainly much point in identifying those features of its activity which can be seen in terms of the earlier trade and in stressing elements of continuity with the pre-European period. But there is also point in drawing attention to elements of change and discontinuity. C. R. Boxer examined closely the impact of the Portuguese commercial system, and M. A. P. Meilink-Roelofsz saw considerable changes following from the intrusion of Portuguese and Dutch into the trade of the region. Even van Leur himself conceded that, by the end of the eighteenth century and the beginning of the nineteenth, the sheer power of the European intruders into Southeast

[80] 'Inlandsche Staten in den Oosterschen Archipel, 1873–1915', BKI, 116 (1960), translated as 'Native States of the Eastern Archipelago, 1873–1915', in Resink, *Indonesian History between the Myths*, The Hague, 1958.

Asia was such as to create a watershed in Southeast Asian history. And, since much of the work of modern historians has been directed to the study of the nineteenth and twentieth centuries, the period of greatest Western impact, it has been difficult for historians, either from within the region or outside it, to avoid interpretations couched in terms of European challenge and Southeast Asian response.

Difficult, but perhaps not impossible. The issues of perspective and autonomy became, for a time, a major focus for discussion. In 1961 John Smail, in an influential article, indicated a variety of meanings which the idea of Eurocentrism could have.[81] It could refer to the angle of the historian's vision: was the history of the region to be seen from the point of view of the outside observer or of the indigenous people? Or it could reflect the preferences and values of the historians: whose side were they on, as it were, in their account of events? Third, it could refer to a judgment of historical significance: what were the decisive factors in shaping the course of history? The three meanings, of course, often went together. If the angle of vision was that of the European intruder (and there was always a danger of this, given that the historian's sources were often those created by the intruder), it was perhaps likely that the value judgments would support the role played by the European and that the European would be placed in the foreground of the analysis as the shaper of events. Smail argued that the thought-world of modern scientific inquiry—both in the natural sciences and the humanities—was now a universal thought-world, and all serious historians, whether Western or Eastern, worked within it. In these circumstances his own concern was with the moral viewpoints and the perspectives of historians. By perspectives he seems to have meant judgments about causal significance. He noted that a new generation of nationalist historians had, in effect, reversed the moral position of the old colonial historians, 'exchanging one systematic bias for another', while preserving a perspective which tended to see the European still as the effective agent of change. By contrast Smail's aim was to achieve a morally neutral viewpoint and an Asiacentric perspective, an aim which might be achieved, he believed, by adopting a sociological method. If one focused on fundamental cultural patterns, the actions of the colonial ruler were likely to appear, if not superficial and transitory, at least less important. Local cultures were resilient, resistant to change, and readily able to absorb stimuli from outside. And even when the European intrusion had seemed most obviously to have promoted change—in stimulating the emergence of new élites or of urban working classes, for example—that could still be seen as part of a local evolution. His conclusion was that the antithesis between Eurocentric and Asiacentric was a false one. The goal should be, not the writing of an Asiacentric history, but the writing of an 'autonomous' history.

A retrospective look at this discussion makes it seem clearer that the question of perspective is very much a function of the issues that interest the historian and of the ways in which central questions are posed. The

81 'On the Possibility of an Autonomous History of Modern Southeast Asia', JSEAH, 2, 2 (1961).

motives and policies of metropolitan powers are a legitimate subject of enquiry and impose a different framework from that appropriate for studies of what happened in Southeast Asia during the period of European expansion. The debate, however, undoubtedly affected the way in which historians framed their questions. Even studies which continued to concentrate on the colonial period no longer saw it almost as a part of European history as their predecessors had tended to do. On the contrary, they reflected a deliberate attempt to achieve a shift of perspective. Milton Osborne, for example, attempted to see both sides of the colonial equation in dealing with French rule in Indochina.[82] So did David Marr, whose *Vietnamese Anticolonialism 1885–1925* (Berkeley, 1971) placed evolving Vietnamese political thought firmly in a local setting. Both drew on *quoc-ngu* (Vietnamese) as well as French sources. And in dealing with Thailand, the one country that avoided the fate of colonial rule, David Wyatt portrayed Chulalongkorn's educational reforms, not in terms of the initiative of a Westernized absolute monarch, but as a response to the West 'which flowed painfully but naturally out of Thai history, society and culture'.[83]

The coming of Islam to Southeast Asia, and its impact on the societies of the region, formed a further major theme of historians in the post-war period, though the discussion was conducted in different terms from those of the debate about Indianization and the autonomy of Southeast Asian history. Van Leur, of course, had extended his analysis of the nature of Indian influence, and the comparative superficiality of its impact, to cover the penetration of Islam, but he had done so more or less in passing and as a consequence of the methodological position he had adopted. The coming of Islam did not, in his eyes, constitute a new phase or period of Southeast Asian history. He argued that Muslim trade introduced no significant change in economic forms; and culturally he saw Islam as being received and absorbed, not imposed on those who were converted. In general, however, the arguments by which he supported these conclusions were less developed than those relating to Indianization; it was rather a matter of bringing it within his general conceptual framework than of presenting new evidence or revising the old.

There was no major challenge to that general picture in the 1950s and 1960s. Broadly, historians of Islam in Southeast Asia addressed themselves to three types of enquiry: to the diffusion points from which Islam reached the peninsula and archipelago; to the nature of its initial impact; and to the evolution of Islamic thought and organization in that environment.

The issues in the debate about the method of Muslim penetration were threefold: whether it was carried by traders from Gujerat in the thirteenth and fourteenth centuries; or whether an earlier source was to be found in South India; or whether Bengal was the principal point of origin. Amongst the participants in the discussion were G. E. Marrison and G. W. J. Drewes, who inclined to the view that Southeast Asian Islam

82 *The French Presence in Cochin China and Cambodia: Rule and Response, 1859–1905*, Ithaca, 1969.
83 *The Politics of Reform in Thailand*, vii.

came from the Coromandel coast of India.[84] By contrast, S. Q. Fatimi argued for Bengal as the diffusion point though he allowed that, at different times, different diffusion points might have played a part.[85]

Side by side with the question of origins went the second type of discussion: that concerned with the particular character of the Islam which established itself in Southeast Asia and the way in which it adapted to, or transformed, the local scene. Did it stimulate extensive social changes or was it, as van Leur asserted, adapted, domesticated and assimilated? There were obvious elements of change, both in belief and social order, with the coming of Islam. The almost universal observance of Islamic ritual in the societies converted, attendance at the mosque, the call to prayer, the fast, the pilgrimage, all appear to testify to a universal conversion. But it was an uneven conversion. The religion had a stronger foothold in those parts of the archipelago most directly involved in international trade—Aceh, the west coast of Sumatra, Melaka, the north coast of Java, Makassar—but the penetration of Islam in the inland agrarian society of Java, with its hierarchical tradition and its ability to blend Islam with older customary beliefs, was apparently less profound. This would seem to point to differences in Islam's transforming role. There were clearly incipient tensions between the new religion and an earlier tradition, which varied from place to place, and which became acute in certain areas from time to time.

Historians have stressed both continuity and change. A. H. Johns emphasized the role of members of Sufi orders in bringing to Southeast Asia a mystically tinged Islam. Sufi readiness to accept and use elements of non-Islamic culture was precisely what was important in making Islam acceptable in the Southeast Asian environment.[86]

However, while emphasizing the acceptability of Sufism, Johns was perhaps more concerned with the network of links connecting the city states of Southeast Asia with the centres of Islamic learning in Cairo, Medina and Mecca, and with diverse schools and a variety of influential teachers, than with the impact of the new religion on the society that received it. He noted the absence of a 'central, stable core of Islamic civilization and learning' within the region,[87] and drew attention to the theological and intellectual traditions of a wider Muslim world on which the Muslim leaders of Melaka, Aceh and other port cities were able to draw. He emphasized that it was 'not a single tradition, but a complex web'.[88] Within that diversity Sufism provided the main current until the rise of the Wahhabi movement in the eighteenth century stimulated a fundamentalist attempt to cut through 'the accretions and innovations' of the intervening centuries and return to what was seen as the original faith.

If Johns was concerned with the doctrinal world of the *ulamā* (learned

[84] Drewes, 'New Light on the Coming of Islam to Indonesia?' BKI, 124 (1968), 433ff. Marrison, 'The Coming of Islam to the East Indies', JMBRAS, 24 (1951).

[85] *Islam Comes to Malaysia*, Singapore, 1963, 53.

[86] 'Sufism as a Category in Indonesian Literature and History', JSEAH, 2, 2 (1961).

[87] 'Islam in Southeast Asia: Reflections and New Directions', *Indonesia*, 19 (1975) 33.

[88] ibid, 42. See also Johns, 'Islam in Southeast Asia: Problems of Perspective', in Cowan and Wolters, eds, *Southeast Asian History and Historiography*.

men), other writers have focused more on the processes by which Islam was accommodated. Soemarsaid Moertono explored the resilience and persistence of Hindu-Javanese forms and ideas even after the conversion of the inland Javanese kingdom of Mataram.[89] Amongst the populace Islam provided a base for resistance to oppression, but at the court level old Javanese elements continued. A. C. Milner, who also focused on kingship, stressed the way in which local rulers adopted Islamic ideas selectively, adopting those aspects with which they could 'empathize'—the Persian tradition of kingship, or the mystical idea of the 'perfect man'—and thus fitting them into the local scene, rather than transforming it.[90] This kind of compromise became more difficult to maintain with changes in the character of Islam and the growth of '*sharī'a*-mindedness' in the nineteenth century.

The third type of enquiry—that concerned with the later evolution of Muslim thought and action—was prompted in part by the general concern of post-war students of Southeast Asia with the contemporary scene. Students of politics, sociology and economic development were drawn, amongst other interests, to examine, in particular, the current strength and the social and political role of Islam in Indonesia and Malaysia, where tensions between Muslims and non-Muslims, among different types of Muslim, and between Muslims and the state are a central part of today's political conflicts. While in Malaysia the state itself has sought an Islamization of society, in Indonesia Islam has provided a basis for opposition to the Suharto regime. But to distinguish between those two situations in such simple terms is to obscure the complexity, in both situations, of differences within the Islamic community. In West Malaysia there are shifting intra-élite rivalries within the Malay community, where at one time an aristocratic élite, centred round the courts of Malay rulers, was in incipient conflict with *ulamā* leaders, and at another time a Western-educated élite, nominally Muslim, nevertheless did not share the desire of religious leaders for a *sharī'a*-based political order. In Indonesia the picture is complicated by regional differences. Orthodox Islam (though what is orthodox might be a matter of dispute) has established itself more strongly in Sumatra, south Sulawesi and west Java than in central and east Java, and even in those regions there is some tension between strict observance and the pull of custom. In central and east Java a division exists between what might be called 'nominal' Muslims (*abangan*), whose religion has developed on the basis of a syncretist accommodation with earlier beliefs, and the *santri* community whose members profess a stricter adherence to orthodoxy. Differences of this kind have had an impact on political alignments and conflict. Whether the issues at stake are religious and theological, or whether economic and social conflicts have taken on a religious garb, may be a matter of debate, but either way the religious dimension remains a fact of modern politics.

Historians have played their part in this type of enquiry by focusing on nineteenth- and twentieth-century developments in Muslim thought and

89 *State and Statecraft in Old Java: A Study of the Later Mataram Period, 16th to 19th century*, Ithaca, 1968.

90 'Islam and the Muslim State', in M. B. Hooker ed., *Islam in Southeast Asia*, Leiden, 1983.

action, concerning themselves with classical issues of Islamic debate and with conflicts between competing orthodoxies. The nineteenth century saw the development of fundamentalist doctrines stemming from the wider Muslim world, and challenging existing practice in one way or another. The Wahhābi movement, for example, originating in Arabia, attacked the compromises that Islam had made with custom and called for a return to the original simplicity and austerity of the faith. Towards the end of the century the Modernist movement, with its centre in Cairo, presented a challenge of a somewhat different kind. It, too, was concerned to strip the faith of the scholastic accretions which, it believed, had come to obscure the teachings of the prophet, but it also sought an accommodation between Islam and the forces of the modern world, believing that a purified—and rational—faith could be reconciled with science and contemporary thought.

Historians have tackled the question from a variety of angles. Christine Dobbin and Taufik Abdullah have considered the special circumstances of Minangkabau. Dobbin focused on revivalism in the eighteenth and early nineteenth centuries which culminated in the Padri movement.[91] Taufik Abdullah's concern was the relation of religion and custom in the early twentieth century. Minangkabau custom, in his argument, embodied the idea of interaction with peoples, ideas and mores outside the Minangkabau heartland. Custom thus contained within itself the idea of its own transformation. Against that background he examined the conflict—in part generational, in part theological, and in part ideological—between reforming and conservative forces within the Islamic community.[92] Deliar Noer charted the growth of the Modernist movement in the twentieth century, the formation of the reformist organization, Muhammadiyah, in 1912, and the development of a political role for Islam in the closing decades of Dutch rule.[93] Though he did explore questions of doctrine—for example, the right of individual interpretation, and the role of reason—his particular focus was on the consequences of religious teaching for the exercise of political authority. A political role for Islam would, indeed, seem inevitable, given its absolute claims, summed up in Noer's view that Islam is 'both a religious and a civil and political society' (p. 1). Muslims are nevertheless likely to differ about how such claims should be implemented. W. R. Roff's study of the origins of Malay nationalism was concerned with the Islamic dimension of the emerging élites he was able to identify.[94] For Indonesia, B. J. Boland examined the way in which the relations of religion and the state took political form in the history of the independent republic.[95] A special case was that of the Muslim community in the Philippines whose role was surveyed by C. A. Majul.[96]

[91] *Islamic Revivalism in a Changing Peasant Economy: Central Sumatra, 1784–1847*, London and Malmö, 1983.

[92] 'Modernization in the Minangkabau World: West Sumatra in the Early Decades of the Twentieth Century', in Claire Holt, B. R. O'G. Anderson and James Siegel, eds, *Culture and Politics in Indonesia*, Ithaca, 1972.

[93] *The Modernist Muslim Movement, 1900–1942*, Singapore and Kuala Lumpur, 1973.

[94] *The Origins of Malay Nationalism*, New York and London, 1967.

[95] *The Struggle of Islam in Modern Indonesia*, The Hague, 1971.

[96] *Muslims in the Philippines*, Quezon City, 1973.

While some scholars have focused on the political role of Muslims, others have directed their enquiry towards their economic activities. Clifford Geertz threw out the suggestion that the austerity of Islam, and its insistence on the equality of believers, made it an appropriate faith for an embryo bourgeoisie, and hinted at a comparison between the role of Islam in Southeast Asia and that ascribed by Weber to Protestantism in Europe—the role of sacralizing commercial behaviour and thus assisting the development of a commercial class.[97] This suggestion was taken up by at least one historian, Lance Castles, whose study[98] of the cigarette industry in Kudus, on the north coast of central Java, attempted to test the Geertz hypothesis. James Siegel's study of Acehnese traders discussed the Islamic notion of reason (*akal*) as possibly contributing to the individualism of a commercial class.[99]

On the whole it can be said that the main thrust of historical enquiry into Islam in Southeast Asia was directed to what could be described as the political and economic behaviour of Muslims in the present and more or less recent past, rather than to matters of doctrine and belief. And such a focus was, of course, in line with the general preoccupations of post-war scholarship.

Another subject of increasing interest to historians was the character of traditional authority and social order—of ruler and realm, state and statecraft, to borrow the titles of two significant contributions[1]—and of the ideas which appeared to support that authority.

As described by Robert Heine-Geldern in an influential article of 1942,[2] the classical states of Southeast Asia were in theory highly centralized, and embodied ideas, derived from Indian influence, of a divine kingship and of parallelism between the universe and the terrestrial order. The capital of the ruler was the magical centre of the realm, and at its centre, in turn, a temple or the royal palace, whose towers and terraces and orientation were designed in accordance with an elaborate symbolism, represented Mt Meru, the abode of the gods. As the kingdom was a microcosm of the universe so the king in his capital, a descendant of a god or an incarnation of a god—Śiva or Viṣṇu, Indra or Brahmā—maintained the harmony of the kingdom, matching the harmony of the universe. The political reality was, of course, very different from the doctrine of the exemplary centre and it was, no doubt, precisely because of the facts of balance and division that the theory was so firmly centralist in character. T. Pigeaud, writing of Java, emphasized the precarious nature of royal power and saw the

97 *The Development of the Javanese Economy*, Boston, 1956, 91.

98 *Religion, Politics and Economic Behaviour in Java: The Kudus Cigarette Industry*, New Haven, 1967.

99 *The Rope of God*, Berkeley and Los Angeles, 1969.

1 B. J. O. Schrieke, *Ruler and Realm in Early Java*, The Hague, 1957, being a collection of papers on which Schrieke was working at the time of his death in 1942; and Moertono, *State and Statecraft*.

2 'Conceptions of State and Kingship in Southeast Asia', *Far Eastern Quarterly*, 2, 1 (November 1942).

'perennial division and reunion of the realm' as an inherent part of the system.[3]

In the 1960s and early 1970s the interest in traditional political order and political theory sprang in part from the focus on recent and contemporary history. The political behaviour of the so-called 'new states' could be illuminated, perhaps, by the exploration of older forms and perceptions. That was essentially the thrust of B. R. O'G. Anderson's essay on 'The Idea of Power in Javanese Culture'.[4] Though probing traditional Javanese culture, and seeking to establish that that culture included a coherent political theory, its main concern was with the way in which these conclusions might sustain a better understanding of contemporary Indonesian politics, illuminating, for example, Sukarno's leadership style, the tension between centre and periphery, or the role of ideology in political action. Clifford Geertz's notion of the 'theatre, State', proposed in his *Islam Observed* (New Haven, 1968) and developed in his later study of the nature of the nineteenth-century Balinese principality,[5] served a similar function. Other studies, perhaps more strictly historical in character, have been concerned either to explore traditional concepts of authority for their own sake or to examine particular polities in particular periods.

As an example of the former approach, I. W. Mabbett re-examined conclusions about the nature of Khmer kingship by d'Aymonier, Finot, Cœdès and others, and asked whether the notion of divine kingship represented a literal or a metaphorical claim. He demonstrated the ambiguity of epigraphical references to the 'Devarāja', and of the expressions of that concept in ritual and in architectural forms.[6] He concluded that the symbolism of the Devarāja cult was a kind of language in which statements about the moral and political order were expressed. In similar vein, Hermann Kulke argued that the *devarāja* cult related to the worship of Śiva as king of the gods rather than to the worship of a god king, though kings may have been 'participants' in divine rule.[7]

In the second category are works such as M. C. Ricklefs' study of the reign of Sultan Mangkubumi in Yogyakarta, an account of the division of the realm and a consideration of Javanese ideas about the nature of the realm—and about its indivisibility.[8] In Ricklefs' account, the centralist nature of Javanese political theory masked, or was perhaps a response to, a reality in which power was in fact divided. Moertono's work was also directed to a particular period of Javanese history, the later Mataram period from the sixteenth to the nineteenth century. More sociological in approach and method was Akin Rabibhadana's examination of Thai social

[3] *Java in the Fourteenth Century: A Study in Cultural History: The Nagara-Kertagama by Rakawi Prapañca of Majapahit, 1365 AD*, The Hague, 1960, IV. 122.

[4] In Holt et al., eds, *Culture and Politics in Indonesia*.

[5] *Negara: The Theatre State in Nineteenth-Century Bali*, Princeton, 1980.

[6] 'Devarāja', in JSEAH, 10, 2 (1969).

[7] *The Devarāja Cult*, 1974, translated from the German, Ithaca, 1978. For further exploration of the question see J. Filliozat, 'Sur le Çivaisme et le Bouddhisme du Cambodge', BEFEO, 70 (1980), and Claude Jacques, 'The Kamraten Jagad in Ancient Cambodia', in Norobu Karashima, ed., *Indus Valley to Mekong Delta: Explorations in Epigraphy*, Madras, 1985.

[8] *Jogjakarta Under Sultan Mangkubumi, 1749–1792*, London, 1974.

order and its stratification according to formal and informal patron–client relations.[9] Victor Lieberman's account of dynastic cycles in Burma between the sixteenth and eighteenth centuries sought the explanation of the phenomenon of division and reunification in the administrative structure of the kingdom. Though sticking closely to his chosen case, Lieberman threw out the suggestion that there was a basic coherence in administrative processes throughout agrarian Southeast Asia and he concluded his work with a comparision of the Burmese case with those of Siam and Mataram.[10]

Part of the same general concern with social order and authority was the interest in peasant society and its occasional disturbances, uprisings and movements of resistance. These have sometimes been seen as early manifestations of nationalist revolt, but increasingly scholars have focused on the millenarian character of such movements and on the way they combined protest at specific grievances with elements of traditional belief and practice. For example the Javanese idea of a Just Ruler (*Ratu Adil*) who could restore harmony and prosperity to a disturbed society was a common element in the movements described by Sartono Kartodirdjo in his attempt to classify different types of peasant protest in Java. Sartono drew attention to the syncretistic nature of the ideologies to be found in his case studies where anti-extortion protests were apt to take on a messianic flavour, mixed with nativistic longings for a return to a pristine culture and with Holy War ideas.[11] Others have explored similar themes in other cases. Yoneo Ishii and Chattip Nartsupha have described the leadership of 'men of merit' and 'Holy Men' in revolts in Thailand.[12] David Chandler has observed a similar phenomenon in Cambodia,[13] and Reynaldo Ileto has shown how Catholic ideas were appropriated and incorporated into local ideology in the Philippines.[14] Michael Adas has attempted a bold comparative study, taking five different cases of millenarian revolts in Africa, India, Southeast Asia and Oceania. In the general setting of accelerated social change and dislocation under colonial rule, he emphasized the special role of prophetic leadership in shaping these revolts.[15]

These themes have been explored through a number of specific case studies, as in Sartono's study of the Banten Revolt in 1888;[16] and in the

[9] *The Organization of Thai Society in the Early Bangkok Period, 1782–1873*, Ithaca, 1969, and 'Clientship and Class Structure in the Early Bangkok Period', in G. William Skinner and A. Thomas Kirsch, eds, *Change and Persistence in Thai Society: Essays in Honor of Lauriston Sharp*, Ithaca, 1975.

[10] *Burmese Administrative Cycles*, 6 and 271ff.

[11] *Protest Movements*, Ch. 1. See also his 'Agrarian Radicalism in Java', in Holt et al., eds, *Culture and Politics in Indonesia*.

[12] Yoneo Ishii, 'A Note on Buddhistic Millenarian Revolts in North-eastern Siam', JSEAH, 6, 2 (1975), and Nartsupha, 'The Ideology of Holy Men Revolts in North East Thailand', in Andrew Turton and Shigeharu Tanabe, eds, *History and Peasant Consciousness in South East Asia*, Osaka, 1984.

[13] 'An Anti-Vietnamese Rebellion in Early Nineteenth-Century Cambodia: Pre-Colonial Imperialism and a Pre-Nationalist Response', JSEAH, 6, 1 (1975).

[14] *Pasyon and Revolution: Popular Movements in the Philippines, 1840–1910*, Quezon City, 1979.

[15] *Prophets of Rebellion: Millenarian Protest Movements against the European Colonial Order*, Chapel Hill, 1979.

[16] Sartono *The Peasants' Revolt of Banten in 1888*, The Hague, 1966.

study of H. J. Benda and Lance Castles of the Samin movement in Java.[17] In this as in other fields, historians have been influenced by anthropological studies such as James Scott's exploration of peasant order and resistance in Malaya.[18]

The autonomy debate, changing emphases in the approach to the study of Islam, the increasing interest in the remoter past, the focus on the nature of social structure and political authority were but some of the matters commanding the attention of historians. Of importance, too, was the study of emerging élites, their role in movements of nationalist resistance to colonial rule, the institutions developed for the government of new states, questions of ethnicity and class.[19] A Marxist framework of analysis has been employed by some Thai historians and by Vietnamese historians, though in both cases it has been shaped by indigenous perspectives.[20] Local history has also become an important field of enquiry. Carried out by graduate students, by their teachers and by enthusiastic amateurs, it can be expected, in time, to provide an extended base for comparative studies. While biography has not yet been a major feature of historical writing about Southeast Asia, there have been a number of examples both of comparatively recent political figures (Poeze's study of Tan Malaka and Dahm's of the formative years of Sukarno are examples)[21] and text-based studies of earlier figures.[22] And a significant new approach to the history of the region is provided by Anthony Reid's attempt to apply the methods of the French *Annales* School to the study of the region. Reid aims at a 'total history' of Southeast Asia of the kind represented by Fernand Braudel's study of the Mediterranean world.[23]

17 'The Samin Movement', BKI, 125 (1969), republished in H. J. Benda, *Continuity and Change*, New Haven, 1972.

18 *The Moral Economy of the Peasant: Rebellion and Subsistence in Southeast Asia*, New Haven, 1976, and *Weapons of the Weak*, New Haven, 1985.

19 The literature on nationalism is extensive. Examples, almost at random, are J. E. Ingleson, *The Road to Exile: The Indonesian Nationalism Movement, 1927–1934*, Kuala Lumpur, 1979; R. T. McVey, *The Rise of Indonesian Communism*, Ithaca, 1965; C. A. Majul, *The Political and Constitutional Ideas of the Philippine Revolution*, Quezon City, 1967; David Marr, *Vietnamese Anti-Colonialism*, Berkeley, 1971; W. R. Roff, *The Origins of Malay Nationalism*, New Haven and London, 1967; R. van Niel, *The Rise of the Modern Indonesian Elite*, The Hague and Bandung, 1960; Alexander Woodside, *Community and Revolution in Modern Vietnam*, Boston, 1976.

20 Reynolds, 'Marxism in Thai Historical Studies'; J. K. Whitmore, 'Communism and History in Vietnam', in W. S. Turley, ed., *Vietnamese Communism in Comparative Perspective*, Boulder, 1980.

21 Harry A. Poeze, *Tan Malaka: Strijden voor Indonesie's vrijheid*, I: *Levensloop van 1897 tot 1945*, The Hague, 1976; and Bernhard Dahm, *Sukarnos Kampf um Indonesiens Unabhangigkeit*, Hamburg, 1966, trans. Mary F. Somers Heidhues as *Sukarno and the Struggle for Indonesian Independence*, Ithaca, 1969. See also J. D. Legge, *Sukarno: A Political Biography*, London, 1972, 2nd edn, Sydney, 1985.

22 Anne Kumar, *Surapati, Man and Legend: A Study of Three Babad Traditions*, Leiden, 1976, and Peter Carey's assessment, in his edition of the *Babad Dipanagara*, of Diponegoro's leadership in the Java War of 1825, *Babad Dipanagara: An Account of the Outbreak of the Java War, 1825–1830*, a transliteration and translation of the Surakarta Court version of the *Babad*, Kuala Lumpur, 1981.

23 Reid, *Southeast Asia in the Age of Commerce, 1450–1680*, I: *The Lands Below the Winds*, New Haven, 1988. Braudel, *The Mediterranean and the Mediterranean World in the Age of Philip II*, trans. S. Reynolds, New York, 1976.

In the study of these and other themes it is possible to discern certain shifts in the way historians of the region have handled and presented their subject matter. It might be appropriate to speak of changing fashions of interpretation or of changing views as to what constituted a satisfactory explanation of events. This is not to say that there was any sharp dividing line between successive types of approach or between successive periods. What is in question is rather the subtle alterations of emphasis or focus that take place within a continuing discourse. Before exploring these further, however, it may be appropriate to give consideration, first, to political developments which helped to shape changing perspectives both of the present and of the past of the region. For the most part, Western students of the contemporary scene after World War II had optimistic expectations for the future of the new states that were emerging. For Indonesia it seemed possible that the transfer of sovereignty by the Dutch would open the way to a democratic independent future. A peaceful transition to independence for Malaya and the Philippines held similar promise, though prospects for Burma and Vietnam were more clouded. The emerging reality was, however, to be different. Indonesia's constitutional experiment 'declined', to use Feith's term; authoritarian tendencies were to appear in the Philippines; and Burma turned inwards to a particular version of socialism. These developments necessarily affected the perspectives of later students, with respect both to the character of the forces at work in the immediate post-war scene and to the longer historical processes which had produced those forces. But of overwhelming importance for a whole generation of observers was the direction taken by events in Vietnam. Just as World War II had created a dramatically new environment for the study of Southeast Asia by Western and indigenous scholars alike, so the Vietnam conflict altered the framework of enquiry and affected perceptions of the very foundations of scholarship.

The post-war conflict between the French, anxious to reassert their control over Indochina, and the Vietnamese nationalist movement in some ways paralleled Indonesia's struggle for independence, but there were special complicating factors, in particular the increasing intervention of the United States as Vietnam came to be seen more and more in global Cold War terms.

This is not the place to consider the course of the struggle, the issues involved or the bitterly divisive consequences for the United States and its allies, as opposing perceptions of the situation came into conflict with each other. Was American action a matter of supporting South Vietnam in its resistance to aggression from the North and, indeed, a defence of the free world? Or was intervention really a case of supporting one side in what was really a civil war within Vietnam? Were those differences in perspective insignificant in the light of the fact that the Hanoi regime was a communist régime supported by China? The fusing of ideological considerations and considerations of global balance was associated with fears of the consequences of a northern victory—the expectation that it would lead to the fall of the neighbouring dominoes. For our purposes here it is sufficient to notice the types of response evoked by the conflict from students of the region. There were committed approaches sympathetic to one side or the other in Vietnam. As examples could be cited Douglas Pike's detailed study of the organization and techniques of the NLF in South Vietnam, *Viet Cong* (Cambridge, Mass., 1966) which, in spite of its attempt to be dispassionate and 'affectively neutral', was clearly hostile to the NLF, and Jeffrey Race's *War Comes to Long An: Revolutionary Conflict in a Vietnamese Province* (Berkeley, 1972), which attempted a more sympathetic explanation of the resilence of the Viet Cong. The perspectives of these works carried implied judgments on the validity of American intervention. Other works focused more directly on the intervention itself. George Kahin and John W. Lewis launched a sustained criticism in their book *The United States in Vietnam* (1967). So did Gabriel Kolko in his later *Anatomy of a War* (New York, 1985). A slightly more sympathetic, though still critical, assessment of American policy was G. Lewy's *America in Vietnam* (New York, 1978). There were many significant works of reportage and of serious journalistic comment. Bernard Fall's *Street Without Joy* has already been mentioned. Robert Shaplen's *The Lost Revolution* (London, 1966) is another example. Other studies attempted to see the conflict against the background of French colonial rule. Donald Lancaster, for example, in *The Emancipation of French Indochina* (London, 1966), set the post-war struggle, occupying about three-quarters of the book, in the context of French rule in Indochina. Finally reference should be made to George Kahin's massive study of the steps by which America became locked into a position of continuing commitment, *Intervention: How America Became Involved in Vietnam* (New York, 1986). It is part of the framework of Kahin's approach that until 1966, where his story ends, there were other choices that might have been made.

The Vietnam War thus evoked a great deal of serious enquiry at a number of levels. Much of it may be described as scholarly analysis, of the contemporary scene or of the immediate background or of the longer-term history of the conflict and the setting in which it took place. And much of it was passionate criticism or defence of policy. Scholarly enquiry and passion are not necessarily mutually exclusive, and a considerable part of the scholarly work was indeed prompted by moral considerations and was directed to an examination of evidence bearing on the political issues. This was the rationale of the Committee of Concerned Asian Scholars and of its *Bulletin*. Such enquiry was thus linked closely to the currents of passion and bitterness that ripped through American campuses and moved other sections of American society.

As we have seen, the post-war expansion of Asian studies had reflected a general concern with issues of national and international policy. The Vietnam War provided a focus for those issues. But whereas, in the 1950s and 1960s, there was a confidence that the accumulation of knowledge of Southeast Asian countries could provide a sound and agreed basis for policy, by the late 1960s and early 1970s it would be true to say that observers were disposed, not only to criticize the thrust of Western policies towards Southeast Asia, but to call into question the basic assumptions on which those policies had rested. And associated with such criticisms was a recognition of the difficulty of acquiring any real understanding of the processes of change transforming Southeast Asia societies.

## CHANGES IN INTERPRETATION

This leads us back to the suggestion that a gradual shift was to be observed, discernible perhaps from the early 1960s, in the interpretative modes of historians.

This is a complex matter, involving a variety of levels of analysis and interpretation. For the purposes of the present argument one may distinguish at least four aspects of the question. There have been, first of all, changes of perspective or changes in the angle from which the events of the past were perceived. Second, there have been changes in perceptions of what it was important to study, i.e. judgments about subject matter. Third, there have been changes in the categories of explanation—in ideas about what would constitute a satisfactory account of past events and processes. And finally there have been sharp and major changes in the actual circumstances of modern Southeast Asia which must affect the way in which the past is interpreted. Van Leur's realignment of concepts of Asian trade is a prime example of the first of these categories. The second category is well illustrated, for example, by Jean Gelman Taylor's posing of new questions about lineage and family relations in the mestizo society of the Indies which gave a different shape to the social history of the Indies in the eighteenth and nineteenth centuries, and by James Warren's essay in 'history from below' in his study of Singapore rickshaw drivers as an integral part of the society and economy of Singapore.[24] But it is intended to focus here on the third and fourth categories.

The readiness of many historians to adopt the conceptual models of the social sciences—of politics, or sociology or anthropology—in illuminating aspects of the region's past has already been noticed, and this was part of the shift taking place in modes of historical thought; but what is referred to here goes beyond specific methodological borrowing. It involves a general and growing disposition to move from interpretation in narrowly political terms toward a consideration of what were seen as more fundamental cultural patterns. The immediate problems of the post-war world which, as we have noticed, were important in stimulating the enormous expansion of Southeast Asian studies were seen, to a considerable extent, as political. They were to do, that is to say, with international balances of power, with the shape, character and politics of the 'new states' which affected that balance, with constitutional forms and leadership styles. And to a great extent they were explored at a political level: in terms of parties, emergent élites and political pressures, and of concepts such as statehood, nationalism, democracy, communism, with their implied comparisons with Western situations. These emphases were to change. As the new generation of scholars who came to the study of Southeast Asia gradually made their way, learning the necessary languages, acquiring through doctoral training and fieldwork a closer knowledge of the societies with which they were dealing, they came to a greater sense of difference rather than similarity, to an awareness of the deeper dimensions of local tradition

[24] Taylor, *The Social World of Batavia: European and Eurasian in Dutch Asia*, Madison, 1983; Warren, *Rickshaw Coolie: A People's History of Singapore, 1880–1940*, Singapore, 1986.

and culture and to a recognition of their effect upon patterns of political action. In attempting to come to grips with such levels of interpretation, students of the modern world perhaps also became more alive to the sheer difficulty of grasping the 'inwardness' of other societies and, philosophically, of dealing with the problem of knowing 'the other'.

These changes in the commonly accepted frameworks of interpretation may have been due, in part, to the influence of the particular social scientists specifically concerned with the interpretation of cultures, the anthropologists. Observers such as Clifford Geertz, through their exploration of the social context of political action in Southeast Asia, have done much to illuminate the contemporary scene in a way that is of direct relevance for the work both of political scientists and historians. For students of Indonesia the seminal work of Geertz was of particular importance. His notions of agricultural involution, shared poverty, primordial loyalties, *aliran* (cultural streams) and theatre state, though subject to criticism by later students, combined to alter the way in which political events were perceived and understood in their cultural setting. The extent to which such categories became part of the conceptual equipment of historians might be seen, for instance, in Benedict Anderson's interpretation of the first year of the Indonesian Revolution in terms of fundamental configurations of Javanese society;[25] in his essay, already noticed, on the Javanese concept of power; in Ruth McVey's exploration of the way in which the Indonesian Communist Party appealed to the Javanese peasantry through its ability to tap traditional perceptions;[26] in Heather Sutherland's account of the impact of colonial rule on the Javanese aristocracy;[27] or in Bernhard Dahm's study of Sukarno whom he saw, for all his appearance as the modern leader of a twentieth-century state, as displaying the characteristic traits and modes of thought of the Javanese culture from which he sprang.[28] It was clearly no longer possible to see Indonesian political interactions primarily in terms of parties, pressures and institutions. In a similar way David Marr's essay in the intellectual history of Vietnam, *Vietnamese Tradition on Trial, 1920–1945* (Berkeley, 1981), examined changes in Vietnamese outlooks and values, but also saw intellectuals as engaged in a dialogue with traditional ideas.

In broad terms, and in the light of what has already been said about the study of classical political theory and social order, it might be possible to describe the change in terms of an appeal to tradition as an explanatory factor, and an accompanying tendency to emphasize the inertia of tradition. Observers were increasingly disposed to switch their attention from the things that appeared to be in process of rapid change—political forces, in brief—to those that appeared to be stable, deeply rooted in the past and persistent. This focus, of course, fitted the emphasis placed, since the work of van Leur, on the essential autonomy of Southeast Asian history. If activities and institutions which seemed to owe most to the modernization

25 *Java in a Time of Revolution*, Ithaca, 1972.

26 *The Rise of the Indonesian Communist Party*, Ithaca, 1965.

27 *The Making of a Modern Bureaucratic Elite: The Colonial Transformation of the Javanese Priyayi*, Kuala Lumpur, 1979.

28 *Sukarno and the Struggle for Indonesian Independence*.

processes set in motion by European imperialism, and to have been carried further by the radical transformation of the post-colonial era, were, on closer analysis, still really embedded in profound traditional patterns, the colonial era itself could be regarded not only as an interlude in the longer history of the region, but as an interlude which did not fundamentally alter indigenous patterns. Something of this way of looking at things was present in Harry Benda's idea of 'decolonization', which was not just a matter of ending colonial rule but of ending also the way it was perceived by Western historians, and of rejecting the excessive weight of influence they had tended to ascribe to it.[29]

The appeal to tradition as providing an explanatory framework for the analysis of 'modern' conflicts, however, had its own difficulties. Modernity and tradition are abstract concepts and are likely to distort the complexity of reality if used as simple antitheses in the examination of present-day societies. The very notion of tradition implies a judgment made now about past patterns of belief and behaviour. It tends to imply, further, if not a static past, at least a stable and slowly changing past. The idea of the 'inertia' of tradition is an integral part of the notion. There are enormous conceptual and analytical problems here. What is to be regarded as 'the tradition' and what is to be seen as change must depend in part on where observers take their stand. In Southeast Asia, for example, were Indian influences from the second and third centuries onwards to be seen as external to a more basic local tradition? And what of Islam? As we have seen, van Leur was in no doubt that the 'sheen of the world religions' was a 'thin and flaking glaze'. But other observers would tend to see these elements as absorbed and made an integral part of Southeast Asia's own patterns. A similar argument could be brought to bear when assessing the rapid currents of change of the nineteenth and twentieth centuries. Should emerging élites be categorized unquestioningly as 'modern' or regarded as a part of a continuously evolving local adaptation? There are no absolute criteria to be applied. The contrast between tradition and modernity may sometimes serve a useful analytical purpose, but only for particular ends and within the framework of a particular enquiry. It must also be remembered that the application of these categories is made in the present and may, indeed, be seen as a modern construction—a modern perception of what was the case in a more or less distant past. To that extent the tradition becomes the creation of the modern observer.[30]

Perceptions of tradition went hand in hand, of course, with recognition of the enormous upheavals that were transforming Southeast Asian societies. Terms like 'underdeveloped' came to be replaced by 'developing' or 'transitional' as adjectives to describe societies such as these, and attention was given to particular elements of change and to the analytical modes which could best express them. Was class an appropriate analytical cat-

[29] 'Decolonization in Indonesia: The Problem of Continuity and Change', *American Historical Review*, 70 (1965).

[30] For a discussion of these issues see S. N. Eisenstadt, 'Reflections on a Theory of Modernization', J. C. Heesterman, 'Political Modernization in India' and J. R. Gusfield, 'The Social Construction of Tradition: An Interactionist View of Social Change', in J. D. Legge, Convenor, *Traditional Attitudes and Modern Styles in Political Leadership*, Sydney, 1973.

egory for Southeast Asian societies for example? To what extent was it useful to speak of new class formation? Were peasants in process of becoming proletarian as a result of the introduction of export commodities within a traditional agricultural framework? Were there signs of emergent middle classes within what were predominantly agricultural social orders?[31]

In a discussion of this kind it is necessary to distinguish between the 'real' changes occurring and investigators' perceptions of them, or at least to notice the theoretical necessity of such a distinction, even if, in practice, it is difficult to make with confidence. Questions such as those just listed cannot be taken as neutral and 'scientific' in character. They are loaded with values, and the way in which they are answered may reflect the attitudes of the observer rather than the reality that is observed. Even if that could be avoided, the use of a particular analytical framework might well influence what is seen and introduce its own unsuspected values. The placing of an analytical emphasis on the inertia of tradition, for example, may have the conservative effect of turning the attention of participants and observers alike away from elements of change. Similarly, to focus on the vertical divisions of society, divisions, perhaps, between ethnic groups or between competing regions, may be to play down elements of class conflict and emphasize the barriers in the way of any fundamental restructuring of society, and thus serve the interests of existing élites which are reluctant to accept changes that might possibly threaten their dominance. (And, of course, even to point this out may serve a purpose.)

Modern Thai historiography provides an example of the presence of such hidden perspectives. Thailand did not have to develop a nationalist history to cope with the colonial experience, and some recent Thai historians have argued that their predecessors, Prince Damrong amongst them, placed too much emphasis on the continuity of Thai history, and on the reforming role of the monarchy, perhaps to the point where the notion of continuity became one of the weapons whereby a traditional élite was helped to perpetuate its rule.[32] A similar view was argued by B. R. O'G. Anderson,[33] who drew attention to the emphasis placed by Western as well as Thai students on the uniqueness of Thai culture and on the role of the Thai monarchy, in the nineteenth and twentieth centuries, as a modernizing and national institution. That focus, said Anderson, had strong value implications. To view the monarchy as a modernizing institution is to regard it as performing a national role. He argued that the monarchy should be seen more properly as comparable with the *colonial*

[31] See, e.g., discussions of the nature of labour engaged in the sugar industry in Java and the Philippines: G. R. Knight, 'Capitalism and Commodity Production in Java', in H. Alavi ed., *Capitalism and Colonial Production*, London, 1982; Knight, 'Peasant Labour and Capitalist Production in Late Colonial Indonesia: The "Campaign" at a North Java Sugar Factory, 1840–1870', JSEAS, 19, 2 (1988); J. A. Larkin, *The Pampangans*, Berkeley, 1972; A. W. McCoy, 'A Queen Dies Slowly: The Rise and Decline of Iloilo City', in McCoy and De Jesus, eds, *Philippine Social History*. See also Rex Mortimer, 'Class, Social Cleavage and Indonesian Communism', *Indonesia*, 8 (1969).

[32] See Charnvit Kasetsiri, 'Thai Historiography from Ancient Times to the Modern Period', in Reid and Marr, 166.

[33] 'Studies of the Thai State: The State of Thai Studies', in Eliezer B. Ayal, *The Study of Thailand: Analyses of Knowledge, Approaches and Prospects in Anthropology, Art History, Economics, History and Political Science*, Athens, Ohio, 1978.

régimes of Southeast Asia, which were also modernizing régimes in their way, and not, as had been the case, as representative of the national leadership of a stable society. The Thai socialist, Jit Poumisak, challenged that perspective in 1957, and his work, said C. J. Reynolds, marked 'a seismic change in the semiotic code' by which Thai society was understood in both European and Thai historiography.[34] And after 1973, when Jit's work was rediscovered, other approaches, though still focusing on the continuity of Thai culture, did so for different purposes, using it either as a means of explaining Thailand's resistance to change or of emphasizing the adaptability of that culture and its capacity to incorporate external influences.[35]

Awareness of the presence of such value dimensions is a further element in the interpretative shifts that we are discussing. Historians and other social scientists became increasingly sensitive to the value positions and political assumptions embedded in what were apparently the most dispassionate of analyses, and that self-consciousness has simultaneously sharpened the tools of investigation and undermined some of the confidence with which those tools were formerly applied. Sometimes, of course, the values of investigators were proudly displayed. A new generation of nationalist historians, while anxious to maintain the rigorous standards of the discipline, were nevertheless naturally concerned to develop indigenous perspectives on the past, in order to sustain the identity of new nations. And it would be possible to describe most Western students of Southeast Asia in the early post-war period as representing a liberal orthodoxy. Reference has already been made to the way in which they were disposed to sympathize with the movements of emancipation to be observed in Asia and to be optimistic about the future political and economic progress of the new states once the imperial yoke had been thrown off. The rise of the theory of underdevelopment and dependency during the 1970s provided a further example of scholarly commitment to an open value position. The exponents of that approach were concerned with Third World poverty in general and argued in a variety of ways that there was an inbuilt and systematic inequality in the relations between underdeveloped and developed economies. This inequality could be removed, not, as orthodox growth theory had it, by aid and foreign investment but by alternative strategies aimed at achieving rural reform.[36] Such strategies, however, were unlikely to be chosen by existing power holders; the solution, in consequence, was conceivable only in a situation where the power of entrenched interests, anxious to

[34] *Thai Radical Discourse*, 139, 150.

[35] See Chatthip Nartsupha, 'Thai Studies by Thai Scholars since 1973', Paper presented to the 36th Congress of the Japan Association of Historians of Southeast Asia, 7 December 1986. Chatthip gives Chai-anan Samudvanija and Chusit Chuchart as examples of the first view and Nidhi Aeusrivongse as an example of the second. See also Reynolds, *Thai Radical Discourse*, 9–10, on the construction of continuities in Thai history.

[36] There is an extensive literature on underdevelopment/dependency theory (UDT). Major works include Andre Gunder Frank, *Capitalism and Underdevelopment in Latin America*, New York and London, 1969, M. Barratt Brown, *Essays on Imperialism*, Nottingham, 1972, Samir Amin, *Accumulation on a World Scale*, New York and London, 1974 and *Imperialism and Unequal Development*, New York and London, 1977, Immanuel Wallerstein, *The Modern World System*, New York, 1974.

preserve the status quo, had been broken. Dependency theory presupposed, that is to say, major social revolution. In other words, what appeared at first to be a technical criticism of conventional growth theory seemed on closer inspection to contain a moral criticism of existing orders of power and to represent a direct and frank advocacy of, possibly violent, political and social change.

Not all students of Southeast Asia have been as open and frank about their preferences, or as aware of them. Values may be concealed in the way questions are posed, in the analytical models by which they are explored, or in the vocabulary that is used to present them; and historians have become conscious, as a matter of course, that this is so, with profound consequences for their perceptions of their enterprise. In the past they were aware of the dangers of concealed bias, but there was nevertheless a conviction that, in spite of the dangers, truth was attainable in principle. More recently there has developed a sense that, since the meaning perceived in the events of the past is necessarily that of the observer, the notion of truth is hardly applicable. All one can hope to achieve are competing perceptions. The excitement which stimulating teachers like Benda managed to convey to their students as they set themselves to understand the world about them has, perhaps, given way to caution and hesitation.

The effect of these considerations will be the main focus of the remaining sections of this chapter.

## DECONSTRUCTING SOUTHEAST ASIAN HISTORY

For Southeast Asian historians of Southeast Asia who were also, perforce, participants in the struggles of the day, the problem was yet more complex than for others. For Indonesian historians the nature of their dilemma was explored in considerable detail in a major seminar organized jointly by Gadjah Mada University and the University of Indonesia in 1957, which led, some years later, to the preparation of a stocktaking symposium designed to identify the problems of writing Indonesian history and to chart possible directions for the future. Contributions were made by Europeans, Asians and one American, and the papers were published by Cornell University Press.[37] In the concluding essay Soedjatmoko attempted to bring into focus the peculiar problems of the modern Indonesian historian and, by extension, the modern historians of other Southeast Asian nations. Like scientific historians in general they must have 'a loving concern with the past in all its uniqueness', but at the same time they are caught up in an emotional involvement in the present. Their interest in the past is expected to serve the needs of that present which, in Indonesia's case, means providing a nationalist perspective and perhaps inventing new myths—or at least images of the past—to sustain a sense of identity and self-understanding for the nation in the present. Yet the new

[37] Soedjatmoko, Mohammad Ali, G. J. Resink and G. McT. Kahin, eds, *An Introduction to Indonesian Historiography*, Ithaca, 1965.

images must be scientifically defensible.[38] Is this a contradiction in terms or can the two be reconciled? Soedjatmoko referred to the 'polyinterpretability' of historical reality and the elusiveness of the search for objectivity. And he drew attention to other problems. Historians of today are operating in a period of rapid change, 'of shifting historical images the world over'. In a transitional situation our awareness, even of the present from which the past is viewed, is constantly changing. In all that transience how can one pin down a pattern of meaning in the events of the past? In these circumstances historians, because of their professional training, have lost the historical innocence which would enable them to write the patriotic history that their society wants.

Soedjatmoko advanced a moderately optimistic response to this cluster of dilemmas. Historical knowledge is at best provisional, and historians have to accept that limitation and recognize that they can work only for a 'new, but still limited' understanding of their situation. In so doing they remain participants in the events of the day, with the freedom and the responsibility that entails. But a strict adherence to the disciplinary requirements of the study will help to save them from the distorting effects of the surrounding culture.

In this way Soedjatmoko attempted to reconcile the idea of scientific history with that of participation. Others have been less sure of the possibility of any such reconciliation, or rather have been acutely conscious of the cultural determinants of any perception of the past and, in consequence, of the imperfect and partial character of any historical account. If, as has been suggested above, traditional writings are cultural artefacts, the same can surely be said about so-called 'scientific' history. What is seen from a privileged vantage-point in the present, what is taken for granted and what is selected for comment, is necessarily shaped by interest, purpose and culture and, at a more general level, will reflect fundamental assumptions about how the world is constituted.

One critic of Western studies of Asia, Edward Said, has detected an all-embracing framework within which Asia has been observed, a framework which he called 'Orientalism'. By this he did not mean simply studies of an objectively existing East. Certainly, though arguing that the 'Orient' was almost a European invention, he allowed the real existence of an Orient; but he was concerned, not with that reality, but with the way in which it had been perceived, with the special place that Asia had occupied in European experience and imagination, with Orientalism as a discourse. For Said, Western perceptions were a way of coming to terms with—and managing—the East. Orientalism was a 'corporate institution' for dealing with the East, 'dealing with it by making statements about it, authorizing views of it, describing it, by teaching it, settling it, ruling over it'. In short Orientalism was 'a western style for dominating, restructuring and having authority over the Orient'.[39]

The idea of hegemony was central to Said's analysis, a hegemony which

[38] Indonesia's national history project attempted to give just such a combination of scientific method and national perspective. See Sartono Kartodirdjo, Djoened Poesponegoro, Nugroho Notosusanto, eds, *Sejarah Nasional Indonesia*, 6 vols, Jakarta, 1973.

[39] *Orientalism*, London, 1978, 3.

he claimed was expressed in the structure of the disciplines—history, language, sociology, economics and others—by which the Orient was examined and in the assumptions which informed those disciplines. For him the idea of hegemony was the defining characteristic of Orientalism—and simultaneously an empirical conclusion about it. In illuminating fashion he detected that hegemony in both academic and imaginative accounts, in language, in artistic conventions and in the categories by which Asian societies and cultures were analysed, carrying his account from the eighteenth century to the present day. There is no doubt that there is substance in his argument, though it might be said that it needs to be demonstrated more carefully, and argued case by case, rather than by the development of the all-embracing category of 'Orientalism', which is itself a value-laden weapon designed for a counterattack. Once it was defined, innumerable examples could be fitted into the general picture. It is a question whether Orientalism is one phenomenon, or many; and even Said admits the possibility of 'a scholarship which is not as corrupt . . . as the kind I have been mainly depicting'.[40] It would indeed be odd if European perceptions of Asia in the eighteenth century and those of the twentieth century were so uniform and unchanging as to be satisfactorily covered by the one term, or if the linguist's Orient of the twentieth century were really part of the same Orient as that of the economist or the historian or the political scientist. And are Western students of China part of the same phenomenon as Western students of India? And what of Indian students of Indonesia or Japanese students of Thailand? Working within an international tradition of scholarship, are they too Orientalists in Said's sense? One might well doubt whether all these parts do form part of the 'larger whole' to which he refers.[41]

However, in setting up the problem as he did, and in drawing attention to elements of cultural hegemony, Said did emphasize in a dramatic form the way in which all social and historical enquiry is likely to be culture-bound. The framework within which it is carried out is a constructed framework and is therefore open to deconstruction, and to the laying bare of the influences and the interests that have shaped it in one way rather than another, and of the political functions it may be seen to perform. In general terms he was giving one formulation of the problem of coming to terms with the 'other'. It is not merely a cultural 'other' that is in question, of course. Certainly cross-cultural studies present their own significant difficulties of symbols and meanings; but those difficulties apply by extension to attempts to understand subcultures within the one society, to understand classes or social groups other than one's own, to understand, for that matter, other individuals—and, of course, other times. As L. P. Hartley remarked, 'The past is a foreign country: they do things differently there.'

The uncertainties and hesitations arising from the recognition of those difficulties have been accentuated over recent years by developments in

[40] ibid., 326.

[41] ibid., 24. Said, p. 25, specifically warns Asian students of Asia against the dangers of employing the structure of cultural domination upon themselves and others.

the realm of literary theory, which were seen to have implications for the study of Asian texts: implications which went far beyond textual study in the narrow sense.

An example of a new approach to textual analysis was provided in the early post-war period by the work of C. C. Berg, who mounted a systematic criticism of the apparent certainties of early Javanese history as they had been presented by pre-war Dutch scholars. Berg's fire was directed especially at the work of Krom. In a series of articles, written from an essentially structuralist point of view, he argued that the so-called historical writings of Java, the fourteenth-century *Nāgarakĕrtāgama*, the possibly older *Pararaton* and the later *Babad Tanah Jawi*, were not works of history at all and could only be understood if read within the framework of the society which produced them.[42] Krom had assumed that such texts contained a substratum of fact. His method was to subject the texts to rigorous internal criticism but to proceed, nevertheless, on the assumption that they could provide evidence of an actual past. As Berg put it, his approach was 'to put aside intrinsically improbable assertions, in the case of conflicting assertions to select the most probable one, and to reject the others, for the time being'.[43] Instead, said Berg, the scholar should recognize the function—often the magical function—which the text performed, perhaps supplying a legitimate ancestry for a usurper, or transmitting myths about the past which sustained a subsequent world view. Following his own method, Berg advanced a radical reading of these texts and called into question the political history which Krom had been prepared to accept. He rejected, for example, the story of Airlangga's division of his kingdom between his two sons, he questioned the existence of the first two rulers of the thirteenth-century Singhasari dynasty in Java, and he argued that the *Nāgarakĕrtāgama's* account of the extent of the empire of Majapahit was no more than a display of geographical knowledge. In brief, the literary sources from which Krom drew much of his account of Hindu-Javanese history from the ninth to the mid-thirteenth centuries offered evidence not for events but only, if properly read, for the cultural configurations of Javanese society.

Notwithstanding their seminal effect on the assumptions underlying textual analysis, Berg's views did not entirely change the findings of scholarship. Later scholars have inclined to the view that Berg had overstated his case. F. D. K. Bosch, in an article in the *Bijdragen* in 1956, argued that, while the evidence for the political chronology accepted by Krom might be weak, firm evidence for Berg's alternative reading was lacking also.[44] He accused Berg of proceeding from an 'intuitive' brainwave on which he built 'an extremely unstable tower of hypotheses piled on top of each other'.[45] De Casparis, writing at about the same time, was equally

[42] 'Kartanegara, de Miskende Empirebuilder', *Orientatie*, 1950; 'De Sadang-Oorlog en de Mythe van Groot-Majapahit', *Indonesie*, 5 (1951); 'De Geschiedenis van Pril Majapahit', *Indonesie*, 4 and 5 (1950 and 1951); 'The Work of Professor Krom', in Hall, ed., *Historians*, 164ff.

[43] 'The Work of Professor Krom', in Hall, 167.

[44] C. C. Berg and Ancient Javanese History', BKI, 1956, 112.

[45] Bosch's critique, amongst other things, considered in detail the substance of Berg's argument with regard to the first two rulers of Singhasari and the extent of Majapahit's empire.

emphatic. Arguing from an epigrapher's point of view, he insisted that the reading of at least some inscriptions was really beyond doubt and that this kind of evidence could not be brushed aside so easily by an attempt at alternative hypotheses based on a 'weak or even imaginary foundation'.[46]

What is important for the present discussion, however, is the confidence with which Berg put forward his alternative readings. Clearly, both he and his critics saw themselves as concerned with what might be called matters of fact. What was the political chronology of thirteenth-century Java? Was Majapahit an extensive realm? And they shared a belief that, if handled properly, textual study could illuminate some sort of reality. They disagreed about what constituted proper handling; but that there was a reality to be discovered by an examination of this kind of evidence was not in question. Later theorists were to raise more fundamental doubts about such a possibility.

The theorists in question were those adopting structuralist and semiological approaches to the reading of indigenous texts. The structuralist and post-structuralist enterprise has operated simultaneously at a number of levels. In part it has been an exploration of the nature of language, signs and meaning, of the links between linguistic systems and social order, and of the ways in which meaning is encoded in symbol and metaphor. In part it has focused on the relationship between reader and text, suggesting in some formulations that meaning is a function of that relationship and cannot exist independently of it. The reader creates the reading and there is no further criterion of reality, no external meaning to be ascertained. And it has also implied conclusions about the nature of reality and the grounds of knowledge. The evolving discussion of these and related ideas by Saussure, Lévi-Strauss, Jakobsen, Barthes, Culler, Derrida and many others over the years has had revolutionary implications for literary criticism. It sharpened the awareness not only of students of literature but indeed of those engaged in considering human behaviour in whatever form. And amongst others it has influenced modern students of the textual sources of Southeast Asian history, whose work has come to represent a renewed interest in the early history of the region, in its literary forms and cultural expressions.

In focus and method the work of this later generation of textual scholars differs sharply from the largely contemporary concerns, and the social science modes, of the 1950s and 1960s. Even where the attention of historians in the immediate post-war period was directed to early history—to a consideration, for example, of the structure of authority of the classical kingdoms—they tended to deal in terms of such generalized categories as patrimonial states, bureaucratic élites, patron–client relationships, status systems, and social stratification, rather than examining the cultural expressions of those periods for their own sake. Moreover, as we have seen, their primary interest was often in the light that traditional order might throw on modern political behaviour. It differs also from the earlier 'Orientalist' tradition. At first glance the growing interest in textual study may appear as a swing back to the linguistic, literary and philosophical

46 'Historical Writing on Indonesia (Early Period)' in Hall, ed., *Historians*, 160.

concerns of classical scholarship, but, in fact, its application of structuralist theory has led it into new paths of enquiry. By an examination of basic formal patterns, inner relationships, codes and symbols embedded in the literatures, inscriptions and other records of the Southeast Asian past, it seeks to uncover meanings below the surface of the texts and to gain some perception of the cultural conventions and shared knowledge within which the creators of the sources unselfconsciously existed: to attain, that, is to say, insights into how these societies, perhaps unconsciously, saw themselves. And the language is now the language of image and myth, discourse, signs and symbols, codes and emplotment.

Examples of such an approach are provided by James Siegel's examination of Acehnese historical thinking, Shelley Errington's essay on assumptions about history in Malay writings, Anthony Day's exploration of Javanese concepts of time, prophecy and change, Michael Aung-Thwin's consideration of prophecies, omens and dialogue in Burmese historiography, A. C. Milner's study of the political ideas implied in certain Malay texts, Keith W. Taylor's use of texts to catch the voices of eleventh-century Vietnam, and Michael Vickery's attempt to discern the nature of state formation in Cambodia.[47] An example of the application of the same sort of approach to more recent history may be found in Craig Reynolds' consideration of modern Thai historiography.[48]

Of considerable importance in fostering this type of approach is the work of O. W. Wolters, whose attempt to detect the subtle implications that lie within the structure of thirteenth- and fourteenth-century Vietnamese texts is a model of its kind.[49] It is a hallmark of his work that he has been more concerned than many other practitioners are to stay strictly within the texts he is reading. In the application of the method, he seeks, as a matter of principle, not to appeal for explanation to matters outside the text or to use the text as evidence of a reality external to it.[50]

Though much of the work done under structuralist influence has been directed to the study of texts in the literal sense—chronicles, inscriptions, poems and other literary creations—the same type of approach may be applied to texts of a different kind, texts by analogy. Cultural traits, patterns of behaviour, events in the normally accepted sense of the term

[47] Siegel, *Shadow and Sound*, Chicago, 1979; Errington, 'Some comments on Style in the Meanings of the Past', in Reid and Marr; Day, 'Ranggawarsita's Prophecy of Mystery', in David K. Wyatt and Alexander Woodside, eds, *Moral Order and the Question of Change: Essays on Southeast Asian Thought*, New Haven, 1982; Michael Aung-Thwin, 'Prophecies, Omens and Dialogue: Tools of the Trade in Burmese Historiography', in Wyatt and Woodside; Milner, *Kerajaan: Malay Political Culture on the Eve of Colonial Rule*, Tucson, 1982; Taylor, 'Authority and Legitimacy in 11th-Century Vietnam' and Michael Vickery, 'Some Remarks on Early State Formation in Cambodia' in Marr and Milner, eds, *Southeast Asia*.

[48] *Thai Radical Discourse*.

[49] 'Possibilities for a Reading of the 1293–1357 Period in the Vietnamese Annals', in Reid and Marr; Wolters, *History, Culture and Region*; 'Narrating the Fall of the Ly and the Rise of the Tran Dynasties', *ASAA Review*, 10, 2 (November 1986); *Two Essays on Dai-Viet in the Fourteenth Century*, New Haven: Yale Southeast Asia Studies, 1988.

[50] Note his distinction between a 'textual' and a documentary approach to a text: Wolters, *History, Culture and Region*, 69. One might compare this with Victor Lieberman who also bases much of his work on textual analysis but who focuses more on the historical events evidenced by the texts than on the structure of the texts themselves: Lieberman, *Burmese Administrative Cycles*.

may also be regarded, in their own way, as texts to be read. They are like language, with internal relationships to be observed. Human actions themselves reflect the sign systems of those who perform them. To put it another way, culture is not merely 'like' language. It is in large measure shaped by its language, and indeed social behaviour is itself a language. There is no objective, external, 'innocent', world to be perceived. The student of society can only perceive the system of signs and language habits by which that society is encountered. These may be so private that an outside observer has little hope of really entering that society; and they may be distorted in the very process of being observed. But, by being attentive to the forms, the student of texts, both written and acted, may hope in some measure to penetrate the linguistic system and, as it were, to crack the codes within which meanings are concealed. Reynaldo Ileto's decoding of the language and gestures of peasant rebels in the Philippines, for example, was concerned with texts both written and acted.

Closely connected with the theoretical underpinnings of the textualist approach was the temper displayed in its practice. It involved careful, scrupulous and attentive consideration of words and actions. Wolters, in his study of thirteenth- and fourteenth-century Vietnam, makes a distinction between 'choosing to do something to the past' and 'doing something with the past'.[51] The former involves constructing the shape of the past, with the danger that the shape might 'be influenced by preconceptions of the nature of the past in question'. The latter involves 'following directions and messages provided by the linguistic and structural systems that generate the sources' meaning when they are read as texts'. One might question the validity of the distinction. (Might not preconceptions of the nature of the past affect one's perceptions of the directions and messages? And is not the reading of the messages in a sense a construction of the shape of the past?) Nevertheless the distinction does convey a sense of the care, subtlety and sensitivity with which the sources are to be studied.

The method has been fruitful, though the ideas that sometimes accompany it and underpin it may be disturbing. The idea that texts are self-regarding, that they are not referential—that they refer only to themselves and not to a reality outside themselves, and that they may be open to an infinite multiplicity of readings—may seem to lead to an absolute relativism. Are the patterns and structures to be discerned in texts objectively there or are they merely the constructs of the reader, and as such open to deconstruction? Is there such a thing as a valid reading? Or must there be, as Derrida argues, a constant deferment of judgment, a continuing deconstruction of the rhetoric that is always present in a text and in any reading of it? Is the textual scholar, including the student of texts by analogy, to be left, in the end, with an inescapable indeterminacy of meaning?

Questions of this kind have become part of the general methodological discourse of the human sciences and have contributed to a recognition on the part of historians in general, and not merely of historians studying cultures other than their own, of the enormous difficulties facing their

[51] *Dai-Viet in the Fourteenth Century*, ix.

enterprise. The difficulties are, of course, present in any enquiry in which human beings study themselves. Such a recognition has affected the fundamental assumptions on the basis of which historical study is conducted. For historians of Southeast Asia, the change of atmosphere which has taken place since the London seminars of the 1950s is apparent. No longer would they speak, with quite the same confidence, of the possibility of a 'real' history, whether of Southeast Asia or anywhere else, or of an attempt 'to arrive at a real world-history sense of values'.[52]

This is not the place to seek answers to the questions raised above, though a short response may be to suggest that many of the assertions that are to be found in structuralist theory are epistemological rather than practical assertions, concerned with the nature and grounds of knowledge rather than with the world as it may be perceived. Though students of history must certainly be aware of language as a social construct, and of the rhetoric built into their readings of texts, what matters, in the end, is how they might defend the statements that they make. They are anchored in the contingent world and must cope with it as best they can, describing and analysing it with the tools at their disposal. Even if they stay within the texts, the statements they make must be defended by reference to the texts. To that extent, and contrary to structuralist principle in at least some of its formulations, the texts are indeed referential. Historians may never succeed in capturing reality, but that is not to say that there is no reality to be captured.

The self-reflexive aspect of structuralist thought does not necessarily lead, it is suggested, to a paralysing relativism. Certainly the self-awareness it has brought, and the recognition of the difficulty of getting some kind of grasp of other cultures may appear to represent a retreat from the confidence which, according to the present argument, marked the study of Southeast Asian history in the early post-war years. But perhaps it should be described as an advance rather than a retreat? If it makes historians more cautious and self-critical than before, and more alert to the difficulties lying in the way of understanding other cultures, it leaves them still with the responsibility of grasping, as well as they can, the nature of the past of the societies with which they deal.

[52] Hall, ed., *Historians*, 7 and 9.

# From Early Times to c. 1500

# INTRODUCTION

This section of the work gives an account of the region up to the fifteenth century of the Common Era. The opening chapter, drawing on archaeological, anthropological and linguistic evidence, is concerned with the prehistory of its peoples. The next three have parallels in subsequent sections of the work. An account of the political structures of the region is followed by accounts of its economic and social history, and of its religious experience and popular beliefs.

Chapter 2 considers the environment of the region through time and it then attempts to integrate data from a range of disciplines in order to deal with a broad range of hypotheses on its prehistory. It discusses the extent of distributional correlation among human biological groupings, cultures and languages before the rise of the first historical states.

This is the subject of Chapter 3. It begins with an account of the Vietnamese polity and of its unique relationships with the Chinese empire. It then considers the development of other Southeast Asian polities. A comparative approach is attempted, limited by the relative paucity of material. But that in itself is connected with the attitude to history prevailing in the several polities concerned, and in turn that is a guide to understanding their nature. Champa, it is concluded, is not a kingdom in the conventional sense of the word. The Khmer polity at Angkor, dependent on ricefields, differed again. Pagan is compared with Angkor. In the Irrawaddy basin, more culturally diverse and competitive, the need to affirm the ethical nature of political authority was the greater. Both polities came to an end at the time of the advent of the Tai peoples into lowland Southeast Asia. Tai polities emerged, including Lan Na, Lan Sang and Ayutthaya, the last of which was the most enduring.

The history of the Malay world is a modern reconstruction, based on Chinese and Arabo-Persian texts, inscriptions and archaeological evidence: the Malays preserved almost no memory of Śrīvijaya, the south Sumatra polity or polities of the seventh to the fourteenth centuries. Malay ambitions were limited by the advance of Siamese power on the peninsula and the rise of Majapahit in Java, and then revived with the development of Melaka as a new commercial entrepôt.

Either maritime trade, rice-growing, or both, formed the economic basis of these polities. These activities are described in Chapter 4, together with their relationship to the political dynamics of the various states. The chapter gives special attention to the Javanese kingdoms and to Majapahit, but it also discusses Angkor and Pagan, and the very different Cham and Vietnamese realms. Though more impersonal structures were emerging in Majapahit, their political economies remained rather similar than dissimilar to those elsewhere in the region.

Religion, though spiritually motivated, was also a basis of political power and resource mobilization. Indeed, as Chapter 5 shows, it was integrated with social and cultural life rather than being seen, as in modern Western societies, as something separate. The sources for its study are richer than for other aspects of Southeast Asian civilization, but are unequally distributed, in terms of region, period and social level. They show the assimilation of Indian culture and Indian religions and their adaptation to or accommodation of Southeast Asian beliefs and practices. They also show the divergent experience of mainland and archipelago. In the former, Theravāda Buddhism, disseminated from Burma, came to predominate. In Java, the worship of Śiva was the prevalent form of Hindu religion, while Mahāyāna Buddhism flourished in Sumatra, the Malay peninsula and western Kalimantan. Islam appeared in the region six centuries after its foundation, and Islamization was at first slow. The conversion of the ruler of Melaka at the beginning of the fifteenth century was a crucial step. By the end of the century Islam was firmly established in northern Sumatra, the peninsula, northern Java and western Kalimantan.

CHAPTER
# 2

# SOUTHEAST ASIA BEFORE HISTORY

Southeast Asia is a region of anthropological and archaeological complexity, remarkable for the sheer variety of cultural expression which it has nourished since very early times. Geographically, it comprises an environmental patchwork of highlands, lowlands and intervening seas extending across tropical latitudes for about 5000 kilometres southeastwards from Burma (Myanmar) to eastern Indonesia. Throughout this region were represented, before the appearance of the first historical records about 2000 years ago, societies of many socio-economic levels—from hunters and gatherers, through tribal agriculturalists, to socially ranked chiefdoms fully conversant with the manufacture of artefacts of bronze and iron. Cutting across these socio-economic levels were considerable variations in language and human biology, all reflecting many millennia of adaptation, innovation, colonization and contact between populations.

The prehistory of Southeast Asia is of importance to the world for several reasons. In terms of remotest human ancestry, the area holds important evidence for the expansion of hominids from Africa into Asia around one million years ago. It also witnessed the earliest known human sea crossings anywhere in the world—into the western Pacific and Australia beginning at least 40,000 years ago. Its northern regions may also hold the key to the domestication of rice, one of the modern world's most important plant foods, and the area as a whole may have witnessed the domestication of many other major species, including certain yams, aroids (especially taro), bananas, and perhaps sugarcane. Southeast Asia also provided the source-region and early environmental backdrop for the most extensive diaspora of a single ethnolinguistic group in the history of mankind—that of the speakers of Austronesian languages, who by the early centuries CE had spread more than halfway around the world to Madagascar and Easter Island.

Research in the prehistory of Southeast Asia is currently at an exciting stage, with new discoveries and interpretations appearing almost annually. It may thus be apposite to recall a tendency on the part of many scholars writing before the mid-1960s to regard the region in prehistory as little more than a backward appendage of the more advanced cultures of India and China. It is now clear that this view was far too simple, and that Southeast Asia has a prehistory as complex and as indigenously creative as any other major region of Eurasia. It also served, over a timespan of at least

40,000 years, as the ultimate source-region for the populations of Australia and the Pacific Islands; populations as diverse and as anthropologically significant today as the Aboriginal Australians, the Melanesians, the Micronesians and the Polynesians.

In order to write a coherent account of the prehistory of Southeast Asia, one which goes beyond the minutiæ of the archaeological record, it is necessary to consider the results of many separate disciplinary fields of study. A major task is to consider the environment of the region and to examine how it may have changed through time. Beyond this, in order to identify hypotheses of real human significance, one must compare and integrate data from the independent disciplines of biological anthropology, comparative linguistics, and archaeology. It will be evident that few immutable interpretations of the prehistoric record are accepted by all scholars, and one must instead deal with a broad range of hypotheses which reflect the disciplinary and cultural backgrounds of their authors as much as the mechanical calculations of scientific objectivity. There are, however, certain points of agreement, a major one being that there is considerable overlapping of human biological groupings, cultures and languages. Especially when one takes a broad geographic scale, it becomes impossible to construct watertight categories. Even a cursory survey of the ethnographic record reveals that people who appear biologically to be quite different may speak languages in the same family (for instance, Negritos and Southern Mongoloids in the Philippines), and peoples with strong physical similarities may be quite different in terms of language and cultural background.

Such circumstances, however, should not lead to the view that all biological, linguistic and cultural variation is entirely uncorrelated. This is not the case even in the modern world with its unprecedented rate of biological and cultural mixing, and it may be better to infer relatively high correlations, especially on a local scale, amongst the majority of the pre-urbanized populations who inhabited Southeast Asia before the rise of the first historical states. Individual explanations may then be sought for those contrary situations which obviously will occur from time to time in real life, as a result of the normal processes of contact and intermarriage which occur between adjacent human groups.

## PRESENT-DAY ENVIRONMENTS OF SOUTHEAST ASIA

In a purely geographical sense, Southeast Asia falls conveniently into two parts: mainland, comprising China south of the Yangtze,[1] Burma (Myanmar), Thailand, Indochina and peninsular Malaysia; and island,

[1] It must not be forgotten that the incorporation of southern China into the political and cultural boundaries of Han Chinese civilization did not occur until the first millennium BC. South China before this was an integral part of Southeast Asia in cultural and linguistic terms, and many millions of speakers of languages in the Tai, Tibeto-Burman, Miao-Yao and Austroasiatic families still live north of the southern Chinese border today. It is impossible to understand the later stages of Southeast Asian prehistory without reference to southern China.

comprising Indonesia, East Malaysia, Brunei, the Philippines and Taiwan. Biogeographically, however, the major division lies much further to the east, since the islands of Sumatra, Java, Borneo, Bali and Palawan lie on the once-exposed continental Sunda Shelf (Sundaland), a geologically stable and now partly drowned extension of the Asian landmass (Map 2.1). During glacial periods of low sea-level, much of Sundaland was joined as dry land to the rest of Asia—a recurring circumstance with profound implications for the origins of the flora and fauna and the most ancient human inhabitants of the area.

To the east of Bali and Borneo, across Huxley's Line of biogeographers, lie the deep seas and islands of the Philippines and the region of Wallacea, the latter (Sulawesi, Nusa Tenggara and Maluku) named after the nineteenth-century naturalist Alfred Russel Wallace. This region has never been crossed by a continuous land connection: its colonization by plants, animals and humans required, for the most part, the crossing of ocean divides. Eastwards again, and mostly beyond the concern of this chapter, lies the continental Sahul Shelf which joins Australia and New Guinea.

In terms of geology and geomorphology, the major part of the mainland of Southeast Asia is formed by the roughly north–south trending basins of the Irrawaddy, Salween, Chao Phraya, Mekong and Red (Hong) rivers and their tributaries, and by the intervening areas of high relief such as the Truong Son spine of Indochina and the mountains which separate Thailand from Burma. The major environmental distinction within this region is therefore that between the low-lying and broad riverine plains and alluvial plateaux, the latter including the archaeologically-important Khorat Plateau of northeastern Thailand, and the intervening uplands. It is this environmental distinction which correlates most closely with the anthropological division of mainland Southeast Asian societies into the coastal/riverine civilizations of the lowlands and the inland/upland 'hill peoples'.

The land masses which lie on the Sunda Shelf proper, that is the Thai-Malay peninsula and the islands of western Indonesia, have survived the post-glacial rise in sea level as enclaves of varied relief which necessarily have much shorter river systems than the non-peninsular parts of the mainland. Although the distinction between riverine/coastal plains and interior uplands is still of major cultural importance, the major environmental differentiation in this zone lies between terrain which is stable and volcanically inactive (Malay peninsula, Borneo, eastern Sumatra) and that produced by the awe-inspiring Sunda–Banda volcanic arc. This spectacular alignment of volcanoes, which includes the famous Krakatoa between Java and Sumatra, has been wrought by subduction of the bed of the Indian Ocean around the southern side of Indonesia from western Sumatra, past Java and Bali, to Maluku. Further volcanic arcs run northwards through Sulawesi and the Philippines and onwards to Japan. Certain of these volcanic regions, with their fertile soils and monsoonal climates, support some of the greatest agricultural population densities on earth, while the geologically stable and relatively infertile interiors of Borneo and parts of eastern Sumatra until recently supported some of the sparsest.

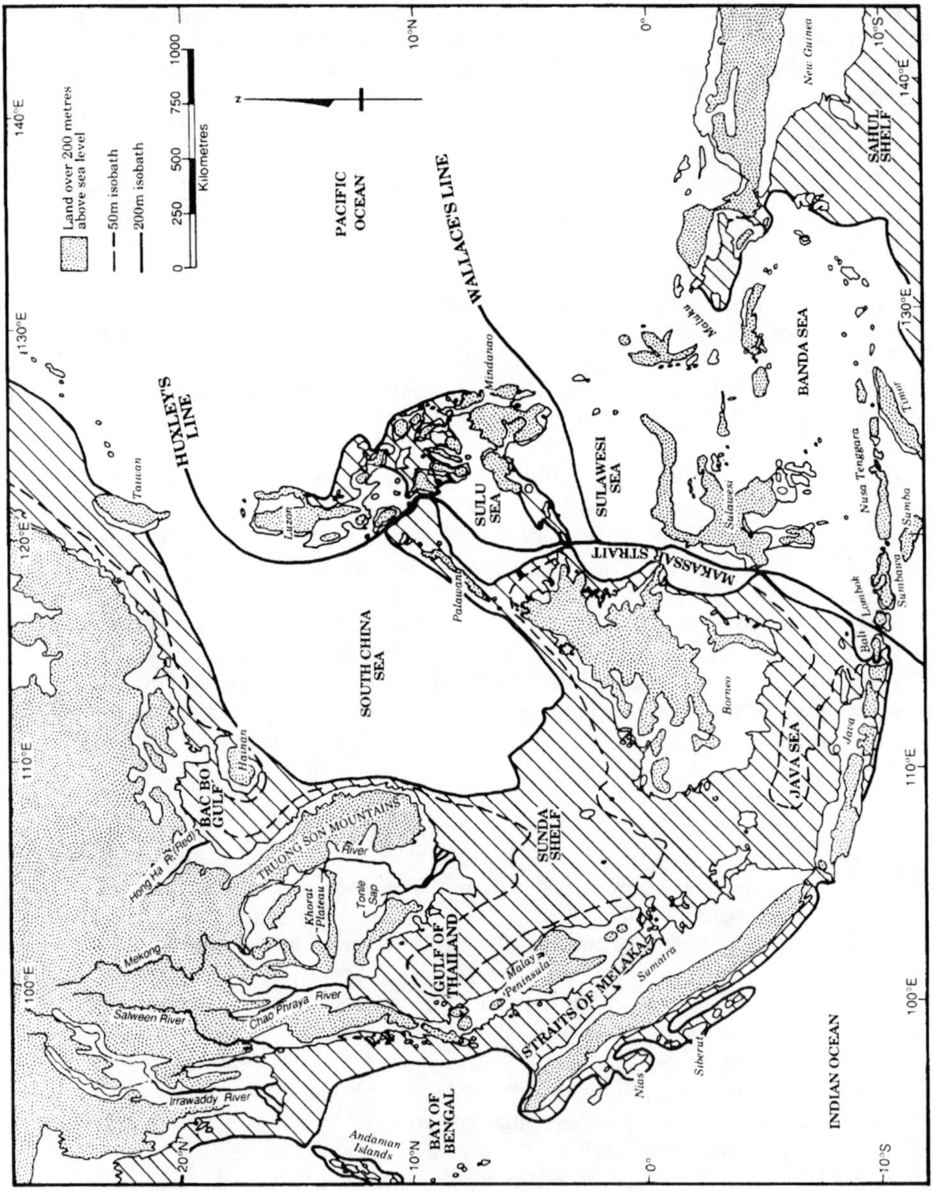


Map 2.1 The physical geography.

The biogeographical zone of Wallacea between the Sunda and Sahul Shelves is also partially the result of volcanic arc formation, here in open and deep seas rather than against a continental shelf in the way that the western part of the Sunda–Banda arc impinges on Sundaland. Hence the Wallacean islands are smaller than those of Sundaland, and have also been more isolated through geological time. The Philippine islands are similarly of volcanic origin and have apparently never been joined in entirety to the Asian mainland, with the exception of Palawan which lies on the Sunda Shelf. The absence of major land bridges joining these regions has caused distinctive flora and fauna to evolve, and may also have barred any eastward dispersal of hominids beyond Bali and Borneo prior to the Late Pleistocene.

## The Climate and Vegetation of Southeast Asia

The whole of Southeast Asia lies within the tropics and is therefore in a zone of uniformly high temperature, except at high altitude. However, the annual pattern of rainfall in the equatorial zone is different from that in the flanking intermediate tropical zone (Map 2.2). The equatorial zone lies mainly in Indonesia and Malaysia within about five degrees of the equator (there is also a northwards extension in the eastern Philippines) and it has a non-seasonal climate with heavy rainfall occurring throughout the year. In contrast, the intermediate tropical (or intertropical) zone beyond is characterized by a 'winter' dry season which increases to almost half the year as one moves southwards towards Australia and northwards towards southern China.

The significance of this climatic zonation for human prehistory is considerable. The equatorial zone demonstrates several environmental features which might be deemed hostile towards easy human colonization, whether by foraging or agricultural groups.[2] Soils tend to be infertile clays, especially outside zones of recent volcanic activity, and most nutrients are cycled within the enormous rainforest biomass rather than in the topsoil. Equatorial forests present few edible wild plants or animals; numbers of species of course proliferate, but large stands of plant foods suitable for human consumption do not, and the fauna is also dispersed or arboreal, and difficult to hunt. Even with agricultural production, the labour of clearing forest in such constantly humid conditions with rapid weed growth did not encourage dense populations in preindustrial times, and many of the equatorial regions are still strikingly underpopulated today.

[2] It has recently been suggested that inland equatorial rainforest would have provided insufficient food for a human population to live by hunting and gathering alone. If this view is correct, much of the interior equatorial rainforest of Southeast Asia might have been totally uninhabited until the development of agriculture. The coastal zones, however, certainly did support some habitation according to the archaeological evidence, as did the interior of peninsular Malaysia (see page 129). The situation is therefore quite complex. See T. N. Headland, 'The wild yam question: how well could independent hunter-gatherers live in a tropical rain forest ecosystem?', *Human Ecology*, 15 (1987); R. C. Bailey et al., 'Hunting and gathering in tropical rainforest: is it possible?', *American Anthropologist*, 91 (1989); P. Bellwood, 'From Late Pleistocene to Early Holocene in Sundaland', in C. Gamble and O. Soffer, eds, *The Late Palaeolithic Global Record*, II, London, 1990.

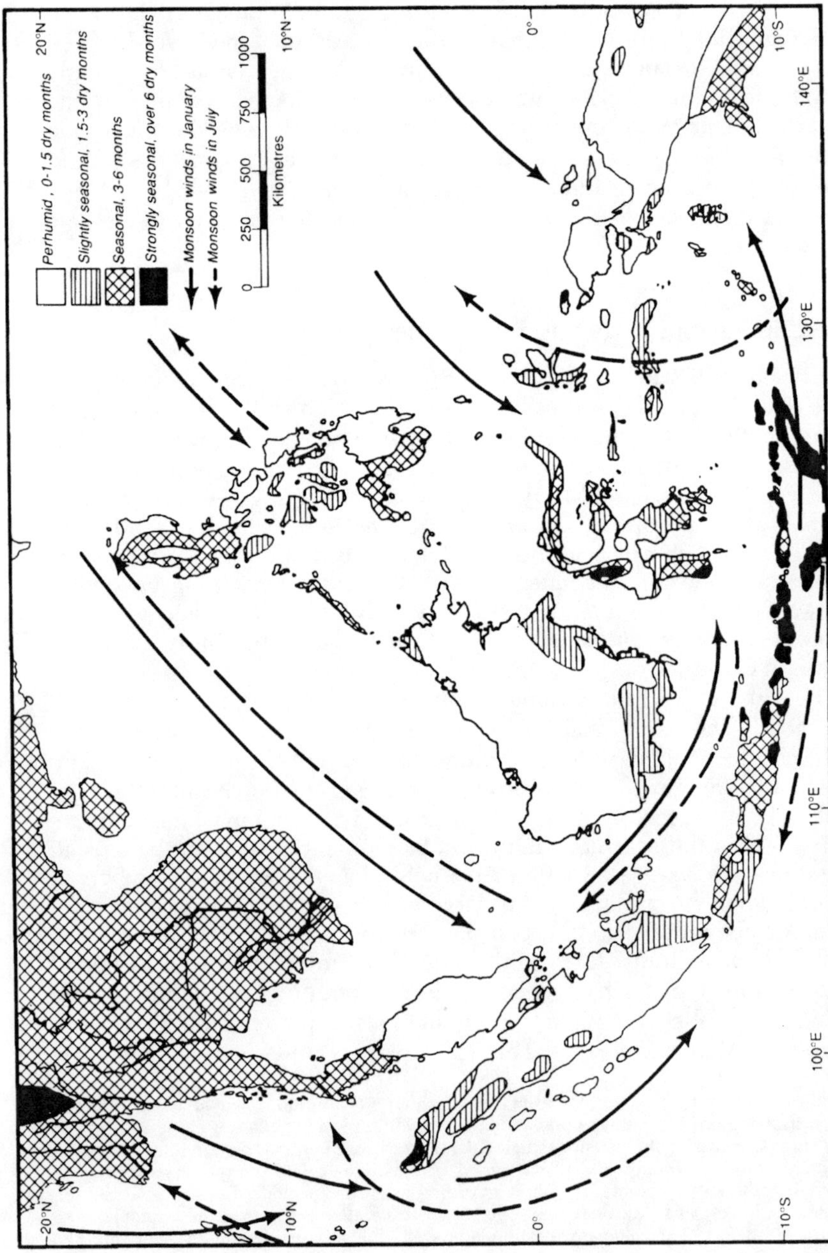


Map 2.2 Rainfall and monsoon patterns.

In contrast, those regions which lie within the intertropical zone, especially where the dry season is reliable and three months or more in duration, support more open monsoonal forests with a deciduous tendency during the driest periods. This zone, which of course exists both north and south of the equator, includes most of mainland Southeast Asia north of Malaysia, the islands of southeast Indonesia from Java to Timor, and parts of Sulawesi and the western Philippines. Many of these regions also have very fertile soils, and the resulting combination of good soil and sufficient dry season sun for the ripening of rice has led in some areas to intensive irrigation agriculture and the growth of dense populations. Even from the viewpoint of prehistoric hunting and collecting, the animal biomass of the intertropical zone, when not curtailed by island isolation and poverty of species, should have been higher than that of the equatorial rainforests. This observation would apply especially to the large browsing mammals of mainland Southeast Asia and the islands of Sundaland.[3]

The distributions of large mammals, however, and fauna and flora in general, are not determined simply by good soil and the incidence of rainfall. Southeast Asia straddles one of the most ancient zones of biogeographical transition in the world—that which has generally kept apart the placental mammals of Eurasia and the marsupial fauna of Australia and New Guinea. The Sunda Shelf islands west of Huxley's Line form the true eastern limit of Asia, and contain (ignoring instances of local extinction) Asian species such as cattle, deer, pigs, elephants, tigers, monkeys, gibbons, and orang utan. The only native placental mammals in Australia and New Guinea are species of rodents and bats which managed to reach these areas across sea gaps in pre-human times.

The islands of Wallacea have few endemic large mammals, and those which do occur are mostly of Sundaland as opposed to Australasian origin. Sulawesi, for instance, has the endemic pig-like *babirusa* and the buffalo-like *anoa*, and also three species of marsupial phalangers, small tree-dwelling mammals whose ancestors presumably island-hopped in pre-human times from the Sahul zone. The simple fact that Sundaland and Sahul-land were never directly joined by a continuous land bridge is obviously one of great importance for the story of human expansion eastwards.

## THE CHANGING NATURE OF THE SOUTHEAST ASIAN ENVIRONMENT

The record of human settlement in Southeast Asia extends back in time for about one million years. During that time the landscapes and climates of the region have fluctuated considerably, according to the cyclical rhythm of changes associated with the Pleistocene glaciations in temperate

[3] For instance, wild *banteng* cattle occur at densities of 1–2 animals per hundred hectares in primary rainforest, but up to 10–15 animals per hundred hectares in savanna grasslands in eastern Java (where herds of up to 246 animals have been recorded). See P. Pfeffer, 'Fauna of humid tropical Asia', in *Natural Resources of Humid Tropical Asia*, Paris: Unesco, 1974.

latitudes. Some understanding of the magnitude of these changes is necessary before the human prehistoric record can be presented. The data will be discussed according to the standard chronological subdivisions of Early Pleistocene (c.1.6 million to 700,000 years ago), Middle Pleistocene (700,000 to 125,000 years ago) and Late Pleistocene (125,000 to 10,000 years ago). The Late Pleistocene corresponds to the last interglacial and last glacial periods, and is succeeded by the Holocene, the present period of warm interglacial climate within which all human developments beyond the Palaeolithic appear to have taken place.

It is now known, as a result of the study of pollen sequences and the documentation of changing oxygen isotope ratios in the shells of marine micro-organisms, that approximately seven episodes of temperate latitude glaciation have occurred since the beginning of the Middle Pleistocene. Others, perhaps of lesser magnitude and shorter duration, extend back into the Pliocene. True glacial low points in temperature were quite short (c.10,000 years), as were true interglacial high points. For example, the generalized 'shape' of the last full glacial cycle (which is the one best understood) consisted of a very rapid rise out of the penultimate glacial into the last interglacial, and then a very long-term and erratic downward slide in temperature from the last interglacial (c.120,000 years ago) into the last maximum cold stage (c.18,000 years ago). The phenomenon of rapid amelioration of the climate in post-glacial phases is particularly important since the last one was clearly associated, perhaps via increasing temperature and rainfall and a greater degree of rainfall seasonality, with the origins of cereal and tuber agriculture.

In tropical Southeast Asia, of course, true continental glaciations did not occur, although ice caps are known to have expanded dramatically in the high mountains of New Guinea, and to a much lesser extent on Mount Kinabalu in Sabah and some of the high volcanoes in Sumatra. Tree lines and vegetation zones were correspondingly depressed, in some cases by more than 1500 metres of altitude. The main results of glaciations for humans in the Southeast Asian tropics would have been a lowering of average annual temperature,[4] a major decrease in annual rainfall, changes in vegetation patterns, and a lowering of sea level to as much as 130 metres below the present as enormous quantities of water became progressively trapped in the high-latitude ice sheets. The sea-level changes would probably have had dramatic effects on human migration and expansion, and they will be examined first.

The Sunda Shelf is the largest area of shallowly submerged continental shelf on earth. When it was almost fully exposed as dry land during glacials it would have formed a subcontinent over four million square kilometres in extent. The terrestrial deposits which now form the beds of the South China and Java Seas give ample evidence of this, as do several

[4] By up to 8 degrees Celsius in highlands, but probably much less in lowlands and at sea level. See J. R. Flenley, 'Late Quaternary changes of vegetation and climate in the Malesian mountains', *Erdwissenschaftliche Forschung*, 18 (1984); D. Walker and Sun Xiangjun, 'Vegetational and climatic changes at the Pleistocene-Holocene transition across the eastern tropics', in *The Palaeoenvironment of East Asia from the Mid-Tertiary*, I, Centre of Asian Studies, University of Hong Kong, 1988.

drowned river valleys and frequent records of mangrove pollen in cores drilled into the sea bed. Full exposure of the shelf, however, so that all the islands which now rise from it were joined together by dry land extending to the shelf edge, need not have been a particularly common circumstance. The last time it occurred was for a few millennia around 18,000 years ago, prior to that around 135,000 years ago,[5] and then possibly at intervals of between 90,000 and 120,000 years back into the Middle Pleistocene (Figure 2.1). Drowning of the Sunda Shelf to the level of the present ocean surface would have occurred at similarly spaced intervals, with the most recent peaks occurring at 6000, 125,000 and possibly about 210,000 years ago. Sea level was probably slightly higher than now about 6000 years ago, following a very rapid post-glacial rise which drowned about two million square kilometres of low-lying Sundaland terrain in about 8000 years.

Prior to half a million years ago there is far less agreement about cycles of Sundaland submergence and emergence. Not only may the cycles of sea-level change have differed in amplitude and chronology, but the geological and faunal records are both open to differing interpretations. Some authors favour a fairly continuous emergence and continental character for Sundaland until about 500,000 years ago, and others stress the significance of episodes of island isolation, especially for Java.[6] Despite these uncertainties it is apparent that during the Middle and Late Pleistocene the sea level would have oscillated for most of the time between 20 and 80 metres below the present level. This prompts some very important observations in respect of human dispersal.

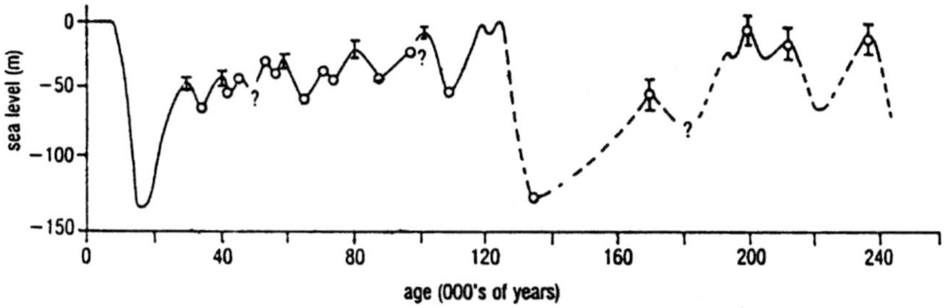


Figure 2.1 A sea-level curve for the past 250,000 years based on data from the Huon Peninsula, northeastern Papua New Guinea.

Redrawn from J. Chappell and N. J. Shackleton, 'Oxygen isotopes and sea level', *Nature*, 324 (1986), 137–40.

[5] Sea-level changes have been well studied for the Pleistocene in Australia and New Guinea, and these results may generally be applied to Southeast Asia, despite some variation in isostatic crustal movements. For current views, see J. Chappell and N. J. Shackleton, 'Oxygen isotopes and sea level', *Nature*, 324 (1986); and chapters in M. J. Tooley and Ian Shennan, eds, *Sea Level Changes*, Oxford, 1987.

[6] See discussion in my *Prehistory of the Indo-Malaysian Archipelago*, Sydney, 1985 (hereafter PIMA), 30–1. For the view that Java was an island around one million years ago, see J. M. Leinders, F. Azis, P. Y. Sondaar and J. de Vos, 'The age of the hominid-bearing deposits of Java', *Geologie en Mijnbouw*, 64 (1985). A contrary view based on faunal composition is expressed by L. R. Heaney, 'Zoogeographic evidence for Middle and Late Pleistocene land bridges to the Philippine Islands', MQRSEA, 9 (1985).

The Malay peninsula, Sumatra and Java, for instance, would all be joined to each other and to Asia at a sea level of 20 metres below present. Borneo would be joined as well at 50 metres below present. This means that Java and Sumatra may have been joined to Asia for well over half and possibly even 90 per cent of Middle and Late Pleistocene time, Borneo for perhaps less.[7] However, when high sea levels did separate islands they certainly led to a dramatic increase in the rate of extinction of terrestrial mammals.[8] One can only guess what biological effects they would have had on the sparse populations of *Homo erectus*, who presumably would have lacked the ability to cross sea to maintain their links with the Asian gene pool to which they originally belonged.

Within Wallacea the fluctuating Pleistocene sea levels would not have produced any major land bridges, although most of the Philippine islands excluding Palawan could have been joined together as one or two major islands in the Middle Pleistocene, as may some of the Nusa Tenggara chain from Lombok eastwards. However, it seems that neither of these regions was ever joined by dry land to Sundaland during the timespan of hominid settlement in the region, despite many past claims for various land-bridge possibilities.[9] At present, all indications are that the first hominids to cross Huxley's Line did so by crossing sea, and the available evidence suggests that these first intrepid migrants were members of the modern species *Homo sapiens* at a date around or a little prior to 40,000 years ago.

The other effects of glaciation in the tropics referred to above, namely reduced rainfall and a consequent change from closed rainforest to more open vegetation, would have had effects on human dispersal additional to those caused by changes in sea level. Since human foragers can maintain only very small numbers in rainforests,[10] pre-agricultural human ranges and population densities in equatorial Southeast Asia might have been much greater during full glacials than in interglacials. There is evidence from many disciplines which suggests that Southeast Asian climates during periods of glacial low sea level were drier than now, and that rainfall was perhaps significantly reduced in some parts of the area now occupied by ever-wet rainforest.[11] Major results of such changes might

[7] These estimates are reflected to some extent in the percentages of endemic mammal species which these islands support today. Only 4.5 per cent of the terrestrial mammal species of Malaya are endemic, while the percentages for Sumatra, Java, Borneo and Palawan are, respectively, 10.3, 23.0, 32.5 and 63.3. Sulawesi terrestrial mammal species are 100 per cent endemic. See C. Groves, 'Plio-Pleistocene mammals in Island Southeast Asia', MQRSEA, 9 (1985).

[8] See L. R. Heaney, 'Biogeography of mammals in Southeast Asia: estimates of rates of colonization, extinction and speciation', *Biological Journal of the Linnean Society*, 28 (1986).

[9] For recent arguments against land bridges to the Philippines (excluding Palawan) and Sulawesi during the Pleistocene, see L. R. Heaney, 'Zoogeographic evidence . . . ', MQRSEA, 9 (1985) and G. Musser, 'The mammals of Sulawesi', in T. C. Whitmore, ed., *Biogeographical Evolution of the Malay Archipelago*, Oxford, 1987. The Pleistocene mammal faunas of these islands and of Nusa Tenggara to as far east as Timor include a variety of mammals ranging in size up to the elephant-like stegodonts. Their dispersal, which may long predate that of humans, can be explained by invoking Late Pliocene (rather than Pleistocene) land bridges, or they may have swum across short sea gaps. See PIMA, 23–6.

[10] See footnote 2, above.

[11] See, for instance, R. J. Morley and J. R. Flenley, 'Late Cainozoic vegetational and environmental changes in the Malay archipelago, in Whitmore, ed., *Biogeographical Evolution*; W. S.

have been corridors of relatively open forest or parkland vegetation, crossing Sundaland from the northern hemisphere into the southern. Such corridors would help to explain how the earliest *Homo erectus* pioneers managed to reach Java, given that this species has no record of rainforest adaptation during its evolution in Africa. However, there is no evidence that the great belt of rainforest which now occupies most of the Malay peninsula, Borneo, Sumatra and Sulawesi was ever completely broken up or replaced. It has always existed, but perhaps not always as extensively as it does today.

## HUMAN PREHISTORY: THE FIRST MILLION YEARS

Remains of early humans of the species *Homo erectus* have been recovered extensively in Java and China, and to a lesser extent in northern Vietnam;[12] in this section the focus will be mainly on Java (Map 2.3). There is a general consensus amongst biological anthropologists that the early evolution of humanity took place in Africa, and that hominids expanded into the tropical latitudes of Asia around one million years ago. The species *Homo erectus* was fully developed in East Africa by at least 1.6 million years ago, and there is no compelling evidence at present for any existence outside Africa of earlier hominids of the genus *Australopithecus*.

By 750,000 years ago *Homo erectus* had spread into temperate climatic zones in Europe and China, and the species as a whole underwent some degree of geographical differentiation, at least in terms of cranial variation. Research with respect to the species as a whole has concentrated on interpreting this observed regional variation, and explaining the slow pre-*sapiens* chronological tempos of biological and cultural evolution. An even more significant question concerns genetic continuity: were Asian *Homo erectus* populations the direct ancestors of modern Asians, or were they replaced and consigned to an eventual fate of extinction by incoming modern *Homo sapiens*, ultimately from Africa? The origin of modern humans is one of the most contentious and important issues in anthropology today, and the Southeast Asian fossil record has potentially much to contribute to this debate.

Before examining current opinions on the issue of continuity versus replacement, it is necessary to review some of the facts, especially for Java, confused and disputed as they may be. The modern discovery of 'Java Man' began in 1891 when Eugene Dubois found part of the skull-cap of *Homo erectus* (for many years better-known as '*Pithecanthropus*') in deposits cut by the Solo River at Trinil, central Java. Other locations which have

Broecker et al., 'New evidence from the South China Sea for an abrupt termination of the last glacial period', *Nature*, 33 (1988); Earl of Cranbrook, 'The contribution of archaeology to the zoogeography of Borneo', *Fieldiana, Zoology*, 42 (1988).

12 Teeth and partial jaws of *Homo erectus* are believed to occur in a fossiliferous cave breccia in the cave of Tham Khuyen in northern Vietnam, but no detailed report is available. See Le Krung Ha, 'First remarks on the Quaternary fossil fauna of northern Viet Nam', *Vietnamese Studies*, 46 (1978); R. L. Ciochon and J. W. Olsen, 'Palaeoanthropological and archaeological research in the Socialist Republic of Vietnam', *Journal of Human Evolution*, 15 (1986).

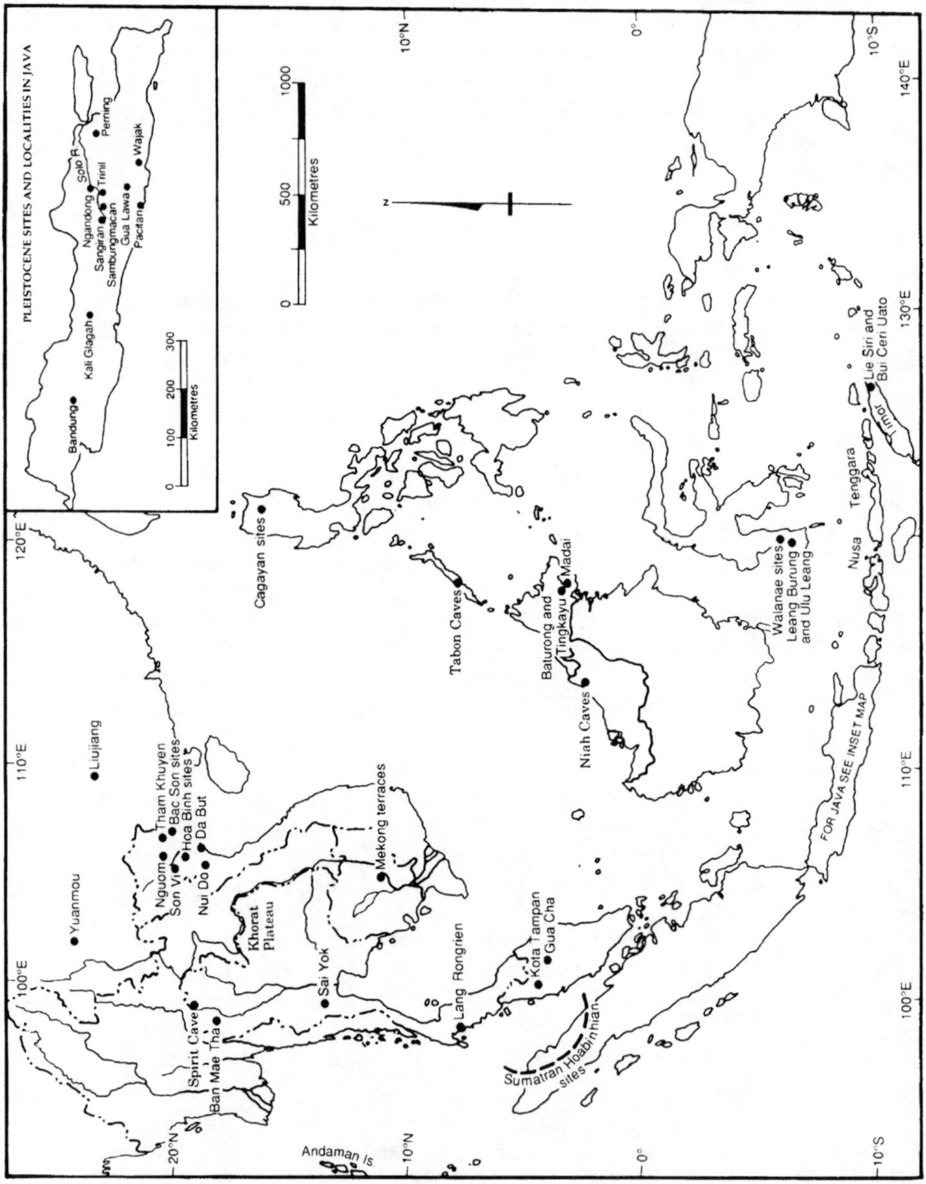


Map 2.3 Major Pleistocene and early Holocene sites.

yielded human fossils this century include Ngandong and Sambungmacan, also on the Solo River, Perning near Mojokerto in eastern Java, and the important site of Sangiran where the Cemoro River, a small tributary of the Solo, has cut into an anticlinal dome exposing layers dating from the Pliocene to the Middle and Late Pleistocene.

Sangiran holds the most reliable information recovered so far on the dates, faunal and environmental associations of the Javanese hominids. The deposits provide excellent environmental conditions for fossilization and begin with Pliocene marine and estuarine sediments at the base, grading up through lacustrine, fluvial and volcanic deposits which probably span most of the Pleistocene. A major phase of uplift and erosion set in during the Late Pleistocene causing an erosional disconformity, above which lie Late Pleistocene river terrace gravels. Sangiran has recently been subjected to a detailed programme of interdisciplinary research, and the major lithostratigraphic divisions recognized are shown in Figure 2.2, together with their apparent correlations with the earth's magnetic reversal record.[13] The absolute chronology is supported by fission track and potassium-argon dates on volcanic materials and fluorine measurements on animal bones. It is sufficient here to state that the major *Homo erectus* finds from the sites of Sangiran, Trinil and Perning are agreed by most authorities to date between about 1.3 and 0.5 million years ago, with a maximum (but perhaps unlikely) age of around 1.7 million years. The Ngandong and Sambungmacan remains are considerably younger and fall very close to the transition to *Homo sapiens*.

The faunal sequence presented in Figure 2.2 is currently disputed. The traditional view, as developed by von Koenigswald and Hooijer, suggests that the Jetis 'Sino-Malayan' fauna (Late Pliocene–Early Pleistocene) already contained ancestral species of gibbon, orang utan, elephant, cattle, deer, pig, hippopotamus, tiger, bear, panther and dogs of the *Cuon* genus, as well as the now-extinct *Stegodon* and, of course, *Homo erectus*. This traditional scheme has recently been criticized and rearranged[14] into a new scheme which places a number of these species later in time, especially the rainforest forms such as gibbon and orang utan, which are claimed to have appeared in Java only during the last interglacial period. These problems have arisen because of uncertainties about the exact find-places of animal

[13] Reported in N. Watanabe and D. Kadar, eds., *Quaternary Geology of the Hominid Fossil Bearing Formations in Java*, Bandung: Geological Research and Development Centre, 1985. Other references used in compiling Figure 2.2 are D. A. Hooijer, 'The Middle Pleistocene fauna of Java', in G. Kurth, ed., *Evolution und Hominization*, Stuttgart, 1968; S. Sartono, 'the stratigraphy of the Sambung Mekan site in Central Java', MQRSEA, 5 (1979); A. Sémah, 'A preliminary report on a Sangiran pollen diagram', ibid., 7 (1982); S. Matsu'ura, 'A chronological framing for the Sangiran hominids', *Bulletin of the National Science Museum, Tokyo*, Series D, 8 (1982); F. Sémah, 'Le peuplement ancien de Java: ébauche d'un cadre chronologique', *L'Anthropologie*, 90 (1986); G.-J. Bartstra et al., 'Ngandong Man, age and artifacts', *Journal of Human Evolution*, 17 (1988); G. Pope, 'Recent advances in Far Eastern Palaeoanthropology', *Annual Review of Anthropology*, 17 (1988).

[14] By J. J. M. Leinders et al., 'The age of the hominid-bearing deposits of Java: state of the art', *Geologie en Mijnbouw*, 64, (1985). The traditional scheme is still supported strongly by G.-J. Bartstra, 'The vertebrate-bearing deposits of Kedungbrubus and Trinil, Java, Indonesia', ibid., 62 (1983); and by D. A. Hooijer, 'Facts and fiction around the fossil mammals of Java', ibid., 62 (1983).

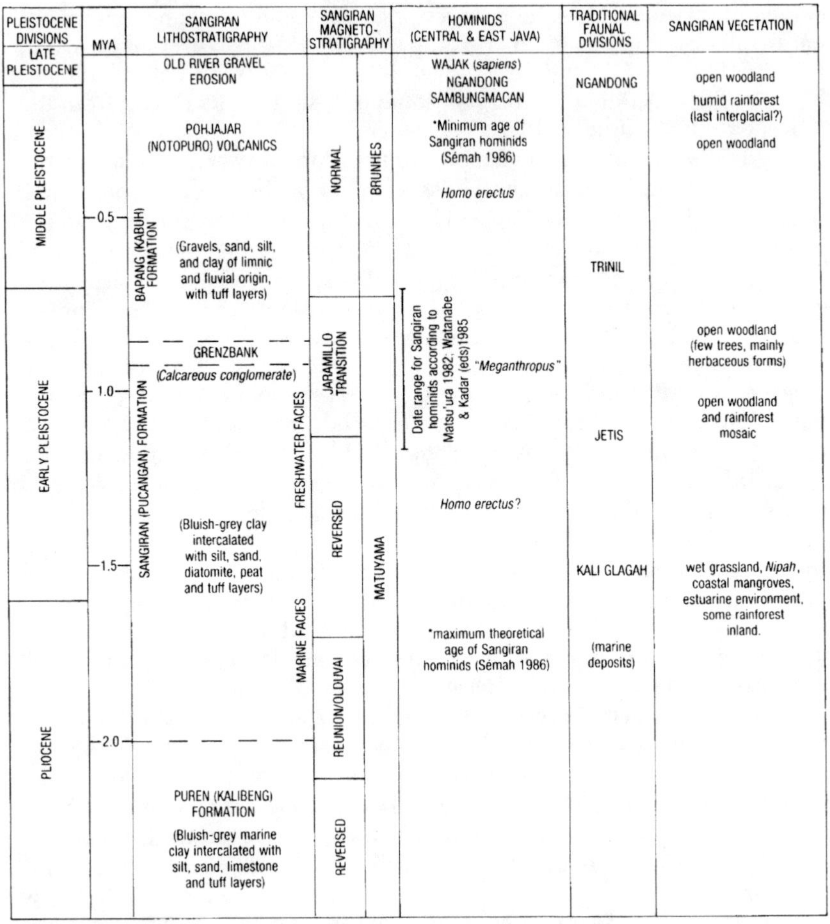


*MYA=millions of years ago*

Figure 2.2 The Sangiran sequence of geological formations, hominids, faunas and vegetations since the Late Pliocene.

bone assemblages—a problem which also applies to the find-places of many of the human fossils, which were originally collected by villagers rather than by professional scientists. It need hardly be stressed that the study of human evolution in Java is still affected by a great deal of stratigraphic and chronological disagreement.

The oldest Javanese fossil hominids come from the upper part of the Sangiran (or Pucangan) formation at Sangiran, whereas the majority from Sangiran, and also the crania from Trinil and Perning, appear to belong to the overlying Bapang (or Kabuh) beds. The oldest specimens are the most robust, and the species overall has an average cranial capacity of about 950 cubic centimetres, thick skull bones, a broad face with large teeth and a low skull broadest at its base. Stature perhaps ranged up to 160 centimetres, weight to 80 kilograms, and the species had an upright posture and bipedal gait quite similar to modern humans. Sexual dimorphism in size and musculature is generally assumed to have been greater than amongst ourselves.

Although most fossils found in Java fit comfortably within the acceptable morphological limits of *Homo erectus*, there has been sporadic but continuing debate with respect to the mandible fragments of a particularly massive-toothed hominid found close to the Grenzbank layer in Sangiran. These were originally named *Meganthropus*, and several authorities during the past twenty years have claimed Australopithecine affinities for them. Most today consider them to be within the range of tooth-size allowable for *erectus*. Nevertheless, the African evidence has shown how two separate hominid lines could and did exist contemporaneously in the same part of the continent for about one million years (*Homo* and the robust Australopithecines). So while it seems very unlikely that Australopithecines *sensu stricto* did reach Indonesia, mainly because the fossil record begins there too late in time, the possibility of two successive *erectus* immigrations cannot yet be ruled out entirely. Indeed, the whole question of population replacement arises in a far more controversial context in the transition from *erectus* to *sapiens*.

The great mystery over *Homo erectus* in Southeast Asia concerns its fate. The view most widely accepted until recently has been that formulated originally by Weidenreich, and more recently supported by A. G. Thorne and M. Wolpoff,[15] that the Javanese remains all belong to a recognizable and regional morphological lineage which lies in the ancestral line of at least some of the *Homo sapiens* populations of early Australian prehistory. The Chinese fossils may likewise be considered to lie in the direct ancestry of the modern Mongoloids of eastern and Southeast Asia. Wolpoff has more recently claimed, in partial support of this view, that *Homo erectus* across the Old World underwent specific evolutionary changes during the 1.5 million years of its existence. These changes include increasing brain size, reductions in muscularity and tooth size, and decreasing sexual dimorphism. They suggest that the species was not a static and extinct dead-end outside Africa and that it could have evolved into, or at least transmitted many genes to, modern populations over many regions of the Old World.[16]

The major opposition to the regional continuity school comes from those who favour a punctuational or 'Noah's Ark' model of evolution; in their view, the ancestors of modern *sapiens*, ultimately derived from an *erectus* population in Africa, spread out over the Old World at some uncertain time before about 40,000 years ago.[17] In this view, speciation is regarded as

[15] 'Regional continuity in Pleistocene hominid evolution', *American Journal of Physical Anthropology*, 55 (1981); Wolpoff, 'Human evolution at the peripheries: the pattern at the eastern edge', in P. V. Tobias, ed., *Hominid evolution: past, present and future*, New York, 1985.

[16] M. Wolpoff, 'Evolution in *Homo erectus*: the question of stasis', *Paleobiology*, 10, 4 (1984). See also A. Fisher, 'The emergence of humanness', *Mosaic*, 19, 1 (1988).

[17] R. L. Cann, M. Stoneking and A. C. Wilson, 'Mitochondrial DNA and human evolution', *Nature*, 325 (1987); C. B. Stringer and P. Andrews, 'Genetic and fossil evidence for the origin of modern humans', *Science*, 239 (1988); G. P. Rightmire, '*Homo erectus* and later Middle Pleistocene humans', *Annual Review of Anthropology*, 17 (1988).

a local rather than a continent-wide event; novel adaptations arise locally, and their bearers then spread more widely. This model regards *Homo erectus* as static in an evolutionary sense and, except in Africa, without genetic issue.

This debate has, of course, been of importance for many years in Europe, a region which may (like Southeast Asia) be regarded as a fairly remote peninsula of the Eurasian super-continent. In Europe the debate is over replacement of Neanderthals by modern humans versus the possibility of genetic continuity. It is significant to note that the debate changes in character with the area under consideration; Neanderthal replacement and extinction seem to be favoured explanations in France, but not necessarily in eastern Europe where transitional forms between Neanderthals and modern humans are claimed by several researchers. Unfortunately, in Southeast Asia there is simply insufficient fossil evidence to allow a proper evaluation of the two theories, and it may be simplistic to regard them as all-or-nothing alternatives. Indeed, there are biologists who favour both a radiation of modern humans into Southeast Asia and some degree of genetic assimilation of pre-existing populations;[18] one can hardly deny that both processes have operated on an enormous scale within the recent millennia of agricultural and colonial population expansion. But the recent human experience has involved one species capable of interbreeding throughout its range; one can only guess if this would have been true for late *erectus* and incoming *sapiens* populations in China and Java, for whom the remoteness of common ancestry might have been much greater than that which binds modern populations.

It is my suspicion, albeit without the benefit of formal proof, that Asian *Homo erectus* was not simply replaced without issue. The morphological similarities of the cranium and skeleton which link *erectus* in Java and China with the younger *sapiens* populations of the eastern Old World are hard to explain simply as the identical results of natural selection on successive and unrelated species, although the 'Noah's Ark' model in its purest form demands such an explanation. Furthermore, the youngest remains of *Homo erectus* from Java, those from Ngandong and Sambungmacan, show clear signs of evolution beyond the earlier series from Sangiran and Trinil. The eleven crania found together with a dense accumulation of animal bones in the lower part of the Late Pleistocene terrace at Ngandong, recently dated by the uranium-thorium method on bone to about 100,000 years ago,[19] have large (1160 cubic centimetres) and broad braincases and yet are clearly the direct and regional descendants of the earlier Javanese populations in terms of skull morphology and facial robusticity. They are, however, sufficiently advanced for some authors to regard them as early *sapiens*, and they are the first Javanese hominids for whom there is strong circumstantial evidence for stone-tool use. It is therefore not impossible that tool-using hominids approaching the *sapiens*

[18] For instance, G. Brauer, 'The "Afro-European *sapiens* hypothesis", and hominid evolution in East Asia', in P. Andrews and J. L. Franzen, eds., *The Early Evolution of Man*, Frankfurt: Senckenberg Institute, 1984.

[19] G.-J. Bartstra, S. Soegondho and A. van der Wijk, 'Ngandong man: age and artefacts', *Journal of Human Evolution*, 17 (1988).

grade, living some 60,000 years before the first truly modern populations in Southeast Asia, should have been at least partially ancestral to their ultimate successors.

Like the debate over the fate of *Homo erectus*, the issue of the cultural standing of this species in Southeast Asia is also very contentious. There are no known primary living sites older than about 40,000 years in Southeast Asia, and all of the *erectus* fossils from Java have been found in situations suggesting secondary deposition, without direct and unequivocal associations with stone tools. For instance, the Ngandong remains occurred with very large numbers of animal bones in a situation which suggests movement by river action,[20] and the earlier fossils all come from alluvial or lacustrine deposits. Hence the Sangiran and Trinil hominids have no stone tools in proper association, and debates about the tool-using abilities of these particular hominids are unlikely to be productive at the present time.[21]

However, it is clear that, like the other pre-*sapiens* populations of Africa and Eurasia, the Javanese hominids favoured fairly open parkland or monsoonal forest landscapes with high mammal biomasses, and generally avoided the equatorial rainforests. The much fuller archaeological records of Africa and China clearly indicate stone-tool use and meat-eating throughout the timespan of *Homo erectus*, and back beyond two million years ago in East Africa, although there is still considerable debate over whether the meat was hunted or simply scavenged from carnivore kills. The Southeast Asian evidence cannot yet contribute to this debate, and one analyst has recently suggested that the teeth of the Java fossils suggest a vegetarian rather than a meat diet.[22] This could explain the absence of stone tools, if the absence is real. On the other hand, stone tools are certainly found in association with Middle Pleistocene hominid fossils in India and China, so a complete absence of them in Java would be unprecedented. Only further fieldwork is likely to solve this problem.

Despite the absence of stone tools in direct association with any Southeast Asian pre-*sapiens* hominids, there have been numerous discoveries of tools in geological contexts for which Middle Pleistocene dates have been claimed. None of these claims is secure, but a brief review is warranted. Most of these industries are based on large pebble and flake tools which have become popularly known as 'chopper/chopping-tools'. They contrast in a very general way with the Acheulian handaxe industries of Africa, Europe and India, although it must be remembered that bifacial handaxes often do occur in the chopper/chopping-tool industries, especially in Vietnam and Java. The problem in the past, however, has been that researchers have often assumed that large and crude tool industries of this type are necessarily 'Lower Palaeolithic' and of Early or Middle Pleistocene age. Modern research has shown that they need have no particular

20 A. P. Santa Luca, *The Ngandong Fossil Hominids*, New Haven, 1980.

21 R. P. Soejono, 'New data on the Palaeolithic industry in Indonesia', *Congrès Internationale de Paléontologie Humaine*, Pretirage Tome 2, Nice, 1982, states that a single stone tool has been excavated from Bapang (Kabuh) deposits at Ngebung near Sangiran. A single find such as this clearly needs more confirmation.

22 P. F. Puech, 'Tooth wear, diet and the artifacts of Java Man', *Current Anthropology*, 24 (1983).

chronological focus—they can indeed be Holocene in many instances—and in no case is an antiquity older than Late Pleistocene absolutely secure.

On the mainland of Southeast Asia pebble-tool industries of this type have been reported from many sites over the years; from the terraces of the middle Irrawaddy in Burma (the 'Anyathian' industry), from the Mekong terraces of Cambodia, and from sites such as Nui Do in Thanh Hoa Province of northern Vietnam. None of these assemblages has absolute dates, but it has recently been claimed that stone tools found at Ban Mae Tha in Lampang Province, northern Thailand, originate from beneath a basalt flow dated by the potassium-argon method to between 600,000 and 800,000 years ago.[23] If the claims are correct these tools would certainly be the oldest dated ones in Southeast Asia, but this still requires confirmation. The only other important mainland industry once thought to date from the Middle Pleistocene, the so-called 'Tampanian' pebble and flake industry from Kota Tampan in Perak, Malaysia, is now believed to date only to about 30,000 years ago.[24] Hence, it may well turn out to be an early facies of the Hoabinhian, to be described below.

In island Southeast Asia the best-known of these chopper/chopping-tool industries is the Pacitanian, recovered from non-fossiliferous colluvial and alluvial valley deposits in south central Java. This industry, which contains handaxes, steep-edged scrapers and 'horsehoof' cores as well as large flake tools, is now believed, as a result of geological research by G.-J. Bartstra, to be less than 50,000 years old. This researcher, however, has recently suggested that a much smaller flake industry found in water-rolled condition in Late Pleistocene river gravels at Ngebung near Sangiran and at Ngandong may represent the handiwork of the late *Homo erectus* population represented by the fossils from Ngandong and Sambungmacan.[25] These tools are, potentially at least, the oldest in Indonesia.

Elsewhere in the islands, pebble and flake industries have also been attributed to periods before the Late Pleistocene from the Cagayan Valley in northern Luzon and the Walanae valley in south Sulawesi. Clearly, if these attributions are correct, then views about the seaborne dispersal of early hominids across Huxley's Line would be revolutionized. Regrettably, however, the data are not secure, and the same applies to the many industries of this type reported down the Nusa Tenggara chain from Lombok to Timor,[26] in some cases in apparent but probably secondary association with the bones of stegodonts.[27] The reasons for all this uncertainty over the dating of Southeast Asian stone tools are fairly clear: no

[23] G. Pope, 'Evidence of Early Pleistocene hominid activity from Lampang, northern Thailand', BIPPA, 6 (1985); P. Sorensen, 'The prehistory of Thailand', in C. Flon, ed., *The World Atlas of Archaeology*, London, 1985.

[24] Zuraina Majid and H. D. Tjia, 'Kota Tampan, Perak', JMBRAS, 61, 2 (1988).

[25] 'Sangiran, the stone implements of Ngebung, and the Palaeolithic of Java', MQRSEA, 9 (1985); G.-J. Bartstra et al., 'Ngandong Man' *Journal of Human Evolution*, 17 (1988).

[26] For recent discoveries in Wallacea see R. P. Soejono, 'Stone tools of Palaeolithic type from Lombok', *Man and Culture in Oceania*, 3 (1987).

[27] However, since many of the Lesser Sundas would have been visible from one another, starting from Bali across to Lombok, it is clear that the possibility of pre-*sapiens* settlement as far east as Timor must be considered seriously. The water gaps would have been narrower during glacial periods.

cave deposits are known with an antiquity greater than about 40,000 years, perhaps due to the very rapid rate of limestone solution and erosion in the humid tropics. All the industries just described come from open sites, mainly alluvial, where secondary deposition has frequently occurred and where no absolute dating method has so far been applicable. It is not surprising, therefore, that the archaeological record in Southeast Asia takes on a remarkable clarity after 40,000 years ago—from this time onwards there are stratified cave deposits with ample opportunity for radiocarbon dating. Figuratively at least we enter a world of light, inhabited by tool-making and ocean-crossing members of our own species, *Homo sapiens*. The record takes on recognizable and meaningful links with the present, and begins to relate sensibly to the origins of living peoples.

## ANCESTORS FOR THE LIVING

The archaeological record of stone tools does, of course, continue on from the industries just described into the recent past. Before describing it, however, the peoples of Southeast Asia themselves, descendants of the early *sapiens* populations of the eastern Old World, must be introduced. The question of the origins of *Homo sapiens* in Asia, whether directly from local *erectus* predecessors or by a replacement radiation, has been discussed above. What should be stressed here is that the task of documenting the origins of modern human physical differentiation is a biological one which depends on studies of genetic characteristics, ancient and recent skeletal materials (especially crania), and comparative studies of phenotypic features in modern populations. Linguistic and archaeological reconstructions of prehistory can give only ambiguous hints about biological differentiation, and it is important that the results of the three disciplines be granted the independence which they deserve.

The great majority of the 400 million inhabitants of Southeast Asia today belong to a biological grouping which may be termed Southern Mongoloid. There is a degree of variation within this population, expressed most visibly in darkening skin pigmentation and increasing face and jaw size as one moves from north to south, and also from west to east within Indonesia. The only indigenous populations in Southeast Asia who are outside the Southern Mongoloid grouping are the Negritos of central peninsular Malaysia and the Philippines, and the Melanesians focused in and around New Guinea. Much of eastern Indonesia, especially Maluku and Nusa Tenggara, is an area of gentle biological gradation between Southern Mongoloids and Melanesians. There is no sharp boundary here, although major phenotypic differences are apparent if one compares populations from opposite ends of the cline, such as Timorese and Balinese.

The cline which links Indonesians and lowland Melanesians probably represents the results of gene flow over many millennia through intermarriage between populations who were ultimately of different origin. The opposite hypothesis, that the observed cline represents the results of evolutionary processes of natural selection operating on a once-unified and geographically static population, is much less satisfactory. This is because one would have to explain which selective factor could have produced such relatively lightly-pigmented and straight-haired Southern Mongoloid populations in tropical latitudes, especially along the equator in Indonesia, when elsewhere at this latitude in the Old World, and particularly in Melanesia and Africa, the trend is generally for very dark pigmentation and curled hair.[28] Indeed, there are strong but complex grounds for regarding the Southern Mongoloids as mainly the heirs to a population expansion from southern China and northern mainland Southeast Asia, for the most part within the past seven thousand years of agriculture and consequent population growth. Evolution never ceases, however, and new clines form constantly as new populations enter a region, or as existing ones adapt to new evolutionary circumstances. It would be most unwise to claim that the Southern Mongoloid populations migrated southwards in one vast, identical and unchanging wave, even though the writings of some earlier authorities suggest that they visualized such a scenario.

The most acceptable model for Southeast Asian biological prehistory therefore postulates a gradual and complex replacement of an indigenous Australo-Melanesian population by expanding Southern Mongoloids. The Negritos, who have probably undergone localized and independent selection for their relatively short stature, are thus the only Southeast Asian survivors of the original Australo-Melanesian continuum outside the eastern Indonesian clinal zone. The early expansion of the Southern Mongoloid population was due in part to the demographic advantages provided by an agricultural as opposed to a foraging economy, together with the inter-island mobility encouraged by the development of advanced seagoing and navigational skills.

The Negritos are thus of great significance in Southeast Asia: they seem to represent the modern members of an Australo-Melanesian population which may once have occupied much of the region, perhaps even to as far north as Cambodia and Taiwan if some admittedly ambiguous historical records are taken into consideration. Today, they occupy only the Andaman Islands, parts of peninsular Malaysia and Thailand, and parts of the central and northern Philippines. Most of the Philippine Negritos have now adopted sporadic agricultural practices and all have adopted, within recent millennia, Austronesian languages from neighbouring cultivators. The Semang of Malaysia, while still primarily hunter-gatherers and forest collectors-for-trade, have at some time adopted Austroasiatic languages related to ancestral Mon and Khmer. The few remaining Andamanese, some of whom live in virtual island isolation, are the only ones to have

[28] On the general correlation of skin pigmentation with latitude see G. L. Tasa et al., 'Reflectometer reports on human pigmentation', *Current Anthropology*, 26 (1985). The only other large indigenous equatorial population which has not developed dark skin pigmentation is that in the Americas. Since the ancestors of these American Mongoloids crossed from Asia at least 10,000 years ago, it is clear that differences in skin pigmentation may take tens of thousands of years to develop; see J. S. Friedlaender, ed., *The Solomon Islands Project*, Oxford, 1987, 357. Likewise, Australia has been settled for at least 40,000 years by a dark-pigmented population of ultimate tropical Indonesian origin, but it seems that only a slight loss of pigmentation occurred in the cool temperate south of the continent and Tasmania.

retained a relatively pure foraging economy together with their original languages, unrelated to any outside major grouping.

The major point about the Negritos, one which has often been overlooked, is that none live close to the equator. As far as can be detected, the inland equatorial rainforests of Sumatra, Borneo and possibly Sulawesi seem to have been virtually uninhabited, except within reach of coastal resources, until they were entered by the ancestors of the present Southern Mongoloid agricultural inhabitants. The Negritos, therefore, may stem ultimately from the larger Australo-Melanesian populations who inhabited the more widespread monsoonal forest environments of the Pleistocene intertropical zone. The relatively short stature characteristic of modern Negritos may be the result of adaptation to the warmer and more humid climatic conditions of the Holocene, adaptations mediated by the lowered availability of protein and the value of small body size for easy movement in closed rainforests.

Modern genetic data also help to support the above picture of recent (mainly post-Pleistocene) Southern Mongoloid expansion in Southeast Asia. Blood groups alone are no longer considered reliable indicators of population origins owing to their tendency to undergo rapid changes in frequency, but there are other genetically controlled systems which seem to be much more stable in this regard, perhaps because their frequencies reflect mutation alone and not the biasing effects of selection and drift. These, therefore, may record aspects of shared ancestry between populations rather than just similar environmental adaptations. Population-specific variants which appear to distinguish Asian Mongoloids (including Southern Mongoloids) from Aboriginal Australians and Melanesians occur in the transferrin, immunoglobulin, and Gc serum protein systems, the Diego red cell and human leukocyte antigen systems, and the mitochondrial genome.[29] In addition, the transferrin variants seem to undergo a clinical change of frequency along the Nusa Tenggara chain which corresponds with the visible phenotypic situation in eastern Indonesia.

Abnormal haemoglobin E is also common amongst Southeast Asian populations as far east as Timor and virtually absent beyond; Melanesians have other genetic abnormalities which give resistance to malaria, such as thalassemia, G6PD deficiency and the ovalocytosis red-cell variant. Unlike the genetic variants discussed above, the genes for these abnormalities must have been highly susceptible to natural selection when carriers first entered a malarial region. However, as pointed out by R. L. Kirk,[30] once the effective protective gene was established, the chance of a new mutation entering the population would be reduced, so in this respect a high frequency of haemoglobin E could be an important and ancient marker for many Southeast Asian Mongoloids, dating back at least to the period of agricultural expansion into tropical latitudes.

[29] See R. L. Kirk, 'Human genetic diversity in south-east Asia and the western Pacific', in D. F. Roberts and G. F. de Stefano, eds., *Genetic Variation and its Maintenance*, Cambridge, 1986; A. V. S. Hill and S. Serjeantson, eds., *The Colonization of the Pacific: a Genetic Trail*, Oxford, 1989.

[30] 'Human genetic diversity', 116.

Another interesting observation about Indonesian genetics has been made by A. Sofro.[31] His analysis of genetic distances based on eighteen polymorphic loci shows that Indonesian populations fall into western and eastern clusters, with the Bimanese of Sumbawa occupying an approximate mid-point, and that the eastern cluster reflects the most internal variation. This may be a very important observation, since the Melanesian region to the east seems to have been a focus of early agricultural development and a presumed centre of genetic gravity since at least the early Holocene. One might expect that Australo-Melanesian populations were always denser in Holocene times in eastern Indonesia than in the west, hence the impressive length and complexity of the Mongoloid–Melanesian cline in the east.

Despite the many important observations which can be made from genetic evidence, however, the most direct evidence for ancient human ancestry comes not from the living, but from the dead. Skeletal remains are often poorly dated, fragmentary, and frankly ambiguous when questions of population origin are under consideration, but they certainly cannot be ignored. Skeletal remains tend to add complexity to the picture; nowhere is there clear-cut evidence from them for rapid population replacement, and we must allow for millennia of intermarriage and local evolution. The important concept is that human biological history of Southeast Asia has involved not a swift replacement of some populations by others, but a gradual southwards and eastwards shift in the structure and centre of gravity of a cline between Southern Mongoloids and Australo-Melanesians.

As discussed above, there is considerable disagreement amongst biological anthropologists concerning the presence or absence of continuity from *erectus* to *sapiens* in East and Southeast Asia. In China the arguments for a continuous local evolution of Mongoloids are quite strong, and many linking skeletal remains of Late Pleistocene age are now reported. In Southeast Asia the oldest cranial and mandibular remains which can be referred to as putatively Australo-Melanesian come from Niah Cave in Sarawak and Tabon Cave on Palawan (Philippines), both dated loosely within the range 40,000 to 20,000 years ago. In addition, a very large series of skeletal remains of Australoids *sensu stricto* dates from about 30,000 years ago and onwards in Australia.

No Pleistocene fossils from Southeast Asia have yet been claimed as unequivocally Mongoloid, although the Late Pleistocene skulls from Wajak in Java are stated to have certain Mongoloid facial features by T. Jacob.[32] In addition, it has recently been claimed that certain Australian and Southeast Asian skulls of Late Pleistocene age have affinities with some contemporary or older Chinese skulls, such as that from Liujiang in Guangxi.[33] The basic conclusion to be drawn from this is that not all 'Mongolization' of Southeast Asia necessarily occurred with the develop-

[31] 'Population Genetic Studies in Indonesia', Ph.D. thesis, Australian National University, 1982.

[32] *Some Problems Pertaining to the Racial History of the Indonesian Region*, Utrecht, 1967.

[33] M. H. Wolpoff, X. J. Wu and A. G. Thorne, 'Modern *Homo sapiens* origins . . . ', in F. H. Smith and F. Spencer, eds., *The Origins of Modern Humans*, New York, 1984.

ment of agriculture in the Holocene, and some gene flow from more northerly sources may well have been entering the region long before the end of the Pleistocene. Unfortunately, available data do not allow greater specificity.

During the Holocene there is an increasingly widespread occurrence of Southern Mongoloid skeletal material during the past 7000 years, except in regions such as the central Malay peninsula and eastern Indonesia where modern populations still demonstrate a great deal of Australo-Melanesian inheritance. An overall reduction in tooth size in Southeast Asia seems also to be associated with these changes, presumably linked with the availability of softer foods through agricultural processing.[34] This gene flow trend has been gradual, however, and even in regions as far north as northern Vietnam and southern China the prevailing phenotype in early Neolithic times appears to have been considerably less Mongoloid than is the case today. Indeed, it is quite clear that a great deal of the Mongoloid expansion which is evident in Southeast Asia, whether replacing Australo-Melanesian hunter-gatherers or assimilating populations of 'Proto-Malays',[35] has taken place squarely within the historical period. It is still happening today, as Filipino agriculturalists impinge on the hunting territories of Negritos and Indonesian transmigrants leave Java for the hinterlands of Irian Jaya and Maluku.

Apart from the timing of Mongoloid gene flow into Southeast Asia, another important question concerns its general source-region. Simple geographical logic would of course point to adjacent parts of southern China, as well as northern Southeast Asia itself. This logic is supported by the dental analyses of Turner, who has proposed that the dentitions of Southeast Asians (including Negritos) belong, in terms of tooth morphology, to a grouping termed Sundadont. He distinguishes Sundadont teeth from those of Sinodonts (north-east Asian Mongoloids) and Australo-Melanesians, and points out that all prehistoric teeth from Southeast Asia, even the most ancient such as those of the Niah and Wajak skulls, are Sundadont. Hence, no case for a southerly expansion of northeast Asian Mongoloids can be seriously entertained, and the teeth of Aboriginal Australians and Melanesians clearly began to diverge away in morphological terms from their Southeast Asian Sundadont cousins at least 40,000 years ago. Since Sundadont teeth were probably universal throughout southern China during the Late Pleistocene and early Holocene, all sources of direct gene flow into Southeast Asia are likely to lie south of the Yangtze River.[36]

In summarizing this section, the main features of Southeast Asian

[34] C. L. Brace, 'Tooth size and Austronesian origins', in P. Naylor, ed., *Austronesian Studies*, Ann Arbor, 1980.

[35] The terms 'Proto-Malay' and 'Deutero-Malay', as used by previous generations of physical anthropologists, mean little in the light of modern knowledge of Southeast Asian prehistory. They suggest two separate Mongoloid strata, a concept unsupported by any other evidence.

[36] See C. G. Turner II, 'Teeth and prehistory in Asia', *Scientific American*, February 1989. For a related view emphasizing evolution within Southeast Asia, see D. Bulbeck, 'A re-evaluation of possible evolutionary processes in Southeast Asia since the Late Pleistocene', BIPPA, 3 (1982).

biological evolution within *Homo sapiens* populations may be presented as follows:

1 The population of Southeast Asia around 40,000 years ago may have been predominantly Australo-Melanesian, with some Southern Mongoloid features developing in the northern part of the region. Founders moved away to settle Australia and New Guinea at this time, if not before, and these have since evolved in relative isolation from their Southeast Asian contemporaries.

2 The continuing populations of Southeast Asia underwent widespread cranial and facial gracilization, due partly to local selection and partly to southerly gene flow from regions of Mongoloid development in southern China. Southerly populations probably remained predominantly Australo-Melanesian in many aspects of phenotype until well into the Holocene.

3 During the Holocene, and especially within the past 7000 years, continuing southerly and easterly expansions of Southern Mongoloid populations have occurred. Today these movements can most easily be identified in the linguistic and historical records of peoples speaking Austroasiatic, Tai-Kadai, Tibeto-Burman and Austronesian languages. Perhaps the most significant of them can be postulated to have occurred during the early millennia of agriculture, when expansionary processes began which ultimately were to carry people of Mongoloid affinity right across the Indian and Pacific Oceans, to places as far as Madagascar and Easter Island.

## THE ARCHAEOLOGICAL RECORD—LATE PLEISTOCENE TO MID-HOLOCENE

Radiocarbon dating can be utilized from about 40,000 years ago. From that time down to the appearance of agriculture, mainly between 6000 and 3000 years ago depending on locality, the archaeological record is focused on tools of flaked stone and circumstantial evidence for a fairly mobile foraging lifestyle. The record is a simple one in lithic terms, since blade and microlithic tools did not appear in the region until well into the Holocene. Furthermore, the rising sea levels of the post-glacial period have probably destroyed the vast majority of coastal sites which may have existed prior to about 9000 years ago, especially in the western part of Sundaland.

The artefact assemblages to be described in this section belong to a period when the hunting and collection of food, as opposed to systematic agricultural production, may be presumed to have been the sole form of subsistence. The transition to the latter mode was in most regions relatively sharp, the implication being that most of the original hunters and gatherers of Southeast Asia were assimilated fairly rapidly in areas favourable for cultivation. In some regions they may have developed or adopted cultivation practices themselves, but the archaeological record alone is generally ambiguous on this point. Whatever the mechanisms behind this economic change, it is clear that the remnant hunters and gatherers who survive today have undergone considerable contact with agriculturalists and can give only very ambiguous information about life in the Late Pleistocene.[37]

For instance, the Negritos have probably survived assimilation only because they occupy remote and relatively unproductive environments which until recently were of little interest to expanding agriculturalists. The only Negritos who may be considered relatively uninfluenced by contact with alien cultural traditions are the Little Andamanese, but even these had probably acquired pigs and pottery manufacture by about 2000 years ago, and like all other Negrito groups had stopped making stone tools well before European contact.[38] The Philippine Negritos have virtually all adopted some kind of cultivation, albeit reluctantly,[39] and the Semang of Malaysia have also been in contact with neighbouring cultivators for millennia, although they have been able to retain a mobile hunting and collecting lifestyle more successfully than their Philippine counterparts. It would be presumptuous, therefore, to assume that these groups can reveal very much about the details of Late Pleistocene life in Southeast Asia, apart from the generalizations which one might make about the likelihood that societies of that time were egalitarian, of low population density, and built around small numbers of independent and mobile nuclear families.

The situation is even less helpful with the Southern Mongoloid hunters and gatherers. These include Austronesian-speaking groups such as the Punan of interior Borneo, Kubu of Sumatra and Tasaday of Mindanao,[40] and the Austroasiatic-speaking Yumbri of northern Thailand and Shompen of Great Nicobar. With these there are some very grave questions to be asked concerning the lengths of time for which their present lifestyles, dominated by hunting and gathering, have been practised. The Punan and Kubu, for instance, must almost certainly be derived from original populations of cultivators. Their ancestors possibly entered the forests gradually and voluntarily, partially as hunters and partially as collectors of forest products for trade.[41] These groups may well have little to tell us about 'pristine' and pre-agricultural hunting and gathering in the region.

The conclusion to be drawn is that Late Pleistocene life can be reconstructed only from Late Pleistocene data. The linguistic and ethnographic records cannot be extended back this far, and comparative cultural observations of present-day peoples are likely to have little relevance. It is also becoming more apparent that Late Pleistocene people inhabited environments which

[37] See T. N. Headland and L. A. Reid, 'Hunter-gatherers and their neighbours from prehistory to the present', *Current Anthropology*, 30 (1989).

[38] Z. Cooper, 'Archaeological explorations in the Andaman Islands', BIPPA, 6 (1985).

[39] T. Headland, *Why Foragers do not Become Farmers*, University Microfilms International, 1986. A reluctance amongst hunters and gatherers to develop agriculture if they can exchange or work in return for cultivated produce is also reported from Africa; see J. D. Clark and S. A. Brandt, eds., *From Hunters to Farmers*, Berkeley, 1984, 5.

[40] The Tasaday, according to many recent media statements, are reputed to be fakes. I think it may be better to regard them as the last survivors of a short-lived and relatively unsuccessful attempt to colonize what was once a large block of rainforest, without investing the labour input demanded by agriculture.

[41] For a clear statement of this argument see C. L. Hoffman, 'Punan foragers in the trading networks of Southeast Asia', in C. Schrire, ed., *Past and Present in Hunter Gatherer Studies*, Orlando, 1984.

were often very different from those of today, and which probably underwent dramatic changes over fairly short periods of time. Some of these changes have already been discussed; they include sea-level fluctuations, changes in vegetation and rainfall, and animal extinctions. At 40,000 years ago the sea level was around 50 metres below present; sufficient to join Borneo, Sumatra and Java to the Asian mainland. By 18,000 years ago the sea was at its lowest, perhaps 130 metres below the present level, and Sundaland would have been exposed as a vast and probably rather dry subcontinent with a vegetational cover comprising less rainforest than now, but probably more seasonal monsoon forest and mangrove. With the coming of the Holocene the rainfall increased, and equatorial rainforests expanded to occupy virtually the whole of the equatorial region.

The results of these changes on humans are still rather obscure. It has been suggested, for instance, that the rapidly rising sea levels of the period between 18,000 and 6000 years ago would have forced people to migrate away from Sundaland, eastwards into the Pacific, as they lost their lands.[42] However, as pointed out by F. L. and D. F. Dunn,[43] the coastlines of Sundaland increased in length by about 46 per cent as the sea level rose from minus 120 metres to the present level, so the conditions for coastal occupation may actually have improved and people could have survived individual episodes of rapid inundation by simply retreating inland. Thus the changes in sea level need not have impacted directly on sparse groups of human foragers, although there may have been other indirect and minor impacts.

As one example, the terminal Pleistocene severing of land links to Borneo, combined with increasing forest cover as the climate became warmer and wetter, seems to have led to a number of local animal extinctions (tiger, Javan rhinoceros, dhole, tapir and possibly giant pangolin) and probably also many instances of species reduction in size.[44] The earlier shift into drier conditions leading up to the last glacial maximum may also have taken a toll of forest animals; the orang utan made its final appearance on the Asian mainland in cave deposits in northern Vietnam about 18,000 years ago,[45] and may have succumbed to the cool, dry and relatively deforested conditions of this period. The precise timings and reasons for animal extinctions in Southeast Asia are poorly understood, but most zoologists favour natural causes rather than over-hunting by humans; all the evidence for this period suggests that human populations were fairly sparse, and for the most part avoiding the

42 J. Gibbons and F. Clunie, 'Sea level changes and Pacific prehistory', *Journal of Pacific History*, 21 (1986); and reply by P. Bellwood, 'The impact of sea level changes on Pacific prehistory', *Journal of Pacific History*, 22 (1987).

43 'Maritime adaptations and exploitation of marine resources in Sundaic Southeast Asian prehistory; MQRSEA, 3 (1977).

44 Earl of Cranbrook, 'The contribution of archaeology to the zoogeography of Borneo', *Fieldiana, Zoology*, 42 (1988); L. R. Heaney, 'Mammalian species richness on the Sunda Shelf', *Oecologia*, 61 (1984).

45 Ha Van Tan, 'The Late Pleistocene climate in Southeast Asia; new data from Vietnam', MQRSEA, 9 (1985).

rainforests until the Holocene, by which time better methods of trapping might have allowed more hunting success.

In general, it must be accepted that there is no convincing evidence of any major impact of the Late Pleistocene environmental changes on the human cultures of Southeast Asia, a clear contrast with the situation in many temperate zones of Europe and Asia. This contrast, however, may simply reflect poor knowledge of Southeast Asia compared with the rest of the Old World, and also the relatively inimical conditions for survival there of the Late Pleistocene archaeological record.

This record, as it is currently understood, comprises a very basic flake industry, with sundry core and pebble-tool components, which occurs virtually everywhere from about 40,000 years ago until well into the metal-using period (variously between c. 2000 BC and the first millennium CE). Basic forms were also carried east by some of the early settlers of Australia and New Guinea. This fundamental flake industry is diversified in some places with elaborations such as biface, prepared-core, blade and microlithic technologies (Figure 2.3), but overall patterning is hard to discern; Southeast Asia does not have widespread horizon-marking tool forms, and the flaked-stone industries of the region still tell little about any zones of stylistic or ethnic differentiation which may have existed during the pre-agricultural period. Neither do they record in any clear fashion the Holocene economic changes centred on agriculture.

The basic flake industry occurs chiefly on fine-grained rocks such as chert, jasper and obsidian in the islands of Southeast Asia, and generally on coarser-grained rocks of river pebble origin on the mainland. Most flakes are unretouched and simply used as struck, and they occur together with a range of cores (sometimes of a distinctive horsehoof shape which also occurs commonly in Australia and New Guinea), pebble tools, and debitage. The well-known 'Hoabinhian' stone tool industries of mainland Southeast Asia are focused more on pebble-tool production, but these are almost entirely a Holocene phenomenon, as are the blade and microlith industries of Java and Sulawesi.

On the Southeast Asian mainland the oldest reliably-dated flake industry (excluding those listed above as possibly connected with *Homo erectus*) comes from basal layers dated between 37,000 and 27,000 years ago at Lang Rongrien cave in Krabi Province, southern Thailand. These tools occur with remains of land tortoises and rodents, but marine shells are absent; the cave is twelve kilometres inland now, and was probably much further inland during lower sea-level conditions. Above this tool-bearing layer is a layer of roof-fall 1.5 metres thick, and the cave appears not to have been inhabited again until Hoabinhian pebble tools first appeared about 9600 years ago.[46] The older Lang Rongrien industry lacks pebble tools (although the sample is very small), but these are present in the lower layers of Sai Yok cave in Kanchanaburi Province, where pebble tools and horsehoof or 'flat-iron' shaped cores occur towards the base of the

[46] D. Anderson, 'A Pleistocene–early Holocene rock shelter in Peninsular Thailand', *National Geographic Research*, 3 (1987).

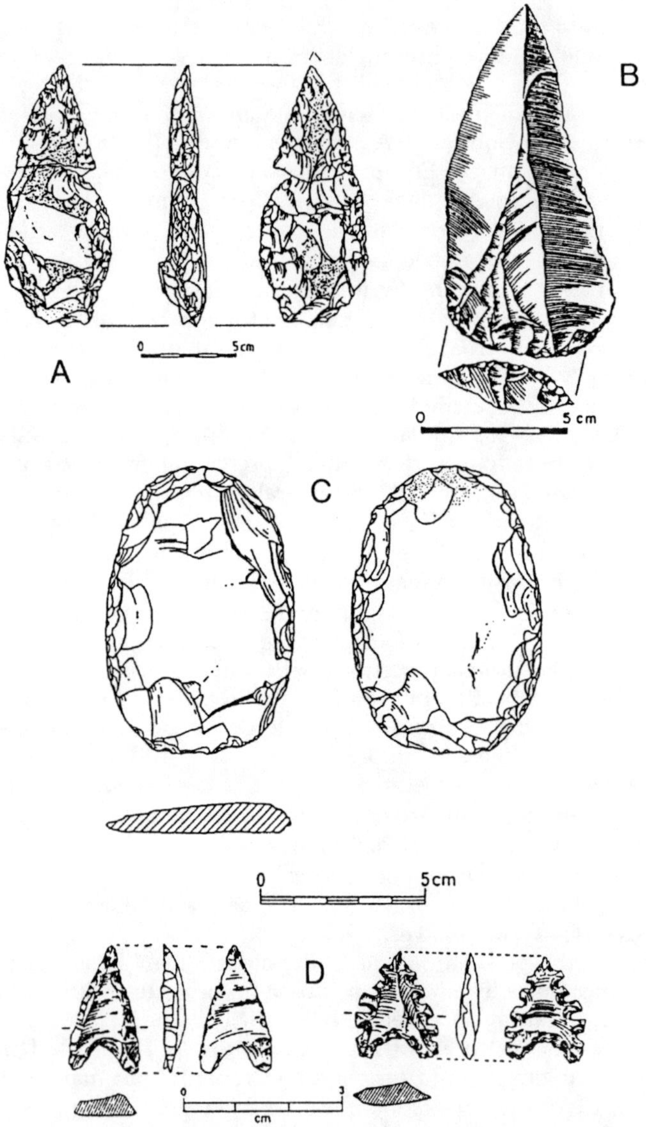


Figure 2.3 Distinctive types of stone tools from Late Pleistocene and Holocene Southeast Asian assemblages.
**A.** Late Pleistocene chert biface from Tingkayu, Sabah, northern Borneo.
**B.** Late Pleistocene chert blade with faceted striking platform from Leang Burun shelter 2, south Sulawesi.
**C.** Early Holocene Hoabinhian pebble biface from Gua Cha, Kelantan, Malaysia.
**D.** Mid-Holocene Maros Points (top) and backed microliths (below) from Ulu Leng shelter, south Sulawesi.
B and D, courtesy Ian Glover, Institute of Archaeology, London; C courtesy Adi Haji Taha, National Museum, Kuala Lumpur.

4.75 metre sequence. Although Sai Yok has no absolute dates, a Late Pleistocene antiquity may be expected.[47]

In northern Vietnam an industry termed the Sonviian is reported from open sites on elevated terrain around the inland edge of the Red River deltaic plains, and also from several caves where it is stratified beneath Hoabinhian layers. Sonviian pebble tools tend to be flaked peripherally, rather than over the whole of one or both faces as were many later Hoabinhian tools, and in Nguom rock shelter in Bac Thai Province they are dated between about 23,000 and 18,000 years ago. They occur here with bones of pig, cattle, porcupine, macaque monkey, and also the locally-extinct orang utan.[48] Below the true Sonviian industry as recognized by Vietnamese archaeologists there is a layer in Nguom shelter with only small flakes, but as with Lang Rongrien the sample size appears to be small. More evidence is needed before it can be accepted that a small flake industry preceded a large pebble one in Southeast Asia—a sequence which would be entirely the reverse of that in most other regions of the Old World.[49]

After about 13,000 years ago these earlier mainland industries graded into a fairly classic form of pebble-tool Hoabinhian in many regions, and widespread evidence for rainforest occupation, particularly in the Thai-Malaysian peninsula, commenced. To this we will return, after a brief survey of Late Pleistocene industries in island Southeast Asia, where the record is seemingly more variable than on the mainland. Flake-tool industries of Late Pleistocene data are now known from many sites, including the Niah Caves in Sarawak, the Madai-Baturong region in Sabah, Tabon Cave on Palawan, and Leang Burung shelter 2 in southern Sulawesi.

Inside the huge 60-metre-high West Mouth of the Niah Caves in Sarawak an industry of flake and pebble tools, together with bone spatulae and points, appears to date back to between 30,000 and 40,000 years ago.[50] The early modern skull from the lower levels of this site has been referred to above; this is potentially the oldest of this evolutionary grade so far recovered from Southeast Asia, although its date is not very secure. Niah is also of interest because it has produced edge-ground axes made on pebbles which may be over 10,000 years old; these represent an important technological innovation which also appeared, presumably independently, in Late Pleistocene contexts in Japan, northern Australia and the New Guinea Highlands. The edge-grinding of axes might also go back into the terminal Pleistocene in the Bacsonian of northern Vietnam, and it is

[47] It is impossible to give a reference for every archaeological site mentioned from here onwards. Further descriptions for most will be found in PIMA, and P. Bellwood, *Man's Conquest of the Pacific*, Auckland, 1978; also C. Higham, *The Archaeology of Mainland Southeast Asia*, Cambridge, UK, 1989.

[48] Ha Van Tan, 'The Late Pleistocene climate'.

[49] It should be noted, however, that Bartstra has recently claimed this to be the case for Java, with small flakes from Ngebung predating the larger pebble and flake Pacitanian industries; 'Sangiran, the stone implements of Ngebung, and the Palaeolithic of Java', MQRSEA 9 (1985).

[50] Z. Majid, 'The West Mouth, Niah, in the prehistory of Southeast Asia', *Sarawak Museum Journal*, 32 (1982).

of interest that the appearance of this technology long predates the appearance of systematic agriculture in this part of the world. In most other regions of the Old World such tools are normally found in agricultural contexts.

The West Mouth has also yielded a large series of human burials in flexed or sitting postures dated between 14,000 and 8000 years ago. Some of these were coated with haematite, one had a rhinoceros femur as a pillow, and another was apparently buried with an edge-ground pebble tool. As with Hoabinhian burials on the mainland of Southeast Asia, a fully extended burial posture is rare and only becomes dominant in the later agricultural stage. The cave inhabitants were also able to hunt or scavenge meat from no less than fifty-eight species of mammals, including primates, carnivores, and herbivores ranging in size from small rodents to rhinoceros and cattle. The economy here was clearly opportunistic: anything available was caught and eaten, although pigs, porcupines and monkeys were the most common animals, perhaps reflecting their easier availability. The fauna suggests that, while there may have been more open glades within the forest during the Late Pleistocene, the region around Niah was essentially under rainforest not too different from that of today. This means that some degree of occupation in near-coastal equatorial rainforest is of great antiquity in this part of Sundaland. As yet there is no evidence for any long-term interior rainforest occupation by pre-agricultural foragers, as already noted.

Further north in eastern Sabah recent archaeological research has focused on a series of caves and open sites in the Madai and Baturong limestone massifs and the Tingkayu valley, slightly inland from Lahad Datu Bay.[51] The Tingkayu open sites are believed to have been situated near the outlet of a lava-dammed lake of 75 square kilometres which existed between 28,000 and 17,000 years ago, and include a well-preserved working floor for a wide range of pointed or ovate bifacially-flaked tools made on slabs of chert (Figure 2.3A). Unfortunately these sites cannot be directly dated, and they contain nothing apart from the debitage left by biface manufacture. However, the tools are so far unique in Southeast Asia, with only distant and possibly coincidental parallels in Late Pleistocene northeast Asia and Japan. They remain something of a mystery.

Following the draining of the Tingkayu lake, the Sabah biface industry occurred no more, and caves in the Baturong and Madai massifs contain a simple industry of chert flakes and cores dating between 18,000 and 7000 years ago. These tools occur in freshwater shellfish middens (marine species were absent until the coastline moved inland towards its present position early in the Holocene), together with bones of pig, deer, cattle, porcupine, orang utan, monkey, rat, snakes and reptiles. Bones of the Javan rhinoceros and dhole, both now extinct in Borneo, occur in layers dating to about 10,000 years ago, and from this period there is also a number of large hollowed anvils or mortars with smoothly ground surfaces.

[51] P. Bellwood, *Archaeological Research in South-eastern Sabah*, Sabah Museum Monograph 2, Kota Kinabalu, 1988.

On Palawan Island in the southern Philippines a chert flake and pebble industry similar to that from the Sabah sites has been excavated from several of the Tabon caves. This seems to have commenced at least 30,000 years ago, and like that from the Sabah sites is unassociated with marine shellfish until the Holocene; the Tabon caves would have been at least thirty-five kilometres from the sea during the last glacial maximum. Another assemblage of definite Late Pleistocene age is that from the rock shelter of Leang Burung 2 in the Maros limestone region of southern Sulawesi, north of Ujung Pandang (Makassar). Here layers dated to between approximately 30,000 and 20,000 years ago have produced a few elongated blade-like flakes with faceted striking platforms (Figure 2.3B), representing a prepared-core technology similar to the Levalloisian of western Eurasia.[52] In this case the development seems to be localized and independent, as does a similar appearance of the technique in north-western Australia at a much later Holocene date, about 4000 years ago. Some of the Leang Burung flakes also have silica glosses on their cutting edges, perhaps resulting from the cutting of grasses or rattans, and haematite pieces are present, perhaps witnesses to some long-vanished tradition of artistic expression.[53]

Apart from the above, the only other well-reported industry which commenced during the Late Pleistocene consists of steep-edged scrapers and knives made on flakes and thick blades at least 13,000 years ago in eastern Timor. This is associated with a rather sparse Wallacean faunal assemblage of bats, extinct giant rats and reptiles,[54] together with plant fragments of Job's tears (a perennial cereal), betel vine and *Areca* nut (the ingredients of betel chewing), and candlenut (*Aleurites*). There is no reason, however, to assume that these plants were domesticated rather than simply collected and perhaps protected in the wild.

## Holocene Stone Industries and the Transition to Agriculture

The Late Pleistocene industries of Southeast Asia give an impression of uniformity with sporadic localized innovation. During the Holocene the picture becomes more variable in the islands, with the appearance of localized microlithic and blade technologies. Such small tool classes seem to have been absent on the mainland of Southeast Asia, where the pebble-tool industries generally termed Hoabinhian attained a seemingly universal distribution. The Hoabinhian, however, may have witnessed the

52 I. Glover, 'Leang Burung 2', MQRSEA, 6 (1981).

53 Some of the Maros caves have negative hand stencils outlined with red pigment, and drawings of pig or babirusa also occur. While these are undated, there seems no reason why some hand stencils at least should not be Late Pleistocene. See H. R. van Heekeren, *The Stone Age of Indonesia*, The Hague, 1972, 118–20.

54 The fauna of some of the Lesser Sunda Islands today includes non-native mammals such as macaque monkey, civet cat, pig, deer (*Cervus timorensis*) and porcupine. The marsupial phalanger also occurs archaeologically on Timor. The archaeological record for Timor, and zoological opinions in general, suggest that all these animals were introduced during the agricultural period (post–3000 BC). However, some of the non-domesticated species could have been introduced by earlier hunting and gathering populations. See G. Musser, 'The Giant Rat of Flores and its Relatives East of Borneo and Bali', *Bulletin of the American Museum of Natural History*, 169 (1981); I. Glover, *Archaeology in Eastern Timor*, Terra Australis II, Canberra, 1986.

development of edge grinding in Vietnam by the beginning of the Holocene.

It is important to note that these industries in some (but certainly not all) regions of both mainland and island Southeast Asia continued with little morphological change well into the era of agriculture and pottery, occasionally even into the first millennium CE, as perhaps in inland parts of Cambodia-Thailand and southern Sulawesi. One suspects here that the hunting and gathering populations who originally developed these flaked-stone industries continued to use them until they were eventually assimilated to an agricultural lifestyle, or until stone was replaced by iron for tools and weapons. The early agricultural populations appear to have used flaked-stone tools on a much lesser scale than their hunting and gathering predecessors, and concentrated more widely on the manufacture and use of ground-stone tools, especially adzes and knives.

On the mainland of Southeast Asia, from Burma and southern China southwards to Malaysia and parts of northern Sumatra, the dominant industry from about 13,000 years ago until the arrival of agriculture is termed the Hoabinhian, after discoveries made in the 1920s in the former Hoa Binh (now Ha Son Binh) Province of northern Vietnam.[55] The Hoabinhian has acquired a certain notoriety amongst Southeast Asian archaeologists because of claimed associations with the origins of agriculture and pottery manufacture. These associations still lack definite proof, mainly because most of the data come from poorly excavated and probably disturbed cave deposits. The term Hoabinhian also hides a great deal of local and regional variation which still remains to be documented; the use of such a term for all early Holocene assemblages of mainland Southeast Asia from beyond the Tropic of Cancer almost to the equator does not imply technological homogeneity, or that the makers were necessarily closely related in linguistic or biological terms. Indeed, the only clear observations about Hoabinhian identity come from the Malay peninsula, where the Hoabinhian foragers were almost certainly the ancestors of the Austroasiatic-speaking Negritos, and in part also of the Senoi agriculturalists. Whether the Hoabinhian also has a place in the ancestry of other mainland groups such as the Vietnamese, Thais and Burmese is simply unknown, given the difficulty of determining how much population expansion and replacement occurred throughout the region with the spread of agriculture. What is clear, however, is that many skulls from Hoabinhian sites have been accorded a degree of Australo-Melanesian affinity by Vietnamese, French and Indonesian researchers,[56] and these observations, while often vague, can hardly be ignored.

One of the most significant points about the Hoabinhian is that it seems to represent the colonization of the wet Holocene rainforests of the Malay

[55] Detailed and referenced surveys of the Hoabinhian can be found in PIMA, 162–75; Bellwood, *Man's Conquest*, 64–71; Higham, *Archaeology*, 31–65; Ha Van Tan, Nouvelles recherches préhistoriques et protohistoriques au Viêt Nam', BEFEO, 68, (1980); Ha Van Tan, 'The Hoabinhian in the context of Viet Nam', *Vietnamese Studies*, 46 (1978).

[56] See, for instance, Nguyen Lang Cuong, 'An early Hoabinhian skull from Vietnam', BIPPA, 7 (1986–7); S. Budisampurno, 'Kerangka manusia dari Bukit Kelambai Stabat, Sumatera Utara', *Pertemuan Ilmiah Arkeologi ke-III*, Jakarta, 1985.

peninsula and northern Sumatra. It also suggests a considerable increase in population density in certain more northerly zones of seasonal rainfall distribution, especially western Thailand and northern Vietnam. Demographically, therefore, it appears to represent some degree of success in the forging of new adaptations to post-glacial environments. However, there are also areas where archaeological survey has failed to find any occupation of this period, for instance the Khorat Plateau of northeastern Thailand, which for some unknown reason appears to have been almost uninhabited when settled by agriculturalists after 5000 years ago.

In terms of basic archaeological data, evidence for Hoabinhian occupation and burial activities occurs mainly in limestone caves and shelters. There are also a few coastal shell middens dating from after 8000 years ago in northern Sumatra, western peninsular Malaysia and northern Vietnam; any older than this would have been destroyed by rising sea levels. Many of the sites with marine shell deposits, both caves and open middens, occur well inland today, and this presumably reflects the higher sea levels during the middle Holocene combined with the massive effects of coastal and estuarine aggradation caused by subsequent forest clearance for agriculture. Many of the Sumatran middens, for instance, lie on an old shoreline 10–15 kilometres inland and are totally buried under alluvium. A few other non-midden inland and riverine open sites have also been reported from Sumatra, the Malay peninsula and northern Thailand.

Hoabinhian tools are characteristically made on flat, oval or elongated river pebbles flaked around their peripheries and over one or both surfaces. Bifaces dominate in parts of the Malay peninsula (Figure 2.3C), and unifaces (so-called 'Sumatraliths') elsewhere. They occur sporadically with other flake tools, grindstones, bone points and bone spatulae. In one region of northern Vietnam north of Hanoi there is an interesting regional variant of the Hoabinhian known as the Bacsonian which has a marked emphasis on the edge-grinding of pebble tools. This seems to have commenced about 10,000 years ago. Hoabinhian burials are mostly flexed or contracted, and often dusted with haematite; definite instances of the placement of grave goods are rare.

In the upper levels of many Hoabinhian cave sites there are also potsherds; these are plain or impressed with vines or mats in Vietnam, cord-marked in most other areas. There are problems in explaining the presence of pottery amongst presumably mobile foraging societies. Cave disturbance, for instance, cannot be invoked as the sole explanation, since pottery does appear to be well tied to a Bacsonian context in the shell midden of Da But, Thanh Hoa province (7000 years ago), and it may also date to about 8000 years ago in the upper layer of Spirit Cave in northwestern Thailand (but see page 97). There also seems to be an overlap in time between pottery and Hoabinhian tools at certain caves in Cambodia and the Malay peninsula, although at the site of Gua Cha in Malaysia there was a much sharper change from the aceramic Hoabinhian to a Neolithic layer with richly furnished burials about 3300 years ago. The overall picture is by no means simple, and the big question remains: did the makers of the Hoabinhian stone industry play any role in the development of agriculture and Neolithic technology in mainland Southeast Asia?

This is not a question which can be easily answered. It is clear from most sites that the Hoabinhians were hunters. Bones of a wide range of mammal species are found; pig and deer predominate, but large mammals including elephant, rhinoceros and cattle occur as well, as of course do small ones like rats and squirrels. None of these species appear to have been domesticated, although bones of dog, certainly a non-native and domesticated introduction into Southeast Asia from the Indian subcontinent or China, are reported from the Da But midden. Plant remains, on the other hand, are scarce, with the most important coming from early Holocene contexts in Spirit Cave, northwest Thailand. These include parts of food plants (almond, and possibly some legumes), stimulants (betel nut), poisons (butternut kernels), and other useful plants including bamboo and gourd. No remains of cereals such as rice or millet were found, although rice does occur in the nearby Banyan Valley Cave in contexts which postdate 5500 years ago, and hence may reflect contact with adjacent agriculturalists. In general, none of the plant remains found in early Holocene Spirit Cave can be proved to be from domesticated plants, and it seems that they may belong to a stable and broad-spectrum hunter-gatherer adaptation which may have lasted in this remote region to the first millennium CE, albeit with earlier sporadic contact with lowland agricultural groups.[57]

The Hoabinhian thus poses many questions for future research, not least concerning the existence of regional facies, its role (if any) in agricultural developments, and its role in the ancestry of the modern cultures and populations of the region. At the present time it exists as little more than a classificatory pigeonhole for pebble tools; it clearly merits far more serious attention.

In island Southeast Asia there is no true pebble-tool Hoabinhian beyond northern Sumatra, although variants have been claimed for Taiwan and Luzon. In most regions the flake industries of Late Pleistocene type, as exemplified in sites such as the Tabon, Niah and Madai caves, simply continued without technological change until flaked stone gradually faded away with the development of polished Neolithic adze technology and eventually metal tools. Holocene industries of this continuing type have been reported from regions as far apart as southern Sumatra, Java, northern Luzon, northern Sulawesi, Flores and Timor, and also eastwards into New Guinea and the western Pacific.

As a variation on this basic theme there was an emphasis in parts of the Philippines, Sulawesi and Java on the production of small blades and blade-like flakes after about 7000 years ago. By far the best-known elaboration along these lines is the microlithic technology which appeared in the Toalian industry of southern Sulawesi from about 8000 years ago, also in parts of Java, and from 6000 years ago across much of the Australian continent. This distribution has to be explained to some extent by diffusion, but whether the microlithic tool forms were first developed within

[57] For discussions of the Spirit Cave evidence, see C. Gorman, 'The Hoabinhian and after', *World Archaeology*, 2 (1971); D. E. Yen, 'Hoabinhian horticulture', in J. Allen et al., eds, *Sunda and Sahul*, London, 1977; Higham, *Archaeology*, 45–61.

Southeast Asia or introduced from some outside region remains unknown.

The Toalian, the most important of these industries in Southeast Asia, occurs in caves, rock shelters, and in open sites on slightly raised alluvial deposits in the southwestern peninsula of Sulawesi. The best sequence comes from the excavated shelter of Ulu Leang in the Maros limestone district, where small elongated or geometric-backed microliths appeared after 8000 years ago, to which were added remarkable and distinctive hollow-based and serrated projectile points ('Maros points') after about 6000 years ago (Figure 2.3D).[58] Other artefacts found in Toalian levels include glossed flakes, small bipolar cores, bone points, and possible bivalve shell scrapers. Pebble tools and edge-ground tools seemingly do not occur in this region, but it must be remembered that the microliths make up only a small percentage of the total of flaked stone in Toalian sites —the background core and flake industry continued throughout with little change. The Toalian also continued in a morphologically simplified form in the southern part of the south Sulawesi peninsula until about 1000 CE. It is quite possible that hunters and gatherers survived in this remote region until well after this time, although in Ulu Leang itself, further north in the Maros region, rice appeared in a level dated to 500 CE, perhaps indicating exchange with nearby agriculturalists. Plain potsherds also became quite numerous in Ulu Leang in association with Toalian tools after about 4000 years ago.

The Toalian economy involved the hunting of native Sulawesi mammals—phalanger, macaque monkey, civet cat, *anoa*, *babirusa* and pig (*Sus celebensis*). In perhaps contemporary (mid-Holocene?) deposits in the cave of Gua Lawa in central Java were found bones of cattle, elephant, water buffalo, clouded leopard, pig and deer, together with bone points, bone spatulae, and hollow-based but unserrated arrowheads similar to the Maros points. Backed blades, points and geometrics have also been reported in obsidian from the Bandung region in western Java, and an overall picture emerges of bands of hunters with microlith-tipped projectiles (arrows or spears) roaming the open monsoonal forest landscapes of Java, southern Sulawesi, and probably many of the Lesser Sunda Islands before and during the gradual spread of agricultural communities throughout the region.

No signs have yet appeared of any such industries north of the equator or in the equatorial rainforests of Sumatra, Borneo, central Sulawesi or New Guinea, and in this respect southern Indonesia had its closest early and mid-Holocene cultural affinities with Australia. All this began to change as Austronesian-speaking agriculturalists expanded right through and ultimately dominated the whole of island Southeast Asia, just as the speakers of Austroasiatic languages appear to have replaced or assimilated many of the original Hoabinhian foraging communities of mainland Southeast Asia. To this new era, and to the agricultural foundations of all complex societies in Southeast Asia, we now turn.

[58] I. Glover and G. Presland, 'Microliths in Indonesian flaked stone industries', in V. N. Misra and P. Bellwood, eds, *Recent Advances in Indo-Pacific Prehistory*, New Delhi, 1985.

## THE RISE AND EXPANSION OF AGRICULTURAL COMMUNITIES

With the rise of agriculture, the Southeast Asian archaeological record takes on a new level of complexity, owing to the increasing range of technological and economic categories of evidence which survives. Fairly obvious examples include pottery, remains of houses and villages, elaborate burial practices, bones of domesticated animals, and the tools and plant remains associated with agriculture. This does not mean that early agricultural societies were necessarily more complex in all respects than foraging ones, but they have left behind, at least in the Southeast Asian context, an archaeological record which is more suitable for the making of inferences about culture, history and lifestyle. The record of agricultural societies is also closer to us in time and can be related more easily to the linguistic and ethnological records of present-day populations.

As well as having increased material complexity, agricultural populations also tend to have much greater population densities than hunters and gatherers—by factors of ten or more with even the simplest systems of shifting cultivation, and factors of hundreds with the very intensive wet-rice systems of the historical civilizations. Early agriculturalists created more substantial and more numerous archaeological sites than foragers, an obvious fact which is very evident in the Neolithic and Early Metal phase records of Thailand and Vietnam. In the equatorial zone, however, ancient open sites can be notoriously difficult to locate in the densely-vegetated conditions, and far less evidence about the actual settlements of early agriculturalists is available.

Why did human societies first adopt agriculture, evidently independently in several parts of the world, just after the beginning of the Holocene? There is no simple answer to this question, but there are some logical observations which can be emphasized. By the time that agricultural techniques were successful enough to support the considerable increases of population evident in the Neolithic records of China and mainland Southeast Asia, the system as a whole would have required an annual cycle of labour investment and settlement stability very different from that practised by contemporary foragers. Unless the incentives or pressures for accepting such social and economic upheaval were strong, it is hard to understand why successful early Holocene foragers who had sufficient food and experienced no pressure on their resources would have wanted to change. Modern hunter-gatherers in Southeast Asia generally resist the total adoption of agriculture unless shrinking land resources leave them with few other options, and many hunters and gatherers of the Holocene probably did not switch their economies simply because concepts of food production entered their lives. Modern ethnography also suggests that those who did ultimately adopt agriculture would hardly have done so via 'affluent forager' leisure-time experimenting.

Despite the complexities behind the acquisition by foragers of an integrated and successful agricultural lifestyle, the fact remains that some of them, in certain localities such as western Asia, central and southern

China, the New Guinea highlands and the Mexican and Peruvian highlands, did at one time develop agriculture from an economic base of hunting and gathering. There is an important distinction to be made here between the concepts of primary indigenous development in isolation, and secondary adoption through various processes of borrowing. Agriculture has only rarely been adopted by borrowing with conscious and willing intent—if the ethnographic record is any guide—and could have developed indigenously out of a foraging economic base only in regions where suitable high-yielding plants occurred, and where human societies were perhaps nudged towards a greater investment in cultivation by various stress factors. These might have included seasonal uncertainty of wild food supplies, reductions in food supplies caused by environmental changes, and even crude population growth. True and primary developments of agriculture did not occur commonly, but once they had occurred the populations behind them were offered substantial demographic advantages over their foraging neighbours. Hence some of the great ethnolinguistic expansions of prehistoric times—of the Indo-Europeans, Bantu, and in Southeast Asia the speakers of Austroasiatic and Austronesian languages—occurred when populations who had recently developed systematic and productive methods of agriculture expanded slowly, but continuously and inexorably, into territories held only by foragers. Such processes are continuing today on a much smaller geographical scale as the last of the foraging peoples across the world face historically unprecedented pressures to give up their old ways of life.

In most of Southeast Asia (excluding southern China and possibly coastal northern Vietnam) there is no evidence to suggest that any primary development of agriculture occurred, and it seems basically to have been introduced by people already acquainted with the cultivation of rice, millet and other subtropical crops like yams, taro and sugarcane. They also kept domesticated pigs, chickens, dogs, and perhaps cattle. All evidence to hand suggests that this expansion into Southeast Asia commenced mainly from the coastal regions of southern China. However, it is very important to emphasize that many tropical fruits and tubers native to Southeast Asia were brought into cultivation systems as they expanded southwards, and existing foraging populations may well have contributed useful knowledge of such plants to agricultural groups. Futhermore, recent research indicates that a separate and primary centre of plant cultivation, perhaps associated with such crops as taro, sugarcane, pandanus and Australimusa bananas, was developing in the New Guinea highlands by at least 6000 years ago. The agricultural developments in this region had no apparent impact on Southeast Asia beyond the eastern part of Indonesia, but they did have the crucial result for Pacific prehistory of making New Guinea mainly impervious, presumably for demographic reasons, to Austronesian colonists.

The view which I state here clearly ignores the possibility of an early and indigenous stratum of agriculture in Southeast Asia based purely on fruits and tubers, which was favoured at one time by a number of geographers and ethnologists. I find it impossible to identify any evidence for such a stratum west of New Guinea and the Pacific islands (where cereals were not grown in prehistoric times), and in the absence of such supporting evidence it seems wiser at this time to focus on the importance of the high-yielding annual cereals, particularly rice. It is rice which has yielded the bulk of the positive archaeological record for ancient agriculture in Southeast Asia.

The annual cereals—in particular wheat, barley, maize, rice and the millets—have formed the economic bases for the great majority of the densely-populated complex societies on record. Annual cereals have by definition evolved in subtropical or temperate regions with alternating wet and dry (or warm and cold) seasons of growth and dormancy. They tend to have large grains, and—after selection for increased grain size and yield, loss of shattering habit when ripe, and synchronous ripening—they are capable of yielding very large quantities of nutritious food per unit of land. Rice (*Oryza sativa*) and foxtail millet (*Setaria italica*) were first cultivated from annual forebears in China, the latter north of the Yangtze where it supported the oldest Chinese Neolithic cultures from 6000 BC onwards. According to current archaeological evidence, rice was first cultivated somewhere in the lower Yangtze region under the warmer climatic conditions of the early Holocene,[59] and it was supporting the inhabitants of impressive timber villages such as Hemudu in Zhejiang Province by 5000 BC. The wealth of technology associated with these developments in central coastal China includes pottery, carpentry, stone adzes, wooden and bone agricultural tools, boats, paddles, spindle whorls for weaving (of cotton?), matting and rope, together with the evidence for domesticated pigs, dogs, chicken and possibly for cattle and water buffalo. This all suggests changes away from a former forager lifestyle, which can only be described as revolutionary.

The problem, however, is that the Chinese archaeological record does not yet tell in fine detail how and why these developments took place. The absence of convincing evidence for agriculture anywhere in the world during the Pleistocene suggests very strongly that the post-glacial climatic amelioration had a role to play, perhaps in allowing a radiation of large-grained annual cereals throughout many zones of Eurasia between about 15 and 35 degrees north latitude.[60] Foraging populations perhaps began to utilize and depend upon these wild cereals for food, until situations of stress obliged them to systematize cultivation practices in order to maintain regular supplies. In the case of southern coastal China, the stress factors may have been related to periodic temperature coolings during the early Holocene[61] which caused a lowering of yield or even a local

[59] Average annual temperatures were 2–4 degrees Celsius warmer than now over much of China between 6000 and 2000 BC: K. C. Chang, *Archaeology of Ancient China*, New Haven, 1986, 74–9.

[60] According to R. O. Whyte, annual cereals evolved around the fringes of central Asia with increasing dry-season stress and higher temperatures around the end of the last glaciation: 'Annual crops of South and Southeast Asia', in Misra and Bellwood eds, *Recent Advances*. Recent palynological research in Yunnan provides some support for this view; see D. Walker, 'Late Pleistocene–early Holocene vegetational and climatic changes in Yunnan Province, southwest China', *Journal of Biogeography*, 13 (1986).

[61] According to Yang Huairen and Xie Zhiren, 'Sea level changes in east China over the past 20,000 years', in R. O. Whyte, ed., *The Evolution of the East Asian Environment*, Hong Kong, 1984, there were cool stages from pollen evidence at 8200 and 5800 BP.

disappearance of wild rice stands. We really do not know the answers here, however, and precise causal explanations for agricultural origins in all parts of the world still remain elusive.

Once successful cereal agriculture was established, with a stable annual round of cultivation activities and storage techniques, then expansion of the system began. Here we come to an area of some disagreement, since agricultural expansion has been related by some authors to population pressure. It must be stated, however, that large-scale pressure of people on land is not evidenced in the archaeological or pre-modern ethnographic records for Southeast Asia or even southern China. It cannot even be invoked to explain renowned ethnographic cases of agricultural expansion such as that of the Iban of Sarawak, where the opening of new lands last century offered status as well as more cultivation space for ambitious and warlike young men. The same, of course, applied to the great Pacific migrations of the Polynesians, if we are to believe some of their legends. New frontiers, new wealth and the chance to escape difficulties at home have always been attractive lures, as recent colonial history attests.

The reason why early rice cultivation spread very quickly, at least in the intermediate tropical zone where it yielded best,[62] was perhaps that the swampy and alluvial environments most suited to it (and also to the taro tuber) were of limited geographical extent. Under conditions of low population density people might have preferred to seek new natural swamps along rivers which flooded during the wet season, rather than to create their own by laborious processes of damming, bunding and water transport. Rice and taro, therefore, may both have been grown in natural wet fields of a simple and seasonal kind from the very beginning, and dry-land shifting cultivation in most areas may be a secondary development.[63] Swamps and low-lying seasonally flooded alluvial soils, particularly in thickly forested habitats, can also produce higher and more stable yields than dry swiddens without markedly higher labour inputs.[64] Environments of this kind were perhaps actively sought by early Neolithic colonists, with or without the stimulus provided by localized population pressure on resources.

Before leaving this background discussion of agricultural origins and dispersals, it is necessary to emphasize the major shifts which took place in agricultural economies as they expanded southwards towards the equator, and on into the Pacific islands. The agricultural economy which developed in southern China and northern mainland Southeast Asia, and which came eventually to dominate the intermediate tropical regions both north

[62] Prehistoric rices probably grew best in intermediate tropical latitudes for a complex series of reasons connected with photoperiodicity (i.e. growth cycles are synchronized with changes in day length), the need for reliable dry-season sun for ripening, and increased grain size and protein content in these environments. Humid equatorial climates were probably unsuitable for rice until considerable selection within the species had taken place. See discussion with references in PIMA, ch. 7.

[63] See T. T. Chang, 'The ethnobotany of rice in Island Southeast Asia', AP, 26 (1988); Joyce White, 'Origins of plant domestication in Southeast Asia', in D. Bayard, ed., *Southeast Asian Archaeology at the XV Pacific Science Congress*, Dunedin, 1984.

[64] For example, see M. R. Dove, *Swidden Agriculture in Indonesia*, Berlin, 1985, 299; C. Padoch, 'Labor efficiency and intensity of land use in rice production: an example from Kalimantan', *Human Ecology*, 13 (1985).

and south of the equator, was focused on the cultivation of cereals such as rice, foxtail and other millets (*Panicum* and *Echinochloa*), and the perennial Job's tears. Cotton (*Gossypium arboreum*[65]), sugarcane, greater yam (*Dioscorea alata*) and perhaps taro (*Colocasia esculenta*) were also of considerable importance in these latitudes.

Within the equatorial zone of Indonesia and Malaysia, however, the prevailing climatic conditions were clearly unsuitable for the cultivation of the photoperiodic rices introduced by early Austronesians. The result was that rice declined to relative insignificance, and was indeed never taken into the Pacific islands, with the minor exception of the Marianas (which, not surprisingly, are outside the equatorial zone). The later prehistory of equatorial Southeast Asia was focused more on the cultivation of millet, tubers (yams, taro and other aroids), sago palms for starch, and tree fruits such as coconut, banana and breadfruit.[66] Rice is now dominant in many parts of equatorial Indonesia, but there are indications that this dominance may have developed subsequent to the initial millennia of agriculture as the rice plant itself became better adapted to equatorial conditions. On the other hand, some of the intermediate tropical islands of the southern hemisphere, such as Java and Bali, would have been suited to rice from the very beginning, as soon as the plant was transmitted to them through the equatorial zone.

## THE ARCHAEOLOGY OF EARLY AGRICULTURAL SOCIETIES

Societies with a Neolithic mode of technology appeared almost everywhere in lowland and coastal regions of Southeast Asia between approximately 4000 and 1000 BC (Map 2.4), except in those ever-decreasing territories which remained the preserve of hunters and gatherers. Bronze became widespread in the northern part of mainland Southeast Asia during the second millennium BC, and iron after 500 BC; both first appeared together towards the end of the first millennium BC in Malaysia and island Southeast Asia. In this section I will discuss those cultures and assemblages which can be termed Neolithic[67] before turning to the essen-

[65] See R. K. Johnson and B. G. Decker, 'Implications of the distribution of native names for cotton (*Gossypium* spp.) in the Indo-Pacific', AP, 23 (1983).

[66] P. Bellwood, 'Plants, climate and people; the early horticultural prehistory of Indonesia', in J. J. Fox, ed., *Indonesia: the Making of a Culture*, Canberra, 1980.

[67] The term 'Neolithic' is no more than a convenient pigeon-hole, implying the existence of agriculture and the absence of metal, and should not be taken to refer to any particular grade of cultural evolution. Many Neolithic societies (such as the Maya) were undoubtedly far larger and more complex than many metal-using ones in Southeast Asia. However, circumlocutions such as 'Era of Early Agriculture' or 'Pre-Metal Agricultural Period' beg many questions and serve no useful purpose. D. Bayard, 'A tentative regional phase chronology for northeast Thailand' in Bayard, ed., *Southeast Asian Archaeology*, and Higham, *Archaeology*, have recently divided the archaeology of non-peninsular mainland Southeast Asia into four General Periods lettered A to D, but the cultural characteristics used for these periods cannot yet be applied in equatorial regions such as Malaysia or Indonesia. I will therefore retain a traditional terminology which will be more appropriate for the non-specialist reader.

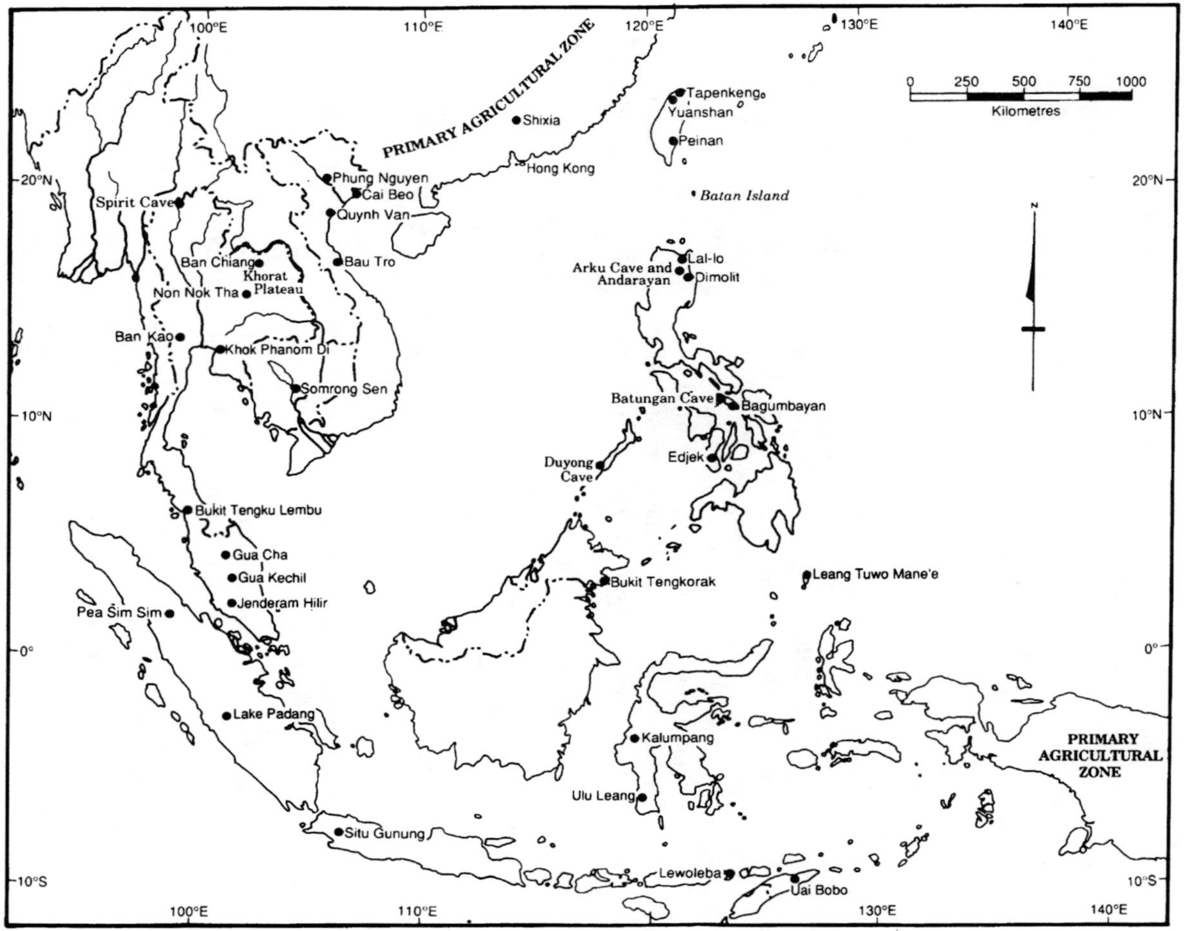


Map 2.4 Major Neolithic and early agricultural sites.

tial linguistic record which allows them to be interpreted in a culture-historical framework. These Neolithic assemblages are oldest in southern China and the northern parts of Southeast Asia, and they seem to become younger in age as one moves southwards and eastwards through Indonesia. New Guinea appears to have been the focus of an independent origin of agriculture as old as that in China.

The wealth of southern Chinese coastal cultures in Neolithic times has already been alluded to in connection with the site of Hemudu in Zhejiang Province. The quantity of rice found here should be emphasized; not only were rice husks used for tempering pottery, but the site also yielded a waterlogged layer of husks, grain, straw and leaves up to fifty centimetres thick. Much further south, at Shixia in Guangdong Province, rice remains have been found in cooking pits and store pits, and apparently used as a temper for building daub, in a 3-hectare settlement site dating to about 3000 BC.[68] It is apparent that the whole southern coast of China became inhabited by pottery-using and rice-cultivating peoples between 5000 and 3000 BC, and even earlier dates are quite conceivable.[69]

Recent research in the coastal regions of northern Vietnam has yielded a number of sites, often shell middens, with a rather confusing array of Neolithic material culture dating from the fifth millennium BC onwards.[70] This includes pottery with pointed or round bases, decorated by cord-making, red-slipping, basket or mat impressions, or incision. Untanged or shouldered stone adzes, flexed burials, and bones of deer, cattle, pig and dog are also found in some of these sites, but it is not clear whether any of these animals were domesticated (presumably pigs and dogs were). Few data about subsistence are available, although the situation improves slightly with the Phung Nguyen culture of the middle Red River valley above Hanoi, dated to the late third or early second millennium BC. This, the immediate precursor of the first bronze-using cultures in northern Vietnam, does have evidence for the cultivation of rice, together with a broader range of material culture. This includes stone arrowheads and knives, baked clay spindle whorls and bow pellets, and pottery with incised and comb-stamped decoration which Vietnamese archaeologists consider to be directly ancestral to the pottery of the Dong-son civilization of the first millennium BC.

More information is available about the prehistory of Thailand than any other country in Southeast Asia, mainly because a succession of large

[68] A. E. Dien et al., eds, *Chinese Archaeological Abstracts*, Los Angeles: University of California Institute of Archaeology, 1985, II. 121–3.

[69] For instance, pottery, generally associated with agricultural rather than foraging societies, could be as much as 12,000 years old in southern Japan and nearby Jiangsu Province in central coastal China. W. Meacham, 'C-14 dating of pottery', *Journal of the Hong Kong Archaeological Society*, 11 (1984–5), discusses several dates as old as 5000 BC for pottery in Hong Kong and Macao. C. L. Brace et al. have also suggested that the smallness of south Chinese tooth sizes favours very early agricultural origins in this region: 'Prehistoric and modern tooth size in China', in F. H. Smith and F. Spencer, eds, *The Origins of Modern Humans*, New York, 1984.

[70] Relevant sites include Quynh Van, Bau Tro and Cai Beo. See Ha Van Tan, 'Nouvelles recherches'; and 'Prehistoric pottery in Viet Nam and its relationships with Southeast Asia', AP, 26 (1988). Cord-marked pottery has apparently been found with edge-ground ('Bacsonian') tools dating from about 5000 BC in the Da But shell mound (see page 87).

multidisciplinary projects have occurred there in recent years. However, general understanding has been confused by suggestions that agriculture and bronze-working arose in Thailand at very early dates, earlier perhaps than anywhere else in the world.[71] Recent research has placed these discoveries in their proper contexts, and although sporadic disagreements still erupt it is now clear that some of the earlier claims were exaggerated. One of these claims was that plant remains recovered from contexts dated prior to 7000 BC in the Hoabinhian layers of Spirit Cave in northwest Thailand were domesticated—a claim since rendered unlikely by the botanical analyses of Yen.[72] Spirit Cave also produced, from an upper layer, pottery with cord-marked or net-impressed decoration, some with a resin surface coat, together with untanged stone adzes and slate knives. The date of 6000 BC originally published for these items would make them the oldest of their kind by at least a millennium in Southeast Asia, but similar artefacts found with remains of rice (believed to be wild) in the nearby Banyan Valley Cave date only to some time after 3500 BC. Given the difficulties of dating artefacts from shallow cave deposits such as those in Spirit Cave it seems that the date for the Neolithic assemblage from the site will have to be held in abeyance for the time being, at least until more data are available to allow a surer assessment. As noted above, Higham's general view of the sequence represented by the northwest Thailand cave sites is that they represent a broad-spectrum foraging economy which may have survived well into the first millennium CE,[73] albeit perhaps with contact with nearby agriculturalists after about 3500 BC.

This rather negative conclusion, however, certainly does not apply to the broad and fertile floodplains which cross the Khorat Plateau of northeast Thailand. Agricultural societies were firmly established here by about 3000 BC, evidently in a region which was almost totally devoid of any preceding settlement by foragers if the results of recent archaeological surveys are accepted at face value. The first of these sites to be excavated, in 1966 and 1968, was Non Nok Tha, a low mound on the western side of the Khorat Plateau which contained many extended burials spanning both the Neolithic and Early Metal phases. The older graves contained untanged adzes, shell beads, and cord-marked and rare painted pottery, and also yielded bones of domesticated cattle, pig and dog together with rice husks used as a temper for the pottery. The dates proposed by the main excavator of the site suggested an initial settlement during the fourth millennium BC. This date has since been challenged, but a foundation of the site during the third or second millennium BC still seems likely.[74]

The results from Non Nok Tha were soon paralleled by the excavations

[71] See summaries in Bellwood, *Man's Conquest*, 161–5; W. G. Solheim II, 'Reworking Southeast Asian prehistory', *Paideuma*, 15 (1969).

[72] C. Gorman, 'Hoabinhian: a pebble-tool complex with early plant associations in Southeast Asia', *Science*, 163 (1969); Yen, 'Hoabinhian horticulture; as in footnote 57.

[73] *Archaeology*, 61.

[74] For a preliminary excavation report see D. T. Bayard, *Non Nok Tha: the 1968 excavations*, Dunedin, 1972. On chronology, see D. Bayard, 'A tentative regional phase chronology for northeast Thailand', in Bayard, ed., *Southeast Asian Archaeology*. Higham favours a commencement date for Non Nok Tha only in the second millennium BC ('The Ban Chiang culture in wider perspective', *Proceedings of the British Academy*, 69 (1983) 249).

at the more famous site of Ban Chiang about 120 kilometres to the northeast. Ban Chiang rose to prominence in the 1970s owing to the appearance on the antiquities market of very fine red-on-buff pottery dug illegally from graves: pottery which is now dated at about 2000 years ago. The lower occupation of the site, however, commenced by at least 3000 BC. While the exact cultural contents of these lower layers are uncertain (they certainly did not contain bronze, which appears in this site after 2000 BC), likely components include extended and flexed burials, infant burials in pottery jars, the pottery with fairly elaborate cord-marked, incised and burnished decoration.[75] Significant economic information from the site includes, as from Non Nok Tha, evidence for rice chaff temper in sherds, and bones of domesticated pig, dog, chicken, and cattle (probably of gaur or banteng stock, rather than the Indian zebu). There is also a very wide range of hunted and collected meat resources, including shellfish, turtles, crocodiles, and mammals ranging in size up to large deer and rhinoceros.[76] These people probably practised rice cultivation in low-lying and seasonally flooded soils, but analysis of their skeletal remains by M. Pietrusewsky indicates that their life expectancy was fairly short, averaging only thirty-one years for a sample of 112 individuals.[77] The analyses also indicated a likelihood that malaria was a significant disease by this time.

Despite problems in interpreting the sites of Non Nok Tha and Ban Chiang, they are both of great potential significance for the period prior to the appearance of bronze, which enters the record in northeast Thailand at some time between the late third millennium and 1500 BC (the precise date for the appearance of cupreous metallurgy in Thailand is still uncertain). Indeed, Ban Chiang is still the only excavated site in northeast Thailand for which there is a base deposit which is pre-bronze but putatively agricultural. It seems reasonable to assume that the earliest inhabitants during the late fourth millennium BC were migrants into the region, which appears to have been only very sparsely inhabited up to that time. They brought in a fully agricultural economy and Neolithic technology, the latter different only in a few stylistic details from contemporary assemblages in southern China and Vietnam. Unhappily, the Thailand sites have yielded only very limited evidence for settlement or house plans;[78] this was not the fault of the excavators, but reflects the fact that ephemeral timber architecture rarely survives in readily-identifiable post-hole patterns in the tropics, a circumstance which puts this region at an

75 Joyce White, *Ban Chiang*, Philadelphia, 1982; *A Revision of the Chronology of Ban Chiang*, University Microfilms International, 1987; 'Ban Chiang and charcoal in hypothetical hindsight', BIPPA, 8 (1988).

76 C. Higham and A. Kijngam, 'New evidence for agriculture and stock-raising in monsoonal Southeast Asia', in Misra and Bellwood, eds, *Recent Advances*.

77 'The ancient inhabitants of Ban Chiang', *Expedition*, 24, 4 (1982). For Ban Chiang rice (which still had certain wild characteristics) see D. Yen, 'Ban Chiang pottery and rice', *Expedition*, 24 4 (1982).

78 Presumably these people lived in nucleated villages, and the Ban Chiang mound may indeed represent a prehistoric village with an uncertain area of at least 3.5 and possibly as much as 8 hectares. Non Nok Tha, however, might have had a more specialized function as a cemetery for several small and scattered settlements; see R. N. Wilen, *Excavations at Non Pa Kluay, North-east Thailand*, Oxford, 1989, 152–4.

archaeological disadvantage compared with more temperate environments in China and Europe. In terms of the natures of these societies it can only be emphasized that grave goods give no clear indications of the existence of ranking or stratification prior to the mid-second millennium BC, by which time bronze was in common circulation.

Meanwhile, of course, there remains the question of where the first agricultural inhabitants of northeast Thailand came from. My own preference is for the coastal regions of northern Vietnam and southern China, but Higham has recently suggested that movements inland occurred from an early centre of agricultural development, sedentism and population growth around the head of the Gulf of Thailand.[79] No agricultural sites have yet been found here which predate 2000 BC, but new reports suggest their presence a little further north near Lopburi by the late third millennium.[80] Evidence for an increase in charcoal and grass pollen from cores taken near the site of Khok Phanom Di suggests that some incipiently agricultural activities could have been practised in the region as early as the fifth millennium BC.

The huge habitation and burial mound of Khok Phanom Di[81] is one of the richest and most impressive pre-bronze sites ever excavated in Southeast Asia, although it may have a parallel in the remarkable but poorly-recorded site of Somrong Sen in Cambodia, excavated earlier this century. Khok Phanom Di is 200 metres in diameter and has almost seven metres of archaeological deposit dating between 2000 and 1400 BC. When first occupied it lay on an estuary close to a mangrove shore, perhaps with freshwater ponds where wild rice grew, but today the site is far inland as a result of a slight fall in sea level combined with alluviation resulting from inland forest clearance for agriculture. The basal of the three major excavated levels yielded 104 burials (mostly extended) in clusters, some wrapped in barkcloth and dusted with red ochre. Grave goods of this phase included shell beads and bracelets, stone adzes, and well-crafted pottery of which the finest vessels have black burnished surfaces and horizontal zones of incised decoration. The people grew or collected rice, which occurs as husk temper and impressions in pottery, used harpoons and fishhooks of bone, and ate large quantities of marine foods such as fish, shellfish, crabs and turtles.

In the middle level of Khok Phanom Di, dating presumably to early in the second millennium BC, a number of richly-provided burials made an appearance. Two women were buried under an apparent mortuary hut with a floor which was replastered forty-three times. Another woman was buried under a large pile of the clay cylinders from which pots are made, together with strings of beads—120,000 shell disc beads in total—over her chest, and lots of fine pottery vessels. Evidently she was a potter of high

[79] *Archaeology*, 86–7.

[80] Here with copper-casting crucibles and slag, perhaps the earliest dates for metallurgy in Thailand if the dates are correct. See V. Pigott and S. Natapintu, 'The Thailand Archaeometallurgy Project: 1984–7', paper presented to Conference on Ancient Chinese and Southeast Asian Bronze Age Cultures, Kioloa, Australia, February 1988.

[81] C. Higham et al., 'Khok Phanom Di: the results of the 1984–5 season', BIPPA, 7 (1986–7); Higham, *Archaeology*, 65–89; C. Higham, 'Social organisation at Khok Phanom Di, central Thailand, 2000–1500 BC', *Arts Asiatiques*, 44 (1989).

status. A child, perhaps a member of the same family, was buried near her with similar high-status goods. These wealthy burial assemblages could indicate that the society was perhaps ranked on a genealogical basis, and females in particular appear to have enjoyed high positions. Individual burial zones seem also to have been used by members of the same family through several generations, according to skeletal analyses. But while this picture of burgeoning Neolithic wealth could indicate an attractive source region for a gradual fissioning of population inland to the Khorat Plateau, the main problem is that the dates are simply too late in time. An independent development of rice cultivation by foragers at this latitude is certainly not impossible, but more evidence to support such a hypothesis is clearly essential.

Apart from the sites mentioned there are few other coherent Neolithic cultures known from the northern mainland of Southeast Asia. Burma, Cambodia and Laos offer few data which can be incorporated into a modern archaeological narrative. Southern Vietnam belongs to the Austronesian story, to which we will return. The long peninsula of southern Thailand and Malaysia, however, does have an intriguing and very widely spread series of Neolithic assemblages dating between about 2000 and 500 BC. These have been termed the Ban Kao culture after the site of this name in Kanchanaburi Province, and the pottery of this culture does have some similarities with that from Khok Phanom Di, which lies only about 200 kilometres to the east of Ban Kao.

The burial assemblage from Ban Kao itself dates from the middle of the second millennium BC; it comprises extended burials with a range of grave goods, including untanged stone adzes, barbed bone harpoon or spear points, shell beads and bracelets, and finely made cord-marked pottery with an unusual predilection for high pedestal or tripod supports. The habitation layers of the site have also produced many other important categories of Neolithic technology, including shouldered adzes, stone bracelets, bone fishhooks and combs, and baked clay barkcloth beaters and spindle whorls (the latter for spinning, possibly cotton thread?). One site south of Ban Kao has yielded the post-holes of a small house with a raised floor, and there is some evidence that these people may have had domesticated pigs, chicken and cattle. So far there is no direct evidence for rice, but its presence must be assumed given its importance at Khok Phanom Di.[82]

Perhaps the most remarkable point about the Ban Kao culture is its expansion southwards for 1500 kilometres into central peninsular Malaysia. Pottery of Ban Kao type has been found right down the peninsula to as far as Selangor, occasionally with other distinctive artefact types such as T-sectioned stone bracelets and stone cylindrical barkcloth beaters. The most striking type of Ban Kao vessel is a carinated cooking pot supported on cord-marked tripod legs. Complete or broken examples of such tripods have now been found at about twenty sites overall, from Ban Kao itself right down to Jenderam Hilir in Selangor, where many such tripods found during tin-mining operations have recently been radiocarbon dated to the

[82] For a good illustrated summary of Ban Kao see P. Sorensen, 'Agricultural civilizations', in C. Flon, ed., *The World Atlas of Archaeology*, London, 1985.

early second millennium BC.[83] At the cave of Gua Cha in Kelantan the upper layers contained extended burials with excellent pottery of Ban Kao type (but here without tripods), together with stone bracelets and adzes, shell bead necklaces and a cylindrical stone barkcloth beater. This Gua Cha assemblage dates to around 1000 BC, and intruded fairly sharply over an earlier Hoabinhian assemblage of bifacial pebble tools.[84] Another cave in Bukit Tengku Lembu, Perlis, produced similar pottery in association with a sherd believed to be Northern Black Polished Ware from India (mid to late first millennium BC), although this site was destroyed by fertilizer diggers and the exact associations of the artefacts found are unclear. Nevertheless, if all the dates[85] are taken at face value it appears that the Ban Kao culture as a whole may date from 2000 BC to the late first millennium BC.

Explanations for the Ban Kao culture in anthropological and historical terms will necessarily be rather complex, given the very high degree of anthropological and biological variation still found in the peninsula. Prior to 2000 BC the region was occupied by Hoabinhian foragers who may be considered ancestral to both the Semang Negritos and perhaps to a lesser degree the Senoi, who have a greater degree of Southern Mongoloid biological affinity than the Semang. The southward expansion of the Ban Kao culture, most probably by movement of people rather than by trade or superficial diffusion, appears to have led to three major introductions into southern Thailand and Malaysia: agriculture, Austroasiatic languages, and gene flow of Southern Mongoloid origin. The Semang have clearly at some time in their past adopted Austroasiatic languages, and the languages of both the Semang and the Senoi populations are today classified in a subgroup termed Aslian which retains distant relationships with Mon and Khmer.[86]

The ancestry of the Senoi, if this historical reconstruction is accepted, may thus be quite closely correlated with the expansion of the Ban Kao Neolithic culture. Continuity from local populations cannot be ignored, however, and skeletons from both Hoabinhian and Neolithic contexts at Gua Cha show no marked signs of any phenotypic population change across the cultural boundary. Presumably, therefore, the skeletons from

83 Leang Sau Heng, 'A tripod pottery complex in Peninsula Malaysia', in I. C. and E. A. Glover, eds, *Southeast Asian Archaeology 1986*, Oxford, 1990; P. Bellwood, 'Cultural and biological differentiation in Peninsular Malaysia; the last 10,000 years', paper presented at 2nd International Conference on Malay Civilization, Kuala Lumpur, August 1989.

84 For a reanalysis of the earlier results obtained from this site by G. de G. Sieveking, see Adi Haji Taha, 'The re-excavation of the rockshelter of Gua Cha, Ulu Kelantan, West Malaysia', FMJ, 30 (1985).

85 Owing to its chronological isolation, I am not here accepting the fourth millennium BC date for pottery from the shelter of Gua Kechil in Pahang. See F. Dunn, 'Radiocarbon dating of the Malayan Neolithic' *Proceedings of the Prehistoric Society*, 32 (1966).

86 For a good discussion of Asian linguistic prehistory, see G. Benjamin, 'Austroasiatic subgroupings and prehistory in the Malay Peninsula', in P. N. Jenner, et al., eds, *Austroasiatic Studies*, Honolulu, 1976; 'In the long term; three themes in Malayan cultural ecology', in K. Hutterer, A. T. Rambo and G. Lovelace, eds, *Cultural Values and Human Ecology in Southeast Asia*, Ann Arbor, 1985; 'Ethnohistorical perspectives on Kelantan's prehistory', in Nik Hassan Shuhaimi, ed., *Kelantan Zaman Awal*, Kota Bharu, 1987. From my own theoretical viewpoint it is quite unnecessary to postulate that Austroasiatic languages were spoken in the peninsula in Hoabinhian times, and no traces of earlier pre-Austroasiatic languages remain.

both periods at Gua Cha can be considered ancestral Senoi, although this is a remote site and one might expect the evidence for biological change to be a little sharper in more accessible and densely populated coastal regions. Whatever the exact situation, it is clear that, prior to the first arrival of Austronesian-speaking peoples in peninsular Malaysia, perhaps during the first millennium BC, the populations of the lowlands were firmly established in an agricultural mode of production.

## Island Southeast Asia

The archaeological record of Neolithic societies in the islands of Southeast Asia, like that of the mainland, seems to commence increasingly later in time as one moves generally southwards. The pattern of agricultural expansion into the islands should correlate to a high degree with the pattern of expansion of the Austronesian-speaking peoples, simply because these are today the only occupants of the area, apart from some small groups of Papuan-speakers in Halmahera and the eastern part of Nusa Tenggara (especially Timor). However, the pattern of Austronesian expansion can be reconstructed formally only from linguistic and not from archaeological evidence, and the linguistic aspects of the historical narrative will be covered in the following section. The archaeological record is necessarily rather unspecific on ethnolinguistic matters, but it does give a very important record of dates, material culture and economic adaptations to equatorial latitudes.

In southern China, it will be recalled, societies with rice cultivation and highly developed Neolithic technological characteristics existed in coastal regions south of the Yangtze from about 5000 BC onwards. The plentiful evidence for rice in some of these cultures must be emphasized, as too should many features of artefact design and economy which characterize a great many Neolithic cultures in island Southeast Asia and Oceania. These include the use of a red slip to decorate pottery, bent knee-shaped adze handles, untanged or stepped stone adzes, art styles emphasizing the uses of spirals and circles, and domestication of pigs, dogs and chickens. The list can be continued with items of less widespread distribution such as the cord-marking of pottery, pottery pedestals with cut-out decorations, baked-clay spindle whorls, slate reaping knives and slate spear points, all common or present in the Neolithic cultures of southern China, Taiwan and the northern Philippines, but increasingly rare further south.[87]

I should make my opinions on the significance of southern China clear from the outset, however, since I do not wish to suggest that all Austronesian-speaking peoples of island Southeast Asia and Oceania descend from Neolithic populations in this region, both linguistically and

[87] In the Chinese context I am here referring particularly to the Hemudu, Majiabang and Liangzhu cultures of the southern Lower Yangtze region; the record further south on the Chinese coast is more attenuated. Interestingly, layer 4 at Hemudu (c. 5000 BC) has produced a pottery stove, now on display in the Zhejiang Provincial Museum, almost identical to ethnographic examples used by the Bajaus of the southern Philippines and Sabah. The Bajaus use their stoves on boats; perhaps the people of Hemudu did likewise, since the site has produced a wooden paddle and a pottery boat model.

genetically, via some kind of sealed impervious tube. It is obvious that the past 5000 years have seen much interaction between different populations throughout the whole region from China to Melanesia, and also continuous biological and cultural change on a local scale. The main significance of southern China, and one which becomes ever firmer as the archaeological record unfolds, is that it was the zone where first developed the Neolithic technological and economic 'package' which fuelled all later population expansions into mainland and island Southeast Asia. It is quite possible that no more than a few families actually moved out of this region across to Taiwan, but those that did clearly began a process which had profound long-term cultural repercussions.[88]

The Neolithic cultures of Taiwan, from which ultimately were to be derived those in the islands to the south, commenced at some uncertain time between 5000 and 3500 BC,[89] with no apparent later survival of the preceding Hoabinhian-like flaked-stone assemblages of the island. The oldest Neolithic assemblages belong to the Tapenkeng culture, and they include cord-marked pots with incised rims, untanged and stepped stone adzes, polished slate spear points and a possible stone barkcloth beater. No plant remains have yet been reported from early Tapenkeng contexts, but rice remains and impressions are known from at least two other Taiwanese sites which probably predate 2000 BC. A pollen core from Sun-Moon Lake in the mountainous centre of the island also records an increase in grass pollen, perhaps as a result of agricultural clearance, from about 2800 BC onwards. The Austronesian-speaking peoples who survive in highland Taiwan still cultivate millet, yam, taro, sugarcane and gourd, and these must all, like rice, be of considerable antiquity as cultivars.

After about 2000 BC the archaeological assemblages of Taiwan seem to have divided into two separate style zones. That of the western side of the island retained a strong Chinese affinity, but the Yuanshan culture of eastern Taiwan is of more significance for island Southeast Asia since it reveals many characteristics found in the early Neolithic assemblages of the Philippines. Cord-marking had faded away by the early Yuanshan as a method of finishing pottery surfaces, and most decorated Yuanshan vessels are either slipped in red or brown, or decorated with incised or dentate-stamped patterns. Slate reaping knives and spear points; untanged, stepped or shouldered stone adzes; stone barkcloth beaters; and spindle whorls of baked clay are also characteristic of the Yuanshan culture, which seems to occur to as far south as Batan Island, between Taiwan and Luzon. The most dramatic Yuanshan discovery, however, has occurred recently as a result of railway construction in the town of Peinan in southeast Taiwan. No less than 1025 stone cist graves for extended burials have been excavated, often under the stone-paved floors of what appear to have been houses with walls and yards constructed of slate slabs.

88 W. Meacham, 'On the improbability of Austronesian origins in South China', AP, 26 (1988), has suggested that no early Neolithic archaeological links existed between Taiwan and the south Chinese mainland. I have published a detailed reply to this: 'A hypothesis for Austronesian origins', AP, 26 (1988).

89 Dates for island Southeast Asian Neolithic cultures have recently been reviewed by M. Spriggs, 'The dating of the Island South East Asian Neolithic', *Antiquity*, 63 (1989). See also PIMA, 214.

The contents of the Peinan graves are quite astonishing. They include perforated rectangular or curved slate reaping knives, tanged or straight-based slate spear points, stone fishing-net sinkers, baked-clay spindle whorls and bracelets, and a fine range of footed and handled pottery of Yuanshan affinity with occasional incised or punctate decoration. Nephrite split earrings are also common, including the important ling-ling-o type with four circumferential projections which has a remarkable distribution from southern Thailand, through southern Vietnam, and across to the Philippines, Sarawak, Taiwan and the Guangdong region of southern China.[90] The excavators of the Peinan site[91] date the graves to between 3000 and 500 BC, although the most reliable radiocarbon determinations seem to cluster around 3000 years ago.

The southwards expansion of agricultural subsistence into the equatorial latitudes of island Southeast Asia is not as clearly traceable as it is in Taiwan or southern China. This is partly because the perhumid environmental conditions are more inimical to coherent preservation of archaeological remains, and also because the nature of the agricultural economy itself changed. Plants like rice and cotton were not initially taken beyond intermediate tropical latitudes (if current archaeological and botanical evidence can be relied upon); as a result, many important artefact types such as stone reaping knives and baked-clay spindle whorls were simply dropped from cultural inventories.[92] The same applies to stone adzes, perhaps because early systems of tuber and fruit horticulture did not require such complete land clearance as the light-demanding cereals. The result of all these changes was that from the central Philippines southwards into Indonesia and east Malaysia the Early Neolithic archaeological record consists mainly of pottery, flaked-stone tools, very rare adzes, and little else. Indeed, the firmest evidence for the spread of agricultural communities into island Southeast Asia comes from the comparative study of the Austronesian languages, rather than from the primary archaeological record.

The archaeological evidence, however, does show very clear links between Taiwan and the northern Philippines, where many sites of the third and second millennia BC have been found with red-slipped pottery which resembles that of the Yuanshan culture.[93] They include Dimolit on the eastern coast of Luzon, where the postholes of two ground-level

[90] Most of these objects date from the first millennium BC, although it is quite possible that some are earlier. See H. Loofs-Wissowa, 'Prehistoric and photohistoric links between the Indochinese Peninsula and the Philippines', *Journal of the Hong Kong Archaeological Society*, 9 (1980–1).

[91] Wen-Hsun Sung and Chao-Mei Lien, *An Archaeological Report on the 9th–10th Terms of the Excavation at the Peinan Site. Taiwan*, Taipei: Department of Anthropology, National Taiwan University, 1987.

[92] Spindle whorls are reported from late prehistoric contexts in Mindanao, but this seems to be about their southerly limit. A shift towards the use of barkcloth amongst early agricultural communities presumably occurred in the equatorial zone, although by the first millennium CE the backstrap loom would have been known to most populations and the growing of cotton would perhaps have been extended to regions such as Borneo, where its production occurs on a local scale today.

[93] See B. Thiel, 'Austronesian origins and expansion; the Philippines archaeological data', AP, 26 (1988).

houses were excavated, each about three square metres in size; Arku Cave in the Cagayan Valley, which has also yielded shell bracelets, baked-clay spindle whorls, and shell and stone ling-ling-o earrings; the Lal-Lo shell middens near the mouth of the Cagayan Valley; and the Andarayan site near Arku Cave, which has produced rice-husk temper in red-slipped pottery dated by the accelerator radiocarbon method to the mid-second millennium BC.[94] In general, these assemblages support a hypothesis of a Neolithic settlement of Luzon from Taiwan, by people with rice (doubtless amongst other crops), commencing perhaps in the early third millennium BC.

Beyond Luzon, a horizon of plain or red-slipped pottery (otherwise undecorated) appears to continue southwards during the late third and early second millennia BC. It can be traced with reasonable certainty in the Bagumbayan site on Masbate and the Edjek site on Negros (both central Philippines), the Leang Tuwo Mane's shelter in the Talaud Islands, the Ulu Leang shelter in southern Sulawesi (where it occurs at c. 2500 BC with a continuing Toalian industry of Maros points), and the Uai Bobo 2 shelter in eastern Timor.[95] All of these assemblages are rather limited in artefact variety compared to those of Taiwan and northern Luzon, and, as already stressed, generally lack stone adzes (many have continuing flake industries in association) or any evidence for rice cultivation or weaving. One stone adze and four of *Tridacna* shell, however, were found in a burial of the third millennium BC in Duyong Cave on Palawan Island, but unfortunately this burial had no pottery in association. Another point of some interest is that the introduction of pig into Timor about 2500 BC may have been associated with the arrival of the first pottery-using peoples, as also might the introduction of wild populations of phalangers, civet cats and macaque monkeys.[96]

The archaeological record, therefore, suggests that pottery-using peoples, circumstantially with varied agricultural economies, settled large parts of island Southeast Asia during the third millennium BC. The archaeological record alone cannot prove the existence of agriculture but, when the palynological record is considered in support, the hypothesis of an expanding agricultural population becomes convincing. This record of forest clearance and burning comes mainly from cores drilled in highland swamps in Java and Sumatra.[97] Unfortunately these regions have no archaeological records in direct association, but the results are of great

[94] See B. E. Snow et al., 'Evidence of early rice cultivation in the Philippines', *Philippine Quarterly of Culture and Society*, 14 (1986).

[95] References for all these sites will be found in PIMA, 223–30.

[96] But see also footnote 54, above; the wild species together with *Rattus exulans* (the Polynesian rat) could have been introduced by hunters and gatherers prior to the arrival of agriculture, and the available radiocarbon dates do not allow an exact resolution of the chronology. The overall result of so many new animal arrivals was the eventual extinction, by perhaps 1500 years ago, of the large native murid rodents of the island.

[97] See B. K. Maloney, 'Man's impact on the rainforest of West Malesia; the palynological record', *Journal of Biogeography*, 12 (1985); J. Flenley, 'Palynological evidence for land use changes in Southeast Asia', ibid., 15 (1988). Unfortunately, cultivated cereals, tubers and fruits do not produce pollens which are generally identifiable to species, so the pollen record can normally identify only the activities of forest clearance and burning. In addition, foragers as well as agriculturalists can burn forest, although rarely in the humid tropics.

interest nevertheless. For instance, a pollen core from Pea Sim Sim swamp near Lake Toba in northern Sumatra (1320 metres above sea level) indicates that some minor forest clearance could have started as early as 4500 BC, but the major phase, evidenced by an increase in large grass pollen, began during the first millennium BC. The Lake Padang core from central Sumatra (950 metres above sea level) indicates swamp vegetation clearance and burning by about 2000 BC, and there is evidence here for an increasing protection of the useful *Arenga* tree palm species by 2000 years ago. At Situ Gunung in western Java there is an increase of pandanus and fern spores, perhaps indicating forest clearance, at about 3000 BC.

The overall pollen record seems to suggest some intermittent forest clearance in Sumatra and Java starting during the fourth and third millennia BC, with an intensification after about 3000 years ago. Since these records are all from highland areas it may be reasonable to expect that cultivation in coastal lowlands began slightly earlier, but this remains uncertain. It is also apparent that the Pea Sim Sim dates for initial forest clearance are a little earlier than would be expected from the archaeological record alone. Given the evidence from the Malay peninsula and Indonesia generally, it seems unlikely that systematic forest clearance for agriculture would have begun in Java and Sumatra much prior to 2500 BC, but new data could change this view.[98] It is not impossible that Sumatra was settled by agricultural groups from southern Thailand or Malaysia before Austronesian settlement commenced.

The archaeological record has now been considered to the eve of bronze working on the Southeast Asian mainland, variously between 2000 and 500 BC, and to the end of a rather loosely defined 'Early Neolithic' phase in island Southeast Asia, at approximately 1500 BC. After this date in the eastern island regions, especially the Philippines, Sulawesi, Sabah and Timor, new Neolithic fashions in pottery and other artefacts developed which had links with contemporary cultures extending almost 5000 kilometres into the Pacific. Before examining these later cultural phases, however, it is necessary to clarify the record of early agricultural expansion, both on the mainland and in the islands, by considering the evidence from comparative linguistics.

## THE LINGUISTIC RECORDS

As I have stated elsewhere,[99] the record from comparative linguistic research is essential for tracing the origins and subsequent histories of populations defined according to linguistic criteria. The concept of a group of people who share a common language for essential day-to-day communication is an important one, given that the main channels of trans-generational transmission of a language flow via birth and kinship. In

[98] For instance, Flenley ('Palynological evidence' 186) claims a decline of forest before 4800 BC from the Lake Diatas core from Sumatra, followed by forest recovery and then further disturbance at about 2500 BC.

[99] 'The Great Pacific Migration', *Yearbook of Science and the Future* (1984); 'A hypothesis for Austronesian origins', AP, 26 (1988).

small-scale societies the possession of a common language gives people one of their most important guarantees of group membership.

While a great many individual languages associated with major political units have been learnt deliberately by millions of non-native speakers (for instance, Latin, Malay, Spanish and English), these secondary learning processes cannot explain the great extents of certain major language families (as opposed to single dominant languages) across millions of square kilometres of the earth's surface. Many of these very wide distributions can best be explained as the results of demographic expansions which occurred after agriculture was first developed in different parts of the world. This explanation, of course, is unlikely to be universal for all language families, and it is clear that major language similarities can also develop through various processes of areal diffusion, as perhaps happened with the languages of the Aboriginal Australian hunters and gatherers. However, such processes are not convincing as sole explanations of the enormous and deep-seated geographical extensions of language families such as Austronesian,[1] Austroasiatic or Sino-Tibetan (Maps 2.5, 2.6).

There are two important corollaries in terms of the geographical patterning of languages which arise from this theoretical viewpoint. One is that areas where agriculture developed in a primary sense should also be areas where there is high linguisitic diversity, expressed in terms of the existence of more than one major language family. The second is that there should also be in such areas a high degree of lingusitic diversity between the individual languages within the families themselves.[2] Southern China, for instance, contains languages in four separate families (excluding Chinese), these being Austroasiatic (now confined to parts of Yunnan), Tai-Kadai, Miao-Yao, and Tibeto-Burman (a branch of the larger Sino-Tibetan family). In addition, each of these language families also has its area of greatest diversity in the general region of southern China and immediately-adjacent parts of northern Southeast Asia. The Tai languages offer an especially clear example of this, since Thai itself has expanded southwards into most of what is now Thailand within historical times.[3] The focus of Tai linguistic diversity occurs today north and east of Thailand, in Laos, northern Vietnam and southern China.

Within the Southeast Asian region there are two language families which appear to represent a primary dispersal of agricultural populations

[1] W. Meacham ('On the improbability', 93) has recently suggested that Austronesian languages arose by a process akin to areal diffusion from a stage of 'New Guinea-like linguistic diversity' over most of island Southeast Asia. I am unable to visualize such a process, given that very intricate patterns of linguistic diffusion via trade in New Guinea itself have certainly never had such a homogenizing effect.

[2] The reason for this is that those populations who developed agriculture first will have been able to resist linguistic assimilation, owing to their increasing population sizes, for the longest periods of time: diversity correlates to a large extent with time depth of development. It should be emphasized, however, that the concept of 'diversity' requires very careful definition: attempts by linguistics in the past to define it in terms of lexicon alone (via the technique of lexicostatistics) have not always met with convincing success. In addition, the reverse corollary to the one stated here, that areas of high linguistic diversity are necessarily areas of agricultural origin, can easily be shown to be untrue.

[3] Tai is the name of the language subgroup to which Thai, the modern national language of Thailand, belongs.

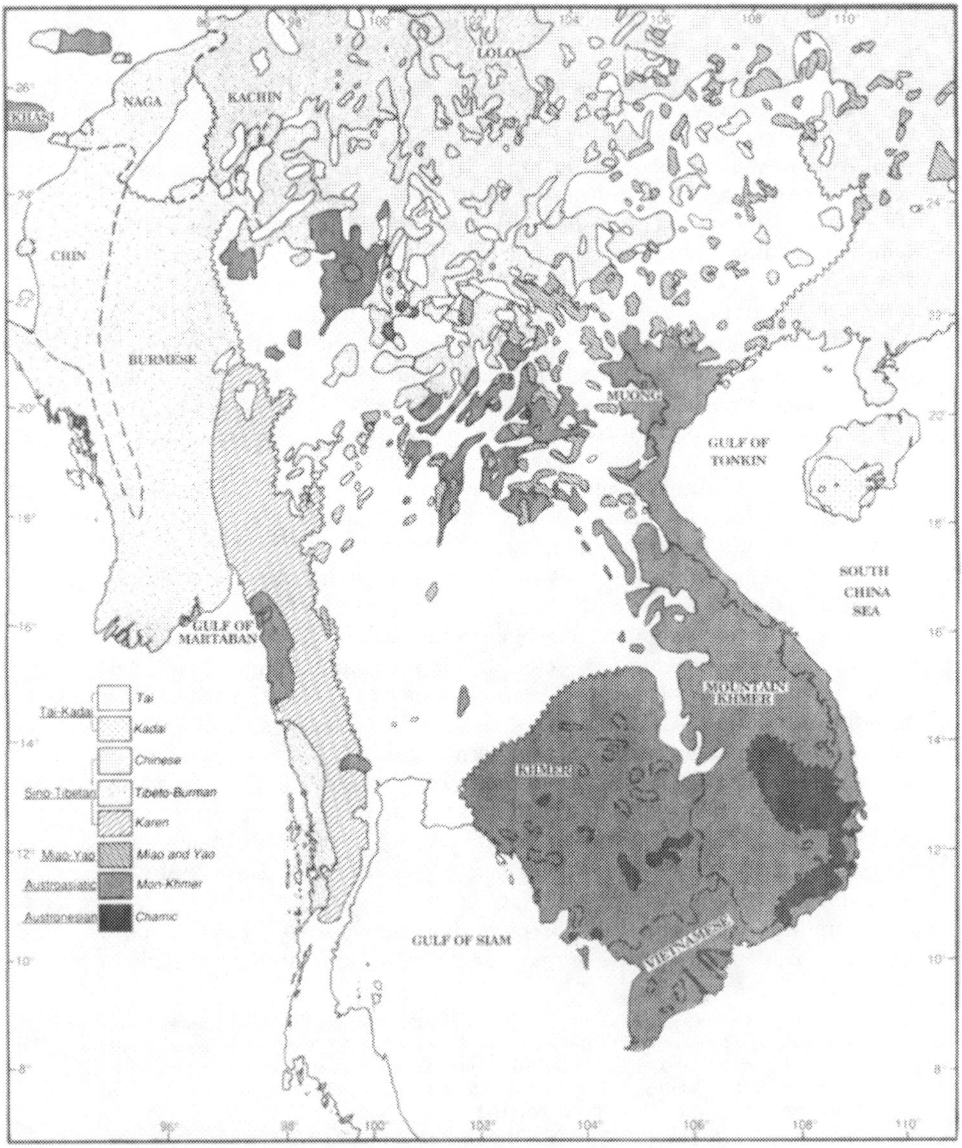


Map 2.5 Distribution of language families and major languages.

through landscapes which were mostly occupied previously only by foraging groups. These are the Austroasiatic and Austronesian families. The other two major families represented in the region, Tibeto-Burman and Tai-Kadai, undoubtedly also underwent initial expansion at the same time, but the greatest expansions of these occurred when the Burmese and Thai languages were distributed over very large areas due to historical conquests and processes of state formation within the last millennium. Khmer and Vietnamese, both members of the Austroasiatic family, also expanded historically for similar reasons, as have Malay and Javanese within the Austronesian family.

The Austroasiatic language family, the most widespread and also the most geographically fragmented in mainland Southeast Asia, includes approximately 150 languages in two major subgroups: Mon-Khmer of Southeast Asia, and Munda of Northeastern India.[4] The Mon-Khmer subgroup is the largest and contains Mon, Khmer, Vietnamese and—besides many other tribal languages—the far-flung outliers of Khasi in Assam, the Aslian languages of Malaya, and Nicobarese. The Munda languages of Bihar, Orissa and West Bengal are even more far-flung, which probably explains their divergence over time (at least four millennia?) into a separate first-order subgroup of Austroasiatic.

To date, no one has attempted to write a combined account of Austroasiatic prehistory from the linguistic and archaeological perspectives, but it is probable that many of the prehistoric sites of northeast Thailand, such as Non Nok Tha and Ban Chiang, were inhabited by speakers of Austroasiatic languages which eventually fell victim to the assimilatory tendencies of the historical Thai kingdoms after the thirteenth century CE. Another observation of great interest is that the reconstructed vocabulary of Proto-Austroasiatic suggests a knowledge of rice,[5] a circumstance in perfect accord with the Neolithic archaeology of the region from northeast India across to southern China and northern Vietnam. The possibility that Austroasiatic languages were also once spoken very widely in southern China, with linguistic traces even as far north as the Yangtze River,[6] is also worthy of note; it is quite apparent that a once-continuous distribution of Austroasiatic languages over most of mainland Southeast Asia, and even across into the Nicobars and possibly northern Sumatra, has been broken up by the historical expansions of the Chinese, Tai, Vietnamese, Burman and Austronesian (Malay and Cham) peoples.

It is not possible at this stage of research to make any sensible correlations between the Tibeto-Burman or Miao-Yao languages and the archaeological record, mainly owing to the lack of archaeology in the regions

[4] G. Diffloth, 'Austro-Asiatic languages', *Encyclopaedia Britannica*, 15th edn, Macropaedia, 2, 1974; 'Asian languages and Southeast Asian prehistory', FMJ, 24 (1979). See also M. Ruhlen, *A Guide to the World's Languages*, Stanford, 1987, 156. The Andamanese languages do not belong to Austroasiatic or any other major family and have presumably been evolving in isolation since far back in the Pleistocene.

[5] A. and N. Zide, 'Proto-Munda cultural vocabulary: evidence for early agriculture', in P. N. Jenner, et al., eds, *Austroasiatic Studies*, Honolulu, 1976, II. 1295–334.

[6] The word 'Yangtze' (Yangzi) itself is even of Austroasiatic origin according to J. Norman and T.-L. Mei, 'The Austroasiatics in ancient South China, some lexical evidence', *Monumenta Serica*, 32 (1976).

of concern. The Tibeto-Burman subgroup, which includes such major languages as Burmese, Chin, Naga and Kachin (with Karen belonging to a separate but co-ordinate subgroup of Sino-Tibetan), has a more north-westerly centre of gravity than Austroasiatic and may reflect for the most part a more recent record of expansion. The Miao-Yao languages of southern China are still expanding into the Golden Triangle region of northern Thailand today, and in prehistoric times were perhaps confined to north of the Chinese border. The Tai-Kadai and Austronesian groups, however, can provide much more detailed information, and the Austronesian languages have witnessed decades of intensive archaeological and linguistic research which gives them an interdisciplinary relevance almost equal to that of the Indo-European languages.

Let us look first at the distributions of these two language families. The Tai-Kadai (or Daic) family includes Thai itself, Lao, Shan of northern Burma, and many languages in the Guizhou and Guangxi provinces of southern China. The Kelao language of Guizhou and Li of Hainan Island form the Kadai subgroup. The distribution of this language family allows one to infer an origin zone in southeastern China; it was presumably once much more widespread there before being overlain, especially in Guangdong province, by Chinese.

The Austronesian family is far more widespread (Map 2.6), although it has never been represented on the southern Chinese mainland. The history of the Austronesian languages reflects one of the most phenomenal records of colonization and dispersal in the history of humanity. Austronesian languages are now spoken in Taiwan, parts of southern Vietnam, Malaysia, the Philippines, and all of Indonesia except for the Papuan-speaking regions of Irian Jaya and parts of Timor, Alor, Pantar and Halmahera. In southern Vietnam the Austronesian Chamic languages probably replaced earlier Austroasiatic languages, and have been replaced in turn by Vietnamese expansion down the coast after the release of the latter from Chinese domination in the tenth century CE. Everywhere else in the Austronesian world (including the Pacific islands and Madagascar) the Austronesian languages show few signs of post-expansion replacement, mainly because they have suffered no linguistic competition from non-Austronesian languages, with the singular and important exception of the Papuan languages of western Melanesia. This region has seen very rapid rates of linguistic interdigitation and change, undoubtedly because the Papuan-speaking peoples were the only ones beyond the mainland of Asia to develop their own indigenous systems of food production and demographic resistance to later colonists.

Because of the wealth of comparative research carried out on the Austronesian languages, it is possible to draw some very sound conclusions, using purely linguistic evidence, concerning the region of origin of the family, the directions of its subsequent spread, and also the vocabularies of important early proto-languages, particularly Proto-Austronesian and its close successor Proto-Malayo-Polynesian. The Malayo-Polynesian languages do not include those of Taiwan, but incorporate the vast remaining distribution of the family from Madagascar to Easter Island.

If we commence at the earliest time, it is necessary to refer to the

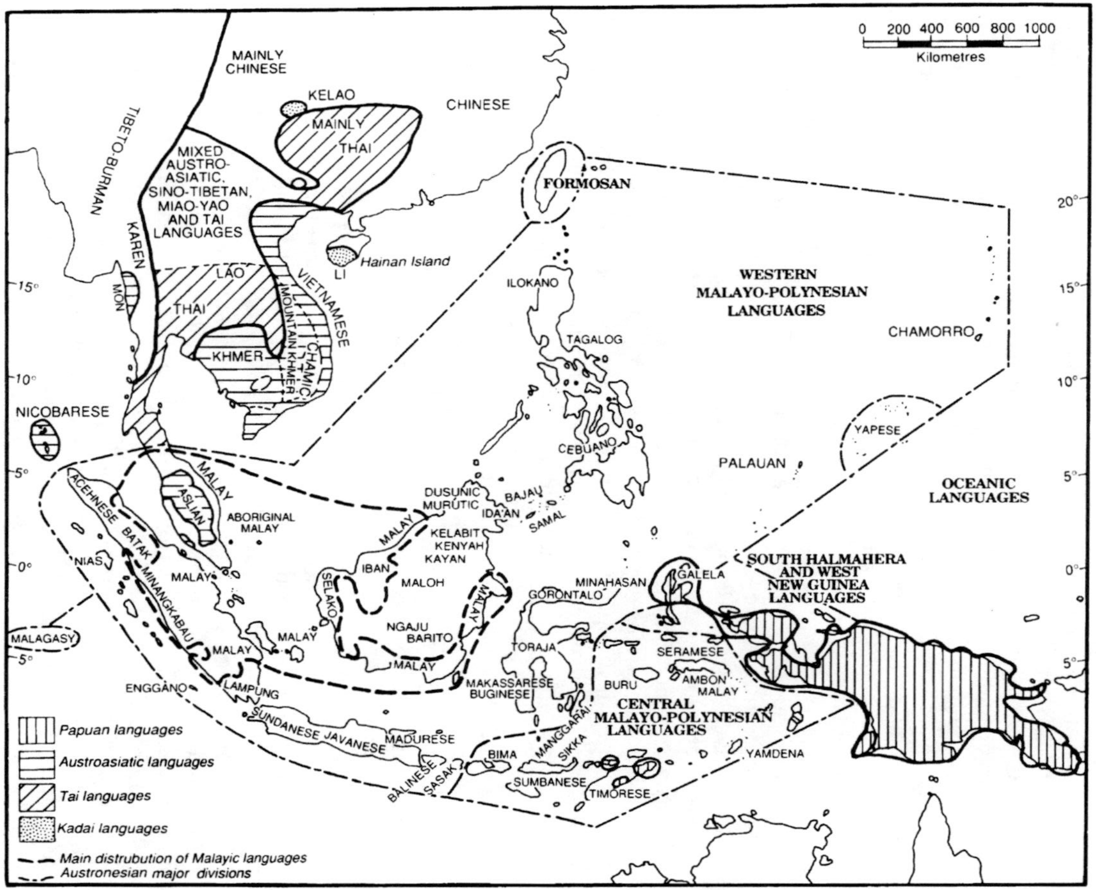


Map 2.6 Distribution of Austronesian languages.

hypothesis of P. Benedict, recently given strong support by L. R. Reid,[7] that the Tai-Kadai and Austronesian languages form a superfamily called Austro-Tai, with a common ancestral language or chain of languages (Proto-Austro-Tai) once spoken on the southern Chinese mainland. Benedict has recently attempted to include the Miao-Yao language family in Austro-Tai, and has also suggested a number of important vocabulary reconstructions for Proto-Austro-Tai, including terms for field, wet field (for rice or taro), garden, plough, rice, sugarcane, the betel nut complex, cattle, water buffalo, axe, and canoe. If Benedict is correct, and no convincing refutation has yet been presented, then one has to consider seriously the possibility that the initial expansions of these two great language families (or three with Miao-Yao) began among Neolithic rice-cultivating communities in south China. It may be no coincidence that the Austroasiatic languages also originated in the same general region. The archaeological record, of course, agrees very well with these reconstructions of linguistic dispersal, and even provides a date range between 5000 and 3000 BC; comparative studies of unwritten languages are quite unable by themselves to provide acceptable absolute dates since there is no universal rate of linguistic divergence between all pairs of languages.

Moving beyond Austro-Tai into Austronesian, the reconstruction of overall linguistic prehistory which is most acceptable today, and which fits best with all independent sources of evidence, is that favoured by R. Blust.[8] This is based on a postulated family tree of subgrouping relationships with a connected hierarchy of proto-languages extending from Proto-Austronesian forwards in time (see Figure 2.4). Reduced to its essentials, this reconstruction favours a geographical expansion beginning in Taiwan (the location of Proto-Austronesian), then encompassing the Philippines, Borneo and Sulawesi, and finally spreading in two branches, one moving west to Java, Sumatra and the Malay peninsula, the other moving east into Oceania.

A wealth of linguistic detail can, of course, be added to this rather bare framework, but I will restrict myself to some points of broad historical and cultural significance. During the linguistic stage termed Proto-Austro-Tai (c.4500 BC?) it would appear that some colonists with an agricultural economy moved across the Formosa Strait to settle in Taiwan. Here they established the Initial Austronesian languages, increased their population and occupied many regions of the island, until, after perhaps another millennium (c.3500 BC?), their linguistic descendants made the first moves into Luzon. This movement to the Philippines precipitated the break-up of the Initial Austronesian linguistic continuum in Taiwan into two major subgroups, Formosan and Malayo-Polynesian, and corresponds with the Proto-Austronesian stage of linguists.[9] The Proto-Austronesian vocabulary

[7] See Benedict, *Austro-Thai Language and Culture*, New Haven, 1976; G. Thurgood, 'Benedict's work: past and present', in G. Thurgood, J. A. Matisoff and D. Bradley, eds, *Linguistics of the Sino-Tibetan Area: the State of the Art*, Canberra 1985; Reid, 'Benedict's Austro-Tai hypothesis; an evaluation', *AP*, 26 (1988).

[8] 'The Austronesian homeland; a linguistic perspective', *AP*, 26 (1988). See also PIMA, 102–29.

[9] Austro-Tai likewise split into its two major 'subgroups' (now of course regarded as separate language families) of Tai-Kadai and Austronesian when populations became separated by

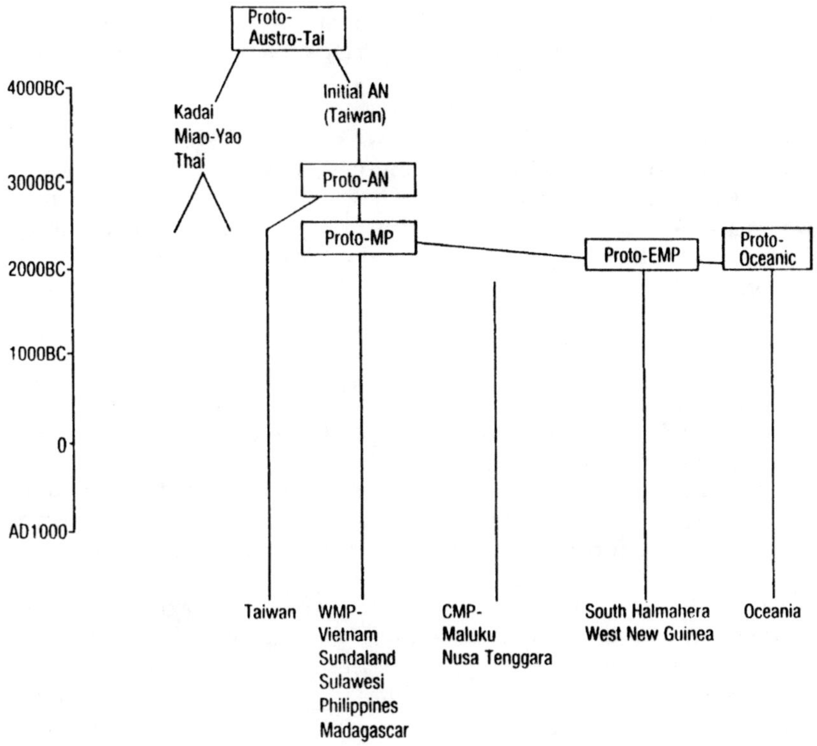


Figure 2.4 A family 'tree' (here shown inverted) for the Austronesian languages.

AN = Austronesian; MP = Malayo-Polynesian; WMP = Western Malayo-Polynesian; CMP = Central Malayo-Polynesian; EMP = Eastern Malayo-Polynesian.

indicates an economy well suited to marginal tropical latitudes, with cultivation of rice, millet, sugarcane, presence of domesticated dogs and pigs, and the use of canoes. This listing, of course, refers only to what has survived linguistically in terms of recognizable shared inheritances, and many other items recognizable in the archaeological record (such as pottery and domesticated fowls) do not have such well-documented linguistic histories.

As a result of further colonizing movements through the Philippines into Borneo, Sulawesi and Maluku, the Malayo-Polynesian subgroup eventually separated into its several constituent Western and Central-Eastern subgroups. The divergence of Central-Eastern Malayo-Polynesian commenced in Maluku or Nusa Tenggara, and this group also contains all

the Formosa Strait. Austronesian languages have never been spoken in southern China, for the simple reason that they did not begin to differentiate from Austro-Tai until after founder populations of speakers moved into isolation in Taiwan.

the Austronesian languages of the Pacific islands, apart from some in western Micronesia. The vocabulary of Proto-Malayo-Polynesian, a linguistic entity which may have been located in the general region of the lands bordering the Sulawesi Sea, is of great interest because it contains a number of tropical economic indicators which were absent in the earlier Proto-Austronesian stage. These include taro, breadfruit, banana, yam, sago and coconut, and their presence reflects the shift away from rice towards a greater dependence on tubers and fruits in equatorial latitudes.

The record of the initial expansion of the Western Malayo-Polynesian languages into Java, Sumatra and Malaya may be masked partly by the expansions of the Malayic and Javanese languages within the past fifteen hundred years. B. Nothofer believes that the oldest Austronesian settlement of this region is represented today by the languages spoken in the small islands off the west coast of Sumatra and in the northern Sumatran highlands (his Barrier Island-Batak group).[10] There is also evidence in the Aslian languages for borrowing from now-extinct Austronesian languages in the Malay peninsula.[11] Evidence from the pollen record in the Sumatran highlands (pages 105–6) could also be taken to indicate an initial expansion of Austronesian agriculturalists before 1000 BC, but this correlation can only be surmise.

Most of the major Western Malayo-Polynesian languages, however, including those of the Malayic subgroup (Malay, Minangkabau, Iban, and several other languages of Sumatra and western Borneo), together with Acehnese, Chamic, Javanese and Balinese, have been separating only since the first millennium BC or later.[12] A great deal of the expansion of Malay as a lingua franca around the coasts of Borneo and into eastern Indonesia has occurred since the seventh century with the development of major trading states such as Śrīvijaya and Melaka, and dialects of Malay now dominate almost the whole of peninsular Malaysia. This phenomenon of linguistic levelling is to be expected in a region which has witnessed a succession of major political formations at the state level, just as it has occurred in the histories of Thai and Vietnamese.

In eastern Indonesia the degree of linguistic diversity is greater than in the western regions, perhaps reflecting the lesser degree of political integration in this area in historical times. Another cause of diversity, especially close to New Guinea, has been a process of strong mutual influence between languages in the Austronesian and Papuan families; these processes have been particularly important in Melanesia itself, and have led to such rapid lexical diversification that some linguists have even claimed western Melanesia to be the homeland region of Proto-

[10] 'The Barrier Island languages in the Austronesian family', in P. Geraghty, L. Carrington and S. A. Wurm, eds, *Focal II: Papers from the Fourth International Conference on Austronesian Linguistics*, Canberra, 1986.

[11] G. Benjamin, 'Ethnohistorical perspectives on Kelantan's prehistory', in Nik Hassan Shuhaimi, ed., *Kelantan Zaman Awal*, Kota Bharu, 1987.

[12] Blust, 'The Austronesian homeland', 57. On the Malayic languages see the papers by Blust, Nothofer and Adelaar in M. T. Ahmad and Z. M. Zain, eds, *Rekonstruksi dan Cabang-Cabang Bahasa Melayu Induk*', Kuala Lumpur, 1988; K. A. Adelaar, *Proto-Malayic*, Alblasserdam, Netherlands, 1985.

Austronesian.[13] This opinion, however, does not agree with the results of comparative phonological or grammatical research.

The completeness of Austronesian domination in island Southeast Asia is as striking as its inability to make any sizeable impact on the linguistic situation in the island of New Guinea. It is this domination in island Southeast Asia which makes so clear the conclusion that the archipelago cannot have supported any major agricultural population, if indeed any at all, before the period of Austronesian colonization. Even the Philippine Negritos, who have obviously been able to resist major assimilation until very recently, were converted to Austronesian speech from some unknown original languages quite early in the Austronesian sequence.[14] However, the Austronesians seem also to have borrowed a number of taboo concepts from the Negritos,[15] so the acculturation process was not entirely one-way.

The linguistic picture presented here of the origin and dispersal of the Austronesian languages clearly has some fairly convincing points of overlap with the archaeological record in its broadest sense. There is always an element of circularity in linguistic reconstruction, in that the reconstructions of proto-language vocabularies depend precisely on the shape of the family tree; if there are errors in the formulation of the latter, they will clearly affect the former. The family tree championed by most modern linguists, however, does have independent support from the Neolithic archaeological record in island Southeast Asia as it is currently understood, and this is not true for other hypotheses, such as that of an Austronesian homeland in Melanesia, or an Austronesian route of major expansion through the Malay peninsula into Indonesia. The identification of a homeland region in south China and Taiwan, however, does not mean that all worthwhile features of Austronesian prehistory evolved in this region and then spread southwards in a monolithic wave. The expansion process was highly complex, and the Austronesian lifestyle as a whole probably owes as much to the past 5000 years of adaptation and change in island Southeast Asia and the Pacific islands as it does to its original Proto-Austronesian roots.

## THE EARLY METAL PHASE

Having described the evidence for the expansion of agricultural societies over much of Southeast Asia, I now examine the developments that occurred between the introduction of bronze, initially perhaps during the earlier second millennium BC in northern Thailand and Vietnam, and the spread of Indic and Chinese influences through parts of the region from about 2000 years ago. The period of gradation from prehistory into

[13] For instance, I. Dyen, *'A Lexicostatistical Classification of the Austronesian languages'*, International Journal of American Linguistics, Memoir 19, 1965.

[14] L. A. Reid, 'The early switch hypothesis: linguistic evidence for contact between Negritos and Austronesians', *Man and Culture in Oceania*, 3 (1987).

[15] R. A. Blust,'Linguistic evidence for some early Austronesian taboos', *American Anthropologist*, 83 (1981).

history is poorly documented in Southeast Asia, and many societies which were completely without historical records continued well into the last two thousand years in remote regions. These included not only foragers, but also metal-using agriculturalists in remote mountainous interiors. This means that no early historical 'horizon' extends right across the region, and I do not propose to adhere to a fixed termination date for prehistory in this chapter.

In the interests of simplicity I will simply refer to the late prehistoric metal-using phase across Southeast Asia as the 'Early Metal phase', a term which is intended to have no more than technological connotations. On the mainland of Southeast Asia north of the Thai-Malayan peninsula there clearly was a separate 'Bronze Age' which lasted to the coming of iron, after which bronze and iron continued in use side-by-side. In island Southeast Asia, however, bronze and iron appeared together from about 500 BC onwards. I will also describe later in this section certain Late Neolithic assemblages from the eastern regions of island Southeast Asia which are contemporary with the use of bronze on the mainland.

A number of other general observations about the Early Metal phase will be made here, before the archaeological record is considered in more detail. First, Southeast Asia had no early period when only copper was in use; bronze (an alloy of copper and tin) was present from the beginning, and although pure copper items have been identified from various times and places they seem to have been rare. There is indeed no good evidence to suggest that bronze was invented independently in Southeast Asia, and a Chinese source is likely but still unproved. It must be remembered that the Yellow (Huang He) River Neolithic cultures (such as the Yangshao) were possessed of a high-temperature kiln technology for firing pottery from about 5000 BC onwards, and in recent years there have been reports of both copper and bronze industries from contexts of the third millennium BC in Gansu Province, western China.[16] However, the problem of the origin of bronze-working in eastern Asia, one which has provoked lively debate in recent years, still defies a clear solution.

The value of bronze to those societies which acquired it was not restricted simply to technological improvements. The metal also became associated with concepts of status and wealth, for obvious reasons connected with the skills, labour resources and trading connections all required for its production and ownership. Bronze, all over Southeast Asia, does appear to have had a significant correlation with the rise of ranked societies in pre-Indic times, and weapons, vessels and ornaments of the metal were probably exchanged between regional élites for purposes of alliance and intermarriage. Iron, which appeared widely after 500 BC, was clearly easier to obtain and manufacture. Yet, while not such a prized symbol of status as bronze, it did play a different but equally important role, mainly by improving the efficiency of productive labour, especially in agriculture and war. It is not surprising, therefore, that several authors

[16] K. C. Chang, *The Archaeology of Ancient China*, 143, 282; An Zhimin, 'Some problems concerning China's early copper and bronze artefacts', *Early China*, 8 (1982–3); Sun Shuyun and Han Rubin, 'A preliminary study of early Chinese copper and bronze artefacts', ibid., 9–10 (1983–5).

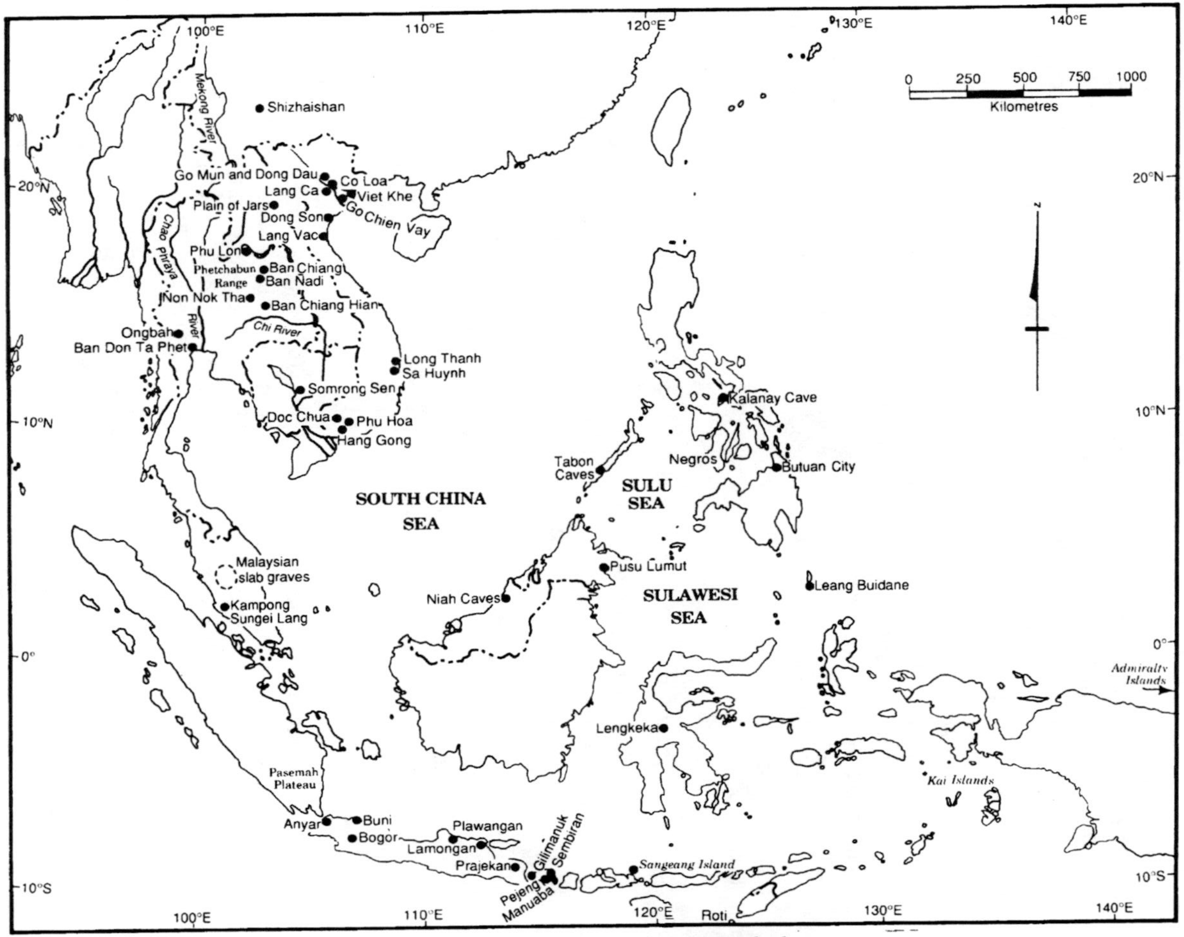


Map 2.7 Major sites of the Early Metal phase.

have correlated the arrival of iron with significant rises in the complexity and extent of pre-Indic or pre-Chinese political integration in Thailand and Vietnam.

Iron, like bronze, has uncertain origins in Southeast Asia. Again a Chinese source seems most likely, albeit with the proviso that contacts between littoral Southeast Asia and India after about 200 BC are now being increasingly documented, and some transfer of technology from India cannot entirely be ruled out. Although much Chinese iron was cast after about 400 BC, it is apparent that the simpler smelting methods used in Southeast Asia were present there, as also in India, from the early part of the first millennium BC.[17]

With the coming of metal and the continuing increases in population numbers and cultural complexity throughout Southeast Asia, the archaeological record necessarily becomes more detailed, especially in terms of the categories of artefacts represented and the stylistic variations found within them. The record is therefore more difficult to summarize briefly, and in this final section I will concentrate on particular sites or cultures which are relatively well understood, perhaps at the expense of complete regional coverage.

## Northern Thailand

On the Khorat Plateau of northern Thailand the agricultural societies represented in the lower layers of Ban Chiang appear to have continued their general lifestyle with no sharp change after the appearance of bronze, which probably had little immediate impact on agricultural production. The best record of such societies for the period after 1500 BC comes from the burial and habitation mound of Ban Na Di, about twenty kilometres southwest of Ban Chiang.[18] The lowest layer of this site dates to the late second millennium BC, and contains bronze from the beginning. This seems to have been brought in ready-smelted, the copper possibly from a source such as that recently investigated at Phu Lon, near Nong Khai on the Mekong River, where high-quality malachite ore was obtained from excavated shafts and smelted on site during the first millennium BC.[19] The inhabitants of Ban Na Di cast the copper and tin alloy (the tin perhaps from northwest Thailand or Laos) using both the lost-wax technique and bivalve moulds of baked clay or stone. Items produced included socketed axes, spearheads, bracelets, beads, fishhooks, bells and bowls. The metal was

[17] See J. Needham, 'Iron and steel technology in East and Southeast Asia', in T. A. Wertime and J. D. Muhly, eds, *The Coming of the Age of Iron*, New Haven, 1980. As in India and China, many Southeast Asian iron tools or weapons were carburized by intentional heating in charcoal followed by quenching, in order to increase the hardness and strength of the edge.

[18] C. Higham and A. Kijngam, *Prehistoric Investigations in Northeastern Thailand*, Oxford, 1984; C. Higham, 'Prehistoric metallurgy in Southeast Asia', in R. Maddin, ed., *The Beginning of the Use of Metals and Alloys*, Cambridge, Mass., 1988; J. Pilditch, 'The typology of the Ban Na Di jewellery, *Proceedings of the International Conference on Thai Studies*, Canberra, 1987, II. 277–90; B. Vincent, *Prehistoric Ceramics of Northeastern Thailand*, Oxford, 1988.

[19] V. Pigott, 'Pre-industrial mineral exploitation and metal production in Thailand', *MASCA Journal*, 3 (1986); S. Natapintu, 'Current research on ancient copper-base metallurgy in Thailand', in Pisit Charoenwongsa and Bennet Bronson, eds, *Prehistoric Studies: the Stone and Metal Ages in Thailand*, Bangkok. 1988.

melted in open hearth-type furnaces, probably with the assistance of bellows with clay nozzles, and poured from crucibles made of clay tempered with rice chaff. Similar chaff-tempered crucibles have been reported from other sites in both the Khorat Plateau and the Chao Phraya Basin, in the latter region with prolific evidence for copper ore preparation and casting at recently excavated sites in the Khao Wong Prachan Valley.[20]

Many burials were also found in cemetery groupings in Ban Na Di, often wrapped in mats or, in the case of one child, placed under a crocodile skin. The grave goods included bronze items, small shell beads (7850 found with one burial alone), trochus-shell bracelets, and stone bracelets with T-shaped cross-sections almost identical to specimens found in contemporary sites of the Ban Kao culture far to the south (page 100). Some of these bracelets had been deliberately cut into pieces and then reassembled with bronze wire, perhaps as their owners grew from youth into adulthood. Large numbers of unbaked clay figurines of cattle, pigs, dogs, other animals and humans were also found in the graves, together with cord-marked and painted pottery similar to that found in the Middle Period layers of Ban Chiang. A remarkable finding from contexts of the early to mid-first millennium BC at Ban Na Di is of silk impressions in the corroded surfaces of bronze items; whether the silk was made in Thailand or imported from China still remains unknown.

Iron made its first appearance in Ban Na Di at about 300 BC, as in the site of Ban Chiang Hian some 150 kilometres to the south, and probably also in Ban Chiang itself. Artefacts made of iron include neck rings, spearheads, bracelets and knives, and in the same iron-bearing layers at both Ban Chiang and Ban Na Di were found elaborately carved clay rollers similar to those found at Somrong Sen in Cambodia. While the functions of these items are disputed, I suspect they were strung as ornaments over body and clothing; other more exotic explanations include the view that they were used in systems of accounting.[21] The early iron-bearing layers in Ban Chiang have also produced the remarkable red-painted pottery with its outstanding repertoire of curvilinear designs, a style which seems to have been absent from Ban Na Di despite the geographical closeness of the two sites.

In economic terms, the pre-iron period at Ban Na Di, Ban Chiang and Ban Chiang Hian continued the Neolithic pattern, with evidence for domesticated cattle, pigs, fowl and dogs, together with the cultivation of rice in seasonally flooded fields in alluvial lowlands, perhaps bunded to encourage water retention. True canal irrigation to allow double cropping has not been suggested for this period, so only one harvest was probably taken per year, as remains the case generally today in this region. It has been suggested, however, that rice fields were perhaps used on a more

[20] According to V. Pigott ('Prehistoric copper production in Southeast Asia; new evidence from central Thailand', paper presented to the Circum-Pacific Prehistory Conference, Seattle, August 1989) the Khao Wong Prachan sites, which could date as early as the late third millennium BC, have produced copper slag and ore, crucibles, ceramic casting moulds (some for cup-shaped or conical ingots of copper), and several burials with copper artefacts.

[21] W. J. Folan and B. H. Hyde, 'The significance of the clay rollers of the Ban Chiang culture, Thailand', AP, 23 (1980).

permanent and intensive basis in the iron-using period, together with domesticated water buffaloes for trampling and possibly even plough traction (although metal ploughshares are known only from northern Vietnam). Whatever the details of agricultural change might have been, it does seem likely that more intensive production was developing during the first millennium BC in order to stabilize yields through good and bad years, and to feed the increasing populations in the fertile riverine lowlands.

In the more mountainous zones the picture may have been different from that on the alluvial plains. So far, no major signs of agricultural settlement predating the introduction of iron have been found in the Phetchabun Range west of the Khorat Plateau, despite intensive survey and excavation programmes there by three separate teams.[22] This could suggest that most agricultural settlement before about 500 BC was focused in the low-lying alluvial basins, and that the 'hill-tribe' phenomenon of mainland Southeast Asia—the expansion into high altitudes from the north of shifting agriculturalists—is a relatively recent development mainly limited to the historical period.[23]

The transition to a common use of iron in northern Thailand, or from General Period B to General Period C in the regional terminology favoured by Bayard and Higham,[24] may have witnessed a number of important social and economic changes. I have referred already to increases in the efficiency of labour and food production, and Higham has also suggested that these developments may have caused a shift from a gently ranked lineage type of social organization, evidently with a fairly elaborate network of exchange of prestige goods, to one with truly stratified classes and a ruling echelon controlling considerable amounts of wealth, labour and perhaps military force and tribute. Such a shift may be recognizable in changes in settlement sizes; while pre-iron settlements on the Khorat Plateau appear to have averaged around three hectares in size and to have been relatively independent of each other in social terms (as suggested by a marked regionality in pottery styles), those of General Period C were evidently ranked in size, with an upper echelon of 'central places' in some cases exceeding twenty hectares in size. Some of these very large settlements may have been partly encircled by 'moats', perhaps for water storage as much as defence, although none have yet been thoroughly investigated archaeologically.[25] Some degree of political aggrandizement may also have occurred during this period, with political influences from the Chi Valley of the central Khorat Plateau moving northwards to correlate with relatively sharp shifts in pottery styles at sites such as Ban Na Di and Ban Chiang.

[22] See D. Bayard, *The Pa Mong Archaeological Survey Programme, 1973–5*, Dunedin: Otago University Department of Anthropology, 1980; J. Penny, *The Petchabun Piedmont Survey*, University Microfilms International, 1986; S. Rutnin, 'Prehistory of Western Udon Thani and Udon region, northeast Thailand', *Proceedings of the International Conference on Thai Studies*, Canberra, 1987, III, part 2.

[23] This interpretation assumes that the site of Spirit Cave does not reflect early agricultural activities; see page 88.

[24] See footnote 67, above.

[25] Many moated sites are described from aerial photographs by E. Moore, *Moated Sites in Early North East Thailand*, Oxford, 1988.

It is worth noting also that these developments towards greater levels of political integration in northern Thailand appear to have occurred quite independently of any influences from India or China. For instance, glass and precious stone beads, fairly sure indicators of trade contact with India, do not seem to be present in Khorat Plateau sites much before 200 BC and do not become common until after 1 CE. However, it would be most unrealistic to think that the inland regions of Thailand were totally isolated from the outside world before this time. For instance, one indication of a very widespread exchange of metallurgical knowledge during the first millennium BC is provided by a number of bimetallic artefacts of both bronze and iron found in many sites across Southern and Eastern Asia. Ban Chiang has yielded two spearheads with iron blades and cast-on bronze sockets; similar bimetallic artefacts, including iron daggers with copper or bronze hilts, have also been reported from mid to late first millennium BC contexts as far apart as Mahurjhari in Madhya Pradesh, Shizhaishan and related sites in Yunnan, Gilimanuk in Bali, Prajekan in east Java and Dong-son in northern Vietnam. A bimetallic axe is even reported from a late Shang dynasty context in China. While the real meaning of these unusual artefacts in terms of trade or the diffusion of metal-working techniques is not yet clear, it does seem unlikely that they represent totally independent centres of innovation.

## Northern Vietnam

Bronze working in Vietnam, as in Thailand, seems to have commenced during the early to middle second millennium BC. Items such as arrowheads, spearheads, knives, fishhooks and socketed axes were first manufactured in the Dong Dau phase, beginning about 1500 BC, and certain new forms such as shaft-hole sickles appeared in the Go Mun phase, after 1000 BC.[26] The site of Doc Chua in southern Vietnam has also yielded socketed axes, spearheads and sandstone bivalve moulds from layers contemporary with Dong Dau in the north. The most outstanding metal assemblages from Vietnam, however, belong to the bronze- and iron-using phase named after the major settlement excavated at Dong-son, in Thanh Hoa Province. The Dong-son repertoire with its splendid bronze drums marks the apogee of indigenous Southeast Asian metalworking achievement, despite the fact that northern Vietnam itself was politically influenced by China from the mid-third century BC onwards, and eventually became a Chinese protectorate in 111 BC and a province of the Han empire in 43 CE.

The roots of the Dong-son metallurgical style appear to go back into the decoration on Neolithic and Early Metal phase pottery in Vietnam, and to the invention, perhaps a little before 600 BC, of the unique shape of drum which characterizes the style. These roots seem to be fundamentally Southeast Asian, although it has long been known that some of the motifs on the drums are paralleled on late Zhou bronzes of the middle Yangtze region, and some interaction with outside centres of metalworking is only

[26] Ha Van Tan, 'Nouvelles recherches'.

to be expected. The classical Dong-son bronze drum itself, however, termed the Heger type I by art historians was clearly not a form borrowed from Zhou or Han China; it seems to have been developed in either Yunnan or northern Vietnam by about 500 BC. This is a matter of some debate at present, and it appears that a recently-identified pre-Heger I type, considered the main ancestral form by some authorities,[27] might have appeared first in Yunnan. Despite this, the major centre of manufacture of the true Heger I drums seems to have been located in northern Vietnam; a divergent tradition evolved in Yunnan whereby many of the drums were modified into lidded cowrie containers and provided with three-dimensional scenes of human activities on their tops. These are amongst the most evocative and outstanding examples of bronze casting in non-Chinese East Asia, and portray scenes which include human sacrifice, horse riding, offering of allegiance to a lord, women weaving with back-strap looms, house models, and many species of animals.[28]

The cultural heart of the Dong-son world from perhaps 400 BC onwards was the Red River valley and adjacent coastal regions of Vietnam. The Heger I drums, of which more than two hundred are known from throughout Southeast Asia (apart from a total absence in Borneo, north-eastern Indonesia and the Philippines),[29] have flat tympana, bulbous upper sides and splayed feet, and were cast in one piece, complete with their decoration, by the lost-wax method. The largest are almost one metre high, and can weigh up to 100 kilograms. The decorative zones which encircle these drums are full of remarkable detail, showing friezes of birds, deer and other animals, warriors with feather headdresses, houses with raised floors, and a range of intricate running geometric patterns. The upper sides of the drums contain scenes of warriors in long boats, sometimes with a drum in a cabin or being beaten amidships. These were originally interpreted by Victor Goloubew in 1929 as boats to take the dead into the afterlife, using analogies from recent art and beliefs in south-eastern Kalimantan which he believed represented a survival of Dong-son traditions. This interpretation has recently been supported in the most recent authoritative survey of Heger I drums by Bernet Kempers,[30] but it must not be assumed that these drums were made only for funerary purposes, despite their common occurrence in burials. H. Loofs-Wissowa has recently surveyed a number of possible functions, including the possibility that they were bestowed as legitimizing 'regalia' on local chiefs

[27] Eiji Nitta, 'Pre-Heger I bronze drums from Yunnan', *Shiroku*, 18 (1985); D. Hollman and D. H. R. Spennemann, 'A note on the metallurgy of Southeast Asian kettle-drums', BIPPA, 6 (1985); M. von Dewall, 'New evidence on the ancient bronze kettle-drum of South East Asia from recent Chinese finds' in B. Allchin, ed., *South Asian Archaeology 1981*, Cambridge, UK, 1984; P. Sorensen, 'The kettledrums from the Ongbah Cave' in Sorensen, ed, *Archaeological Excavations in Thailand: Surface Finds and Minor Excavations*, London, 1988.

[28] See J. Rawson, ed., *The Chinese Bronzes of Yunnan*, London, 1983.

[29] 133 have been found in Vietnam alone according to Nguyen Duy Hinh, 'The birth of the first state in Vietnam', in Bayard, ed., *Southeast Asian Archaeology*, 185. A. J. Bernet Kempers (*The Kettledrums of Southeast Asia*, Rotterdam, 1988) mentions 55 from island Southeast Asia, and many others are known from elsewhere in Southeast Asia and southern China, especially Yunnan.

[30] *Kettledrums of Southeast Asia*.

by a religious authority in northern Indochina.[31] The distribution of these Heger I drums through the countries of Southeast Asia and right along the Sunda Chain almost to New Guinea is a truly remarkably phenomenon, to which I will return.

The manufacture of the Heger I drums, as noted above, was by the lost-wax method, most recently reviewed and described by Bernet Kempers. The wax model was evidently made around a hollow clay core, and the standardized geometric and animal decoration was impressed into the wax by using incised stone moulds, so that the designs appeared in low relief on the drum surfaces. The more detailed figurative designs, such as the houses with people and drums inside, appear to have been carved into the wax individually, and thus emerged incised rather than in relief in their final cast forms. Some of the Indonesian drums have four frogs cast in relief on their tympana, but these seem to be rather rare in mainland Southeast Asia, a circumstance which may reflect manufacture to order, to suit local tastes and preferences.

The oldest drums are generally considered to be the most naturalistic in their decoration: excellent examples include those from Ngoc Lu and Hoang Ha in northern Vietnam (Figure 2.5). In many later ones some of the standardized zonal decoration became highly schematized, and the feathered warriors broke down into almost illegible networks of lines and eye motifs. Surprisingly, however, this did not happen with the figurative scenes, which were incised in remarkable detail until the end of the tradition, as shown by the Sangeang drum from Indonesia, which may have been made as late as the third century CE. The Sangeang drum also shows figures in houses in Han Chinese and Indian (Kushan?) costumes, and one from the Kai Islands near New Guinea has an inscription in Chinese characters which also dates to about the third century CE. The significance of these historical connections, of course, is that many of the Heger I drums were made in Vietnam when it was fully a province of the Chinese empire, unless (and this has never been demonstrated) some of the later centres of Heger I manufacture moved southwards into Fu-nan or Java. Even if they did, the fact remains that many drums were still being traded in Indonesia well into the period of early Indian political and religious influence, so the Dong-son stylistic distribution cannot be considered entirely prehistoric in time.

The range of other Dong-son bronze goods, excavated from such sites as the pile-dwelling village of Dong-son itself on the lower Ma River, and more recently from burials at Viet Khe, Lang Ca and Lang Vac, includes bowls and situlae, miniature drums and bells, a range of mostly socketed tools and projectile points, bracelets, belt hooks, and some remarkable daggers with hilts cast as human figures in the round. As in Yunnan the techniques of lost-wax casting of human and other figures merit great admiration, and a clay crucible capable of holding twelve kilograms of molten bronze was found in the Lang Ca cemetery. The

[31] 'The distribution of Dongson drums: some thoughts', in P. Snoy, ed., *Ethnologie und Geschichte*, Wiesbaden, 1983.

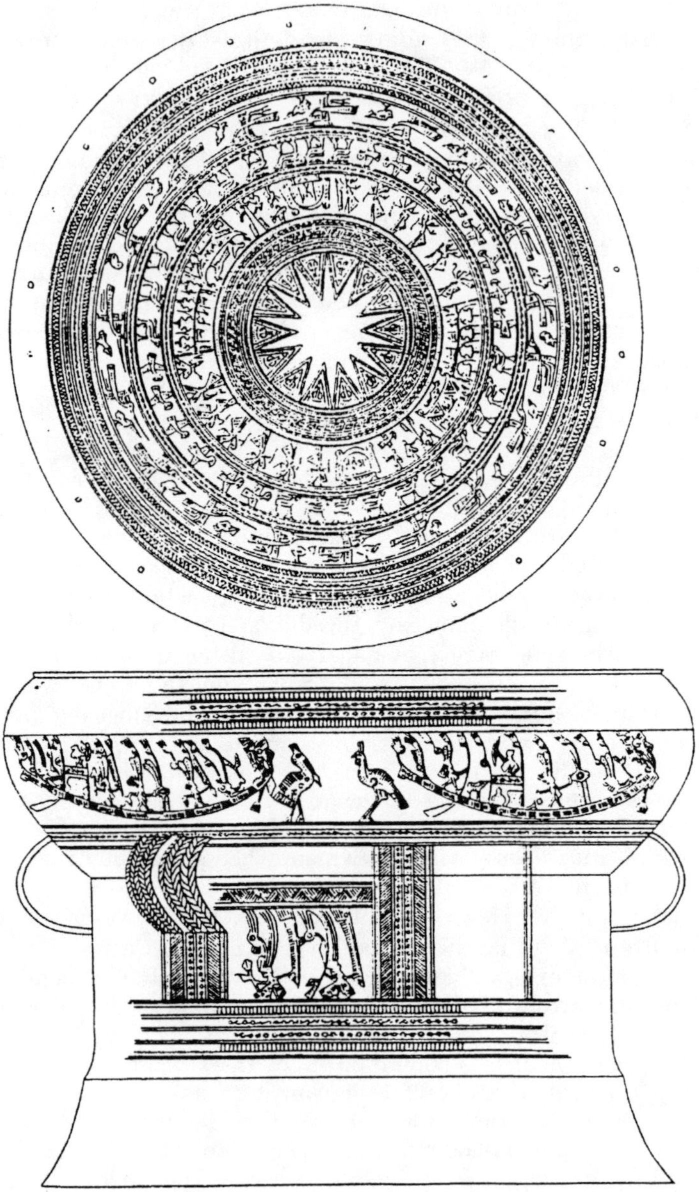

Figure 2.5 An early type of Heger I drum from Ngoc Lu, northern Vietnam. The tympanum is decorated with concentric bands showing birds, deer, warriors with head-dresses and perhaps loin-cloths, houses with raised floors and saddle-shaped roofs, possible reed-ornamented shrines, pairs of people pounding rice, and what may be raised floors with drums stored on posts beneath. The sides show boats carrying warriors and drums.

From A. J. Bernet Kempers, *The Kettledrums of Southeast Asia*, Rotterdam, 1988, plate 11.30 a and c

earthen-ramparted enceinte of Co Loa[32] near Hanoi, six square kilometres in extent, which was the traditional capital of the Au Lac kingdom from 257 BC, has also yielded a 72-kilogram bronze drum with over 100 socketed bronze ploughshares inside.

Iron artefacts are generally rare in northern Vietnam. The site of Dong-son has produced some spearheads, and a Chinese cast-iron hoe claimed to be associated with a radiocarbon date of about 400 BC was found at the site of Go Chien Vay. Indeed, it is quite possible that much Dong-son iron was imported from China, together with many bronze items including a Warring States sword from Viet Khe, and Han dynasty coins, a sword and mirror from Dong-son itself. The pottery from Dong-son sites also has strong parallels with the Geometric paddle-impressed pottery of this period in southern China, and constant interaction between this region and Vietnam can probably be taken for granted after about 300 BC.

The social and historical evidence for the Dong-son phase suggests, of course, the existence of a stratified society, perhaps under the rule of a single state centred on Co Loa if we are to believe traditional history. Indeed, the Au Lac kingdom of the third century BC had a traditional predecessor in the Van Lang kingdom, which may have commenced as early as the seventh century BC.[33] The burial sites themselves reveal marked stratification in the distribution of wealth; one burial at Viet Khe, for instance, included more than one hundred bronzes, and a few wealthy people seem to have been buried in coffins of lacquered wood; the Viet Khe burials are radiocarbon dated to between 550 and 350 BC. There is also evidence in Chinese records to the effect that canal-irrigated rice fields were present in northern Vietnam before 111 BC, which suggests the possibility of intensive double-cropping. In addition, a Chinese census of 2 CE records a population of almost one million people in northern Vietnam, and this in turn suggests that the population prior to the period of Chinese political control may also have been very large; large enough, perhaps, to demand some degree of centralized government.

Elsewhere on the mainland of Southeast Asia the archaeological record of the Early Metal phase is not as well known as in northern Vietnam or Thailand. For Burma and Cambodia the record is virtually blank, and while Laos has the splendid monuments of the Plain of Jars (at least those which have survived recent military activity) it appears that no systematic research has been done there since the 1930s.[34] The stone jars themselves, averaging about 1.5 metres in height, appear to have been used for burial purposes during the first few centuries CE. Heger I drums have been reported from scattered localities across Cambodia, Thailand, and down into the Malay portion of the peninsula where one, buried under a plank within a possible burial mound at Kampong Sungei Lang in Selangor, has been radiocarbon dated rather loosely to between 500 BC and 200 CE. The Malayan drums, like the Indonesian ones, have generally high lead and tin

[32] Details about Co Loa are regrettably few, but a plan of the site can be found in L. Bezacier, *La Viêtnam: de la Prehistoire à la Fin de L'Occupation Chinoise*, Paris, 1972, fig. 121.

[33] K. Taylor, *The Birth of Vietnam*, Berkeley, 1983.

[34] An account of the Plain of Jars can be found in my *Man's Conquest*, 195–8. For the results of recent bombing see P. T. White, 'Laos', *National Geographic*, 171, 6 (1987).

contents and seem to be relatively late in the typological sequence.

The later prehistory of peninsular Malaysia, however, as well as that of the Chamic province of southern Vietnam, belongs properly with the Early Metal phase of island Southeast Asia. To this world, the heartland of the Austronesians, we now turn.

## THE LATE NEOLITHIC AND EARLY METAL PHASES IN THE AUSTRONESIAN WORLD

The late prehistoric archaeological record from the islands of Southeast Asia differs markedly from that of the northern mainland. The record in Thailand and Vietnam consists almost entirely of large settlement and burial sites which encourage debate on such matters as the rise of social complexity, the growth of settlement hierarchies and the evolution of skills in metalworking. The mainland tradition of tight settlement nucleation in a relatively dry environment with good conditions for site preservation (despite the common occurrence of leaching, bioturbation and agricultural disturbance) has clearly aided research into these questions.

In the islands, however, especially those with equatorial climates, the record has only rarely yielded coherent settlement and social evidence, despite the relatively frequent discovery and excavation of cemetery assemblages. Large, stable and nucleated settlements seem to have been rare in these latitudes in both prehistoric and historic times, and conditions for survival of a fine-grained archaeological record outside caves are poor. Perhaps because of this, interpretations of island Southeast Asian late prehistory tend to focus more on supra-settlement phenomena such as population expansion, style diffusion and trade. The history of social complexity before the Indic civilizations is basically unknown; so far none of the relevant prehistoric burial assemblages have been analysed or published in sufficient detail for many observations to be made. We are thrown back on the evidence from comparative linguistics to suggest that some Austronesian societies on the eve of Indic state formation were at least lightly ranked, especially in Java where Austronesian chiefly titles such as *ratu* or *raka* are presumed to have been retained from prehistoric times.[35]

This need not, of course, suggest that all societies of 2000 years ago in island Southeast Asia were actively developing systems of ranking. It is likely that the relatively egalitarian type of bilateral society which still exists in parts of the Philippines, Borneo and the remoter parts of Indonesia was also well represented in late prehistoric times, especially in regions of low population density. Indeed, it may be that the most intensive Indian contacts were attracted to islands such as Bali and Java precisely because they did have the highest levels of rice production, the largest populations and the greatest degrees of social stratification, just as they have had throughout much of historical time.

[35] J. Wisseman-Christie, 'Raja and Rama: the classical state in early Java', in L. Gesick, ed., *Centers, Symbols and Hierarchies*, New Haven, Yale University Southeast Asian Studies Monograph 26, 1983, 9–44.

## The Late Neolithic

We now return to continue the Neolithic record in the central and eastern parts of island Southeast Asia (the record for the western part of Indonesia in this phase is still uncertain), by repeating the main points of pages 102–6. A horizon marked by the quite sudden appearance of plain or red-slipped pottery can be followed, generally during the third millennium BC, through the southern Philippines into Sulawesi and to as far as Timor. According to linguistic observations, this most probably records the expansion of speakers of Austronesian languages with agriculture through this part of the archipelago—a process which appears to have taken place fairly rapidly, perhaps covering the 3500 kilometres from Taiwan to Timor in less than one millennium. It is likely that this initial expansion was a rapid coastal process, followed by much later 'filling in' of island interiors, a process which still of course continues today.

After about 1500 BC there are hints of change, both in island Southeast Asia and in Melanesia, which was first settled by pottery-making peoples a little before this date. In my *Prehistory of the Indo-Malaysian Archipelago*, chapter 8, I have termed the phase between about 1500 and 200 BC (when metal first appeared in dated contexts in island Southeast Asia) the Late Neolithic, mainly in recognition of an apparent shift in pottery decoration towards an increasing use of geometric and curvilinear zoned incision, and away from the earlier plain or simple red-slipped styles. This shift is by no means well plotted in time and space and does not occur in all sites, but it is my opinion that the Late Neolithic phase in central and eastern island Southeast Asia was connected in some way with a very important episode of Austronesian expansion into the Pacific islands.

The pottery evidence is intriguing, with a wide range of incised, punctate and stamped styles of decoration documented after 1500 BC in the Philippines (sites in the Cagayan Valley on Luzon, Batungan Cave on Masbate, and the Tabon caves on Palawan), western Sulawesi (the Kalumpang site with its remarkable repertoire of decorated pottery), eastern Timor (several cave assemblages), and perhaps the coastal site of Lewoleba on Lomblen (Lembata) Island between Flores and Alor.[36] Kalumpang itself is not dated, but some of the pottery resembles that found in the first millennium BC levels of the Bukit Tengkorak cave site in Sabah (to be described below), and it occurs together with a range of stone adzes, a stone barkcloth beater, slate projectile points like those found commonly in Taiwan, and some possible stone reaping knives. The caves in eastern Timor have also yielded a small but interesting collection of shell and stone artefacts dating approximately from the Late Neolithic phase as here defined. These include shell one-piece fishhooks, beads and bracelet fragments, and, after 500 BC, an unusual industry of tanged stone points.

Some of the pottery and shell artefacts in the sites just listed have parallels of a generalized kind with artefacts characteristic of the Lapita cultural complex in the western Pacific. The Lapita story involved the

[36] For details see ibid.; I. Glover, *Archaeology in Eastern Timor*, 211; D. D. Bintarti, 'Lewoleba, sebuah situs masa presejarah di Pulau Lembata' in *Pertemuan Ilmiah Arkeologi*, ke—IV. vol. IIa, Jakarta: Pusat Penelitian Arkeologi Nasional, 1986, 73–91.

colonization of a 5000-kilometre spread of islands from the vicinity of New Guinea through to Samoa during the late second millennium BC. The islands of western Melanesia, particularly New Guinea, the Bismarck Archipelago and the Solomons, had already been settled by Melanesian populations during the Late Pleistocene, whereas the islands from Santa Cruz through to Tonga and Samoa in western Polynesia were now reached for the first time. Although no true Lapita sites have yet been found west of Papua New Guinea, there can be little doubt from linguistic and biological evidence that the makers of Lapita pottery were the ancestors of the Austronesian-speaking peoples of Melanesia and Polynesia, and thus to a major extent of island Southeast Asian derivation.

The most remarkable features of Lapita assemblages include striking dentate-stamped or incised pottery, a range of tools, body ornaments and fishhooks made of shell, and a far-flung exchange network involving obsidian from sources in the Admiralty Islands and New Britain. These features, especially the early Lapita decorated pottery, may reflect conscious innovation by a population of highly mobile colonists settling the fringes of a western Melanesia already inhabited by food producers of equal or greater population density. Perhaps the Lapita communities needed to emphasize consciously their cultural identity vis-à-vis other unrelated Melanesian populations through the use of a kind of tattoo-style decoration on their pottery, and almost certainly on their bodies as well.[37]

The immediate origins of the Lapita colonists of Melanesia clearly lay somewhere in the eastern part of island Southeast Asia, presumably amongst populations who had already abandoned the cultivation of rice under equatorial conditions and who had developed an economy based on tubers, fruits, marine resources, and the domesticated triad of pigs, dogs and fowls. Archaeologically, there are no specific regions or assemblages which can be isolated as definite ancestors for Lapita, and it is likely that the Lapita complex as a whole developed many of its most distinctive style characteristics during the actual process of expansion through the Melanesian region. Nevertheless, one recent discovery in east Malaysia has cast a clearer light on the question of Lapita relationships with island Southeast Asia, and this comes from the Bukit Tengkorak rock shelter in Sabah, northern Borneo. The shelter yielded, from a layer dated between approximately 1000 and 300 BC, sherds of red-slipped and incised pottery, shell beads and a fishhook fragment, an agate microblade industry used mainly for drilling shell and, most surprising of all, numerous flakes of obsidian from the Talasea source on New Britain in western Melanesia.[38] The finding of Talasea obsidian on Borneo doubles the extent of distribution of this commodity, which is now reported from Sabah to Fiji, a distance of 6500 kilometres. While the people of Bukit Tengkorak themselves probably had no direct involvement at all in Lapita origins, they were certainly part

[37] Most peoples of Polynesia, island Melanesia and Micronesia (and indeed most Austronesians) practised tattooing until recently, although the custom seems to have been rare amongst the Papuan-speaking populations of western Melanesia.

[38] See P. Bellwood and P. Koon, 'Lapita colonists leave boats unburned! The question of Lapita links with Island Southeast Asia', *Antiquity*, 63 (1989).

of the network of communities which was in touch in some way with the distant arena of colonization far to the east.

The whole Lapita saga provides one of the most exciting arenas for research in the Pacific region at present, mainly because it represents one of the fastest episodes of prehistoric human colonization on record. The rate of Neolithic colonization across Europe has recently been estimated to have occurred at an average of approximately one kilometre per annum.[39] I estimate, from current archaeological evidence, that the rate from Taiwan to Timor was possibly three kilometres per annum, allowing 1000 years for initial agricultural settlements to expand, and a phenomenal thirteen kilometres per annum from the Admiralty Islands to Tonga, allowing 300 years for settlement expansion as indicated by the Lapita radiocarbon dates. Of course, one can hardly make a direct comparison of a continental area such as Europe with an area of small islands such as Melanesia beyond New Guinea, but the figures are striking nevertheless. Finally, it is interesting to note that this very rapid rate of colonizing movement for early Polynesian-related populations in the western Pacific is supported to some extent by the results of recent genetic research.[40]

## The Early Metal Phase

The remainder of the prehistoric record in southern Vietnam, peninsular Malaysia and island Southeast Asia falls into the Early Metal phase. In the last two regions it appears that copper, bronze and iron made their appearances together, between perhaps 500 and 200 BC according to dated finds from Malaya, Java, Sabah, the Philippines, Timor, and the Admiralty Islands of Melanesia.[41] The immediate source for the introduction of metalworking techniques into these southern regions is unknown, if indeed there was a single source, but the very broad distribution of Heger I drums throughout peninsular Malaysia and the Sunda Chain suggests that northern Vietnam played a large role in the dissemination of bronze-working technology. In addition, there are other items of possible Dong-son manufacture from Indonesia, of which the finest is perhaps a male statuette from Satus near Bogor in western Java which resembles the figurines on Dong-son anthropomorphic bronze dagger handles.[42]

While it is not known exactly how the tradition of bronze casting first became established in the island regions, it is clear that flourishing local industries were established in at least Java and Bali by early in the first millennium CE. These industries were responsible for the numerous 'swallow-tail' socketed bronze axes of Java, the splendid series of Pejeng style bronze drums from Java and Bali, the series of spiral-decorated bronze flasks and clapperless bells from Cambodia, peninsular Malaysia

39 A. J. Ammerman and L. L. Cavalli-Sforza, *The Neolithic Transition and the Genetics of Populations in Europe*, Princeton, 1984.

40 See A. Hill and S. Serjeantson, eds, *The Colonization of the Pacific: a Genetic Trail*, Oxford, 1989.

41 For the Admiralty find see W. Ambrose, 'An early bronze artefact from Papua New Guinea', *Antiquity*, 62 (1988).

42 PIMA, fig. 9.10.

and western Indonesia, and the flamboyant and unique ceremonial axes of Roti. The Pejeng drums, unlike the original Heger I specimens, were made in two pieces with mantles and tympana cast separately by the lost-wax method. Negatively-incised moulds such as the ones found at Manuaba in Bali were used to form the relief decoration on the wax surface, and the Manuaba stone mould pieces have a human face motif precisely like those around the side of the massive drum from Pejeng itself. During excavations by I. W. Ardika in 1989, the site of Sembiran in northeastern Bali produced a small fragment of a mould for casting a Pejeng type drum, here in association with Indian Rouletted Ware of the first two centuries CE (see page 133). In addition, villagers some years ago dug up a Pejeng-style drum in the nearby village of Pacung, which also seems to have been buried close to a horizon which has produced Rouletted Ware.[43] A local manufacture of bronze drums and other bronze artefacts in Bali from at least 2000 years ago is thus confirmed.

In terms of the introduction of ironworking techniques into island Southeast Asia we should look perhaps not to Dong-son, where evidence for local ironworking is sparse, but instead southwards to the Sa Huynh tradition of southern Vietnam. The Sa Huynh culture can circumstantially be associated with the Austronesian-speaking settlement of Vietnam from Borneo, perhaps late in the second millennium BC.[44] The Sa Huynh pottery from southern Vietnam has definite similarities with that of the Late Neolithic and Early Metal phases in the Philippines and Borneo, as stressed in many papers by W. G. Solheim II.[45] In addition, the evidence that jar burial was already in vogue in the Tabon Caves in the Philippines and in Niah Cave in Sarawak by the beginning of the first millennium BC, as well as at the Long Thanh site in Nghia Binh Province, southern Vietnam, does suggest that important cultural contacts were occurring across the South China Sea at this time. These contacts may have assisted the Chams to settle their portion of mainland Southeast Asia, and perhaps to interact on an equal basis with the previously-established Austro-asiatic-speaking inhabitants, many of whom would certainly have been fully-fledged rice agriculturalists by this time.

The Sa Huynh jar burial tradition is best known from Early Metal phase sites in southern Vietnam which presumably long postdate the period of initial Chamic expansion. They date to the period between about 600 BC and 500 CE, and probably overlap considerably with the foundation of the

43 Ardika is currently writing his Ph.D. thesis at the Australian National University on these discoveries. On locally-manufactured Indonesian bronzes generally, see H. R. van Heekeren, *The Bronze-Iron Age of Indonesia*, The Hague, 1958; PIMA, 282–9. The Pacung drum is described by J. McConnell, 'Preliminary report on a newly found bronze drum from Bali, Indonesia', *Indonesia Circle*, 40 (1986). A Heger I and Pejeng-type drum were both placed vertically and base to base at the site of Lamongan in eastern Java in order to contain a child skeleton with gold beads, a bronze vessel and lots of other bronze and iron artefacts; this circumstance of course confirms a certain degree of contemporaneity for the two forms: D. D. Bintarti, 'Analisis fungsional nekara perunggu dari Lamongan, Jawa Timur', *Pertemuan Ilmiah Arkeologi ke-III*, Jakarta: Pusat Penelitian Arkeologi Nasional, 1985.

44 According to Blust ('The Austronesian homeland', 57), the Chamic languages are most closely related to those of western Borneo. Acehnese of north Sumatra is also closely related to Chamic.

45 For instance, 'Pottery and the Malayo-Polynesians', *Current Anthropology*, 5 (1964).

Indic state of Champa. Good examples include Sa Huynh itself, Hang Gon and Phu Hoa, all open (non-cave) jar burial sites which have produced large lidded burial jars containing fragmentary human bone (some possibly cremated), small accessory vessels with finely-executed incised and shell-edge stamped decoration, stone ling-ling-o earrings, and glass and carnelian beads which may be of Indian origin, thus confirming a protohistorical date for much of the material. The Sa Huynh sites have also produced many iron artefacts, mostly socketed tools of various kinds, but including a few bracelets, bells and small vessels of bronze. An iron sword of possible Chinese manufacture was also found at Hang Gon.[46]

The significance of the Sa Huynh tradition of southern Vietnam is thus its presumed association with an Austronesian settlement from Borneo or some nearby area, and then its secondary role in the acquisition of iron metallurgy and perhaps the transmission of this crucial aspect of technology back into island Southeast Asia. One rather puzzling observation, however, is that southern Vietnam at this time had very few significant contacts with the Dong-son world and its immediate predecessors to the north. Only two Heger I drums have ever been found in this part of the country, and the main links of Sa Huynh as far as iron metallurgy is concerned seem to have lain more to the west, with the contemporary iron-using societies of southern Thailand and Malaysia. As noted above (page 118) the origins of iron-working in Southeast Asia generally still remain something of a mystery.

The earliest iron-using societies of peninsular Malaysia are well represented in Perak, Pahang and Selangor, where a number of slab graves and other find-places have produced an unusual industry of long-necked iron tools with shaft holes for handles. There are also contemporary assemblages in western Thailand from Ongbah Cave and Ban Don Ta Phet. Both at Ongbah and at Kampong Sungei Lang in Selangor the iron industry was associated in burial contexts with the remains of Heger I drums, and Ban Don Ta Phet has produced a fine range of Indian agate and carnelian beads which appears to date from the final centuries BC, thus reinforcing the observation that much of what passes for 'Early Metal phase' in the archaeological record does, in fact, overlap well and truly with the beginnings of Indian contact.[47]

This observation is even more true for the islands of Southeast Asia, where the nebulous beginnings of 'history' occupied a labyrinthine spatial and temporal trajectory. This circumstance makes it difficult to order the record systematically; normal practice is to classify objects of Indic inspiration as 'Classical', and objects which lack such pedigree as 'prehistoric'. In reality, however, the Indic traditions were centred on courts and temples, and many peasant and tribal populations undoubtedly continued to use traditional types of artefacts for centuries after the first appearance of historical records and inscriptions. The result is that many assemblages

[46] See my *Man's Conquest*, 191–4, with references; also H. Fontaine and Hoang Thi Than, 'Nouvelle note sur le champ de jarres funeraires de Phu Hoa', *Bulletin de la Societé des Études Indochinoises*, 51 (1975); H. Fontaine, 'A note on the Iron Age in southern Vietnam', *Journal of the Hong Kong Archaeological Society*, 8 (1979).

[47] I. C. Glover, *Early Trade between India and South-East Asia*, Hull, 1989.

of late prehistoric appearance, even from islands such as Sumatra, Java and Bali where Indic states developed fairly rapidly, are likely to be contemporary with nearby historical civilizations.

In this final section we will pass over such problems, and examine a number of quite striking, if localized, expressions of late prehistoric and early historic cultural activity which seem to represent fully indigenous Southeast Asian traditions. These occur especially around the Sulu and Sulawesi Seas and in various places along the Sunda Chain. Many in the latter region fall under the general heading of 'megalithic cultures', a category which has lent itself to some rather bizarre hyper-diffusionist thinking in the past, but which still offers many interesting questions for interpretation.

The most famous megalithic traditions of Southeast Asia are, of course, known only from the ethnographic record. They occur in northern Sumatra (the Bataks), Nias, the Nusa Tenggara islands (especially Sumba, Flores and Timor), and parts of interior Sulawesi and Borneo.[48] Such cultures are rightly famous for the wealth of funerary and prestige ritual associated with the stone monuments which they have constructed in the recent past, and there can be no doubt that such practices in some form go back deeply into the Austronesian past in both Southeast Asia and in the Pacific islands. This is suggested by the existence of many prehistoric megalithic complexes in the region, of which the oldest seem to be the slab graves and associated house structures of south-eastern Taiwan (page 103). Most other examples belong to the Early Metal phase and, while none can be linked in any coherent way with the megalithic traditions of ethnographic times, there can be little doubt that many served similar prestige-related and funerary functions.

Perhaps the most striking Indonesian complex of prehistoric large stone monuments lies around Pageralam on the Pasemah Plateau of southern Sumatra. This includes large underground slab-lined burial chambers, some of which were once decorated on their inside surfaces with polychrome paintings of humans and buffaloes; a series of remarkable carved standing stones and boulders; and a range of more utilitarian carved stone items such as mortars and troughs. The slab-lined burial chambers contained a few glass beads and fragments of bronze and iron, and the most interesting of the carved boulders show men wearing a variety of ornaments and items of clothing, such as bracelets, anklets, necklaces, earplugs, helmets with peaks at the rear, loincloths, and tunics. Two of these carvings, the Airpurah and Batugajah reliefs, show men carrying or holding Heger I drums, a circumstance which could suggest a date for the whole complex during the early first millenium CE.

Further to the east, the slab graves of parts of Java and the unique lidded sarcophagi carved out of volcanic ash in southern Bali have also produced assemblages of both iron and bronze, together with glass and carnelian beads of kinds likely to have originated in India. The Balinese sarcophagi in particular have a very wide range of bronzes in association, and are

48 For recent surveys see J. Feldman, ed., *The Eloquent Dead*, Los Angeles, 1985; J. P. Barbier and D. Newton, eds, *Islands and ancestors; indigenous styles of Southeast Asia*, New York, 1988; Janet Hoskins, 'So my name shall live', BKI, 142 (1986).

surely in themselves indicators of a complex and stratified society which, like that of contemporary Java, seems to have attracted Indian traders from perhaps as early as 2000 years ago.

Some recent and rather dramatic evidence of this has come to light in the form of sherds of Indian Rouletted Ware of the first and second centuries CE found in northwest Java (the Buni complex of sites) and at Sembiran in northeast Bali. The Buni finds include at least one complete vessel of Rouletted Ware which appears to have been retrieved, together with complete locally-manufactured vessels, from burials discovered by local villagers. The Sembiran finds come from habitation levels buried beneath more than three metres of alluvium just behind the beach on the narrow coastal plain which fringes the northeastern part of Bali. They are especially important because they have been excavated scientifically by Indonesian archaeologists under the direction of I. W. Ardika.

The artefacts recovered at Sembiran, from a presumed trading station visited by Indian as well as Indonesian vessels, include many sherds of Indian pottery of types paralleled precisely at Arikamedu, an Indo-Roman trading station near Pondicherry in south India. They include not only Rouletted Ware, but also the very distinctive Arikamedu type 10 stamped ware.[49] One sherd has three characters in Kharoshti script scratched on its surface. There are also a small fragment of blue glass which might have been intended for bead-making, a gold bead, and many small monochrome glass beads of various colours (mainly reds, greens, blues and yellows) which are presumably of Indian origin; these are still undergoing chemical investigation. In addition, the Sembiran finds are associated with the bronze drum mould fragment and perhaps also the Pejeng type drum from nearby Pacung, as described on page 130.

Although the Sembiran Indian finds are so far unique in Bali, the important burial assemblage of Gilimanuk in the western part of the island has produced a lot of very similar Early Metal phase local pottery, as well as an Indian type of gold foil funerary eye cover similar to ones also reported from Buni in northwest Java.[50] When all these finds are put together, they hint very strongly at the oldest direct evidence from Southeast Asia for the trade in spices which linked the Roman empire, India and Southeast Asia in the first centuries of our era.[51] They also give a

[49] For the Buni finds see M. J. Walker and S. Santoso, 'Romano-Indian rouletted pottery in Indonesia', AP, 20 (1977). The Sembiran research by I. W. Ardika (see also footnote 43) is a project currently under completion at the Australian National University. On Arikamedu and the Indo-Roman trade in general, see R. E. M. Wheeler, A. Ghosh and K. Deva, 'Arikamedu', *Ancient India*, 2 (1946); V. Begley, 'Arikamedu reconsidered', *American Journal of Archaeology*, 87 (1983); J. I. Miller, *The Spice Trade of the Roman Empire*, Oxford, 1969. Rouletted Ware may generally date between 150 BC and 200 CE in India. Concerning spices and timbers possibly involved in the trade, none have survived in the Sembiran excavations but Miller's investigations point to cinnamon, cloves, nutmegs, sandalwood and many other tropical tree products, all known to Roman authors of the first century CE.

[50] R. P. Soejono, 'The significance of excavations at Gilimanuk (Bali)', in R. B. Smith and W. Watson, eds, *Early South East Asia: Essays in Archaeology, History and Historical Geography*, London and New York, 1979.

[51] Although certain mainland Southeast Asian sites such as Chansen, Ban Don Thapet and Oc-eo have evidence for some form of Indian contact from the first century CE, Sembiran differs because of the quantity of Indian sherdage found there. This implies an actual Indian trader presence which cannot be so easily inferred from 'luxury' items such as beads or seals.

picture of flourishing Early Metal phase societies from western Java across to Bali sharing a similar range of local pottery styles, rich in iron and bronze, and having access, at least in coastal locations, to certain Indian status markers—fine pottery, glass and carnelian beads, and gold accoutrements. The evidence indicates that this was occurring perhaps 300 years before the first Sanskrit inscriptions in Indonesia, and perhaps even 600 years before the first surviving stone temples, so these societies are still essentially within prehistoric time. Their economic bases are still uncertain, although one could make an informed guess that the combination of wet-rice grown in bunded *sawahs* and the buffalo for ploughing were by now well established in both islands.[52]

Further to the east the Early Metal phase is best understood around the Sulu and Sulawesi Seas, where many assemblages dating between about 200 BC and 1000 CE have been excavated both in caves and in open sites. A distinctive feature of this region was the popularity of jar burial, usually involving the placing of secondary burials in large jars together with small and finely decorated accessory vessels, bronze and iron objects, glass and cornelian beads, shell bracelets, and (particularly in the Philippines) occasional earrings of the ling-ling-o type. Jar burials also occur quite frequently in Java and Bali, but usually in association with other primary earth burials as at the Anyar, Plawangan and Gilimanuk sites. Also worthy of mention are the impressive groups of stone burial jars and stone statues in central Sulawesi; although these are still undated, recent excavations around some of the stone jars at a site called Lengkeka in the Bada Valley have produced paddle-impressed pottery and iron fragments, thus suggesting a date in the Early Metal phase.[53]

The most important jar burial sites around the Sulawesi and Sulu Seas include the cave of Leang Buidane in the Talaud Islands, the caves of Pusu Semang Tas and Pusu Lumut in eastern Sabah, and a large number of sites in the central and southern Philippines, including Kalanay Cave on Masbate and several of the Tabon caves on Palawan. Most of these jar burial assemblages were smashed in antiquity and the bones and grave goods inextricably intermixed. It seems that most jars contained only one secondary burial, and the human remains, where studied, are always similar to those of the present Southern Mongoloid populations. Most of these sites date mainly within the first millennium CE; some have very specific kinds of Indian beads which can be traced back as far as 200 BC in the subcontinent itself; and virtually all have iron and bronze objects. Baked-clay bivalve casting moulds for axes were found in Leang Buidane and Pusu Lumut, evident signs that local casting was being carried out during this period, although perhaps using imported metal in the form of scrap or ingots.[54]

One remarkable open jar burial site at Magsuhot on Negros Island is

[52] For some discussion of this see N. C. van der Meer, *Sawah Cultivation in Ancient Java*, Canberra, 1979.

[53] H. Sukendar, *Laporan Penelitian Kepurbakalaan di Sulawesi Tengah*, Jakarta: Pusat Penelitian Arkeologi Nasional, 1980.

[54] For general descriptions of these sites see PIMA, 304–17; and P. Bellwood, *Archaeological Research in South-eastern Sabah*, Kota Kinabalu, 1988.

unique and deserves special mention. Three large burial jars were placed side by side in a large pit lined with broken sherds, associated with two baked-clay figurines of a woman and a calf, as well as the bones of a woman and two children. A jar weighing fifty-two kilograms was buried separately in an adjacent pit with no less than seventy small accessory vessels in association, and was connected to the ground by a tube of stacked pots, apparently to allow the pouring of libations or some kind of communication with the dead. All bone, unfortunately, seems to have dissolved in this particular jar (a common fate in open sites in the tropics), but it did contain an iron knife and some glass beads, and the pottery is generally of the first millennium CE Kalanay type characteristic of the central Philippines.[55]

Since the late prehistory of the Philippine-Sabah-Sulawesi region is best known from burials, as indeed is that of the remainder of Indonesia, little information has been recovered which can be related directly to matters of economy and food production. Such economic evidence as has been recovered is of varying reliability, and it would be less than honest to claim any clear knowledge of agricultural crops and techniques or settlement details during this period. What is clear, however, is that most of the Early Metal phase assemblages of island Southeast Asia, including those of southern Vietnam, share so many idiosyncratic features of artefact style and burial ritual that we must be seeing the results of some very frequent inter-island contact and trade, already well developed before any direct impact from the Indian, Chinese or Islamic traditions. My own expectation is that most of this contact between islands, especially in the Philippines, Borneo and eastern Indonesia during the first millennium CE, was probably following inter-island links established as much as two thousand years earlier when Lapita colonists first sailed their canoes into the western Pacific.

No chapter on prehistory is ever complete, and this one has had to leave out a large range of topics which fall on the borderline of history during the second millenium CE. Such topics, which have immediate roots in late prehistory, include the rise and expansion of the Malays and Makassarese, both of whom now have good archaeological pedigrees,[56] and the rise of trade entrepôts in the Philippines, as revealed by archaeological research on Chinese trade wares in Luzon and Cebu. Another late prehistoric find of great importance made recently is that of the remains of eight edge-pegged and sewn-plank boats of the early second millennium CE, together with evidence for local gold working at Butuan City on Mindanao.[57]

Finally, it is clear that the commencement of historical records, however important they may appear from our twentieth-century vantage point, did

[55] R. Tenazas, 'A progress report on the Magsuhot excavations . . .', *Philippine Quarterly of Culture and Society*, 2 (1974).

[56] On pottery associated with Malay expansion, see P. Bellwood and M. Omar, 'Trade patterns and political developments in Brunei and adjacent areas, AD 700–1500', *Brunei Museum Journal*, 4, 4 (1980). On the archaeology of the rise of the Gowa-Tallo kingdom (Makassar), see D. Bulbeck, 'Survey of open archaeological sites in South Sulawesi, 1986–7', BIPPA, 7 (1986–7).

[57] For the Philippines, see K. Hutterer, 'The evolution of Philippine lowland societies', *Mankind*, 9 (1974); J. Peralta, 'Ancient mariners of the Philippines', *Archaeology*, 33, 5 (1980).

not correlate with any sudden change in the daily lives of the vast majority of Southeast Asian people. Neither, as I have shown, are historical records alone sufficient to explain many of the deep-seated cultural, biological and linguistic characteristics which make Southeast Asia such a fascinating arena for study.

## BIBLIOGRAPHIC ESSAY

Those looking for recent overviews of the prehistory of Southeast Asia will find them in two books recently published: P. Bellwood, *Prehistory of the Indo-Malaysian Archipelago*, Sydney, 1985, and C. Higham, *The Archaeology of Mainland Southeast Asia*, Cambridge, UK, 1989. Both authors have published shorter summaries in the *Journal of World Prehistory* (Bellwood, 'The prehistory of Island Southeast Asia', 1 (1987); Higham, 'The later prehistory of Mainland Southeast Asia', 3 (1989)).

Older general works, now rather outmoded but still useful, include the two books on Indonesia by H. R. van Heekeren (*The Stone Age of Indonesia*, The Hague, 1972, and *The Bronze-Iron Age of Indonesia*, The Hague, 1958). There is also the general survey by P. S. Bellwood, *Man's Conquest of the Pacific*, Auckland, 1978. Several volumes of conference papers covering many regions and topics across Southeast Asia have also been published in recent years; the most useful include R. B. Smith and W. Watson, eds, *Early South East Asia: Essays in Archaeology, History and Historical Geography*, New York, 1979; V. N. Misra and P. S. Bellwood, eds, *Recent Advances in Indo-Pacific Prehistory*, New Delhi, 1985; D. Bayard, ed., *Southeast Asian Archaeology at the XV Pacific Science Congress*, Dunedin, 1985; and K. C. Chang et al., eds, *Anthropological Studies of the Taiwan Area*, Taipei, 1989.

The most active journals devoted mainly or wholly to Southeast Asian prehistory and archaeology include *Asian Perspectives* (Hawaii), *Bulletin of the Indo-Pacific Prehistory Association* (Canberra), *Jurnal Arkeologi Malaysia* (Kuala Lumpur) and *Modern Quaternary Research in Southeast Asia* (Groningen). Other useful publications include *Amerta* and *Berita Penelitian Arkeologi* (Jakarta; both in Indonesian), *Federation Museums Journal* (Kuala Lumpur), *Journal of the Hong Kong Archaeological Society*, *Philippine Quarterly of Culture and Society* (Manila), *Sarawak Museum Journal* (Kuching) and the *SPAFA Digest* (Bangkok).

Recent publications include C. Higham, *The Bronze Age of Southeast Asia*, Cambridge, 1996; P. Bellwood, *Prehistory of the Indo-Malaysian Archipelago*, revised edition, Honolulu, 1997; and *Indo-Pacific Prehistory: the Chiang Mai Papers*, Bulletins of the Indo-Pacific Prehistory Association, Canberra, 1996–7.

CHAPTER

# 3

# THE EARLY KINGDOMS

The historical record for Southeast Asia begins with the arrival of Chinese soldiers and officials along the shores of the South China Sea towards the end of the third century BC. Archaeological evidence reveals the existence of many polities distributed across the terrain of Southeast Asia at that time.

## VIETNAM

The one most directly encountered by record-keeping Chinese officials lay in the plain of the Hong (Red) River, in what is today northern Vietnam. Han Chinese armies conquered this area in the first century CE and, by the end of the third century, the efforts of Chinese frontier administrators and leading local clans had produced a relatively stable provincial polity, sensitive to Chinese imperial interests while at the same time representing a local system of power capable of taking initiative on behalf of its own interests when Chinese dynastic power was weak or in transition.

In the sixth century, provincial leaders renounced the overlordship of feeble Chinese dynasties, but in the early seventh century they gave no effective resistance to the arrival of Sui and Tang dynastic authority. During the seventh and eighth centuries, Tang administrators established the Protectorate of An Nam in northern Vietnam; the Protectorate was a type of frontier polity designed for remote, strategic areas inhabited by non-Chinese peoples. Establishment of the Protectorate of An Nam was accompanied by the absorption of the local ruling class into the hierarchy of imperial officialdom. So long as Tang dynastic power remained strong, the region remained relatively peaceful. But the late eighth and the ninth centuries were a time of political instability, with newly emergent local powers struggling for supremacy as partisans or opponents of an increasingly ineffective Tang rule; by the end of the ninth century, the imperial court was reduced to sending military expeditions into the region simply to maintain the integrity of the frontier.

One significant development during the Tang era was that the site of modern Hanoi became the political centre of the Vietnamese lands. The earliest-known political centres in the Hong River plain were along the northwestern and northern edge of the plain; by the seventh century,

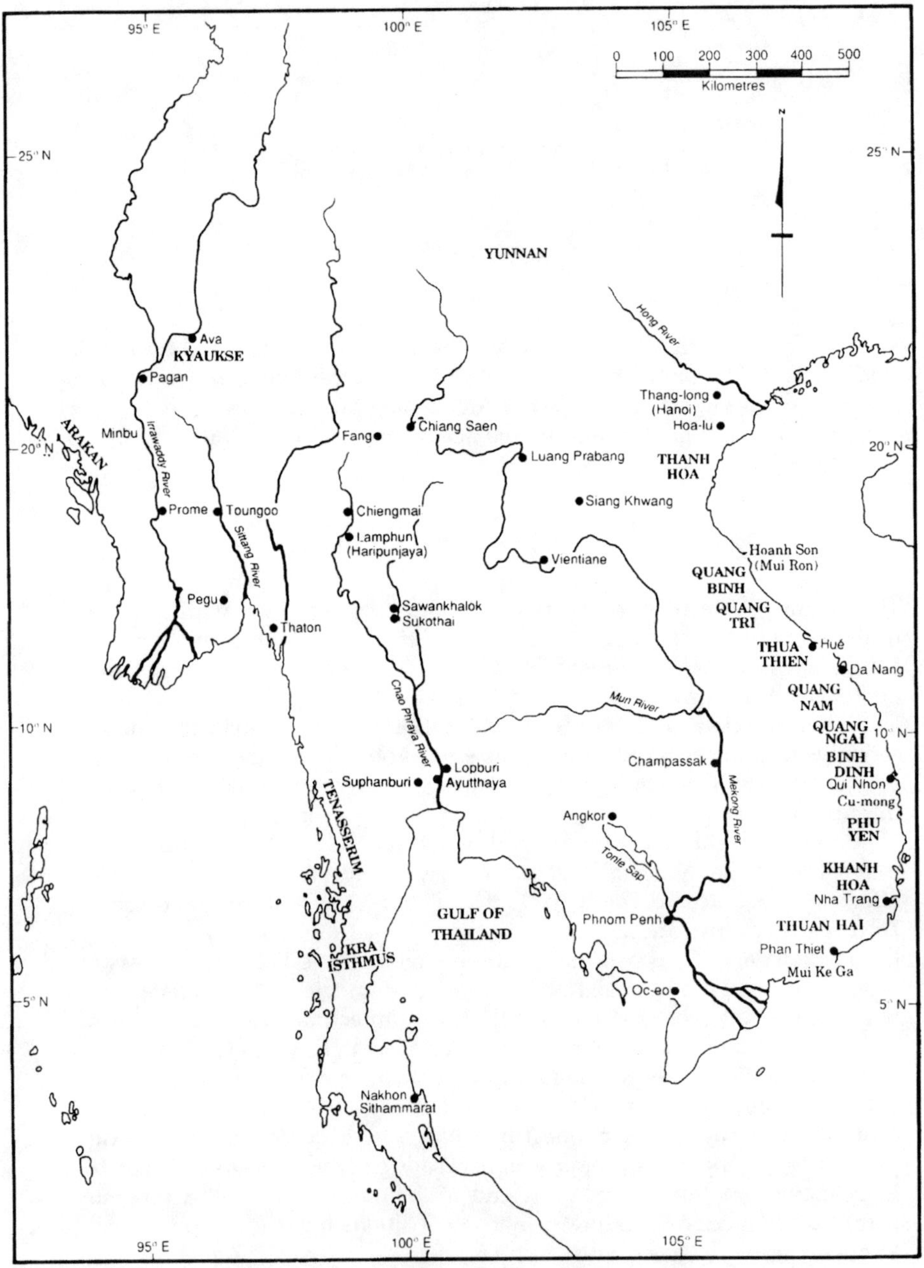


Map 3.1 Early mainland kingdoms.

the settlement of the plain had advanced to the point where Hanoi became the seat of authority. The centre of the Vietnamese polity would thereafter remain at Hanoi except during relatively brief periods of transition. Hanoi lies at the centre of the riverine network that links it to all parts of the roughly triangular-shaped plain; it is situated on the Hong River just beyond tidal influence.

In the tenth century, after the fall of Tang, efforts by ruling-class people in Vietnam to establish a monarchy failed, despite success in defeating an expedition from the Southern Han dynasty at Canton in 939. By the 960s, peasant armies led by a rustic named Dinh Bo Linh imposed a modicum of order from their headquarters at Hoa-lu, a natural redoubt among the rocky outcroppings that mark the southern edge of the Hong River plain. Early in the eleventh century, an emerging aristocratic leadership, allied with the Buddhist monkhood, moved the royal court to the site of modern Hanoi, which they named Thang-long; they proclaimed the Ly dynasty and established the realm of Dai Viet. Subsequent Chinese dynasties were unsuccessful in their efforts to enforce a lasting conquest of the Hong River plain, and the Viets emerged as custodians of the political and strategic wisdom accumulated during the previous centuries of participation in China's imperial system.

The Viet kings who ruled at Hoa-lu from the 960s until 1009 asserted their authority over all the localities inhabited by Viets and gained Chinese recognition of their regional authority. These two achievements were fundamental prerequisites for establishing a Viet polity, yet they were not enough, and Hoa-lu kingship was transitional. In the 960s, Dinh Bo Linh gained military supremacy over the plains of northern Vietnam, suppressing the claims and ambitions of several rivals; in 980–1, Le Hoan defeated a Sung Chinese expeditionary force, thereby earning Chinese acknowledgment of him as a vassal. But these were primarily military accomplishments. The extent to which they were translated into long-term diplomatic gains was due to the efforts of Buddhist monks employed by these rustic warriors of Hoa-lu.

The monks understood that the achievements of Hoa-lu were precarious because the Hoa-lu kings ruled chiefly by threat of violence, and the death of each one was followed by a war of succession. The monks made themselves indispensable to the volatile warrior-kings as learned experts capable of dealing with China and as mobilizers of labour, wealth, and popular opinion in the most populous parts of the Hong River plain, where Buddhist temples and monasteries were numerous. The monks perceived that the military achievements of Dinh Bo Linh and Le Hoan would not endure without corresponding achievements in political organization and cultural development; they further perceived that the kind of authority at Hoa-lu, limited by a warlord mentality, was incapable of moving toward these larger goals. Using their skills of persuasion, introducing their protégés into positions of influence and authority, and shaping public sentiment, the monks eventually succeeded in effecting a relatively peaceful transfer of power to a clan that was either allied with the Buddhist leaders or was simply their secular arm.

Ly Cong Uan was born in 974; raised and educated by monks as a temple orphan, he acquired a reputation as a devout Buddhist, a student of history, and a soldier. When an unpopular king died at Hoa-lu in 1009, he was commander of the palace guard. Advised and assisted by his patron, the monk Van Hanh, and by the efforts of the entire Buddhist establishment, he was proclaimed king by general acclamation and, in 1010, shifted the capital to the site of the Tang-era administrative centre, renamed Thang-long, surrounded by the temples and paddyfields of the Hong River plain.

During the nineteen years of his reign (1009–28), Ly Cong Uan (known posthumously as Ly Thai To) appears to have successively entertained three preoccupations. During the early years, he built his capital, organized the tax system, and led soldiers to the southern and northern frontiers of his realm, subduing rebels and upland tribespeople. After establishing suitable relationships with the terrestrial powers, he showed an interest in establishing proper relationships with the supernatural powers, patronizing the Buddhist religion and local cults, thereby cultivating a cultural basis for his authority. During his final years, he appears to have withdrawn from public life to meditate and to prepare for death, delegating authority to his talented sons, especially to his eldest son and designated heir, Ly Phat Ma.

There is considerable evidence that Ly Cong Uan was governed by an idea of restoring harmonious relationships between rulers and ruled, and between rulers and the supernatural powers. He criticized the Hoa-lu kings for ignoring 'the will of heaven', 'plundering and injuring' the people, and he pronounced the judgment that during the reigns of his predecessors 'all things in creation were improper'.[1] He affirmed a golden age during the Shang and Chou dynasties of antiquity, when rulers respected both heaven above and the people below, and he affirmed his intention to restore that state of affairs in his own lifetime. He was remembered as both devout in his attention to religion and merciful in his attention to the common people. He repeatedly cancelled tax debts or remitted tax due. Four of the six taxes he is recorded as having collected covered items of trade with the peoples in the upland areas (salt, rhinoceros horn, elephant tusk, aromatic wood, lumber, fruit, flowers). Lowland taxes were levied on ponds (fish and pearls), fields (rice), and mulberry trees (silk), and it appears that these taxes were collected only in the royal estates that surrounded the capital, leaving the agrarian wealth of most of the country in the hands of local powers.

Vietnamese historians remembered him as having 'made the people happy' and as having made 'far-sighted plans' for a stable dynastic institution.[2] Although he took vigorous action along the frontiers, attacking 'rebels' and establishing trading relations, he appears to have tolerated the prerogatives of local clans so long as they remained loyal; this was undoubtedly a 'happy' improvement for local clans in comparison with the rough-shod Hoa-lu régime. In preparing his son Ly Phat Ma to be his successor, he arranged for him to reside outside the gates of the capital so that he would be familiar with the common people, and sent him to lead

[1] Ngo, Si Lien, comp., *Dai Viet su ky toan thu*, Tokyo 1984–6, ban ky 2, 207–8.

soldiers against frontier peoples. In fact, it appears that Ly Cong Uan was not a strong personality and was very much under the influence of his mentor Van Hanh, who preceded him in death by only three years. Yet he played his assigned role with competence, and his place in history grew with the fortunes of the dynasty of which he became the founder.

Ly Phat Ma (posthumously known as Ly Thai Tong, r. 1028–54) was born in the year 1000 and had been carefully groomed to be a king. Many omens and portents are associated with his birth and youth, suggesting that, far from being simply an heir of his father, he had a destiny of his own. His achievement was to institutionalize Ly dynastic power, and he is accordingly understood as the greatest of the Ly kings and as one of the greatest kings in all Vietnamese history. A study of his 26-year reign is, among other things, a study of a complex and intelligent mind in the process of growth. More than any other ruler in early Vietnam, Ly Phat Ma is revealed in the sources as a living personality interacting with his advisers in a dynamic relationship of mutual stimulation. While Ly Cong Uan had proclaimed but one reign title during the years of his rule, Ly Phat Ma successively proclaimed six reign titles, each representing a phase in his intellectual growth and a corresponding style of leadership.

During the first five years of his reign, Phat Ma was relatively dependent upon advisers inherited from his father. He watched his father's officers put down an uprising by two of his brothers contesting his accession, and led an expedition against a third rebellious brother at Hoa-lu. After his succession was assured, he supervised court appointments, a reorganization of the palace guard, and a reform of the monkhood, these being three of the four main hierarchies at the capital; the fourth hierarchy was that of the palace women. In addition to attending to the ceremonial duties of kingship, he also led soldiers to pacify the southern and northern borders. He ably maintained his patrimony but did not show much of his own mind.

In 1034, Phat Ma changed his reign title in response to 'auspicious omens'[3] and for the next five years revealed a personalized style of authority that at times astonished and offended his officials. He insisted that his officers address him in a more exalted form. He ignored convention and promoted a favourite concubine to royal status, thereby provoking a rebellion, which he crushed. He reorganized administration on the borders and built ocean-going junks. He apparently attempted to reform the system of justice and prisons at Thang-long by placing it under the protection of the cult of a tenth-century hero. He ignored the objections of his advisers and insisted on personally conducting the spring ploughing ceremony. He captured the leaders of a rebellious clan in the northern mountains and publicly executed them at Thang-long, publishing an edict full of self-righteous pride and indignation. When, in 1039, his advisers requested that the reign title be changed, he argued heatedly with them, ordered them to cease the discussion, and acquiesced only after they had 'obstinately' insisted.[4] During these years, Phat Ma was running ahead

[2] ibid., ban ky 1, 188–9, and ban ky 2, 207.
[3] ibid, ban ky 2, 224.
[4] ibid., 228.

of his officials, exploring his own capacity for initiative, and refusing passively to accept their advice.

The argument of 1039, according to what survives in the sources, was about whether good government was the result of personal leadership or the observance of proper procedure. Phat Ma insisted that good government depended upon his own efforts as king, and resisted what he saw as a move by his officials to appropriate some of the initiative he had won in recent years. For their part, the officials were apparently simply endeavouring to take up the slack between their ruler's vigorous personality and the ramshackle administration with which he was trying to rule. Their argument over changing the reign title was their way of gaining Phat Ma's attention. Phat Ma's strong personal leadership had advanced beyond his court's institutional capability to follow. His advisers saw this sooner than he did. They did not want to restrain him so much as to increase the institutional efficiency of the government in order that it would support his vigorous style rather than fall apart under the rude tugs of his breakneck pace.

Phat Ma apparently came to understand his officials' point of view, and there followed a period of institution building, of concern with law and organization. The system of justice and prisons in Thang-long was reorganized along more practical lines, in contrast to the earlier attempt to improve it by appealing to the cult of a deceased hero. The hierarchy of palace women was reorganized, provoking an unsuccessful uprising, and was probably an effort to reduce influence from the clans of these women; palace women, except for those born into the royal family, were both tokens and facilitators of the relationships existing between their families and royal authority. An assembly of monks was convened after a period of lavish royal acts of Buddhist piety, apparently as a way of bringing the monkhood into a more explicity collaborative role with the court. The most distinctive endeavour of this era, however, resulted in the publication of the Minh-dao ('clear way') law book in 1042.

According to the edict announcing the new law book, the old laws, almost certainly of Tang origin or inspiration, were oppressive and fostered injustice. The new laws were written by officials charged by Phat Ma to 'deliberate about what was suitable to the contemporary age'.[5] The Minh-dao law book has not survived, but nine edicts dated within a few months of its publication have survived and may suggest some of the problems addressed by it. Most of these edicts are aimed at increasing the throne's control over the human and material resources of the state. They concern military discipline, the annual oath of loyalty to the king required of all officials and soldiers, theft of livestock from royal estates, the unlawful selling of taxpaying males into slavery, corrupt tax collectors, famine relief, the rights of ruling-class men to protect their women, and a definition of pardonable and unpardonable crimes, the latter being offences against royal authority.

The Minh-dao reign period, although short (1042–4), was significant because, at this time, Phat Ma's unusual ability as a leader was joined with

[5] ibid., 231.

a supportive and responsive institutional framework. His officials no longer stood back in astonishment as they had in earlier years. Now they were harnessed to his vigorous style of leadership by a more rationalized and disciplined scheme of government. Phat Ma and his advisers had translated his outstanding personal energy into a more energetic government at all levels of administration. An institutional foundation was raised capable of bearing the strains of a strong hand. An episode attributed to the year 1043 has Phat Ma visiting a ruined temple and causing a sagging pillar to straighten by mere thought; court officials subsequently 'composed a rhyming narrative to publish this extraordinary supernatural event'.[6] A few months later, amidst preparations for war, Phat Ma's battle shield moved of its own accord as it hung in a public hall; his officials advised him that this was 'a sign that divine beings have secretly united all classes of things to respond to your will'.[7] These stories suggest that Phat Ma had not stopped doing astonishing things, but rather that his officials had stopped being astonished by them.

The main activity of the Minh-dao era, made possible by the recently achieved institutional capabilities, was preparation for a seaborne expedition 950 kilometres south to the city of the Cham king, whose punishment was thought by Phat Ma to be necessary for the proper exercise of his authority along the southern coasts. Ships were built, soldiers trained, weapons put in readiness, rice stockpiled, coins minted, rebels chastised.

The expedition to Champa in 1044, led personally by Phat Ma, was a great success. Phat Ma returned laden with plunder, inaugurating a period of general well-being and prosperous ease. Taxes were reduced, foreign merchants were accommodated, markets were opened in the mountains.

A new reign period was proclaimed in 1049, marking a decline in Phat Ma's personal vigour and a new reliance on ceremonial formalities. This coincided with the rebellion of a vassal on the northern frontier and the uncovering of a conspiracy at court. These events appear to have turned Phat Ma's thoughts toward his own mortality and the fact that, no matter how great his achievements had been, he could not live forever, nor could he find permanent solutions to all the problems of government. He began to take personal comfort in religion, dreaming of the Bodhisattva Avalokitesvara and having the 'One-Pillar Temple' (Chua Mot Cot) built with elaborate gardens and fishponds. His final years were occupied with promoting and bestowing gifts upon meritorious officials, putting his family affairs in order, and, finally, a few months before his death in 1054, handing authority to his 31-year-old son Ly Nhat Ton.

Ly Phat Ma established the Ly dynasty upon an institutional foundation that endured for more than a century. All later Ly kings stood in his shadow. His personal style of leadership embodied a new independence from the constraints imposed by the anarchy and disunity that were revealed in the tenth century with the breakdown of the Tang heritage of government. Phat Ma's son and heir, Ly Nhat Ton, was the first Vietnamese king of the post-Tang era to enjoy an uneventful succession, a

[6] ibid., 232.
[7] ibid., 233.

clear indication that Phat Ma had firmly established a dynastic institution.

Ly Nhat Ton (posthumously known as Ly Thanh Tong, r. 1054–72) was a competent steward of his father's achievements, which he endeavoured to re-enact, but he did not advance beyond them. He further institutionalized and formalized the power gathered by Phat Ma, but tended to rest securely upon it, finding few opportunities to exercise initiative. Yet, benefiting from what his father had done, he entertained a grander conception of his power than any previous king. Surviving evidence does not afford a well-rounded view of his personality, as it appears to do for his father. His lavish building projects were criticized as wasteful and oppressive by later historians, who nonetheless praised his compassionate attitude toward the common people. What is clear from the sources is that he was a sophisticated and cultured man who was at once a scholar and a judge, a musician and a warrior, a devout Buddhist and a ruthless dynast. Furthermore, his imperial pretensions and fearless approach to the northern border attracted the concerned attention of the Sung court of China.

Chinese sources identify Ly Nhat Ton as the Viet king that dared to claim imperial status, which for the Chinese was a direct challenge to their view of the world. This Chinese perception may simply be a piece of historiographical debris from the Sino-Vietnamese war of the 1070s, a formula for justifying a later decision to send soldiers against Dai Viet. But even if this be so, there is corroborating evidence from the Vietnamese side that Ly Nhat Ton adopted many of the formalities of China's imperial court, from the official name of the realm, to the attire of his officials, to the ranks and titles conferred upon officials, upon members of the royal family, and upon the royal ancestors. It appears that it was Ly Nhat Ton who first conferred upon Ly Cong Uan and Ly Phat Ma posthumous titles derived from Chinese dynastic usage. But aside from these academic particulars, it was during the reign of Ly Nhat Ton that the Sino-Vietnamese border became the scene of confrontation.

During the reign of Ly Cong Uan, a buffer zone inhabited by upland tribespeople separated the lands under Thang-long's effective control and Sung border jurisdictions. Ly Phat Ma extended his power over this buffer zone through military conquest and marriage alliance with local chieftains, bringing Thang-long's power face to face with Sung's border outposts. The Sung court took a relatively passive attitude toward Phat Ma's success in eliminating the buffer of local chieftains, for it was then more concerned with Sung's northern frontier and did not want to provoke trouble in the south. But some Sung border officials took a more positive attitude and agitated for military action against Thang-long while secretly training local military units and sheltering refugees, including army deserters, from the Viet side of the border. The seeming contradiction between the benign pronouncements of the Sung court and the devious policy of some Sung border officials provoked Ly Nhat Ton to launch a punitive attack across the border in 1059, declaring his 'hate' for 'Sung's untrustworthiness'.[8] After a year or so of attacks and counter-attacks, in which the local Sung officials fared poorly, a parley between Sung and Vietnamese envoys

[8] ibid., ban ky 3, 242.

produced a temporary calm as some activist Sung officials were dismissed and the Sung court officially accepted Thang-long's explanation of events. But new incidents soon occurred, and Sung border officials went so far as to conspire with Champa to put pressure on Thang-long. However, official Sung policy remained opposed to any provocative action in the south. Consequently, during the 1060s, Sung border officials were divided in their opinions: some conspired to engineer a military expedition against Thang-long, while others denounced these efforts as foolhardy. Meanwhile, Nhat Ton allowed his subordinates to maintain pressure on the border and seems not to have understood the inherent danger in Sino-Vietnamese relations. This volatile border situation would not explode until after Ly Nhat Ton's death; he seems not to have given it much thought as his attention was focused elsewhere.

Ly Nhat Ton's chief preoccupation during the first twelve years of his reign was to father a son. Year after year, he orchestrated prayer recitations at shrines and temples throughout the land in quest of an heir. Finally, in 1066, a son, Ly Can Duc, was born to a concubine of commoner origin, the Lady Y-lan. This event was the watershed of Nhat Ton's reign. Before this, he was essentially waiting, seemingly constrained by the fear of dying without issue. With the birth of Ly Can Duc, he sprang into action, and the remaining six years of his life were an echo of his father's vigorous style. He decided to re-enact the crowning achievement of his father, the expedition to Champa. Both tactically and psychologically, Nhat Ton's 1069 expedition to Champa was a duplication of Phat Ma's expedition of 1044. The ritual of preparation, the omens, the itinerary were virtually identical to those recorded for Phat Ma. One difference was that while the Cham King was killed in 1044, his life was spared in 1069. Phat Ma had been asserting Thang-long's power and no quarter was given; Nhat Ton was simply reaffirming Thang-long's power and there was space to extend mercy to a defeated king.

Behind these expeditions to Champa lay a contest for maritime pre-eminence in the South China Sea. Thang-long was quick to perceive the importance of sea power and of dominating the southern coasts. Although agriculture defined power, trade adorned it, and Vietnamese chronicles record eleventh-century contacts with merchants from other parts of Southeast Asia, in particular Java. Ly Nhat Ton paid an enormous sum to a Javanese merchant for a pearl that 'glowed in the dark'.[9] Champa was in a position to block the access of Thang-long to the markets of the south seas and apparently attempted to do so. The Vietnamese took to the sea with alacrity and did not shrink from the rigour of long-distance military expeditions.

The reigns of Ly Cong Uan, Ly Phat Ma, and Ly Nhat Ton comprise a distinct era not only in the development of Vietnamese political organization but also in the development of Vietnamese culture and intellectual life. These kings mobilized the material resources available to them in ways that are not entirely clear from the sources. Their highly personalized style of rule was reinforced from the 1040s by a rudimentary dynastic

[9] ibid., 244.

institution, which appears to have been a court-based command hierarchy for governing royal estates, managing soldiers, and administering the frontiers where the soldiers were assigned; royal authority over regional Vietnamese leaders appears to have been based on mutual consent, reinforced with the threat of punitive action. Oaths of loyalty were sworn annually to the king, and all the kings held elaborate birthday celebrations to feast and reward the important people in their realm. Perhaps as important as threats, oaths, and rewards was the development of a common Vietnamese cultural point of view, a process in which the first three Ly kings played large roles.

Each of these kings took an interest in local spirit cults and was keen to bring them under the umbrellas of royal patronage and the Buddhist religion. They cultivated an image of themselves as men of virtue capable of interceding with supernatural powers on behalf of their followers. Furthermore, the virtue of these kings was understood as a positive force arousing supernatural powers to bring prosperity and martial success to the kingdom. After centuries of Chinese dynastic overlordship, this was a time of self-discovery when local traditions were assembled to form a common Vietnamese tradition associated with the Ly dynastic achievement. The process of exploring the limits of Vietnamese cultural sensibilities reveals a confident, self-absorbed attitude that was matched by expanding military power. This era of formulating a royal definition of what it meant to be Vietnamese came to an end in the 1070s with a serious military encounter with China and the awareness of limits imposed by this encounter.

When Ly Nhat Ton died in 1072, new policies at the Sung Chinese court were being initiated by Wang An-shih, an activist who promoted like-minded officials throughout the Sung bureaucracy and disdained traditional policies as 'passive'. Although his leadership provoked resistance and severe factional conflict, he was trusted by the emperor. He had endorsed aggressive policies formulated by activist officials on China's western border and elsewhere to 'nibble away' the power of upland tribal chieftains; these policies had been successful. He apparently perceived the Vietnamese border as a similar case, and so endorsed preparations for military operations by activist officials there.[10]

Ly Can Duc was enthroned in 1072 at the age of six, a clear indication that the dynastic concept had been effectively institutionalized. As Sung military preparations progressed on the border, the Vietnamese military commander, Ly Thuong Kiet, decided to make a pre-emptive strike; in 1075, he launched a surprise attack on Sung border provinces by both land and sea. The Sung fleet, several cities, and accumulated military supplies were destroyed by the Vietnamese before they withdrew. The Vietnamese were aware of the factional conflict in China, and left placards designed to appeal to Wang An-shih's enemies in the Sung bureaucracy.

Wang An-shih, surprised and angry, was stung into hastily organizing a punitive expedition against Thang-long, brushing aside cautionary admonitions advanced by his bureaucratic rivals. The Sung expedition of 1076–7,

[10] Kawahara Masahiro, 'Richō to Sō tono kankei (1009–1225)' [Relations between the Lý dynasty and the Sung], in Yamamoto Tatsurō, ed., *Betonamu Chūgoku kankeishi* [A history of international relations between Vietnam and China], Tokyo, 1975.

unlike Chinese campaigns before the tenth century, was led by officers on a short bureaucratic leash without sufficient preparation or the authority to take initiative. The Sung fleet failed to penetrate Vietnamese waters; the army was stalled at a river several miles northeast of Thang-long and withdrew after three months of fighting. After a few years of negotiations, Sung and Vietnamese officials agreed upon a common border, which has remained essentially unchanged to the present day.

This war forced the Chinese to recognize Thang-long as a special type of vassal that could not be 'nibbled away'; it forced the Vietnamese to recognize China as a power best left unprovoked. The border, clearly drawn across the terrain and understood by the Vietnamese as both a limitation and a protection, was an unusual feature of organizing political space in Southeast Asia, where traditional borders were never so firmly fixed. An awareness of this border, the importance of defending it and of maintaining relations with the power beyond it, became a large part of Vietnamese cultural consciousness from this time.

Without the personal authority of an adult king, Vietnamese leaders, at the height of the war crisis during the years 1075–7, legitimized court appointments by a series of 'examinations' to select suitable men from among those who could read and write; these examinations appear to have been a ritual of appointment in a time of emergency, and there is no further evidence of them after the 1080s. The leaders of the court at this time, Ly Dao Thanh (d. 1081), an official who had first risen to prominence under Ly Phat Ma, and his protégé Le Van Thinh, responded to Ly Can Duc's minority by trying to formalize the dynastic institution. Eventually, however, Ly Can Duc cut short this trend, banishing Le Van Thinh in 1096 and reaffirming the personalized style of leadership that was expected of Ly kings.

Ly Can Duc reigned until his death in 1127. He was childless, and, during the last years of his life, the maternal clan of his designated heir, a nephew, gained ascendancy at court. Thereafter, the Ly kings were simply figureheads for their mothers' clansmen and custodians of the cultural synthesis achieved by the early Ly kings. At this time, Vietnamese sources emphasize the role of loyal ministers rather than virtuous kings. In the twelfth century, Thang-long successfully resisted Khmer invasions in the south and promoted its status at the Southern Sung court of China. But internally, the Ly dynastic consensus that depended upon the strong personal leadership of kings faded into a series of confrontations between the maternal clans of potential kings, who controlled different regions of the realm. By the beginning of the thirteenth century, Dai Viet was in a state of chronic civil war.

The Ly dynasty made three major contributions to traditional Vietnamese culture. First, Buddhism was affirmed as the measure of civilized behaviour for both kings and subjects. Second, a pantheon of indigenous 'Vietnamese' spirits was identified as guardians of royal power. Third, a Vietnamized version of Chinese political theory was developed to affirm that Thang-long was the seat of a 'southern emperor' who ruled the 'southern kingdom' by heavenly mandate; the mandate of the 'northern emperor' of China extended only to the border, and the border was under the protection of 'Heaven' and the supernatural powers of the land.[11] The tributary relationship with China was nurtured as the only alternative to confrontation and war.

The Tran clan eventually succeeded in subduing all their enemies and proclaiming a new dynasty in 1225. This clan was from the coast of the Hong River plain, and an important element in their military success was their naval power, which enabled them to dominate the riverine channels of the plain. The architect of the Tran dynasty was Tran Thu Do. Although he never took the throne, he dominated the Tran clan during the period of its establishment as a dynasty. He endeavoured to remedy the weaknesses of the Ly political system that had allowed the Tran to seize power, and he achieved an unprecedented degree of centralized control over the royal clan, the court and administration, and the economy.

To avoid the danger of maternal clans intruding with their ambitions into the court, the Tran kings were to take queens only from the Tran clan; for four generations, Tran kings made queens of their cousins or, in one case, a half-sister. To avoid the dangers of a royal minority or a succession dispute, Tran kings abdicated the throne to their chosen adult heirs upon the death of their predecessors, thereafter ruling as 'senior' kings. At the peak of Tran power, kings made decisions in consultation with their uncles, brothers, and cousins, thereby fostering solidarity within the royal clan. The Tran dynasty eventually began to collapse when these rules were no longer observed.

To break the power of regional clans, Tran clan members were made lords of strategic areas, and a trend of royal estates growing at the expense of local powers in the Hong River plain gave the Tran control of a higher percentage of the rice surplus than had been available to the Ly. The Tran were so successful in eliminating potential rivals in the Hong River plain that, when dynastic power began to fade in the late fourteenth century, it was a clan from the Ma River plain, further south, that stepped forward to claim the throne.

In the 1230s, the Tran began using an examination system to recruit officials to staff a larger, more disciplined, adminstrative service than had existed under the Ly. The examination system was inevitably modelled upon Chinese precedents, and aspiring candidates prepared themselves by studying the classics, histories, and literature of China. Although the Tran were devout Buddhists and espoused their version of the Ly cultural achievement, from this time there began to appear a small but articulate class of literati, drawn from an emerging class of wealthy landowners, who cultivated an image of learning, loyalty, and competence derived from their classical, Confucian, education. When the royal clan faltered in the fourteenth century, this class strove to maintain order and eventually emerged in the fifteenth century as spokesmen for royal authority, definers of public morality, and guardians of the court.

The kind of centralizing policies pursued by Tran Thu Do became an asset to the generation of Tran clan leaders that followed him when Thang-long was challenged by military encounters with Mongol-Yuan forces.

[11] Ngo Si Lien, ban ky 3, 249.

Mongol forces conquered Yunnan in the mid-1250s and attempted to enter Dai Viet to encircle Southern Sung. The Tran resisted during the dry season of 1257–8 and forced Mongol forces to retire to Yunnan. After Khubilai Khan conquered Southern Sung in the late 1270s, he sent envoys to Thang-long demanding submission. The Vietnamese resisted this demand. At this time, the Tran king commissioned a history to be written demonstrating that he had inherited an imperial status equivalent to the Chinese emperor and was therefore not obligated to submit to the conqueror of the Chinese emperor.[12] The Tran court was also interested in the pantheon of Vietnamese spirits thought capable of turning their supernatural power against invaders, and when hostilities ceased in the late 1280s these spirits were recognized with imperial appointments.

When Mongol-Yuan forces flooded into Dai Viet in 1284 from four directions, the Tran were ably led by a group of princes, the most prominent being Tran Quoc Tuan (also known as Tran Hung Dao). After six months of fighting, during which Thang-long was abandoned to the invaders, a series of battles was fought along the lower Hong River in which the Vietnamese prevented a link-up between a Mongol army that had landed in Champa and marched north and the Mongol forces that had arrived directly from China. In the last of these encounters, the southern Mongol army was destroyed and its commander killed. The Mongol forces subsequently withdrew. In 1287–8, a final Mongol-Yuan invasion was defeated after Vietnamese naval forces seized the Mongol supply fleet. Mongol forces were trapped when they attempted to withdraw, and suffered defeats in battles that entered Vietnamese lore.

In the generations following the Mongol wars, the Tran clan gradually lost its taste for leadership. There is evidence of social unrest in the fourteenth century that is not yet well understood; a series of rebellions broke out, beginning in the 1340s. Tran Minh Tong, who ruled from the 1320s until his death in 1357, married a Tran kinswoman, but also had sons by two women of the Ho clan, the leader of which, Ho Quy Ly, thereby began to insinuate himself into the court. Tran Minh Tong's successor, reputedly decadent and incompetent, had no children and failed to abdicate in favour of a designated heir. Upon his death in 1369, a succession dispute resulted in the royal kinsmen of Ho Quy Ly gaining control of the throne. The ensuing two decades formed a time of acute crisis as the Chams, led by one of their most remarkable kings, known to the Vietnamese as Che Bong Nga, repeatedly ravaged the kingdom and sacked Thang-long. Not until the 1390s, after the death of Che Bong Nga, was Ho Quy Ly able to restore order.

Ho Quy Ly presided over the collapse of the aristocratic Buddhist world of the Ly and Tran dynasties and the initial stirrings of the literati-gentry class. He appealed to the classical histories to justify his authority, finally proclaiming his own dynasty in 1400. Striving to bring an end to prolonged disorder, he gained a reputation as a harsh and arbitrary ruler, and many

[12] O. W. Wolters, 'Historians and Emperors in Vietnam and China: comments arising out of Le Van Huu's History, presented to the Tran court in 1272', in Anthony Reid and David Marr, eds, *Perceptions of the past in Southeast Asia*, Singapore, 1979.

members of the Vietnamese ruling class resisted him.[13] The Yung-lo emperor of Ming China did not ignore the opportunity to intervene, and, in 1406, Ming armies, posing as restorers of the Tran dynasty, occupied Dai Viet, capturing Ho Quy Ly after a series of battles. Ming officials endeavoured during the course of the following two decades to transform Dai Viet into a Chinese province. However, their policies were hindered by three contradictions that ultimately led to failure.

First, there was a strategic contradiction in the Ming policy of sinicizing a frontier era; efforts to sinicize a resisting population undermined the order and security that was the goal of frontier policy. Second, there was a bureaucratic contradiction between the ideal of civilizing barbarians that was used to justify the occupation and the underworld of exploitation that characterized the actual attempt of Ming officialdom to govern the Vietnamese; the quality of Ming personnel available to be sent to the Vietnamese lands subverted the stated goal of the occupation. Finally, there was a fiscal contradiction between the private fortunes being made by corrupt officials and the local government deficit that was a continual drain on the imperial treasury; imperial troops were enforcing opportunities for private enrichment while revenue shortfalls required annual subsidies from the central government. These contradictions, combined with a new Vietnamese resistance movement that could not be overcome without major new investments, led to the abandonment of the occupation policy within a few years after the death of the Yung-lo emperor in 1424. The Chinese were constrained to recognize that, while Vietnam was within reach of Chinese armies, it was beyond the reach of China's sinicizing influence. The lesson for the Chinese of their effort to occupy Vietnam was that tributary relations represented a higher wisdom than did a policy of conquest and assimilation.[14]

Vietnamese resistance to the Ming occupation eventually gathered behind the leadership of Le Loi, a wealthy landowner from Thanh Hoa, in the plain of the Ma River, south of the Hong River plain. Raising his standard of resistance in 1418, he survived a series of Ming operations against him and was eventually joined by a swelling entourage of talented Vietnamese, most prominent of whom was Nguyen Trai, destined to be recognized as a great statesman and the most gifted poet of his age. By the end of 1426, Ming forces, including recently arrived reinforcements, were besieged in Thang-long. Two Ming relief armies were defeated and turned back in 1427. In 1428, surviving Ming forces were allowed to evacuate, and Le Loi proclaimed the Le dynasty.

Le Loi died after only five years as king. He was succeeded by a son and a grandson, both of whom reigned as minors under regencies dominated by men who had served as Le Loi's officers during the anti-Ming resistance. A regicide and failed coup by a prince in 1459 led to the accession of another grandson of Le Loi in 1460. The new king was Le Thanh Ton, and his relatively long reign, to 1497, would be remembered as one of the most

[13] John K. Whitmore, *Vietnam, Ho Quy Ly, and the Ming (1371–1421)*, New Haven, 1985.

[14] Alexander B. Woodside, 'Early Ming Expansionism (1406–1427): China's abortive conquest of Vietnam', *Papers on China*, 17.

famous in all of Vietnamese history. Agrarian, legal, and ideological reforms of earlier Le reigns culminated in the reign of Le Thanh Ton with the establishment of a bureaucratic form of government that became the model for Vietnamese rulers during the ensuing five centuries. This was an unprecedented age of scholarship and literature: important works of poetry, folklore, history, law, and government were written and have survived. It was also an age of military power, as expeditions into Laos and against Champa in the 1470s resulted in territorial acquisitions. The paradox of Le Thanh Ton's reign is that, although it was notable for its bureaucratic achievements, within ten years of his death the dynasty was plunged into a crisis of leadership from which it never emerged.

The Ming occupation and the establishment of the Le dynasty are conventionally understood as signposts of deep and significant change in Vietnamese history. The effects of the occupation were not casual. In addition to the physical destruction of Buddhist temples and much of the literary heritage of the Ly and Tran dynasties, there was also an experience among educated Vietnamese of psychological challenge, of being forced to redefine what it meant to be Vietnamese. The aristocratic Buddhist order of Ly and Tran had been swept away. The new ruling class was a mix of militarized clans from the southern provinces and of gentry literati educated with ideas of neo-Confucian rationalism and activism. Vietnamese society appears to have been disoriented by the decades of violence attending the collapse of Tran and the Ming occupation; and this is generally seen as giving meaning to the efforts of the early Le kings to enact a broad range of reforms leading to an altogether new conceptualization of government under Le Thanh Ton.

But Le Thanh Ton's reign was followed by a crisis that was more profound than the crisis that preceded the founding of the Le dynasty, for it led to something new in Vietnamese history: prolonged civil wars, internal divisions, and an expanding southern frontier. There are good reasons for seeing the collapse of Le leadership in the early sixteenth century as a more significant marker of discontinuity than the troubles attending the collapse of Tran. Le Thanh Ton had more in common with earlier Vietnamese kings than he had with any Vietnamese king that followed him. He ruled a realm that would have been recognizable to Ly and Tran kings in its geographical extent and in its dynastic integrity. Vietnamese rulers in later centuries would never again enjoy the security of such a well-defined space and of such unambiguous claims upon the loyalty of all Vietnamese.

Yet a comparison of Le Thanh Ton with the Ly and Tran kings is deceptive, for it risks ignoring the possibility that Le Thanh Ton's bureaucratic achievements were an indication of weakness rather than of strength: an indication that the popular cultural foundations of Vietnamese kingship, as developed under the Ly and Tran, had crumbled and that authority was thereafter rationalized within a ruling-class culture that lacked a solid base in the indigenous society. Constructing a bureaucracy may have been an effort to gain objective control over a society with which the ruling class no longer enjoyed a subjective sympathy. Such an approach would make Le Thanh Ton a transitional figure, a remarkable man in whom intelligence and energy, rather than institutional achievements, were the source of authority.

Comparing the Dai Viet case to other Southeast Asian polities of that time raises a serious problem. The quantity of information available about people and events at Thang-long is greatly out of proportion to what is known about Champa, Angkor, Pagan, the early Tai kingdoms, Śrīvijaya, and Majapahit. At least two responses can be made to this state of affairs. Attention can be focused upon a conjectural reconstruction of events and cultural trends that is understood as standing apart from disparities in the quantity and character of sources available for each polity. This approach is seemingly 'scientific', and furthermore 'democratic', but it is also relatively superficial and eschews any curiosity about whether or not the nature and amount of evidence available about a certain piece of the past may reveal a history of a particular kind. Any comparative exercise about histories of particular kinds will move beyond the collation of 'data' to the question of what history 'means' in each context.

Does the quantity and quality of information available about a particular polity in the past carry a message above and beyond the 'bare facts'? Does Vietnamese history, for example, mean something different from Khmer history in the respective Vietnamese and Khmer cultural traditions? If we answer these questions in the affirmative, as I am inclined to do, then how does this affect comparative analysis? This topic will appear jejune for those whose eyes are fixed on 'facts' and nothing more. But the 'facts' of one polity may turn out to be part of a well-developed historiographical tradition that has been shaped by a centuries-long process from one generation to the next in service to a particular historical point of view; whereas the 'facts' of another polity may come out of a very different process and experience, or may turn out to be part of a twentieth-century scholarly reconstruction of bits and pieces without the matrix of a shared living memory. We must ask, are these different kinds of 'facts' comparable? If they are, then the comparison is truly academic, which may be as far as it can be taken. But if they are not, then we are authorized to ask what exactly is being compared—relatively abstract models of polities in the past, or 'histories' of these polities. 'Histories' imply a point of view established by historical experience that lends a criterion for assigning value to stories remembered and recorded about the past, and this includes the collective decision about whether or not stories about the past should be or will be remembered or recorded.

History of a particular kind was relatively important to the Vietnamese, perhaps because they had no choice but to hold up their end of a relationship with China that demanded serious attention to the past. Judging by what has been remembered and recorded about Champa, Angkor, Pagan, the early Tai kingdoms, Śrīvijaya, and Majapahit, history of the Vietnamese kind was less important to these polities; this does not mean that history was less important in the cultural perspectives of these polities, but it could mean that their history meant something different from what Vietnamese history meant to the Vietnamese. Vietnamese history was largely an argument about the Sino-Vietnamese relationship, a story with a clear and urgent purpose, the acceptance of which was an important part of being Vietnamese. Have the Chams, Khmers, Burmans, Tai-speakers, Malays, and Javanese made a similar use of history, or have they been governed by entirely different notions of what history is 'for'? With this question in mind, let us turn to narratives of Champa, Angkor, Pagan, the early Tai kingdoms, Śrīvijaya, and Majapahit.

## CHAMPA

Champa is a generic term for the polities organized by Austronesian-speaking peoples along what is now the central coast of Vietnam. Chinese perceptions of these polities have been preserved and have ascribed to Champa greater coherence and continuity than other evidence will support. What is generally understood as Cham history is a twentieth-century rationalization of scraps of evidence from inscriptions and Chinese sources. The time has come to set this rationalization aside and to take a fresh look. It immediately becomes apparent that the very concept of Champa must be redefined. Rather than signifying a 'kingdom' in the conventional sense of the word, Champa should more properly be understood as an archipelagically-defined cultural-political space. Two clues will provide entry into this unusual case, one geographical and one cultural-linguistic.[15]

The land of Champa at its maximum extent stretched along the central coast of what is now modern Vietnam from the Hoanh Son massif (Mui Ron) in the north to Phan Thiet (Mui Ke Ga) in the south, a distance of almost 1000 kilometres. Champa was comprised of small island-like enclaves defined by the sea and the mountains. It was the closest that a continental terrain could approximate the morphology of an archipelago. The 'islands' were relatively isolated from the continent by a thick band of mountains to the west, open to the sea on the east, and separated from each other by lines of mountains that ran out into the sea. Bearing this in mind, it is no accident that this is the one place (apart from the Malay peninsula, which approximates a large island), where Malayo-Polynesian peoples appropriated continental terrain.

The peoples of Champa, the lowland Chams and the upland Rhade and Jarai, are ethnolinguistically Malay. Their organization of political space can best be understood as a form of Malayo-Polynesian polity, quite different from the polities we are accustomed to find in continental settings or even on densely-populated islands such as Java. Political authority in traditional Malayo-Polynesian culture grew out of maritime nomadism; it was accordingly dispersed, with a preference for small groups enjoying relative freedom to move about as they pleased. The land of Champa offered opportunities for this type of organization, being broken up into many small coastal enclaves with an extended mountainous hinterland.

Champa can be best understood as a kind of archipelago where ambitious leaders repeatedly established centres of authority, simultaneously

[15] My understanding of Champa and of new directions in Cham studies is indebted to discussions with Nora Taylor. She bears no responsibility for my errors.

and in different places. In lieu of constructing a schematic and meaningless 'narrative' of Cham 'history', I propose to look at five regions that may be understood as 'island-clusters' within the larger archipelago. The evidence sits more comfortably in such a framework than it does in the conventional category of a unified kingdom.

Beginning in the north, Quang Binh, Quang Tri and Thua Thien Provinces correspond with what the Chinese called Lin-yi. Lin-yi, as something in the vicinity of Hué, held the attention of Chinese record-keepers from the late second century to the mid-fifth century, after which the Chinese appear to have applied the name to something further south in the vicinity of Da Nang. The outstanding feature of Lin-yi from the Chinese point of view was that it appeared out of the debris of the crumbling southern border of the Han empire and was a source of incessant frontier raids until 446 when a Sino-Vietnamese expedition destroyed its centre at Hué. The Chinese continued to apply the name Lin-yi to something they perceived further south for another three centuries. Instead of presuming that 'the Chams moved their capital further south', it appears more likely that whatever had been happening in this region was in some unknown way altered after 446 and that regions further south simply continued along lines of development already established.

The so-called Lin-yi that existed from the late second century to 446 cannot be verified with architectural or inscriptional evidence. According to the Chinese sources, this region was the southernmost frontier jurisdiction of the Han empire for three centuries before someone identified as a son of a local Han magistrate proclaimed himself king in the waning years of the Han dynasty. For the next two and a half centuries, the dominant feature of this Lin-yi is that its kings appear to have defined their ambitions in response to the rhythms of dynastic power in China; they seem to have been preoccupied with the Sino-Vietnamese frontier and with opportunities for plunder and expansion beyond that frontier. This perception can be attributed to the priorities of Chinese annalists. In fact, warfare along the border during this time increased in times of Chinese dynastic strength, when Sino-Vietnamese armies were most active, and decreased when Chinese dynasties were weak and least able to project military power into the far south.[16] This suggests that warfare may have been as much a factor of initiative from the north as from the south. The border was unstable and powers both in the north and in the south endeavoured to maximize their control of terrain. The modern territories of Quang Binh, Quang Tri and Thua Thien would in fact be a contested frontier zone until the fifteenth century when the arena of contention shifted further south.

After 446, Sino-Vietnamese annalists perceived kings of polities beyond the southern border as being situated in the vicinity of the modern city of Da Nang, in the modern province of Quang Nam. These annalists stopped using the name Lin-yi after 758, and from 875 began to use the name Chan-ch'eng, understood as equivalent to Champāpura or 'City of Champa'. This region is rich in architecture, statuary, and inscriptions in Sanskrit and Cham. The major archaeological sites are Mi-son, Dong Duong, and

[16] K. W. Taylor, *The Birth of Vietnam*, Berkeley, 1983, 106–9, 115–18.

Tra Kieu, each of which represents a distinctive artistic tradition.[17] The name Amarāvatī has been applied to some of the artistic remains by French scholars on the basis of a presumed relationship with the Indian style of that name. The name Indrapura has also been applied to this region. The task of absorbing the vast amount of archaeological evidence already found and still being found has barely begun. Inscriptions reveal a rhythm of political life centred on an aspiring leader's ability to erect a linga and to protect it from rivals.[18] According to the usual reading of the Sino-Vietnamese annalists, Cham–Viet warfare in the late tenth century led to the abandonment of the Quang Nam region as an arena for aspiring Cham kings, though in fact the annalists can be read as being ambiguous on that point.[19] This coincided with the appearance of a new Vietnamese kingdom separate from the Chinese imperial system and may suggest that the process by which the Vietnamese established their position of separation with regard to China also involved the assertion of a greater measure of military ascendancy in the south. However, inscriptional evidence reveals that Cham kings continued to be active in this region into the late twelfth century,[20] and the Sino-Vietnamese annalists themselves do not deny that this territory belonged to Cham kings until the late fifteenth century.

From the eleventh to the fifteenth centuries, Vietnamese annalists locate the kings they call Cham in the vicinity of the modern city of Qui Nhon. The Cham capital, often identified by the name Vijaya, was twice sacked by Vietnamese seaborne armies in the eleventh century as part of the process by which the Vietnamese were developing their dynastic space and exploring the limits of their maritime power. In the twelfth and early thirteenth centuries, Khmer armies, with Angkor at the peak of its power, repeatedly occupied parts of the Cham territories and endeavoured to establish an overlordship over the Cham kings; Cham kings remained active, however, and even managed to sack Angkor in 1177. In the late thirteenth century, Chams and Viets allied against the Mongol-Yuan invasions; the momentum of this alliance eventually led to the visit of a Vietnamese king to Champa in the early fourteenth century, and the marriage of a Vietnamese princess to the Cham king. According to Vietnamese annalists, however, territorial quarrels over the region of Quang Binh, Quang Tri and Thua Thien eventually led to hostilities, and, during the era of Tran dynastic decline in the late fourteenth century, as we have seen, an able Cham king, known to the Vietnamese as Che Bong Nga, repeatedly invaded and plundered the Vietnamese lands, thrice sacking the Vietnamese capital. Following the death of Che Bong Nga in 1390, Ho Quy Ly, and then the fifteenth-century Le kings, presided over new assertions of Vietnamese power in the Cham territories. In 1471, according to Vietnamese annalists, a Vietnamese army seized the Cham capital at Vijaya and the Vietnamese annexed everything north of what is today the southern border of Binh Dinh Province.

17 Jean Boisselier, *La Statuaire Du Champa*, Paris, 1963.

18 L. Finot, 'Notes d'epigraphie: les inscriptions de Mi-son', BEFEO, 4 (1904), inscriptions no. 4, 12, 14, & 15.

19 G. Cœdès, *The Indianized States of Southeast Asia*, ed. Walter Vella, trans. Susan Brown Cowing, Honolulu, 1968, 124–5; Ngo Si Lien, ban ky 1, 189–94 passim.

20 Finot, 'Les inscriptions de Mi-son', inscription no. 25.

The status of the region of Quang Binh, Quang Tri and Thua Thien during the thousand years after the so-called kings of Lin-yi ceased to rule there in the fifth century and until an unambiguous and final Vietnamese authority appears to have been established in the fifteenth century has yet to be carefully studied. It was clearly a border zone in which Viet and Cham peoples mingled. The Vietnamese annalists claim that northern portions of this region were annexed in the eleventh century and southern portions were obtained by marriage alliance in the early fourteenth century. But Ho Quy Ly's campaigns against Champa at the turn of the fifteenth century reveal that this was still a contested area. Similarly, the status of the Quang Nam region after the tenth century and until the Vietnamese annexation of 1471, has yet to be clearly understood. This was recognized by the Vietnamese as Cham territory, and Cham kings continued to rule from there, some of them emplaced by Khmer armies, but overall it appears to have been a less propitious place for Cham kingship after the tenth century than it had been before.

This should not lead to the conclusion that the Quang Binh, Quang Tri and Thua Thien region after the fifth century and the Quang Nam region after the tenth century were simply absorbed by Cham polities farther south. On the contrary, it is more likely that, exceptional periods of Cham leadership aside, such as the case of Che Bong Nga, regional leaders exercised a kind of autonomous authority appropriate to local circumstances. The information from the Vietnamese annals about Cham–Viet relations must be treated carefully, for surely it reflects presumptions about interstate relations derived from experience with Vietnam's northern neighbour. Vietnamese-style historical narrative was not adequate to describe the relatively diffuse, personalized kind of authority that must have characterized Cham political experience.

The Vietnamese annexation of the coast down to Cu-mong in the late fifteenth century was not the end of Champa. A fourth Cham region centred in the vicinity of the modern city of Nha Trang, in the modern province of Khanh Hoa, had been the home of kings from the beginning of Cham history and has archaeological and inscriptional evidence comparable to the Quang Nam region in terms of chronology, quantity, and sophistication. Scholars sometimes apply the name Kauthara to this region. Sino-Vietnamese annalists recorded what appears to have been a perception of this region in the eighth and ninth centuries under the name Huan-wang. Cham kings ruled here until the end of the seventeenth century. Thereafter, Cham kings continued to rule under Vietnamese overlordship in what is the modern province of Thuan Hai until 1832.[21] In this region, often referred to by scholars as Pāṇḍuranga, Cham kings had been ruling for centuries. The majority of Chams living in Vietnam today are in Thuan Hai.[22]

One of the wonders of Cham history is that a Malayo-Polynesian people was able to compete for space in a continental environment for so long. The archipelagic, maritime nature of this continental terrain is one way to

[21] Po Dharma, *Le-Panduranga (Campa) 1802–1835, ses rapports avec le Vietnam*, Paris, 1987.
[22] Vien khoa hoc xa hoi thanh pho Ho Chi Minh, *Nguoi Cham o Thuan Hai*, Thuan Hai, 1989.

understand this. Another dimension that deserves further consideration is the participation of the upland peoples in the Cham story. Temples and other archaeological remains can be found in the mountains, at least one king ruled from the mountains, and there is evidence of close relations between upland and coastal leadership groups. Much scholarly attention has been spent on lists and genealogies of kings as metaphors for a kingdom, but now it is clear that there were many kings ruling simultaneously in different places. Who were these kings? They were never called Cham; rather, they were called kings of Champa. It is in fact difficult to get a clear sense of who the Chams were. Judging from surviving Cham populations, we are encouraged to speak of there being several kinds of Cham peoples. And it is increasingly clear that the participation of peoples from the mountains, the Rhade and the Jarai, as soldiers and even kings, is more than a possibility. Furthermore, the significance of Champa as a network, or series of networks, of ethnic, religious, political, and commercial relationships connecting the Cham territories with the Malay world of peninsular and insular Southeast Asia is still poorly understood. There is in fact much evidence from Champa that has yet to be studied; what is meant by Champa appears to be on the threshold of a major revision.[23] The construction of Cham history will have a significant impact upon the development of Vietnamese historiography, which is at present in a preliminary phase of making space for Cham voices to be heard in the earlier history of the terrain now part of Vietnam.

## ANGKOR

Turning to the lower Mekong basin, we find a very different historical experience from that of the Viets or the Chams. Here there was no experience with the soldiers and officials of a neighbouring empire, nor the awareness of boundaries, in terrain and in culture, that such an experience produced among the Viets and Chams. Information about the outside world available to Khmer leaders arrived as news about Hindu gods and forms of Hindu and Buddhist devotion as well as cosmological notions of political space that were expounded in the Sanskrit language. This news arrived, we assume, chiefly by way of maritime trade, and encouraged openness and receptivity toward distant contacts and awareness of being part of a borderless world. Early Khmer leaders learned to justify their authority by placing it in a universal context of devotion that could fully absorb the religious aspirations and compel the loyalty of their followers. In a process of developing the theory and practice of an increasingly centralized political space, warfare among rival hegemons was rationalized as corresponding to deified moral conflict on a universal scale. The emergence of the Angkor polity from the ninth century represents the accumulated political and cultural wisdom from generations of efforts to organize a political order in a relatively diffuse socio-economic environment.

Unlike the Viets, who developed their polity in a relatively confined

[23] Finot, 'Les inscriptions de Mi-son', inscription no. 21. T. Quach-Langlet, 'Le cadre géographique de l'ancien Campa', in *Actes du seminaire sur le Campa*, Paris, 1988, 36.

locale that was densely populated from an early time, and the Chams, whose ambitions were for the most part defined by coastal enclaves, other peoples in Southeast Asia inhabited more expansive landscapes where human settlement remained an important variable for a longer time. The Khmers inhabited the lower Mekong basin, which included the Tonle Sap, or Great Lake, a natural reservoir for the annual monsoon floods of the Mekong. During the earliest, or pre-Angkorean, centuries of Khmer history, there was no fixed centre, nor can it even be said that there was a single Khmer polity. Khmer leaders strove to promote and enforce their authority by demonstrations of battlefield and devotional prowess, the effectiveness of which seldom had any enduring value beyond their individual lifetimes.[24] However, in the ninth century, Khmer political life became centred at Angkor. Angkor is located near the northwest shore of the Tonle Sap, with good water transport from all the ricefields in the drainage basin of that lake as well as the lower Mekong plain. At the same time, it is well situated for land contact with the basins of the Mun and Chao Phraya, where more ricefields could be found. Once Khmer settlement had exploited the rice-growing potential of this region to a minimally-necessary level, and once Khmer leaders found ways of organizing their authority over much of this region, Angkor was the favoured site as long as agriculture remained the primary source of wealth. Pre-Angkorean and post-Angkorean Khmer centres were located to the east and south, along the Mekong with direct access to the sea and the commerce-generated wealth that this access afforded; but Angkor depended upon rice.

The establishment of the Angkorean polity is associated with the career of Jayavarman II during the first half of the ninth century. Prior to this time, there was a multiplicity of polities in the lower Mekong basin, relatively small and transitory realms representing the personal achievements of particular individuals rather than institutionalized political systems. Chinese record-keepers organized their information about these polities in the shape of two successive kingdoms, which they called Fu-nan, from the second to the sixth centuries, and Chen-la, from the sixth through to the eighth centuries. The Chinese perception of a change from 'Fu-nan' to 'Chen-la' in the sixth century appears to correspond to a transition from coastal or riverine entrepôts linked to the trade route between India and China to a more inland focus upon ricefields.

The earliest known maritime trade route between India and China followed the coasts, except for land transit across the Kra isthmus and transit through the natural and man-made channels of the lower Mekong plain. The archaeological site of Oc-eo, in southern Vietnam near the Cambodian border, appears to have been situated at a strategic junction of canals that linked the Gulf of Siam with the main channels of the Mekong.[25] Oc-eo was an entrepôt from the second to the sixth centuries, and is generally associated with the 'Fu-nan' era of pre-Angkorean history. But, beginning in the fourth century, an all-sea route was pioneered

[24] O. W. Wolters, 'Khmer "Hinduism" in the seventh century', in R. B. Smith and W. Watson, eds, *Early South East Asia: Essays in Archaeology, History and Historical Geography*, London and New York, 1979.

[25] Paul Wheatley, *Nagara and Commandery*, Chicago, 1983, 119–46.

between India and China via the Straits of Melaka (Malacca); by the sixth century this was the preferred route, and the old coastal route was neglected.[26]

In Cambodia, this shift in the trade route coincided with the appearance of conquerors from the mid-Mekong region in the north, the brothers Bhavavarman (who was active during the last half of the sixth century) and Mahendravarman (who was active during the first decade of the seventh century). They did not unite all of the Khmer lands under their rule, but their activities covered more of the Cambodian landscape than those of any previous aspiring hegemon. Furthermore, their careers were oriented toward the inland rice-growing areas of the Mekong basin rather than toward the old coastal entrepôts. Their conquests did not survive their deaths, but, later in the seventh century, the king remembered as Jayavarman I briefly reassembled his version of their conquests. Thereafter, until the eighth century, local Khmer leaders pursued their ambitions without any successfully laying claim to a hegemonic role.

The conquests of Bhavavarman, Mahendravarman, and Jayavarman I reveal an unprecedented interest in northwestern Cambodia, the future site of Angkor, and this suggests that conquerors were beginning to understand the significance of rice, in contrast to international commerce, and to value a site that would allow them to control areas where rice could be or already was being grown.[27] Jayavarman II began his career in the southeast of modern Cambodia, but his conquests were not completed until he had established himself near the future site of Angkor. This locality would remain the seat of Khmer kings for the next six centuries. On a nearby mountain, Sanskrit-educated priests performed a ceremony in the year 802 that nullified all prior oaths of vassalage and proclaimed Jayavarman II a universal monarch.

Jayavarman II is believed to have died in 850 and to have been succeeded by his son Jayavarman III, who reigned until his death in 877. Very little information survives about these two kings. They were followed by Indravarman, who reigned from 877 to 889, and his son Yaśovarman I, who reigned from 889 to around 900. There is no firm evidence that these kings were related to the two Jayavarmans, though later genealogists endeavoured to establish a connection. We have no information about the method of determining succession, but most probably the ability to lead soldiers and gather followers was an important part of enforcing one's claim to rule. Some kind of institutionalized officialdom was developed, apparently to oversee agrarian workers on behalf of the temples established throughout the realm by royal charter, but this did not include any strict notion of dynasty. Genealogies and claims of blood relationship with previous kings were part of the legitimizing process, but the mechanism of succession remained sensitive to the ability of claimants to assume command at Angkor.[28]

26 O. W. Wolters, *Early Indonesian Commerce: A Study of the Origins of Sri Vijaya*, Ithaca, 1967, 71–85.

27 O. W. Wolters, 'North-western Cambodia in the seventh century', BSOAS, 37, 2 (1974).

28 Michael Vickery, 'The reign of Sūryavarman I and royal factionalism at Angkor', JSEAS, 16, 2 (1985).

Yaśovarman I was the first king to reside at the actual site of Angkor, and is known as a great builder. He built sanctuaries at Angkor as well as about one hundred monasteries throughout the realm, each apparently serving as a royal outpost in the locality where it was located. These monasteries were for monks who variously worshipped the three chief deities of Angkor: Śiva, Viṣṇu, and Buddha. All three cults favoured royal power and benefited from the patronage of kings.

Evidence permits only a few observations about the economic, social, and political organization of the Angkorean polity. It is certain that the economy was based upon wet-rice agriculture, that temples were prominent custodians of land and peasants, and that royal authority was expressed through a relatively well-developed hierarchy that included priests and religious sanctions. The degree of centralized control enjoyed by the kings over temples, ricefields, and available labour can only be conjectured, but it was sufficient to realize large building and excavation projects and, periodically, to sustain long-distance military expeditions. Judging from the vicissitudes of Angkorean history, it appears that, whatever the mechanism of hierarchical control available to the kings, orderly conditions and glorious deeds were more the result of their personal abilities than of an institutionalized command system.

Yaśovarman's death was followed by the unremarkable and relatively brief reigns of two of his sons. In the 920s, a brother-in-law of Yaśovarman, known as Jayavarman IV, established himself as king on a site about one hundred kilometres northeast of Angkor. In the 940s, Rājendravarman, identified in genealogies as a nephew of both Yaśovarman and Jayavarman IV, gained ascendancy and resided at Angkor, where he is credited with many architectural achievements. He appears to have been something of a conqueror, and is thought to have plundered a Cham temple near the modern city of Nha Trang. His accomplishments must have been considerable, because it appears that he was able to arrange that after his death, in 968, a high court dignitary, possibly a greatgrandson of Yaśovarman, ruled on behalf of his son, Jayavarman V, who did not complete his studies until 974. Inscriptional evidence indicates that, during the reign of Rājendravarman and Jayavarman V, a group of powerful families, typically claiming kinship by marriage with previous kings, succeeded in entrenching themselves near the centre of authority. Very little is known of Jayavarman V's reign. He apparently presided with success over the hierarchy of loyalties built up by his predecessors. But his death in 1001 was followed by a war of succession in which his nephew was pushed aside by another royal claimant who, in 1006, was in turn defeated by Sūryavarman I.

Sūryavarman I appears to have begun his career in northeastern Cambodia. His exact relationship with previous kings is unclear, but he established a successful claim to the throne, the concept of usurper not being appropriate to the Khmer situation. Sūryavarman I is known for extending his authority over the Lopburi region of the lower Chao Phraya plain in modern Thailand. Other than that, very few details survive from his reign, the most notable being the oath-taking ceremony of 1011, the earliest surviving evidence of such a ceremony in Cambodia. Some scholars believe that Sūryavarman I showed special favour to a Buddhist cult, but, if so, this seems not to have prejudiced the Śaivite and Vaiṣṇavite cults. It is generally assumed that Sūryavarman I was a strong ruler under whose leadership the Khmers expanded to the north and west. He died in 1050 and was succeeded by one of his sons, Udayādityavarman II.

The sixteen-year reign of Udayādityavarman II was marked by three major rebellions and military pressure from the Chams. Despite this evidence of warfare during his reign, Udayādityavarman II contributed one of the great Śaivite temples at Angkor, the Baphuon, as well as the large artificial lake known as the Western Baray with a Vaiṣṇavite temple. He was succeeded by a brother, Harshavarman III, of whom little is known. The last half of the eleventh century appears as a time when the kings of Angkor were challenged by aspiring local powers. Perhaps this development is related to the rise of families of high dignitaries in the tenth century whose ambitions could be woven into royal authority only by a strong figure such as Sūryavarman I.

In 1080, kingship was claimed by a family thought to have been established in northern Cambodia; some scholars believe that the descendants of Sūryavarman I continued to resist this family from a base in southern Cambodia for over thirty years. In 1113, Sūryavarman II, described as a grandnephew of the leader of the northern family, defeated two kings, one of whom may have been his great-uncle, to claim the throne.

Sūryavarman II is famed as a great conqueror. For several years his soldiers dominated the northern Chams, whom he recruited as allies in a series of unsuccessful invasions of Dai Viet. The Khmers communicated with the northern Cham territories through mountain passes from the Mekong Valley, and, interestingly, the southern Cham territories appear not to have felt the power of Sūryavarman II. Lopburi, which appears to have shaken off Khmer overlordship after the reign of Sūryavarman I, was again placed under the authority of Angkor. Evidence of unsuccessful Khmer attacks on the Mon polity at Haripunjaya, near modern Chiengmai in northern Thailand, may be dated to the general time of Sūryavarman II. There are indications that Sūryavarman II was also active in the Mun River basin and adjacent portions of the Mekong basin in modern Laos and Thailand.

The most famous of all Angkorean edifices, the Angkor Wat, was built by Sūryavarman II as his personal funerary temple. It reveals devotion to the cult of Viṣṇu at a time when Viṣṇu cults were also prominent in India and Java. This may reflect an alert interest in intellectual and religious trends in the Sanskritic world and a continuing sensitivity to the cultural authority of this world. At the same time, Sūryavarman II successfully conducted diplomatic relations with the Southern Sung court of China, posing as a vassal and promoting trade. Sūryavarman II disappears from the evidence around 1150, after which Angkor suffered internal discord and Cham raids for thirty years.

Sūryavarman II's immediate successors are undistinguished. The first of them, Dharaṇūrndravarman II, a cousin of Sūryavarman II, was married to a granddaughter of Sūryavarman I. This marriage produced the king later known as Jayavarman VII. Jayavarman VII's early career was spent on the sidelines as other contenders struggled for supremacy. In the 1170s, a trend of Cham raids, perhaps facilitated by Angkor's internal difficulties, culminated in 1177 when a Cham water-borne expedition sacked Angkor.

In the wake of this event, with the Khmer lands at the mercy of the Chams, Jayavarman VII stepped forward to lead resistance to the invaders. In the 1180s, he completed the expulsion of the Chams and established his authority at Angkor. In the 1190s he began to send expeditions into Champa, with the eventual result that Champa was ruled as a province of Angkor for nearly twenty years in the early thirteenth century. At the same time, Jayavarman VII sent armies to the north and west; there is evidence of his authority as far north as the modern site of Vientiane.

In addition to his conquests, Jayavarman VII is known for the many impressive buildings completed during his reign, including temples dedicated to each of his parents, and the Bayon, a Mahāyāna Buddhist temple in the centre of the Angkor Thom walled enclosure designed at that time. He is also credited with the building of roads, 121 rest houses, and 102 hospitals throughout Angkorean territory. Jayavarman VII favoured Mahạyāna Buddhism, and this, along with his reported conquests, the apparently hasty construction of his monuments, and the seemingly intense level of activity that characterized the thirty to forty years of his rule, has contributed to his reputation as an improviser in an age of decay, a man of energy searching for some new form of thought and organization capable of pushing the Angkorean polity into a fresh trajectory. But the momentum imparted to the Angkorean polity by Jayavarman VII appears to have come from his personality rather than his organizing achievements, and he has the distinction of being the last important king of Angkor. The manner in which his reign came to an end is unknown, but it is generally dated around 1220, when the Chams threw off Khmer overlordship.

Angkorean history in the eleventh, twelfth, and thirteenth centuries reveals a pattern of strong kings followed by disorder. Sūryavarman I, Sūryavarman II, and Jayavarman VII all enjoyed relatively long and distinguished reigns. All three were apparently men of unusual ability. But they were unable to translate their personal achievements into any sort of long-term institutional stability, as, for example, Ly Phat Ma had been able to do at Thang-long during the 1030s and 1040s. The reasons for this are probably related to the relative lack of threat perceived by the Khmers and the accompanying lack of incentive to affirm orthodox patterns, whether in terms of religious thought or of royal succession. The Chams did not pose the same order of threat to the Khmers as Chinese dynasties did to the Vietnamese. When the formation of Thai polities in the Chao Phraya and Mekong basins posed a higher level of threat to Angkor in the thirteenth century, the Khmers adapted with fundamental economic and cultural changes; they did not respond as if they had irrevocably invested themselves in any particular political or cultural heritage.

Following the Mahāyāna Buddhist fervour of Jayavarman VII, there was a brief revival of royal Śaivism, but by the end of the thirteenth century Theravāda Buddhism had spread widely among the Khmers, opening a new post-Angkorean age in Khmer culture. The building of monuments came to an end. Sanskrit inscriptions were replaced by Pāli scriptures; the old brahmanical priestly class was replaced by peripatetic monks with begging bowls. Beginning in the late thirteenth century, Thai military pressure posed serious problems; by the late fourteenth century, the site of Angkor could only with difficulty be defended against Ayutthaya. Rice-fields were neglected as trade and commerce grew in importance as a source of wealth. During the first half of the fifteenth century, Khmer kings abandoned Angkor in favour of sites further east and south, in the vicinity of modern Phnom Penh, with greater access to the maritime trade routes that were being invigorated at that time in response to new commercial initiatives from China.

The end of Angkorean history came not with a dramatic collapse but rather as a reorientation of the Khmer polity: from dependence on rice-fields to greater reliance upon wealth generated by trade and commerce; from continental empire to maritime entrepôt; from a religious culture that was priestly to one that was monastic. It is incorrect to attribute the abandonment of Angkor simply to Tai pressure. For one thing, the pattern of Angkorean history reveals an unstable and seemingly irremediable reliance upon personality that made it progressively more difficult for an aspiring ruler to enforce his royal claims. The final abandonment of Angkor in the 1430s appears to have resulted from conflicts that cannot be strictly defined as resulting from either internal rivalry or external interests, but were rather a more complicated aspect of the relationship that had developed between Ayutthaya and Angkor. Angkor had for centuries served as the focus of hierarchy in the lower Chao Phraya and Mekong basins. This was a political fact for the new Thai polity of Ayutthaya as well as for the Khmers; and Ayutthaya kings, no less than the Khmer kings, endeavoured to appropriate Angkorean traditions. Furthermore, the attraction of a site more accessible to seaborne foreign merchants appears to have been at least as important as the distraction of a site vulnerable to a rival power. Ayutthaya and Phnom Penh resembled one another both in their focus upon maritime trading contacts and in their investment in the legacy of Angkor.[29]

The appropriation of Angkor by modern Khmers as an important part of their history is based upon relatively recent reconstructions of the past. Between the days of Angkor and the twentieth century were generations of Khmers for whom Angkor, if not unknown, was nonetheless without the significance now attached to it.[30] Unlike the case of the Viets, who never abandoned Thang-long despite successive efforts by Chinese dynasties to wrest it away, the Khmer world offered options that did not require the retention of Angkor. Exercising the option to relocate the Khmer polity, both geographically and culturally, offered the possibility of leaving behind a particular historical experience. That this experience should be retrieved in modern times reflects a case of shrinking options. In a world of multiplying predators, the Khmers have begun to need Angkor.

[29] Michael Vickery, 'Cambodia after Angkor, the chronicular evidence from the 14th to 16th centuries', 2 vols, Ph.D. thesis, Yale University, 1977, 1. 513–22.

[30] Michael Vickery, 'Some remarks on early state formation in Cambodia', in David G. Marr and A. C. Milner, eds, *Southeast Asia in the 9th to 14th centuries*, Singapore, 1986.

# PAGAN

A historical experience that may be usefully compared with those of the Viets and Khmers occurred in the Irrawaddy basin. Here, the selection of items from the cultural repertoire of ancient India was not the same as the news that made a difference to the Khmers. The universalized vision of authority that was credible among the Khmers, relatively isolated from alien threats in the lower Mekong basin, was too catholic, too indiscriminate, and too amoral for the political and intellectual process that evolved in the Irrawaddy basin. There the mood was more culturally diverse and competitive, and the need to affirm the ethical nature of political authority was accordingly greater. The Sarvāstivādin Buddhism of the Pyus and the Theravāda Buddhism of the Mons and the Burmans provided a more clearly defined programme for moral action and a correspondingly greater emphasis upon means for demonstrating merit to vindicate one's place in society. The cities of the Pyus, the Mons, and the Burmans shared a single lowland geo-strategic site, were vulnerable to mountain-based powers, were in close land contact with the borderlands of the Indian world (the Arakanese and Bengali coasts and the Assam basin), and were in regular maritime contact with the eastern coast of the Indian subcontinent and with Sri Lanka. The rulers of Pagan who aspired to unite these cities under their authority from the eleventh century claimed a superior measure of merit as defined by the religious ideas that united the different ethno-cultural (and socio-economic) patterns of that time and place. They showed an ability to synthesize, to affirm a centre amidst the clamour of competing languages (Pyu, Mon, Burman), competing economies (the trading cities of the monsoon coast and the ricelands of the dry zone in the north), and competing enemies (Pagan history tells of invasions from both the mountains and the sea). This focus came to be based upon a well-developed notion of a moral centre as defined by the Pāli canon of Theravāda Buddhism. In contrast, the Angkorean achievement contained fewer contradictions, being measured less by the moral quality of the ruler than by the amoral power of the god whom the ruler worshipped.

A casual visitor to Pagan may be puzzled by such impressive architectural remains in the midst of what is essentially a desert in the dry zone of northern Burma, shielded from the monsoon rains by the surrounding mountains. Its location on the Irrawaddy River, however, is roughly equidistant from the regions of Minbu downriver and Kyaukse upriver. Minbu and Kyaukse emerged in early times as important rice-producing areas through the development of extensive irrigation systems. Pagan was the ideal site to concentrate the rice surplus of these two regions. Pagan's success as the first documented polity to extend its authority throughout the Irrawaddy basin is primarily a measure of the ability to mobilize the agrarian resources of Minbu and Kyaukse made possible by its location. Lower Burma, Arakan, and Tenasserim were all significant centres of trade and culture, but the history of Pagan reveals that, in that time and place, an inland agrarian polity was better able to concentrate people and wealth than were coastal entrepôts.

The history of Pagan reveals an interesting comparison with Angkor from at least three vantages. Like Angkor, Pagan was an inland agrarian polity that enforced its authority over coastal areas; both Angkor and Pagan are impressive centres of monumental architecture; and the history of each came to an end contemporaneously with the advent of Tai peoples into lowland Southeast Asia. Pagan history is much shorter than Angkorean history, but, for the better part of three centuries, these two polities gave direction to most of the intellectual and material resources of mainland Southeast Asia.

Pagan reportedly appeared as a walled city in the mid-ninth century. The kings of Pagan were Burmans, relatively recent arrivals in the Irrawaddy basin, which had been inhabited for several centuries by Pyus and Mons. The Burmans appear to have gained entry into the basin in conjunction with expeditionary operations of the kingdom of Nanchao, located in modern Yunnan, which early in the ninth century seems to have broken the power of the Pyus. In the ninth and tenth centuries, Pagan developed as a regional power in northern Burma, while further south a Mon kingdom, based at Thaton, was in maritime contact with Sri Lanka and the Indian subcontinent and was a centre for both overseas trade and Buddhism.

The history of Pagan as a major polity began with the reign of Anawrahta, dated from 1044 to 1077. He is famous for his conquests, the most important being Thaton, in 1057, which resulted in a massive infusion of Mon culture into Pagan. Burmese historiography has portrayed Anawrahta as a king whose conquests were motivated by his piety, either to gain possession of Buddhist relics and scriptures or to spread the Buddhist religion. His conquests included parts of Tenasserim and Arakan, and he is credited with an expedition into Yunnan; his votive tablets have been found throughout the Irrawaddy basin. But more significant than the extent of Anawrahta's conquests was the impact of Mon culture upon the Burmans after their conquest of Thaton and the removal of Mon ruling-class people and other skilled elements of the Mon population to Pagan.

Evidence suggests that Anawrahta's conquest of Thaton may have been in response to Khmer conquests in the lower Chao Phraya basin during the reign of Sūryavarman I, which disturbed the Mon populations there and threatened lower Burma. One result of Anawrahta's activities in lower Burma and the peninsula was to bring Pagan into the maritime trading network that linked the coasts along the Bay of Bengal. In the 1060s and 1070s, Anawrahta maintained friendly contact with the Sri Lankan conqueror Vijayabāhu I, including exchanges of monks and Pāli Buddhist texts. The larger world opened up by Anawrahta's conquests was for a century defined by the imagination of Pagan's kings; evidence of serious external threat and internal contradiction does not appear until the last half of the twelfth century.

The second prominent king of Pagan was Kyanzittha, who ruled from 1084 to around 1112. Remembered as a somewhat disreputable prince with a talent for leading soldiers, Kyanzittha suppressed a Mon uprising that had claimed the life of Anawrahta's son and successor. He was a great admirer of Mon culture and has left inscriptions in the Mon language as well as art and architecture in the Mon style. The Mons appear to have dominated the religious and intellectual life of Pagan at this time, and their language was widely used among ruling-class people. The language of the Pyu continued to be a cultural force as well, seemingly as the repository for the legacy of the Pyu cities of earlier times. Pāli became the language of scripture and liturgy as the Theravāda monkhood flourished under royal patronage. The Burmans themselves learned to write their language in a Mon script. Their initial contribution was, of course, military, for it was their battlefield prowess that had made of Pagan an assembly of such diverse cultural elements; but the story of Pagan eventually is concerned with how the Burmans assimilated these elements and went on to establish a Burman cultural tradition. The reign of Kyanzittha is generally understood as the time when this process of assimilation began to reach a level of maturity; the term 'synthesis' is often applied to cultural developments inspired by Kyanzittha's leadership. A fitting symbol for Kyanzittha is the Myazedi pillar, erected near the end of his reign, with identical inscriptions in four languages: Burman, Mon, Pāli, and Pyu.

The Shwezigon stupa and the Nanda temple were completed during Kyanzittha's reign; both are jewels in the rich architectural legacy of Pagan and both reveal an effort to direct popular religious sentiment toward Theravāda Buddhism through what can be described as architectural pedagogy. It was at this time that Theravāda Buddhism was implanted at the centre of Burmese cultural life.

Kyanzittha was succeeded by a grandson, Alaungsithu, who ruled for more than half a century, into the late 1160s. Alaungsithu presided over the beginning of a transition away from the conventions of Mon culture toward the expression of a distinctive Burman style. The temples built during this time include the last examples of Mon architecture at Pagan as well as the earliest efforts to construct Burman-style temples, the most famous example of which is the Thatbyinnyu.

Surviving evidence portrays Alaungsithu as a peripatetic king travelling extensively through his realm, building monuments and nurturing Buddhism with acts of piety. His travels also included punitive expeditions to Arakan and Tenasserim. Efforts by Pagan to control Tenasserim appear to have threatened trade between Angkor and Sri Lanka and to have elicited a Sri Lankan raid. Evidence suggests that Alaungsithu enjoyed a prosperous reign.

Narapatisithu, who reigned from around 1173 until 1211, was the last of the important kings of Pagan. By this time, according to the most recent study of Pagan, a contradiction in the system of land control required attention. The legitimacy of Pagan's kings had become dependent upon their ability to demonstrate superior merit by endowing temples and monasteries with tax-exempt lands. In the late twelfth century, land was no longer readily available for this purpose, and the revenue base of the kings had shrunk relative to the monastic lands. The authority of the throne being thus threatened by the growing wealth of the monks, Narapatisithu carried out an ecclesiastical reform as an acceptable means of depriving the monkhood of its wealth by way of 'purifying' it. The monkhood was pronounced corrupt, its ordination was declared invalid, and its possessions were confiscated. Monks were sent to Sri Lanka to be properly ordained, and returned with the recognized authority to ordain a new, 'purified' monkhood. Narapatisithu's successful reform of the monkhood allowed him to increase the amount of land available for taxation, and brought Pagan to the peak of its power.[31]

Narapatisithu's reign appears to have been a time of general peace and prosperity. Many great temples and other monuments were built. Art, architecture, and inscriptions reflected a confident Burman idiom. Mon influence was not as significant as it had been a century earlier.

The problem of land control that Narapatisihu had temporarily solved reappeared after his death as kings continued to transfer land to the monkhood to demonstrate the merit upon which their legitimacy and moral authority was based. Narapatisithu's successors, however, were unsuccessful in their attempts to reform the monkhood, and their ability to direct events began to fail as the monkhood found ways to protect its wealth. As royal authority shrank, outlying areas began to go their own way. A new Mon kingdom was established at Pegu in 1281. A king appeared in Arakan.

This unwinding of the internal hierarchy of Pagan was already in an advanced stage when Tai peoples known as Shans began to enter the lowlands from the mountains to the east and north. They were enticed by the opportunity offered by Pagan's weakness, and stimulated by the Mongol conquest of Yunnan in the 1250s and by subsequent Mongol expeditions in the direction of Pagan beginning in the late 1270s. When Mongol expeditions penetrated into the Irrawaddy basin and reached as far as Pagan during the period 1283–1301, Shan chieftains provided the leadership that eventually forced the Mongols to evacuate the lowlands, and the kings of Pagan were forced into a subordinate, mainly ceremonial, role. Pagan was thereafter of only local significance as a political centre.

After a period of disorder attending the assertion of Shan military and political leadership in northern Burma during the first half of the fourteenth century, Burmanized Shans established a regional polity at Ava, on the Irrawaddy River adjacent to the irrigated ricelands of Kyaukse. At the same time, Burmans fleeing from these disorders established a polity at Toungoo, further south on the Sittang River. Meanwhile, the Mon kingdom at Pegu prospered as a centre of commerce on the southern coast, an independent kingdom developed in Arakan, and Prome, in the central Irrawaddy basin, endeavoured to assert regional autonomy against both Ava and Pegu. The Pagan polity was thus partitioned among several regional powers. For the next two centuries, these powers pursued their ambitions through cycles of diplomacy and warfare.

The kings of Pagan appear to have comprised a dynasty in a sense that was not true at Angkor. Succession to Pagan was usually from father to son, while succession at Angkor included a wider horizon of brothers, uncles, nephews, cousins, and others with distant claims of kinship to earlier kings. Wars of succession appear to have been as common at Pagan as they were at Angkor, yet at Pagan these conflicts appear to have taken

[31] Michael Aung-Thwin, *Pagan: the origins of modern Burma*, Honolulu, 1985, 169–98.

their course within a more strictly defined circle of claimants than at Angkor. The reason for this may be related to the role of the monkhood at Pagan as a parallel hierarchy with an interest in stable royal authority.

On the other hand, the dynastic concept at Pagan was never institutionalized to the extent that it was at Thang-long, where, in the thirteenth century, royal marriage policy, the practice of royal abdication, and rules governing the status of collateral lines produced a highly controlled, relatively conflict-free version of dynastic organization. In addition to a politically active monkhood, Thang-long political life was also influenced by a group of officials educated in Chinese political thought and by the necessity of presenting to Chinese dynasties an image of stable dynastic rule consonant with Chinese ideas about good government. The Vietnamese dynastic concept was conditioned by the imperatives of a relatively intense tributary relationship with China that were not felt in other Southeast Asian polities.

The history of Pagan is not a twentieth-century reconstruction to the extent that Angkor's is; it is also not integrated into a continuous historiographical tradition to the same extent as that of Dai Viet. Although the vicissitudes of Burman, Mon, Shan, and Arakanese interaction offered a repertoire of possibilities that have given Burmese history its great variety and interest, the cultural achievement of Pagan has endured as a compelling, according to some the definitive, statement of what it means to be Burmese. This is different from both the case of Angkor, whose cultural achievements were not continued by later generations of Khmers, and Dai Viet, whose ideological, if not cultural, orientation was transformed without loss of continuity in the historico-political tradition. The greatest moments of Pagan's history grew out of a syncretic attitude that made space for non-Burman peoples; the effort by Burmans to appropriate Pagan appears to have led to alienation of the Mons and subsequent loss of lower Burma. Ethnic conflict should probably be placed beside the problem of land control in analysing Pagan's collapse. This makes ironic the idea of Pagan as the paradigm of what it means to be Burmese.

## AYUTTHAYA

In the thirteenth century, the outer edge of authority enjoyed by Angkor and Pagan recoiled from the ambitions of Tai-speaking chieftains. The Tai peoples had for many generations inhabited the valleys leading from the Southeast Asian lowlands to the Yunnan plateau. They were peripheral participants in the Tibeto-Burman-led realm of Nanchao that, from its headquarters in Yunnan, mobilized upland peoples in the eighth and ninth centuries. By the eleventh and twelfth centuries, Tai leaders were organizing new centres of authority in the valleys of the upper Mekong as well as offering their military skills to lowland rulers. The Mongol conquest of Nanchao in the 1250s led to major Mongol expeditions against Dai Viet and Pagan. Angkor was too far off to experience such direct Mongol attention, but the Tai leaders of the upper Mekong were not, and in the space between Mongol activism and Angkorean passivity these leaders assembled conquests and jostled for status.

The most prominent of these northern Tai leaders was Mangrai, born in 1239 at Chiang Saen where, in 1259, he began his career as a ruler, subsequently shifting to Fang. He formed alliances with neighbouring Tai rulers, and in 1281 he conquered the kingdom of Haripuñjaya at Lamphun, thereby suppressing the last Mon-Khmer outpost in the region. When Pagan collapsed in 1289, Mangrai sent an expedition to the Irrawaddy, established relations with the Shan there, and formed a marriage alliance with the new ruler of Mon Pegu. In the 1290s he began building a city at Chiengmai to be the centre of his realm. For nearly two decades he led resistance to Mongol pressure from the north. He is credited with a book of laws inspired by Buddhist norms of civilized behaviour. He died in 1317, and has been remembered as the founder of the kingdom of Lan Na. Mangrai's career vibrates with creative energy and is comparable to that of his ally and most illustratious contemporary, Ramkamhaeng of Sukothai.

Ramkamhaeng's grandfather had, in the 1240s, overthrown the regional Angkorean outpost in the central Chao Phraya plain, Sukothai. The Mon-Khmer population of this area had already been modified by generations of Tai settlers. When he became king of Sukothai in 1279, Ramkamhaeng initiated a policy of gathering vassals that eventually allowed him to claim suzerainty from Luang Prabang in the north to Nakhon Sithammarat in the south and from Vientiane in the east to Pegu in the west. The success of this enterprise owed much to Ramkamhaeng's battlefield reputation; accordingly, Ramkamhaeng's military and political achievements did not survive his lifetime. More enduring were the cultural developments stimulated by Ramkamhaeng's authority in the area of religion, literature, and sculpture. The type of Tai culture destined to be generalized under the rubric Siamese or Thai can be distinguished from this time at Sukothai. Ramkamhaeng died in 1298, and the far-flung bonds of vassalage that he had pulled together at Sukothai quickly unravelled. His successors ruled a small, local power that was absorbed by Ayutthaya within a century and a half.

The vigorous responses of Mangrai and Ramkamhaeng to the opportunities of their age were an indication of even more significant possibilities closer to the Angkorean heartland. Their ambitions were exercised along the periphery of Angkorean influence, but their cities created large inland markets that attracted the interest of littoral merchants. This was a time when Chinese merchants, enjoying the cosmopolitan atmosphere of the Mongol-Yuan dynasty, were especially active in the region. Chinese potters immigrated to Sawankhalok near Sukothai, which became a major centre of ceramics production. Within a few years, Chinese merchant interests in the lower plain of the Chao Phraya played a role in the founding of Ayutthaya.

By the mid-thirteenth century, the Angkorean administrative centre in the lower Chao Phraya plain, Lopburi, had become independent of Angkor. By the end of the century, the western parts of the plain were under the control of Tai rulers who bowed to Ramkamhaeng but after his death looked for other options; most prominent among these were those who ruled from Suphanburi. Ayutthaya, located between Lopburi and Suphanburi on an island in the Chao Phraya, offered the prospect of an entrepôt to those with commercial skills and resources. The initiative for establishing a new kingdom at Ayutthaya is attributed to a man from a Chinese merchant family named U Thong who managed to marry into the ruling families of both Lopburi and Suphanburi. In 1351, he founded Ayutthaya as a united kingdom of Lopburi and Suphanburi, taking the name Ramathibodi and ruling until his death in 1369. This achievement is generally understood as a bringing together of the Angkorean-style administrative skills of the Mons and Khmers of Lopburi, the manpower and the martial skills of the Tais of Suphanburi, and the wealth and commercial skills of the local Chinese merchant communities.

One of the earliest discernible priorities of Ramathibodi was confrontation with Angkor. The border between Ayutthaya and Angkor was in dispute, as was control of the people who lived in the borderlands. There is evidence indicating that the Ayutthayans briefly seized Angkor during the time of Ramathibodi. This reveals that, at its inception, Ayutthaya was fighting to appropriate the claim to regional overlordship that had been held for many generations by Angkor. It would be only sixty years before the logic of Ayutthaya's advantage as an entrepôt of maritime commerce would lead to the abandonment of Angkor.

The urgency of Ramathibodi's contest with Angkor was not shared by the king who followed him, Borommaracha I (r. 1370–88), who was from Suphanburi and accordingly perceived Sukothai as a greater threat and a more natural enemy than Angkor. As former vassals of Sukothai, the Tai of Suphanburi were keen to appropriate Ramkamhaeng's claim to supremacy among the Siamese Tai. Borommaracha I appears to have focused all his energies upon the goal of subduing Sukothai, yet without conclusive results.

The next two rulers were a son of Ramathibodi, Ramesuan (r. 1388–95), and a grandson, Ramaracha (r. 1395–1409); these kings were from Lopburi and they resumed Ramathibodi's policy of pressing against Angkor while paying less attention to Sukothai. While it appears that the Ayutthayans under Ramesuan may have succeeded in sacking Angkor a second time, Tai Ayutthayans wanted a more assertive policy toward Sukothai; at least this is how historians have understood the coup of 1409 when Ramaracha was forced to flee and a son of Borommarcha I gained the throne.

The new king was Intharacha (r. 1409–24), and under his leadership Sukothai was decisively reduced to vassalage. With the Sukothai affair settled, the Ayutthayans were finally prepared to turn their full attention to Angkor. Intharacha's son and successor, Borommaracha II (r. 1424–48), sent an expedition to sack Angkor in 1431, after which, as we have seen, it was abandoned by Khmer kings. The next rival on the horizon was Lan Na, and in the 1440s Borommaracha II initiated a policy of attempting to reduce the kings at Chiengmai.

The successors of Mangrai had maintained a resilient system of military and administrative control and, in the reign of Ku Na (1355–85), established the basis for a distinctive regional cultural identity, called Tai Yuan or Northern Tai. Ku Na was unusually well-educated for a king; he promoted a scholarly sect of Buddhist monks that, for many generations, became the leading religious, literary, and cultural influence in the region.

Ku Na's successors were troubled by factional strife for more than half a century, although they managed to pull together enough soldiers to repel Ming Chinese invasions in 1404 and 1405. Not until around 1450 did King Tilokaracha or Tilok (r. 1441–87), secure internal order Tilok has been remembered as Lan Na's greatest king because during his long reign the kingdom was stable and prosperous; alien threats were successfully dealt with; and new symbols of cultural glory were raised, most famous of which was the Maha Chedi Luang, a massive Buddhist reliquary at Chiengmai.

Tilok's most famous enemy was Borommatrailokanat or Trailok, remembered as one of the greatest of Ayutthaya's kings (r. 1448–88). Trailok pursued the policy of attacking Lan Na that had been set by his father, Borommaracha II. Tilok and Trailok duelled repeatedly during their long reigns. The Ayutthaya–Lan Na warfare of this time is often labelled a stalemate, yet this is not precisely true, for it was decisive in that Lan Na successfully repelled Ayutthayan armies and grew stronger and more cohesive in the process; the Ayutthayan threat surely facilitated Tilok's efforts to enforce more centralized authority from Chiengmai and reinforced a Tai Yuan cultural identity separate from the Sukothai-Ayutthaya version of being Tai. Tilok never entertained the idea of conquering Ayutthaya, so he can be seen as having been successful in a way that Trailok was not, for Trailok failed in his endeavours to conquer Lan Na. Far from being inconclusive, this warfare determined that Lan Na would continue as a regional power beyond the reach of Ayutthaya for centuries to come.

Even more than his vain efforts to subdue Lan Na, Trailok is remembered for administrative reforms that began a process of extending bureaucratic control over labour. This can be interpreted as, at least partially, a result of his mobilizations against Lan Na. The progressive elaboration of the system of labour control conceived during his reign became the basis for the regenerative if not enduring strength of Ayutthaya in following centuries. One idea was essentially a hierarchical numbering system that was applied to everyone from the lowest slave to the king; this fixed each individual's rights and obligations under the law. Another idea was the division and subdivision of officialdom into units charged with specific functions. It is not clear to what degree these ideas were implemented during the reign of Trailok; but the significance of initiating such a reform is very great. It meant that the traditional Tai practice of personal patron-client relationships would henceforth be interacting with a more bureaucratic and impersonal system of control. Very likely, the administrative reforms of Trailok were inspired by the legacy of Angkor.

In addition to Lan Na and Ayutthaya, a third Tai power appeared at this time among the Lao along the middle Mekong. Ramkamhaeng had claimed Luang Prabang and Vientiane as vassals. Legends tell of the son of a former king of Luang Prabang in exile at Angkor named Fa Ngum who conquered his way up the Mekong valley to become King of Lan Sang at Luang Prabang in 1353. Fa Ngum departed from Angkor on his fateful venture in the same year that Ayutthaya was founded by Ramathibodi, but there appears to be no connection to be drawn between these episodes without excessive conjecture, except that the shrinking Angkorean frontiers and the collapse of Ramkamhaeng's network of vassalage offered opportunities to men of imagination and daring.

Lan Sang never achieved the level of organization enjoyed by Lan Na or Ayutthaya. It covered a huge area, from Luang Prabang in the north to Champassak in the south and most of what is today northeastern Thailand. It never advanced far beyond a simple mechanism for mobilizing soldiers. Fa Ngum's successor, Un Hüan (r. 1373–1416) successfully managed marriage alliances with Lan Na and Ayutthaya, but his death was followed by a quarter-century of factional conflict, coinciding with the disorders in Lan Na. Relative peace was restored during the reign of Sainyachakkaphat (1442–79), a contemporary of Tilok and Trailok.

In the 1470s, Le Thanh Ton of Dai Viet was endeavouring to establish more direct administrative control over his vassals among the Tai chieftains of Siang Khwang (Plain of Jars or Tran-ninh Plateau). These chieftains were two-headed birds who also posed as vassals of Lan Sang. When Vietnamese demands became too vexing, they appealed to Sainyachakkaphat, whose assistance emboldened them to rebel openly against Le Thanh Ton. The Vietnamese responded with a large expedition that seized Luang Prabang and sent Sainyachakkaphat fleeing westward. The Vietnamese subsequently withdrew as a younger brother of Sainyachakkaphat named Suvanna Banlang (r. 1479–86) organized resistance and restored order in Lan Sang. This was the only time before the twentieth century that Vietnamese armies marched beyond the mountains down to the mid-Mekong plain. The fact that Dai Viet was exceptionally strong during the reign of Le Thanh Ton helps account for this episode. But it also reveals the strategic significance of Siang Khwang to both Viet and Lao kings. The rulers of Siang Khwang would continue to balance their loyalties between Viet and Lao authority into modern times.

We have glimpsed the early Tai kingdoms in the formative stage of their development. What resulted from the first few generations of Tai leadership in the valleys of the Mekong and Chao Phraya rivers were two inland kingdoms, Lan Na and Lan Sang, and Ayutthaya. Lan Na was destined to experience many years of Burmese vassalage before eventually being incorporated into the nineteenth-century empire of the Chakri kings of Bangkok. Lan Sang eventually devolved into small regional powers who in varying degrees felt the touch of Bangkok's supremacy prior to the arrival of the French. Only Ayutthaya would continue to prosper and, despite recurring troubles with Burmese empire-builders, make good its claim to leadership among the Tai peoples of the region. This claim, however, was made possible by reasons beyond the Tai frame of reference. In appropriating the administrative legacy of Angkor, Ayutthaya moved beyond the skill of juggling vassals that was the glory of Sukothai. In linking up with the commercial networks of resident Chinese, Ayutthaya stepped beyond the narrow options of an inland valley economy. The syncretic achievement that marked the rise of Ayutthaya is similar to that which marked the rise of Pagan, but while the Burmese lost patience with the ambiguities of syncretism, the Ayutthayans continued to cultivate a cosmopolitan outlook. Modern Thai historiography is anchored in perceptions of the

Ayutthayan experience and in the assertion that this experience established a claim of authority among Tai peoples that continues to deserve honour.

## ŚRĪVIJAYA

So far we have considered the histories of mainland polities whose sense of space was defined by mountains, plains, and sometimes coasts. When we shift our attention down the Malay peninsula to the islands beyond, terrain fades into the sea, and the history of the Malay peoples that we situate there has come to signify our understanding of the rhythms of maritime commerce that passed between western and eastern Asia, both changing and being changed by the region. The history we are talking about is a modern reconstruction based mainly upon Chinese and Arabo-Persian texts, a few inscriptions, and, increasingly and most promisingly, archaeological evidence. The Malays themselves have preserved virtually no memory of what we now call Śrīvijaya, a generic term for the succession of thalassocracies centred in southeastern Sumatra from the seventh to the fourteenth centuries. Affirming a particular version of the past was never an urgent priority in a culture with a relatively diffuse awareness of authority, where the sea offered countless options for people who were at home in boats and where agriculturalists were dispersed in many small riverine enclaves.

The earliest trade routes passed through the region overland or, if by water transport, along the coasts, save for Kra isthmus portages. This situation changed from the fourth century as the Malays responded to opportunities for direct maritime trade between southern China and western Asia via the Straits of Melaka. These opportunities have been conventionally explained by the division of China and the consequent growth of southern Chinese interest in seaborne access to west Asian markets, but this is a passive indicator. Malay initiatives in exploiting the possibilities also bear scrutiny. The Malays participated as carriers and also by substituting local products for established items of trade. The process of political organization set in motion among Malay leaders by this new source of wealth reached a critical phase during the last half of the seventh century when rulers near Palembang, on the Musi river of southeastern Sumatra, achieved a position of paramountcy.

Three inscriptions dating from the 680s and testimony of I Ching, the Chinese pilgrim, dating from the 670s to the 690s reveal a prosperous entrepôt where ships going to and coming from China and India gathered while waiting for the winds to change. The ruler was a great patron of Buddhism, and a large international community of monks resided nearby; Chinese monks came here to study with Indian teachers. In a more prosaic vein, ships with fighting men were being sent to intimidate potential rivals along the Straits of Melaka and of Sunda. During the first half of the eighth century, the ruler of Śrīvijaya sent several missions to China; beyond whatever commercial significance these missions may have had, they were primarily demonstrations of diplomatic prowess in the arena of Malay politics.[32] These smudges of evidence from the late seventh and early eighth centuries have been the object of much study and speculation. Their significance for the purposes of our narrative is that they reveal the emergence of the Palembang-based Śrīvijayan polity as a pyramidal network of loyalties among Malay rulers; these rulers were united by a common interest in wealth to be gained from the passage of merchant ships through the region.

Very little is known about Śrīvijayan history but all indications are that something like what we have just described continued to exist as the dominant political force on the Malay peninsula, Sumatra, and western Java for most of the next five hundred years. In the mid-ninth century, a ruler of Śrīvijaya was a prince of the Śailendra line that had ruled in central Java during the preceding century; evidence suggests that this monarch financed the building of a Buddhist monastery at Nālandā in Bengal. In the late tenth century, Śrīvijaya was challenged by Javanese invasions, in response to which it appears that a Śrīvijayan expedition destroyed the Javanese capital in 1016. During this time, the Cōḷa dynasty of Tamil Nadu in southern India developed a fleet and took an interest in Southeast Asia; in 1025, a Cōḷa expedition sacked the Śrīvijayan capital and raided other Malay centres. The earliest evidence of Chinese merchants appearing in Southeast Asia aboard their own ships comes from the tenth century. These sparse bits of information have given rise to theories about diplomatic relations during the tenth and eleventh centuries among the rulers of Tamil Nadu, Śrīvijaya, Java, and China.

The underlying plot of this tale seems to be that the benefits to Śrīvijaya of its supervision of commerce through the region inspired acquisitive instincts among other powers. The Cōḷas oversaw commerce in the western waters of the Bay of Bengal. The Javanese directed commerce in the Java Sea and points east. But opportunities in these areas were peripheral in comparison with Śrīvijaya's splendid position at the throat of the trade routes. Śrīvijaya could not be destroyed by its rivals, but it could be plundered and, for short periods of time, pressed into vassalage. Any power that could dominate the Straits of Melaka stood to benefit enormously from the commerce that passed through. What appears to be new from the tenth century is that the politics of control in the straits was no longer simply a Malay affair; other powers were now in a position to challenge and modify Śrīvijaya's hegemony at the centre of regional trade routes.

What ultimately affected the fate of Śrīvijaya more than military expeditions from Java or southern India was the growing presence of Chinese shipping. The importance of China to the international market ensured that Chinese ships were treated well, even without a Chinese threat of force. But the expansion of Chinese shipping, particularly during the twelfth century when Southern Sung looked south for trade with west Asia, greatly reduced the importance of Malay shipping, and with it the leverage of Malay rulers upon the flow of commerce. The effect of

[32] O. W. Wolters, 'Restudying some Chinese writings on Srivijaya', *Indonesia*, 42 (1986).

increased Chinese shipping was to disperse authority in the Malay world. Rather than there being a single Malay overlord, as the Śrīvijayan ruler had been, several local ports were now able to stand independently of other Malay powers by dealing directly with the Chinese. As the Śrīvijayan system of paramountcy unravelled, the position of Palembang receded to the level of other ports with access to the Straits of Melaka. In the twelfth century, rulers claiming the Śrīvijayan tradition of authority were located at Jambi, northwest of Palembang on the Batang Hari River, closer to the straits.

In the thirteenth and fourteenth centuries, new regional powers further reduced the options of Malay rulers. Sukothai and then Ayutthaya expanded Siamese military activities down the Malay peninsula, ultimately reaching the Straits of Melaka. A new expansionary momentum arose from Java in the thirteenth century and reached a peak in the fourteenth century under the leadership of Majapahit. Malay ambitions were ultimately squeezed out of the Śrīvijayan tradition by the weight of Ayutthaya and Majapahit. Siamese and Javanese expeditions competed to throw nets of vassalage over the Malay rulers of the straits region. This situation changed rapidly when Ming Chinese fleets patrolled Southeast Asian waters at the beginning of the fifteenth century, sponsoring the rise of Melaka and providing a new focus for Malay political activity.

The founder of Melaka, a Malay prince known as Parameśvara, first appears as a vassal of Majapahit at Palembang. In the 1390s he sought to escape Javanese overlordship by shifting to Tumasik (modern Singapore); recent archaeological work in Singapore reveals the late fourteenth century as an especially prosperous time for commercial activity.[33] Tumasik, however, was too exposed to Ayutthaya, and Siamese pressure forced Parameśvara to shift to Melaka, where he presided over a rebirth of Malay political authority under the protection of the Chinese. Parameśvara's close relations with China were the key to his success in competing with Ayutthaya for space on the Malay peninsula.

The newly established Ming dynasty of China took an unprecedented interest in Southeast Asia, and it supported this interest with large naval patrols during the first two decades of the fifteenth century. Parameśvara of Melaka took full advantage of this opportunity to place himself under Chinese protection. He welcomed the Chinese fleets, sent envoys to China, and in 1411 personally went to the Chinese capital to demonstrate his loyalty. Melaka quickly became a new version of the Śrīvijayan model of a Malay-led international entrepôt. Its relationship with China provided protection from Ayutthayan claims, and Majapahit, in the fifteenth century, was already in decline. Melaka established its supremacy over other centres of Malay authority along the coasts of the peninsula and the northeastern coast of Sumatra, thereby guaranteeing control of all trade passing through the straits. Firm relationships were developed with Gujerati and Tamil merchants having access to Western markets and with the north Javanese ports that enjoyed access to Maluku (the Moluccas),

[33] John N. Miksic, *Archaeological research on the 'forbidden hill' of Singapore: excavation at Fort Canning 1984*, Singapore, 1985.

the spice islands to the east. For the next century, Melaka was the central entrepôt for trade in and through Southeast Asia. Even after the Ming fleets ceased patrolling, the momentum of Melaka's initial emergence did not soon diminish, revealing both an increasingly diffuse political environment in the Southeast Asian archipelago and the relative advantage of Melaka's position as the regional entrepôt. Melaka also enjoyed effective leadership; in particular, Tun Perak, brother-in-law of one of Parameśvara's successors, has been remembered among Malays as a hero of the first order for his battlefield prowess against the Siamese during the last half of the fifteenth century.

During the fifteenth century, Islam was adopted by the rulers of Melaka, and from there it spread to other parts of the region. The founding of Melaka and the emergence of Islam mark the beginning of Malay history as it has been traditionally remembered in recent centuries. The Malay annals are informed by an Islamic historiographical perspective and do not consider the pre-Islamic Malay past to be of interest. While Malay history, as a collective memory, can thus be said to begin with Melaka, evidence allows us to say that Melaka was a new version of a very old tradition of behaviour among Malay rulers, a tradition of concentrating the benefits of trade.

The case of Melaka further shows a network of authority within which foreigners played functional roles in governing foreign merchant communities and overseeing port activities. Malay merchants were always at a disadvantage, because, unlike vulnerable rich foreigners, they could pose a political threat to Malay rulers from within their own society and were accordingly targets of suspicion and discrimination. Paradoxically, the supervision of commerce by Malay rulers could not lead to a commercial ethos among the Malays without undermining indigenous Malay authority.[34]

Śrīvijaya's role in Southeast Asian history as a regional entrepôt arose from conditions of geography more than from any quality particular to the Malays. Śrīvijaya was the result of Malay nautical skill and organizing initiative, and of opportunity. But history has shown that the exercise of leadership in the Śrīvijayan mode has not been confined to the Malays; Singapore can be understood as a modern version of the Śrīvijayan achievement of using a favourable location to concentrate commercial wealth.

## MAJAPAHIT

The island of Java became the demographic centre of insular Southeast Asia because of its large fertile plains and rainfall suitable for growing rice. The earliest Javanese centres that have left a conspicuous mark on the landscape were located in upland plains, valleys, and plateaux nestled among the volcanic peaks of south-central Java. But population growth, the search for land suitable for ricefields, and efforts to escape from the cramped contradictions of political life as it developed in that region

[34] A. C. Milner, *Kerajaan*, Tucson, 1982, 14–28.

eventually shifted the focus of political authority eastward into the plains of the Solo and Brantas Rivers. Majapahit was admirably located to concentrate the rice surplus of the Brantas River plain and of the island of Madura. The rise of Majapahit from the end of the thirteenth century reveals that human settlement had by then reached a level sufficient to enable political authority to enact the logic of available terrain.

Evidence sufficient to begin a narrative of political events in Java dates from the first half of the eighth century when a ruler known as Sanjaya appears as a conquering Śaivite king who established himself at Mataram in south central Java. Kings who associated themselves with his achievement appear to have spent the next century as vassals of a line of Mahāyāna Buddhist kings called Śailendra. The Śailendras are credited with the Borobuḍur, a huge stupa-like monument of terraces built upon a hill in the Kedu plain. The walls of the terraces are covered with bas-relief sculpture illustrating Mahāyāna texts in a distinctive Javanese style based upon Guptan prototypes; this suggests a pedagogical intent. Aside from their architectural accomplishments, virtually nothing is known of the Śailendras, though there are indications that they were active not only in Java but also in Sumatra and along the coasts of what are today Cambodia and Vietnam. They were expelled from Java in the mid-ninth century by a Śaivite king of Sanjaya's line known in inscriptions by at least three names, the most common being Pikatan.

Later inscriptions describe Pikatan's career according to a three-phase pattern of hermit-like ascetic preparation, warfare leading to victory, and withdrawal from worldly affairs into ascetic resignation. The careers of later important Javanese kings were also remembered in terms of this pattern, which suggests a tradition of seeing the coercive violence necessary for political achievement as a manifestation of divine energy concentrated in certain individuals who then restore cosmic harmony through renunciation. The Śaivite temple complex at Prambanan, built by Pikatan or one of his successors and variously dated to the late ninth or early tenth century, appears to be a Śaivite answer to the Borobuḍur as a pedagogical centre.

Java in the eighth and ninth centuries thus presents two lines of kings, one Mahāyāna Buddhist and one Śaivite, each credited with the construction of impressive monuments whose dimensions were never again matched by later generations. The Borobuḍur and Prambanan were clearly designed to attract attention, to inspire awe, and to lend material substance to stories suitable for mass indoctrination. This suggests a time in which new religious ideas were being popularized and manpower was being mobilized with an unprecedented degree of central direction and cultural focus.

Evidence suggests that the structure of political authority at that time was essentially a realm of competing localities. The builders of the Borobuḍur and the Prambanan were apparently the two most prominent of these local powers. Their architectural achievements probably represent an enjoyment of momentary ascendancy over neighbouring powers.[35] Political ambitions appear to have gained religious sanction through association with the spread of Buddhist or Śaivite thought.

[35] Jan Wisseman-Christie, 'Negara, Mandala, and Despotic State: images of early Java', in Marr and Milner, eds, *Southeast Asia*.

In the tenth century, literature, drama, and music developed rapidly to produce a Javanized Hindu worldview that included both Buddhism and Śaivism and evolved into modern times with a remarkable degree of continuity. What appears to be religious dissonance in the eighth and ninth centuries should more correctly be interpreted as an early phase of Javanizing non-indigenous religious symbols from more than one source. By the end of the tenth century, Sanskrit texts were being translated into Javanese.

In the mid-tenth century, the royal seat was shifted eastward into the Brantas River plain where rulers could command a larger base of ricefields. The change of locale may also have been an important factor in the process of harmonizing Buddhism and Śaivism with a Javanese perspective. This new vantage afforded wider horizons, with access to the Java Sea and contact with Bali, Maluku, Sumatra, and the peninsula. As Javanese rulers began to explore this larger world, they appear to have come into conflict with the maritime trading polity of Śrīvijaya based in southeast Sumatra. In 1016, the Javanese polity was overtaken by some kind of military disaster, generally assumed to have been related to the rivalry with Śrīvijaya. Java appears to have thereupon fallen into a state of disorder until the rise of Airlangga, son of a Balinese king and a Javanese princess, who was active from the 1020s until his death in 1049.

Airlangga is remembered as one of the great kings of early Java. His career is recorded in conformity with the pattern of ascetic meditation, warfare with victory, and renunciation that has already been noted with reference to Pikatan. After suppressing local powers so as to reaffirm royal authority, he established a place for Java in the regional maritime world. Śrīvijaya having been humbled by an expedition from Cōḷa India in 1025, Airlangga obtained a marriage alliance with the ruler of Śrīvijaya, and Javanese ports thereafter began to emerge as maritime trading centres. Airlangga patronized Śaivites, Mahāyāna Buddhists, and people known in a generic fashion as 'ascetics', while he personally favoured Viṣṇu. Old Javanese literature flourished.

Before his death, Airlangga divided his realm between his two sons. Very little information survives about events during the remainder of the eleventh century, the twelfth century, and into the first two decades of the thirteenth century. By the late twelfth century, the eastern portion of Airlangga's realm, known as Janggala, had been absorbed by the western portion, known as Kaḍiri (originally Panjalu). Old Javanese literature continued to develop, with the writing of epic poems and Javanese versions of stories based upon episodes in the *Mahābhārata*. Javanese ports established commercial relations with spice-producing islands in Maluku and attracted merchants from Gujerat. This period of about a century and a half is generally referred to as the time of Kaḍiri; more is known of cultural and commercial developments than of political events.

Kaḍiri was overthrown in 1222 by a man called Ken Angrok, meaning 'he who upsets everything'. The legends and stories which contain information about Ken Angrok indicate a hero of lowly birth who flouted conventional rules of behaviour, thereby revealing his superior destiny. He attacked Kaḍiri, posing as the champion of Janggala, which Kaḍiri had swallowed a generation or two before; he set his capital in Janggala. The kingdom he established has been remembered as Singhasari, the name later given to his capital. He died in 1227, but his career marked the beginning of what, a century and a half later, became the prologue in the historical memory of Majapahit.[36]

During the Singhasari era of the thirteenth century, the process of Javanizing non-indigenous cultural influences entered an advanced stage in both poetry and bas-relief sculpture. The cultural basis of what, in the following century, became Majapahit was achieved at this time. The most famous king of Singhasari and the king who appears to have first perceived the possibilities that later became Majapahit was Kĕrtanagara (r. 1268–92).

Kĕrtanagara was an aspiring empire builder whose achievements stimulated the rise of Majapahit. He endeavoured to assert Javanese supremacy over a declining Śrīvijaya and despatched naval forces around the Java Sea. The extent of his conquests is not clear, but his ambitions included the islands of Madura and Bali as well as Java. In him can be detected for the first time the idea of a great archipelagic empire ruled by Javanese, which came to be expressed in the term *nusantara*. He practised a form of Śaivite-Buddhist Tantrism that he may have understood as a means of entering a new, more potent arena of spiritual power commensurate with his unprecedented ambition.

Kĕrtanagara was murdered and supplanted by a vassal in 1292, but in the following year his son-in-law, later known as Kĕrtarājasa, gained control and established his capital at Majapahit. Kĕrtarājasa's seizure of power was facilitated by the arrival of a Mongol expeditionary force, with which he first allied against his father-in-law's murderer, and which he subsequently drove back into the sea.

Kĕrtarājasa and his successors stood in the tradition of empire conceived by Kĕrtanagara, and, for the next hundred years, Majapahit claimed hegemony over most of insular and peninsular Southeast Asia. This claim was largely rhetorical: at the peak of its power in the mid-fourteenth century, Majapahit dominated eastern Java, Bali, and Madura, while exercising a punitive influence over western Java, portions of southern Borneo, Celebes, and Sumbawa. Majapahit was also capable for a time of projecting its power into the Straits of Melaka. But the moment of glory for Majapahit was relatively brief and depended upon the vision, determination, and skill of a single man, the minister Gaja Mada who conducted affairs from around 1330 until his death in 1364.

The first two reigns of Majapahit, that of Kĕrtarājasa (1293–1309) and his son Jayanagara (1309–28), appear to have been mostly occupied with suppressing rebellions and asserting military control over eastern Java. Jayanagara died without a male heir, so the throne was assigned to a daughter of Kĕrtanagara who had also been a wife of Kĕrtarājasa. She took no public role, however, and her eldest daughter was chosen to act as a regent on her behalf. This daughter, in 1334, gave birth to a son who

[36] Theodore G. Th. Pigeaud, *Java in the 14th century. A Study in Cultural History*, The Hague, 1962, III. 45ff.

became king in 1350, called Rājasanagara or Hayam Wuruk. Such an intricate arrangement of formal authority suggests a strong hand in the background, the hand of Gaja Mada.

The details of Gaja Mada's activities are known but imprecisely. It is clear that he conquered Bali; there is a story about how he trapped and killed a visiting Sundanese king; and there are indications that he ordered the compilation of a law book and established some kind of administrative system; but all else is obscure. The momentum of his achievements appears to have continued through to the end of Rājasanagara's reign, in 1389. The glory of Majapahit is celebrated in an epic poem, the *Nāgarakĕrtāgama*, written in praise of Rājasanagara in 1365.

After Rājasanagara's death, Majapahit rapidly declined in importance, torn by warfare between rival lords and challenged by the rise of Melaka for control of regional entrepôt trade. Evidence from the fifteenth century is sparse and incoherent, but it is clear that by the beginning of the sixteenth century Majapahit had fallen to the level of a local polity, and shortly thereafter ceased to play any significant role in the affairs of Java. Majapahit faded from view as Muslim polities on the north coast of Java appeared and seized the initiative.

Early Javanese history is much richer than this brief narrative can convey. The relative seclusion of Java from the purview of predatory powers appears to have allowed Javanese rulers the luxury of savouring cultural and religious diversity and the intricate symbolisms that embraced this diversity. An island surrounded by islands, Java was the centre of its own world, able to define itself without the mutual pushing and shoving that shaped continental historical identities. Of course, Java and neighbouring islands contained a diversity of local perspectives, but there appears to have always been space for these perspectives within the larger Javanese tradition. The early encounter of Buddhism and Śaivism, represented in the Borobuḍur and Prambanan, was a critically important event in the formation of Javanese culture. Subsequently, space was made for Islam in the Javanese tradition with relatively little disruption. Perhaps these synthesizing achievements were possible because none of the new religions embodied a non-Javanese political or military threat.

The vision of Javanese paramountcy over the islands that inspired the rulers of Majapahit, and which is enshrined in the term *nusantara*, has in modern times been realized to a degree far beyond the capabilities of those rulers. In the twentieth century, Majapahit became the historical model and legitimation for the dreams of Javanese leaders. Its moment of glory has been frozen in the imaginations of recent generations as an enduring goal to achieve and preserve.

The diverse narratives we have constructed remind us that the attempt to schematize early Southeast Asia history is bound to be unrewarding. The peoples of Southeast Asia experienced a remarkable range of options in organizing their societies and polities. The choices they exercised upon these options reveal a region that continues to resist any convincing simplification. Southeast Asia's imperviousness to all-encompassing historiographical agendas that endeavour to construct a total regional vision of the past may be an indication of what is less perceptible under the heavy layers of scholarship in which our knowledge of other parts of the globe is embedded, or it may reflect distinctive regional conditions. Historians of Southeast Asia benefit from the lack of a coercive interpretative tradition. My intention in writing this essay has been to strengthen resistance to any such tradition.

## BIBLIOGRAPHIC ESSAY

For many years the standard references for early Southeast Asian history have been G. Cœdès, *The Indianized States of Southeast Asia*, ed. Walter F. Vella, trans. Susan Brown Cowing, Honolulu, 1968, and D. G. E. Hall, *A History of Southeast Asia*, 4th edn, Macmillan, 1981. Although scholarship has advanced beyond these works, nothing has yet appeared with which to replace them as serviceable introductions. The most important and up-to-date discussion of conceptual themes in early Southeast Asia is O. W. Wolters, *History, Culture, and Region in Southeast Asian Perspectives*, Singapore, 1982. Collections of essays that are worthy and have significant implications are R. B. Smith and W. Watson, eds, *Early South East Asia: Essays in Archaeology, History and Historical Geography*, London, 1979, and D. G. Marr and A. C. Milner, eds, *Southeast Asia in the 9th to 14th Centuries*, Singapore, 1986. Other useful summaries of evidence are P. Wheatley, *Nagara and Commandery*, Chicago, 1983; C. Higham, *The Archaeology of Mainland Southeast Asia*, Cambridge, UK, 1989; and K. R. Hall, *Maritime Trade and State Development in Early Southeast Asia*, Honolulu, 1985.

An introduction to early Vietnamese history as far as the tenth century is K. W. Taylor, *The Birth of Vietnam*, Berkeley, 1983. For excellent discussions of methodological issues in reading early Vietnamese texts and of Vietnamese Buddhism, see O. W. Wolters, *Two Essays on Dai Viet in the Fourteenth Century*, New Haven, 1988. J. K. Whitmore, *Vietnam, Ho Quy Ly, and the Ming*, New Haven, 1985, is a study of the late fourteenth and early fifteenth centuries. There is no single scholarly treatment of early Vietnam in the English language; readers of French may consult Lê Thanh Khôi, *Le Viêt-Nam, Histoire et Civilisation*, Paris, 1955.

For Champa, J. Boisselier, *La Statuaire du Champa*, Paris, 1963, remains very useful. Cham inscriptions were studied by L. Finot in BEFEO, 4 (1904). Recent works of note on Cham studies are P. Y. Manguin, 'L'introduction de l'Islam au Campa', BEFEO, 66 (1979); D. Lombard, 'Le Campa vu du sud', BEFEO, 76 (1987); Po Dharma, *Le Panduranga (Campa) 1802–1835, ses rapports avec le Vietnam*, Paris, 1987; Centre d'Histoire et Civilisations de la Peninsule Indochinoise, *Actes du Seminaire sur le Campa organisé a l'University de Copenhague le 23 Mai 1987*, Paris, 1988; Po Dharma and P. D. LaFont, *Bibliographie Cam et Campa*, Paris, 1989, and Vien khoa hoc xa hoi thanh pho Ho Chi Minh, *Nguoi Cham o Thuan Hai*, Thuan Hai, 1989.

Any study of Angkor continues to rest upon the inscriptions, for which see G. Cœdès, *Inscriptions du Cambodge*, 6 vols, Hanoi, 1937–56. For an early synthesis, see L. P. Briggs, *The Ancient Khmer Empire*, Philadelphia,

1951. A brief narrative can be found in D. P. Chandler, *A History of Cambodia*, Westview, 1983. H. Kulke, *The Devaraja Cult*, Ithaca, 1978, advanced discussion of religion and politics at Angkor. E. Moran, 'Configuration of Time and Space at Angkor Wat', *Studies in Indo-Asian Art and Culture*, vol. 5 (1977), advanced understanding of the architectural features of Angkor Wat. Several articles by O. W. Wolters have proposed new ways of reading evidence, in particular 'Yayavarman II's Military Power: The Territorial Foundations of the Angkor Empire', JRAS, (1973), 'North-Western Cambodia in the Seventh Century', BSOAS, 37, 2 (1974), and 'Khmer "Hinduism" in the Seventh Century', in Smith and Watson, *Early South East Asia*. On Sūryavarman I, see M. T. Vickery, 'The Reign of Sūryavarman I and Royal Factionalism at Angkor', JSEAS, 16, 2 (1985). On the collapse of Angkor, see M. T. Vickery, 'Cambodia after Angkor, the Chronicular Evidence from the 14th to 16th centuries', Ph.D. thesis, Yale University, 1977.

For Pagan, most of the inscriptional evidence is available in G. H. Luce and Pe Maung Tin, *Inscriptions of Burma*, 5 vols, Rangoon, 1933–56. A classic introduction to Pagan studies is G. H. Luce, *Old Burma–Early Pagan*, 3 vols, New York, 1969–70. See P. J. Bennett, *Conference Under the Tamarind Tree: Three Essays in Burmese History*, New Haven, 1971, for discussions of the immediate post-Pagan period. For a stimulating synthesis of Pagan history based upon a model of interaction between ideology and economics, see Michael Aung-Thwin, *Pagan: The Origins of Modern Burma*, Honolulu, 1985.

For the early Tai kingdoms, one cannot do better than to consult D. K. Wyatt, *Thailand: A Short History*, New Haven, 1984.

On Śrīvijayan history, see O. W. Wolters, *Early Indonesian Commerce*, Ithaca, 1967, and *The Fall of Srivijaya in Malay History*, Ithaca, 1970. For a recent review of the state of Śrīvijayan scholarship, see O. W. Wolters, 'Restudying some Chinese Writings on Srivijaya', *Indonesia*, 42 (1986). On Śrīvijayan archaeology, see P. Y. Manguin, 'Étude Sumatranaise N. 1, Palembang et Srivijaya: ancien hypothese recherches nouvelles', BEFEO, 76 (1987).

For Javanese inscriptions see J. G. de Casparis, *Prasasti Indonesia II: Selected Inscriptions from the Seventh to the Ninth Century A.D.*, Bandung, 1956. On the Borobuḍur, see L. Gomez and H. W. Woodward, Jr, eds, *Barabudur: History and Significance of a Buddhist Monument*, Berkeley, 1981. Other important studies of early Java are J. G. de Casparis, 'Pour une histoire sociale de l'ancienne Java principale au Xème s.', *Archipel*, 21 (1981), and J. W. Christie, 'Raja and Rama: The Classical State in Early Java', in L. Gesick, ed., *Centers, Symbols, and Hierarchies: Essays on the Classical States of Southeast Asia*, New Haven, 1983. For Majapahit, see T. G. Th. Pigeaud, *Java in the Fourteenth Century*, 4 vols, Hague, 1962.

CHAPTER

4

# ECONOMIC HISTORY OF EARLY SOUTHEAST ASIA

In the pre-nineteenth-century world, the Southeast Asian region was eulogized as a land of immense wealth; developments there were of crucial importance to the entirety of world history in the pre-1600 period. Writers, travelers, sailors, merchants, and officials from every continent of the eastern hemisphere knew of Southeast Asia's wealth, and by the second millennium of the Christian era, most were aware of its power and prestige. By contrast, the early history of Southeast Asia and its international significance is not appreciated in the contemporary age.

In the early centuries CE Indians and Westerners called Southeast Asia the 'Golden Khersonese', the 'Land of Gold', and it was not long thereafter that the region became known for its pepper and the products of its rainforests, first aromatic woods and resins, and then the finest and rarest of spices.[1] From the seventh to the tenth centuries Arabs and Chinese thought of Southeast Asia's gold, as well as the spices that created it; by the fifteenth century sailors from ports on the Atlantic, at the opposite side of the hemisphere, would sail into unknown oceans in order to find these Spice Islands. They all knew that Southeast Asia was the spice capital of the world. From roughly 1000 CE until the nineteenth-century 'industrial age', all world trade was more or less governed by the ebb and flow of spices in and out of Southeast Asia.

Throughout these centuries the region and its products never lost their siren quality. Palm trees, gentle surf, wide beaches, steep mountain slopes covered with lush vegetation, birds and flowers of brilliant colours, as well as orange and golden tropical sunsets have enchanted its visitors as well as its own people through the ages. Indeed, it is said that when in the last years of the sixteenth century the first Dutch ship arrived at one of the islands of the Indonesian archipelago, the entire crew jumped ship, and it took their captain two years to gather them for the return trip to Holland.

[1] Paul Wheatley, *The Golden Khersonese: Studies in the Historical Geography of the Malay Peninsula before A.D. 1500*, Kuala Lumpur, 1959.

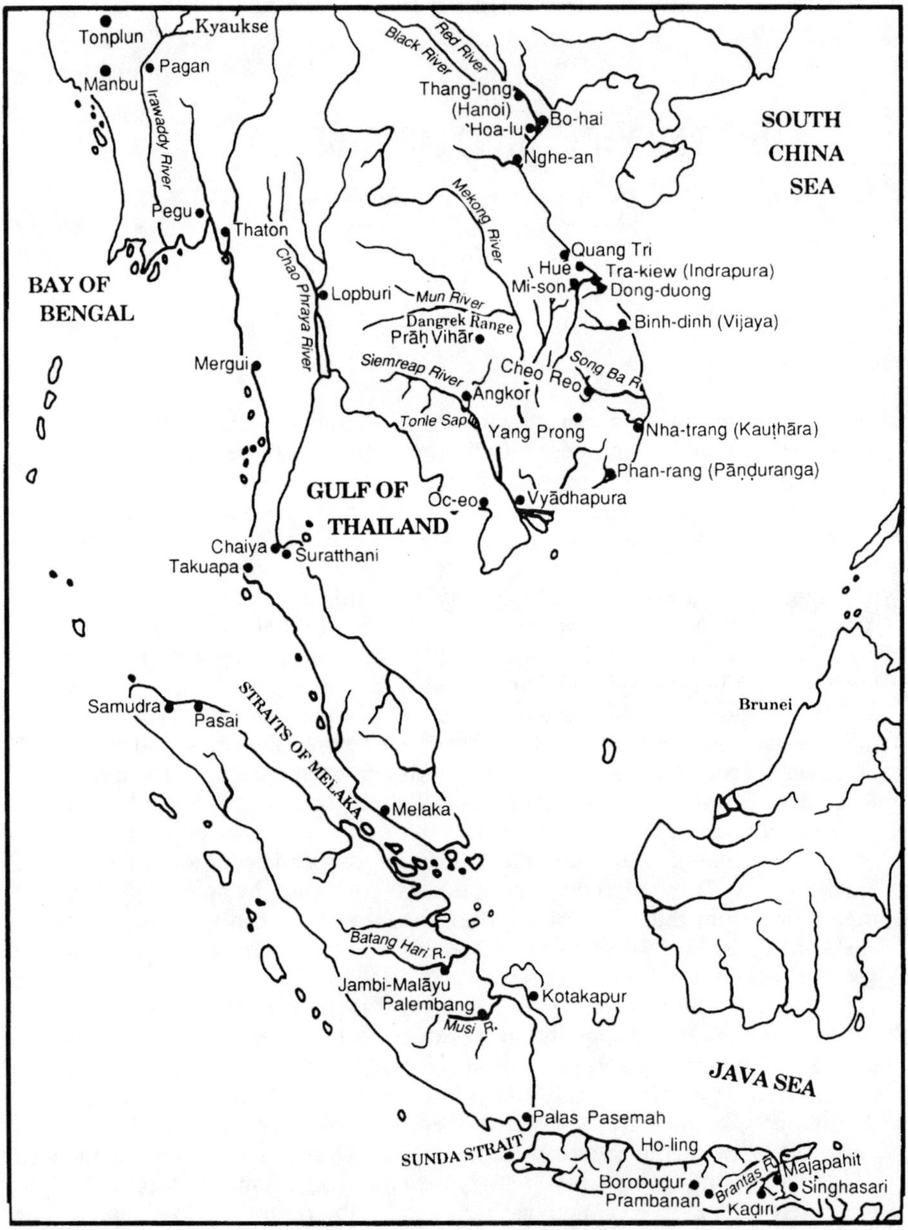


Map 4.1 Early economic centres.

## EARLY ECONOMIC DEVELOPMENT

The story of economic development in early Southeast Asia begins long before the Christian era. Southeast Asia had already been for centuries a region with a distinct cultural identity. By the early Christian era, Southeast Asia had skilled farmers, musicians, metallurgists, and mariners. Even though they had no written language, no large urban concentrations, and no bureaucratic 'states' of recognizable proportions, they were nevertheless a highly accomplished people who had already assumed a significant role in the cultural development of the southern oceans of the eastern hemisphere.

Their expertise was in three general areas. First, they were innovative farmers. It is possible that Southeast Asians were the first to domesticate rice and to develop wet-rice cultivation. Early archaeological data for rice culture, as early as 2000 BC, have come from Southeast Asian sites (notably northeastern Thailand), and archaeologists have found evidence of a rice plant that could be classified as an intermediate stage between wild and domesticated rice that has been dated to 3000 BC. But they were never a rice monoculture. In addition to rice, they also harvested a number of other crops, including sugarcane, yams, sago, bananas, and coconuts. And they apparently were among the first (if not the first) to domesticate the chicken and the pig.

It may be that Southeast Asians independently discovered bronze and developed their own sophisticated metallurgical techniques based on the special qualities of bamboo. Since the trunk of this plant grows in hollow segments, they were able to use it to fashion a fire-piston that produced the heat required to liquefy metal. Archaeologists have dated bronze objects uncovered in northeast Thailand to 1500 BC, and iron bracelets and spearheads to about 500 BC. By 200 BC many peoples in the region possessed a sophisticated metal technology that included bronze, brass, tin, and iron. Beautiful large bronze ceremonial drums from Dong-son (in modern Vietnam) could be found all over Southeast Asia. That these drums were so widely dispersed throughout the region is clear evidence that there existed an extensive and efficient exchange mechanism within the Southeast Asian world prior to any significant trade with imperial India or China.

Their third area of expertise, that of sailing, may explain in part how these drums, among other things, became so widely dispersed. The people of the maritime realm were the pioneers of early watercraft developed on the southern oceans. From before the historic period, they knew how to ride the monsoons, the seasonal winds that pulled on to the continent during the hot months of the Central Asian summer and pushed away during the cold Central Asian winter. This basic rhythm of the Central Asian bellows offered an opportunity that the seaborne nomads of Southeast Asia seized. They sailed thousands of kilometres from their homes, navigating by means of swell and wave patterns, cloud formations, winds, birds and sea life. This sophisticated and complex knowledge was passed orally from generation to generation. They measured their peoples by 'boatloads', and on the slightest pretext, boatloads would leave islands where they were already concentrated and sail off to set up new communities on uninhabited islands, so that these 'Malayo-Polynesian' peoples eventually stretched halfway around the globe, from Madagascar on the East African coast to Easter Island in the Pacific.

They were the nomads of the Southern Ocean, and they played a role in history that in some ways resembles that of the nomads of the northern steppe. They were prime movers in the links created between larger centres, as well as potential impediments to those links once they were created. Exactly when this far-reaching maritime activity began is unknown, but 'Malay' (*Kunlun*) sailors were known in China by the third century BC, and there is evidence that they were settling along the East African coast by the first century CE. By the time of the Roman empire, there were permanent communities of Malayo-Polynesian speaking peoples on the coast of Malagasy, where they remain to this day.[2]

The Malay sailors did not cover these routes empty-handed, and in the process of sailing across the thousands of kilometres of southern ocean from Africa to Easter Island, they moved the specialties of one place to others. Cinnamon, a product that originally came from the South China coast, may also have reached the markets of India on the vessels of these sailors, and the markets of Southwest Asia and the Mediterranean through Malay trading stations in East Africa. The Roman historian Pliny, writing in the first century CE, described cinnamon traders between Africa and Asia who rode the winds 'from gulf to gulf'. Pliny describes their craft as 'rafts'. What he was no doubt referring to was the double outrigger canoe of the Malays. This same craft is still used today along the routes that these ancient mariners sailed. The cinnamon they brought was then traded north by the Africans until it reached Ethiopia, where the Europeans obtained it.

Bananas, too, may have made this journey from Southeast Asia to India to Africa with the Malays, and then spread across the continent to West Africa along internal, overland trade routes. But it was not only food that made the journey. The tuning scales of the Malayo-Polynesian xylophone also spread over the African continent and can still be heard today in West Africa, more than halfway around the world from their islands of origin.

Since Malay sailors were known in China by the third century BC, it was probably not long after that that they began to sail through the Straits of Melaka (Malacca) and Sunda into the Indian Ocean and on to India; and thus it is quite possible that the Southeast Asians themselves were responsible for the earliest contacts between Southeast Asia and South Asia. Historians do not know exactly when the first Indian ships went to Southeast Asia, but many believe that it was sometime in the last two centuries BC. It has been suggested that during the Mauryan period India's supply of gold had come from Siberia, from the northern reaches of Central Asia, but that after the Mauryans had fallen, the movements of

[2] Keith W. Taylor, 'Madagascar in the Ancient Malayo-Polynesian Myths' in Kenneth R. Hall and John K. Whitmore, eds, *Explorations in Early Southeast Asian History, The Origins of Southeast Asian Statecraft*, Ann Arbor, 1976. On early Southeast Asian seamanship, see Pierre-Yves Manguin, 'The Southeast Asian Ship: An Historical Approach', JSEAS, 11, 2 (1980).

steppe nomads cut them off from these sources and forced them to look elsewhere. It was then, they think, that merchants from India began to sail into Southeast Asian waters, looking for the 'Islands of Gold'.[3]

The early Southeast Asian population shared a relatively common physical geography, wherein ample and readily available productive land was available to support the basic economic needs of the indigenous society. The exceptions were the several dry and infertile islands of the eastern Indonesian archipelago, like Timor and northern Maluku (the Moluccas). Southeast Asia had no substantial grasslands, no pastoral tradition, and thus low dependency upon animal protein; meat and milk products had little importance in the traditional diet. Houses were constructed from the seemingly inexhaustible local supply of wood, palm, and bamboo; they were usually elevated on poles above the annual floods of the lowlands, and human and animal predators in the highlands. The ease of building and rebuilding and the abundance of unoccupied fertile land meant that the population was inherently mobile. Indeed, the shortage of labour relative to land produced a social pattern in which additional labour rather than land became the object of competition.

Traditional household-based production in early Southeast Asia consisted of clearing woods, planting, weeding, harvesting, cooking, feeding pigs and chickens, and fishing. Men and women performed daily chores according to local tradition, but everyone participated in food production. As more stratified societies emerged, productive activities became more differentiated. Work was often assigned by local leaders ('big men/women', chiefs, or religious élites who tended to distance themselves from food production) to their social subordinates, as well as to prisoners of war and debt slaves. When states began to emerge there was a corresponding dissociation of a small or large group of state élite, inclusive of religious functionaries; courtiers; musicians, dancers, and dramatists; as well as craftsmen and traders.

Millet, or dry rice, was highly adaptable and predates Southeast Asian wet-rice as the staple grain. The late Roman-era geographer Ptolemy's reference to *Yāvadvīpa* probably equates with *Yawadvipa*, 'millet island'. But millet (dry) and *sawah* (wet) cultivation were incompatible; as *sawah* agriculture spread, millet production was displaced.[4]

Initially, millet probably was produced in the uplands, by means of what is commonly called 'slash-and-burn' or 'shifting' cultivation. Shifting cultivation of rice was ideal for sloping highland areas with adequate drainage. It required little labour, and was able to produce a substantial surplus relative to the size of the workforce. A new patch of forest was cleared and burned each year. Planting normally consisted of using pointed sticks to make holes, into which two or three grains were placed. Nutrients added to the soil in the initial burn-off were washed away by rain within two seasons, thus necessitating the shifting cultivation cycle. Slash-and-burn

[3] Paul Wheatley, *Nagara and Commandery: Origins of the Southeast Asian Urban Traditions*, Chicago, 1983.

[4] N. C. van Setten van der Meer, *Sawah Cultivation in Ancient Java: Aspects of Development during the Indo-Javanese Period, 5th to 15th Century*, Canberra, 1979; Paul Wheatley, 'Agricultural Terracing', *Pacific Viewpoint*, 6, 2 (1965).

regions could usually produce a stable food supply, but their populations were not usually as spatially confined as were their lowland neighbours. Fields, rivers, and lake productive centres might be some distance apart rather than coincident, thereby making their aggregate revenue potential less. Local migration cycles, together with the relatively low yield per hectare, limited highland population density to twenty to thirty persons per square kilometre, and made it difficult to collect surplus for urban development or for export.

Transition from upland shifting to settled lowland rice cultivation may have been induced by population pressure, but was more likely due to a supportive physical environment. It is generally believed that wet-rice cultivation was becoming common in the early Christian era, although surviving records can definitively substantiate only that wet-rice agriculture in permanent fields was practised in eastern Java and the Kyaukse area of Burma by the eighth century. On the mainland (Cambodia, Thailand, and Burma), seed was more commonly broadcast on a bunded and ploughed floodplain, and grew quickly and needed little work. In Java, however, the transplanting method came to be preferred; this gave higher yields per land used, though not the highest per labour input. By either the broadcast or seedling method, a Southeast Asian lowland wet-rice farmer could normally expect an annual output of twenty to twenty-five bushels of grain per acre. In early times one rice crop proved adequate to supply local needs, although a second could be harvested, if weather and irrigation facilities permitted and there were incentive to produce a surplus for external consumption.

On Java, seed was annually sown in small seedling beds at the approach of the rainy season. While seedlings took root, farmers and family prepared nearby fields; they weeded and broke up soil with wooden, stone, or metal-tipped hoes until the monsoon rains soaked the earth. Then seedlings were transplanted by hand, with enough space between for each plant to grow. As the crops matured, farmers repaired the local irrigation system and regulated the flow of water as rains reached their peak. As water receded, fields were drained, and the sun ripened the grain. At harvest, the entire community worked side-by-side. Javanese women harvested using a finger-knife that cut only one stalk at a time, rather than use a sickle, which might offend the local rice spirit and thus jeopardize future production. During the subsequent dry season, fields were cleared, tools repaired, and feasts, festivals, and marriages were celebrated.

*Sawah* cultivation was effectively maintained only where dissolved volcanic matter was brought into the fields with irrigated water, in rich alluvial plains, or where fertilizer (such as water-buffalo excrement) was added. Initial Southeast Asian wet-rice may have been cultivated without ploughs, but by the late first millennium CE water-buffaloes were being driven into the irrigated fields to make the land suitable for the reception of seeds or seedlings. Ploughing with wooden or metal-tipped ploughs puddled the flooded soil and turned it into a creamy mud; it also produced a dense layer of soil at a depth of 30–50 centimetres, which reduced the percolation of irrigated water. As the water-buffalo worked the fields, their droppings added to soil fertility.

In *sawah* regions there were three food staples: rice, fish, and coconut. Rice might be affected by periodic disease and plagues; mice plagues are shown in Borobuḍur and Angkor Wat reliefs. But fish (from rivers, tanks, or *sawah* fields) and coconut (when properly maintained) were virtually free of pests and diseases. Rice was eaten by preference. Reliance upon other staples was looked down upon except during rice famines when *sawah* cultivators could normally turn to tubers (taro, which grew in *sawah* areas) and yams (which were gathered from nearby forests or were grown in the rain-fed fields), as well as to sago palms, which were another stable source of starch. The three staples were supplemented by a wide variety of vegetables, pigs, and fowl that could not be stored. Properly prepared, rice and fish—which was usually dried or fermented and was the major garnish to rice—could be stored more than a year; coconuts (the source of fruit, sugar, oil and palm wine) could not be stored as long, but were available at three-month intervals.

*Sawah* agriculture could thus support a high population density and high yields from small areas—a field of one hectare (2½ acres) could well support a household. But large population centres in the early *sawah* regions were the exception. Small housing clusters (one house and one field, or several houses and nearby fields) were more practical for flooding and draining of the fields. Too much water flow would damage the dykes, while too little would result in algae growth. Rights to occupy and use land were characterized by long-term commitment to a soil plot.

Such a stable food source was ideal to feed non-food-producers, i.e. state functionaries and traders. There is thus a general coincidence of *sawah* cultivation and state development in early Southeast Asia. *Sawah* cultivators could occupy the same lands for generations; because they had little need to move, they were ideal producers of surplus. Taxing the early small and scattered productive units must have been a time-consuming task for emergent states, yet *sawah* cultivators could not easily escape their revenue cesses. Leaving their fields uncontrolled was not an option among *sawah* cultivators, except just after harvest, and developing new lands for cultivation (bunding, etc.) might take several seasons. But early armies and state bureaucratic corps were not large enough constantly to threaten *sawah* producers. Instead, would-be élites had to offer inducements, such as protection (although this was not always needed in areas where population centres were geographically isolated from their neighbours or foreigners, as in central Java, Angkor, and Pagan). More commonly material rewards (foreign luxury goods) or ideological rewards (titles, temples) were bestowed to secure food and labour from subordinate *sawah* cultivators.

Control of water was important in dry areas, but in regions where rainfall was plentiful, or where there were too many rivers useful for irrigation, an élite would have had to employ too many functionaries to control a water system. Even in eastern Java, where there was a stronger seasonality than western Java, water control as the basis of the indigenous agrarian system does not seem to have been a major factor, although rulers based in east Java did build hydraulic networks that gave them better control of agricultural production. One incentive to develop this control was the more significant position that long-distance trade assumed in the east Java economy, particularly the rice-based trade to the eastern Indonesian archipelago via the Solo and Brantas Rivers. In contrast, in central Java, overland transport from the Kedu plain heartland to north coast harbours was more difficult.

Early Southeast Asian trade involved highland hunters and gatherers who exchanged their forest products (woods, bamboo, lacquer) and services with lowland rice cultivators. Salt from the coast was a key commodity in this upland–lowland exchange. Another type of exchange network encompassed hinterland populations and coastal peoples; the hinterland supplied local agricultural or forest products that were in turn dispensed externally to international traders. Coastal-based traders returned goods of foreign origin or specialized services (for example, transport) to the hinterland producers. In exceptional cases merchants worked from a coastal base to organize the necessary trade mechanisms that allowed them to extract local products from their hinterlands. In normal trade, agricultural and imported commodities entered the markets and trading system either laterally, through direct barter between producers and consumers, or vertically, through political or religious institutions or developing hierarchical commercial networks, and only rarely through monetized commercial transaction.

As is the case today, women assumed a significant role in the local market systems. Chinese sources report that women were in charge of trade in Khmer territories as well as elsewhere in the region.[5] While males normally dominated port-based and large-scale wholesale trade, there are counter examples. The most notable is that of Nyai Gede Pinateh, a Muslim from Palembang, China, or the Khmer realm who was the harbour master (*syahbandar*) of the major port of Gresik on the north Java coast around 1500; between 1405 and 1434, two queens ruled over Pasai just before Melaka eclipsed the Sumatra coast port as the paramount port of trade in the Straits of Melaka.[6]

Because land was plentiful in the Southeast Asian region, and additional labour was always in demand, women enjoyed a high degree of economic and social status—certainly by contrast with the low economic and social status of Chinese and Indian women. Our ability precisely to define the role of women in early Southeast Asian society is clouded by the epigraphic records that were preponderantly recorded on Indic temples, and were initiated by an élite who were emulating Indic culture. True to the Indian epics and religions that promoted male superiority and female dependency, there are infrequent references to women, and the inscriptional vocabulary is male or universal generic. A discrepancy between court ideal and reality is conspicuous in contemporary temple reliefs that portray everyday life, wherein females are participants in scenes that involve not only agriculture and home, but also market, trade, diplomacy, warfare, entertainment, literature, and even statecraft.

5 Paul Pelliot, *Mémoires sur les coutumes du Cambodge de Tcheou Ta-Kouan*, Paris, 1951, 20; and J. V. G. Mills, *Ying-yai Sheng-lan of Ma Huan* (1433), Cambridge, 1970, 104.

6 M. A. P. Meilink-Roelofsz, *Asian Trade and European Influence in the Indonesian Archipelago between 1500 and about 1630*, The Hague, 1962, 108.

In everyday life, male work included ploughing, felling trees, hunting, metalwork, house building, statecraft, and formal (Indic or Sinic-based) religion; females transplanted, harvested, grew vegetables, prepared food, wove cloth, made pottery, and marketed local produce. Because of their control over birth and crop growth, women were believed to have magical powers relative to fertility. Women were deemed to have special capacity to mediate between mankind and the spirit world, and were called upon to heal the sick, and to change unfavourable weather conditions.

A common feature of the early Southeast Asian socio-economy was the practice of bilateral kinship. In determining inheritance, for instance, equal value was accorded the maternal and paternal lines, and sons and daughters usually received equal rights to their parents' estates (including land). The value of daughters was never questioned in early Southeast Asia. Bride wealth passed from male to female at marriage (the reverse of the European dowry custom), and it was normal practice for a married couple to reside with the family of the bride. Contemporary iconography as well as the earliest literary records portray the marriage ritual as involving the escort of the male, with his bride price, to the residence of the female for the marriage ceremony. Should the husband leave his wife, the bridal wealth, as well as their mutual resources (including their land), remained in her possession. From the perspective of the woman's family an absent husband created no substantial hardship, as the abandoned wife and children were quickly assimilated into the family work unit.

While the conjugal relationship tended to be strong, and the woman's predominance in the family gave her a major sense of responsibility for its survival, divorce was relatively easy. The Chinese envoy Chou Ta-kuan, reporting daily life in the Khmer realm around 1300, writes, 'If the husband is called away for more than ten days, the wife is apt to say, "I am not a spirit; how am I supposed to sleep alone?"'[7] Another display of the power and autonomy of women was the widespread practice among men of painful surgical implants of penis balls to enhance the sexual pleasure of their women. For example, two fifteenth-century temples near modern Surakarta in Java display lingas with three or four small ball implants.[8] The Chinese Muslim Ma Huan (1433) provides the earliest written record, reporting that among the Thai:

> when a man attained his twentieth year, they take the skin which surrounds the *membrum virile*, and with a fine knife . . . they open it up and insert a dozen tin beads inside the skin; they close it up and protect it with medicinal herbs . . . The beads look like a cluster of grapes . . . If it is the king . . . or a great chief or a wealthy man, they use gold to make hollow beads, inside which a grain of sand is placed . . . They make a tinkling sound, and this is regarded as beautiful.[9]

In the Khmer state, inheritance of the throne of the Angkor-based realm has been shown to be neither patrilocal nor matrilocal. Although males held monarchical authority, when they assumed power they would record

[7] Chou Ta-kuan (1297) in Pelliot, *Mémoires*, 17.
[8] W. I. Stutterheim, *Gids voor de oudheden van Soekoeh en Tjeta*, Surakarta, 1930, 31.
[9] Ma Huan (1433) in Mills, 104.

their official descent from either their father's or their mother's family, dependent upon which genealogical faction was most critical to their successful acquisition of the throne. With considerable royal polygamy, wherein marital alliances to regionally-powerful families were an important source of political stability, there were numerous offspring who might step forward to assert their claims of rightful descent, backed by their armed maternal relatives. That this was the case is documented in the frequent epigraphic references to the female links of Khmer monarchs, and corresponding failure in such cases to mention the male lineage.[10]

## THE AGE OF FU-NAN: THE EMERGENCE OF THE SOUTHEAST ASIAN POLITICAL-ECONOMY IN THE EARLY CHRISTIAN ERA

The first known polity to emerge in Southeast Asia was a place the Chinese called Fu-nan. Its seaport at the present-day town called Oc-eo, was originally located in the Mekong River delta in what is now Vietnam, very near the Cambodian border, at the point where the Gulf of Thailand coast recedes closest to the river. Its capital Vyādapura was near Ba Phnom in what is now Prei Veng Province, Cambodia. Although Fu-nan's date of origin is obscure, it is usually dated from the first century CE. During this century there was an unprecedented Roman market for Asian goods, especially Chinese silk, and, most importantly, the enhancement of a maritime route between India and China that passed through Southeast Asia.

That this first Southeast Asian polity emerged several hundred kilometres north of Java and the straits region was due to the fact that prior to about 350 CE the international traffic between India and China avoided the trip around the 1600-kilometre length of the Malay peninsula. Travellers on their way to China ended their voyage around the Bay of Bengal at the Isthmus of Kra, the peninsula's narrowest point, and moved their goods overland to the Gulf of Thailand where their maritime journey resumed.

Although it might seem strange at first glance that Fu-nan emerged on the eastern shore of the Gulf of Thailand, on the opposite shore from the Kra and the portage, there was a most important reason. What distinguished Fu-nan's site from a number of other small coastal enclaves around the Gulf of Thailand was its agricultural productivity. The area around Oc-eo is the only place near the coast west of the Mekong where a particular kind of topography and soil enabled its people to grow significant amounts of rice with the existing pre-canal irrigation wet-rice methods of cultivation—they used the natural flooding of the river to water their rice fields. The ability to amass ample amounts of rice and other foodstuffs for themselves as well as for those who arrived on the ships gave them a

[10] A. Thomas Kirsch, 'Kinship, Genealogical Claims, and Societal Integration in Ancient Khmer Society: An Interpretation', in C. D. Cowan and O. W. Wolters, eds., *Southeast Asian History and Historiography*, Ithaca, 1976, 190–202. I have found similar bilateral succession patterns among the rulers of Śailendra-era Java. See Kenneth R. Hall, *Maritime Trade and State Development in Early Southeast Asia*, Honolulu, 1985, 110–11.

crucial advantage over would-be coastal entrepôts on the gulf that did not have such productive hinterlands.

But it was not simply the feeding of passers-by that made rice important. Oc-eo was nestled on a coastline that offered sailors protection from the troubled seas at the tip of southern Vietnam. Because of the winds, the travellers could not simply pass through. For half the year, when the winds blew off the continent, one could sail to Southeast Asian ports from either China or India. But one could not go on to either one until the winds had shifted and begun to blow toward the continent. Thus, the ships all tended to arrive at the same time and leave at the same time, regardless of which way the travellers were going. Indeed, their arrivals and departures became so predictable that the local people began to call them 'the migratory birds'. Furthermore, they were often obliged to remain in port, sometimes for as long as five months, waiting for the winds to shift. This meant that the Southeast Asian port often had to feed the travellers for months on end. It was this reality that ensured that a port's access to agricultural surpluses was one of the most important variables in its success.

Given the number of travellers coming from India and the length of time they were in port, it is not surprising that a cultural dialogue of profound importance to Southeast Asia generally developed between Fu-nan and India. The local explanation and legitimation of this dialogue are found in a legend that was already old when Chinese visitors recorded it in the 240s CE. According to this legend, the process began when a local princess (whom the Chinese called Lin-yeh) led a raid on a passing ship of unspecified nationality. The ship's passengers and crew managed to defeat the raiders and make a landing. One of the passengers was Kauṇḍinya, an Indian brahmin. And Lin-yeh subsequently married him, after he drank of the local waters. Thereafter Fu-nan set about to attract merchant ships by providing facilities and harbour improvements. The couple inherited the realm, which consisted of several settlements principally along the Mekong, each with its own local chief. Seven of these they transferred to the realm of their son, and the rest they retained as their own domain.

One cannot take legends of this sort too literally. There was already an ancient myth among the Malayo-Polynesian peoples that described a marriage between a sky-god and a foam-born princess (or sometimes a princess born from a bamboo shoot), and this story seems to be an updated version of that legend. There may never have been such a marriage. What this myth explains is that the rulers of Fu-nan began a cultural dialogue with India, and that the political integration of larger domains was contemporary with this dialogue.

It is important to note that the Malay princess married this foreigner and thus established for him a place within local society, and that he 'drank the waters', which suggests that he took an oath of loyalty to the local ruler, i.e. he entered his service, or that he in some way assisted in the development of the local wet-rice agriculture system. There is also an important moral to this story, that good things come not from attacking and plundering passing ships, but from befriending and servicing them.

Such a legend might also have been useful in maintaining good relations with both Indian traders and religious pilgrims, since it emphasized a friendly link between local rulers and Indian brahmins. It might also have been used to legitimize Fu-nan's expansion. Chinese accounts report that by the beginning of the third century, Fu-nan had conquered the entire northern rim of the gulf, all the way from the Mekong delta to the Isthmus of Kra, and a legend that claimed a special, Indian origin for its rulers would have been useful in distinguishing it from those it subordinated.

By the second or third century CE, Fu-nan was both rich and powerful, and foreign visitors were numerous. Not only were there Indians and Chinese, but by the third century Persian Gulf sailors from the Sassanid empire in Persia could also be found in Fu-nan. The third-century Chinese visitors, Kang Tai and Zhu Ying, were impressed and reported back to their ruler that the people of Fu-nan

> live in walled cities, palaces, and houses. . . . They devote themselves to agriculture. In one year they sow and harvest for three [i.e., they leave it in and it will grow back three years before they have to replant]. [Customs] taxes are paid in gold, silver, pearls, and perfumes . . . There are books and depositories of archives and other things. Their characters for writing resemble those of the Hu [a people whose alphabet was of Indian origin].[11]

Fu-nan was also importing goods brought to it by Malay sailors from other Southeast Asian ports. Copper and tin were transported downriver from the uplands of modern Thailand to supply the workshops of Oc-eo in Fu-nan, where, according to the results of excavations, there was no lack of raw materials.[12]

Fu-nan appears to have reached the peak of its fortunes sometime in the fourth century, prior to the instigation of a competitive, all-sea route from India to China that went through the Straits of Melaka. Although Fa Xian's early-fifth-century account is the earliest record of a traveller going through the straits region and laying over in the northwestern Indonesian archipelago for five months, he makes it clear that the route was not new when he took it; historians have dated this new route to China to about 350 CE.

Even during the time of Fu-nan's best years there had been a number of ports in the Sunda Strait region, east of the Straits of Melaka, that had already assumed some importance, and sailors from these ports had frequented the ports of Fu-nan. They were also engaged in a direct trade with India. The third-century visitors from China heard, for example, that in 'Zhiaying' (on the southeastern coast of Sumatra) there was a king who imported horses from the Yuezhi (the Kushana realm of northwestern India) and that in 'Sitiao' (central Java), there was a fertile land that possessed cities with streets.[13] Sanskrit inscriptions carved in stone on the east coast and Hindu and Buddhist archaeological remains on the west coast of Borneo indicate that ports there, too, were already engaged in a dialogue with India.

[11] Quoted in P. Pelliot, 'Le Fou-nan', BEFEO, 3 (1903) 252.
[12] O. W. Wolters, *Early Indonesian Commerce: A Study of the Origins of Sri Vijaya*, Ithaca, 1967, 52.
[13] ibid., 62–61.

These southern sailors had also played a large part in the introduction of Southeast Asian products to the international markets. Originally neither the Indians nor the international traders using the ports of Fu-nan were interested in Southeast Asian specialties. The traders at Fu-nan went to China in order to exchange Mediterranean, Indian, Middle Eastern, and African goods (items such as frankincense and myrrh, other plant resins, and other substances used to manufacture perfumes and incense) for China's silk. But, given the opportunity that the presence of the international transit trade at Fu-nan created, sailors from the Sunda Strait area responded with entrepreneurial skill and began to introduce their own products, beginning with those that might be construed as substitutes for products destined for the China market. Sumatran pine resins were substituted for frankincense, and benzoin (a resin from a plant related to the laurel family, also known as benjamin gum) was substituted for bdellium myrrh.

But it was not long before the sailors from the western Indonesian archipelago introduced their own unique products to the ports of Fu-nan and India. One of the most important was camphor, a resin that crystallized in wood and that was valued as a medicine, as incense, and as an ingredient in varnish. Throughout the ages the most highly prized camphor has been that of Barus, a port on Sumatra's northwestern coast. Aromatic woods such as gharuwood and sandalwood (a specialty of Timor) became important commodities, and the fine spices of Maluku also began to appear in international markets at this time. Charaka, who is believed to have been the court physician of the northwest Indian monarch Kaṇishka at the end of the first century CE, mentions in his medical text cloves, for example, as does one of the plays written by the Gupta court poet Kālidāsa, which was more or less contemporary with Fa Xian's travels.[14]

As long as the sailors from the ports near the straits brought their goods that were destined for the China market into Fu-nan's ports, they were no threat to the interests of Fu-nan. However, by the fourth century CE they had begun to bypass Fu-nan and were taking their products directly to China; if they stopped at any ports on the way, they were not those of Fu-nan but ports on the eastern coast of Vietnam. 'Malay' sailors had for centuries known the way to China, and once the Chinese market for their products made it worth their while to make the trip, they went. They could bring back goods from China to their own ports and could, furthermore, pass these along to Western marketplaces via their own Sunda Strait entrepôt.

During the fifth century, due to disturbances on the overland caravan routes still used by the majority of the silk traders, the maritime route became even more significant. And although some of the increased traffic still used the ports of Fu-nan, it was the ports of the Sunda Strait region that were the primary beneficiaries.[15]

After the fall of the Han dynasty in the third century CE, China was divided; and in the fourth century northern China was overrun by nomadic steppe peoples. This caused a massive flight of population from the north

[14] ibid., 66.
[15] O. W. Wolters, 'Studying Srivijaya', JMBRAS, 52, 2 (1979).

to the south. Since those who could afford to relocate were usually the more privileged, this group predominated among the refugees. Some historians claim that as many as 60 to 70 per cent of the northern upper classes moved south of the Yangtze River. These people had well-established tastes for the products that came from the West—from India, Southwestern Asia, the eastern Mediterranean, and the East African coast.

Prior to 439 this southern market had been supplied, for the most part, by the overland routes. Goods had continued to come overland through northern China to the south even after the fall of the Han dynasty and the steppe invasion. However, after 439, this source of foreign products was completely blocked when the Gansu corridor, the major road from China's population centres to the western boundaries, was captured by a hostile northern kingdom, and Chinese in the south for the first time were completely cut off from what they called 'the western regions'.

South China, however, did not wither on the vine. On the contrary, it witnessed an unprecedented commercial development. It could be defended more easily than the northern plains, since its rice paddies inhibited horse-riding steppe invaders, and it became the seat of two successful Buddhist kingdoms, the Liu Sung dynasty (420–79) and the Southern Qi (Nan Ch'i) (479–502). This China market was irresistible, and the seamen of the Sunda Strait region rose to the challenge, picking up the goods from the West in India and Sri Lanka, bringing them through Southeast Asia and then delivering them to this southern Chinese market.

These southern Chinese, too, developed a desire for Southeast Asian products, and not only for the resins and aromatic woods of the rainforest. China became an inexhaustible market for rhinoceros horn which was used as a tonic in China, guaranteed to overcome the male fear of sexual inadequacy in middle and old age, and as a bedroom charm in Japan. The Chinese also became important purchasers of kingfish and other bird feathers, as well as tortoiseshell, among other exotic things. And, by the late fifth or early sixth century, Chinese consumers were well acquainted with pepper and other spices, including cloves, nutmeg, and mace, items that they valued not only for their flavour, but for their medicinal properties as well.

The competition from the south, from the seamen of the ports of the Sunda Strait region, eventually deprived Fu-nan of its predominance in the international trade, and by the sixth century its realm was contracting. Its vulnerability was exposed in the middle of the sixth century when it was taken over by Zhenla, a name given by the Chinese to the Khmer people who lived along the middle reaches of the Mekong River. Although some traders continued to use the Kra portage, its special position was gone.

## THE AGE OF THE ŚRĪVIJAYAN MARITIME EMPIRE (670–1025)

Among the most significant factors in the rise of the Melaka-Sunda Strait region as the pre-eminent Southeast Asian maritime trade centre was its rulers' political acumen: their ability both to consolidate their own Sumatran hinterland and to dominate rival ports and thus indirectly their hinterlands. This control enabled the emergent Śrīvijaya polity to concentrate the agricultural, forest, and ocean products of the Indonesian archipelago in its own ports, both those goods that came by sea from neighbouring islands in relatively small ships carrying some twenty-five to fifty people, and those goods that moved downriver by way of mountain trails and the tributaries of Sumatra rivers. The creation of this realm was a political feat achieved not simply by force but, of equal importance, by the adroit merging of both local Malay and imported and adapted Buddhist symbols of power and authority.

The founders and rulers of the Śrīvijayan realm were local Malay chiefs who ruled the port area that the Chinese Buddhist pilgrim I Ching visited in the latter part of the seventh century on his return voyage from India, now generally accepted to have been at or near the modern city of Palembang, a port city in southeastern Sumatra.[16] It was this area that became the core of Śrīvijayan hegemony. In the traditional Malay view of the world there was a powerful duality, a landscape dominated by high and steep mountains and seas whose horizons seemed unreachable. Both the mountain heights and the depths of the sea were the loci of powerful forces that shaped the lives of the people, forces that were both generous and devastating. The same volcanoes that provided the most fertile land could and did on occasion destroy the villages that grew up on them. The sea, too, was a bountiful provider and a major means of communication, but its storms could also destroy the lives and livelihood of those dependent upon it.

In traditional Malay belief, both the source of the river waters and the home of the ancestral spirits were high on the mountain slopes; the highest reaches of the mountains were thus thought of as holy places and the source of beneficent forces that bestowed well-being upon the people. The Śrīvijayan king drew upon these beliefs as he took the title 'Lord of the Mountain'. He was also 'Lord of the Isles', and able to commune with the 'Spirit of the Waters of the Sea', a dangerous force that had to be propitiated and whose powers had to be absorbed by the king. It was for this purpose that the king blithely threw gold bricks daily into the Palembang estuary.

The critical link between these two forces of mountain and sea were the rivers, for they were the channels through which the rainwater that fell on the mountains flowed down, ultimately to merge with the sea. These river basins contained the earliest polities of island Southeast Asia, and shaped the political dynamic between them. The king's magical powers, closely associated with fertility, were also linked with the river. The magic of the association between the king and the water was so strong that it was dangerous for the king to bathe in ordinary water for fear of causing a flood. His bath water had to be treated with flower petals before it was safe. And there were other fertility taboos. On a specific day each year the

[16] E. Edward McKinnon, 'A Note on the Discovery of Spur-Marked Yueh-Type Sherds at Bukit Seguntang Palembang', JMBRAS, 52, 2 (1979) 35.

king could not eat grain. If he did, there might be a crop failure. Nor was he able to leave his realm, for if he did, the sun's rays might go with him, the skies would darken, and the crops would fail.

Palembang's significance as a port probably dates back to the prehistoric period when the metal culture of the mainland was spread about by the Malay sailors from the more easterly islands.[17] Sailors moving down the 1600-kilometre length of the Malay peninsula to the islands would have found both Palembang on the Musi and Jambi-Malāyu on the Batang Hari River were near the tip of the peninsula. As river-mouth ports, they offered the sailors access not only to those people who lived near the coast but indirectly to Sumatra's sizeable hinterland and to all those who lived along the banks of these two rivers' many tributaries. Thus, both of these ports probably began as small trading centres near the mouths of rivers that linked the peoples of the mountains with the sailors of the seas. There the sailors could exchange their goods, including metals, for the produce of the island.

When the international trade began to grow between the Fu-nan region and India sometime around the first century CE, these Sumatran ports emerged as small political centres that concentrated the resources of their river's drainage basin near the coast in order to attract traders. They could then use imported goods to enhance their own resources and as gifts or trade goods to be exchanged for the products of their hinterland. Since the maritime realm of Southeast Asia possessed many river systems that were separated by mountains, this dynamic led to the creation of many small riverine polities based at their mouths. These coastal centres tended to look back toward the mountains and forward to the sea, but they did not look kindly to their sides; they saw their neighbouring river systems as rivals and enemies. And some of them by about 350 CE had already begun their dialogue with Indian culture.

For centuries there had been many independent ports and polities in the southern maritime realm, but in the early part of the seventh century, one of them, Śrīvijaya, emerged victorious in a contest to dominate the others and thus become the core of an emergent state system. Why it was the local ruler of Palembang who became the paramount power in the region is not immediately apparent. Although its location about halfway between the Straits of Melaka and the Sunda Strait was significant, there were a number of other ports that enjoyed locations with similar advantages. Nor was either of the two major southeastern Sumatran ports, Palembang and its chief rival Jambi-Malāyu, located near those places that produced the items most desired by international traders. Camphor, the Sumatran forest product most sought after in this early period, came from more northern and western parts of the island. Although some pepper was locally grown, it was also a product of west Java across the Sunda Strait. Sandalwood, another product popular from the earliest period, came from Timor, which was about 2500 kilometres to Sumatra's east. The cloves, nutmeg, and mace that would eventually become the maritime realm's most famous

[17] R. B. Smith and W. Watson, eds, *Early South East Asia: Essays in Archaeology, History and Historical Geography*, London, 1976.

products came from other islands that were equally far away to the east.

Further, archaeological data currently available indicate a general absence of intensive rice cultivation near the early Sumatran ports. Unlike Java, where centres of power were in the vicinity of production centres, Sumatra's early downriver ports depended upon less direct means of collecting food and upland products. Unless food was imported from Java, which seems unlikely until later times when the volume of trade increased substantially, early Sumatra entrepôts would have drawn upon lower river basin deep-water rice (*lebak*) and tidal irrigated rice (*pasang surut*) to feed transients. Palembang's hinterland consisted of the Pasemah Highlands and the upper Musi, areas well-known today for their rice and very similar in natural conditions to Java's wet-rice areas; volcanic activity in these regions supplied fertile material for rice cultivation. Megalithic archaeological remains in south Sumatra come from Pasemah in what are now ricelands. One carved stone depicts a man riding on an elephant and carrying a drum of the Dong-son type. Such a stone monument, or at least its inspiration, may have been a present to Pasemah populations in return for their products. Bronze bowls and bells found in the same area suggest early foreign relations and downriver contacts. Similarly, in the Jambi-Malāyu upriver heartland, stone sculptures of the early Christian era depict male figures standing on somebody, a traditional Indonesian symbol of power, which would also indicate downriver contact.[18]

There were, no doubt, numerous factors that accounted for Palembang's victory over its rivals, but one of them probably was the agricultural productivity of the fields in the valleys of the Musi River and its tributaries. Although none of the river-mouth ports of the island realm had agricultural resources comparable to those of Fu-nan in the Mekong delta, Palembang did have the unusually wide, slow, and silt-rich Musi River behind it, a better agricultural base than any of its competitors had. A local legend claimed that civilization was founded at Palembang only after the waters of the various rivers were weighed, and it was determined that those of the Musi were heaviest. Obviously its founders were searching for a silt-laden river that could be depended upon continually to deposit the fertile silt on fields adjacent to the river. Today, the best rice land in the area is quite near modern Palembang, at Bukit Seguntang. It is on and around this hill that some of the richest finds of archaeological remains from the Śrīvijayan period have been made, and this hill appears to have been the location of the ceremonial centre described in the account of I Ching where 1000 priests resided and where gold and silver Buddhas were offered golden vessels shaped like lotus flowers. These bowls were known to be a specialty of Śrīvijaya, and as late as 1082 there is a Chinese record of Śrīvijayan envoys bringing lotus bowls filled with pearls and other precious objects as presents for the Sung emperor.[19]

Palembang also offered a fine natural harbour and a river that was

[18] F. M. Schnitger, *The Archeology of Hindoo Sumatra*, Leiden, 1937.

[19] Recent aerial photographic surveys of the Palembang region surrounding Bukit Seguntang reveal the existence of earth dock networks which substantiate that the Bukit Seguntang area was the centre of early commerce. Hermann Kulke and Pierre-Yves Manguin have graciously shared this information.

navigable for long distances. Even in the nineteenth century, the largest ocean-going steamers had no difficulty in reaching the city, which is 80 kilometres inland from the mouth of the Musi. Even above Palembang the river and its tributaries remain navigable by small boats for many miles. This gave the Palembang area unusually good access to the Sumatran hinterland and the island's valuable forest products.

In terms of indigenous understanding, the initial motivation for conquest most likely emerged from internal Malay politics, an attempt to unite the surrounding Malay peoples, and not necessarily from a desire to control the straits. The earliest image we have of the Śrīvijayan founder comes from a stone inscription dated 683 CE. What is revealed is a traditional Sumatran war chief, a local ruler who after assembling the surrounding chiefs and their forces, selected from 20,000 a force of 2000 men, which he led against Jambi-Malāyu, the rival to the north and the only other important river system on this strategic coast. Śrīvijaya defeated its rivals; the ruler had proved himself in battle, and thus he could claim in this inscription to possess supernatural power that allowed him to bestow prosperity upon his new subjects.

> The king expressed his concern that all the clearances and gardens made by them [his subjects] should be full [of crops]. That the cattle of all species raised by them and the bondsmen they possess should prosper . . . that all their servants shall be faithful and devoted to them . . . that, wherever they may find themselves, there be in that place no thieves, no ruffians and no adulterers . . . that there arise among them the thought of Bodhi [wisdom] and the love of the 'Three Jewels' [the Buddha, the Doctrines, and the monkhood].[20]

I Ching's account of Śrīvijaya suggests that Palembang's subjugation of Jambi-Malāyu and thus the Batang Hari River system occurred between 671 and 685 CE.

The realm that Śrīvijaya ultimately commanded can be divided into three parts: the core area around Palembang; its Musi River hinterland, upriver and downriver; and those river-mouth ports and their hinterlands that had previously been its rivals. In each of these three parts, the manner in which they ruled was somewhat different. The urban core centred at Palembang was directly administered by the monarch and his family. The monarch was assisted by royal judges, revenue collectors, land administrators, and various other officials. The king referred to the cultivators of the royal domain as 'my bondsmen', and they were also the nucleus of his imperial army.

The second part of the empire, the Musi River hinterland, was ruled by more indirect means, through alliances with local chiefs who swore allegiance to the kings at the Palembang core. This relationship between the royal centre and its upriver and downriver hinterland was based on what was in reality a mutual self-interest. These relationships had to be consolidated and could not be neglected or abused, for it did sometimes happen that peoples in the hinterland took over river-mouth ports and made them their own. The relationship between coast and hinterland was crucial since it was necessary to maintain the downriver flow of manpower

[20] Quoted in Hall, *Maritime Trade*, 163.

(with its military implications), agricultural resources (which could provision the port), and forest products such as the resins that were exported overseas, in order to uphold the royal centre's special position.

Although Śrīvijaya was not reluctant to use military means when it had to, it more often secured hinterland alliances through the offering of benefits, material and spiritual, to all who attached themselves to its centre. In return for their loyalty and their products, the leaders of these upriver and downriver populations received redistributions of wealth and provision of goods derived from the trade route, as well as the prestige and the reflected power of the Śrīvijayan centre. And the king's Buddhist advisers also played a strategic role in the hinterland. The king sent them out from the centre to make periodic contact with the local élite; to encourage them to hold local religious ceremonies and social pageantry that honoured both the king and the Buddhist faith; and to persuade them to participate in the royal cults at the centre, where public and religious edifices proliferated, and where oath-taking ceremonies were held.

At the same time that the Śrīvijayan centre offered benefits, it also resorted to traditional oaths and threats of dire consequences to those who broke them. One of the stone inscriptions found in the Śrīvijayan hinterland combined the traditional Malay water oath with Buddhist images of power. On the upper edge of the stone was a seven-headed snake, an Indian motif that evokes the cobra as protector of the Lord Buddha. This image may have been particularly effective in the Malay world, since Malay rulers, too, prior to any Buddhist presence, invoked the power of snakes to protect themselves and their realms. Below the snake was an oath of loyalty to the king, and below the oath was a funnel. During the oath-taking ceremony, water was poured over the snakes and the oath, and then drained out through the funnel. The water must have been drunk by the oath-takers, for the text said, in part, that anyone who was insincere in the oath would be killed by the water he drank (literally, his insides would rot). On the other hand, if the oath-taker remained faithful, he would receive not only a secret formula for the final (Buddhist) liberation of his soul, but also the pledge, 'You will not be swallowed with your children and wives', a reference either to snakes, which it was believed could swallow men, or to the possibility of being swallowed up by flood waters.[21]

In dealing with the third part of the Śrīvijayan realm, the other river-mouth ports and their hinterlands, the element of force played a much larger role. Although Indian-inspired formalities and techniques were employed and material advantages were shared, the crucial element in Śrīvijaya's control was force. Arab accounts claim that the Śrīvijayan monarch had bewitched the crocodiles in order to ensure safe navigation into the realm's ports, but the truth of the matter was that they had bewitched the sea nomads of the straits region.

During the heyday of Fu-nan, foreign sailors had feared Śrīvijaya's waters. Strong currents and hidden rocks and shoals made the straits area dangerous, and so did these sea nomads. They often engaged in piracy

[21] ibid., 166.

and preyed upon any merchant ship that happened to come their way. The Śrīvijayan monarchs, unable to suppress these nomads, essentially bought them out. The kings made an agreement with some of them that in return for a portion of the port's revenues, they would not raid the ships at sea. The kings could also use their seaborne allies to patrol the local waters and ensure the safe movement of trading vessels. They could also enlist their services as peaceful carriers in the trade. But in order to succeed in this manoeuvre, the kings had to have sufficient trade goods and revenues to make it worth the sailors' while, which meant that they had to attract a steady stream of foreign traders into their ports. If their ability to provide on a regular basis were ever to decline, the sailors could strike new alliances with rival ports, or revert to piracy. Śrīvijaya's rulers depended upon this navy in order to ensure Palembang's predominance and its development as the major international port and the central treasury for the entire realm.

Śrīvijaya's power overseas was also marked by monasteries patronized by its kings and by inscriptions. One 775 CE inscription on the east coast of the Malay peninsula commemorated the dedication by a Śrīvijayan king of a Buddhist monastery at the site, and also referred to the king as 'the patron of the snakes', a more traditional image of power. Śrīvijayan inscriptions with Buddhist elements can also be found at various strategic points along the Sumatran coast, including two places that overlook the Sunda Strait between Sumatra and Java.

Śrīvijaya's success was, no doubt, related to its good location on a major international trade route, its fine harbour, its 'heavy' and navigable river, and the political and economic talents of its rulers. But it may well be that the most important secret in Śrīvijaya's success was something not yet discussed: its curious relationship with the Buddhist Śailendras, a royal lineage located well outside Śrīvijaya's realm in central Java. Not only did the royal family of Śrīvijaya intermarry with the Śailendras; for public purposes, especially in India, they seem to have preferred to emphasize their descent from the Javanese lineage, rather than their more powerful Sumatran ancestors.

The marriage between the two was certainly convenient. During the days of Śrīvijaya, central Java was the most productive rice bowl in the island realm, and Śrīvijaya's ability to control the international trade that was crucial to its power was dependent upon its ability to provision the ships and feed the travellers who remained in its ports while waiting on the winds. While it is most likely that Palembang's agricultural resources were superior to those of any other river-mouth port within its realm, it is unlikely that they were equal to this task. Thus, any picture of Śrīvijaya would be incomplete without a view of the temple realm of central Java, the realm to which the Śailendras belonged.

## THE TEMPLE REALM OF CENTRAL JAVA (570–927)

Central Java, generally known as Mataram, was already home to distinguished and important polities by 570 CE, a hundred years before the rise of Śrīvijaya. Indeed, some historians would trace the development of important centres back to the first centuries CE. Chinese dynastic records suggested that Sitiao, a place of fertile land and cities with streets reported by Fu-nan's third-century Chinese visitors, was in central Java. Ho-ling, based in central Java, was one of two fifth-century Java coastal centres with which the Chinese court interacted (Ho-lo-tan in the Tarum River basin near modern Jakarta was the other).[22]

When in the seventh century the kings of Śrīvijaya created their polity, they subordinated and incorporated into their realm a number of previously independent river-mouth ports on the northern and western coasts of Java, but they made no effort to include the rest of the island. In particular, they made no effort to subordinate central Java and its Kedu Plain, a unique and valuable part of the maritime realm. The relationship that developed between Śrīvijaya and central Java was a mutually advantageous, symbiotic linkage between a state dependent on the control of international trade and a rice-plain that remained somewhat distant from that trade.

The Kedu Plain was created by repeated volcanic eruptions; its rich soil and its size, combined with the region's year-round growing season, created an interior rice bowl unrivalled in the maritime realm of Southeast Asia. The prosperity of the rice plain, especially during its heyday in the eighth and ninth centuries, was related to the market for rice created by those Southeast Asian ports that serviced the international traders, and yet the rulers of this plain remained remarkably aloof from that trade. The Merapi-Perahu Mountains isolate the area from the ports on Java's north and east coasts, and its rivers flow south, away from the routes of international trade. Its royal centres and its pilgrimage sites always remained distant even from the small local ports on the nearby southern coast.

The relationship between the village-based producers of the rice plain and international traders was always indirect and mediated by other communities more directly related to international commerce. Local produce reached the international ports only through an intricate, multi-layered system of markets. The farmers and artisans of the villages took their produce, principally rice, salt, beans, and dyestuffs, to a periodic farmers' market that came to them every so many days, according to a fixed schedule. There they could find merchants who travelled with this market from place to place. The travelling merchants bought the local produce and passed it along in exchanges with intermediary wholesalers. Then merchants from the ports of Java's north coast purchased the produce from the wholesalers and sold it to merchants who travelled the seas, who delivered it to the ports where international merchants congregated. There were thus at least four layers of merchants and of markets between central Java's rice producers and the international traders.[23]

[22] W. J. van der Meulen, S. J., 'In Search of Ho-ling', *Indonesia*, 23 (1977).

[23] Jan Wisseman-Christie, 'Negara, Mandala and Despotic State: Images of Early Java' in David G. Marr and A. C. Milner, eds, *Southeast Asia in the 9th to 14th Centuries*, Singapore, 1986, 80–3. Wisseman-Christie argues that the Javanese trade system today is very similar to that of at least the tenth century. The key participant is the *bakul*, a market-based trader who buys from farmers and pedlars and sells both locally and to carriers moving on to other

Because this marketing system provided the international ports with the provisions they needed and did not compete with them for the international trade, the river-mouth ports, up to and including Śrīvijaya, had never felt a need to subordinate central Java. Furthermore, this same system acted as a buffer between the land-based élites on the rice plain and the region's merchants; the latter congregated in ports frequented by international traders and thus allowed the social coherence of the rice plain to remain largely undisturbed and its population's orientation to remain internally focused.

Clifford Geertz once described the attitude of Bali's post-1600 élites toward international trade, a description that is apt for central Java as well.

> [International trade] was connected to political life eccentrically—through a set of extremely specialized institutions designed at once to contain its dynamic and to capture its returns. The lords were not unmindful of the material advantages to be got from trade; but they were not unmindful either that, in reaching for them, they risked the very foundations of their power. Grasping by habit, they were autarchic by instinct, and the result was a certain baroqueness of economic arrangement.[24]

That there was no direct relationship between the élites of central Java and the international traders did not inhibit in any way their enthusiastic incorporation of Indian religions, ideas, architecture, or arts or crafts. Quite the opposite: they were just as enthusiastic users of things Indian and, compared to other places in the maritime realm, their monuments and their aesthetics tended to be more orthodox, more like those of India. The most spectacular results of this enthusiasm for Indian ways were the great temples of central Java.

During the heyday of Śrīvijaya, from the early eighth century until the middle of the tenth century, central Java witnessed a construction boom. In a little more than 200 years, the mountain-sides and plains of central Java were covered with monuments (mostly temples) of exquisite design and execution. This construction apparently began with a Hindu temple complex on the Dieng Plateau high in the mountains, and culminated with another Hindu temple complex at Prambanan. In between, in both time and space, was the Buddhist monument called Borobudur, which was built by the Śailendras, the closest allies of Śrīvijaya.

The temple boom of central Java marked the growing importance of a different sort of polity in Southeast Asia. While Śrīvijaya represents the river-mouth port system, with its dynamic of inter-port rivalry, the development of central Java points to the emergence of rice-plain polities whose political dynamics were quite different from those of the river-mouth ports.

One might expect that political centralization would have been relatively easier to accomplish on a rice plain than in the steep rainforest-covered

markets. The *bakul* is both a wholesaler and retailer, bulking goods for more distant markets, and breaking down lots that arrive from the outside. Wisseman-Christie argues that the *bakul* allowed the Javanese trade system to operate in the absence of large urban-supply markets. Jan Wisseman-Christie, 'States without Cities: Strategies of Decentralization in Early Java', *Indonesia* (Oct. 1991).

24 *Negara: The Theater-State in Nineteenth Century Bali*, Princeton, 1980, 87.

valleys where the riverine states of the island realm emerged. Travel and communication across this plain were easier, and presumably a political network, like the marketing network that knitted it together, would have faced few physical obstacles. Nevertheless, political integration was not as easy as the plain's geography would suggest, for a great number of local élites, based in what have been called eco-regions, were firmly entrenched.

In the various phases of wet-rice growing, the need for water varies widely. When the crop is first planted, the fields must be flooded. But as it matures, the fields are gradually drained and are allowed to dry out by the time of the harvest. Thus, it was advantageous for all those whose water came from the same stream to co-ordinate their planting, to stagger it through the year so that not everyone was drawing off water at the same time. The need for co-ordination led to the creation of 'eco-region' water boards, organizations made up of representatives from all those villages that used the same source of water. The village leaders who participated on these water boards, members of special lineages, played a highly responsible role in the everyday lives of the people, and this gave them great power.

These eco-regions shared not only the same water, but the same gods, and the jurisdiction of the local water-board tended to overlap the jurisdiction of the local shrine. The behaviour of the gods, like the behaviour of the farmers, was shaped by the human planting cycles, for they came down to inhabit their shrines only on special days, usually related to the planting schedule. Both the operation of this intricate irrigation system and the habits of their gods instilled in the Javanese people an acute awareness of complex cyclical intersections based not so much on the cycles of heavens as on the cycles of the earth, the human-made intersections of ricefield and river.

Throughout the heyday of central Java, the heads of those lineages in charge of the eco-region water boards were always the most important political actors. The roots of the irrigation-based eco-regions grew deep and held tenaciously, and the political élites of these relatively small units were anxious not to give up their own local prerogatives even though they themselves might entertain notions of expansion that required others to relinquish theirs. For any one of them to distinguish himself from the others and emerge as king was not a simple matter, for their resource bases and their lineage-based legitimacies were similar.

The kingdoms that began to form on the central Javanese rice plain sometime in the sixth century were essentially alliance structures in which one local eco-region lineage managed to elevate itself over a larger area, to establish its superiority as a royal lineage, and to establish a centre with which other local eco-region lineages were willing to ally. Thus, these aspiring leaders had somehow to acquire a superior legitimacy that would distinguish them from the others and enable them to prevail. It was in this respect that the Indian religions and their temples came to play such a significant and prominent role in central Javanese statecraft. Those who became Hindus or Buddhists could claim a relationship to higher gods, a relationship fitting for higher kings.

In the same manner that local shrines marked the centres of eco-region networks, it was the remarkable temples and monuments of Indian inspiration that were to mark the new larger spiritual (and political) network that subsumed the local shrines and the networks they represented. The temples and the monuments served as centres where a king could demonstrate his spiritual superiority, his connection to these higher gods and to a higher knowledge, through elaborate rituals and state ceremonies conducted by Buddhist or Hindu holy men. Indeed, the sculpture that covered the walls of the temples was evidence of a higher learning and a principal means of imparting that knowledge to the people. The temples and especially the Borobuḍur, with its explicit Buddhist message, and the Prambanan complex, which expoused subsequent rulers' devotion to a syncretic Hindu tradition, were thus 'teaching' devices.

Moreover, the temples enjoyed the practical benefits that came from the special learning that the holy men possessed. The Sanskrit writing skills of the court-based priests had secular uses such as bookkeeping that assisted in the administration of the temples and the larger realms they represented. And they provided the kings with a royal Sanskrit vocabulary that assisted them in magnifying their status relative to that of other local leaders. The Śailendras in the eighth century were the first rulers in Java to adopt the title *Mahārāja*, the Sanskrit word for Great King, and to proclaim themselves rulers of a Javanese state.[25]

The purpose of the temples was to honour royal lineages, as well as the higher gods, but they were built by regional coalitions, each local constituent contributing a part of the complex. Much of the funding came from donations that bestowed religious merit upon the donors. Brahmins or monks laid out the temple designs and supervised. Royal 'bondsmen' moved the stones and did the rough shaping and chipping. Professional artisans then carved the statues and reliefs. In no case did royal labour demands exceed the king's customary labour rights. The sculptors' work demonstrates an exuberant creativity. Humorous improvisations can be found on many central Javanese monuments, including the two largest at Borobuḍur and Prambanan.

The temple complexes and royal centres grew to be the centres of a political-religious redistribution system that operated apart from the ordinary market. Temples usually had rights to a share of local production and local labour, and thus became collectors and marketers of agricultural produce, and could use the labour to construct not only religious edifices, but bridges, dams, or roads that contributed to the well-being of the temple, as well as the community. Like the temples, the kings, too, were the recipients of tribute (often rice) from their allies, tribute that they could exchange for imported goods that came from the north coast ports. These

[25] Earlier rulers, including the early monarchs of Śrīvijaya, ruled *bhumi*, a sphere of authority or realm, which was a more ambiguous statement of territorial authority than *rajya*. The earliest dated eighth-century Sailendra inscriptions speak of the *rajya*/state, ruled by a *maharāja* who defeated neighbouring *rāja*. The *rajya*/state was administered by a well-established hierarchy of state ministers, local lords, and superintendents of subordinate areas who linked the central court with intermediary, territorially-defined administrative units and villages. See, for example, the Kalasan Sanskrit inscription of 778, as discussed in Hermann Kulke, 'The "City" and the "State" in Early Indonesia', *Indonesia* (Oct. 1991).

rare and precious items, such as gold, silver, and textiles, especially Indian cottons, were then redistributed with great ceremony by the kings to their allies.

The kingdoms of central Java relied on alliances, often cemented by marriage, and on mutually beneficial exchange relationships. The kings never became superior landholders. Nor were their realms bureaucratic or highly institutionalized states that deprived local units of their separate identities. Theirs was a 'ritual sovereignty' marked by the temple complexes and the patronage of monks and priests steeped in Indian learning who endowed the king with sacred powers and reinforced an aura of divine majesty. They created ceremonial centres, centres of religion, art, and learning that drew their allies and held them in their orbit.

The Śailendras were only one of the kingly lineages of central Java. They were predominant from about 760 to 860, and it was during this time that they constructed the Borobuḍur, which became the focal point of the Śailendra monarchs' cult of legitimacy. They were different from other central Javanese royal lineages in large part because they, like their allies the rulers of Śrīvijaya, were patrons of Mahāyāna Buddhism rather than Hinduism.

When the Śailendras lost their predominance to a Hindu lineage of kings in the middle of the ninth century, royal refugees from the Śailendra realm went to Sumatra where they became incorporated into the Śrīvijayan royal house. Their arrival coincides in time with a Śrīvijayan decision to endow the funds for a monk's abode at the Nālandā pilgrimage centre in northeastern India. The inscription on this building recorded the benevolence of the Śrīvijayan monarch in a place where it would be visible not only to Indians, but to a wide variety of international visitors. In the early eleventh century another monk's abode was endowed by Śrīvijayan monarchs at Nāgapaṭṭinam, the centre of the Śaivite Hindu Cōḷa realm that was located on India's southeastern, Tamil-speaking Coromandel coast. What is most curious about these two endowments is that, in both cases, the royal donors of Śrīvijaya chose to identify themselves as Śailendras, even after this Javanese lineage had taken refuge on Sumatra.

The Śailendras had prevailed in central Java for a hundred years. After their demise, other royal lineages, patrons of Hinduism, including the builders of the Prambanan temples, replaced the Śailendras as hegemons of central Java, and they, too, came to enjoy a commercial relationship with Śrīvijaya. Indeed, temple building in the area did not slow until about 900 CE. Neither the ascendancy of Śrīvijaya nor the heyday of central Java came to an end until the early eleventh century. And it was a combination of three events that occurred almost simultaneously that marked the end of their great epoch.

First, Śrīvijaya's hegemony over trade within the maritime realm of Southeast Asia was challenged by a new power that had emerged in east Java, and from 990 to 1007 there was periodic war between the two. Then in 1025 Śrīvijaya suffered a devastating attack from the Cōḷas, based in South India. And in that same year a king based in east Java consolidated his authority over central Java and by 1037 had apparently severed his realm's ties to Śrīvijaya. Thereafter, both Śrīvijaya and the temple realm of central Java were overshadowed by the expanding power of a new realm based in east Java.

During this era there were significant increases in the volume of trade and more sailors (especially Chinese) were penetrating the archipelago; a single Southeast Asian entrepôt could no longer dominate trade. International traders were moving toward the sources of supply. Java, and especially east Java, was better suited to facilitate this new level of commerce. With its rivers that flowed from the heartland to the north coast, east Java could more adequately provide the rice for export that was required in an exchange for spices from the eastern archipelago.

## EAST JAVA, 927–1222

When Marco Polo, a merchant of Venice, the port city that had grown rich while marketing Asian spices in Western Europe, travelled through Southeast Asia in the last decade of the thirteenth century, he was convinced that Java was unspeakably rich.

> [Java] is of surpassing wealth, producing . . . all . . . kinds of spices, . . . frequented by a vast amount of shipping, and by merchants who buy and sell costly goods from which they reap great profit. Indeed, the treasure of this island is so great as to be past telling.[26]

The Java that Marco Polo described was neither the realm of Śrīvijaya nor that of central Java. He was speaking of east Java, the site of kingdoms that replaced Śrīvijaya in international importance in the early part of the eleventh century, in spite of the fact that they were located somewhat east of the routes that the traffic between India and China usually took. It was not their location, but their control of spices that drew international traders to them. Contrary to what Marco Polo and many other foreigners thought, east Java was not a producer of spices. The greatness of the centres that developed there was ultimately based on their ability to stockpile rice, which they traded for the spices and other rainforest products harvested in the other parts of the eastern archipelago.

It was in east Java that, for the first time in the island realm, kings emerged who combined within one realm a trading position equal to that of Śrīvijaya with a control over agricultural resources comparable to those of central Java, and who furthermore created what was tantamount to a monopoly on the marketing of the fine spices, the rarest and most expensive. Along with this eastward shift in the geographical locus of power came changes in economic and political structures, and in aesthetics and worldview that marked a major transition in the political-economy of early Southeast Asia.

East Javanese polities grew up within the basin of the Brantas River. This is an unusually long river in the island realm, since it practically encircles a tangle of mountains before finding its way to the sea. Its headwaters

[26] Henry Yule, trans., *The Book of Ser Marco Polo*, London, 1903, 272–4.

converge on the slopes of Mount Arjuna and flow from there in a clockwise direction, first south, then west, then north, and finally east to the sea. As a result, it was rather more unruly than the straighter streams of the plains of central Java.

But of equal significance, the Brantas, unlike the rivers of central Java, empties on the island's northeast coast. Although its ports were a long way from the Straits of Melaka and Sunda where the transit traffic between India and China flowed, its waters did in the end flow north into the Java Sea. In fact, it was ideally situated to play a strategic role in the growing trade in fine spices, since it was located at an intermediate point between what is now called Maluku (the Moluccas), islands that included those where these spices were harvested, and the Straits of Melaka, where these spices had met the international trade routes during the time of Śrīvijaya's hegemony. It is quite possible that the earlier marketers of these spices had stopped off in East Java's ports to take on provisions on their way to the ports of Śrīvijaya, thus creating an east Javanese interest in the trade.

That the distribution of these spices could fall under what amounted to monopoly control by the east Javanese was due to the fact that the trees from which these fine spices came could be found in one place, and one place only, at the far eastern end of the hemisphere. There were three spices in particular that were of great importance to east Java: cloves from the clove tree; and nutmeg and mace, both from the nutmeg tree. Before 1600 the clove tree, an evergreen of the tropical rainforest, grew only on five tiny volcanic islands immediately off the western coast of Halmahera: Ternate, Tidore, Motir, Makian, and Batjan. The spice that we call cloves is the dried unopened flower-bud of this tree. The nutmeg tree, also a tropical evergreen, was equally rare. It grew only on some of the Banda Islands (of which there are ten), which occupy a total of forty-four square kilometres in the midst of the Banda Sea. What we call nutmeg is the kernel found inside the seed, and the spice known as mace is the thin membrane of a chewy rind that covers the kernel.

Given the value of these spices throughout the hemisphere, it is remarkable that prior to the modern period, the trees were never transplanted to other locations. No doubt, this was not from any lack of trying. The islanders kept a close watch on visitors to make sure that they did not smuggle out any plants or seeds; even if a few managed to get out, they apparently did not take root in foreign soils. The seeds of these trees do not remain viable for long. Probably of most importance, these trees require highly-skilled tending to make them produce, and they are particular about where they will grow and under what conditions. One common saying declares, 'nutmegs must be able to smell the sea, and cloves must see it'.

Furthermore, the winds conspired to keep international traders from meeting the real Spice Islanders, the sailors who brought the spices from Maluku. Those who delivered the spices sailed home with their cargoes of rice and other goods on the same west wind that delivered the international traders. While the international traders were in Java waiting for the wind to shift, these Spice Islanders were at home, 1600 kilometres east of Java.

They would return to Java with their precious cargoes of nutmeg, mace, and cloves, on the same east wind that carried the international traders back toward home. The winds thus kept these two groups apart, which no doubt worked to the advantage of the rulers of east Java and may have contributed to the mistaken notion that all spices were produced on Java.

Unlike the rulers of central Java, the monarchs of east Java sat in proximity to coastal ports, and became directly involved in stimulating the international trade. A 927 inscription found at Palebuhan describes a river-mouth port called Goreng Gareng (not yet located) and a local ruler, in what was essentially a frontier area, intent both on developing a port under royal patronage and on enticing farmers into his realm. Already in these early years, 135 vessels were based at the king's port, and he was sending not only Javanese port merchants, but also foreign merchants from Sri Lanka (Sinhalese), southern India, and Burma into the countryside to collect taxes.

Since the new east Javanese kingdom began to compete for a share in international commerce and for the rice surpluses of central Java, its relationship with Śrīvijaya soon became hostile. Between 990 and 1007 there was periodic war between the two, a matter that was settled not by east Java, but by the Cōḷas when they decimated Palembang in 1025. On the other hand, the issue of hegemony over central Java was settled by King Airlangga.

Airlangga (c.991–1049), eulogized as the founder of a new world, ruled for more than thirty years, from 1016 to 1049. His capital was at a place called Kahuripari. Since most of the inscriptions concerning him are found in the delta region around modern Surabaya, historians are confident that this royal centre was somewhere on the Brantas River delta, about 60 or 80 kilometres from the river's mouth, although its exact location has not yet been determined.

Airlangga's first acquisition outside east Java was the island of Bali, which he had managed to subordinate by 1025. Bali, located just two kilometres off the east coast of Java, was an important rice producer. Although it lacks Java's flat plains, it does have good volcanic soil, and rice was planted on the terraced hillsides. The relationship between east Java and Bali must have already been one of long standing, for Airlangga, who grew up in east Java, was the child of a royal marriage between an east Javanese princess and a Balinese prince.

According to tradition, his hegemony over central Java was achieved only after a struggle with 'demons' in central Java, a struggle that lasted from 1025 to 1037. These 'demons', like the kingdoms of central Java, were portrayed as allies of Śrīvijaya. But Airlangga, who generally relied on Javanese versions of Hindu images of statecraft, was able to overcome the demons due to the powers of meditation he developed only after an initial retreat. Like Arjuna in the Javanese version of the *Mahābhārata*, he was able to concentrate his mind and his powers on the defeat of his enemies. Airlangga also saw himself as an earthly manifestation of the Indic god Viṣṇu, who had appeared to Arjuna as Kṛiṣṇa. Although his direct administration was probably limited to the lower reaches of the Brantas River, he had by 1037 established a 'new Mataram', and at least a ritual hegemony over both Bali and central Java.[27]

Another aspect of Airlangga's greatness lay in his successful damming of the Brantas River. Although its basin has rich volcanic soil, farmers had apparently remained reluctant to settle there because of periodic floods. An inscription of 1037 reveals that the river had burst its dykes, flooded villages, and impeded the progress of ships up the river to the royal port. Not only was there devastation and hardship for the people, but the king was losing revenue. Local villages were unable to deal with the problem; and thus, Airlangga assumed the responsibility. He decided upon a royal project that constructed dams at strategic points on the river. The dams not only reduced the hazard from floods, but also enhanced the possibilities of irrigation. Some sources suggest that Airlangga then transferred vanquished peasant population from central to east Java, presumably to populate the basin.

The water control project also provided a better harbour for international shipping at the royal port of Hujung Galah, a site that is presumed to be in the vicinity of Surabaya. The new port facilities serviced a growing international trade. It was not long before east Java had gained a dominant position in the international spice market, a market that grew to include most of the eastern hemisphere.

Airlangga thus transformed what had been disadvantages within his realm into advantages. The solution to the initial problems that the basin faced required more extensive organization and thus required a greater degree of direction by a supra-local authority. As a result, those monarchs based in the east were able to assume powers beyond those possible for their counterparts based in central Java to achieve. The increasing centralization is also reflected in a tradition that claims that Airlangga codified Javanese law by drawing together the various regional traditions into one 'Javanese' code, although it is no longer extant.

The international economic climate was favourable. The Tang dynasty in China had fallen in 906, but by 960, a few decades before Airlangga's birth, the Sung dynasty had once again united China; and, unlike previous empire-wide dynasties, it was more oriented toward its southern, commercial coast. Technological innovations also contributed to an increase in China's commercial and maritime interests, and after 1127 this trend accelerated even more when the Sung dynasty lost much of the north to invaders and moved its capital to Hangzhou, south of the Yangtze River. China's orientation toward the southern oceans would not be reversed until about 1430. It was during the Sung dynasty that Chinese porcelain gained an overseas market comparable to the one silk enjoyed, and large

[27] Kulke, regards Airlangga as an exception to the normal patterns of early Javanese statecraft. Through military conquest, not administrative accomplishment, Airlangga established a more direct Javanese royal authority than had previously been the case, and was appropriately the first Javanese monarch to have the title *ratu cakravartin*, 'universal monarch', bestowed upon him in epigraphic references. See also Wisseman-Christie, 'Negara, Mandala and Despotic State', 74–5. Majapahit-era monarchs assumed the title *bhatara* ('god'), which was appropriate to their enhanced status.

quantities began to move out on the maritime routes of the Southern Ocean.

Prior to the rise of east Java, the Abbasid Caliphate at Baghdad had been experiencing grave difficulties in controlling its empire. Ever since the latter part of the ninth century, the Persian Gulf area experienced rebellions and civil wars, a problem that compounded the difficulties on the routes from the Indian Ocean to the Mediterranean since the Red Sea area had been disturbed for even longer. However, by 973, the Fatimid Caliphate (909–1171, a Shi'ite power first based in present-day Tunisia) had secured its hold over Egypt and thus brought peace to the Red Sea route. Thus, once again the spices had good access to the Mediterranean market.

During the time of Airlangga, east Java's ports grew in importance. Like earlier east Javanese kings, he gave royal charters (metal plates that recorded agreements between the king and his subjects) to port-based merchants who participated in indigenous exchange networks that traded between the ports and the hinterland. Local market lists indicate that non-prestige goods of foreign origin, specifically metals and dyes, were traded for local products, especially rice, which the traders brought back to the port.

The charters also provided for what was essentially a royal tax on commerce, since they ensured that the king would receive his share of any commercial profits. Indeed, the largest percentage of royal charters issued during the tenth to twelfth centuries concerned port or coastal settlements in the Brantas delta region. Java's port-based merchants also played a role in collecting the king's tax on local agriculture since they also served as tax farmers, a role apparently no longer played by foreign merchants after the time of Airlangga.

The kings used their revenues to promote trade. Much was invested in the development of additional farmland in order to produce the all-important rice surpluses. The monarch provided for foreign visitors' lodging, harbourage, and board, expenses that he could afford since he received a percentage of all the gold, silver, and other metals paid in exchange for the merchandise in his ports. Royal revenues were also drawn upon to pay soldiers and seamen who went out in the monarch's name to force the subjugation of formerly autonomous coastal and hinterland religions, and to police the realm, to eliminate pirates and bandits who might prey on travellers or villagers. This security was an important factor in the traders' decision to use a certain port or not. For example, during this era the Chinese were aware that they could get a superior variety of pepper (or a better price) in the Sunda Strait region, but did not bother to go there since it had a reputation for brigandage.

Airlangga and the east Javanese kings who followed him also used their share of the realm's wealth to enhance their sovereignty, remitting tribute for the construction of temples, the performance of ritual, and the patronage of scholars, all to enhance the monarch's superior status and the centre's prestige. During this era there was a shift in the legitimization of the centres of power and their returns to their subject populations from huge religious buildings to much smaller ones, and from religious returns to prestige goods. It appears that east Java's kings controlled the importation of prestigious foreign goods and redistributed these luxury items throughout their realm, including the hinterland, through alliance-making or other sorts of gift-giving. Chinese sources indicate that quantities of these goods were shipped to Java and quantities of contemporary Chinese ceramic sherds have been found throughout the realm, and yet these goods are not mentioned in local market-related inscriptions. The most likely explanation for this apparent contradiction is that the kings controlled luxury goods such as Chinese ceramics and used them as political capital.

One of the puzzles in early Javanese history is why east Java between the ninth and thirteenth centuries—where population, wealth, and transport infrastructures were sufficient to have produced permanent urban centres beyond the coast—did not develop large-scale hinterland centres of permanent trade. One explanation, as we have seen, is that the Javanese wet-rice economy functioned most efficiently when its population was clustered in small productive communities that were encompassed within decentralized eco-regions. Another explanation is that royal policy purposefully nourished this decentralization. That this was the case at the inception of east Java hegemony is reflected in the inscriptions that record royal initiatives, such as those of Airlangga, that amplified the state revenue base, by means of state-encouraged development of previously uncultivated peripheral lands as well as taxable trade. Between 900 and 1060, for example, there were more than forty new enclaves established by direct royal intervention in the developing Brantas delta region.[28] While the economic returns from the development of the Brantas delta are undeniable, these and other royal initiatives were ultimately undertaken to promote the king's authority vis-à-vis other élites and rival institutions during an era in which monarchs based in east Java were asserting their sovereignty over their previously decentralized polity.

In the period from the ninth to the thirteenth century, prior to the establishment of the Majapahit state, royal grants known as *sīma* ('tax transfers') were the centrepiece of the royal offensive. These were not gifts of land: Javanese monarchs did not normally have local land rights, and even their tax rights were subject to social restraint. When title to land was to be transferred, that land was purchased first from those villages affected. *Sīma* were thus transfers of all or a denoted portion of the income rights (there was frequently a ceiling placed on the amount of tax the state was willing to forgo) due to a superior political authority from designated land.

*Sīma* grants were a means of encouraging territorial expansion and the pioneering of previously uncultivated peripheral areas, but they were also a means by which farmers and non-farmers were incorporated and subordinated to the prevailing agrarian order. *Sīma* land, which was designated to provide prescribed income to a religious institution—especially ancestor temples that honoured past monarchs, members of local élites or village ancestors—as well as a favoured individual or group, was considered to be outside the administrative authority of the king. In addition to *sīma* tax

[28] There were undoubtedly more for which no epigraphic records remain. See Wisseman-Christie, 'States without Cities'.

transfers made by those claiming monarch status, regional authorities (*rakai*) also issued *sīma* charters that ceded their rights to tax (usually with the approval of an 'overlord' king), and normally relinquished their local administrative rights over *sīma* land coincident with a monarch's tax transfers. Yet a ceremony that dedicated the *sīma* tax transfer, whether that of a king or a regional authority, emphasized that the grantee was expected to remain loyal to the Javanese state. This ritual involved an oath in which the recipient pledged fidelity, and it culminated with the pronouncement of a curse by a religious official threatening those present who were not faithful to the monarch. Usually a great public festival was held in honour of a new *sīma* foundation. These ceremonies and festivals must have served as a means of redistributing wealth that might otherwise have been used in ways disruptive to society—and to the king's sovereignty. *Sīma* were held in perpetuity, as evinced by inscriptional records of court cases in which *sīma* rights granted by defunct ruling families were upheld.[29]

*Sīma* grants were thereby used to free designated lands from numerous demands for taxes and services. In an age in which tax-farming was the norm, *sīma* grants also prohibited various tax collectors and officials, who were often also working for local magnates and village authorities, from entering *sīma* domains to extract payments on their own or others' behalf. Thus, while on the surface *sīma* 'tax transfers' would seem to have entailed the relinquishing of royal power locally, they instead subtracted a portion of the wealth directly available to a local élite (who were, however, compensated for their lost income with 'presents' of gold, silver, or cloth) and established a stable institutional foothold from which east Javanese rulers could attempt to extend their political and economic power beyond their shifting centres of royal power.

The *sīma* tax transfer system also acted as a brake on the growth of population clusters in the hinterland. Non-farmers, including merchants, were incorporated into rural communities rather than advancing the evolution of separate commercial enclaves. In a clear assertion of royal authority, *sīma* charters included limits on the amount of trade that could be carried on by resident professionals free of state taxes, as well as the number of professionals who could operate free-of-tax in a *sīma* community.[30] The *sīma* tax concessions would have encouraged economic activity in a community until it reached the tax transfer ceiling. But this would have also discouraged professional commercial activity beyond that ceiling. The *sīma* system thus reduced the level of local competition, and also ensured the dispersal of professional trading activity. Farming communities were themselves similarly affected by the prevailing state revenue collection system that taxed larger communities more heavily, which also encouraged community division rather than consolidation. Rather than demonstrating an increasing concentration of population, the epigraphic records of this age document the proliferation of small residential clusters; instead of forming larger housing assemblies, numerous villages subdivided into

[29] Wisseman-Christie, 'Negara, Mandala and Despotic State', 72; J. G. de Casparis, 'Pour une histoire sociale de l'ancienne Java, principalement au Xième S.', *Archipel*, 21 (1981) 128–30.

[30] Wisseman-Christie, 'States without Cities'.

hamlets and developed multiple sets of officials who were incorporated into an increasingly hierarchical state administrative structure.

When Airlangga died in 1049, his realm was divided between two of his sons and Bali was left again to its own devices. This decision to divide the empire was later blamed on the counsel of one of the king's advisers, a Hindu ascetic known as Bharada. In the east was Janggala/Singhasari and in the west Panjalu/Kaḍiri.[31] This bipolarity remained until the thirteenth century, for almost 200 years. That the realm was divided, however, did not in any way inhibit the further development of east Java's commercial position. It grew to be one of the world's richest lands, as bullion, gold and silver vessels, silk, and the world's best porcelain, lacquerware, chemicals, and metal manufacturers poured in.

Compelling testimony regarding the commercialization of Java comes from a 1225 report by Zhao Rugua, the Commissioner of Foreign Trade at the Chinese port of Quanzhou. He indicates that during the Sung Dynasty (960–1279) the Chinese were buying so much spice (especially pepper) from eastern Java that copper coinage was flowing out of the country at an alarming rate. Zhao reported that Java's own coins were mixtures of silver, tin, lead, and copper, and that, like Chinese coins, they had square holes in the middle so that they could be strung together (it is not clear whether Java was using Chinese coins or making coins similar to those of China). Finally, in an effort to protect its currency, the Chinese government banned trade with Java. The Javanese traders, however, tried to circumvent this prohibition by saying that they came from 'Sukadana' (*Su-ki-tan* in Chinese), a name that they apparently made up.[32]

## SINGHASARI (1222–1292) AND MAJAPAHIT (1293–1528)

Majapahit was the last and the greatest of the empires in the pre-1500 Southeast Asia island realm. Its kings came to possess a degree of central control in East Java that went beyond previous precedent, and they furthermore created a state centre that established varying degrees of hegemony over central Java and an overseas realm almost three times the size of what had been Śrīvijaya's, a realm that included all the islands that are now Indonesia's, and more. The roots of Majapahit and its ambitions were in Singhasari. The Singhasari ruler Viṣṇuvardhana (r. 1248–68) had subordinated the Kaḍiri population centre and thereby become the preeminent political authority in east Java, a position Singhasari's rulers maintained until 1292. But it was his son Kĕrtanagara (r. 1268–92) who laid the foundations for Majapahit. Indeed, the *Nāgarakĕrtāgama*, an epic poem and chronicle composed in 1365 by the Buddhist monk Prapanca in order to glorify the rulers of Majapahit, actually begins its story with the reign of

31 The alleged division of the whole of eastern Java by Airlangga into Janggala and Panjalu has been shown to be only a division of his own core realm in the delta region: Boechari, 'Sri Maharaja Garasakan, a new evidence on the problem of Airlangga's partition of his kingdom', *Madjalah ilmu-ilmu Sastra Indonesia*, 4 (1968).

32 F. Hirth and W. W. Rockhill, *Chau Ju-kua: His Work on the Chinese and Arab trade in the twelfth and thirteenth centuries, entitled* Chu-fan-chi, St Petersburg, 1911, 78, 81–3.

this mysterious and highly controversial Singhasari king. Kĕrtanagara, who came to the throne only after destroying 'a wicked man', claimed to have been initiated into secret Tantric rites that gave him extraordinary powers against demonic force. And in order to maintain these powers, he was obliged to bring on his own ecstasy through Tantric rituals involving the consumption of intoxicating drink and the performance of sexual acts.

Although a later fifteenth-century chronicler hostile to Tantric rituals characterized him as a drunkard who was brought to ruin by his lust, the *Nāgarakĕrtāgama* described him as a saint and ascetic, free of all passion. To end despair (and the difficulties that Airlangga's legendary division of the realm seem to have caused), Kĕrtanagara erected a statue depicting himself as Aksubhya, the meditative Buddha, on the spot where Bharada (the ascetic blamed for the partition of the meditating Airlangga's kingdom) had lived. He also confirmed his father's patronage and synthesis of the indigenous Javanese religious traditions (Śaivite, Hindu, Mahāyāna Buddhist, and Tantric). Viṣṇuvardhana's ashes were divided between two shrines; at one he was worshipped as an incarnation of Śiva, at the second as Amoghapāśa, the Bodhisattva of Compassion. The *Nāgarakĕrtāgama* viewed Kĕrtanagara's religious purification of Java as the cause of his and his descendants' glory as divine kings and reuniters of the realm.

Indeed, Kĕrtanagara would need all the powers he could summon, for it was he, and then his son-in-law, who would face the Mongols, the Central Asian conquerors whose steppe cavalries had overrun much of the continents of Asia and Europe. By the time that Kĕrtanagara came to power in 1268, southern China and mainland Southeast Asia had already suffered the invasion of these armies. Nanchao, an independent kingdom in what is now China's southern Yunnan Province, had been invaded in 1253, setting in motion a stream of refugees. The Thais felt the brunt of the refugees; they expanded out, infringing upon what had been Burmese Pagan to the west and Cambodian Angkor to the east. They then started to expand down the Malay peninsula into territory that east Java's rulers at Singhasari considered to be within their sphere of interest.

The Mongols followed up their occupation of Nanchao with an invasion of Vietnam in 1257 (an invasion that the Vietnamese resisted for some twenty-seven years, after which they forced the Mongols out). And in 1267, the year before Kĕrtanagara came to power, Khubilai Khan made a direct attack on the Southern Sung. There followed an invasion of Burma in 1271 (where sporadic fighting did not end until 1300), and in 1274 for the first time the Mongols took to the seas and launched a naval attack against Japan.

In 1275 Kĕrtanagara made east Java's first significant move overseas, after both Thai expansion on to the Malay peninsula and Khubilai Khan's naval attack on Japan. He sent an expedition to occupy Jambi-Malāyu, the old Sumatran port that had been Śrīvijaya's first conquest. Up to this point in time, there is no record of an east Javanese presence in the straits region. At most, their concern had been to keep the Straits of Melaka open for international shipping.

However, that attitude soon changed. In 1271 Khubilai Khan had established the Mongol version of a Chinese dynasty, the Yuan; and in

1276 the Southern Sung capital, Hangzhou, fell to his armies. Apparently ports in Sumatra lost no time in applying to the new Yuan dynasty. In 1277 Palembang, in 1281 Jambi-Malāyu, and in 1282 Samudra-Pasai (a pepper depot on the northern tip of the island) sent envoys to Khubilai's capital. Presumably they were seeking Mongol recognition as special ports of trade with China, the old preferred-port status that Śrīvijaya had enjoyed.

These Sumatran appeals to the Mongol ruler of China were followed by the first sustained expansionist phase in east Java's history. After subjugating Bali in 1284, Kĕrtanagara again sent his armies westward, and by 1286 he had established Javanese hegemony over the straits region. It was in that year that he erected a statue of his father at Jambi-Malāyu.

Khubilai Khan, however, was not pleased by Javanese hegemony in the straits. In 1289 he sent envoys to Kĕrtanagara to confront him and demand that the tribute missions be sent from Java to the Khan's capital. Kĕrtanagara replied by disfiguring and tattooing the faces of the Mongol envoys, and sending them back in this disgraced fashion. His impudence so enraged Khubilai Khan that the Mongol sent 1000 warships to chastise Java.

However, before the fleet arrived, the previously subordinated ruler of Kaḍiri defeated Singhasari in 1292, and during the occupation of the royal residence of Singhasari, King Kĕrtanagara died. After this calamity in the last months of 1292 or early 1293, Kĕrtanagara's son-in-law Raden Vijaya cleared a new capital site from the forest, and named it Majapahit. This royal city, which gave its name to the realm, was located about fifty kilometres upriver from Surabaya, a little southeast of present-day Majakerta (near where Airlangga's capital had been).

When the Mongol warships arrived, the son-in-law managed to persuade them that Singhasari was gone and that since Kĕrtanagara had died, which was punishment enough, that they should help him chastise Kaḍiri's ruler instead. It was only after he had destroyed his local rivals and enemies with the help of the expeditionary army, that he turned on the Mongols and forced them to evacuate from Java.

After the founder of Majapahit defeated the Mongols in 1293, not only did Java manage to make peace with the Mongols and re-establish commercial relations with China; it also acquired, at the opposite end of the hemisphere, an expanding market of great significance, that of Western Europe. After undergoing an agricultural and commercial revolution and crusading in the eastern Mediterranean for some two hundred years, the Western Europeans had begun to consume meat in quantity, and had developed a taste for and subsequently a need for Asian spices to flavour dried or salted meat and preserved vegetables and fruits.

Venice was the principal supplier of this market. The city-state had taken over much of Byzantium's Mediterranean trade, had developed a sea route to Flanders and England, and eventually controlled about 70 per cent of Western Europe's spice market. And as a result of the Pax Mongolica, Venetian merchants, like the family of Marco Polo, had created their own trade links to the East. But the principal suppliers of Venice were the Mameluke rulers of Egypt (1250–1511) who had held the Mongols back and once again secured the Red Sea route to the Mediterranean.

The realm of Majapahit was to meet this demand and be changed in the process. Java's own marketing network benefited from the growth in international demand, the internal peace and security provided by Majapahit's hegemony, and from the kings' efforts to remove obstacles between hinterland producers and ports.

The relationship between Majapahit's kings and its merchants grew so close that some sources, both local and foreign, considered Java's spice merchants to be little more than the monarch's 'trade agents'. Although this was an exaggeration, it was certainly true that the kings were paid for the use of the ports, controlled the bullion and luxury goods that flowed in, and received a share of the profits made from the exchange and transportation of local and international products.

By 1331 the kings at Majapahit had secured all of eastern Java as well as the island of Madura. Placing his own relatives or, in a few cases, deserving members of the court at the head of each of these 'provinces', the king maintained firm control at the centre. By 1343 Bali had been secured, and thereafter was ruled by Javanese princes. In 1347 the kings began subordinating ports to their north and east, a process that culminated with their ritual hegemony over places as far away as the southern Philippines and New Guinea.

Majapahit was apparently content with the situation in the straits region until 1377. Although it had on occasion punished local rulers who became too ambitious (such as a Sunda Strait ruler in 1357), it does not seem to have made any attempt to establish a presence there until 1377. Exactly what prompted the king to move then is not clear, but it may have been the threat of a new alliance between ports in the Straits of Melaka and China. In 1368 the Chinese had succeeded in expelling the Mongols and had established the Ming dynasty. In 1371 this new dynasty had sent an imperial invitation to Palembang, whose rulers had responded with a tribute mission to China. Majapahit's 1377 expedition against these ambitious ports was apparently successful, for soon thereafter representatives of the ports in the straits region were participating in its central ceremonies.

Indeed, Majapahit was able to establish a close relationship even with Samudra-Pasai, a pepper depot that lay beyond the Straits of Melaka. A chronicler of that polity remembered the east Java centre at its height.

> The [Majapahit] Emperor was famous for his love of justice. The empire grew prosperous. People in vast numbers thronged the city. At this time every kind of food was in great abundance. There was a ceaseless coming and going of people from the territories overseas which had submitted to the king, to say nothing of places inside Java itself. Of the districts on the coast, from the west came the whole of the west, from the east came the whole of the east. From places inland right down to the shores of the Southern Ocean the people all came for an audience with the Emperor, bringing tribute and offerings . . . The land of Majapahit was supporting a large population. Everywhere one went there were gongs and drums being beaten, people dancing to the strains of all kinds of loud music, entertainments of many kinds like the living theatre, the shadow play, masked-plays, step-dancing, and musical dramas. These were the commonest sights and went on day and night in the land of Majapahit.[33]

[33] A. H. Hill, 'Hikayat Raja-Raja Pasai', JMBRAS. 32, 2 (1960) 161.

Thus, by 1377 Majapahit's realm included ports and their hinterlands from the furthest tip of Sumatra in the west to New Guinea in the east and as far north as the southern islands of the Philippines. The 'navy' with which it exercised its sovereignty over this far-flung peoples was based in ports on Java's north coast; the sailors were paid by the monarchs for their good behaviour and their transportation services. They were essentially mercenaries of trade as well as maritime security, and they served Majapahit only so long as it provided their most profitable opportunity.

The international traveller who came to Majapahit in the latter part of the fourteenth century, at the peak of its glory, would approach on a merchant ship, riding the west wind, and first enter the core region of the realm at the port of Surabaya, a town of about a thousand families (including some that were Chinese). But Surabaya, on the coast, was not the centre of either trade or politics. To reach Majapahit's centres one had to take a small boat from Surabaya up the Brantas River through the flat and fertile delta region.

After going some thirty or fifty kilometres, one would come to Canggu, a ferry crossing and a marketplace. From Canggu it was a half-day's walk further up the river to the 'twin cities', Majapahit and Bubat, a market city located on a wide plain to Majapahit's north. To its east ran the royal highway, and to its north, the Brantas River.

It is unclear from available archaeological and literary evidence whether Bubat (and Canggu, too) was a permanent market centre or a centre of trade that was periodically occupied at times coincident with the Majapahit agricultural and ritual cycle. The *Nāgarakĕrtāgama* tells us that most foreigners would stay at Bubat, a cosmopolitan city of many quarters (ethnic neighbourhoods), of which those of the Chinese and the Indians were most notable. Bubat's market was a square, surrounded on three sides by tall and splendid buildings, panelled with carvings of scenes from the Indian epic, the *Mahābharata*. Here traders from India, China, and mainland Southeast Asia, from the kingdoms of Cambodia, Vietnam, and Thailand among others, gathered to do business with the Majapahit monarch's representatives. Here is where the Majapahit realm's spices and other goods met the goods of China, India, and parts west.

Although it was a market, Bubat had taken on some of the character of a ritual capital due to its relationship to the monarchy. The *Nāgarakĕrtāgama* refers to Bubat as 'the crossroads, sacred, imposing'.[34] And it was here that Majapahit's own suppliers, traders, and artisans gathered, along with the foreign merchants. They came not only to do business, but also to pay homage to the king.

Bubat assumed special prominence as the centre for the celebration of the Caitra festival. This comprised a succession of ceremonies which were critical to Majapahit's sovereignty, and which exemplified the Majapahit state's economic and social life. This festival was held in March or April, soon after the wind had shifted and begun to blow from the west, bringing the international traders.

[34] Th. G. Th. Pigeaud, *Java in the Fourteenth Century: A Study of Cultural History*, The Hague, 1960–3, III. 9.

After initial ceremonies at the Majapahit centre, in which both Hindu brahmins and Buddhist monks prayed for the royal house's prosperity, the princes paraded in golden attire. Brahmins offered the king holy water in finely made ewers, and the scholars, nobles, and judges of the realm moved in stately procession to the beat of ceremonial drums and the blare of conch shells and trumpets, and to the praises of singers and poets. Thus, the court 'came down' for the first seven days of the Caitra festival to participate in public amusements and in ceremony.

At Bubat the men and women of the royal court and their visitors could enjoy all that was offered—not only the music, dancing and drama, but games and gambling and trials of combat. From the special viewing stands, the royal personages and their honoured guests, the holy men, their allies from within the realm, and foreign visitors and traders from many lands, watched as the Javanese fought with weapons, or demonstrated their skills at unarmed combat, or engaged in an elaborate tug-of-war.

But it was not only entertainment that was offered up to the king. It was here in Bubat that the king received various collections in kind and in cash. The court's right to a share of the local specialties produced throughout the realm ensured his supply of rice, salt, sugar, salted meats, cloth, oil, and bamboo. The international traders, too, brought gifts for the king, and thus the king amassed a mountain of both necessities and luxuries.

The king, however, did not hoard all these goods or try to keep them all for himself and the court. A king was measured by his generosity, and the Majapahit ruler was expected to redistribute these goods. Some were given as gifts in return for the services of the artisans who contributed their labour to the festival's preparations (such as those who had built the reviewing stands), and to the musicians and poets and other performers who contributed to the festival's success. Others would be consumed at the feasts that ended the festivities. A portion of local and imported luxury goods (such as silk and porcelain) would be distributed to the king's allies, and thus dispersed throughout the realm. In essence, it was the king's wealth and power that created his prestige and drew his tributaries to him: they expected something in return, something which they deemed equal to their own importance. At the close of the ceremonies at Bubat, as the moon of Caitra waned, the princes of the realm received the representatives of common village communities, and sent them away, too, with presents of clothing and food.

The seven days at Bubat were followed by seven more days of festivities at the royal centre of Majapahit. Here the royal family and its allies, including local village élites, gathered for ceremonies and speeches. These made clear that while the Majapahit monarch ruled both a wet-rice and maritime realm, it was his association with the Javanese wet-rice tradition that was critical to his legitimacy. One main theme in the speeches was the importance of both the farmers and the royal military. Neither the royal house nor the market towns could survive without the produce of the village. Java's international position was based on its rice, the major commodity sought by the harvesters of spice. It was for rice that the Spice Islanders came to Java. Thus, the livelihood of the farmers had to be protected.

On the other hand, the royal court had to have revenue; it had to be supplied. Without the court, its military and its many allies, rival trading centres based on other islands might come to attack. That the commercial élite recognized the importance of the king's military is indicated by the generous contributions (8000 copper cash per day) that market heads made to the commander-in-chief of Majapahit's forces.

The ceremonies culminated in a community meal that once again marked out the relationships between the centre and its allies. Those closest to the royal line were served on gold plates and ate their fill of mutton, water buffalo, poultry, game, wild boar, bees, fish, and ducks. Those of lesser rank and relationship, including the commoners, were served on silver dishes, and offered 'meats innumerable, all there is on the land and in the water', including those that the high-ranking did not eat, worm, tortoise, mouse, and dog.

Along with this food came prodigious quantities of alcoholic beverages made from the fruits of various sorts of palm trees, from sugar and from rice, and one and all drank until they were drunk, 'panting, vomiting, or bewildered'. And along with the food and drink came the best in entertainment, singers and dancers, and a musical play enacted and sung by the princes of the realm and the king himself.

The speeches of the princes at the royal centre of Majapahit also addressed the necessity of maintaining those public works that were under government protection, some of which were built and maintained by the centre, and others by central persuasion of local élites. Among the projects mentioned in these speeches were dams, bridges, fountains, market places, and tree planting.

Also among the royal projects were roads that served as a link with those important locations that lacked a riverine connection with the capital. The road network intersected with the rivers and generally ran perpendicular to them. Wherever the roads crossed the rivers, there were ferries to move carts across.[35] The ruler and his retinue periodically travelled along this road network, making royal progresses to receive the personal homage of the various royal subordinates. In these places he performed royal ceremonies that the local élite had to pay for (an indirect form of taxation). Nevertheless, the money or goods paid for services and supplies went to local people.

Special reference is made to tradesmen and women who accompanied the royal progresses and who camped in open fields near the court's lodging at the conclusion of each day's journey. These carts and tradesmen are well represented in the Majapahit era's temple reliefs. And even when the kings were not travelling, the roads were used to transport rice and other goods. The *Nāgerakĕrtāgama* speaks of 'caravans of carts' along Java's roads and of crowded highways. But the use of the road network was seasonal because of the monsoon rains. Movement on the roads was concentrated in the drier season from March to September. This same epic describes travel on the roads in the wet season: 'The road . . . over the whole length then was difficult, narrow. There followed rains. The incline

[35] There were at least seventy-nine ferry crossing 'districts' in east Java: ibid., II. 215–19, 227–47.

being altogether slippery, several carts were damaged there, colliding one with another.'[36] Thus, in the rainy season the bulk of Javanese rice was conveyed by river from the hinterland to the coast, and foreign goods moved upriver in return.

According to the epigraphical evidence, in the 1330s, shortly before the kings of Majapahit began to consolidate their far-flung maritime empire, they also began to consolidate the royal centre's control over the resources and the people of east Java. The two processes of annexation and the extension of effective hegemony were almost simultaneous.

The trend toward systematic annexation and integration within the Brantas River basin had begun as early as the tenth century, when the early kings had used port merchants and foreigners as royal tax-farmers to ensure that hinterland rice reached the royal port. Airlangga had carried the process a step further when he dammed the Brantas River, and expanded the use of *sīma* tax transfer grants; he thereby enabled east Java's kings to reduce the residual power of local agricultural élites. Apparently Airlangga also dispensed with the use of foreigners as tax-farmers, and used only local port merchants to collect the king's share from the villages in the royal domain. During the Majapahit period, even the tax-farmers were eliminated. Payments of rice due to the royal government were collected by state ministers within the royal domains, and local allies were obliged to deliver their own part of the king's share directly to him.[37]

As is typical in other early Southeast Asian political-economies, even in periods in which a strong central authority existed, the king's supply of agricultural produce came largely from his own domains and the amount of tribute rice expected from allies remained small. For the most part, rice from outside the royal domain continued to move to Java's ports through market mechanisms, not taxation or tribute. Because of their income from the commercial sector, it was not necessary for Majapahit's monarchs to confront the foundation of local autonomy and prosperity by increasing their collection of agricultural produce from their allies. To increase its demands on the agrarian sector, the state would have had to infringe further upon the most basic political rights and socio-economic powers of these entrenched local élites. When the kings sought to enhance royal revenue and authority, they pursued not a larger share of the realm's agricultural resources, but control over wealth generated outside the agricultural sector. They were content to tax local commerce and non-agricultural production; to promote the cause of merchants, artisans, and élite who could best assist in facilitating the flow of goods to and from Java's north coast ports; and in general, to encourage the development of Java's economy.

The principal means by which the Majapahit kings enhanced the royal treasury and royal power was by the issuing of royal charters that redefined the local tax system. Renewed interest in *sīma* tax transfers during the Majapahit era offers testimony to the state's efforts to extend its

[36] Quoted in ibid., III. 23; IV. 497.

[37] Kulke, 'The "City" and the "State" in Early Indonesia'; and J. G. de Casparis in Sartono Kartodirdjo, ed., *Papers of the 4th Indonesian-Dutch History Conference*, Yogyakarta, 1986, I. 3–24.

authority. Inscriptions explain that the state was giving attention to previous *sīma* grants because the original documents had become unreadable, and there was a legitimate need to reissue *sīma* charters. Since there is no evidence that the initial *sīma* tax remissions were altered, there must have been great symbolic importance associated with the Majapahit monarch's confirmation and recertification of the *sīma* charters bestowed by previous rulers.

A new class of *sīma* charters was also issued. These 'investment *sīma*' were coincident with the increase in the number of wealthy families who lacked hereditary landholding rights. These families bought land, built family temples on it, and then applied (with a lump-sum payment) to have the sanctity of their family temple (as well as the legitimacy of their landholding status) validated. Their family temple assumed a subordinate position within a royal ritual network, and their land was declared perpetually tax-exempt. In these charters the Majapahit ruler normally retained a portion of his tax rights (instead of relinquishing almost all his revenue rights, as had been the practice among previous monarchs), and divided the remainder between the temple and the petitioning family. *Sīma* grants of the Majapahit era thereby created a family trust that strengthened the status and position of the newly powerful—the establishment of an ancestor temple and its reception of *sīma*-holding status sanctified the family's élite status. These new *sīma* charters not only confirm the enhanced power of the Majapahit state (and a more public and visible monarchy), but also document a less rigid social hierarchy.[38]

Other royal charters reveal an accelerating trend toward relieving specified non-farmers (mostly merchants and artisans in the eastern part of Java) of their former obligations to local land-based élites by transferring them to royal tax-paying roles. These new royal taxpayers, as a result, gained a revised relationship with the king and his court that was no longer completely mediated by local authorities. Local authorities were thus deprived of some of their non-agricultural revenue as well as their authority over non-agricultural populations.

The Canggu Ferry Charter of 1358 and three charters (dated 1336, 1391, and 1395) addressed to the two neighbouring towns of Bililuk and Tanggulnam suffice to demonstrate how this was accomplished.[39] Prior to the ferry charter of 1358, the people who operated the ferries had no relationship with the royal court. They had been viewed as constituents of the local landed élite, and had paid their taxes to them. The new royal charter, however, relieved them of any obligation to pay taxes or tribute to the local authorities, and instead required them to deliver a quantity of textiles directly to the king and to make a substantial contribution of flowers and cash to help pay for royal ceremonies.

Their new status as royal taxpayers independent of local authorities was only part of the agreement. The charter required them to make a contribution of goods and money for Bubat's Caitra festival, a contribution that entitled them to participate in it along with the royal lineage and its

[38] Wisseman-Christie, 'Negara, Mandala, and Despotic State', 73.
[39] Pigeaud, passim.

distinguished guests. This was an unprecedented recognition, indeed, a display of their economic, political, and military importance in controlling transport in east Java.

The charters from Bililuk and Tanggulnam reveal that the townspeople engaged in making salt (from saline streams), refining sugar, packing water-buffalo meat, pressing oil, and manufacturing rice noodles, and that in the local market they purchased four kinds of spices (probably used in large quantities by the meat packers), iron ware, ceramics, rattan, and cloth.

There were also textile workers who bought cotton cloth and dyes. Most likely they were manufacturing batiks, materials dyed by an elaborate process that was indigenous to Indonesia and predated any Indian influence. There are written references to it in the literature of east Java. Batiks are made by painting designs on a material (now mostly cotton) with wax—the Javanese originally used beeswax. The cloth is then dipped into a dye. Only the unwaxed areas are able to pick up that particular colour. Once that colour has set, the old wax is removed and a new design is painted, and the cloth is dyed in a different colour. This process is repeated until an intricate and many-coloured design is completed. To this day, batiks remain one of the most beautiful products of island Southeast Asia.[40]

Prior to the granting of the royal charters, the local artisans and merchants had been subject to a local 'chief of trade', a representative of the local landed élite. Because he supervised the market in which they purchased their supplies and sold their products, they were obliged to make contributions to him on thirteen different occasions. One obligation concerned contributions that they should make toward his travel and transport costs; five refer to their obligations regarding any births, marriages, or deaths in his family; and seven concerned obligations such as entertaining his guests.

The royal charters abolished all of these obligations, and in their place instituted a fixed tax that was to be shared by both the king and the 'chief of trade'. Although the king probably had received some portion of the artisans' produce previously as a part of the local authorities' contributions to the royal centre, the king would now enjoy direct royal collection of what he considered his share. That the royal tax was a fixed amount also had the benefit of eliminating what had been arbitrary and unpredictable assessments levied by a representative of the local élite.

The royal charters issued to communities throughout east Java often required that local resources be used to pay for or provide the supplies for locally performed ceremonies that honoured the monarch and displayed his powers. Local authority had long been linked to local ceremony, and the king thus ensured that local people would be exposed to ritual enactments of royal power as well. Often the resources due to the king (goods or money) were designated as contributions to royal ritual at the capital, in which representatives of the local community were required to participate.

A temple network, in which local temples became ritual subordinates to

[40] W. Warming and M. Gaworski, *The World of Indonesian Textiles*, London, 1981.

those temples that were administered by royal abbots and priests, was one innovation that provided additional infrastructure and extended the effective core area of the ruler's authority. The first evidence of this consolidation is provided in the account of Kĕrtanagara, noted above, who reconfirmed the special privileges granted to religious domains by his father Viṣṇuvardhana. As explained in Kĕrtanagara's inscriptions, this was done to separate the 'holy domains' of the 'clergy of all kinds' from the 'lands of royal servants'. This would initiate the independence of the holy domains 'in order to render the more firm the Illustrious Great King's sitting on the jewel lion's throne, being considered as the one sunshade of all Java, as the exalted deity among all the honored [neighbouring divinities] of the land of Janggala and Pangjalu'. This realm-wide ritual network is verified a century later in the *Nāgarakĕrtāgama*'s 1365 description of the ancestor commemoration rites (*śrāddha*) performed for the queen Rājapatni at her funeral temple at Bayalangu. The *Nāgarakĕrtāgama* account mentions at least twenty-seven interconnected royal temples that were strategically placed throughout the extended imperial core, and had been established in the hundred years between the mid-thirteenth century and the time the *Nāgarakĕrtāgama* was written.[41]

That increased centralization was manifested in royal rituals is not surprising, given the propensity toward ceremony in early Southeast Asian states. As well as any political leaders today, the kings understood the use of rituals in which they could claim that their special powers, their relationship to illustrious ancestors and to higher gods, was at the root of local prosperity. They could display their families, their allies, and their strategic constituents as well as their own superior rank. Furthermore, there was another equally important political advantage to this method of centralization. It served to defuse possible resistance. Since donations and contributions to these ceremonies bestowed religious merit and the ceremonies ensured general prosperity, it was awkward for local authorities to refuse such levies.

Although new revenues generated by the agreements in the charters did not immediately add substantial income to the royal treasury, they promoted an indirect increase in revenue. Once an artisan community's obligations were fixed on an annual basis by royal decree, it was able to retain a greater or at least a more predictable share of its production. This gave the artisans an incentive to increase production, since any amount produced over the fixed assessment could be sold by them for their own profit. The flow of these goods into coastal ports and their exchange for goods of foreign origin increased the king's revenues, since it was this commerce that was directly taxed by the monarch.

New levels of demand emanating from hinterland and coastal towns for Java's rice, along with the growing foreign demand for spices that were acquired with Java's rice exports, had the effect of encouraging the production and sale of rice surpluses. As demand expanded, local peasants had an opportunity to increase their incomes. There is no doubt that the rice economy of eastern Java as well as the older region of central Java

[41] Kulke, 'The Early and Imperial Kingdom' in Marr and Milner, 16–17.

prospered. The wide distribution and heavy concentration of Chinese ceramics in archaeological sites that date to the Majapahit era, literary and epigraphic references to local consumption of commercial products of nonlocal origin, and archaeological evidence of monetarized exchange at all levels of the Javanese economy, suggest that the desire and the ability to consume imported or luxury goods had spread beyond the élite during this era.[42]

The availability of these 'foreign' goods also provided peasant cultivators with incentives to produce more rice. However, given the importance of religious ritual in early Javanese society, Javanese peasants may not have been responding to new economic opportunity simply for the sake of their own personal or family consumption. Religious ceremonies and temples, too, might have provided incentives. New or expanded sources of incomes may have made it possible for many outside the élite to become sponsors of religious ceremony for the first time. Investment of surplus income in temple construction or religious ritual, especially that directly associated with the king, bestowed significant merit upon the donor and enhanced the status of the benefactor within the traditional system.

The fact that some of the new royal taxes specified in the charters were payable in cash rather than in kind reveals the growing monetarization of the Javanese economy, a consequence of Java's commercial prosperity as a major international centre of trade. Chinese goods and copper cash continued to flow into Java; Mediterranean gold moved through the Middle East and India to Java, along with major export items from these regions. By the time of Majapahit, copper coins (either Chinese or similar to China's) had become the local currency not only in Java but in Sumatra's ports as well. Precious metals such as gold and silver were rarely used to facilitate exchange or make payments (a practice that had been common in the pre-Majapahit period). In Majapahit's realm gold and silver remained important not as currencies but as commodities and merchandise for the market.[43]

## THE SOUTHEAST ASIAN MARITIME REALM, c.1500

Those forces that ultimately weakened Majapahit's control of its realm and the eclipse of its far-flung hegemony were both subtle and large. In short, the Javanese were too successful. The growth and development of the international spice business had fuelled Java's expanding commercial and political pre-eminence from the eleventh to the latter part of the fourteenth century, but the further development of that same market precipitated its

42 Hall, 242–50. R. S. Wicks, 'Monetary Developments in Java Between the Ninth and Sixteenth Centuries: A Numismatic Perspective, *Indonesia*, 42 (1986). It is here implied that the Javanese society would have widely responded to such an opportunity to improve his income. This assumption is somewhat controversial, as scholars also argue that the typical Southeast Asian peasant had other priorities than economic goals in his life. See William C. Scott, *The Moral Economy of the Peasant*, New Haven, 1976; and Samuel L. Popkin, *The Rational Peasant: The Political Economy of Rural Society in Vietnam*, Berkeley, 1980.

43 Wicks, op. cit.

decline, since the spice business grew so great that Majapahit could not contain it. By the early sixteenth century, north Sumatran pepper ports were exporting between 15,000 and 20,000 *bihars* of pepper annually, primarily to China, while the Malabar coast of western India was exporting 20,000 *bihars* of its own and Indonesia's pepper annually to the West. Coastal trading communities proliferated within and without the realm of Majapahit, and ports over which it had held sway became increasingly independent and boisterous. As a mark both of their growing independence and of their newly forged international links, the coastal communities of this Sanskritic island world converted to Islam.

In the first decade of the fifteenth century, a series of Chinese imperial embassies established direct contact with north Sumatran pepper sources. The Ming Dynasty became concerned about security in the strait, and even undertook to police it, with the permission of Majapahit (which was in no position to deny such a request). In 1405 China sent out a fleet under the admiral Ch'eng Ho, a Yunnanese Muslim, to clean out a Chinese pirate nest that had grown up at Palembang; this mission he successfully accomplished.

In that same year the Admiral approached the ruler of Melaka (Malacca), a new port that had been founded only three years before, in 1402. Melaka was on the western coast of the Malay peninsula, on what we now call the Straits of Melaka. Its ruler was a prince who claimed descent from a southeastern Sumatran royal lineage that had been defeated and forced into exile by Singhasari's 1275 attack on the port at Jambi-Malāyu. He offered Melaka a special relationship with China; this relationship protected it for decades, until China's maritime position was abruptly abandoned in the 1430s. Melaka immediately thereafter established a relationship with the commercial communities in Java's ports, and became a distribution point not only for Sumatran, but for Javanese trade goods as well. Thereafter, it was no longer necessary to go to Java for the fine spices. This new port grew rapidly in significance and soon began to return to the straits area the significance that it had had in the days of Śrīvijaya, before the triumph of east Java. Furthermore, the years 1405 and 1406 were marked by a civil war at the heart of the Majapahit realm; from that point on east Java's home base was wracked by political dissension, and the island's power overseas waned.

By 1410 Majapahit had lost its hegemony to the west of Java and by 1428 it had lost control over the western part of Java. By the middle of the fifteenth century, commercial communities in the realm's ports had succeeded in depriving Majapahit's rulers of their control over much of the international trade and much of their political realm besides. But the final battle did not come until 1513 when a coalition of Javanese coastal communities attacked the core area of the realm. By 1528 Majapahit's centre was taken, and the royal family was forced to flee and take refuge on Bali. With the exception of those who lived on Bali and a few other small islands, all those who had been Majapahit's would kneel and pray toward Mecca, the sacred centre of Islam on the Arabian peninsula.

Thus, one could say that the hemisphere-wide access of Majapahit's spice trade was its undoing. And the spices, like the islands themselves, had developed a siren quality that was irresistible. So strong was their allure that men at the opposite end of the hemisphere were willing to sail out into totally unknown oceans in order to find them. It was Iberian-sponsored sailors seeking the Spice Islands who were responsible for the sole possession of the western hemisphere by the Atlantic nations of Europe and also for the circumnavigation of Africa that led to the presence of Atlantic shipping in the Indian Ocean. Since these two feats were responsible for beginning the process by which the global balance of power was altered, one could say that their success was not only their own undoing, but the undoing of the entire balance of power in the hemisphere.

The coastal communities that defeated Majapahit and established the new Mataram state based in central Java were Muslim, but this was by no means an indication that any foreign Muslim power was behind this transition. The Muslims who overthrew Majapahit were local people, not foreigners, and few of their grievances against the old realm were religious in nature. Nor did the motivation to convert to the Islamic faith come from outside the realm, but from within it.

Although Muslim traders, both Arabs and Iranians, had been in Southeast Asia ever since the earliest days of Islam in the seventh century, their religion did not have any immediate impact on the Southeast Asian peoples. Indeed, from the seventh to the tenth centuries, few in Southeast Asia converted to Islam, even though this was the time of Śrīvijaya's hegemony when traders from the Islamic Caliphates predominated on the routes between the Arabian Sea and China, and the Caliphates' *dinar* had become the currency of choice in Śrīvijaya's ports. It was only after the decline of both the Caliphate and Śrīvijaya, and the rise of Islamic mysticism and Turkish and Mongolian power, that Islam began to have appeal to Southeast Asian islanders.[44]

It was Merah Silu, the local ruler of Samudra-Pasai, a small polity in northern Sumatra that controlled both a pepper-producing hinterland and a coastal port, who first converted to Islam at roughly the same time that Majapahit was founded, in the last decade of the thirteenth century. This aspiring leader had first established his credentials, military and economic, in the hinterland near the headwaters of the Pasangan River, and it was from this base that he conquered the coast. Thereafter, according to local tradition, he was converted to Islam, not by a foreign merchant but by his own dream. In this dream none other than the Prophet Mohammed came to convert him and gave him the name Malik al-Salih. When he awoke he could recite the Koran and the Islamic confession of faith. Some forty days later, as Mohammed had prophesied in his dream, a ship arrived from Mecca carrying a Muslim holy man who would serve his realm. It also carried the Sultan of Ma'bar, the major pepper-producing region on India's Malabar coast, and one of the principal places from which pepper was exported to the West.[45]

Samudra-Pasai soon after its conversion became a major centre of

[44] Meilink-Roelofsz, *Asian Trade and European Influence*, 103–15; L. C. Damais, 'L'epigraphie Musulmane dans le Sud-Est Asiatique', BEFEO, 54, 2 (1968).

[45] Kenneth R. Hall, 'The Coming of Islam to the Archipelago: A Reassessment' in Karl L. Hutterer, ed., *Economic Exchange and Social Interaction in Southeast Asia: Perspectives from Prehistory, History, and Ethnography*, Ann Arbor, 1977, 213–31.

Islamic studies, the first within the island realm, but for the first hundred years of its existence, neither this port nor the gradual spread of its religion to other ports had much impact on Majapahit's power. During the fourteenth century when Majapahit extended its hegemony out over the seas, representatives of Samudra-Pasai were among the participants in the ceremonies at its centre, probably because Samudra-Pasai was supplying Majapahit's ports with pepper destined for China.

However, eventually the new and growing ports began to resent what they felt was the unwarranted control of Majapahit. Then the Muslim faith offered them not only a sense of community but a new legitimacy as well. By the end of the fourteenth century, Islam had spread throughout the maritime realm, even to the ports on Java's northern coast (and, apparently, even to a few members of the royal family), and had become a symbol of autonomy, and ultimately a rejection of the aristocratic lineage and special religious connections claimed by Majapahit's rulers.[46] But the irony of it is that today it is only necessary to look at those places in Southeast Asia that are now Muslim to know where ports once loyal to Majapahit were.

## THE TEMPLE-BASED POLITICAL-ECONOMY OF ANGKOR CAMBODIA

Among historians who study Southeast Asia's pre-1500 history, there is substantial disagreement on what constituted a 'state'. Is the standard a unified bureaucratized polity that is consistent with traditional Western understanding of what an advanced civilization should be? This view is reinforced by the accounts of Chinese historians, whose dynastic histories contain highly flattering views of their southern neighbours' accomplishments (and consider several of the early Southeast Asian civilizations to have possessed state systems that were similar to their own). Or could an institutionally weak, yet integrated, society still be considered a major civilization?

One standard by which early Southeast Asian states are measured is the number of stone temple complexes they left—the more impressive the archaeological remains, the more prosperous and accomplished was the state; or so the reasoning goes. Thus, the massive temple complexes of central and eastern Java, as well as Angkor (Cambodia) and Pagan (Burma) on the mainland suggest that accomplished political systems were responsible for their construction, through a central administration that mobilized a realm's wealth and manpower to create these architectural wonders. But historians now are coming to find that broad levels of social, economic, and political integration were not necessary for such construction, and that

[46] The Majapahit state, basically decentralized and agrarian, was inadequately prepared to deal with the wealthy commercial enclaves that it had inadvertently created. The Majapahit rulers had tried to derive maximum benefit from the export of agricultural products without adequately reforming their internal administrative structure and practices.

the building of impressive religious edifices does not necessarily demonstrate the political and economic accomplishments of a society.

In the Angkor era—at its height from the ninth to the thirteenth centuries—inscriptions proclaimed the king as the creator and director of public works that were designed to ensure prosperity. These works irrigated some five million hectares, and were constructed around the Khmer capital at Angkor and in a number of regional domains under Khmer authority. Without this hydraulic system, the water supply was irregular and thus limited agricultural productivity.

Traditional conviction among the Khmer populations was that their monarch was the source of his subjects' economic welfare. The *nāga*, the water spirit, was widely portrayed in Khmer art, and was a central figure of popular religion. Chou Ta-kuan, Mongol envoy to Angkor in 1296, reported that the Khmer people believed that their ruler slept with a *nāga* princess, and that the result of their union was the country's prosperity.[47] This report implies that the Khmer monarch enjoyed a ritual relationship with the spirit of the soil that released the fertility that guaranteed the earth's productivity. In this same tradition Yaśovarman I (r. 889–910) constructed an artificial lake (*baray*) northeast of his new capital city of Yaśodharapura (Angkor) at the end of the ninth century. According to the inscription reporting this event, the king wished to 'facilitate an outlet for his abundant glory in the direction of the underworld'.[48] This underworld, also depicted as the place from which Khmer monarchs judged the dead, was the abode of the *nāgas*, the source of fertility.

A 1980 examination of the Angkor era water-management system demonstrates that Yaśovarman's lake was not a critical source of water for the Angkor region's agricultural production in a technical sense, though as the focus of Khmer religion, it was important symbolically in the Khmer system of 'theocratic hydraulics'.[49] Archaeologists have assumed that water seeped through the dyke base of Yaśovarman's lake (which measured 6.5 kilometres long by 1.5 kilometres wide) into collector channels outside the dyke, which subsequently carried the water to surrounding fields. But studies conducted in the late 1970s found that Angkor-era agriculture was based instead on bunded-field transplanted wet-rice cultivation that allowed the planting of approximately fifty million fields. In the Angkor region floodwaters would slowly rise from the Great Lake, the Tonle Sap, to its tributaries, but would rapidly recede after the rainy season. A network of dams and bunds diverted and retained the receding floodwaters of the Great Lake after the rainy season. The Khmer lacked the technology to build large-scale dams that could have allowed an integrated region-wide hydraulic system; instead they depended on a network of small, simple earthworks on minor streams to retard and spread floodwaters into clay-based ponds, which stored the water for later use.

47 Chou Ta-kuan, *Notes on the Customs of Cambodia translated from the Shuo-fu*, trans. Paul Pelliot (trans. from French into English by J. G. d'Avery Paul), Bangkok, 1967, 31.

48 A. Barth and A. Bergaigne, 'Inscriptions Sanskrites du Cambodge et Campa' in *Académie des Inscription et Belles-Lettres, Notices et extraits des manuscrits de la Bibliothéque du roi et autres bibliothéques* [henceforth ISCC], 27, Paris, 1884, 1893, 407.

49 W. J. van Liere, 'Traditional Water Management in the Lower Mekong Basin', *World Archaeology*, 11, 3 (1980) 274.

Archaeological evidence demonstrates that Angkor itself was not a major centre of this water-management network but rather the hill Phnom Kulen, which was located upriver from Yaśovarman's lake some fifty kilometres northwest of Angkor. Phnom Kulen was near the headwaters of the Siemreap (river), which flowed from that area through Angkor to the Tonle Sap. A network of small earth dams regulated the flow of water downstream from Phnom Kulen to Angkor.

One striking feature of the water-management network at Phnom Kulen is that its dams, in addition to their effectiveness in managing water, were all constructed running east–west and north–south. Similarly, throughout the Angkor region Khmer temples were constructed at the intersection of moats and roads which were oriented east–west and north–south; this was done purposely to project the image of the heaven on earth (*maṇḍala*) that had been initiated by Khmer monarchs. In addition to being consistent with Indian and Khmer cosmological focus on east–west and north–south, the water-management network was consecrated by the traditional symbols of fertility. A number of linga phallic symbols were carved in the rocky riverbed at the mountain source, suggesting the sanctity of the water that flowed from the mountain region to Angkor. It is significant that Jayavarman II (r. 802–50) consecrated his *devarāja* cult (an emblem of the unification of the Khmer realm) at Phnom Kulen, which became the original 'Mount Mahendra', the centre of the Khmer heaven on earth, prior to the establishment of his new capital downriver at Hariharalaya and the consecration of a new Mount Mahendra there.[50] The original Mount Mahendra at Phnom Kulen was thus not only a source of legitimacy for later monarchs who drew upon the protective powers of Jayavarman's *devarāja* cult, but it was also seen quite correctly as the source of the Angkor region's water supply, a fact that enhanced the possibilities for success for the monarch's subjects.

Khmer inscriptions and archaeological evidence well reflect the growing religious sophistication of Khmer society in the Angkor era. The sacred language and symbols of 'Hindu' religious philosophy proclaimed the king's glory and abilities. The king was filled with life-sustaining energy derived from 'Hindu' and indigenous deities, as divinity flowed from the heavens or from the earth and permeated him, endowing him with the power to dispense 'purifying ambrosia' or other less abstract forms of prosperity upon his subjects. While local deities and spirits protected the monarch and his subjects, 'Hindu' gods suffused Khmer monarchs with their superior creative and purifying energy, enhancing further the prospects for prosperity in this and other worlds.

The principal concern of the leaders of early Khmer society was the establishment and endowment of local temples, for which they accrued religious merit and economic return. Key figures in the foundation of these early temples were consensual leaders of local populations, rather than persons claiming royal authority. Inscriptions recording such activities emphasize the religious prowess rather than the physical might of the local élites who were establishing the temples. Regional leaders held official

[50] G. Cœdès, *The Indianized States of Southeast Asia*, ed. Walter F. Vella, trans. Susan Brown Cowing, Honolulu, 1968, 100–3; Hermann Kulke, *The Devarāja Cult*, Ithaca, 1978.

titles; the power of the landed élites was recognized by those claiming the authority to rule over the Khmer people by the bestowal of titles on these pre-existing leaders, giving them 'new' authority as district officers in the state administration. In such a way the landholders, the regional economic, social, and political leadership, were integrated into an emerging state system.

The actions taken by landed élites involved the worship of local and 'state' divinities to 'acquire merit' and to 'exhibit devotion'. Inscriptions celebrated the presentation of gifts made to the temple by local leaders as part of their worship, and the wealth of those making the gifts was stressed and donations were carefully calculated. The landed élites who were responsible for this epigraphy emphasized the giving of gifts to temples as the foremost means to ensure the prosperity of society.

The Khmer aristocracy concentrated economic resources under a temple's administration, whether to acquire the merit associated with such donations, to allow for a more efficient management of an élite's resources, or to avoid the revenue demands of those political élites claiming rights to a share of the local landed élite's possessions. The foremost method of accomplishing this goal was to donate land to temples. Boundaries of donated lands were clearly defined in the inscriptions, usually associated with place names—perhaps a village, an estate, a pond, or the riceland of another landholder. Past and present holders of the assigned lands were enumerated, along with the mode of the property's acquisition and its price if acquired by purchase; the land's productivity (rice yield) was even estimated. Inscriptions reporting assignments of populated land gave the parcel's current occupants and spelled out what portion of the occupants' production was assigned to the temple. If the land was unpopulated, a labour force was assigned the task of working the newly donated lands. These labourers were counted—males, females, females with children—and their ethnic identity (e.g. Mon or Khmer) was recorded.

It is not uncommon to discover that the relatives of donors of such land endowments were members of the priesthood servicing the local temple, who became managers of the assigned property. In many instances the donor family rather than the temple staff managed family land assigned to a temple, the temple receiving only a designated share of the income. What was transferred by donors was not 'ownership' of land, but the right to income from land. Control over labour and production rather than ownership of land was critical for the development of early Southeast Asian states. To Khmer élites, 'landholding' meant rights to the production and labour service of the inhabitants of a parcel of land rather than absolute possession of it. In land donations to temples, only certain rights over the land were transferred; while inhabitants of the assigned land normally continued to farm the land, the recipient temple collected much or all of their production. Donated property was usually subject to a combination of claims, those of the temple receiving the donation as well as those of the donor's family, who retained certain personal rights to the property—for example, the right to a share of the land's production as well as administrative or political rights over the inhabitants.

The economic diversity of local temples is reflected in the variety of donations 'for the service of the property' assigned: domesticated animals, goats, buffaloes, cattle, coconut palms, fruit trees, areca nuts, betel leaves, clothing, a threshing floor, plus numerous individual objects, are examples. The type and size of gifts to temples indicate not only economic specialization within early Khmer society in order to create such wealth, but also the developing institutional capacity to utilize and administer this production. An economic system was emerging, centred in the temple. The assignments of land and its production by Khmer aristocrats turned temples into local storage centres; goods deposited in temple storehouses were a source of social and economic power, reinforcing the prestige of the temples' primary benefactors, the local landed élites, who influenced the redistribution of the temples' stores in support of their followers (including those working for the temple).

The concentration in temples of the authority to manage local resources had a significant impact on the process of local political integration. The implication of such centralization for economic control is reflected in epigraphic references to the 'joining together for the enjoyment of the gods', whereby a single landholder, or several, shifted a share of the income (goods and services) destined to one god or temple to that of another, or amalgamated the administration of one temple's lands with that of another.[51] Through these actions, a pattern of subordination of one local deity to another as well as one local temple to another began to emerge in Khmer society. Regional temple networks came to be sustained and controlled by a secular, landed élite who transferred income from their lands or donated material goods and services to temples in the network.

During the Angkor era amalgamation (*miśrabhoga*) arrangements were normally not undertaken without the approval of the king himself, but in pre-Angkor society private landholders and not a royal authority dominated the concentration of economic resources and the amalgamation of temple administration. Prior to the ninth century Khmer monarchs were concerned only with recruiting as their allies the local landed élites who had initiated such transfers and consolidations, confirming the transactions rather than challenging them. Royal edicts, although expressing concern for land, never claim that the monarchy's authority over land superseded that of the local landed élites.[52]

An inscription of the Angkor-era ruler Jayavarman IV (r. 928–41) speaks of a Khmer monarch's concern for land, forbidding the careless grazing of buffaloes that might destroy good riceland.[53] But in expressing concern, Jayavarman IV still had to take an indirect approach and respect the landholding rights of the local élites. In this instance Jayavarman ordered a royal official to notify the region's political leader (a *khloñ viṣaya*—a district

[51] M. C. Ricklefs, 'Land and the Law in the Epigraphy of Tenth Century Cambodia', JAS, 26, 3 (1967) 411–20.

[52] See O. W. Wolters, 'North-Western Cambodia in the Seventh Century', BSOAS, 37, 2 (1974) 383; and 'Jayavarman II's Military Power: The Territorial Foundation of the Angkorian Empire', JRAS (1973) 21–30. Wolters argues that in early Cambodian history local chiefs dominated. The early Khmer 'state', Wolters holds, was a temporary entity based upon the success of periodic independent leaders. See also Michael Vickery, 'Some Remarks on Early State Formation in Cambodia' in Marr and Milner, 95–115.

[53] G. Cœdès, *Inscriptions du Cambodge*, Hanoi, 1937–42, Paris, 1951–66, VI. 115.

chief) of his wishes; the local leader in turn decided to acknowledge the edict by permitting it to be published in his district. Clearly it was the regional chief's option to acknowledge Jayavarman IV's concern for the local lands; it would appear that the chief equally had the option of ignoring this expression of royal interest. Thus, while Angkor-era kings had a greater involvement in land transfers and assignments, early Khmer rulers could only express interest in the transfers of income and management rights of lands that were part of a regional élite's domain. Even in later times the nonroyal private sector, dominated by landed regional élites, was still strong and functional.

Within the Khmer realm religious foundations (i.e. temples) of powerful local families, who also held official titles in the Khmer state's administration, became a means of integrating the land and its production into the structure of the state. Family temples and their properties were subordinated to central temples placed strategically throughout the realm. A portion of the production collected by private temples was channelled to the state temples. In return, the priests of local family temples received validation through periodic participation in the rituals of the central temples. Local family cults also became legitimized via their worship by Khmer monarchs and their subordination to royal cults. In these times temples were not just religious centres but important links in the state's economic and political network. Religion supplied an ideology and a structure that could organize the populace to produce, tap this production, and secure a region's political subordination, without the aid of separate secular economic or political institutions.

Sūryavarman I's reign (1002–50) represents a critical phase in the development of an integrated Khmer economic and political order, with the Khmer temple network assuming a major role in the developmental process. The prosperity of families in the Khmer realm—a prosperity based upon control over the production of land and manpower—came to depend more and more upon royal favour. This new pattern demonstrates the intensified integration of the regional aristocracy into the Khmer state as 'bureaucrats'.[54] They were given official bureaucratic titles; their authority over land and manpower was recognized; and they were charged with responsibility for the expansion of the Khmer state's economic base. Along with this recognition, however, went the responsibility of sharing their land's production with the state. Land transferred to aristocratic families was assigned specifically for the benefit of family temples, whose staffs assumed responsibility for supervising its development. Because they were subordinated to royal temples, these family temples had to share the local production received with the central temples and thus with the Khmer kings who had made the original assignment.

What developed through this pattern of land assignment and development was a network of private and temple landholding rights that was

[54] Michael Vickery, 'The Reign of Sūryavarman I and the Dynamics of Angkorean Development', paper presented at the Eighth Conference of the International Association of Historians of Asia, Kuala Lumpur, 1980. Vickery notices a 'rapid bureaucratic expansion' in Angkor in the tenth century, which thus preceded Angkor's final 'imperial breakthrough' in the eleventh-century reign of Sūryavarman.

subject to the supervision of the monarchy. Angkor's society was élite-dominated. The king held the power to maintain élites with patronage and at the same time needed to prevent or neutralize the emergence of rival power centres. Élites were linked to the royal court through the Khmer temple network, if not through the bestowal of royal favour. Angkor's rulers were capable of reducing local power centres to subordinate provinces of their government, but in the process of awarding territorial grants or property right transfers they were not able to dispense landholding rights at will. The landed élites subject to the Khmer state did have independent rights and were not subject to the constant demands of the state. In the Angkor era, although local autonomy was assaulted—sometimes with a good deal of energy—the landed aristocracy retained power. The Khmer state system was not highly centralized or 'bureaucratic', nor was it a 'feudal' order in which the king assigned bureaucratic duties to a landed élite who derived their landholding rights and status as a consequence of the king's favour. Records of land assignments to families and their temples during the Angkor era reflect constant friction between the centre and its periphery and provide evidence about the nature of the relationship between the Khmer monarch and his regional élites.[55]

'Ownership' of land in the Khmer realm was thus embedded in a system of rights held by related people. The king in theory held the final authority to validate landholding rights, although this authority was not normally exercised—Sūryavarman I's initiatives were unusual; the Khmer monarch thus assumed the role of patron placing land under the 'exclusive' control of favoured families and their temples. The aristocracy, drawing their livelihood from the land, theoretically owed their continued prosperity directly or indirectly to royal favour.

In their epigraphic records Khmer monarchs reveal two purposes in their dealings with the land endowments of local temples: on the one hand they intervened where possible to limit the power of potential rivals, and on the other hand they desired to enhance the economic strength of their supporters. Avoiding possible conflict, Khmer kings rarely intervened in local temple affairs unless there was a direct threat to royal interests, but adeptly employed their right to assign their supporters' income rights to unsettled lands; rights to previously settled land left vacant could be solicited from the king by a family, the land rights of extinct lineages could be reassigned, and landholding rights to unpopulated and overgrown land

[55] On the application of the term 'feudal' to Khmer statecraft, see I. W. Mabbett, 'Kingship in Angkor', JSS, 66, 2 (1978). The ability of Khmer monarchs from the time of Jayavarman II to Sūryavarman II to wage apparently massive warfare demonstrates the strength and unity of the Khmer state, despite the impression that day-to-day government did not seem to be concerned with anything more extensive than securing the material needs of the centre or mediating local disputes and interests. Mabbett notes that Khmer monarchs created special posts with ceremonial functions and prospects for future favours in order to attract members of traditional landed élites. Khmer kings accommodated powerful kinship groups, each with its own network of relatives and dependants, by giving them administrative responsibilities, while the monarch monopolized divine authority. Subordinate Khmer élites thus flourished under a strong monarch. The Khmer system offset the absence of a strong centralized professional bureaucracy and dynastic institutions that were monopolized by a distinct 'royal family'. See also Mabbett, 'Varṇas in Angkor and the Indian Caste System', JAS, 36, 3 (1977).

could be assigned. Families with existing estates were sometimes encouraged to resettle in new territories.

The extension of agriculture into previously uncultivated lands and the construction of hydraulic networks to facilitate the production of rice surpluses were central to the development schemes of Khmer kings and their subordinates. Khmer temples at the state and regional levels fulfilled three economic functions in the agricultural development process. First, they were centres of investment ('banks'), the source of investment capital and management; donors' gifts were redistributed to individuals or groups of peasant and bondsman cultivators as capital investments (e.g., seeds, livestock, and land to be cultivated), which stimulated the agrarian sector. Second, temples were repositories of technological information and knowledge, directly or indirectly supporting scholars, astrologers, and artisans whose expertise and literacy could be drawn upon by cultivators. Third, Khmer temples were supervisory agencies that involved agricultural labourers in the development process, offering sufficient returns to encourage them to remain on the land.

As noted, lands assigned to temples for development were often unpopulated, requiring the assignment of a labour force (men, women and children are enumerated in the inscriptions) with no previous claim to the land's production. This workforce might be acquired by moving a population, possibly war captives (men and women), from an area peripheral to the state's core domain to the lands to be developed. Labourers assigned to develop new lands were incorporated into the local economic and social system by temples. Lone peasant cultivating families could not easily have borne the economic burdens of shortfalls in production as they brought new land into production or implemented agricultural technology associated with the construction of irrigation projects. Temples, however, could mobilize their storage and redistributive mechanisms to meet the subsistence needs of the labourers in such an event, drawing from material resources assigned for this purpose by kings or regional élites. Temples were also in charge of agricultural development, engaging diggers, scribes, managers, and other specialists, combining the technical expertise and human resources necessary for the extension of agriculture. Furthermore, temples offered labourers emotional security; workers sought not only personal economic profit but also worked for the spiritual gain derived from service to a temple's deity.

If land assigned to a temple was not to be administered by the temple staff, the heads of the family or other members of the lineage might act as property managers on the temple's behalf, utilizing income from the land to erect buildings, construct hydraulic projects, secure additional labour to work the land, or in general ensure that the land's productivity would increase. The dominant landholding families thus also benefited from the development of temple land and the accumulation of wealth by the family temple. This income was tapped for redistribution by the family to its supporters in various forms. Relationships between élite families and the temple were rarely questioned by Khmer monarchs, who instead attempted to obtain a share of the wealth accumulated locally by the right their central temples had to a percentage of the local temples' income. However, income from local temples covered only a small percentage of the royal temples' expenses, and this revenue sharing was more symbolic than critical to the financial well-being of the state temples.

That only limited demands were placed on local family temples is conveyed in the accounts of the Khmer royal temples. The Ta Prohm temple's rice needs during the reign of Jayavarman VII (1181–1218) were said to be 6589 kilograms daily for cooking and 2,512,406 kilograms annually.[56] This rice fed the temple's personnel, who included 18 high priests, 2740 officiants, and 2632 assistants—among whom were 615 female dancers, 439 learned hermits who lived in the temple monastery (*aśrama*), and 970 students. A total of 12,460 people lived within the walls of the temple compound. The sum of rice consumed annually was thus 2,512,406 kilograms, of which only 366,800 kilograms were delivered by villages assigned to the temple and 42,157 kilograms from royal storehouses, together covering less than one-fifth of the temple's rice consumption. Villages assigned to the central temple supplied rice through their local family temples, but in comparison to the total amount of production annually drawn by local temples from their assigned lands, the annual payment of roughly 90 kilograms of rice that these family temples were obliged to pay to a central temple was insignificant. The central temple's primary source of income was the temple's own assigned lands worked by 'bondsmen' (*knum*) at the behest of Khmer monarchs and state élites. State-level central temples thus functioned economically in a fashion similar to the local family temples, but on a much larger scale.

Following the twelfth-century inscription of Jayavarman VII in his Prah Khan temple complex describing the Khmer realm as being composed of 306,372 subjects, male and female, inhabiting 13,500 villages, one historian calculated that Khmer subjects were producing roughly 38,000,000 kilograms of hulled rice annually for 20,000 gold, silver, bronze, and stone gods. Each worker supplied an average of 120 kilograms of hulled rice, or 60 per cent of his productivity.[57] The potential of the flow of production to and the concentration of economic resources in Khmer temples is demonstrated in the Ta Prohm inscription's enumeration of the temple's stores, which contained a set of golden dishes weighing more than 500 kilograms; a silver service of equal size; 35 diamonds; 40,620 pearls; 4540 gems; 523 parasols; 512 sets of silk bedding; 876 Chinese veils; a huge quantity of rice, molasses, oil seeds, wax, sandalwood, and camphor; and 2387 changes of clothing for the adornment of temple statues.

The revenue demands of central temples upon local family temples thus appear to have had more political and social than economic importance. Royal interest in local temples, aside from guaranteeing the financial well-being of allies and limiting the economic resources of potential rivals, was more concerned about a local temple's ritual being in harmony with that of

[56] G. Cœdès, 'La stèle de Ta-prohm', BEFEO, 6 (1906).

[57] L. A. Sedov, 'On the Problem of the Economic System in Angkor, Cambodia in the IX–XII Centuries', *Narody Asii: Afriki, Istoria, Ekonomika, Kul'tura*, 6 (1963), estimates that 366.8 tons of rice were supplied by roughly 66,625 villagers, each of the 3140 villages providing roughly 117 kilograms per year to the central temple.

royal temples than about making a local temple economically subordinate to a royal temple.

Endowments to temples at both the state and local level represented the mobilization, organization, and pooling of economic resources (capital, land, labour, and so forth) to support portions of the overall ritual process of the temple—for example, financing a single event in the temple's religious calendar of ritual, the construction of a building in the temple compound, clothing for a temple image, or a subsidy for a temple priest. While this redistribution of economic capital was central to a temple's existence, the mobilization of 'symbolic capital' was also critical, as temple endowments generated one or more ritual contexts in which honours rather than material returns were distributed to and received by donors. In this way economic capital was converted to culturally symbolic capital, honours that enhanced the status of the donor in the minds of his kin and clients.[58]

An endowment permitted the entry and incorporation of Khmer corporate units (e.g., families and kings) into a temple as temple servants (priests, assistants, and so on) or as donors. The donor represented a social, economic, or political unit; the gift was a means by which the group or its leader could formally and publicly receive recognition. While an endowment supported the deity, and often returned some material advantage to the donor, perhaps more important were the symbolic returns of the 'donation'. Rulers—regional élites or Khmer monarchs—were patrons and protectors of temples, ensuring the continuance of a temple's services, resources, and rules. They were not 'rulers' of temples, however, but were servants of the temple's deity, human agents of the lord of the temple—a stone image that could not arbitrate in the real world on its own behalf—who protected and served the deity.

In the Indian tradition a ruler's relationship with a temple represented a symbolic division of sovereignty, whereby the ruler became the greatest servant of the temple's lord, his patronage of the temple's deity sustaining and displaying his rule over men.[59] Yet kings and others who claimed political authority were subject to challenges by those who perceived their shares and rights—a consequence of other individual or group endowments to a temple—to be independently derived from the sovereign deity. An example of the competition to claim the shared sovereignty of the secular (the ruler) and the sacred (the temple) is provided in the Khmer realm, where local élites and kings each patronized temple deities. The issue of who was the ultimate servant of the temple's lord had political significance and explains the attempts by Angkor's monarchs to subordinate the deities of local temples to those of royal temples or to integrate these local deities into royal cults.

The returns from temple donations thus had both economic as well as political implications, and explain the significant flow of economic resources from rulers at various levels to Khmer temples. If an identification

[58] On symbolic gifting see Pierre Bourdieu, *Outline of a Theory of Practice*, Cambridge, UK, 1977.

[59] Arjun Appadurai and Carol Appadurai Breckenridge, 'The South Indian Temple: Authority, Honour, and Redistribution', *Contributions to Indian Sociology*, NS, 10, 2 (1976), point to the role of temples as centres of symbolic redistributions.

with a deity was essential to legitimize rule, as seems to have been the case in the Khmer realm, then instead of material returns upon one's investment symbolic returns must have been equally desirable, especially to Khmer kings who never reaped substantial material benefit from their assignment of local income rights to local temples. The temple's redistributive role was thus critical to issues of sovereignty in both the secular and sacred Khmer world order, and raises questions of how to equate economic and symbolic capital, if it is really possible to quantify this conversion process, and whether there was any attempt to achieve 'equity'—topics beyond the scope of the available historical records.

The redistributive functions of Khmer temples are summarized in Figure 4.1. In this diagram the state's resources flow as donations or dues (gold, land, livestock, food, and labour) from villages and local and regional temples to the state's central temples. Returns may have been in kind, utilizing the temple as a 'bank'. In such instances the donor received a material return (i.e. 'economic capital') upon his 'investment', either directly via a prescribed rate of return or indirectly through the greater productivity achieved regionally as a consequence of the temple's efficient management of land. Returns might also have been 'symbolic capital', which contributed to the legitimacy of various regional and state aristocrats through the performance of temple ceremonies that emphasized the donor's superior spiritual prowess or through the act of recording the gift in an inscription that perpetually honoured the donor's piety.

Thus, in the Khmer realm temples never became independent of those in political authority, whether at the local or state level. Rivalries and tensions developed, rather, among local and state authorities whose power was based on their control over labour, landholdings, and temple administration. There was never a shift of socio-economic power away from secular authorities to a religious order. However, Khmer monarchs were limited by the very nature of their policy of utilizing temples and temple networks as a means of integrating their domains economically and politically. They never developed a centralized bureaucratic order, depending instead upon assignments of land rights and impressive titles to those in royal favour to elicit the loyalty of semi-autonomous regionally based landed élites. Yet there does not appear to have been a lack of ability to finance major royal projects. In the absence of a bureaucratic system for collecting large amounts of income for the state's treasury, temples were viewed as important centres of economic accumulation that could be tapped to finance the king's patronage of religion. Most conspicuous were temple construction and elaborate temple ceremonies and festivals, which provided a pretext under which the state's economic and social resources could be mobilized to achieve the state's political goals. These goals mainly focused on the construction of a state-dominated political system replacing the previous system, which had been built on a series of personal alliances. In this new system temples assumed major roles in the process of political integration.

The Khmer state's centralized temple complex thus related land and population to the king's capital. Temples controlled land, the labour on the land, and the land's productive output. Religious development was

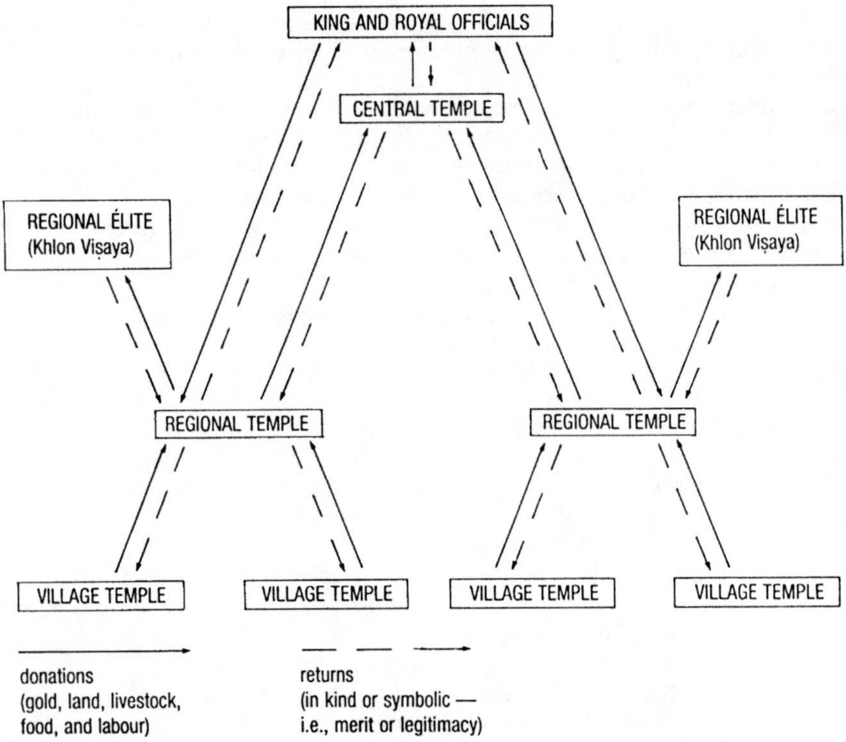


Figure 4.1 The Angkor era temple network.

viewed as an aid to the state's economic development. The extension of cultivated land in the tenth and eleventh centuries was thereby connected to the endowment of religious establishments. Rich temples formed economic bases that were tapped for construction projects, the development of irrigation, rice production, and so on—projects which were healthy for the economy as a whole and which the central government could not always cover financially.

## BUDDHISM AS AN ECONOMIC FORCE IN PAGAN BURMA

The Burmese state of Pagan, at its height from the eleventh to the fourteenth centuries, also drew economic support from a temple network. Early Pagan monarchs had two needs as they established their authority: economic and ideological bases that substantiated their superiority over their political rivals. Buddhism provided the answer. The Buddhist *saṅgha* was able, as an existing body of literati with at least a primary level of technological expertise, to assist in the development of hydro-agricultural systems. In Burma, King Anawrahta (r. 1044–77) resettled skilled and unskilled labour in central and northern Burma during the eleventh century, and also 'imported' Theravāda Buddhism from the Thaton region of southern Burma into the three 'core' agricultural zones (*kharuin*) that surrounded the Pagan royal centre. The Pagan state 'cores' consisted of Kyaukse *kharuin* north of the capital, Toṅplun to the east, and Maṅbu to the west; eighteen secondary 'frontier' settlements (*tuik*) were agrarian communities adjacent to the mountains west of Pagan; forty-three fortified towns were interspersed up the Irrawaddy River from the 'core' to the border of the neighbouring Nanchao realm in the north.[60] Buddhist monasteries and temples were established in critical locations throughout these zones, and upon receiving allocations of rights to land and labour assumed a leadership role in the development of irrigation networks and wet-rice agriculture in each new population centre.

Pagan-era society was organized into professional communities, which in some instances corresponded with ethnic groups (the Mon populations from the Thaton region in lower Burma were resettled in the Pagan economic core during the eleventh-century reign of Anawrahta and were a categorically distinct group in epigraphic records). During the Pagan age, social and political status was determined by one's birth, occupation, and ethnicity. Hereditary status was enforced by the state and the Buddhist Church. Free society was divided into public and private sectors. Public functionaries (*amhū*) served in the military as supervisors of local irrigation and public granaries, and as tax collectors. Private functionaries (*asañ/athi*) included artisans, merchants, and peasants, all of whom were free from service obligations.

During the Pagan age private workers, as seemingly with others, were subject to intensified specialization and became more and more regimented by occupation into specialist groups. Among the Pagan-era working class, those who worked on temples—notably carpenters, masons, wood-carvers, painters, scribes, clerks, artisans, and metal workers—were of higher status than were musicians, dancers, and other performers, food vendors, cooks, hunters, butchers, milkmen, and keepers of game. All such workers were paid for their services rather than providing their labour as a corvée labour tax to the government or temples. Their normal income included gold, silver, lead, land, horses, elephants, clothes, and produce.

Debt bondsmen and women (*kywan*) also figure prominently in the Pagan socio-economy. They pledged their service to a patron for payment in kind, and normally received a share of income from the land they farmed or the work they performed on their patron's behalf. Bondsmen could be assigned to work on a temple's behalf, or they might be transferred with donated land to serve a temple. In early Burmese history bondsmen could easily redeem themselves from servitude; but during the Pagan era, due to the rising complexity of the Burmese political economy and a growing rigidity in the Burmese social hierarchy, it became very difficult for bondsmen to escape their clientage. This is documented in the transition of the common understanding of the word for 'redemption' (*tolhan*), which during Pagan times changed to 'rebellion'.[61] Increasingly a bondsman's only viable option was to enter a monastery as a full-time monk.

Headmen (*sukrī/thugyi*) exercised personal control rather than territorial

[60] Michael Aung-Thwin, *Pagan: The Origins of Modern Burma*, Honolulu, 1985.

[61] Michael Aung-Thwin, 'Kingship, the Sangha, and Society in Pagan' in Hall and Whitmore, *Explorations*, 209.

authority over community occupational groups. They were expected to keep group records, collect and pay revenues to the state, and to enforce hereditary occupation. They pledged their loyalty to a client of the Burmese monarch, who in turn shared locally collected revenues with the king. The king benefited by this regimentation by occupational and ethnic group, and the king and his élite clients provided the linkage among these groups via their sponsorship of monumental architecture, court ceremony, dress that distinguished one group from another, bestowal of titles on loyal subordinates, and the use of a special court language.

Revenue flowed to the centre, and was redistributed as payments and rewards to those favoured by the monarch. However, much local revenue never reached the king or his clients, but instead found its way to the local Buddhist institutions or individual monks as 'in-lieu-of-tax' payments for the upkeep of the *saṅgha*, but also to finance assorted economic development projects that were co-ordinated by the Church. Workers were hired with endowed funds to work temple fields, build and maintain temples, and to service temples. The expenses of monks were paid from temple endowment funds; wells, tanks, and irrigation canals were dug, and palm trees and gardens were planted. Various performances by theatrical and dance troops, festivals, and feasts were financed from revenue assignments to temples. Thus, reassignments of royal revenue collections provided jobs, extended cultivated lands, and financed religion and entertainment.

In Burma status was defined by how much one gave to the Buddhist Church rather than the wealth one accumulated. Kings received merit and consequent legitimacy in return for their generosity. In Burma *kammatic*/*karma* Buddhism, which stressed that salvation was due to one's good works, took precedence over belief that salvation accrued via intellectual attainment (*nibbāṇic*/nirvāṇa Buddhism).[62] From a Burmese perspective, the intellectual quest for salvation was more appropriate to the overly pious; *kammatic* Buddhism was more practical for the average lay person. *Kamma* could be transferred or shared—the merit of one person could enhance the merit of another (usually deceased)—or it could be redistributed, as a rich man could build a temple for the merit of those who could not afford to do so. The king was, ultimately, the one with the most wealth to share. The more a king donated, the more merit he gained. Pagan era kings were considered to be close to Bodhisattva status. Thus, the dilemma of a king was whether to accumulate material or symbolic capital, to maintain the wealth of his kingdom, while being required to give much of his personal wealth away. The Pagan era political-economy may thus be characterized as being based on three mutually related concerns: (1) salvation was achieved through good works and the sharing of merit; (2) religious endowments were a practical means of achieving one's religious as well as social and political goals; and (3) the political-economy depended upon assorted redistributions of material wealth.[63]

[62] Stanley J. Tambiah, *World Conqueror and World Renouncer: A Study of Buddhism and Polity in Thailand against a Historical Background*, Cambridge, UK, 1976.

[63] Michael Aung-Thwin, 'Divinity, Spirit, and Human: Conceptions of Classical Burmese Kingship' in Lorraine Gesick, ed., *Centers, Symbols, and Hierarchies: Essays on the Classical State of Southeast Asia*, New Haven, 1983.

In the absence of a strong centralized political system, Pagan monarchs drew upon the Buddhist religious order to sanctify their authority; by endowing monasteries and temples with land and people, kings set in motion the legacy of royal patronage. Pagan kings were ultimately the individuals with the most wealth to share; by donating more they gained the greatest merit as the chief patrons of the Church. The king was the *kammarāja*, who achieved status by merit and past deeds (*kamma/karma*) as opposed to the Hindu rulers of other early Southeast Asian states who partook of the divine (*dharmarāja*). This system of patronage, however, posed a serious dilemma. The authority of early rulers among their secular subordinates was especially dependent upon periodic redistributions of wealth to maintain bonds of loyalty. Donations to the *saṅgha* by the king and his subordinates began to replace previous material redistributions with redistributions of symbolic capital. Royal allies, by their recognition of the Buddhist *saṅgha* and the king as the chief patron of the *saṅgha*, became participants in the state-sponsored religious system, and enhanced their own personal status as subordinates to the king's 'sacred sovereignty'.

Potential problems in this system were largely emergent in times of political succession, as bonds of personal loyalty could not easily be transferred at the death of a ruler. While a king reigned, there was usually political stability based upon alliance networks that a monarch constructed during his rise to power. Personal bonds of loyalty—titles, position, and even landholding rights—became subject to review when a king died. In such periods of political transition, the hierarchical social structure, the redistribution-based economy, and *kammatic* Buddhism helped to hold the state together.

The history of Pagan demonstrates the pitfalls of this system of *kammatic* kingship, as the *saṅgha* ultimately became the state's major holder of economic resources. The *saṅgha* could, because of the tax-free status of the Church's economic resources, come to control the state's land and labour force. Temple building and religious endowments, initially intended to extend the state's economy and enhance the king's prowess, eventually doomed the monarchy to a status of subservience to the *saṅgha* when the state's economic base fell under its control. To challenge the *saṅgha's* control over the state's economic resources would have led to the negation of the state's image as the Church's leading patron.

Buddhist temples and monasteries became secondary redistribution centres for areas outside the Pagan capital-city palace complex. Burmese monarchs attempted to neutralize the flow of wealth to the *saṅgha*; for example, the king's personal approval was necessary to validate large donations. But the king's authority to restrict donations was neutralized, due to the very nature of Pagan's kingship noted above. As chief patron of religion, the king could not inhibit donations, and, indeed, had to bestow more upon the *saṅgha* than anyone else. Once it had given them, the state was not entitled to take back its income rights to land. In contrast, income rights to land assigned to secular authorities, including royal military and administrators, could be confiscated. To avoid this, royal subordinates frequently reassigned their income rights to the Buddhist *saṅgha*—normally to a specific monk or a local temple rather than to the *saṅgha* in general.

When the monk receiving the income assignment died, property rights reverted to the donor, who could then redonate or retain his property rights, depending on the political climate at that time. Reassignments of income rights to the Church thus were a means by which one could protect personal property from state confiscation.

Overexpansion of the *saṅgha* was thus a major political problem, since the *saṅgha* had the institutional capacity to co-ordinate its affairs over the entire realm, while the state could not. The king's one recourse against the Church's wealth and power was the periodic 'purification' of the religious order, by which the king reduced the Burmese *saṅgha* to small, localized, 'other-worldly' groups with a few material resources, which were under the control of a unified *saṅgha* élite directly appointed and supervised by the king.[64] Pagan monarchs initiated the purification process by publicly accusing the *saṅgha* of being 'corrupt', 'lazy', 'worldly', and thus 'impure'. The ideal *saṅgha* order was one of austerity and asceticism. Thus, to purify the *saṅgha* was an act of piety by the king. In Buddhist tradition there was the expectation that due to the ultimate vulnerability of monks to material corruption (since they were human rather than divine), kings had to purify the religious order periodically to perpetuate the religion.

Burmese rulers followed their public accusation by sending selected monks to Sri Lanka, which was considered to be the centre of Buddhist piety in that era, to be purified (reordained). When they returned, these monks would in turn lead the reordination and purification of all Burmese monks. While the selected monks were gone, the king built an ordination hall for the reordination ceremony. First the ground was ritually cleansed to release the spiritual ties of the local *nat* spirits that might pollute the ceremony; a moat was dug around the hall so that the water in the moat could insulate the grounds of the ordination hall from impurities and all trees that overhung the grounds were cut to prevent their contamination of the grounds.

According to Buddhist tradition, the quality of one's merit was a product of the piety of the monks one donated to. Thus, newly purified Burmese monks, patronized by the king, had the greatest status. Other monks had to subordinate themselves or risk being cut off from state and public funding. Seniority depended upon the order of reordination; detailed accounts were kept to record the minute of ordination/reordination that could demonstrate one's superiority over others in the Burmese *saṅgha* hierarchy. In an era of reordination, the highest-ranking monks thus owed their superior rank to the king, who carefully selected the monks to be sent to be reordained in Sri Lanka and also determined the order of reordination in Burma based upon his perception of a monk's personal loyalty. The king appointed a reordination committee who received applications from those wishing to be reordained. To be worthy of reordination, a monk had to give up his worldly possessions—cattle, land, and manpower. Rights to these could not be transferred to a layman but could only pass to the state.

64 Michael Aung-Thwin, 'The Role of Sasana Reform in Burmese History: Economic Dimensions of a Religious Purification', JAS, 30, 4 (1979).

Those who chose not to give up their material, this-worldly possessions were required to assume lay status, and their property immediately became subject to state tax assessments.

In the Pagan era, strong monarchs were initially capable of instituting periodic purifications of the Burmese *saṅgha*, and thereby re-establishing their right to collect taxes on the formerly tax-free *saṅgha* property. In the thirteenth century the interests of the new landed élite, an artisan class who had become wealthy due to their work on the numerous temple construction projects that had been financed by the state and its secular subordinates, and who had reinvested their wages earned on these projects in land, coincided with the 'impure' *saṅgha*. The large, wealthy *saṅgha* had more wealth to redistribute than did the state—especially to the artisan class who supervised the construction of temples and monasteries. The economic power of this landed artisan class and the *saṅgha* was thus pitted against the political power of the state. Because the *saṅgha* had by that time become closer to this society, its beliefs and its values, than was the old élite, and had also become its economic patrons, there was little public support for the state in its attempts to curb the power of the *saṅgha*.[65]

The thirteenth-century Church supported peasant uprisings and land disputes against the state. It openly bought and sold land and sponsored lavish feasts to celebrate legal victories, where quantities of cattle, pig, and liquor, items normally considered extremely polluting, were consumed.

Pagan's thirteenth-century rulers no longer monopolized wealth, and were no longer able to subjugate the *saṅgha* to their authority. With the continued devolution of land and labour to the *saṅgha*, strong regional socio-economic units rather than a 'unified' state system came to dominate Burma, until fifteenth-century Burmese rulers again found it possible, due to growing public disapproval of an 'impure' and materialistic *saṅgha*, once more to institute a *saṅgha*-wide purification. But following a new purification, the state, needing the economic leadership and merit the *saṅgha* could provide, once again began to make donations of land and labour to the *saṅgha*, and thereby instituted a new cycle of competition between the *saṅgha* and the state.

## INTERNATIONAL TRADE AND COMMERCIAL EXPANSION ON THE MAINLAND, c. 1100–1300

Expansion of the regional agricultural base allowed the dramatic political expansion of both the Khmer and Burmese states during the tenth and eleventh centuries. By the first half of the eleventh century, Khmer monarchs had pushed their control to the west into the Chao Phraya valley of present-day Thailand and toward the Isthmus of Kra of the Malay peninsula. While tenth-century Khmer political interests had been directed toward the eastern portion of the realm, Sūryavarman I (r. 1002–50) reversed this pattern with his activities in the west.[66] Sūryavarman's

[65] Aung-Thwin, *Pagan*. See also G. E. Harvey, *A History of Burma from Earliest Times*, London, 1925.

[66] Hall, *Maritime Trade*, 169–78.

extension of Khmer authority into the Lopburi region had strong economic implications, for control of the lower Chao Phraya provided access to international commerce at Tāmbraliṅga (known as *Tan-liu-mei* to the Chinese), the Chaiya-Suratthani area of southern Thailand, giving the Khmers a more direct contact with the international trade routes than had previously been the case.

Sūryavarman appears to have been especially intent upon establishing a flow of trade from South Indian Cōḷa ports to the Southeast Asian mainland via the Isthmus of Kra and Suratthani area. Goods could then be transported north from the isthmus to Lopburi, where they followed the two exchange networks that evolved in Sūryavarman's reign. The first entered the royal heartland in the Sisophon area; the second encompassed the region north of the Dangrek mountain range, with a link to the core at Prāḥ Vihār and a possible connection to the Mekong River in the east. Under Sūryavarman's rule the commercial economy of the Khmer state achieved such importance that the upper Malay peninsula receded from the patterns of power and trade in the island world and was drawn into those of the mainland. The contacts of this area came to lie not with the international trade route but with a more local route that went across the Bay of Bengal to South India and Sri Lanka. Where previously it had been the locus for outside contact with the islands and the international route for the Mons of lower Burma and southern Thailand, now the isthmus provided a more regional contact for the wet-rice states of Pagan and Angkor and through them to the northern mountain areas where the stirrings of the Tai-speaking peoples were becoming ever more important. This regional trade and communication network rapidly became a path for the spread of Theravāda Buddhism to the western and central sections of the Southeast Asian mainland, establishing a cultural relationship of great significance for later centuries.

As the Khmers were developing commercial contacts with the West, the Burmans were pushing south into the delta of the Irrawaddy and were also moving toward the Isthmus of Kra. After establishing a base at Pagan in the tenth century, the Burmans in an eleventh-century expansion annexed the Mon kingdoms of Pegu and Thaton in lower Burma. Here the Burmans established control over the Mon commercial centres. Around 1050 the Burmans were expanding into the Malay peninsula, where they encountered little resistance from the Khmers. It would appear that after 1050 internal disorder prevented a Khmer presence in the Malay peninsula, leaving the isthmus to the Burmans. The Chams were applying pressure on the eastern Khmer border, Sūryavarman died, and the centre of Khmer political power temporarily shifted north into the Mun River valley beyond the Dangrek mountain range.[67] Angkor-era epigraphy reflects a corresponding lack of interest in commercial affairs until the late twelfth century.

Tenth-century disorder in the region the Chinese knew as the Nanchao region north of the Burman and Khmer realms appears to have blocked

67 Milton Osborne, 'Notes on Early Cambodian Provincial History: Isanapura and Sambhupura', *France Asie/Asia*, 20, 4 (1966), 447.

the overland commercial networks connecting the Irrawaddy plains and China, and thus generated Burman interest in opening commercial channels to the south. Before the closing of the northern route, Burma had served as a centre of exchange between northern India and China; overland trade to Bengal via Arakan had been of major economic importance to the Burmese heartland. Commercial centres on the Malay peninsula provided an alternative source of foreign commodities for this Indian trade after the route to China had been closed. Isthmus ports were located well within the range of Mon coastal shipping, but communication between the Pegu coast of lower Burma and the isthmus was disrupted by a Cōḷa raid in 1024–5.

Under Anawrahta, there was new interest in restoring Burmese commercial intercourse with the isthmus. Around 1057, Anawrahta followed his conquest of Thaton by moving his armies south to Mergui. From Mergui, one historian believed, the Burmese forces crossed the isthmus.[68] Burmese military success in this direction is reflected in a request by King Vijayabāhu I (r. 1055–1110) of Sri Lanka for aid against the Cōḷas, to which the Burmese king responded with 'peninsular products', which were used to pay Vijayabāhu's soldiers. The Cōḷas did not look favourably upon this show of support. In 1067, they launched an expedition against 'Kaḍāram' (Takuapa, the west-coast port terminus of the Persian–Arab trade until the mid-eleventh century), in 'aid of its ruler', who had been forced to flee his country and had sought Cōḷa assistance. Cōḷa administrative problems in Sri Lanka made this intervention short, however; by 1069–70, South Indian control over Sri Lanka had been eliminated. The *Cūlavaṃsa*, the Sri Lankan Buddhist chronicle, records that in 1070, after Vijayabāhu I gained control, many costly treasures were sent to the Pagan king; then in 1075, Buddhist priests from Burma were invited to Sri Lanka to purify the order.[69]

Takuapa's position as the dominant port on the peninsula was dealt a death blow by this second Cōḷa raid; archaeological evidence from the Takuapa area terminates in the second half of the eleventh century, the period corresponding to the raid.[70] The 1025 Cōḷa raid resulted in a loosening of commerce in the straits region, with new ports developing as alternative entrepôts to Śrīvijaya-Palembang. By the late eleventh century the northern Sumatra coast was becoming an important commercial centre. The Kedah coast to the south of Takuapa was more strategically located to be a part of this new pattern of Melaka Straits commerce. A Burmese military presence at Takuapa, followed by the second Cōḷa raid, sealed Takuapa's fate and reinforced the attractiveness of the Kedah coast—Takuapa was no longer a port that could offer security to foreign merchants.

Archaeological remains at Takuapa and Kedah suggest that such a shift occurred, with evidence at Takuapa ceasing and that of Kedah showing a dramatic increase during the second half of the eleventh century. As

[68] G. H. Luce, 'The Career of Htilaing Min (Kyanzittha), the Unifier of Burma A.D. 1084–1113', JRAS (1966), 59.

[69] Wilhelm Geiger, trans., *Cūlavaṃsa*, Colombo, 1929–1930, 58, 8–9; G. H. Luce, *Old Burma—Early Pagan*, New York, 1969–70, I. 40.

[70] Alastair Lamb, 'Takuapa: The Probable Site of a Pre-Malaccan Entrepôt in the Malay Peninsula' in John Bastin and R. Roolvink, eds, *Malayan and Indonesian Studies*, London, 1964.

a consequence of early eleventh-century disorders, the port élites of Takuapa transferred their operations to the new 'preferred port' at Kedah, which explains the Arab geographers' continued use of 'Kalāh' to identify their preferred Malay coastal entrepôt—that is, the Arabs used 'Kalāh' to identify their preferred port wherever it was in the Isthmus of Kra region or the western coast of the Malay peninsula.[71] Similarly, even after Palembang had been replaced by Jambi-Malāyu as the capital of the Śrīvijaya maritime state, the name 'Śrīvijaya' still identified the ports of the southeastern Sumatran coast. It is significant that in 1070 the eastern Isthmus of Kra port of Tāmbraliṅga presented its first tribute to the Chinese court since 1016. This mission may be seen as a response to the events of 1067: while the Cōḷa raid against Takuapa and the shift of Kalāh to the Kedah coast established a new pattern on the west coast, Tāmbraliṅga's mission was sent to reassure the Chinese that its east coast status was unchanged.

After the 1067 Cōḷa raid, the Burmese moved to ensure their external trade connections. The importance of communication networks linking Burma with northern India was recognized by Kyanzittha (r. 1084–1112) in his restoration of the Bodhgāyā shrine in Bengal. An inscription from Bodhgāyā (1105–6) recorded that ships laden with large quantities of jewels had been sent by the Burmese ruler to finance the restoration and the endowment of the Buddhist monument.[72] The fact that this mission was sent by sea is indicative of Pagan's new status as a participant in the regional trade of the Bay of Bengal. An inscription from Pagan records another mission that Kyanzittha sent to either South India or Sri Lanka:

> Then the king wrote of grace of the Buddharatna, Dhammaratna, and Sangharatna [upon a leaf of gold with vermilion ink]. The king sent it to the Chōli prince. The Chōli prince with all his array, hearing of the grace of the Buddha, the Law and the Church, from King Srī Tribhuwanādityadhammarāja's mission . . . he cast off his adherence to fake doctrines, and he adhered straight away to the true doctrine.[73]

Although stated in religious terms, there are strong economic implications in this account. Campaigns that were clearly military in character, and probably economic in purpose, were recorded as religious missions; military campaigns became 'quests for relics'. By triumphantly bringing back relics and sacred treasures, the king could justify the expenses of campaigns whose benefits might remain obscure to the people of the kingdom.

Evidence of such commercial contact is provided in a thirteenth-century Pagan inscription noting that a native of India's Malabar coast made a donation to a temple at Pagan that was connected with an international merchant association based in South India.[74] This thirteenth-century Pagan inscription indicates that the merchants' temple had been present there for

[71] G. R. Tibbetts, *A Study of the Arabic Texts Containing Material on South-East Asia*, Leiden, 1979, 118–228, and passim.

[72] Shwesandaw Pagoda Inscription, *Epigraphia Birmanica* [hereafter EB], I, viii, 163; *Epigraphia Indica* (hereafter EI), 11 (1911–1912) 119.

[73] EB, I, viii, 165, the Shwesandaw Pagoda Inscription.

[74] EI, 7, 197–8. See also Kenneth R. Hall, *Trade and Statecraft in the Age of the Cōḷas*, Delhi, 1980.

some time; the recorded gift provided for the construction of a new shrine (*maṇḍapa*) for the temple compound. Further evidence of a continuing economic relationship between Pagan and South India is reflected in an 1178 Chinese note on the Cōḷas: 'Some say that one can go there by way of the kingdom of P'u-kan [Pagan].'[75]

It thus appears that as Burma came to dominate the Takuapa region and as 'Kalāh' shifted to the Kedah coast, the Burmese empire became a focal point of regional commerce in the late eleventh century. International merchants who were formerly active at Takuapa moved their activities either south to Kedah or north to the regional commercial centres of the Burma coast. In the process the old dominance over international trade enjoyed by Śrīvijaya along the Straits of Melaka was shattered. Java and the northern Sumatra ports drew the major international route south and west, the Burmese drew the regional route of the Bay of Bengal north, and the Isthmus of Kra came to exist essentially as a transition area to the mainland states.

In the following decades, the upper Malay peninsula became the centre of a multipartite interaction among the Sinhalese of Sri Lanka, the Burmese, and the Khmers as the regional trade route developed. Based on his study of Buddhist votive tablets and other evidence, G. H. Luce believed that Pagan controlled the isthmus from 1060 until roughly 1200.[76] Examining the chronicles of Nakhon Sithammarat together with Pāli literature from Sri Lanka, David Wyatt has revised Luce's dating, suggesting that from 1130 to 1176 Tāmbraliṅga was under Sinhalese hegemony.[77] About 1176, King Narapatisithu of Pagan (r. 1174–1211) made an expedition from the Pegu coast into the isthmus and established Pagan's control over the Tāmbraliṅga area 'with the permission of the King of Sri Lanka'.[78]

Burma's twelfth-century influence on the upper peninsula is substantiated by the *Cūlavaṃsa*.[79] When in the 1160s the Burmese refused (or monopolized) the trade in elephants and blocked the way across the peninsula to Angkor, the Sinhalese responded with a retaliatory raid. In this account five ships from Sri Lanka arrived at the port of Bassein in lower Burma. Furthermore, a ship commanded by a government treasurer reached another Mon port, where Sinhalese troops fought their way into the country's interior to the city of Ukkama where they killed the local monarch. This brought the kingdom under Sri Lanka's influence. The people of Burma granted concessions to the Sinhalese and envoys were sent to the community of monks on the island, with the result that the Theravāda monks interceded with the Sri Lankan king on behalf of the Burmese.

Since only six ships reached Burma, this could not have been the record

[75] Hirth and Rockhill, *Chau Ju-kua*, 94, 98.

[76] 'The Early *Syam* in Burma's History: A Supplement', JSS, 47, 1 (1959) 60–1.

[77] 'Mainland Powers on the Malay Peninsula', paper presented at the Third Conference of the International Association of Historians of Asia, Kuala Lumpur, 1968.

[78] 'Episode of the Tooth Relic'. See David K. Wyatt, *The Crystal Sands, Chronicles of Nagara Sri Dharmaraja*, Ithaca, 1975, 26–8, 38–9, 42, 59, 66–71, 72–9; and Wyatt, 'Mainland Powers on the Malay Peninsula', 13–14. The dating of Narapatisithu's reign is based on the research of Aung-Thwin, *Pagan*.

[79] Geiger, *Cūlavaṃsa*, 76, 10–75.

of a large-scale war, but rather of a successful naval raid against lower Burma. Such a plundering expedition was similar to those undertaken by the Cōḷas in the eleventh century, with additional emphasis given to gaining trade concessions. It is unlikely that the raid penetrated to Pagan and killed the Burmese king. Burmese chronicles record that during the reign of Alaungsithu (1113–65) that corresponded with this raid the lower Burma provinces were in a state of 'anarchy' and 'rebellion', suggesting that a local governor had become quite powerful and attempted to assert his independence from Pagan. 'Ukkama', the residence of the 'king' killed by the Sinhalese has been identified as a commercial and administrative centre of lower Burma—possibly Martaban, a later capital of the area—where a local governor could well have been put to death by the raiders. Governors in lower Burma derived considerable income from trade revenues generated by the regional commercial networks. Such an obstruction of commerce may actually have represented an attempt to establish independent control over this lucrative trade. It is notable that one of the attack ships was led by a Sinhalese treasurer, an individual who would have had a great interest in increasing trade revenues. The raid of the Sinhalese on lower Burma can be seen as the high point of the twelfth-century competition for control of the isthmus and is best explained in terms of an interruption and difficulties concerning the patterns of trade and communication in this area.

While the twelfth-century relationship of Sri Lanka and Burma is relatively clear, that between Sri Lanka and the Khmer state is not. As indicated in the *Cūlavaṃsa*, the major reason for the 1160s conflict between Sri Lanka and Burma was Sri Lanka's concern that Burma was preventing free access to the communication channels between Sri Lanka and Angkor. This explanation is indicative of the peninsula's relationship to the Khmer core domain as well. The upper peninsula was significant as the intermediary between Sri Lanka and Angkor, so that it was more important as a source of economic and cultural contact than as an area to be dominated politically. As a result Sri Lanka was willing to risk a war with Burma to preserve the peninsula's neutrality. Of particular interest is the *Cūlavaṃsa's* reference to the interception by the Burmese of a betrothed Sinhalese princess en route to 'Kamboja', a story that is presented as one of the events leading to the 1160s war. This report of a marriage alliance between the Sinhalese and the Khmers suggests that such alliances were a common tool of the Sinhalese royal house. The cross-cousin marriage patterns of the Sinhalese royalty favoured continuing relationships, and to form such an alliance with the Angkor realm would have provided long-range benefits.[80]

Thus, as in the eleventh century, the northern Malay peninsula played an important role in communication between Cambodia and the West. From the other direction, Chinese authors of the Sung period saw the upper east coast of the peninsula as being within the Angkor sphere of influence, and one of them believed that its markets produced some of the best incense available:

[80] Thomas R. Trautmann, 'Consanguineous Marriage in Pali Literature', *Journal of the American Oriental Society*, 93, 2(1973). Such marriage alliances were a common practice of Khmer kings as well. See A. T. Kirsch, 'Kinship, Genealogical Claims, and Societal Integration'.

> Beyond the seas the Teng-liu-mei gharuwood ranks next to that of Hainan [where the price of incense had become too high]. It is first rate. Its trees are a thousand years old . . . It is something belonging to the immortal. Light one stick and the whole house is filled with a fragrant mist which is still there after three days. It is priceless and rarely to be seen in this world. Many of the families of the officials in Kuangtung and Kuangsi and families of the great ones use it.[81]

But by the twelfth century Chinese merchants were dealing directly with the sources of supply on the peninsula, Sumatra, and Java, eliminating their earlier need for a dominant port of the Śrīvijaya type. Tāmbraliṅga, a recognized source of forest products on the east coast of the Isthmus of Kra, was one of their trade partners. Another was the western Chen-la (used consistently by the Chinese to designate the Khmer realm) state of Lo-hu (Lavo), which sent a present of elephants to the Chinese court in 1155. This mission indicates that the Chao Phraya valley (Lo-hu) was then free from Khmer control.

The independence of the formerly subordinate western regions of the Khmer realm corresponds in time to the increasing number of military expeditions that Khmer monarchs despatched against their eastern Vietnamese and Cham neighbours. These expeditions assume an important role in Khmer history from the late eleventh century on, and Khmer inscriptions imply that Khmer monarchs, like their Cham neighbours, began to depend more and more on war booty to finance the activities of their court. Khmer inscriptions eulogize successful expeditions of royal 'conquest' and consequent redistributions of booty to Khmer temples. The increasing importance of these plundering expeditions as a source of state revenue demonstrates that Khmer monarchs were unable or unwilling or did not need to increase the state's direct revenue collections from its agrarian base.

As explained above, the Khmer state's 'ritual sovereignty' statecraft depended on endowing production. The success of this system is reflected in Khmer inscriptions that report the widespread prosperity, general stability, and continuous expansion of the state's agrarian base, despite periodic wars of succession and invasions by the Vietnamese and Chams, which also dominate Khmer history from the eleventh century on and must have placed additional financial burdens on the state. It is puzzling, then, that although the Khmer developed a wet-rice agrarian system that was more than capable of supplying the state's needs, Khmer monarchs pursued plunder anyway. Their obsession with war may have been a necessary response to the periodic Vietnamese and Cham incursions; that is, the best defence was a good offence. A second possibility is that these wars represented a quest for the prowess and personal honour that were bestowed upon a Khmer king who led a successful expedition against the Vietnamese and Chams, and thereby fulfilled the Khmer subjects' expectations of their monarchs. If this were the case, the Khmer military, which appears to have been perpetually active, could have lived off its plunder. It

[81] O. W. Wolters, 'Tāmbraliṅga', BSOAS, 21, 3 (1958) 600, translated from the *Ling-wai-tai-ta* (1178).

is also conceivable, thirdly, that, like the Burmese state of Pagan, Khmer monarchs had so lavishly endowed state temples to promote ritual sovereignty that they had to explore alternative sources of income to provide for their personal activities—for example, to initiate new temple construction and ritual and to pay the various troops that participated in Khmer military campaigns—instead of increasing the assessments of their agricultural producers. A fourth possibility is that, even more than revenue, the Khmer monarchs needed manpower to staff the state's ever-active military and administration and as well to meet the labour needs of the expanding agrarian system and their ambitious construction projects.

As was the case of Java, early Southeast Asian state systems that depended upon income from their agrarian sector alone were limited in their development potential. In a river plain state it was only when those claiming sovereignty became actively involved in external economic affairs that the supreme powers of the state vis-à-vis competing élites and institutions became secure. As in Java, economic leadership in the commercial sphere provided a new source of income that Khmer and Burmese monarchs in the tenth and eleventh centuries utilized to enhance their state's political accomplishments.

Although the evidence discussed above indicates more than casual involvement, participation of the Khmer and the Burmese states in the international commercial routes must be regarded as a secondary concern of their monarchs. Khmer and Burmese rulers were committed to developing their agrarian bases around Angkor and Pagan as well as to overcoming their peripheral relationship, geographically speaking, to the major East–West maritime routes. Thus monarchs expanded their economic base by encouraging their subordinates to bring unused land under cultivation, extending political hegemony from their core domains, while also making diplomatic overtures to their neighbours. But after the twelfth century Angkor and Pagan rulers chose to internalize state polity rather than to promote a stronger interaction in the supraregional trade routes. However, their neighbour to the southeast, the Cham state that controlled the southern portion of present-day Vietnam, had a more compelling desire to penetrate these international commercial channels.

## CHAMPA'S PLUNDER-BASED POLITICAL-ECONOMY

The Cham state that ruled over the southern region of Vietnam from the second to the fifteenth centuries CE, exemplifies the accomplishments of a culturally integrated yet decentralized polity. Like its contemporary Southeast Asian civilizations, Champa, the name by which the realm of the Cham people was known in its epigraphic records as well as in external sources, left impressive temple complexes and numerous inscriptions (composed in both Sanskrit and the Cham language), which are the main source for early Cham history. On the basis of its archaeological remains, Champa has to be classified as a major early Southeast Asian state. Yet Cham epigraphic records reflect a weakly institutionalized state system that depended upon personal alliance networks to integrate a fragmented population.

The Cham realm consisted of scattered communities in river valleys and coastal plains between the South China Sea and the mountains. Chams lived in an environment conducive to a multi-faceted subsistence from agriculture, horticulture, fishing, trade, and piracy. Their capitals were widely separated settlements on different parts of the coast, which took turns assuming hegemony over others—each hegemony was known to the Chinese by a different name. Weakly integrated politically, Cham culture still was highly cosmopolitan and was in constant communication with its neighbours by land and sea to the south and west.[82] A network of lagoons and navigable rivers between Hué and Quang Tri provided protected waterways for internal communication. Cham archaeological remains dot the upriver and highland regions. Cham ruins upriver from Binh-dinh (Vijaya) at Cheo Reo, Yang Prong, and other highland locations especially document Cham presence throughout the Song Ba river network that bends around the Binh-dinh mountains, with mountain pass access beyond the highlands into Laos and Cambodia.[83]

Lowland landholding rights were often shared by several villages, whose leaders co-operated in the control over activities therein. Economic co-ordination between villages included the maintenance of shared water management systems and the provisioning of communal granaries. Cham farmers cultivated paddy fields using relatively sophisticated iron ploughshares and large water wheels for irrigation. Each village had a 'water chief' who organized villagers in the clearance of land and the preparation and maintenance of water channels and dykes. Village chiefs met to co-ordinate overall system maintenance. The Cham realm was especially noted for its 'floating rice', that was quick-growing ('hundred day') and could be grown even under water cover of up to five metres. Cham agricultural settlements were scattered up river valleys and on terraced hillsides and entered an ecological frontier between the highlands and lowlands where wet-rice cultivation was practised in Cham areas, but where swidden shifting (slash-and-burn) cultivation and hunting and gathering predominated among adjacent hill tribes.

Rather than representing shifts from one dynasty's rule to that of another, the periodic movement of the Cham royal centre ('capital') among several river-mouth urban centres bearing Indic titles—Indrapura (Tra-kieu), Vijaya (Binh-dinh), and Kauṭhāra (Nha-trang)—corresponded to transfer of hegemony from the élite of one Cham river valley system to that of another, as one river system's élite became dominant over the other river-mouth urban centres of the Cham coast. As such, the Cham polity was more like the Malay riverine states noted above than its mainland wet-rice plain neighbours to the west and north. Like the rulers of the

82 Paul Mus, *India Seen From the East: Indian and Indigenous Cults of Champa*, trans. I. W. Mabbett and D. P. Chandler, Monash Papers on Southeast Asia no. 3, Clayton, Victoria, 1975; Georges Maspero, *Le Royaume de Champa*, Paris, 1928.

83 Gerald C. Hickey, *Sons of the Mountains*, New Haven, 1982, 460.

84 For extended discussion of 'men of prowess', see O. W. Wolters, *History, Culture, and Region in Southeast Asian Perspectives*, Singapore, 1982.

archipelago riverine-based political-economies, the authority of a Cham monarch was concentrated within his own river-mouth plain; beyond his river-mouth urban centre base, a Cham monarch's sovereignty depended on his ability to construct alliance networks with the leaders of the populations in his upriver hinterland as well as with those of the Cham coast's other riverine systems.

Despite the periodic spatial transfers of authority from one river-mouth urban centre to another, there was one constant. The Cham sacred centre at Mi-son, located on the edge of the highlands and upriver from the Cham urban centre at Indrapura (Tra-kieu) on the coast, served as the locus of Cham royal ceremony that promoted a sense of cultural homogeneity among the disparate populations of the Cham realm. Thus, although Cham society was weakly linked institutionally, the common values expressed in Champa's widely distributed inscriptions demonstrate a high level of societal integration that provided the foundation for a functional Cham polity.

The vocabulary of Cham statecraft as it is portrayed in the inscriptions places stress on the personal achievements of the Cham monarch. Early local belief supported the idea that some individuals (especially the Cham society's leaders) could be superior to others. It was held that there was an uneven distribution of both secular and spiritual prowess. An individual's heroic secular accomplishments confirmed his spiritual superiority. Personal achievements in one's lifetime earned an individual ancestor status.

There were strong traditional concerns for the dead. Just as one allied to those of superior prowess in life, so too one desired a personal bond to 'ancestors of prowess' whom it was believed could bestow material and spiritual substance on their devotees.[84] Those who achieved greatness in life were considered to have contact with the ancestors that was greater than among others of their generation. By establishing a relationship with a successful leader, the follower confirmed his own bond with the ancestors; homage to one's overlord was thus a gesture of obedience to the ancestors.

Subject populations validated their own potential for ancestor status by sharing in their overlord's continuous achievement. The successful overlord projected himself as influencing his supporter's stature in life as well as their hopes for recognition after death. Successful patrons carefully recognized their clients' achievements and meritorious deeds by bestowing 'gifts'—both material (titles and wealth) and spiritual (ritual and death status)—on those whose secular performance on their patron's behalf was noteworthy.

Early Cham society thus rallied behind spiritually endowed leaders who were supported by a blend of local and Indian cultural symbols and values that allowed their leaders to mobilize local populations and their resources for various inter-regional adventures. Specifically, early Cham rulers patronized Śiva, noting his patronage of asceticism and his identification as the lord of the universe and the abode of the dead; they also had affinity for Indra, the Vedic god of war, and in various later times equally identified with Viṣṇu and Buddhist deities.[85] Cham rulers were less

[85] I. W. Mabbett, 'Buddhism in Champa' in Marr and Milner, 289–313.

concerned with developing state institutions, but instead initiated syncretic religious cults that allowed their followers to draw from their leader's spiritual relationship with the ancestors as well as Indian universal divinity.

Ultimately, however, the successful ruler had to generate income for his direct subordinates and secure for his subjects the material well-being that monarchs were expected to provide. With the loss of economic prosperity, serious questions arose regarding the successful magical qualities of the ruler's cults, and the autonomy of regional units soon would be reasserted. Throughout Champa's history, periodic regional autonomy and resistance to the centralizing ambitions of would-be Cham monarchs were coincident with an inability to provide expected economic returns.

While Southeast Asia's early rulers of major wet-rice states based their sovereignty on income derived from a relatively stable agricultural base, the various records of Cham civilization indicate that Cham rulers could not expect a sufficient flow of agricultural surpluses to finance their political ambitions. There is disagreement among historians about the agricultural productivity of the Cham realm. Chinese sources substantiate that the Cham were wet-rice cultivators, and that the Cham territory was especially known to the Chinese as the source of quick-growing 'floating rice' that the Chinese adopted in southern China. But the remaining evidence of Cham civilization, including Chinese sources, does not demonstrate the extensive hinterland agrarian development that is found in the evolving major wet-rice states that were Champa's contemporaries in Cambodia, Burma, Java, and the Red River delta of Vietnam. The comprehensive problem faced by Cham monarchs was that the region between the Mekong delta and Hué where Cham authority was concentrated did not have a broad plain that could serve as a rice bowl to support an elaborate polity.

The king's place, according to Cham inscriptions, was not in managing the day-to-day affairs of his state, but in the battlefield where he protected his subject communities and thereby secured their prosperity. Cham monarchs are never referenced in records of local water management. Nor did Cham monarchs assume a role as supervisors of communal granaries, which in addition to the local water-management networks were the source of unity among local peasant communities. However, Cham monarchs did periodically assign the responsibility for the supervision of new or existing public granaries to newly established temples.

Inscriptions report that, in return for securing his subjects' prosperity, the Cham monarch was entitled to receive one-sixth of local agricultural production. But it is repeatedly proclaimed that due to the ruler's 'benevolence', the state expected to collect only one-tenth. Since such references appear in inscriptions reporting transfers of the ruler's remaining income rights on property to temples (which assume an increasingly significant role as centres for the concentration of economic resources), it can be inferred that the state was either unwilling or unable to collect a share of local production even in its own river system base, and thus assigned its token one-tenth share in the hope that a temple, an institution with local roots, might have better luck making such collections. What was normally assigned were income rights to uncultivated and unpopulated lands, further indication that the state had only limited rights over cultivated lands.

Manpower (war captives or other bondsmen and women) was frequently assigned as well to support the extension of agriculture under the direction of a temple and its temple staff. Such consolidation of control over land and existing granaries and their assignment to temples, which in turn promoted the king's sovereignty in their religious cults, might have provided the Cham king with indirect access to local production that was otherwise inaccessible to the state.

The inherent instability of Cham sovereignty is especially revealed in the inconsistency between the epigraphic stress on the ruler's moral and physical prowess, and their conclusion that this prowess was insufficent to guarantee the future security of endowed temples. Cham inscriptions use curses to protect temples rather than threatening physical retribution to offenders. Cham inscriptions glorify the physical capacity and personal heroism of Cham rulers, but normally end with the proclamation that those who plunder temples (which, based on consistent reference, would seem to have been a common occurrence) were subject to divine retribution —normally a shortened and unprosperous life and the promise of hell as one's destiny in the after-life. For example, a typical endowment inscription ends with the following warning:

> Those who protect all these goods of Indrabhadreśvara in the world, will enjoy the delights of heaven along with the gods. Those who carry them away will fall into hell together with their family, and will suffer the sorrows of hell as long as the sun and moon endure. . . .[86]

One may conclude based on the epigraphic evidence that during a king's reign, but especially after his death, his territory and notably his richly endowed temples were subject to pillage by his various political rivals. Thus, inscriptions of Cham monarchs report their restoration of the temples of previous Cham rulers; these temples had been destroyed by demonic 'foreigners', but also by various Cham chiefs who had attempted to acquire the material resources and labour necessary to proclaim their sovereignty. The act of restoration was a statement of legitimacy, and was a proclamation that the new monarch had sufficient resources to guarantee his subjects' future livelihood.

Since Champa possessed an extensive coastline, one alternative source of income for Cham monarchs was the sea. But here, too, there is little evidence that Cham monarchs depended on trade revenues—port cesses or the returns on royal monopolies on the sale of local commodities to international traders—to finance their sovereignty.

Trade on the Cham coast depended upon the summer monsoon winds, which propelled sea traffic north to China. Prevailing autumn to spring winds from the north made the Cham coast a natural landfall for the merchants of the South China Sea, known collectively as *Yueh*, who were headed for the archipelago and beyond. Despite the Cham coast's favourable position relative to the prevailing seasonal winds, Chinese sources always considered Cham ports to be secondary rather than primary centres of

[86] Barth and Bergaigne, ISCC, 226ff.

international commercial exchange. Yet Cham ports did have important products which the Chinese and other international traders desired—notably luxury items such as ivory, rhinoceros horn, tortoiseshell, pearls, peacock and kingfisher feathers, spices, and aromatic woods.[87]

Chinese and Vietnamese sources enumerate the commodities available at Cham coast ports, and demonstrate the importance of the highlands as the source of Cham trade goods. Elephants and their tusks, for example, were desirable and were included among the tribute gifts the Cham monarch sent to the Chinese court on fourteen separate occasions between 414 and 1050 CE. These elephants came from the highland regions upriver from Vijaya (Binh-dinh) and Pāṇḍuranga (Phan-rang). Rhinoceros horns (ground rhinoceros horn is a prized aphrodisiac among the Chinese), cardamon, beeswax, lacquer, resins, and scented woods (sandalwood, camphor wood, and eagle or aloeswood) were also products of the same upriver region.[88] Areca nuts and betel leaves, the chewing of which gave teeth the distinct red colour, were products of the highlands upriver from Indrapura (Tra-kieu); cinnamon was a product of the region upriver from Vijaya, and gold was said to be mined at a mountain of gold some 30 *li* from modern Hué.[89]

Highland oral histories provide valuable insight into the nature of Cham commercial exchange, which is ignored in all the remaining written sources. In local legend among the highlanders in the Darlac Plateau region near Cheo Reo, the prime source of the highland products enumerated, Cham are reported to have made attempts to integrate highlanders into the Cham political economy by negotiation rather than by force. Highlanders were offered the protection of the Cham armies, as well as the privilege of becoming the trade partners of the Cham.[90] Apparently the most valuable among the trade commodities the Cham offered was salt, which was critical to the highland diet as well as local animal husbandry. In addition to substantiating that the highlands were the source of the trade items enumerated in external sources, highland oral histories report that Cham monarchs were entitled to receive locally woven cloth as tribute.[91]

Among the highland populations in the region north of the Mekong delta the local headmen were said to have organized a band of men to assist the Cham in the search for eaglewood, valued for its fragrance when burned in Cham, Vietnamese, and Chinese ritual. Local tribesmen became Cham vassals and received a Cham sabre, seal, and a title, which roughly translated 'lord/master', that confirmed their leadership status.[92]

87 Paul Wheatley, 'Geographical Notes on Some Commodities involved in Sung Maritime Trade', JMBRAS, 32, 2 (1959).

88 Maspero, *Champa*, 57, 67, 87–8, 99, 120, 133, 138.

89 The Italian adventurer Nicolo de Conti went to Champa via Java in 1435 and reported that Champa was a major dealer in aloes, camphor, and gold. Nicolo Conti, *The Travels of Nicolo Conti in the East in the Early Part of the Fifteenth Century*, London, 1857, 8–9.

90 Hickey, *Sons of the Mountains*, 116.

91 Cloth woven from a variety of local fibres by village women, and generally in rich shades of red, blue, and yellow contrasted with black, white, and grey, worked into stripes or geometric patterns, is still a valuable product of highland groups: ibid., 446.

92 ibid., 117.

An especially close network of cultural dialogue between Champa and Java emerged by the eighth century that included a special trade partnership. During the seventh to the tenth century, there developed what art historians call 'Indo-Javanese architecture' in Champa, which expressed Tantric Mahāyāna Buddhist themes that are similarly depicted in contemporary Javanese art. The reliefs of the temples at the Cham sacred centre at Mi-son are said to resemble those of the Borobuḍur.[93] There was a unique Śiva-Buddhist syncretism at temples downriver from Mi-son at Dong-duong (Indrapura); here there is an inscription dated 911 CE that records the adventures of the tenth-century Cham courtier Rājadvara. Rājadvara twice travelled to Java to study Buddhist magic science; the word used in the inscription is *siddhayātrā*, the same Tantric term used to describe the magical powers of supernatural prowess contained within Buddhism that were pursued by late seventh-century Śrīvijaya monarchs.[94]

The Italian adventurer Nicolo de Conti visited Champa in 1435 on his way from Java to China in the early fifteenth century. During the fourteenth century the Cham monarch, Jayasiṃhavarman II (r. c. 1307), married a Javanese princess, Tapasī. A short time later Che Nang (r. 1312–18), the Cham puppet ruler set up by the Vietnamese conqueror An Huang, asserted his independence by fleeing to Java—perhaps he was the son of the Java princess.[95] There is also the Javanese legend of Dvāravatī, sister of a Cham king, who married the ruler of Majapahit and then promoted the spread of Islam in Java during the late fourteenth century. Cham sources that document an Islamic economic community resident at Pāṇḍuranga in the late tenth century support Javanese belief that the spread of Islam to Java was attributable to Champa.[96]

Despite this evidence that indicates that international trade on the Cham coast could be an important source of income, dependency on sales of local products to an external marketplace was not an adequate economic base upon which to build a state polity. Periodic fluctuations of the sea trade due to disorders at the route's ends in China and the Middle East meant that, like the leaders of the Malay states to the south, Cham monarchs could not depend upon international commerce as a stable and continuous source of royal redistributions. That Cham rulers did not directly control external trade can be concluded from records of Cham coast commerce. These report that the major centre of international trade was at Pāṇḍuranga, at the extreme southern edge of the Cham political domain. The maritime populations of Pāṇḍuranga must have maintained a good deal of autonomy from Cham political control, judging from a description of the community that appears in an eleventh-century inscription, which characterizes the Pāṇḍuranga population as 'demonic, unrespectful, and always in revolt' against the state's authority.

Based on the total omission of reference to merchants in remaining inscriptions from the Cham heartland, it appears that international trade

[93] B. P. Groslier, *Indochina*, Geneva, 1966, 39, 54, 77.

[94] E. Huber, 'La Stele de Dong-duong', BEFEO, 4 (1904) 85ff., verse BXI; Hall, *Maritime Trade*, 79ff.

[95] Maspero, *Champa*, 189.

[96] Hall, *Maritime Trade*, 183.

was confined to Pāṇḍuranga. Here at the extreme southern edge of the Cham realm the 'ferocious' threatening foreigners could be isolated (not unlike China to the north, where seagoing trade with the West was similarly isolated at Canton on the extreme southern edge of the Chinese state). Foreign merchants based at Pāṇḍuranga would have received the enumerated products of the Cham hinterland via active coastal and upriver trade networks that were dominated by a seagoing population permanently resident on the Cham coast.

When they could not depend on the normal flow of commerce to supply them with their livelihood, this seagoing population of the Cham coast was likely to turn to piracy. During such periods of ebb rather than flow, these seamen were likely to pillage neighbouring river-mouth urban centres and their temples. Thus, the eighth-century sack of the Po Nagar temple near modern Nha Trang by 'ferocious, pitiless, dark-skinned sea raiders' may be attributed to the Cham seagoing populations rather than 'foreigners'.

The Chinese court was always trying in vain to compel Cham monarchs to assume responsibility for the behaviour of their coastal populations; judging from the frequency of Chinese demands, it would seem that this coastal population was only marginally under the Cham monarch's control. Cham coast piracy was widely known among the international trade community. Voyagers were often warned to avoid the Cham coast when travelling from the Melaka Straits region to China. This weakened the appeal of Cham ports to international traders and further increased the likelihood that Cham monarchs could not regularly depend on trade revenues to finance their political ambitions.

Being thus unable to secure either sufficient revenue income from their subordinate river valley agricultural communities or consistent return from internal or external trade, Cham monarchs had to seek alternative sources to finance the alliance networks that were critical to their sovereignty. Therefore, it was necessary for Cham rulers to seek wealth beyond their own population centres by leading their allies on periodic military expeditions outside the Cham realm. Plundering raids were thus waged on a regular basis against Champa's neighbours—initially rival river-mouth population centres and later Khmer territories to the west and Vietnamese territories to the north.

This dynamic of plunder explains why Cham history is dominated by seemingly consecutive military expeditions. Periodic Cham raids are reported not only in Cham epigraphy but also in Vietnamese chronicles and from the tenth century on in inscriptions from the Khmer realm to the west. Cham military expeditions acquired plunder and labour—Cham ports were widely known as a major source of slaves, i.e. war captives, who were traded there to various international buyers. The proceeds from successful expeditions were subsequently divided among expedition participants. These included the various warriors who figure so prominently in Cham epigraphy as the monarch's principal political allies and/or the coastal populations, whose navigational skills made them useful participants in raids against Vietnamese coastal settlements to the north as well as against Khmer settlements up the Mekong River in the south—

warriors who in return recognized the Cham monarch's sovereignty.

Successful plundering expeditions were also a means by which the Cham monarch's needed cultural image as the source of his subjects' well-being was validated. Warriors and other key participants in a successful expedition were often assigned jurisdiction over land that was either undeveloped or needed redevelopment. Inscriptions record that one of the first acts of these royal supporters was the lavish endowment of temples, whose staffs subsequently assumed supervision of land development projects. Seemingly these warrior élite were donating, or redistributing, a portion of their share of the successful royal expeditions via their reassignment of various objects, money, and labour that made local development possible.[97]

Royal subordinates also sanctified the development projects by instituting lingas and establishing new temples beyond the royal core that honoured the temple's benefactor, but especially proclaimed the glory of past and present Cham monarchs, for whom the temple lingas were named. Such recognition of the monarch through the endowment and consecration of temples promoted local appreciation of the monarch's accomplishments and encouraged their subordination, in the absence of a direct royal administrative presence, to the sovereignty of the Cham state.

The Cham state may thus be understood as a loose and marginally interdependent polity that encompassed a series of river-mouth urban centres and their upriver hinterlands. In the absence of a sufficient resource base to support their political aspirations, Cham kings by necessity depended on periodic military expeditions to acquire plunder that could be redistributed, directly (sharing booty with their warrior allies) or indirectly (via temple endowments), to maintain the loyalty of the inhabitants of the Cham riverine networks. Cham monarchs maintained the subordination of their direct military allies by keeping them 'in the field' on various plunder expeditions. In the absence of a royal bureaucracy that could directly administer the regions of the Cham realm, Cham monarchs instead depended on the willingness of local élites to recognize the monarch's sovereignty via their participation in his expeditions of conquest and/or by their support of religious cults that proclaimed the ruler's superior prowess. There was an inherent instability in this political-economy that ultimately depended upon redistributions of plunder. The fate of the Cham state was sealed, and Vietnamese retaliatory expeditions finally destroyed the Cham realm in the fifteenth century.[98]

## THE EMERGENCE OF THE VIETNAMESE POLITICAL-ECONOMY

The early maturation of a Vietnamese economy moved spatially from higher, upland areas of the Red River valley into the delta region, and then south into previous Cham territory. Early Vietnamese society consisted of

[97] e.g., Barth and Bergaigne, ISCC, 218, 275.

[98] Maspero, *Champa*, 237–9. For comparison, see George W. Spencer, 'The Politics of Plunder: The Cholas in Eleventh Century Ceylon', JAS, 35, 4 (1976).

small communal groups who farmed the area above the delta, using the natural ebb and flow of the tides of the Red River system to support local irrigation networks. By the tenth century Vietnamese society was based on villages, and had developed elaborate dyke and drainage systems to control the raging monsoon-fed waters of the Red River delta. Staples of Vietnamese life were fish and rice; twelfth-century Chinese writers report that the Vietnamese grew the special early-ripening strain of rice that had come into Vietnam from Champa, although an indigenous type remained of greater preference.[99]

Early Chinese political interest in Vietnam was a consequence of the desire among China's rulers to secure southern trade routes and to gain access to southern luxury goods, which included pearls, incense, drugs, elephant tusk, rhinoceros horn, tortoiseshell, coral, parrots, kingfishers, peacocks, and 'other rare and abundant treasures enough to satisfy all desires'.[1] Han era outposts in Vietnam at the beginning of the Christian era were primarily commercial centres; the Han did not want to develop an elaborate administrative presence, and Vietnam was viewed as being too remote. In this era Vietnamese Lac lords became 'prefectural and district officials' in a chiefly symbolic Chinese political order. They paid tribute and received 'seals and ribbons' from their Han overlords that legitimized them, and in theory added prestige in the eyes of their peers. This Vietnamese élite was more or less allowed to rule in traditional ways, although there were modifications of their social system that the Chinese found inconsistent with a Chinese sense of morality, notably their disregard for Chinese-style patriarchal marriage and their favouring of the less standard bilateral kinship patterns practised throughout the Southeast Asian region. The Lac lords enjoyed labour, comestibles, and craft goods that were supplied by subject communities. Lac lords were in turn expected to pass on some of their normal collections of local produce, but especially 'rare objects and goods' as tribute payments to their Han overlords.

An influx of Han ruling-class refugees during the Wang Mang first-century interlude (9–23 CE) reinforced Han officials, and new patterns of Chinese rule emerged. Of foremost concern to Chinese administrators was their need to pay for their expanded administration. To do this they began to target development of the local agrarian economy as a stable tax base. Chinese administrators promoted greater productive efficiency as well as the extension of agriculture into previously uncultivated lands. Further, they encouraged movement to a formal patriarchal society as a way to increase the role of men in agricultural production. Hunting and fishing, the main focus of male economic activities, produced no taxable surplus; agriculture was a more stable source of tax revenues. Because of the high degree of male mobility in pursuit of game, Vietnamese society in the early Han era seemed, from the Chinese perspective, to have no stable family system. The male role in agriculture, or the lack thereof, and the apparent female control of cultivation, were difficult for Chinese administrators to

[99] John K. Whitmore, 'Elephants Can Actually Swim: Contemporary Chinese Views of Late Ly Dai Viet' in Marr and Milner, 130.

[1] Keith W. Taylor, *The Birth of Vietnam*, Berkeley, 1983, 78, from Hsueh Tsung's early third-century account.

accept. In the first century CE, one Han official tried to combat this by ordering all men aged 20–50 and all women 15–40 to marry; would-be élite were expected to pay for Chinese-style marriage ceremonies. Subsequent registration of new family units made kin groups responsible for tax payments.

Promotion of a stable family unit had further consequences. Unlike some societies that remain settled in one place and have no 'frontier spirit', the Vietnamese developed an intense, culturally supported, desire to hold land—which supported periodic Chinese and Vietnamese government efforts to extend wet-rice cultivation into new territories. In Vietnam possession of land eventually came to be considered synonymous with the well-being of a family, and essential for the perpetuation of the family line. Sons needed to have land to keep the family unit together. Together the family property maintained family ancestor cults. Substantial houses that would endure for generations, rather than makeshift dwellings, become the norm. Ancestors' spirit houses were also constructed, with a central sanctuary honouring ancestors of the patrilineage; this was the centre of family rituals and feasting. Stone tombs, too, were reminders of generations past. Unnourished, ancestral spirits became malevolent errant spirits that ceaselessly wandered in search of offering. Family income had to support ancestors by means of rituals and feasts. Cult lands were farmed by the members of the lineage collectively; guardianship was under the head of the kin group, usually the oldest male. Land thus had social, economic, and religious functions, and the need to hold family land thereby stimulated the migration of the landless.

The Lac lords tried to resist the assertion of Han authority, but were no match for the Han armies. Thereafter Vietnam's Dong-son culture faded. Indigenous landholding patterns, which were initially based on communal usage rather than ownership, were directly assaulted by Chinese bureaucrats. New state-wide revenue systems based on private ownership began to emerge. Han soldiers were settled in newly built 'walled cities' to govern new administrative prefectures and districts. These 'soldier-farmers' supervised the digging of ditches, to irrigate the fields surrounding these new centres that were nearer the Red River delta than the previously developed regions in the upper river plain. Han policy kept soldiers in place, as they settled in and became part of the local social fabric, and thereby removed a potential revenue drain on newly conquered territory (i.e. the resident military was self-sustaining) and further disaffection among the conquered people which additional revenue demands would have brought. Overall, Han rule established a co-ordinated authority over the Giao-chi (as the Vietnam province was then known) irrigation systems, which they helped to extend, and a merging of Chinese and Vietnamese societies began to take place.

Private property rights became important in the areas nearest the urban centres of Han rule. A powerful Han-Viet landlord class came into existence as government tax demands forced peasants to sell land to rich officials and become tenant farmers on their private estates; or, as Han soldiers were given communal lands in return for their service, previous populations who were driven off this newly assigned land began to settle uncultivated lands, based on the same individual holding basis.

This Han-Viet society was based on a clearly defined sense of status and wealth that depended on the private ownership of land. Tomb remains from this era show a material culture of accumulated wealth that was taken to the grave—iron swords, Han coins, glass ornaments, bronze and earthenware vessels, game boards, musical instruments, mirrors, ink-stones, and lampstands. There were even model ceramic farms that well illustrate the local agrarian culture—horses, granaries, wells, and kilns (but with the notable absence of ancestor houses) were encompassed with fortress-like compounds. Great families supported a private community of 'guests' that included scholars, technical experts, spies, assassins, and private armies. The élite ruled by virtue of character seals that were applied in the roofs of their houses, replacing Lac era 'seals and ribbons' as symbols of their authority.

The tombs of the élite reflect a cultural intermix between Chinese and Vietnamese. It was normal for Chinese men to take Vietnamese wives. In the first generation Chinese patterns of life were preponderant, but by the third and fourth generations a substantial synthesis with local culture had taken place, and Vietnamese variations predominate.

As the Han dynasty declined in the late second century, the Han-Viet élite became more interested in seaborne trade as an alternative source of income. Commerce in luxury goods became a major preoccupation of local administrators. The Vietnamese coast in general became an international entrepôt during this period that is coincident with the rise of Fu-nan and Lin-yi, which was founded in the Hué coastal region in 192 by a son of a Han-Viet district official, who killed the local Han magistrate. By the fourth century, Lin-yi's rulers were proclaiming themselves to be kings in the Indic Hindu tradition.[2] The Vietnamese north, under the leadership of the Shih family, turned more toward Buddhist influences.

This Vietnamese devotion to Buddhism became associated with commercial wealth and royal authority. Temples were founded for guardian deities of agricultural fertility. Buddhism represented a new 'other-worldly' method of controlling nature for the benefit of local agriculture. Buddhist temples were dedicated to local spiritual manifestations of the monsoon season, which became syncretic incarnations of the Buddha: the Buddha of the Clouds, Rain, Thunder, and Lightning. Local pre-existing values were thus reinforced with the authority of this new international religion. Art historians note that Vietnamese architecture from this period was more like that of the Javanese Borobuḍur than the northwest Indian Gandhāran style favoured in northwestern China. This substantiates Vietnamese participation in the wide-ranging Buddhist communication network that was coincident with the southern seas trade route between China and India, and especially indicates interaction with the straits region to the south.

During the Sui and Tang era the power of the great landowning Han-Viet families that had emerged in the Han age was partially countered by

[2] Taylor, *Vietnam*, 196–9; Hall, *Maritime Trade*, 71–7, 178–9.

the introduction of the Chinese 'equal-field' system. In its ideal form, state bureaucrats assigned all able-bodied adults a certain amount of land (which was in theory all the property of the emperor) for the duration of their lifetimes. This was intended to stabilize the state revenue base by blocking the drift of free, taxpaying farmers off the tax rolls into great private estates. Since the Chinese collected taxes on a per capita basis, farmers who became tenants on great estates were not counted for taxation; they were thereafter encompassed within assessments of the estate, which was better able to neutralize the state's revenue demands. Thus the equal-field system was an attempt to keep farmers in a free, taxpaying status that would enhance the state's tax revenues. In the Tang era the 'equal-field' system acknowledged the special rights of great families by the assignment of perpetual landholding rights, theoretically no more than one hundred times the amount assigned to a free farmer.[3]

Seventh-century Tang rule in Vietnam was coincident with the initial development of the Hanoi area as the first Vietnamese urban centre south of the Hong River. This era was also marked by the extension of the dyking system down the Hong River into the delta lowlands. The Hanoi region emerged as the new power base of Chinese rule outside the traditional provincial heartland where great families and their estates predominated, and was part of a general Tang assault upon the powers of the old élite. The 'equal-field' system was applied to the newly opened delta lands, and free farmers were assigned to initiate cultivation. To counter the power of the great families, these free farmers were provided with military training and were organized into militia units. By the ninth century, however, a new class of great landlords began to emerge in the newly developed territory due to a 'double-tax' reform that was adopted by the Tang in 780, which based tax collection on land ownership rather than the number of cultivators. Further attempts to implement the 'equal-field' system of land distribution were abandoned and there was no longer a legal barrier to the accumulation of land into estates by men of wealth.[4]

A Tang centre of civil administration was rebuilt near modern Hanoi after a sea raid in 767, and defensive ramparts were built, which were repaired and enlarged in the ninth century. To validate this transfer of political authority to the new urban centre, the Tang consecrated the Kaiyuan cult that associated the Chinese emperor Xuanzong (r. 712–56) with a local earth spirit of the Hanoi area; this union symbolically guaranteed local prosperity, and attributed this success to Chinese rule.

Before the Tang, no Chinese dynasty was strong enough to enforce their land systems. The Chinese land system was based on private ownership that was not uniformly applicable to Vietnam, where communal ownership remained strong; and great estates remained largely beyond the effective reach of the imperial revenue-gathering capabilities. The effectiveness of attempted Chinese reforms to landownership and tax collection depended on proximity to an administrative centre. Tax collection was not due to any theory or law, but was a specialized skill developed by Chinese

[3] E. O. Reischauer and J. K. Fairbank, *East Asia*, Boston, 1989, 100–2, 118–19.
[4] Taylor, *Vietnam*, 209–15.

bureaucrats to extract revenue in particular circumstances within Vietnamese society. Imperial land taxation in Vietnam was thus unorthodox and underwent constant evolution. Since it depended on the personal skill of the bureaucrat, the system was inherently vulnerable to personal greed and corruption. The Chinese government would on occasion police itself, as for example in the Han era when two officials were executed for extorting bribes and filling a storehouse with improperly seized possessions, which were subsequently redistributed among local court officials.[5]

Due to administrative incapacity, Chinese revenue interest in Vietnam before the seventh century was directed more at the control of lucrative international markets on the Vietnamese coast, which were viewed as an important source of enrichment. Chin officials were said to have normally extorted 20–30 per cent of merchandise value at Vietnamese coast ports.[6] There was a fine line between piracy, corruption, and appropriate state service. In 446, war booty from the plunder of Lin-yi was an 'economic inspiration'.[7] Among the Sui era records is a statement that 'men who go to Giao abandon the thankless task of government for more lucrative occupations of commerce'. This account further notes that 'barbarians of Giao often assemble for plunder'.[8] The Sui, eager to secure the luxuries of the Vietnamese coast, gave special titles to local 'leaders' who helped them collect slaves, pearls, kingfishers, elephant tusks, and rhinoceros horns.[9] In 863, Tang officials confiscated merchant vessels and seized their cargo to finance a war with the Nanchao realm to the north.

Development of the delta environment was important not only for its additional agricultural productivity, but also because of its proximity to the sea. The Dai Viet state that established its independence from Chinese sovereignty in the tenth century, like its Southeast Asian contemporaries, depended on the production of its wet-rice economy. Sung rule in China was a great boon to international commerce, and like the neighbouring mainland wet-rice states to its west, the Dai Viet state became increasingly involved in contacts with the international route. Dai Viet rulers enhanced their resource base by promoting contacts initiated by the lords assigned to rule the outer territories—the delta, the south, and the highlands—to acquire trade goods.

Khmer rulers at Angkor were in diplomatic contact with the new Vietnamese state in the early eleventh century, and these embassies had economic purpose. Increasing commercialization of interstate contacts undoubtedly contributed to rising tensions on the eastern mainland. During the period between 1120 and 1210 Angkor, Champa, and the Dai Viet state were frequently at war. One cause, at least from a Cham point of view, was the emergence of a new trading route across the Gulf of Tonkin to Nghe-an, south of the Red River delta; from there, goods could be transported across the mountains to the Mekong River valley and Angkor

[5] ibid., 59, quoting the *Le Tac*, Hué, 1961, 86.
[6] ibid., 107, from the *Chin shu*, 5, 9b.
[7] ibid., 121, from the *Sung shu*, 5, 14b.
[8] ibid., 148, from the *Ch'en shu*, 34, 24a.
[9] ibid., 167, quoting Katakura Minoru, 'Chūgoku Shihaika no Betonamu', *Rekishigaku Kenkyū*, 381 (February 1972) 31, a study of law and taxation in Vietnam under Chinese rule.

via the Ha-trai Pass, thereby bypassing access to Angkor by the lower Mekong and consequently threatening Cham control of the coastal trade.

The route across the Gulf of Tonkin from China also brought numerous Chinese settlers into the lower Red River delta and the lowland areas south of the delta in Thanh-hoa and Nghe-an.[10] One result of this thriving Chinese community was a flow of labour and copper cash out of China into Dai Viet, which must have helped the local economy to develop rapidly. Zhao Rugua's account of southern ocean commerce in the early thirteenth century demonstrates Dai Viet's role as a source of goods for the international trade, especially metals. Vietnamese gold and silver went to Angkor (probably via Nghe-an and the Mekong), to Kelantan on the east coast of the Malay peninsula, to the Jambi-based Śrīvijaya realm on the east coast of Sumatra, and also to Java. In return, the Vietnamese received spices and other local and international products. Vietnamese dynastic records report that Van-don on the coast east of their capital at Thang-long was the major port during the twelfth to the fourteenth century, and had contact with the area around the Gulf of Thailand as well as parts of the island world, especially Majapahit Java.[11]

Another Chinese source confirms the Dai Viet international trade in precious metals, and also reports that the Vietnamese had seized mountain territory in the south that had been Khmer, and was a rich source of the aromatic woods much desired by international traders. Control of this highland trade in aromatic woods, which had previously been a major export of Cham ports, must have been another source of contention among the Vietnamese, Khmer, and Chams.

Li Cho, ninth-century Tang protector-general of the Vietnamese territory, was said to have changed the terms of trade between the Vietnamese lowlands and the mountain chiefs, who had been bartering horses and cattle for salt. He took control of salt production of villages in the tidewaters, and hoped thereby to obtain a larger number of horses that he could sell to accumulate a fortune. An efficient local official is quoted: 'If we cut off the salt and iron trade on the southern coast [we would] cause the ruination of their market . . . after two years they can be crushed in a single battle.'[12] These sources reflect the importance of Vietnamese expansion into the delta, which gave them access to salt, the key commodity in lowland–highland exchange.

Administratively, the Vietnamese and Chinese were both uninterested in the southern highlands because the upland region lacked sufficient land and water sources to allow paddy farming on a scale necessary for Vietnamese agriculture. Further, there was a Vietnamese traditional antipathy for the highlands since they were thought to be the home of evil spirits, as well as the source of poisoned water that caused malaria. But commercial and revenue needs forced the Vietnamese to re-evaluate their traditional distaste.

[10] Two inscriptions dated 1161 and 1207 report well-to-do Chinese families resident at Thanh-hoa. Whitmore, 'Elephants', 131.

[11] John K. Whitmore, 'Vietnam and the Monetary Flow of Eastern Asia, Thirteenth to Eighteenth Centuries', in J. F. Richards, *Precious Metals in the Late Medieval and Early Modern World*, Durham, N.C., 1983, 374.

[12] Taylor, *Vietnam*, 239–40; 96, from the *Chin shu*, 67, 5a.

To gain control over the highland sources of numerous trade goods, the Vietnamese needed to establish their political presence in the Cham territory to the south, which provided access to the highlands via the river systems of the Cham coast. A nineteenth-century Vietnamese document explains that the highlands had been part of the kingdom of Champa, but after his final victory over the Chams in 1471, Le Thanh Ton (r. 1460–97) resettled this coastal plain with Vietnamese. By the early sixteenth century the highlands had been loosely incorporated into the Vietnamese state; initially a local chief was recognized as being in charge of highland civil administration, although several minor Vietnamese bureaucrats were sent to regulate trade with the highland populations. Commercial agents from the lowlands traded with designated highlanders who held licences to trade; those licensed paid taxes to the commercial agents, who in turn passed a specified amount along to the assigned bureaucrats.[13]

Control of trade products naturally enhanced a state's place in international commerce and the wealth and power that derived therefrom. But the Thanh-long government was caught between its own cultural policy and its economic needs. On the one hand the government believed that the highland barbarians might pollute the superior Vietnamese way of life—the Chams were thought of as only a little better than the highlanders. Yet highland products were necessary to enhance Vietnamese participation in international trade. Thus the Vietnamese government tried to restrict highland contact, and Vietnamese traders, who were themselves described in the Vietnamese records as 'rootless errants', were nevertheless honoured as hardy pioneers who preceded the later 'pacification' and 'social education' of highland people.

The tenth and eleventh centuries were especially critical in the transition to a more externally focused Vietnamese economy, which, significantly, was coincident with the emergence of an independent Vietnamese state. The new Vietnamese court at Hoa-lu, on the southern edge of the Hong River plain, was a market for trade as well as promoting it. It is reported that in 976 merchant boats from different nations beyond the sea arrived and presented the goods of their countries.[14] A new port at Bo-hai, near the mouth of the Hong River, where inland trade met the southbound seaborne trade, grew in importance. Economic reorientation toward the sea routes leading south paralleled the rising power of the Dai Viet state in the southern delta, and an alliance between the two centres of Hoa-lu and Bo-hai, one political and the other commercial, supported the political unification of Vietnamese lands.

The political unity achieved by Dinh Bo Linh, the first Vietnamese emperor, made large regional markets possible. This encouraged commercial expansion and attracted foreign merchants. The Hoa-lu court provided a new market for the luxury goods in which foreign merchants specialized. In an edict of 975 Bo Linh prescribed types of clothing to be worn by civil and military officials at the court. To meet these clothing needs, as well as the other material requirements of the emergent Vietnamese court, foreign trade was a necessity. Envoys were sent to China with many gifts,

[13] Hickey, *Sons of the Mountain*, 155.

[14] Taylor, *Vietnam*, 287–8, from the *Ngo Si Lien Dai Viet su'ky toan thu*, 1, 46.

presumably to proclaim Vietnam as an international marketplace as well as to secure political recognition. The Vietnamese economy was thus transformed to serve the needs of a strong king from a hitherto insignificant place.

Other economic development projects were initiated in the eleventh century. In 1048, Ly Thai Tong (r. 1028–54) revived a China-inspired cult of culture, in which the monarch was the highest officiant. As the symbolic source of fertility, the Vietnamese emperor led springtime rites in which he would plough the first furrows, and he also symbolically assisted in the gathering of rice at harvest. At the south gate of the Hoa-lu capital, offerings were made to bring rain and to guarantee crops at the Esplanade of the Gods of the Soil and Harvest. In 1044, a road construction programme linked the capital and the regions in a realm-wide communication network that would have had a favourable impact on commercial transport. In 1042, 5000 Cham war captives were assigned land and resettled in undeveloped unpopulated areas of the southern Hung Hoa Province, and were allowed to name their new communities after their native Cham settlements.[15]

New villages received names selected by villagers and approved by the emperor, who appointed guardian spirits to watch over the village and bring it prosperity. As the Khmer and Majapahit systems used temple networks to integrate outlying areas into the state, so Vietnamese villages were expected to construct communal temples (*dinh*) as repositories for new imperial documents that named the village guardian spirit. Further, local lands had to be designated to support the temple, which was subject to continuing government regulation to assure proper maintenance and ritual performance; this guaranteed local prosperity, which was the self-proclaimed responsibility of the monarch.

During the thirteenth century great estates (*trang-dien*) began to emerge. In 1266, Emperor Tran Thanh Tong authorized nobles to press vagabonds and those without work into bondage, to have them clear land and to farm unused land. Aristocrats dominated southern expansion that began in earnest during the fifteenth century.[16] Conflict emerged at the local level between new Vietnamese settlers and the old Cham residents in the Amarāvatī region. During the reign of Le Thai To (1428–32) there was an attempted socio-economic reform that included a general land redistribution of the sort intended in the Chinese 'equal-field' system. All were to receive a land share, from high-ranking officials to the elderly and orphans, 'isolated persons' (widows and widowers, i.e., those without families), as well as youths. To prevent the re-emergence of powerful estates, large landholding units were forbidden. Communal lands, normally periodically redistributed according to social ranks, were declared inalienable.

Le Thanh Ton decreed that those convicted of crimes should be sent to remote parts of Quang Binh Province in the south. Under his general economic development programme, there was again a ban on large landholdings. Southern settlement in the Nghe-an and Ha Tinh provinces was encouraged by the establishment of fortifications to protect newly developed

[15] Le Thanh Khoi, *Le Viet-Nam*, Paris, 1955, 164.
[16] ibid., 173.

paddy fields. Land was to be cleared—a decree forbade the waste of any land. Prisoners and criminals were sent to settle the new lands. Military officers in local posts were rewarded with plots of land that would not revert to the state at their death. Bureaus were organized in every province to supervise the digging of dykes and canals. State representatives were also charged to provide information that would improve animal husbandry and the cultivation of mulberry trees. After two years of settlement, officials were to be sent to establish appropriate taxes, and to promote the new patriarchal family-focused Confucian moral code.

At the dawn of the sixteenth century, Vietnamese civilization was in a position to prosper due to the political and economic initiatives taken by Le Thanh Ton. Faced with perpetually contracting tax rolls, the consequence of the repeated devolution of revenue-collection authority from the state to land-based military and aristocratic élite, the Vietnamese state authorities of the past had continuously attempted to extend their economic base. Conquest of the Cham territories in 1471 provided ample opportunity for the future.

Cham plunder raids on Vietnamese territory had challenged the theoretical base of Vietnamese imperial authority, which in its cults of legitimacy proclaimed the emperor's ability to guarantee his subjects' prosperity. These raids also depleted the state of needed resources. While the Vietnamese state had itself benefited economically from its various military expeditions against the Chams over the centuries, such actions had been justified as acts of reciprocity; they were also seen as necessary to initiate the future security of the Vietnamese people. Periodic Cham raids against Vietnamese territory forced the Dai Viet state to fund the elaborate preparations that these 'defensive' acts of reciprocity necessitated; to lose against the 'barbarian' Chams was unthinkable. Final victory against the Chams stabilized the Dai Viet state's wet-rice economy not only by removing this financial drain, but also by supplying prime territory for agricultural expansion, together with some 30,000 Cham prisoners (including the Cham monarch and fifty members of the Cham royal family) to settle it. The victory over Champa also put the Vietnamese state in a position to monopolize the coastal access to the highland products most desired by international traders—although highlanders still had the option of trading overland with their Khmer neighbours to the west instead.

The Vietnamese state leadership could not, like their Cham neighbours, turn to plundering raids as a regular source of state financing. This would have been inconsistent with the developing Vietnamese bureaucratic administration that depended upon its land-based military and aristocratic élite to support a harmonious state system modelled on that of China. Yet, in the late fifteenth and early sixteenth centuries, the Vietnamese state actively pursued participation in and facilitation of the East–West sea trade as an acceptable source of state finances. This was like its fellow rulers of Southeast Asian wet-rice states in that same era, who equally found trade-derived revenues an attractive alternative to squeezing additional tax revenue from the land; as in Dai Viet, the bureaucratic capacity among these states was insufficiently developed to guarantee the regular collection of revenue cesses beyond the court's immediate agrarian core.

## THE EARLY SOUTHEAST ASIAN SOCIO-ECONOMY: A CONCLUDING OVERVIEW

It has been posited in the above discussion that major structural changes were taking place in Southeast Asian society during the era from the first century to the fifteenth that were associated with an expanding Southeast Asian socio-economy. Political and economic ties between major 'higher order' centres and their subordinate regions or hinterlands were enhanced during this era, as specifically evinced in inscriptions and other internal and external primary sources that demonstrate the emergence of hierarchical political and economic networks. But was there a change of institutions taking place, characterized by a new administrative capacity eminating from centres of power; or was there a structural change relative to the wider acceptance of new ideas about political and economic activity in general, the creation of a new popularly accepted idiom that made participation in political and economic activities beyond one's immediate locale, and regular interaction with major economic centres, culturally appropriate? Expressed in contemporary anthropological jargon, to define political and economic transition in Southeast Asia one might determine whether early Southeast Asia centres were 'centres of status' or 'centres of power'.[17] Critical to study of this perceived era of change are two parallel questions: (1) how does one define an economic centre ('city') in early Southeast Asia and (2) how does one define an economic network?

In keeping with most contemporary Western understanding of the terms 'city' and 'network', one may study early Southeast Asian history by focusing on administrative institutions that made cities and networks possible. Specifically, one may examine the evolution of religious institutions (temples) and political institutions that could administer the populations of urban centres, and could subsequently utilize this bureaucratic capacity to draw in ('mobilize') the surplus production of their subordinate hinterland populations.[18]

In contrast, the economic development of early Southeast Asia may be equally understood as a consequence of the sequential pooling of economic resources that took place in the process of the establishment of socially recognized cultural centres.[19] Herein economic resources were valuable not for their material content or relative to profit goals as appropriate to a modern economy, but as resources that could enhance the status of an individual or of a ceremonial centre. Cultural centres (or individuals who claimed superior status) drew in the resources of their realm to support culturally significant ceremony, to build impressive buildings (including temples), to accumulate manpower, to finance elaborate gift-giving, or to amass wealth, all in the hopes of impressing surrounding populations into submission rather than in building raw power resources. Such a stockpile of wealth could also finance a centre's participation in external commerce. The centre acted as a societally approved negotiator on behalf of its population vis-à-vis outsiders. In such a role the centre insulated its

[17] Geertz, *Negara*.
[18] Wheatley, *Nagara*.
[19] Wolters, *History, Culture, Region*.

followers from the hardships of the outside world, where local cultural requirements were of little concern. In this external realm, personal gain was a foremost goal, in contrast to the local population's preference for cultural and social well-being.

The majority of the early Southeast Asian political-economies gave cultural and social goals precedence. Economic resources flowed by choice of the producer to a cultural centre, and then were redistributed outward (both internally as well as externally to the local system) to benefit the indigenous population through gifting strategies that enhanced the status of the centre. As such an economy expanded or as the cultural centre widened its realm, the centre could begin to mobilize resources at a less personal level, but with the culturally approved goals. In this transition, temples—whether Hindu or Buddhist—assumed enhanced roles as economic centres, and new ritual networks that focused on the centre of royal power provided additional infrastructure that did not exist in earlier kingdoms.

Consequent to this expansion, a movement from a political-economy of 'cultural redistribution' to a political-economy of 'culturally mobilized wealth' could take place. Despite significant bureaucratic initiatives undertaken by the leaders of some states (notably the post-1300 Majapahit and Dai Viet states, which have been characterized in this overview of the pre-1500 era as the most fully integrated among their archipelago and mainland contemporary polities), the gathering of material resources at a centre continued to be justified through reference to traditional symbols and values. Widespread popular opinion still held that such accumulation allowed the centre leadership to accomplish culturally approved goals, but there was increasing personal distance between the centre and its subordinate population. These developing polities continued to depend on voluntary subordination and contributions rather than upon the administrative draw of resources by a bureaucracy based at the centre. The 'mobilizing centre' of each state did not have an effective bureaucratic capacity upon which it could draw, but depended as in the past on the belief that granting legitimacy to centre or leader was important relative to the bestowal of cultural well-being upon subordinate populations.

In these 'mobilizing economies' there were also traditional competitions for power, as land-based rivals continued to pool resources in their attempts to build new cultural centres. Trade was significant in this competitive process as a source of material wealth that could endow the awe-inspiring centres and their leaders, who dispensed power and bestowed economic and psychological well-being on populations that chose to become subordinate to the centre. Such traditional focus thus continued at a higher level of productivity and exchange, but with the ever-present threat that economic activity could become increasingly impersonal, including less sympathetic manipulation and direct control (administration) of a population by the centre. Another possibility was that new coastal centres of commercial activity, whose development was initially encouraged, might break away from the more internally focused and culturally-defined hinterland centres that remained bound to a more personalized agrarian-based order. Yet another option was that the religious institutions that had initially enhanced the centre's power might themselves become a wealthy and popularly supported rival against an increasingly impersonal polity.

Beyond this 'mobilizing political-economy' is a political and economic order in which wealth allowed the development of less personal bureaucratic, military, or religious administrations and networks that managed lands and economic resources. Agricultural areas increasingly interacted with centre-based administrators in contrast to the earlier age in which local contact with the centre was insulated by a locally-based élite. There were more direct centre-based collections of local surplus (as opposed to earlier stress on donations of local production to the centre) as well as more direct centre-based dispersements to the outside and to the lower levels of the socio-economic order. Market networks would be controlled by political élites, or even by merchants—commercial specialists whose behaviour was largely inconsistent with traditional values. Previously, merchants had been forced to transact their affairs in ways subordinate to local cultural norms; but as political systems with stronger administrative centres developed, this might offer consequent mobility to those whose way of life demonstrated less personal commitment to their fellows. In this new order, the merchant could assume a more significant role as the direct mobilizer of surplus production, orchestrating the flow and return of external goods and services to and from the local producer—as the agent of centre-based cultural brokers, of a power-holding monarch, or as a participant in a developing free-trade economy.

It is the view of this essay on the early Southeast Asian economy that this impersonal order was not appropriate to pre-1500 Southeast Asia. While in the Majapahit, Angkor, Pagan, and Dai Viet states there were emergent patterns consistent with this latter characterization, political-economies retained their internally-focused and traditional agrarian-based structures, which were more similar than dissimilar to those of other archipelago and mainland polities in this period before 1500.

## BIBLIOGRAPHIC ESSAY

Scholarly interest in Southeast Asia's early economic history has largely been a by-product of the development of interdisciplinary and multidisciplinary studies since World War II. The pioneering scholarship on Southeast Asia's history in the West was the product of well-trained Dutch, French, and British historians whose research was an extension of their countries' colonial experience. These early twentieth-century scholars tended to highlight the external forces that shaped Southeast Asia, and the court-based religious and political aspects of the epigraphic and literary sources. In this pre-World War II vision, Southeast Asia was viewed as a region of passage for foreign merchants and other travellers, which provided shelter for ships and seamen based in India, West Asia, and China. As an intermediate region, Southeast Asia developed either 'Indianized' or 'Sinicized' civilizations that had their origin outside the region, or were deeply influenced by external elements. This historiography, which provided important reconstructions of dynastic chronologies, is well reflected in the impressive works of G. Cœdès (*The Making of Southeast Asia*, English edition, 1966, and *The Indianized States of Southeast Asia*, ed. Walter Vella, trans. Susan Brown Cowing, Honolulu, 1968), and D. G. E. Hall (*A History of South-East Asia*, 1955).

A new view of the region wherein integrated local state entities existed prior to the coming into contact with foreign cultural elements, and outside ideas were accepted, adapted, and adopted based on local needs, first surfaced in the English translation of the writings of J. C. van Leur (*Indonesian Trade and Society: Essays in Asian Social and Economic History*, 1955). During the 1950s a new generation of scholars arose, notably the Indonesian epigraphers Boechari, L. C. Damais, and J. G. de Casparis (*Prasasti Indonesia*, 1950, 1956); the Indonesian philologist Th. G. Th. Pigeaud (*Java in the Fourteenth Century*, 1960–3); and the historians Paul Wheatley ('Geographical Notes on Some Commodities Involved in Sung Maritime Trade', JMBRAS, 1959; *The Golden Khersonese*, 1961), Wang Gungwu ('The Nanhai Trade', JMBRAS, 1958) and O. W. Wolters ('Tambalinga', BSOAS, 1958); they began to explore the history of early Southeast Asia by expanding their scope beyond the more traditional use of the epigraphic and philological sources. These scholars not only re-examined the old sources with a new set of questions, but they also tested these texts against new archaeological data that were becoming available, and began to define Southeast Asia as a distinct entity apart from the Indic and Sinic worlds.

Representative of the published reports of this archaeological research are Alastair Lamb in FMJ (1961) and Louis Malleret, *L'archeologie du delta du Mekong* (1959–63). Important studies of agricultural and peasant economies were also taking place during the 1950s and early 1960s, among these: D. H. Burger, *Structural Changes in Javanese Society* (1956); Robbins Burling, *Hill Farms and Padi Fields (1965); Alice Dewey, Peasant Marketing in Java* (1962); Raymong Firth, *Malay Fishermen* (1966); Clifford Geertz, *Agricultural Involution* (1963); Pierre Gourou, *The Tropical World* (1953); Gerald C. Hickey, *Village in Vietnam* (1964); Karl J. Pelzer, *Pioneer Settlement in the Asiatic Tropics* (1948); and David E. Sopher, *The Sea Nomads* (1965).

By the late 1960s and early 1970s Southeast Asian historians were able to incorporate the developments in the scholarly fields of archaeology, social anthropology, linguistics, art history, and the natural and biological sciences. Their work included Wolters' *Early Indonesian Commerce* (1967) and *The Fall of Srivijaya in Malay History* (1970); Wheatley's 'Satyānṛta in Suvarnadvīpa: From Reciprocity to Redistribution in Ancient Southeast Asia' (1975); L. A. Sedov's 'On the Problem of the Economic System in Angkor, Cambodia in the IX-XII Centuries' (1963); M. C. Ricklefs' 'Land and the Law in the Epigraphy of Tenth Century Cambodia' (1967); Brian Colless' 'Traders of the Pearl' (*Abr Nahrain*, 1970–74); G. H. Luce's *Old Burma—Early Pagan* (1969–70); J. Noorduyn's series of articles in BKI; and Anthony Reid's 'Trade and the Problem of Royal Power in Aceh' (1975); and they began to ask specific questions about early Southeast Asian economic systems. The status of the field, so to speak, was summarized in

R. B. Smith and W. Watson, eds, *Early Southeast Asia: Essays in Archaeology, History and Historical Geography* (1979).

During the 1980s a new generation of historians, most of whom were trained by the aforementioned scholars, carried the new historiography further. As previously noted, the continuing research of Wheatley (*Nagara and Commandery*, 1983) and Wolters (*History, Culture, and Region in Southeast Asian Perspectives*, 1982), established the context for historical inquiry. Among those who responded were Pierre-Yves Manguin, Jan Wisseman-Christie, and Hermann Kulke, who focused on Indonesia's early history; Michael Aung-Thwin on Burma, Keith W. Taylor and John K. Whitmore on Vietnam; Claude Jacques and Michael Vickery on Cambodia; and David K. Wyatt on Thailand. A sample of the work of each of these and others is encompassed in David G. Marr and A. C. Milner, eds, *Southeast Asia in the 9th to 14th Centuries* (1986).

In economic history, which places so much emphasis on statistical analysis, the early Southeast Asianist is too often placed on the defensive. Facing a paucity of sources, the historian of Southeast Asia's early economy must be broadly trained and imaginative. The current task of the Southeast Asian economic historian remains that of bridging the gap between the archaeological and written sources. There are continuing problems of fit where the constantly changing archaeological picture does not quite correspond with the written records. Widening the range of questions asked of these sources, the economic historian must move from the pre-tenth century forward, largely drawing upon archaeological data, while constantly looking backward from post-tenth-century written sources and societies.

The economic historian needs to consider especially how a people lived in a particular time and place, how they viewed the world around them, and how they communicated their ideas. There is a need to know more about the meaning and context of their words as well as their archaeological remains, to understand the environment that produced these artefacts. While most current historical emphasis is on local initiative, there must be care not to underestimate the external. In a region of great cultural diversity, the indigenous needs to be more clearly distinguished from the foreign elements in the integrated cultures that emerged in the early centuries of the Christian era. The economic historian may contribute to this delineation through the study of ecological differences, and through determining distances and proximities of populations from urban centres—as well as coming to terms with what an early urban centre was, and discussing the economic importance of existing kinship structures; the interactive economic role of spiritual beliefs, ritual, and regalia; as well as the level of technology and productivity among the early populations, not only cultivators, but also fishermen, artisans/craftsmen, bondsmen/slaves, and non-village-based producers.

There are problems of periodization—are dates relevant to an understanding of the region during this era, and is it possible to accept certain dates as universally important? The mapping of economic activity would better identify economic centres and peripheries, the flow of goods and services, the consideration of overland non-maritime communication and connection, and the understanding of eastern edges of the region (including the Philippines)—areas conspicuously absent in the above discussion of Southeast Asia's early economy, in relation to the Southeast Asian world as well as that beyond.

Despite the awareness among Southeast Asia scholars of early regional traditions of economic activity, there has still been little systematic study of the early economic system. Authors of the colonial era, seemingly concerned more with practical issues of their contemporary political-economy, focused on land tenure rather than on regional gastronomy, indigenous systems of product availability, or intra-household exchange. More recent ethnographically inspired literature has considered the 'structure' and 'function' of economic activity within a local community, or changing systems of exchange, rather than address the system in total.

There is need to come to terms more fully with the empirical data currently available, especially in the epigraphic records; there is equally need for new micro and macro studies in which goods 'flow' freely (transform, transvalue, transfigure) within a recognized natural-cultural whole. Economic activity is not static: it is a medium for communication that both reinforces and shapes the local social reality and individual welfare. Economic activity is a socially bonding experience with interpersonal emotions lacing each transaction, yet it is especially a personal expression wherein an individual asserts control over goods and services (what is received or consumed) as a personally responsible act. With this in mind, there are four sets of critical questions for future study:

1. What were the uses and meaning of economic activity to those who participated?
2. Where did goods and services come from and to whom did they go?
3. How did exchange maintain the health and welfare and improve and prolong life?
4. How did societies cope with scarcity and abundance?

Existing 'embedded' description of transactional behaviour needs more fully to evolve into issue-specific discussions of the regional socio-economy in the early age. Wider variables and variations relative to continuing study will require new and different combinations of economic data on classification, categorization, use, and interpretation. Moreover, one may postulate that the study of the past patterns of production, distribution, and consumption will move us to a more comprehensive understanding of early Southeast Asia, and will lead us to become more broadly sensitive to socio-cultural and ethno-historical issues.

CHAPTER
5

# RELIGION AND POPULAR BELIEFS OF SOUTHEAST ASIA BEFORE c. 1500

The world of Southeast Asia presents a variegated cultural pattern. Geographically, the area can be divided into mainland and maritime Southeast Asia with the Malay peninsula as the dividing line, the southern part of which belongs to the island world, whereas its northern part is more continental in nature. As to maritime Southeast Asia, the motto of the modern Republic of Indonesia: *Bhinneka Tunggal Ika*, freely translated as Unity in Diversity, can be applied to the area as a whole. For, although numerous different languages are used in this vast area, they all belong to the family of Austronesian languages—apart from small pockets of tribal areas. Culturally, too, there is an underlying concept of unity despite the astounding diversity in almost every aspect. The conception of Indonesia as a 'field of ethnological study', as formulated by Dutch anthropologists, can be applied to the entire area.[1]

As far as religion is concerned, the diversity is less pronounced since Islam strongly predominates in Malaysia, Indonesia, Brunei and the southern Philippines, and Catholic Christianity in the major part of the Philippines. In mainland Southeast Asia, on the other hand, Theravāda Buddhism is the established religion of all states except Vietnam, where both Mahāyāna Buddhism and Confucianism predominate. Yet Hindu-Buddhist religion prevails in Bali, and tribal religions have persisted almost everywhere in the more remote areas. Moreover, the great religions have been influenced by earlier tribal beliefs. It is the task of the historian to describe and, if possible, to elucidate the religious developments in order to enable us to look at the present conditions against their historical background.

The study of religious developments is, however, beset with difficulties. These are essentially of two kinds: the nature of religion in the context of Southeast Asia; and the condition of our sources. In Western societies religion is generally felt to be clearly separated from other fields of social and political life, so that it can be studied for its own sake. This is also the case with modern Southeast Asia. In pre-modern Southeast Asia, however, it is hardly possible to separate religion from other fields of socio-economic and cultural life, with which it is closely interwoven. There is not even a

[1] P. E. Josselin de Jong, *Unity in Diversity: Indonesia as a field of Anthropological Study*, Dordrecht, 1964.

real equivalent of our term religion in the pre-modern languages of the area. To study religion one has, as it were, to detach from their social and political contexts those elements that we subsume under religion. These include, for example, various rituals and other forms of the worship of God, of deities or superhuman spirits and powers, as reflected in art and architecture, in literature and inscriptions. These considerations naturally lead us to the second type of difficulty: the nature of our sources.

The sources that have come down to us for the study of religion in Southeast Asia are, on the whole, richer than those available for other aspects of civilization. This is mainly because religious values were considered eternal, so that buildings erected for religious purposes—unlike dwellings for men, including kings—had to be made of durable materials such as stone or brick. Whereas perishable materials could be used for worldly purposes (toys, portraits etc.), effigies of gods and other divine powers required the use of stone or metal. Similarly, texts dealing with religious topics or containing important religious elements were written down for future generations. They were regularly copied as soon as the originals had become difficult to read. Land grants with immunities for the benefit of religious foundations, inalienable 'as long as the sun and the moon illuminate the world', used to be written on stone or bronze. Such documents, classed as inscriptions, are, by and large, the most important sources for the history of religion in Southeast Asia, but, as they are almost always associated with temples or other religious foundations, they are available only for the areas and periods in which such foundations existed. The unequal distribution, rather than the paucity, of sources is indeed one of the most serious problems facing the historian of the ancient period. Thus, the epigraphic sources are rich for Burma from the eleventh century, for Thailand from the thirteenth, for Cambodia and Champa (southern Vietnam) from the fifth, for central Java from the eighth century to the tenth, for eastern Java and Bali from the tenth century; but they are scarce or non-existent for the remaining areas and periods. Thus, nearly all Sumatran inscriptions are either from the end of the seventh or from the end of the thirteenth century to the fifteenth, and the situation is even worse for most of the remaining parts of Southeast Asia.

The literary sources are even more unequally distributed over the area and period. In contrast with the rich literary sources for (northern) Vietnam, written in Chinese, we do not possess a single line of literature from ancient Cambodia, nor from Champa or the Philippines. For eastern Java there is a rich literature in Old Javanese from the tenth century, and in Burma from the twelfth century, written in Pāli, the sacred language of the Buddhists of the Theravāda school. For western Malaysia, Sumatra and Thailand, the literary sources begin just before the end of the period under consideration. No literary sources are available for the remaining parts of Southeast Asia. Their absence is only partly compensated for by some foreign, mainly Chinese, references as well as by archaeological data. This distribution of sources is by no means a coincidence, for important source materials for early religion, whether written or archaeological, can be expected mainly in the principal centres of civilization, which were mostly important political and economic centres as well.

These different types of sources may inform us about different aspects of religious thought and institutions. The Old Javanese texts include not only major poetical works and prose literature, but also religious tracts and treatises. The oldest of these can be dated back to the tenth century. This is a compilation of two or more Mahāyāna texts, called *Sang Hyang Kamahāyānikan*. A number of other texts belong to a somewhat later period, in particular a few Śaiva treatises, such as the *Sewasasana, Wrĕhaspatitattwa, Bhuwanakośa, Bhuwanasaṅkṣepa, Tattwa sang hyang Mahājñāna, Agastyaparwa,* and others. In addition, the *Brahmāṇḍapurāṇa*, an Old Javanese encyclopaedic text based on an Indian prototype, is important for our knowledge of brahmanic Hinduism as known in Java.[2] Among the literary works some have a direct bearing on religion. Foremost among these is the *Nāgarakĕrtāgama*, a long poetical text composed in 1365 by a high official at the court of Majapahit.[3] It is important not only for the history of religious, especially Buddhist, ideas but also for religious institutions. Thus, a few cantos give us lists of different kinds of buildings associated with various religious sects. A somewhat later text, the *Śivarātrikalpa*, supplies much detailed information on Śaiva ritual. Whereas such learned and poetical texts inform us mainly about religious ideas and practices among the classes associated with the royal courts, the inscriptions often allow us glimpses of popular beliefs, especially in the long imprecation formulas found at the end of many Old Javanese inscriptions. These texts nearly always deal with the transfer to religious institutions or to certain persons of fiscal revenues and other emoluments. In the latter case it is usually stipulated that all or part of the revenues shall be used to the benefit of some named religious or charitable institution(s). Some such details may supply valuable information on the nature and socio-economic status of religious foundations.[4]

As to mainland Southeast Asia, Burma has left a considerable number of religious, legal and grammatical texts written in Pāli. The oldest of these, inscribed on gold plates, originates from the neighbourhood of modern Prome and dates back to the seventh century or earlier, but a rich Pāli literature, commentaries on Buddhist texts, lawbooks etc., was written at the court of Pagan, central Burma, from the end of the twelfth century. There, too, the inscriptions inform us about many aspects of religion on which the scholastic texts are silent.

The same type of Theravāda Buddhism, originating from Sri Lanka, also flourished in the area of present Thailand, but our sources supply less

[2] For these and other Old Javanese texts the reader is referred to Theodore G. T. Pigeaud, *Literature of Java*, I–IV, The Hague, 1967–80, cf. in particular the general index in vol. III. Five works deserve particular metion: (1) J. Kats, *Sang Hyang Kamahāyānikan*, The Hague, 1910; (2) J. Gonda, *Het Oud-Javaansche Brahmāṇḍa-Purāṇa. Prozatekst en kakawin*, Bandung, 1932; translation, ibid., Bandung, 1933; (3) Sudarshana Devi, *Wṛhaspatitattwa*, Nagpur, 1957; (4) A. Teeuw, S. O. Robson, Th. P. Galestin, P. J. Worsley, and P. J. Zoetmulder, *Śiwarātrikalpa of Mpu Tanakung*, 1969; (5) Haryati Soebadio, *Jñānasiddhānta*, 1971.

[3] Theodore G. T. Pigeaud, *Java in the 14th Century. A Study in Cultural History*, I–V, The Hague, 1960–3.

[4] The most comprehensive collections of Old Javanese inscriptions are J. L. A. Brandes and N. J. Krom, *Oud-Javaansche Oorkonden* (hereafter OJO), 'Batavia'-'s-Hage 1913 (without translations) and H. B. Sarkar, *Corpus of the Inscriptions of Java*, I–II, with translations but only up to 929.

information than on Burma. A considerable number of votive inscriptions from northern and central Thailand, written in Mon, testifies to Buddhist piety in the eleventh century, but long inscriptions, mainly in Thai, start only at the end of the thirteenth century. Buddhist texts in Pāli from the area of present Chiengmai are even considerably later in date, but often supply information on earlier religious history. An example is the *Jinakālamālī*,[5] written in 1516 by the scholar-monk Ratanapañña at Chiengmai. It is, in fact, a kind of Buddhist chronicle comprising pious stories, usually with precise dates. The chronology seems, however, confused: at least we have not yet succeeded in understanding the system that was used. The text mingles facts with legends. For example, it tells the story of a miraculous statue of Buddha brought back from Sri Lanka by king Rocarāja, a name which is, however, unknown from other historical sources. In conjunction with other, roughly contemporary, Buddhist works the story can be placed in the context of turbulent developments in Thailand and Cambodia at the beginning of the eleventh century.[6] For the history of Theravāda Buddhism, rather more valuable information is to be derived from exogenous sources such as the *Mahāvaṃsa*, written in Sri Lanka, which contains a number of references to the religious contacts with Southeast Asia, in particular Burma, or the later *Gandhavaṃsa* (probably seventeenth-century) or the *Sāsanavaṃsa*. More even than for maritime Southeast Asia, Chinese sources, in particular dynastic annals and travel accounts, supply important information on certain periods and areas with which the Chinese came into contact. An example of the first type of sources is the *Liang Shu*, a seventh-century history of the Liang dynasty. Original Chinese travel accounts include the records of Buddhist pilgrims such as Fa Hsien (beginning of the fifth century) and I Ching (seventh century).[7]

A few words should be added on the archaeological sources. In most parts of Southeast Asia there are impressive and beautiful religious monuments of the past, often restored to their pristine glory. The most prestigious monuments can be admired at Pagan (central Burma), Chaiya and Nakhon Sithammarat (southern Thailand), Sukothai and Ayutthaya (central Thailand), Angkor (western Cambodia), central and eastern Java, and Bali. These monuments are visible expressions of piety founded by kings with important contributions by members of the royal families and other court dignitaries, but constructed by compulsory and sometimes voluntary labour of the artisans and of the agricultural masses. This probably explains why the archaeological sources, in contrast to most of the literature, may give us some idea of popular beliefs. These can be expressed in different ways, especially in the iconography and in the reliefs. Thus the reliefs of Borobuḍur in central Java (first half of the ninth

[5] A. P. Buddhadatta, *Jinakālamālī*, London: Pali Text Society, 1962.

[6] G. Cœdès, *Les États Hindouisés d'Indochine et d'Indonésie*, 3rd edn, Paris, 1964, 251f.

[7] W. P. Groeneveldt, *Notes on the Malay Archipelago and Malacca, compiled from Chinese Sources*, Batavia, 1876; E. Chavannes, *Mémoire composé à l'époque de la grande dynastie T'ang sur les religieux éminents qui allèrent chercher la loi dans les pays de l'occident*, Paris, 1894; J. Takakusu, *A record of the Buddhist religion as practised in India and the Malay Archipelago (671–695 A.D.) by I-tsing*, Oxford, 1896.

century) and the Bayòn in Angkor (end of the twelfth century) show many scenes that depict aspects of the daily life of different classes of people. The study of such reliefs may supplement the information obtained from texts, inscriptions and foreign notices.

The study of the less spectacular archaeological data of the historical period has hitherto received little attention, except for sherds of Chinese and other (Thai and Vietnamese) ceramics, which may give valuable chronological data. On the other hand, the study of ancient tools, foundations of non-religious buildings, major irrigation works, coins and other material remains may well contribute to a better understanding of different aspects of daily life, including religion.

One other type of source, though not strictly legitimate as evidence for ancient history, may nevertheless give some insights into the character of the ancient local religious traditions as they existed before Indian or Chinese influence, and that is constituted by our knowledge of the religious practices current in recent times among the upland or montagnard tribal peoples of the area. Such communities have preserved distinctive cultural traditions characteristic of those who, like the ancestors of modern Southeast Asians, live in relatively small scattered groups and lack a written language or full-time religious specialists. It must be emphasized, though, that it is the general character rather than the detail of specific myths and rituals that is relevant.

The montagnards or hill peoples of Vietnam, for example, have (or had, when studied by modern scholars) a rich variety of what may in a loose sense be called animistic cults and beliefs. Some cults are addressed to ancestors, others to spirits of various types—of waters, mountains, and fields—as well as to the wandering spirits who may be encountered anywhere. There is no clear dividing line between such spirits and the local gods of the hearth, or of the earth, fire, sky and thunder. Magic energies are believed to be everywhere potential, and an apparatus of magical procedures has evolved, including the use of amulets. Sorcerers conduct rituals to cure illnesses, speed the spirits of the dead to a safe haven, and procure fortune in tribal war. Chiefs have important ritual functions, especially at harvest time when as representatives of their communities they cut the symbolic first sheaves of grain, and such seasonal rituals are accompanied by feasting and celebrations.

Features of particular groups include the *phi* (spirits of forests, mountains and waters) worshipped by the Lao, the ancestral totem dog Pau Hou from whom the Mau believe themselves to be descended, the cult of the Muong common ancestor who is regarded as the inventor of agriculture, the forest spirits with whom individuals ally themselves among the Jarai, and the offerings to Yang Xo'ri, protectress of the crops, made by the Sedang.[8]

It is the task of the historian to try to reconstruct the Southeast Asian past with the help of these different types of sources, which often confirm or supplement each other, but sometimes appear contradictory. In the latter case the historian has to examine the sources very carefully to make a

[8] Le Than Khoi, *Le Viêtnam, histoire et civilisation*, Paris, 1955, 44–51, 87f.

choice on the basis of relative reliability. Thus contemporary documents are generally more reliable than texts written many centuries after the period that they describe. It should, however, be added that by and large these sources are richer for religion than for political or economic history.[9]

## THE EARLIEST TIMES

This section is concerned with the transitional period from the beginning of the Christian era to the fifth century, in relation to which we dispose of some written sources both from Southeast Asia itself (a few Sanskrit inscriptions) and from outside the area (mainly Chinese notices). This was a decisive period when the first real kingdoms emerged in conjunction with the first contacts with the more ancient civilizations of India and China. In contrast with Chinese influence, which remained confined to Vietnam, Indian cultural influence gradually spread over many parts of the region. In the absence of any direct data on Indian cultural expansion, historians have formulated different theories as to the causes and the nature of this process, which is often termed Indianization. The disadvantage of this term is that it may suggest a conscious effort on the part of Indians to spread their culture over major parts of Southeast Asia. This was indeed the view expressed by most scholars until about half a century ago and is still occasionally found in works by Indian historians. It was based mainly on analogies with Greek, Roman or Western expansion.[10]

As there is, however, no evidence for Indian conquests in Southeast Asia (apart from an occasional raid in the eleventh century), nor for any large-scale Indian emigration or colonization, it is now generally thought that the influence of Indian civilization, including religion, should mainly be attributed to endeavours by some Southeast Asian élites to assimilate important elements of Indian culture. The eclectic nature of Indian influence is a strong argument in favour of this latter view. This applies to religion as much as to other elements of civilization. By the beginning of the Christian era some parts of the region had already reached a high level

[9] No comprehensive history of the religion of Southeast Asia exists. There are, however, many excellent works on specific areas, periods or aspects, for example W. Stöhr and J. Zoetmulder, *Die Religionen Indonesiens*, Stuttgart, 1965, French translation under the title *Les Religions d'Indonésie*, trans. L. Jospin, Paris, 1968. All references given here are to the French edition. Stöhr deals with tribal religions in Indonesia: known only since relatively recent times, they are not directly relevant to this chapter. Zoetmulder's account, on the other hand, is a judicious discussion, based almost entirely on literature, of classical Indonesian religion. The present account owes much to this publication, from which, however, it differs by the inclusion of much archaeological and epigraphic material.

[10] Many accounts tend to overemphasize the importance of these foreign influences on the beginnings of Southeast Asian kingdoms. There can be little doubt that foreign contacts would only have carried significant effects at a time when there already existed ordered societies in Southeast Asia with élites that were capable of assimilating foreign influences and utilizing these to their own advantage. For a discussion of such problems see especially Ina E. Slamet-Velsink, *Emerging hierarchies. Processes of stratification and early state formation in the Indonesian archipelago: prehistory and the ethnographic present*, Leiden, 1986, and C. Higham, *The Archaeology of Mainland Southeast Asia*, Cambridge, UK, 1989, 306–18.

of civilization which enabled local élites to choose, albeit mostly unconsciously, those forms of Indian religion which were consistent with, or could be adapted to, their own beliefs and practices.

Earlier scholars have often assumed that Indian influence was mainly confined to the early centuries of the Christian era, when the first contacts between South and Southeast Asia were established. More recent research has, however, emphasized the continuous nature of such relations, at least until the maritime supremacy of the Western powers rendered such regular contacts more difficult or nearly impossible.

The sources at our disposal mainly reflect the beliefs held by such local élites, but to understand religious history in its social reality, we need to step outside the monastery or temple library and look at the didactic bas-reliefs on the temple walls, shiny from the reverent fondling of the faithful; at the wayside shrines decked with their little offerings of flowers or incense; at the stories told to children of the spirits of heroes who lived long ago; at the whole lore which a community tells itself about the invisible sacred world that surrounds and contains it.

It is from this perspective that we should view the influence of Indian religions on Southeast Asia. Yet, although only a small part of the population was directly influenced by Indian ideas, it should be emphasized that this was the élite which left us ancient literature, architecture and iconography—in other words, the products of high civilizations which we still admire. In addition, the court culture was never completely separated from the rest of the population, and much of it gradually percolated to the agricultural masses. On the other hand, it was inevitable that the court was also influenced by the popular culture.

The manner in which Indian ideas blended with ancient cults must have differed from one area to another. For ancient Champa, a non-Vietnamese kingdom occupying territory that was later absorbed by the southward expansion of the Vietnamese, Paul Mus has proposed an analysis of the way in which Indian cults, notably those of the Hindu god Śiva with the linga (*liṅga*, a phallic symbol) as his icon, were moulded to the tradition of prior cults such as those of the earth gods identified with the territory inhabited by specific communities. In each such cult, the deity was represented by an icon, often a rough stone (easily replaced by the linga of Śiva), and could be approached by the prayers of the faithful only through rituals addressed to this icon. Such rituals were directed especially to the assurance of fertility; the *yoni* (womb) stone on which the linga stood, which received the sacral fluid poured over the linga, was especially apt to symbolize the fertilized earth. Thus a high god of Hinduism was, as happened also in India, adapted to serve the purpose of primal religion, becoming in the process part of a particularistic tradition identifying a community with its territory.[11]

It is possible to see small-scale territorial cults of this sort surviving beneath the mantle of imported Indian religion in other parts of the region.

[11] L. Cadière, 'Croyances et Pratiques Religieuses de Vietnamiens', *Bulletin de la Société des Études Indochinoises*, 33, 1 (1958) 1ff.; P. Mus, *India seen from the East: Indian and Indigenous cults in Champa*, trans. I. W. Mabbett and D. P. Chandler, Monash Papers on Southeast Asia no. 3, Clayton, Vic., 1975, 7.

Cambodian inscriptions of the pre-Angkor period (i.e. before c. 900 CE) include references to many shrines, such as the 'god of the stone pond', which appear to be addressed to local spirits that inhabit or (as Mus argued in the case of the earth god) are identified with features of the landscape. The old Mon states in Burma, which became staunchly Buddhist, had a chthonic cult; kings as representatives of their communities presided over rituals that linked them with their local patron gods, and after their death the rulers would go to join their ancestors in an invisible other-world where they would be united with the earth goddess, a tree or mound serving as the point of contact between the sacred and profane worlds. With the advent of Buddhism, burial mounds turned into Buddhist stupas and the tree spirits, blithely integrated into Buddhist observance, turned into *sotapan*, followers of the Buddhist teaching who were set on the path to salvation.[12] Such practices were in accordance with Buddhist teaching in India, where the oldest stupas were also burial mounds, in which corporeal relics of Lord Buddha or of Buddhist saints were enshrined. Certain trees, including the famous *aśwattha* beneath which Lord Buddha attained Enlightenment, were the abodes of Yakṣas, ferocious giant spirits who became pious protectors of early Buddhism.

The worship of mountains as abodes of gods or of powerful spirits is also well attested in Indian religion where, for example, Śiva is thought to reside on top of mount Kailāsa, identified with one of the highest peaks of the Himalaya, and Mount Mahāmeru or Sumeru (in Pāli Sineru), the mountain of the gods at the centre of the universe, is an important cosmographic motif influential in art and architecture. In Southeast Asia, however, mountain worship developed into important cults. Thus, in Indonesia some volcanoes, conceived of as 'living' mountains, received worship as the abodes of great Hindu gods, such as Śiva, 'Lord of the Mountain(s)' (Girīndra) and Brahmā, who became identified with the (subterranean) fire. One of the most impressive temple complexes in (east) Java, Candi Panataran, which will be briefly discussed later, is devoted to the cult of Śiva Girīndra. The greatest Buddhist monument in Southeast Asia, Borobuḍur in central Java, is not a temple but a complex of terraces and galleries, richly decorated with narrative reliefs and statues, which encloses a natural hill as a kind of mantle in stone.

In Cambodia, more even than in other Southeast Asian kingdoms, mountain symbolism was embodied in monumental architecture. There, a whole series of monuments of the Angkor period (from c. 900) were constructed as large terraced pyramids. Though they were dedicated to Śiva or Viṣṇu or to a Buddhist Bodhisattva (a being destined to become a Buddha in a future life, and in Mahāyāna, which was the prevalent form of Buddhism in Southeast Asia before the thirteenth century, effectively an object of worship in his own right), the magnificence and obsessiveness of their Mahāmeru symbolism went far beyond any Indian models.

Further, there are many evidences of mountain spirit cults that were not Indian in origin. An early example in Cambodia is the site of Ba Phnom, situated on the Mekong River near the Vietnamese border. Though indeed

[12] H. L. Shorto, 'The *dewatau sotapan*, a Mon prototype of the 37 *nats*', BSOAS, 30 (1967).

the evidence identifying it as a major cult site in pre-Angkor times is equivocal, it does appear to have long been a symbolic centre of the kingdom—hence a Mahāmeru—and the scene of sacrificial rituals addressed to a goddess; according to one view this goddess was a fusion of an aboriginal Me Sa (White Mother) with the Indian Umā Mahiṣāsuramardinī, a demon-slaying embodiment of the spouse of Śiva; sacrifice was conducted at the site as recently as the nineteenth century.[13]

Other kingdoms had their mountain spirit sites, where rituals had to be conducted for the sake of the prosperity of the state. In Pagan, it was Mount Popa. In Sukothai in the thirteenth century, it was at the hill site where the spirit, Phra Kapung, resided beside a spring that issued from a mountain:

> If the prince who is sovereign in Muang Sukothai worships this spirit properly and presents it ritual offerings, then this country will be stable and prosperous; but if he does not present ritual offerings, then the spirit of this hill will no longer protect or respect this country, which will fall into decline.[14]

Origin myths, legitimizing kingdoms and giving their peoples a place in the grand scheme of the universe, were sometimes taken from India but often betray local myths. In Vietnam, for example, the story is told of Lac Long Quan, the Dragon Lord, who first civilized the Vietnamese people; from this spirit's union with queen Ao Co came the line of lords who, according to the tradition, first ruled in the Hong (Red) River area.

Archaeological evidence includes, notably, that of the Dong-son culture, northern Vietnam, which reflects aspects of early religion in the late centuries BC. Richly decorated bronze drums were found all over Southeast Asia, for example in Kuala Terengganu on the east coast of west Malaysia, and on the island of Alor in eastern Indonesia. They show incised designs likely to embody symbols current in myth and ritual.[15] Some scholars have associated the Dong-son culture with a speculatively reconstructed complex of cultures characterized by sky spirits, as opposed to another complex represented by the many megalithic remains in the region and characterized by earth gods. However, it is nowadays widely believed that the megaliths do not in fact attest any one coherent culture.

Funerary rituals normally enclosed elements of indigenous religion. The Indian religions favoured cremation, but a wealth of sources vouches for the survival in historical times of other practices, particularly interment, though this was often only partial: a body was first cremated and its remains were subsequently buried, commonly in an urn. Chinese sources assert that in ancient Champa the great men of the land were dealt with in this way, except that the urns were then committed to the sea or to rivers. The kingdom known as Tun-sun, presumably situated on the eastern coast of the Malay peninsula, was claimed to practise exposure, corpses being

[13] D. P. Chandler, 'Royally sponsored human sacrifices in nineteenth century Cambodia: the cult of *nak ta* Me Sa (*Mahiṣāsuramardinī*) at Ba Phnom', JSS, 72 (1974).

[14] Cœdès, *États*, 377f.; cf. also Cœdès, *Recueil des Inscriptions du Siam*, 2nd edn, Bangkok, 1961, 44f.

[15] A. J. Bernet Kempers, *The kettledrums of Southeast Asia: a bronze age world and its aftermath*, Rotterdam, 1988; Higham, *Archaeology*, 201.

offered up to the birds.[16] The earliest state in Cambodia, known by the Chinese appellation of Fu-nan and flourishing from the second to the sixth century, was said to know four practices: cremation, depositing in the sea, grave burial, and exposure. In Burma, in the later Shan states, the remains of a monk were sometimes buried under a post.

Human sacrifice, attested in remote parts of the area until the recent past, may have been more widespread in the ancient period. This type of practice is likely to have attended the antique cults of territorial gods and spirits of tree, river, and mountain. In each case, it was considered that the spirit, dwelling essentially in a placeless, timeless, sacred world, was inaccessible to the community except through special rituals designed to give him the means of communication. It should, however, be added that there is no real evidence as to the prevalence of human sacrifice in the civilized areas of ancient Southeast Asia.

There are many indications of the importance of the worship of local deities. Just as ancient India had its Yakṣa cults, many areas, villages or even impressive trees and other striking points in nature had their guardian spirits. Thus, the cult of the *nats* in Burma acquired official status and was sanctioned by the Buddhist orthodoxy. The same applies to the cults of the *nāgas* (mythical snakes) in many parts of the region. Thus, a five-headed cobra was the main tutelary spirit of the maritime kingdom of Śrīvijaya, while the founder of the earliest kingdom in Cambodia is said to have married a Nāgī (female cobra), from whom later rulers trace their descent.

Except in Vietnam, where Chinese influence predominated, ancestor worship was not common, except again for the royal dynasties where ancestor cults emphasized the continuity of the state. The same applies to totemism, which does not seem to be observed—at least not in the sense that includes the idea of families or communities descending from certain animals which, for that reason, were considered sacred within such communities.[17]

Some animals seem to have enjoyed a kind of worship. Snakes have already been mentioned in connexion with the *nāga* cult, in which Indian influence probably blended with ancient indigenous snake cults. There are scattered references to other animals but, compared with, for instance, India, animal worship was and is relatively unimportant. In addition, most of the references are in the context of religions of Indian origin, such as the special status of the Garuḍa, a mythical eagle and mount of god Viṣṇu, in Indonesia.

In the areas where the influence of Indian religions was strong, we often see complicated patterns in which outside influence is closely interwoven with ancient Southeast Asian beliefs. In many cases one may discern the

[16] P. Wheatley, *The Golden Khersonese: Studies in the Historical Geography of the Malay Peninsula before A.D. 1500*, Kuala Lumpur, 1966; P. Pelliot, 'Le Fou-nan', BEFEO, 3 (1903) 279.

[17] Some scholars, in particular W. H. Rassers and his followers, have found evidence of totemism in Indonesia, but the indications are marginal or unconvincing. Thus, many Javanese authorities during and after the Kaḍiri period (c. 1100–1222 and later) are mentioned by names preceded by a term indicating an animal, such as *macan*, 'tiger', *kĕbo*, 'buffalo', *gajah*, 'elephant', etc., but there are no indications that such names refer to totem animals. It is much more likely that these are warrior names reflecting the animals figuring on their banners, etc.

power of ancient beliefs at the background of apparently Hindu or Buddhist ceremonies. In Pagan, for example, *naga* spirits were regarded as the owners of the site where the palace of King Kyanzittha (c. 1084–1112) was to be built, and had to be propitiated. The rituals involved in the ceremonies attending the dedication of the palace, though accompanied by the recitation of Buddhist texts, were hardly Buddhist.

Amulets, talismans, portents, the whole panoply of apotropaic magic pervaded the religious life of everybody, high or low, monk, ascetic or layman. In mainland Southeast Asia, Buddhist monks, like the ascetics in maritime Southeast Asia, were regarded as a vehicle of a sort of spiritual energy that could operate in the arena of local magic forces. The monks subscribed readily to notions of magic inhering in relics, and impressed laymen with Buddhist miracles. Several such cases belong to Thai tradition; at the shrine of Wat Mahathat in Sukothai, which contained Buddha relics, a neckbone was seen to float out of the stupa.[18] Such prodigies were regarded as signs to the faithful to encourage them to make the pilgrimage to Sri Lanka. It should be added that many of the magic features of Buddhism in Southeast Asia were already inherent in Buddhism before it spread to Southeast Asia, but underwent various forms of adaptation to Southeast Asian beliefs and practices. Similar observations can be made with reference to Śaivism and Vaiṣṇavism in the region, including maritime Southeast Asia. As, however, religious developments in the mainland and in maritime Southeast Asia are quite different in many respects (though agreeing in others), especially during the classical period (from about the fifth to the end of the fifteenth century CE), it is proper to discuss them separately.

## RELIGIONS OF INDIAN ORIGIN ON THE MAINLAND

### Brahmanism

On the mainland of Southeast Asia, it was ultimately Buddhism that came to dominate, but it is important to recognize that, from early times, Brahmanism and Buddhism were mingled in the cultural legacy bequeathed to all the 'Indianized' states. Just as ancient Southeast Asian traditions mingled freely with the observances of imported religion, so did the lore of different imported religions mingle with each other: the orthodoxy of a state would favour one, each king being free to patronize his own favoured cults and divinities, but others persisted, their representatives dotted about the countryside in temples and monasteries.

Persecutions were rare, but not perhaps quite unknown. The seventh-century Chinese traveller I Ching tells us that Buddhism had been persecuted early in that century in Zhenla (Chen La),[19] a Chinese designation of Cambodia, especially in the pre-Angkor period, i.e. before the end of the

[18] Cœdès, *Recueil*, I, 54.

[19] I Ch'ing, *A Record of the Buddhist Religion as practised in India and the Malay Archipelago*, trans. J. Takakusu, Oxford, 1896, 12.

ninth century, and the absence of significant evidence of Buddhism (there is some, but not much) during the reign of Jayavarman I (c. 657–81) may possibly lend some support to the story. Śiva cults, as well as Viṣṇu cults, Mahāyāna Buddhism as well as Hīnayāna, coexisted in most kingdoms during the early centuries, though as time passed a process of polarization gradually skewed the distribution of different sects and schools; after the thirteenth century, and particularly under the influence of the prestige attached to ordination in Sri Lanka, Theravāda Buddhism rapidly rose to prominence in kingdom after kingdom as state orthodoxy. Even then we must not overlook the continuing importance of brahmins in a narrower role: up to the present century, the Buddhist courts have engaged brahmins in astrological and ritual functions.

If such brahmins were Indians (the Indian brahmins are indeed occasionally mentioned in Southeast Asian inscriptions), one wonders how or why they should have left India. This is the more surprising since Indian lawbooks contain prohibitions for brahmins against overseas travel, which was regarded as ritually polluting. These prohibitions may have had little practical effect, and would not have deterred ambitious men lured by the hope of honour and fortune in a distant land. It has been suggested that some learned brahmins were invited by Southeast Asian rulers at a time when commercial relations between Indian and Southeast Asian ports had spread the fame of such brahmins to the courts. It is indeed likely that this happened sometimes, but probably not on a large scale. It is, for example, striking that the Indian *gotra* names, never omitted in Indian inscriptions, are not normally mentioned in Southeast Asia. On the other hand, in the few cases where they are mentioned it is likely that they refer to Indian brahmins. It therefore follows that the great majority of Southeast Asian brahmins would have been Southeast Asians, many of whom had acquired their knowledge of the Sanskrit texts and of brahmanic ritual in Indian ashrams.

Whatever their origin, brahmins had great influence in the Southeast Asian courts in various capacities. As they had access to the sacred texts, the lawbooks and other literature in Sanskrit, they were employed as priests, teachers, ministers and counsellors: the principal advisers of the kings. Government, particularly in early centuries, depended upon such men, who were the chief available sources of literacy and administrative talent and experience. As in the early Indian kingdoms, an important office was that of the *purohita*, a chief priest with ritual and governmental functions. The epigraphic record of the mainland kingdoms demonstrates the powerful influence of *purohitas*, notably in Burma and Cambodia, where they often served under several successive rulers and provided continuity to the government in troubled times. In ninth-century Angkor, for example, Indravarman I had the services of Śivasoma, who was a relative of the earlier king Jayavarman II and was said to have studied in India under the celebrated Vedānta teacher Śaṅkara.[20]

It is noticeable that sacerdotal offices such as that of the *purohita* tend in Cambodia to pass from uncle to nephew in the maternal line. This has

[20] Cœdès, *États*, 205.

often been seen as a persisting influence of indigenous matrilineal social organization. More recently it has been suggested that this type of succession might rather show how a line of kings would seek to ally itself to particular powerful families by marriage, generation after generation; a family thus related would come to have its male members given high office by tradition, which would produce the effect actually observed.[21] Although this was a desirable side-effect, it is unlikely that the kings would have been able to enforce this matrilineal succession unless it was based on tradition among the priestly families.[22]

Not only in the 'Hindu' courts, such as Angkor, but also in the Buddhist courts, such as those of Pagan in Burma and Sukothai in Thailand, the brahmins conducted the great ceremonies, such as the royal consecration, and functioned as ministers and counsellors, but had to share their influence with that of the Buddhist monks. By its very nature Buddhism was concerned with the acquisition of spiritual merit and moral perfection rather than with the rites and ceremonies of a royal court, which were left to the brahmins. The grand ceremonies in Pagan that attended the dedication of Kyanzittha's palace have already been mentioned; they required the services of numerous brahmins, although Theravāda Buddhism was then well established. In Cambodia, as late as the thirteenth century (during the revival of 'Brahmanism' after the extravagant Mahāyāna Buddhism of Jayavarman VII), Jayavarman VIII built a temple for the scholar-priest Jayamaṅgalārtha, and likewise for the brahmin Vidyeśavid, who became court sacrificial priest. The Chinese visitor Chou Ta-kuan refers to the presence of brahmins wearing the traditional sacred thread.[23]

What is shown by the role of such brahmins is that it is appropriate to speak of Brahmanism as distinct from the specific cults of Śiva or Viṣṇu, or any of their innumerable kin: the priests stood for a social order and for the rituals that gave to the political or local community a sense of its unity and its place in the world.

## Śaivism

Cults of Śiva were strong in the ancient kingdoms of Cambodia and Champa. Two major roles played by Śiva need to be distinguished: the political and the devotional.

The political role was as the focus of linga cults: the linga, originally the 'phallus', was the emblem of Śiva as god of creation and fertility for his devotees. Such cults were sponsored by rulers at the central shrines that constituted the ritual hub of their kingdoms. State-sponsored linga cults

21 Thomas A. Kirsch, 'Kinship, Genealogical claims and Societal Integration in Ancient Khmer Society: an Interpretation', in C. D. Cowan and O. W. Wolters, eds, *Southeast Asian History and Historiography: Essays presented to D. G. E. Hall*, Ithaca, 1976.

22 There are interesting parallels suggesting that royal succession could be based on principles different from those followed by other sections of society. This was the case with the old Minangkabau kingdom (Sumatra Barat), where the rulers succeeded one another along patrilineal lines in a society generally based on matrilineal succession. See especially P. E. De Josselin de Jong, *Minangkabau and Negri Sembilan, socio-political structure in Indonesia*, Leiden, 1951, passim.

23 *Mémoires sur les coutumes du Cambodge de Tcheou Takouan*, trans. P. Pelliot (Oeuvres Posthumes de P. Pelliot, vol. III), Paris, 1951, 14.

were maintained in Cambodia till the twelfth century. In Champa, the royal capital at Mi-son in the fourth century (in Quang Nam district of present central Vietnam) had a royal Śiva cult with a linga called Bhadreśvara (combining the king's name, Bhadravarman, with Īśvara, a title of Śiva) as its principal object of worship; the later king Śambhuvarman endowed a linga called Śambhubhadreśvara. In the eighth century this linga, thought to incorporate the essence of the kingdom, was taken away by 'Javanese' raiders.[24] In the late thirteenth and early fourteenth centuries, Jayasiṃhavarman III established a linga cult down in the south, at the shrine of Po Klaung Garai.

In Cambodia many state monuments had Śiva lingas in their central shrines, often with the iconography of other gods (or even Buddhist divinities) represented in the sculpture of surrounding buildings. The rulers of Cambodia favoured great tiered pyramidal masses that became more elaborate as time went on; many of these had lingas in the central towers that stood at their pinnacles. The *devarāja* (either 'god-king' or 'king of the gods') cult, instituted at the beginning of the ninth century, though its precise nature has been debated,[25] was presumably Śaiva nevertheless, and for a number of kings of Angkor it represented for them the sanctification of their role.

But Śiva was not only an emblem of royalty and power; he was also a god of grace; he is referred to as such, for example in a Cambodian inscription of 624, which identifies him with Brahmā and thus represents a sort of mystic theism. One Śaiva sect, represented in Cambodia, was that of the Pāśupatas, who had a doctrine of union with Śiva as the one god.[26]

This form of devotion has been seen as attesting the Śiva cult as a personal form of religion that stepped aside from social and sectarian divisions. Many inscriptions also embody a type of cult that made of Śiva not a possession of brahmanic ritual but a personal god who had a particular relationship with a divinely inspired ruler. The Śiva cult in Cambodia has thus been interpreted as a means of exalting the king as a vehicle of spiritual energy. A rather similar idea of kingship is attested in the Ly dynasty of Vietnam (c. 1010–1225), though with a quite different cultural vocabulary to express it; the ruler is not a god but has in him a concentration of the spiritual energies of the land.[27]

## Vaiṣṇavism

The god Viṣṇu claimed his purlieu from the beginning, though with a few exceptions his dominion was never quite as conspicuous or constant as those of Śiva or of the Buddha. In Cambodia, the inscription of Queen Kulaprabhāvatī, who died in 514, attests that she founded a hermitage and a reservoir for the benefit of brahmins, and the record refers to the

24 For these 'Javanese' raids see Cœdès, *États*, 173.

25 For the *devarāja* cult see pages 324–9.

26 O. W. Wolters, 'Khmer "Hinduism" in the seventh century,' in R. B. Smith and W. Watson, eds, *Early South East Asia: Essays in Archaeology, History and Historical Geography*, London and New York, 1979, 431.

27 K. W. Taylor, 'Authority and legitimacy in eleventh century Vietnam', in D. G. Marr and A. C. Milner, eds, *Southeast Asia in the 9th to 14th Centuries*, Singapore and Canberra, 1986, 143.

Vaiṣṇava myth of Śeṣa, the cosmic serpent on whom Viṣṇu reclines in rest between the world cycles; iconographically Viṣṇu is thus represented recumbent upon the serpent and with a lotus growing from his navel. The inscription of Guṇavarman, likewise, indicates a devotion to Viṣṇu, for whom an image of his footprints was endowed. (Viṣṇu in the form of the sun god spanned the universe in three strides, and, in a related myth, as the dwarf Vāmana, performed the same feat to gain the promised possession of whatever ground he could cover in three steps; Viṣṇu's footprints are thus evocative of power and dominion.)

The association of Viṣṇu with the sun is an important theme in the history of his cult; it was made early in India and influenced the form of religious art and myth in places where Vaiṣṇavism was practised. There may thus have been a fusion of the Viṣṇu cult with the influence of sun worship from Persia and the dynasties established by Persian conquerors. Some early images of Cambodia, belonging to the so-called 'Fu-nan' period (before the seventh century), represent deities with tunics in a Central Asian style, also found on images of Persia and northwestern India. They have been thought to reflect Iranian influence. Inscriptional references to a 'Śakabrāhmaṇa' may similarly reflect an extension of 'Scythian' influence, as Śaka corresponds to our term Scythian; some have even thought that the Śaka dominions in India, which from the second to the end of the fourth century covered much of western India, may have been a major contributor to the 'Indianization' of much of Southeast Asia.[28] Such inferences, though, are speculative.

In southern Burma, the very name of one of the early cities of the Pyu, an ancient people closely related to the Burmans, viz. Viṣṇupura (modern Beikthano), may emphasize the cosmic aspect of Viṣṇu as the heavenly king of the universe. The religious observance at Śrīkṣetra (modern Hmaw-za near Prome) had a place for images of Viṣṇu and his consort Lakṣmī, goddess of royal majesty and of fortune, and the Kagyun cave site has a relief of a recumbent Viṣṇu. It was only in Burma, incidentally, that we find statues portraying the god standing on his mount, the mythical eagle Garuḍa.[29]

In Pagan, Viṣṇu played an important part in the state ritual if not in private devotion; under Kyanzittha Viṣṇu had his own temple, and the myth of Buddhist prophecy promulgated to glorify the king made of Kyanzittha an incarnation of Viṣṇu. Brahmins associated with the building of the palace may have been custodians of an old Vaiṣṇava cult. Lakṣmī was worshipped at Pagan as Kyak Sri.

In Angkor, several rulers such as Jayavarman III (r. c. 850–77) gave honour to Viṣṇu, but by far the most conspicuous success of Vaiṣṇavism in gaining state support was embodied in the construction of Angkor Wat by king Sūryavarman II (r. c. 1113–50). This, the most famous and the most impressive of all the monuments of Angkor, was built as a series of concentric courtyards surrounding a central pyramidal pile on top of which five towers rose in quincunx to place the Mountain of the Gods

[28] K. Bhattacharya, *Les Religions Brahmaniques dans L'Ancien Cambodge*, Paris, 1967, 130.
[29] G. H. Luce, *Old Burma—Early Pagan*, New York, 1969–70, I. 216.

(Mahāmeru) in the centre of the kingdom, and the kingdom in the centre of the universe. The complex measures overall about 1550 by 1800 metres. An outer gallery was decorated with a series of bas-relief carvings over two metres high running in long sections around the complex, extending more than 1600 metres. They depict secular as well as religious scenes, notably including myths of Viṣṇu and his incarnation of Kriṣṇa. The ritual and cosmological symbolism of the monument is richly embodied in every detail of Angkor Wat's art and design, but it has also been claimed to represent a devotional form of Viṣṇu worship. Such cults were strongly developed in India (especially that founded by Rāmānuja) and, to some extent, in Java, where most kings of the Kaḍiri period (c. 1100–1222) were considered incarnations of Viṣṇu. On the other hand, it has been pointed out that the Vaiṣṇava character of Angkor Wat was not pronounced—even to the extent that the monument was later adopted by the Buddhists as their own.

The devotional aspect of Vaiṣṇavism found expression from early times, and the Pāñcarātra sect, whose doctrines crystallized in the first two centuries CE, taught devotion (*bhakti*) to Viṣṇu as the supreme deity. An inscription of the time of Jayavarman I, in seventh-century Cambodia, refers to a Pāñcarātra priest. Ninth- and tenth-century Angkor knew the sect also, displaying a knowledge of metaphysics according to which Viṣṇu had four emanations (*vyūha*) and lay at the basis of the universe in all its forms, himself being without form.[30] Thus Vaiṣṇavism, like Śaivism, included a significant stream of devotional monistic theism.

## Buddhism

Buddha images and votive seals attest the introduction of the Dharma (Buddhist teaching) from early times. The record begins with a number of Buddha statues, found in various parts of Southeast Asia, both on the mainland, especially at Dong-duong (near Danang in central Vietnam), Korat (northeastern Thailand), Vieng-sra (peninsular Thailand), and in the archipelago at Sempaga (south Sulawesi, north of Ujung Pandang), Jěmběr (east Java) and on the Bukit Sěguntang near Palembang (south Sumatra). These Buddhas, usually represented standing and dressed in clinging transparent robes, reflect a style the prototype of which has been found in Amarāvatī, Andhra Pradesh, India, and dated back to the early centuries of the Christian era. It has, however, convincingly been argued that the earliest Southeast Asian Buddhas were not made in or directly inspired by Amarāvatī, but more probably by Anurādhapura in Sri Lanka, which had itself been strongly influenced by Amarāvatī. As a consequence these earliest Buddhas in Southeast Asia must be dated considerably later than had been thought and probably belong to between the fourth and the sixth century CE.[31]

[30] K. Bhattacharya, 96–9; 'The Pāñcarātra sect in ancient Cambodia', *Journal of the Greater India Society*, 14, 1955, 111–16.

[31] J. Boisselier, in his *La Statuaire du Champa*, Paris, 1963 (Publications de l'École Française d'Extrême-Orient, vol. 54), dates the Dong-Duong bronze Buddha to a period ending in the early sixth century; cf. P. Dupont, *L'Archéologie Môme de Dvāravatī*, Paris, EFEO, 1959; L. Malleret, *L'Archéologie du Delta du Mékong*, II, Paris, EFEO, 1960, 202–208 and pl. LXXXV.

Buddhism, with its universal values, came to be embodied perhaps more than brahmanism in the teachings of pilgrims and wandering scholars. Certainly, in the first seven or eight centuries CE, there was a cosmopolitan oecumene of Buddhist culture disseminated across Asia by travelling monks. Our knowledge of these, like that of the earliest states that grew up along the trading routes, depends a great deal upon Chinese texts, which tell of monks from India and the Buddhist lands of central Asia finding their way by the Silk Road to northern China or by sea through Southeast Asia to destinations often in Kiao-chi (Tonkin) or southern China. In the second and third centuries, the monks who in one way or another reached or passed through Tonkin in the course of their teaching and studying included the Parthian An-shih-kao; Mou Po from China, who was converted to Buddhism there; the Sogdian Kang-seng-hui, child of a merchant in Tonkin; the Indo-Scyth Kalyāṅaruci who translated the Lotus Sūtra; and Mārajīvaka, who went from India to Tonkin and later to Canton at the end of the third century.[32]

Such travels criss-crossed the Buddhist world. Most of the monks were scholarly, actuated by the desire to disseminate the Dharma embodied in holy scriptures, or to find and study such scriptures in foreign lands. From the fifth century, the desire of Chinese Buddhists to refresh and purify their scriptural tradition led numbers to make the hazardous journey to India. Fa-hsien was one, at the beginning of the fifth century, and he gained fame by the account he left of his journey; on the return stretch he took the sea route via Sri Lanka and arrived back in China after an adventurous journey; he suffered shipwreck and was obliged to stay in (probably western) Java for five months waiting for another ship to finish his journey.[33]

Quite a few monks passed that way in the following two centuries, some spending long periods or settling down in places like Fu-nan, the Chinese transcription of the earliest kingdom in Cambodia. Nāgasena was a Buddhist monk sent to China by the ruler of that country. He carried two ivory models of stupas and Chinese references suggest a possible Mahāyāna element in the Buddhism he practised. In the seventh century, the great Chinese Hsuan-tsang went to India and back, but he took the land route both ways. At the end of the century, though, I Ching went to India by sea and spent several years in Southeast Asia, notably in Śrīvijaya at or near present Palembang in south Sumatra. His accounts are of great value, especially for the data they contain about the distribution of Buddhist schools and sects in different countries. Thus, he notes that the Saṃmitīya Nikāya, a sect closely related to the Theravādins of Sri Lanka, was well represented in Champa, while the Sarvāstivādins, asserting the reality of the *dharmas* (in this context: elements of existence), had followers in other areas.

I Ching wrote a valuable compilation of short biographies of about sixty monks who set off for India in search of the Buddhist teaching, but some of

[32] Tran Van Giap, 'Le Bouddhisme en Annam des origines au XIIIe siècle', BEFEO, 32 (1932) 211f.

[33] Fa-Hsien, *A Record of Buddhist Kingdoms*, trans. J. Legge, New York, 1965 (reprint); also translated by S. Beal in *Travels of Fa-hien and Sung-Yun*, London, 1964 (reprint).

these died en route.[34] Places in mainland Southeast Asia which they visited include Cambodia and Dvāravatī (in present-day Thailand). At the time of the Tang dynasty (from 618) the Vietnamese were taking an active part in Buddhist traffic; monks such as Mokṣadeva, Khuy Sung, and Hue Diem set off on pilgrimages, and the teacher Van Ki, traditionally supposed to have been a disciple of the Chinese master Hui-ning, brought to Vietnam Buddhist texts translated into Chinese, which was the language of literati in Vietnam until the nineteenth century.

Thus the early stages of Buddhist history in the eastern zone, in 'Indochina', are reasonably well represented in the historical record, even though the rulers of Cambodia and Champa generally favoured Brahmanism for their court cults. Few Chinese sources are, however, available for present-day Burma, then the country of the Mon (especially the coastal areas including the Irawaddy and Salween deltas), the Pyu in south-central Burma, the Burmans in north-central and northern Burma and others. Almost all sources before the eleventh century, inscriptions and monuments, are those of the Pyu with their centres in Srīkṣetra (present Hmaw-za near Prome) and Viṣṇupura (Beikthano). The archaeology of the latter site has suggested to its excavator that Buddhism is represented by undecorated monuments with square bases and drum-shaped superstructures, which are not unlike certain stupas in eastern India; they apparently date back to as early as the second century.[35]

The history, and particularly the architecture, of Śrīkṣetra are much better known. Buddhist architecture of Old Prome was technically advanced, and employed the true arch—a feature which, remarkably, occurs only in Burma among the countries of Southeast Asia. Three great pagodas guarded the city; the best preserved of these is the Bawbawgyi, which is fifty metres high.

Inscriptions on gold plates from Maungun near Prome, probably datable to the seventh century, reflect the Pāli tradition and thus represent the earliest Southeast Asian evidence of Theravāda Buddhism, which gradually, especially from the eleventh century, became the prevalent religion of Burma and, a few centuries later, of most of mainland Southeast Asia. On the other hand, there is much evidence for Mahāyāna Buddhism in Pyu art, which includes various representations of the Bodhisattvas (future Buddhas) Avalokiteśvara and Maitreya, as well as of the Buddha Dīpaṅkara, who was thought to calm the waves. The Pyu were familiar with a Sanskrit Buddhist canon, which perhaps came to them from northeastern India.

The seventh-century Chinese pilgrim Hsuan-tsang mentions Śrīkṣetra as a Buddhist kingdom, as does I Ching in 675. There are Chinese literary references to Pyu embassies to China in 802 and 807; the notice given of their country claims that in it there were more than a hundred Buddhist monasteries, and all boys and girls would serve for a spell as novices in the order.[36]

[34] *Chinese Monks in India*, trans. Latika Lahiri, Delhi, 1986.

[35] Aung Thaw, *Historical Sites in Burma*, Rangoon, 1972; *Report on the Excavations in Beikthano*, Rangoon, 1968.

[36] G. H. Luce, 'The ancient Pyu', JBRS, 27 (1937) 249f.

Thus it is evident that Buddhism was strong among the Pyu; but it was the Mon kingdoms that seem to have become the chief disseminators of Buddhism of the Theravāda school to the later empires which from the eleventh century came to displace them; and the early history of Mon Buddhism is particularly obscure.

It may go back a long way. For example, there is the tantalizing evidence provided by an ivory comb found in Thailand, at Chansen, possibly from the second century, though the radiocarbon datings are discrepant; it bears what appear to be Buddhist symbols.[37] The oldest known Mon Buddhist inscription, near Nakhon Pathom, sixty-five kilometres west of Bangkok, is not much earlier than 600 CE. P. Dupont considered that the influence of the Mon kingdom of Dvāravatī can be seen in the archaeology of Cambodia before the seventh century, but there is no religious sculpture from before the sixth century; when it begins in the following century, it resembles that of Dvāravatī and shows the influence of the Gupta style.[38]

The recent discovery of a Buddhist inscription at Noen Sa Bua in the Prachinburi area of eastern Thailand, dated 761 CE, written in Old Khmer with a quotation of three verses in Pāli,[39] indicates the expansion of Theravāda Buddhism to near the present Thai–Cambodian border in the pre-Angkor period.

The manner in which Buddhism expanded is, however, still far from clear. Dvāravatī may have been no more than a specific Mon kingdom with its heartland in central Thailand and a Buddhist culture quite distinct from that of any of its neighbours, or it may be part of a wider culture that included all the Mon lands of Burma and Thailand and even extended into pre-Angkor Cambodia. The use of Old Khmer in the Prachinburi inscription may be an indication in that direction. Although Indian culture, and Buddhism in particular, seems to have spread predominantly from west to east, the actual pattern may have been much more complicated. The earliest evidence for an Indianized society actually comes from Fu-nan, in particular from the ancient city of Oc-eo on the Gulf of Thailand.[40] On the other hand, little is known of the state of Buddhism among the Mon of present Burma. There, too, the population may have been Buddhist since very early times without leaving any significant traces.

The Buddhism of Dvāravatī is well enough attested, hazy though the political outline of the state may be. Cœdès identified Mon Buddhist sites associated with Dvāravatī culture in the peninsula and in various parts of Thailand, including Haripuñjaya (Lamphun) to the north.[41] The art of Dvāravatī is represented in iconography by a particular style of the Buddha image with a broad face and eyebrows continuing above the nose. Standing

[37] Higham, *Archaeology*, 272; E. Lyons, 'Dvāravatī, a consideration of its formative period', in Smith and Watson, 354; see also B. Bronson, 'The late prehistory and early history of central Thailand', ibid., 330f.

[38] Dupont, *L'Archéologie Mône de Dvāravatī*.

[39] Mendis Rohanadeera, 'Telakatāhagāthā in a Thailand Inscription of 761 A.D.', *Vidyodaya Journal of Social Science*, I, 1 (1987) (with thanks to Dr N. Chutiwongs, who kindly drew our attention to this important inscription).

[40] L. Malleret, *L'Archéologie du Delta du Mekong*, I–IV, Paris, EFEO, 1959–63.

[41] *Le Royaume de Dvāravatī*, Bangkok, 1929; 'Les Mons de Dvāravatī', in Ba Shin, J. Boisselier and A. B. Griswold, *Essays offered to G. H. Luce*, Ascona, 1966, I. 112–16.

Buddha statues are often represented with *both* hands in the attitude of protection (*abhayamudrā*). Another particular feature is the representation of the Buddha descending from heaven attended by Indra and Brahmā. Local artists may have been inspired by models from Amarāvatī and Sri Lanka, as well as from Gupta India, but adapted these to their own aesthetic conventions.

Thaton, centre of an ancient Mon state, certainly knew Buddhism by the eleventh century, when it was conquered by king Anawrahta (Aniruddha) of Pagan (r. c. 1044–77). Perhaps it had been recently influenced by Haripuñjaya, but we may perhaps give credence to the tradition which ascribes the advent of Buddhism in the area to the great fifth-century scholar Buddhaghoṣa, who would have spent his last years in Thaton after a fertile career in Sri Lanka. On the other hand, there are indications that the Buddhist tradition which was passed on to the Burmese may have been derived from Kāñcī (Conjeevaram) in South India. There may be some truth in all of these possibilities; one direction of influence does not exclude others.

At all events, the early Mon states bequeathed their Theravāda Buddhism to the various expanding kingdoms that, from the eleventh century onward, overran their territory. The expansion of Angkor under Sūryavarman I (r. c. 1002–50) brought Dvāravatī within the Khmer empire; Pagan, under Anawrahta, absorbed the culture of Thaton; and later on, with the rise of the Thai kingdoms, these too took as part of their cultural legacy a substantial inheritance from the Mon. In Pagan, a major role is ascribed to Anawrahta in doing away with the corrupt old religious practices and purifying the religious establishment with a graft of Mon Theravāda, but this account belongs to a subsequent rewriting of history in the interest of an orthodox establishment; it is likely that, in identifying Buddhist legitimacy with the actions of a strong king regarded as the founder of Pagan's fortunes, it exaggerates the changes made by Anawrahta. Anyhow, the tradition is that he was converted to Theravāda after his conquest of Thaton in 1057, influenced by the Mon teacher Shin Arahan who then became the court teacher for himself and subsequent kings.[42]

Links with Sri Lanka were certainly important. The Sinhalese king Vijayabāhu I (r. c. 1055–1110) was confronted with the task of restoring the Buddhist faith after the depredations of the South Indian Cōḷas, and in 1071 at his request some Burmese monks were sent to help. This initiated a close relationship between Sri Lanka and mainland Southeast Asia. It worked both ways, the Theravāda communities in each helping those of the other, but for most of the time it was the established Mahavihāra order in Sri Lanka that was regarded in the east as the fountainhead of pure religion, and numerous missions were sent across so that Burmese and other monks could take the higher ordination (*upasampadā*) in the Mahavihāra lineage and transmit successive purifying streams of it to their homelands.

Anawrahta was said to have obtained a set of scriptures from Sri Lanka, and a replica of the Tooth Relic of Lord Buddha. The archaeology of his

[42] Michael Aung-Thwin, *Pagan: the Origins of Modern Burma*, Honolulu, 1985; and 'Kingship, the sangha and society in Pagan', in K. Hall and J. Whitmore, eds, *Explorations in Early Southeast Asian History: the Origins of Southeast Asian Statecraft*, Ann Arbor, 1976.

reign, more trustworthy than such traditions, demonstrates his piety by a large number of votive seals, inscribed variously in Sanskrit and Pāli.[43] It has been debated how far they show the influence of Mahāyāna Buddhism, but they are certainly not deep-dyed Theravāda; it is altogether likely that the real conquest of Theravāda in Pagan came later, under Kyanzittha, whereas Anawrahta's religious allegiance was more eclectic.

Kyanzittha (r. c. 1084–1112) was certainly an active sponsor of Buddhist foundations and activities (but not exclusively Buddhist as we have seen). He endowed the construction of a number of monuments, the most famous of which is the Ānanda or Nanda temple (*Anantapaññā*, 'Endless Wisdom'), completed probably by 1105 and said to be a miraculously inspired copy of the legendary Nandamūla grotto in the Himalayas. It is decorated with reliefs representing scenes based on the life of Lord Buddha, as well as stories of his earlier incarnations (Jātaka). Kyanzittha also completed the famous Shwezigon, and he sent a mission to India to carry out repairs to the Vajrāsana shrine at Bodhgāyā, site of Lord Buddha's Enlightenment. Some scholars have found evidence of Burmese style in some details of the temple.[44] The inscription recording the restoration of the Vajrāsana ends in the well-known wish that the spiritual merit that the king acquired by this pious deed may enable all sentient beings to escape from the cycle of death and rebirth.

Kyanzittha gave special patronage to all forms of the Mon cultural legacy, but like many of his successors, fostered the relations with Sri Lanka. Copies of the Mahavihāra recension of the Scriptures were distributed to monasteries.

Burma was thus the chief power-house in the dissemination of Theravāda Buddhism, which eventually became the dominant orthodoxy in the mainland kingdoms. The status and prestige attached to the spiritual lineages established by the returning monks in their home countries assured a steadily increasing success for the Sīhala (Sinhalese) orders and their offshoots. But we must not allow this Theravāda dominance to obscure the fact that a variety of sects flourished before and even during its ascendancy.

We need to recognize, for example, that Mahāyāna Buddhism long remained influential, and there is evidence of it at many places and times. Bodhisattvas such as Maitreya and Mañjuśrī were popular in Burma before the rise of Pagan. As early as 791 CE an inscription in Cambodia (at Siemreap) refers to an image of Lokeśvara (better known as Avalokiteśvara). Mahāyāna in Angkor has been seen as a continuing thread, whatever the orthodoxies of successive monarchs. Many inscriptions refer to characteristically Mahāyāna doctrines, such as those concerning the Void (*śūnya*), the 'mind-only' (*cittamātra*) and the three bodies of the Buddha. Perhaps most conspicuously, the reign of Jayavarman VII (1181–1218) is a high point of Mahāyāna aspiration.

Under this ruler, Avalokiteśvara was virtually the patron god of the state, in his various forms and associations, including Balaha and the

[43] Than Tun, *History of Buddhism in Burma, A.D. 1000–1300*, Rangoon, 1978 (JBRS, 61.1,2, *separatum*), 4f.

[44] Luce, *Old Burma*, I. 62.

personified Perfection of Wisdom, the goddess Prajñāpāramitā. Compassion is the pre-eminent quality of a Bodhisattva in Mahāyāna perception, and Avalokiteśvara was above all a vessel of grace, making possible a rebirth in heaven for the faithful; as an embodiment of this Bodhisattva, the king sought to present himself as a loving guardian and father figure, building hospitals and caring for the welfare of all his subjects on the Aśokan model.

This currency of Mahāyāna Buddhism, between the eighth and the thirteenth centuries, cannot be understood in isolation from developments in India. In the first place, Buddhism was on the retreat in the land of its birth, yielding to the brahmanical orthodoxy over much of the subcontinent but acquiring strongholds in certain kingdoms on the periphery, especially in Bengal where successive rulers gave lavish patronage to the Mahāyāna foundations, and it was Bengal that was the most conspicuous source of religious influence upon Southeast Asia during this period. Cœdès identified three strands in Bengali Buddhism: a tendency to Tantric practices, syncretism with Hinduism, and accommodation to indigenous traditions such as ancestor cults.[45]

In the second place, from the eleventh and especially in the thirteenth century, Muslim invasions may have prompted the flight of many monks as refugees. Tāranātha, the Tibetan historian of Buddhism, refers to monks travelling to various lands in the east, including Cambodia and perhaps Pagan. Another link between Southeast Asia and Bengal is constituted by the career of Atīśa (982–1054), who is supposed to have spent twelve years in 'Suvarṇabhūmi', probably southern Burma, before going to Tibet to reform the Tantric tradition there.

Evidence of Tantric Buddhism is not wanting in Burma in the period when we would expect it. In official Burmese tradition, as embodied in the '*Glass Palace Chronicle*' (*Hmannan Yazawin*), a corrupt Tantric type of religion represented by the 'Ari' sect was practised among the Burmese in the eleventh century, before the creation of a great empire by Anawrahta; with his conversion to Theravāda and the assistance of Shin Arahan to purify the religion, the degenerate practices were stamped out. However, it appears probable that this account owes more to the desire of the proponents of the later Sinhalese orthodoxy for historical legitimacy in association with the great king than to actual historical fact. Actually, the chief substantial evidence of Tantric-style practices belongs to the thirteenth century, two centuries *after* the reign of Anawrahta. Some temples have decorations such as images of Hayagrīva that are associated with Tantra, and in particular some thirteenth-century inscriptions in the Minnanthu temple southeast of Pagan describe the Samantakuṭṭaka monks who took beef and fermented spirits, heterodox practices suggestive of Tantra.

Who then were the degenerate Aris referred to by the *Glass Palace Chronicle*, who were supposed to wear 'strong beards and untrimmed hair' and, according to one interpretation of the enigmatic relevant passage, to practise a form of *jus primae noctis* with maidens about to be married?[46] There has been much debate over the meaning of the term *ari*, some seeing

[45] *États*, 182.

[46] G. H. Luce cites the *Hmannan* in a review in the JBRS, 9 (1919) 54.

it as representing *āriya*, 'noble' and others as representing *āraññaka*, 'silvan', alluding to the forest monks who meditated in seclusion. The latter interpretation is more generally favoured now. In the thirteenth century, there were inscriptions indicating an āraññavāsi ('forest-dwelling') sect headed by one Mahākassapa, who was perhaps the leader of a powerful and well-endowed community that attracted the rivalry of the orthodox Sīhala school. But in 1248 the head of the Sīhalas returned from Sri Lanka and his school regained favour.

At this point it is necessary to look back at the importance of this link with Sri Lanka, for of course it was not Bengal which made the running; from the eleventh century, inspired by the Mon legacy, rulers of Pagan (and eventually of other kingdoms besides) were more and more interested in acquiring the spiritual status conferred by the prestige of a state-established Mahāvihāra order sanctified by the ordination of its teachers in Sri Lanka.

In the twelfth century, a particularly important episode was the mission of 1170 headed by the patriarch Uttarajīva, which returned in 1180; the monk Capaṭa, however, remained a further ten years and returned with five colleagues (enough to constitute a chapter capable of transmitting the sect's lineage) and re-established the Mahāvihāra order in Burma; this new line was known as the Sīhala *saṅgha* (coming from Sri Lanka), while the older one that had been headed by Shin Arahan was the Mrammā *saṅgha*; by the thirteenth century there were four sects as a result of further splits. A Cambodian prince was, incidentally, supposed to have been one of Capaṭa's party. Sinhalese Buddhism speedily became the major recipient of state support in mainland Southeast Asia.

One influential offshoot of the Sinhalese Mahāvihāra was created in Martaban by the monk Anumati, who returned from Sri Lanka in 1331. The spread of his school thereafter owed much to the interest of the rulers of the new Thai kingdoms, especially Sukothai. Under Lü Thai (acc. 1347), the monks Sumana and Anomadassi went to Martaban and took the higher ordination. On returning Sumana was given his own *Vat* (wat); he performed various Buddhist miracles and later went to Chiengmai, which thus, from 1369, became a major centre for ṭhe Sīhala school.

A further expedition to Sri Lanka in 1423 saw thirty-nine monks from Chiengmai, Lopburi and Burma going to take the higher ordination; on their return they promoted Sinhalese Buddhism in their own countries. In Chiengmai in particular they received considerable favour, but there is evidence of conflict in that state over the rules of monastic discipline. This suggests rivalry between the newer and older schools.

In Angkor, the wave of Sinhalese Theravāda bore fruit in the thirteenth century, when the ostentatious display of Mahāyāna by Jayavarman VII was followed first by a temporary revival of Hinduism and then by the increasing influence of the saffron-robed Theravādin monks observed late in the century by the Chinese visitor Chou Ta-kuan.[47] The oldest Pāli inscription (after that of 761) dates from 1309. The king Indravarman dedicated a Theravāda monastery and Buddha image; the *Khmer Chronicle*,

[47] *Mémoires sur les coutumes de Cambodge*, 14.

which marks a new court tradition wholly influenced by Theravāda, begins its record in the middle of the fourteenth century.

Some have linked the fall of the great Angkorean tradition with Theravāda itself, suggesting that the Sinhalese school, with its emphasis on individual salvation rather than public Bodhisattva worship and with its implied egalitarianism, eroded the ideological foundations of the state. However, there is perhaps no need to appeal to such factors to account for the end of Angkor; economic and social conditions offer less speculative possibilities of interpretation.

In the western part of mainland Southeast Asia, the destruction by the Mongols of Pagan at the end of the thirteenth century did not affect the continued influence of Theravāda Buddhism, for the various successor states continued the tradition of generous patronage of the *saṅgha*. In particular, the fifteenth century witnessed a revival of the Mon state of Pegu under the pious ruler Dhammaceti. He was a former monk who set about reforming the order. According to a sixteenth-century text he codified the pantheon of thirty-six spirits, thus regulating and accommodating to the official Buddhist cosmology the local *nat*-type spirits, re-identifying them as beings destined for Buddhist salvation, just as had been done in Pagan. Most of these beings were in fact tree spirits at Buddhist sites. Further, the king sent a mission to Sri Lanka. The monks who constituted it took their higher ordination by the Kalyāṇī (Kälani) river, and on their return a religious establishment, called the Kalyāṇī Sīma, was built for them; the Kalyāṇī inscription of 1479 records their pilgrimage.

The declaration by the Kalyāṇī inscription that the Buddhist order was corrupt, lazy and impure, and needed immediate action, demonstrates once more the concern of rulers to regulate the affairs of the *saṅgha*, and raises the complicated question of the relationship of the monks to state and society. In theory, they had cut themselves off from society and sought no political influence; they were wholly dedicated to the Buddha's teaching. But how far was this theory embodied in reality?

In the Burmese case, kingdoms such as Pegu and Pagan provide evidence on both sides, and scholars have placed the emphasis some on one side, some on the other. It has been argued that, although royal patronage tended to politicize some sects, there were many other patrons; the various claims to secular authority over the monks tended to cancel each other out. The monks anyway had freedom of conscience. The hold of Buddhist devotion over national culture worked to limit the power of a ruler to regulate the order; when kings tried to confiscate large parts of the *saṅgha's* possessions, popular opinion operated to thwart such attempts.[48]

On the other hand, there is no doubt that monks were in various ways intimately involved in affairs of government and society. Rulers made decisions that governed their concerns. Thus, a revised edition of the Buddhist Pāli canon was written by order of Kyanzittha. In 1154 King Aloncañsu determined that large temple donations would require royal permission. Monks spent time performing ritual functions on behalf of

[48] Than Tun, *History of Buddhism*, 39.

the state, praying for the king and chanting *parittas* for the benefit of royal enterprises. Monks were caught up in the hurly-burly of politics; some were even involved in rebellions. Kings determined which sects or subsects received large endowments and which did not, exploiting all the tendencies to factionalism of a community whose members had plenty of time to sit and think.

Similarly, in Angkor, rulers exercised a preponderating influence upon the economic life of the *saṅgha* by regulating the system of endowments to religious foundations of all sorts; by giving 'royal' status to favoured donations, they effectively bestowed tax exemption privileges upon the donors. By giving or withholding support to Buddhist foundations, they had influence upon the fortunes of the faith. Sūryavarman I (r. c. 1002–50) should not be seen as exclusively a Buddhist ruler, but he gave much emphasis to Buddhism. Jayavarman VII, as already noticed above, gave considerable prominence to the Mahāyāna school.

Conspicuous are the Thai kingdoms which rose on the rubble of Angkor's power. They sent monks on missions to Martaban or Sri Lanka, and provided well-appointed temples for favoured teachers. Ramkamhaeng (r. c. 1280–97),[48] in particular, paid special respect to the *saṅgha*. If his inscription of 1292 is to be given credence, he had a stupa built at Śrī Sajjanālaya (Savankhalok), which took six years to construct, and endowed a number of monasteries.[49] At one, Vat Aranyika, he celebrated *kaṭhina*: the bestowal of robes on monks after the rainy season retreat. Further, the state of Ayutthaya, which succeeded Sukothai as the main Thai power in the fourteenth century, was no less pious. King Paramarāja, for example, built a monastery, the Laṅkārāma, for the benefit of the famous monk Dhammakitti, a Pāli scholar.

Further east, in Champa, the most notable episode of state support for Buddhism is constituted by the Chan Ch'eng kingdom (to use its Chinese name), established at Indrapura in Quang Nam by Indravarman, who made a state shrine to Avalokiteśvara called Lakṣmīndralokeśvara. There was a striking florescence of Buddhist art under this ruler and some of his successors.[50]

In Vietnam, where Buddhism received strong and consistent support—even though this had to be shared with other traditions—the Chinese way of life determined that the influence of the state upon religious organization should be highly regulated by the ruler. Patriarchs of favoured sects were regularly given important advisory positions in the palace, and this inevitably politicized their following.

It is here that we can most appropriately review the influence of Chinese Buddhism upon Vietnam, for the organization is most marked in Chinese tradition.[51] The most influential Chinese sect was the Ch'an (in India,

[49] Cœdès, *États*, 360, 377; A. B. Griswold and Prasert na Nagara, 'The inscription of King Rāma Gaṃheṅ of Sukhodaya (1292 A.D.), Epigraphical and Historical Studies No. 9', JSS, 69 (1971).

[50] I. W. Mabbett, 'Buddhism in Champa', in Marr and Milner, 298–303.

[51] On Buddhism in Vietnam, see Tran Van Giap, 'Le Bouddhisme en Annam'; K. W. Taylor, 'Authority and legitimacy in eleventh century Vietnam', in Marr and Milner, 139–76; K. W. Taylor, *The Birth of Vietnam*, Berkeley, 1983; Thich Thien-An, *Buddhism and Zen in Vietnam in relation to the development of Buddhism in Asia*, Los Angeles, Rutland, Vermont, Tokyo, 1975.

*Dhyāna*, 'meditation'; in Japan, Zen; in Vietnam, Thien). According to Chinese tradition, the first Ch'an patriarch in China was the monk Bodhidharma, about whom legends grew up, and although such a person existed it is difficult to know the true facts about him. He is supposed to have practised 'wall meditation' (sitting meditating in front of a blank wall) for nine years, and to have visited Shao Lin, the monastery which became renowned as the home of various Ch'an practices and martial arts. The line of teachers which he originated was responsible for the dissemination of Ch'an to Vietnam.

Vietnamese tradition codifies and categorizes religious history, identifying a number of specific schools each with its stylized record listing patriarchs and generations of teachers. It is likely that this traditional account makes the pattern seem more organized and institutionalized than it was; there were temples dotted about the settled lands, each largely managing its own affairs under the eye of patrons and benefactors. However, there were certainly lines of teachers acknowledging allegiance to particular schools of Buddhism that traced their origins to a Chinese legitimacy.

The first was the Vinītaruci school (Ty-Ni-Du-Luu-Chi), named after its founder who was supposed to have been an Indian brahmin who went to China in the sixth century and studied under Seng-tsan, third patriarch in the Ch'an school in China. Going to Tonkin, he was installed in the Phap-Van temple, Ha-dong Province. The line of transmission that led from him, proceeding by the Ch'an process of 'mind-seal' (by which the master imprints his spiritual insights upon the disciple), is said to have passed through nineteen generations. Some patriarchs in the school (including, for example, Phap Thuan in the tenth century) were royal counsellors, some were renowned for spiritual attainments, some gained a reputation for scholarship.

The second major Ch'an-derived Vietnamese sect was the Vo Ngon Thong school, which was founded during the T'ang dynasty but found considerable favour from subsequent independent Vietnamese rulers; for example its fourth patriarch Khuong Viet taught at the palace and advised Le Dai-Hanh (980–1005), and the later king Ly Thai Tong was himself a patriarch of the school, representing the symbiosis of dynasty and *saṅgha*, which was conspicuous under the Ly, a dynasty which was brought to power largely through the work of Buddhist monks.

The third major Buddhist sect identified by Vietnamese tradition was that of Thao Dong, founded by a Chinese monk, Ts'ao-t'ang, in Champa, who was caught up in a war and taken to the Vietnamese court as a captive; there however he was given an important ministerial position as *quoc-su*, a largely secular, partly religious, supervisory post. His teaching was based on the *Amitābhasūtra*, stressing the extinction of the individual self; a famous poem he wrote compares the phenomenal world to a flower in the sky—it is unreal, illusory. The line of patriarchs which directed the fortunes of the school he founded included a number of members of the royal family, notably the emperors Ly Anh Tong and Ly Cao Tong in the twelfth century.

As such examples remind us, the Buddhist communities, like the Brahmanical foundations, could not work in a vacuum; they depended upon, and to a great extent were moulded by, the aspirations of the society in which they lived. Inscriptions are in Southeast Asia the chief sources for our knowledge of their organization, and inscriptions, left by pious rulers and laymen, tell us what were the motives of those who were willing to bear the burden of supporting a large and (at first glance) economically unproductive class.

These motives were partly material, and indeed the function of temples and monasteries in society needs to be seen against the background of that society's economic and political organization. But we need also to take account of the spiritual motives, which were real enough. Consider Pagan, a striking embodiment of religious zeal, where three or four thousand temples were built in an area of sixty-five square kilometres. The inscriptions which record the endowment of many of these foundations usually indicate why the donations were made. In most cases the donors hope to achieve *nirvāṇa* (the extinction of all *karma* and release from rebirth), *sambodhi* (the perfect enlightenment which is a condition of this release), or Buddha-hood. Sometimes they express the ambition to have a future life at the time of Maitreya, the next Buddha; thereby, profiting from his teaching, they can hope to attain enlightenment. Women donors sometimes profess the desire to become males in a later life (thus acquiring better means to progress towards salvation), or even to become Buddhas. Some rulers saw themselves as Bodhisattvas; such was Lu Thai in Sukothai, and it was said when he entered religion and embarked upon his spiritual career, the earth trembled.[52]

Notable is the way in which the doctrine of merit is interpreted. Strictly speaking, the good *karma* of an act of merit such as endowing a religious foundation could accrue (in Theravāda at least) only to the agent himself, but loopholes were found in Theravāda traditions just as in Mahāyāna to make possible the transfer of merit to others; donors of property frequently willed the merit of their actions to the benefit of others (of a widow for her husband, or of a temple endowment for the poor). In Angkor, Jayavarman VII could seek to benefit his mother by virtue of the fact that, as a partial cause of his existence, she was partly responsible for his actions and thereby earned a share in his merit.

But it is clear enough that there could be rewards in life on earth for those who endowed temples and monasteries. They did not altogether relinquish any economic interest in the property they made over; the beneficiaries were like lease-holders in some respects, and there are cases in Pagan of disputes between temple and donor over the nature of the interest retained by the latter. An officially recognized endowment would be declared free of all claims by tax collectors and other royal officers, as in Angkor, even though the family of the donor might be continuing to exploit the donated land to some extent, and its members might be abbots or senior monks. Further, property made over to religion was less liable to future depredations of governments, bandits, or relatives, and would earn social status in the measure of its abundance. Donors who wished to maximize the merit they would gain by this spiritual banking system, as it

[52] Cœdès, *Receuil*, I. 111–16 (Inscription palie du bois des manguiers) at 115.

is sometimes called, would seek to emphasize their donations' permanence by solemn imprecations against any who in the future should violate the terms of the endowment. One such imprecation, in Pagan, says: 'Whoever injures these pagoda slaves, may the axe burst his breast! May he fall off a ladder!'[53]

As recipients of so much pious generosity, the religious foundations of places like Pagan or Angkor became more and more prosperous, dotting the landscape everywhere and acquiring a major role in the economic system. Frequently they acquired fresh property by new donations; rarely did they lose property.

The monks, priests and nuns who were supported in them often enjoyed many of the amenities of a comfortable life, with bonded temple servants to look after all their wants. There has been some discussion of the status of such servants, who for many purposes were effectively slaves, and are usually named as such in translations of the sources which refer to them; but we need to take account of the fact that temple 'slavery' could, for some at least, be something of an honour. Not untypical is the case of a queen in Pagan making over three sons as slaves to a monastery, subsequently to be redeemed by a gift of property. Such transactions involve a purely ritual slavery. But plenty of those who toiled on temple lands or looked after the needs of the incumbents were menials descended, quite often, from captives seized from hill tribes.[54]

The riches of the monasteries eventually made them rivals of the royal power of the state. A convincing argument advanced by Michael Aung-Thwin about the role of the wealth of the Buddhist order in the decline of Pagan may apply to other states as well: while land was plentiful, there was room for both state and *saṅgha* to extend their spheres of control and authority, but as time went on available resources became scarcer, and eventually the *saṅgha* became a rival to the state, disposing of abundant land and labour which otherwise should have been available to furnish the economic resources of government. This stage came in the thirteenth century, and prompted rulers to look more and more critically at the possessions of the monasteries, some seeking to 'purify' the Buddhist order—that is, to confiscate its surplus wealth. On one calculation, the *saṅgha* in Pagan came eventually to control 63 per cent of productive land. The attempts at confiscation were not always successful, and the conflict over resources tended to heighten factionalism, for the interest of the monasteries was bound up with that of the great landed families which endowed them, had members in the monkhood, and lived in symbiosis with the monastic estates. Hence centrifugal forces increased and civil war became more likely.[55] It is entirely possible that the same sort of process could be charted for Angkor.

[53] Luce, *Old Burma*, I. 109.

[54] On slavery in Cambodia, see C. Jacques, 'A propos de l'esclavage dans l'ancien Cambodge', in *XXXIXe Congrès International des Orientalistes, Paris, 1973. Proceedings. Asie du Sud-est continentale*; Y. Bongert, 'Note sur l'esclavage en droit khmer ancien', in *Études d'Histoire du Droit Privé Offertes à Pierre Petot*, Paris, 1959; A. K. Chakravarti, 'Sources of slavery in ancient Cambodia', in D. C. Sircar, ed., *Social Life in Ancient India*, Calcutta, 1971.

[55] Aung-Thwin, *Pagan*; and Aung-Thwin, 'Kingship, the sangha and society in Pagan', in Hall and Whitmore, *Explorations*.

In Vietnam, too, there was potential friction between state authority and the independence of religious orders. Chinese tradition supplied an ideology that legitimized state authority over all phases of life and justified it in regulating the affairs of the Buddhist monks to a greater degree than was generally accepted elsewhere. This ideology was Confucianism.

Of course it is questionable how far Confucianism is a religion, but it deserves to be considered alongside the other systems since, like them, it provided a coherent ideology that gave men a view of their place in the universe, prescribed a code of morality and ethics, and furnished a body of rituals that gave expression to the sense of community identity.

Confucianism in independent Vietnam was taken over from China as a form of state orthodoxy, providing a didactic literature that could serve to shape national culture to a considerable extent. Under the Ly, Confucian scholars were required to write commentaries on Confucian texts. Statues of the Duke of Chou and Confucius were set up as icons in a national shrine. Confucianism was a part of the syllabus for state examinations alongside the other religions, but it really came into its own in the revival of the fourteenth and fifteenth centuries, with the sternly political reassertion of national identity: state cults were promoted and Confucianism benefited from the rise of state power. Rulers such as Le Thanh Ton (r. 1460–97) actively promoted Confucianism.[56]

## RELIGIONS OF INDIAN ORIGIN IN THE MARITIME REALM

The religious developments in the island world of Southeast Asia are in many respects similar to those in the mainland, but there are important differences. The island world can be divided into two zones separated by a line running from north to south, west of the Philippines, between the islands Kalimantan and Sulawesi and east of Sumbawa. Very little is known of the early history and religion of the eastern zone before the sixteenth century; our sources are limited to the western zone, or rather to important parts of this zone, in particular large parts of Sumatra, the Malay peninsula, central and eastern Java, Bali and small parts of Kalimantan. These are the very areas where Indian influence made itself felt from the early centuries of the Christian era and where Indian religions were introduced, especially in circles associated with the royal courts.

The geography of maritime Southeast Asia shows important differences from that of the mainland, differences which carry historical implications. Owing to the presence of mountain ranges running mainly north to south, the mainland is split into at least four sub-zones, each with its own language and culture; maritime Southeast Asia, in contrast, presents a much more consistent pattern. Both in language and in culture the islands have much in common. Apparently, the straits and seas separating the islands and the Malay peninsula, easily navigable in general, were not

56 K. W. Taylor, 'Authority and legitimacy in eleventh century Vietnam', in Marr and Milner, 153.

barriers like the mountain ranges of the mainland: they linked, rather than separated, the different parts of the region.

When, in the early centuries of the Christian era, Indian influence began to make itself felt, the population of many areas already enjoyed a high level of civilization, enabling their élites to adopt and adapt those elements of Indian civilization that they regarded as valuable or useful. These naturally included religion: in particular Brahmanic Hinduism, including especially Śaivism, and, apparently at a later stage, Mahāyāna Buddhism. Vaiṣṇavism seems to have had a much more limited appeal, whereas Jainism and Theravāda Buddhism left no traces in maritime Southeast Asia. As to Brahmanic Hinduism it should be stated at the very outset that the use of the term 'Hinduism' may be misleading because one of its most important features, the caste system, existed only in theory.[57] As, however, the brahmins and Brahmanic culture (including, for example, the use of Sanskrit, especially at an early stage before the seventh century) formed the chief element of the forms of Hinduism in Southeast Asia, the term 'Brahmanism' is preferable. As it preceded Śaivism and Buddhism, it is proper to discuss it first.

## Brahmanism

Old Javanese sources from the eleventh century on regularly mention three religious communities (*tripakṣa*): the Śaivas (worshippers of Śiva as the supreme deity, also called Māheśvaras), the Buddhists (also called Saugatas) and the Rĕsis (also called Mahābrāhmaṇas), each under the supervision of a central government official, called *dharmādhikāra* for the first two communities and *mantri er-haji* for the third.[58] The latter, though few in numbers, were by no means unimportant. They included not only different kinds of ascetics but also court brahmins, who were in charge of royal ceremonies, as well as of education.

The oldest inscriptions of the area, those of king Mūlavarman of Kutai in east Kalimantan (end of the fourth century CE) and of Pūrṇavarman of Tārumā (fifth century) are probably non-sectarian. Those of Mūlavarman describe precious gifts to brahmins, including thousands of cattle and large amounts of gold. The terms used for different kinds of gifts are known from the Indian epics and *Purāṇas*, but seem to reflect potlatch ceremonies. Precious gifts to brahmins are also mentioned in Pūrṇavarman's inscriptions, which are, however, of special interest for references to the worship of the footprints of the king and of his elephant. At several sites in west Java we may witness the king's footprints, more than life-size, by the side of his inscriptions, sometimes with curious symbols (such as a spider in front of each of the footprints carved into a large inscribed rock at Ci-aruteun,

57 This is, however, a complicated issue, for the system of four classes (*caturwarṇa*) is occasionally mentioned in Old Javanese texts and inscriptions. There are, however, strong indications that this was a purely theoretical division of society mentioned mainly in stereotyped contexts, without any of the implications of the Indian caste system. See, for example, J. G. de Casparis, 'Pour une Histoire Sociale de l'Ancienne Java, Principalement aux Xème s.', *Archipel*, 21 (1981).

58 See *Nāgarakĕrtāgama* (abbreviated *Nāg*. in the sequel), 81–1–4; Pigeaud, *Java in the Fourteenth Century* IV. 258 and 479–93. Pigeaud uses the term 'the three denominations'.

west of present Bogor). Although the worship of footprints, especially those of Viṣṇu and, much more stylized, of Lord Buddha, is well attested in India and Sri Lanka, there are no examples of the worship of human, let alone elephant, footprints there. In Indonesia, on the other hand, there is good evidence for the worship of footprints of ancestors in some areas, especially on the island of Nias near the west coast of Sumatra. It is therefore likely that in this case, as in the 'potlatch' ceremonies of east Kalimantan, a traditional Austronesian practice was continued in the guise of Sanskrit terms.[59]

Two typically Hindu ceremonies occupied an important place in Indonesian courts: royal consecration (*abhiṣeka*) and funerary rites (*śrāddha*). The term *abhiṣeka* often occurs in Old Javanese sources. Although the oldest epigraphic reference to royal consecration dates back to 1019, the year of Airlangga's *abhiṣeka*, it is likely that the ceremony was performed much earlier, perhaps even at the time of king Pūrṇavarman of Tārumā (fifth century), who dated his Tugu inscription in his twenty-second regnal year. As regnal years are always counted from the year of consecration, this is an implicit indication of the performance of such a ceremony. The use of elaborate Sanskrit names preceded by *śrī*, 'His Majesty', in addition to Old Javanese names and titles in ninth- and tenth-century inscriptions, confirms the performance of consecration ceremonies, since the conferment of such names, usually ending in *uttuṅgadeva*, 'Exalted Majesty' (aptly called *abhiṣekanāma*), has always been an essential part of the ceremony. The 'Calcutta' inscription of King Airlangga (dated 1041) contains the interesting passage *kṛtasaṃskāra pratiṣṭha ring singhāsana*, 'had the consecration ceremony carried out, established on the Lion Throne'. A pilgrimage to Īśānabajra, the shrine dedicated to the memory of King Siṇḍok, Airlangga's great-great-grandfather, and the erection of a rice-pestle (*halu*), symbolizing the king's potency to promote the fertility of the ricefields, completed the ceremony, which was carried out by Buddhist, Śaiva and Brahmanic priests (*mpungku sogata maheśwara mahābrāhmaṇa*, in that order). These details clearly show how much of the ceremony differed from its description in Indian texts.

The second important ceremony is another of the 'rites de passage': the funerary rites, or rather those performed to ensure the liberation of the soul of the deceased. In India such rites are of great importance to all Hindus. According to the texts they involve elaborate ceremonies, which were to take place at regular intervals after death and were performed by six generations in both ascending and descending lines; the presence of a son of the deceased was essential.

In ancient Java, the elaborate description of *śrāddha* in the *Nāgarakĕrtāgama* concerns the purification and liberation of the soul of the 'Rājapatnī' (Spouse of the King), the youngest of the four daughters of King Kĕrtanagara (r. 1268–92), who were also the four queens of King Kĕrtarājasa (r. 1293–1309). She was also grandmother of King Hayam Wuruk (r. 1350–89) and

[59] J. Ph. Vogel, 'The Yūpa inscriptions of king Mūlavarman from Kutei (East Borneo)', BKI, 74 (1918); and 'De Giften van Mūlavarman', ibid., 76 (1920); J. G. de Casparis, 'The Oldest Inscriptions of Indonesia' in C. M. S. Hellwig, and C. D. Grijns, *A Man of Indonesian Letters*, Dordrecht, 1986.

died in the year of her grandson's accession. The great *śrāddha*, performed in 1362, twelve years after her death (which was the usual period in ancient Indonesia), is described in no fewer than seven cantos of the text. This account contains many interesting features, which tend to show that the ceremony differed completely from its description in Sanskrit texts and from contemporary practice in Gaya (Bihar). The participants included not only members of the royal family but also high officials, as well as simple servants with their wives, priests and monks of different denominations, dancers, musicians, story-tellers and others. These details stand in clear contrast to the Indian *śrāddha*, confined to the close relatives of the deceased.[60]

The ceremony itself involved various Tantric rites carried out by both Buddhist monks and by a *purohita*, 'chief court brahmin', all versed in the three Tantras (*Nāg*. 64–3). The centre of veneration was a lion-throne in the middle of a square: the place where the soul of the Rājapatnī was to descend after the completion of the correct rites. If our understanding of the passage is correct, an effigy of the Rājapatnī, made of flowers (*sang hyang puṣpaśarīra*, *Nāg*. 67–2) had been placed on the throne; subsequently the soul (*swah*) of the Rājapatnī was made to enter the 'flower body'. After seven days of ceremonies (which included ritual meals comparable with the *slamĕtan* of modern times) the queen was 'deified' as Prajñāpāramitā, 'Supreme Wisdom', conceived of as the mother of all Buddhas in Tantric thought.[61] In addition to food and drink, money and clothes were distributed, which gave the whole ceremony a 'potlatch' aspect in addition to its animistic background. The analysis of the ceremony is therefore quite complicated. Its formal basis was the *śrāddha*, on to which not only Buddhist, but also ancient Austronesian beliefs were grafted. One could, however, just as well describe it as an essentially Austronesian rite embellished by learned elements from both Sanskrit ritual literature and Buddhist thought.

Such a *śrāddha*, performed on the twelfth anniversary of the death of a king or queen, is also mentioned in one of the last known Old Javanese inscriptions. It deals with a sacred domain called Trailokyapurī and is dated 1486.[62] The text includes an order by King Girīndrawardhana dyaḥ Raṇawijaya addressed to a court brahmin, Brahmarāja of the Bhāradvāja *gotra*, presumably an Indian (such *gotra* names tracing back a brahmin's family to a legendary Rishi are usual in India, as we have seen, but do not seem to occur elsewhere in Indonesia), to perform a *śrāddha* for the benefit of the soul of a king deceased at Indranibhawana. Another inscription mentions the worship of the eminent sage Bhāradvāja and of Lord (*bhaṭāra*) Rāma. As to the above-mentioned brahmin, he is said to have been well-versed in the Four Vedas (*caturvedapāraga*), a common epithet in India but

60 Among the numerous publications on ancient Indian royal consecration are P. V. Kane, *History of Dharmaśāstra*, III. 72ff.; J. C. Heesterman, *The ancient Indian royal consecration*, The Hague, 1957; J. Gonda, *Ancient Indian kingship from the religious point of view*, Leiden, 1966, 79–83.

61 For the *śrāddha* as performed in ancient Java see Pigeaud, *Java*, IV. 171f. Pigeaud rightly compares modern Javanese *ñadran*, 'visiting ancestral tombs in the month of Śaban'.

62 See the translation of this inscription in Md. Yamin, *Tatanegara Madjapahit*, Jakarta, 1962.

unusual in Java, where even *caturveda* occurs only in Old Javanese texts which are closely based on Indian prototypes. Rāma is well-known in Indonesia, but there are no other examples of a foundation (*pratiṣṭhā*) devoted to Rāma as a deity. In South India, on the other hand, such foundations are not rare. Since we know of a revival of Hinduism in its classical form during the time of the South Indian kingdom of Vijayanagara (1336–1565), it is likely that there was a direct relation between the developments in South India and eastern Java at a time when both were confronted with the expansion of Islam.[63]

It should however be emphasized that the influence of Brahmanism is not confined to the earliest or last periods, nor to the performance of certain rituals. In fact, an important feature of the Indian way of life, at least for the higher classes, was the possibility to opt out of ordinary society to choose a life of contemplation—either as a hermit in the forest or as a member of some religious community. Such *āśramas* often became centres of education, since those who had chosen a spiritual vocation were considered to have acquired the wisdom which could attract people from elsewhere.

In some cases there developed a true alternative society. This appears to have happened at the Dieng plateau (*ḍihyang* in the inscriptions) in central Java. Situated at about 2000 metres above sea level on volcanic soil with many solfataras, it breathes an atmosphere of awe in which supernatural forces manifest themselves to mankind. More prosaically, this same atmosphere accounts for the serious weathering of buildings, statues and stone inscriptions. On the basis of important research by Krom, Poerbatjaraka and others, it may be concluded that an archaic form of Brahmanic Hinduism flourished on and around the plateau from early times to at least the eleventh century. There was a community of ascetics and monks with such titles as *pitāmaha*, literally 'grandfather', *guru hyang*, literally 'teacher of the gods' but apparently corresponding to the later term *dewaguru*, 'superior of a religious community'. Some other, more puzzling, titles such as *talahantan* also seem to denote priestly functions.[64]

The most surprising feature of religion as practised there is the worship of a god called Haricandana. This name seems unknown in India as that of a god, but the word itself occurs in the meaning of 'yellow sandalwood'. As Haricandana is often invoked at the beginning of the imprecation formulas in Old Javanese inscriptions, usually in conjunction with the sage Agastya, it has been suggested that Haricandana was an epithet of Agastya indicating an image of the great Rishi made of yellow sandalwood (an Agastya statue made of *black* sandalwood is actually mentioned in the Dinoyo inscription of 760) but this is less likely as we have evidence of a Haricandana cult.[65] Thus a three-yearly and a, probably less elaborate,

63 J. G. de Casparis, *India and Maritime Southeast Asia: a lasting relationship*, Kuala Lumpur, 1983.

64 N. J. Krom, 'Over het Çiwaïsme van Midden-Java', *Mededeelingen der Koninklijke Nederlandsche Akademie van Wetenschappen, Afdeling Letterkunde*, 58, serie B, no. 8 (1929).

65 F. D. K. Bosch, 'De Sanskrit inscriptie op den steen van Dinaja (682 çaka)', TBG, 57 (1916); 'Het Lingga-Heiligdom van Dinaja', ibid., 64 (1924); J. G. de Casparis, 'Nogmaals de Sanskrit-inscriptie op den steen van Dinojo', ibid., 81 (1941).

yearly festival of Haricandana, for which villages had to supply rice and fruits, are mentioned in an inscription of 878. This cult was combined with that of Brahmā, for whom a 'pillar of rice' (*annaliṅga*) had to be prepared.[66] In this connection we also find the archaic Sanskrit term *makha* denoting a sacrifice. A reference to the worship of Haricandana is even found as late as the end of the fifteenth century in the *Tantu Panggĕlaran*, a late Old Javanese text in which brahmins are said to pay homage to this god. Here, as in other cases (such as those concerning Brahmā and Bhaṭāra Guru), we may have examples of ancient Austronesian deities under Indian names, but this remains no more than a plausible hypothesis as long as there is no clue as to the identity of such Austronesian deities.[67]

The imprecation formulas, regularly found at the end of Old Javanese charters, are interesting examples of the manner in which Hinduism was blended with ancient Austronesian beliefs. Sometimes a considerable number of deities are invoked, including the great gods of the Hindu pantheon: Brahmā, Viṣṇu and Mahādeva (or Maheśvara or Śiva, but always in that order), followed by sun and moon, the eight 'elements': earth, water, fire, wind, the sacrificer, ether, time (*kāla*) and death (*mṛtyu*). Subsequently we get a whole list of lower deities, not only the usual kinds (*gaṇa, bhūta, preta* etc.) but also day and night, as well as the two (later three) twilights, the four guardians of the sky, the mysterious *putradewatā* and *rāmadewatā* (may we compare the fifteenth-century reference to Lord Rāma?). The six Vināyakas, forms of Gaṇeśa or deities associated with Gaṇeśa,[68] also figure in these lists, which also includes the eight points of the compass plus below and above (*i sor i ruhur*). Even the goddess Durgā (always as *durggādewī*) occurs among these lower powers. As has been demonstrated by Hariani Santiko, these imprecation formulas mark the beginning of a development leading to the conception of Durgā as a horrific man-eating demon abiding in cemeteries.[69]

The most interesting item in these imprecations is the invocation addressed to the blessed deities (*dewatā prasiddha*) who 'protect the royal residence of the kings in the land of Mataram' (*mangrakṣa kaḍatwan śrī mahārāja ing bhūmi matarām*). This example is taken from the Sugihmanek inscription of King Dakṣa, dated 915—a time when the *kĕraton* was still in central Java. As to these 'blessed deities' there can be no doubt that the royal ancestors, the deified kings of Mataram, are meant, for the corresponding passage in the Mantyasih inscription of 907[70] lists the names and

66 Conical shapes of boiled rice are still commonly used in Javanese *slamĕtan* ceremonies; cf. Clifford Geertz, *The Religion of Java*, London, 1960, 39f.; Pigeaud, *Java*, III. 118 and IV. 178.

67 Haricandana is well known in India as the name of one of the trees in heaven; the authors have, however, not come across any example of this term indicating a divinity in Indian texts.

68 For Ṣaḍwināyaka and other terms found in Old Javanese imprecations see Edi Sedyawati, 'Pengarcaan Gaṇeśa masa Keḍiri dan Siṅhasāri', Ph.D. thesis, Universitas Indonesia, 1985. An English edition of this important work is in preparation at the Koninklijk Instituut voor de Taal- Land- en Volkenkunde, Leiden, Netherlands.

69 Hariani Santiko, 'Kedudukan bhaṭārī Durgā di Jawa pada abad X–XV Masehi', Ph.D. thesis, Universitas Indonesia, 1987, 146ff.: an equally important work of which no English edition is as yet available.

70 W. F. Stutterheim, 'Een belangrijke inscriptie uit de Kedoe', TBG, 58 (1927), in particular 210.

titles of those preceding kings. As to the Sugihmanek inscription,[71] this text adds the puzzling words *umasuk i śarīra ning wang kabeḥ*, 'entering into the bodies of all people', just after the mention of the 'blessed deities'. Apparently the spirit of those former rulers was thought to pervade the minds of the people and lead them to protect the foundation. Protection was the supreme duty of kings, who were supposed to carry on their beneficial activity after their life on earth by pervading, as it were, the intentions of their subjects. The above passage also illustrates the idea of the deification of kings, on which more details will be given below.

Buddhist powers and concepts never figure in these imprecations; and Śaivism is not prominent. There is mention of Mahādeva or Maheśvara (two names of Śiva) and of Durgā (Durgādevī, at a lower level than would have been expected of Śiva's *śakti*), as well as of Nandīśvara and Mahākāla (two subordinate forms of Śiva acting as doorkeepers, *dwārapāla*). There is also an important reference to the saints of the Pāśupatas and related Śaivite sects in the term *pañcakuśika*, sometimes specified as Kuśika, Garga, Maitri, Kuruṣya and Patañjali.[72]

Some typically Austronesian deities or supernatural powers are a crocodile with the name of Si Pamunguan and another aquatic monster called Taṇḍang Luah, perhaps a river spirit for *luah* = river. The latter's name recalls that of Tandrun Luah, invoked at the beginning of the imprecations in the Śrīvijaya inscriptions of Kota Kapur, Karang Brahi, Tĕlaga Batu and Palang Pasĕmah.[73] This Tandrun Luah probably was a special patron deity of Śrīvijaya, perhaps associated with the river Musi. His unexpected reappearance in central Java more than two centuries later may be an example of inter-island borrowing of potent deities. The example occurs in the above-mentioned inscription of 907.[74] On account of its particular importance many more deities are mentioned than usual. There is a crocodile by the name of Manalu, and there are different snakes (*ulāsarpa*) and different fires (*ñāla* and *apuy*). All these terms and names are preceded by *sang hyang*, always indicating deities, animals and objects considered sacred. There are a sacred axe (*sang hyang wadung*), a sacred heart (*sang hyang tĕas*), presumably the centre of the foundation, and a sacred rice block (*sang hyang kulumpang*).

Some rivers were sacred, such as the Bengawan Solo (*sang hyang bhagawān*), as were some mountains. Thus, the fifteenth-century *Tantu Panggĕlaran* records the myth that the Mahāmeru or Sumeru, abode of the gods, was carried to Java and put down in the east of the island: the present Gunung Sĕmeru. The worship of a still active volcano in its neighbourhood, the Bromo, is attested in the tenth century, where it is considered the abode of god Brahmā, who became identified with fire in ancient Java. A much smaller mountain, the Pĕnanggungan, southwest of

71 See Brandes and Krom, OJO, 30, B-27/28.

72 First mentioned in the Mathurā inscription of Candra Gupta II (380 CE), published by D. R. Bhandarkar, *Epigraphia Indica* 21 (1921) 8f.; D. C. Sircar, *Select Inscriptions*, 2nd edn, Calcutta, 1965, I. 277–9; R. C. Agrawala, *Journal of the Historical Society of Baroda* 20 (1970) 355f.

73 G. Cœdès, 'Les inscriptions malaises de Çrīvijaya', BEFEO, 30 (1930); for this term see line 12 on p. 40 and cf. p. 55.

74 See Brandes and Krom, OJO, 30 line B-28/29.

Surabaya, was worshipped on account of its perfect shape: a central peak surrounded by four lower peaks approximately at the four points of the compass, the supposed shape of the mountain of the gods. Numerous smaller temples, mainly of the fifteenth century, have been discovered on its slopes.[75]

Most of these cults, though probably Austronesian, are in harmony with Brahmanic Hinduism. Worship of mountains as abodes of mighty gods is reflected in mythology: for instance, the Himalaya is the father of Pārvatī, Śiva's spouse. The supreme god himself is often described as 'Lord of the Mountain' (Girīndra or synonyms), and royal dynasties often pay homage to one particular mountain, such as the Rajput dynasties worshipping Mount Abu and the Eastern Gāṅgas of Orissa paying homage to Mount Gokarṇa, 'Cow's Ear'. As to the worship of rivers, not only the names of the Gaṅga (Ganges) and Yamunā (and the place of their confluence at Prayāga near Allahabad), but also those of the Kāvērī (the 'Southern Gaṅgā'), the Sarasvatī, Gomatī (Gumti) and others come to mind. Fire was worshipped in the form of the three sacrificial fires of the brahmins, of the god Agni etc., and snakes were worshipped as *nāgas.* Ancient Indian and Indonesian cults are intertwined to such a degree that it is often impossible to decide whether certain elements of religion in maritime Southeast Asia are Austronesian under an Indian name or Indian influenced by Austronesian tradition.

The development of the great religions, especially Śaivism and, to a lesser extent, Vaiṣṇavism and Buddhism, has to be considered against the background of the cults and ceremonies, as well as the ideas and beliefs, described in this section.

## Śaivism and Vaiṣṇavism

The worship of Śiva, as well as the gods and divine symbols associated with Śiva, was the prevalent form of Hindu religion in Java before the sixteenth century. Sects worshipping Viṣṇu as the supreme deity are also mentioned but were less important. (Mahāyāna) Buddhism, on the other hand, strongly prevailed in Sumatra, the Malay peninsula and west Kalimantan. In Java it flourished mainly during the Śailendra period (c.750–850) and again, but by the side of Śaivism, during the Singhasari-Majapahit period (c.1250–1450).

In the areas where Śaivism prevailed it was mainly centred on the royal courts from where, however, it radiated to secondary centres and to the countryside. Its influence on the agricultural communities was probably confined to those elements of Śaivism that were consistent with popular beliefs. Despite such limitations, the importance of Śaivism is considerable mainly because it flourished in those parts of maritime Southeast Asia that left most of the great monuments and pre-Muslim literature.

As to literature, not only the didactic texts mentioned at the beginning of this chapter but most of the Old Javanese literature is inspired or

[75] V. R. van Romondt, *Peninggalan-peninggalan Purbakala di Gunung Penanggungan,* Dinas Purbakala Republik Indonesia, Jakarta, 1951.

influenced by Śaivism. As to archaeology, numerous Śiva temples have been preserved and restored in central and eastern Java and in Bali. Statues of Śiva and associated deities, especially Durgā, Gaṇeśa and the so-called Guru, abound. Most Śiva images represent the god in his majestic Mahādeva form: four-armed with ascetic hairdress (*jaṭāmakuṭa*), third eye, characteristic emblems (trident, rosary, sacred thread in the form of a snake, etc.), royal attire and ornaments. Less frequently the god is represented in his demonic form of Kāla or Bhairava: nude, except for garlands of skulls and other horrific attributes, or else as a 'doorkeeper' (dvārapāla): guardian of the entrance to a temple (Nandīśvara, the god together with his mount, the bull, and Mahākāla, as the destructor of the world). In addition to these iconic forms, Śiva was also worshipped in the shape of his main symbol: the linga, originally a phallus but in a stylized representation as a column with a square base, a hexagonal middle part and roundish top, but with many variations. Other forms of Śiva, which were popular in South India, such as the dancing Naṭarāja and composite sculptures such as Somāskanda (Śiva together with his spouse Umā and Skanda, his little son, in between) are not attested in Java.

The typical Śiva temple has either a linga or a standing Śiva statue in its cella, to which the eastern entrance gives access through a small vestibule. On either side of the entrance there is a shallow niche for the above-mentioned guardian statues. Also in the three other main walls of the temple there are niches or, in the larger temples, secondary cellas. On the southern side is a standing figure of a bearded and corpulent deity, two-armed and soberly dressed, carrying a fly-whisk (*cāmara*) and a water bottle (*kamaṇḍalu*). At the corresponding place in the western wall there is a four-armed elephant-headed Gaṇeśa and, on the north, a Durgā, another form of Śiva's spouse, as *mahiṣamardinī*, 'slaying the buffalo-demon'. The goddess, standing on the back of the buffalo and brandishing many different weapons in her eight arms, is on the point of killing the demon while he tries to escape through the wound in the buffalo's neck.[76]

These details are of great interest, especially because this combination of deities is typical of ancient Java, although the individual images correspond to similar representations in India, except for the image in the southern niche. In South Indian temples this niche is usually occupied by a seated figure of Śiva Dakṣiṇāmūrti, the 'Supreme Guru', but this figure wears a conical crown (*kirīṭa*), is four-armed, carrying various attributes, and is richly decorated. In Java this deity is replaced by the sober figure of a teacher, whose Śaiva association is confined to the presence of a trident. On the analogy with the Dakṣiṇāmūrti, this statue was usually defined as that of the Divine Teacher (Bhaṭāra Guru), but, following R. Ng. Poerbatjaraka,[77] more recent researchers interpret it as a representation of the sage Agastya. It may seem strange that a *ṛṣi*, however wise and powerful he may have been, should be represented on a par with deities like Durgā and Gaṇeśa, but it is known that Agastya, for whom a temple and an image were made in east Java in 760,[78] enjoyed special veneration in Java.

[76] The iconography of Gaṇeśa and Durgā is discussed in the works mentioned in notes 68 and 69 above. No similar study of Agastya (or Bhaṭāra Guru) is available.

[77] *Agastya in den Archipel*, Leiden, 1926.

Whichever is the correct interpretation, there is no doubt that the Guru was one of the most popular representations in ancient Java. This may well reflect the particular awe felt for a teacher in Java till recent times.

The two other deities, Durgā and Gaṇeśa, were also very popular, as appears from the comparatively very large number of statues that have come down to us. It is curious that the goddess Durgā, Śiva's spouse, is most often represented in the bellicose stance described above, whereas Gaṇeśa, though carrying weapons, is rather benevolent. As to the group of four deities: Śiva 'surrounded' by the Guru, Gaṇeśa and Durgā, it has been suggested that it symbolizes, on a divine level, the principal actors on the stage of the world: the king, his spiritual guide, his prime minister and his queen.[79] The view of the world as a stage is well-known in Indonesia. It is, for instance, implied in the first verse of the poem *Arjunavivāha* (Arjuna's Wedding) and in the performances of the Javanese shadow theatre (*wayang kulit*).[80]

In addition to belonging to this group of four deities, Durgā and Gaṇeśa also enjoyed worship by themselves. Whereas Durgā became more and more closely associated with cemeteries. Gaṇeśa was worshipped for his ability to move huge obstacles with his boundless force. Gaṇeśa statues were therefore placed at dangerous spots, such as river crossings or mountain passes. We have also at least one instance of a Gaṇeśa image placed by the side of a highway frequented by robbers, as appears from the inscription, dated 891, written on its back.[81] In addition, Gaṇeśa is regularly invoked at the beginning of manuscripts of literary works.

In India Śiva was associated with Brahmā and Viṣṇu in a Hindu Trinity, the Trimūrti, but this term is not attested in Old Javanese literature. The concept was well known,[82] but received little attention. Both Brahmā and Viṣṇu were held in great veneration. Numerous statues of the four-headed Brahmā have come down to us, comparatively many more than in India or in mainland Southeast Asia. A particular feature of Brahmā in ancient Java is the god's association with fire, including the subterranean fire revealing itself through the active volcanoes.[83] His consort Sarasvatī and his mount

78 See note 38 above. The Dinoyo inscription of 760 CE deals with a temple and image of Agastya (actually the replacement by an image of black stone of an earlier sandalwood (*candana*) image.

79 W. F. Stutterheim, 'De dateering van eenige Oostjavaansche beeldengroepen', TBG, 66 (1936).

80 J. Zoetmulder, *Kalangwan*, The Hague, 1974, 241f.

81 OJO XIX and XX; H. Bh. Sarkar, *Corpus of Inscriptions of Java*, I, Calcutta, 1971, nos. LVI and LVII, in particular the latter, lines 10–11. The first part of the text is written on an ordinary type of stone, the second on the back of a Gaṇeśa image. The most interesting passage in this context is: *makaphalā karakṣāna nikanang hawān gĕng*, 'hopefully resulting in the protection of the highway'.

82 It is, for instance, clearly reflected in the conception of the Loro Jonggrang complex at Prambanan, where the three main temples are devoted to Śiva, Brahmā and Viṣṇu, each with a smaller temple devoted to the cult of their respective mounts (Nandi, Haṃsa and Garuḍa). It should, however, be noted that the central and clearly predominant temple is devoted to Śiva, not to Brahmā. Actually, the worship of 'compound' deities such as Harihara or Ardhanārīśvara has never been popular in Indonesia—in contrast to ancient Cambodia where Hari-hara statues are very common.

83 J. G. de Casparis, 'Oorkonde uit het Singosarische (midden 14e eeuw A.D.)', *Inscr. Ned.-Indië* I (1940). The inscription deals with regulations concerning the worship of the god Brahmā in close association with the volcano Gunung Bromo.

Haṃṣa (the Goose) are rarely represented, although a few images show the god seated on this big bird.

The numerous Viṣṇu images raise, however, a different issue. From several sources it is known that there existed in Java a relatively small, but influential, Vaiṣṇava community. The *Nāgarakĕrtāgama*, after devoting two stanzas to the Śaivas, five to the Buddhists and four to the Rĕsis community of ascetics, continues with one verse, half of which gives the names of eight Vaiṣṇava (*Vangśa Viṣṇu*) foundations (78–5). Compared with the thirty-eight Śaiva institutions this is a small number, but the devotees of Viṣṇu may have had considerable influence, especially in the twelfth century, when poetical works (*kĕkawin*) extolling Viṣṇu or one of his incarnations were composed (*Kṛṣṇāyaṇa, Hariwangśa, Bhomakāwya*, and others). In addition, many of the kings of that period were praised as 'partial incarnations' (*angśāwatāra*) of that god. King Jayanagara of Majapahit (r. 1309–21) is said 'to have returned home to Hari's (Viṣṇu's) estate' (*Nāg*. 48–3a) and was worshipped as a Viṣṇu image (*Nāg*. 48–3c).[84]

Statues of the god, easily identifiable by his main emblems, the wheel (*cakra*) and the conch (*śaṅkha*), were quite common in Java. As a divine prototype of kings, especially in his incarnations as Kṛiṣṇa and Rāma, his cult was probably closely associated with the royal courts. Viṣṇu's spouse, Lakṣmī or Śrī, not only symbolized royal sovereignty but especially became a rice goddess whose activity promoted the fertility of the ricefields. As such she is still worshipped, in particular in west Java under the name Ni Pohaci Sangyang Sri.[85]

More even than the goddess, Viṣṇu's mount, the heavenly bird Garuḍa, who rescued the immortality drink (*amĕrta*) and devoured dangerous snakes, was quite popular. Either as a bird or, more often, partly anthropomorphic, he is represented not only as Viṣṇu's mount but also by himself. An east Javanese fourteenth-century temple, Caṇḍi Kĕḍaton, even has a series of reliefs devoted to the story of Garuḍa (the *Garuḍeya*).[86] In addition, Garuḍa is prominently represented in the coat of arms of the Republic of Indonesia and in the name of its national airline.

Apart from striking differences in emphasis, the worship of Śiva and associated deities shows few significant deviations from Indian tradition. On the other hand, the conceptions lying at the basis of early Indonesian art and architecture were probably quite different. As in India, a temple does not stand by itself but forms part of a group or complex. In Indonesia such complexes may be very large, comprising hundreds of separate buildings. This suggests that the deity to whom the temple complex as a whole is dedicated was conceived of as a heavenly king ruling the cosmos

84 N. Krom, *Hindoe-Javaansche Geschiedenis*, 2nd edn, The Hague, 1931, 170–5. For the poetical works under discussion see J. Zoetmulder, *Kalangwan*, 283–324. For the statues of King Kĕrtanagara see Pigeaud, *Java*, IV. 141: *arcā* is translated by 'statue' and *pratimā* by 'statuette'. In the *Nāgarakĕrtāgama*, Jayanagara (1309–21) is the only *king* identified with Viṣṇu, but among the princes there were others, for instance Hayam Wuruk's brother-in-law Prince of Wĕngkĕr, who was deified as Viṣṇu.

85 K. A. H. Hidding, *Nji Pohatji Sangjang Sri*, Leiden, 1929; V. Sukanda Tessier, 'Le triomphe de Srī en pays soundanais', Publications de l'EFEO, 101 (1977).

86 N. Krom, *Inleiding tot de Hindoe-Javaansche Kunst*, 2nd edn, 1923, II. 223–9; Stutterheim, *Cultuurgeschiedenis van Java in Beeld*, 'Weltevreden', 1926, figs 137–42.

as an earthly king ruled his kingdom (in theory, 'the earth'). In general, the kingdom was conceived of as a *maṇḍala*,[87] consisting of concentric circles with the king as its centre. The innermost circle was reserved for the king and his immediate associates; the middle circle was occupied by dependants and officials considered subordinates of the centre, while the outer part was occupied by (semi-) independent rulers who were obliged to pay homage to the (principal) king. In addition there was a vertical stratification with the king at the apex of a stepped pyramid: the different, hierarchically ordered, groups comprising the society of those times.

In accordance with these ideas, the great Śaiva complex of Roro (Loro) Jonggrang (about twenty-five kilometres east of Yogyakarta) consists of three divisions, each surrounded by its own wall with gateways. In the centre stands the majestic tower-like temple of Śiva; on either side, to the north and the south, are the somewhat lower temples of Viṣṇu and Brahmā. Opposite these main temples there are much smaller temples dedicated to the mounts of the three gods. Finally there are small structures near the gateways giving access to the middle division. The latter consists of about a hundred and fifty small temples arranged in three rows, which were apparently shrines for minor deities. These are again surrounded by a wall enclosing the present site of the monument. There still are, however, traces of a third enclosure, not parallel with the other two. As no remains of buildings have been discovered in the outer section, it is likely that this area was used for dwellings of priests and other temple personnel, schools with dormitories, and perhaps guesthouses.

As to the significance of the many small temples of the middle area, something more may be concluded by analogy with the contemporary Buddhist complex of Plaosan-Lor. There, many of the small temples and stupas surrounding the main building bear small inscriptions with the word *anumoda* followed by a title and name, indicating that the structure was a pious contribution by the authority mentioned there. This suggests that officials or local chiefs in different parts of the kingdom were asked or ordered to contribute to the royal foundation, thus attesting both their piety and their loyalty. Presumably the same applies to Roro Jonggrang, where indeed a few titles, written in black or red paint, have remained vaguely visible. It was probably, as already suggested by Krom,[88] a state temple which mirrored the relationships within the kingdom.

Roro Jonggrang marks a culmination which was followed by more than three centuries without major temple foundations in Java. It has already been mentioned that Buddhism strongly predominated in Sumatra and the Malay peninsula, but there are important exceptions. Thus, the three statues of P'ra Narai (Takuapa, southern Thailand)[89] are Śaiva and so are

87 For the *maṇḍala* concept see the *Arthaśāstra*, ed. R. P. Kangle, Bombay, 1963, 164–7 (text), 364–71 (translation); U. N. Ghoshal, *A History of Political Ideas*, OUP, 1959, 91–9; O. W. Wolters, *History, Culture, and Region in Southeast Asian Perspectives*, Singapore, 1982.

88 *Hindoe-Javaansche Geschiedenis*, 172; de Casparis, *Prasasti Indonesia*, II (1956) 307ff.; 'Short Inscriptions from Tjandi Plaosan-Lor', *Berita Dinas Purbakala*, no. 4 (1958), especially plate I.

89 Alastair Lamb, 'Miscellaneous papers on Early Hindu and Buddhist Settlements in Northern Malaya and Southern Thailand', FMJ, N.S. VI (1961); Stanley J. O'Connor, *Hindu Gods of Peninsular Thailand, Artibus Asiae*, Supplementum 28, Ascona, 1972, 52–88 and figs 28–31; M. C. Subhadradis Diskul, *The Art of Śrīvijaya*, Paris, UNESCO, 1980, 23f.

the numerous sites of the Bujang valley, Kedah, Malaysia. In the absence of iconographic and epigraphic data, the buildings (actually only foundations as the superstructures must have been of perishable materials) are awkward to date, but stray finds of pottery may point to the end of the eleventh century or somewhat later.[90]

From the middle of the thirteenth century Śaivism again flourished, as appears from the numerous sites in east Java and Bali, which can be dated between c.1250 and 1450. Two sites are of particular importance on account of their size and beauty: Singhasari and Panataran. The tower temple (*prāsāda*) at Singhasari is especially remarkable for its marvellous sculptures representing gods of the Śaiva pantheon. In addition to Śiva in his majestic four-armed Maheśvara form, there are statutes of Durgā (as nearly always in Indonesia, as *mahiṣamardinī*, 'killing the buffalo-demon'), of Gaṇeśa and of Guru (or Agastya): the customary Śaiva pantheon. In addition, however, we find a demonic Bhairava with the inscription *cakracakra* as well as statues of Viṣṇu and Brahmā. From the same, or a closely associated, site a famous image of Prajñāpāramitā, 'Perfect Wisdom', represented as a seated, two-armed goddess carrying a manuscript,[91] has been recovered, thus pointing to a close association between Śaivism and Buddhism.

The great temple complex of Panataran near Blitar, east Java, belongs mainly to the fourteenth century, the age of Majapahit, during which it was probably a state sanctuary. Dedicated to Śiva, Lord of the Mountain, it consists of three courtyards with the main entrance gate on the west and the main temple in the eastern courtyard. Such a composition differs fundamentally from those of the central Javanese temple compounds such as Roro Jonggrang. There the secondary structures are all arranged in rows around the principal building. The arrangement as seen at Panataran, on the other hand, reminds one of that of the *kraton*, the Javanese royal residence. Thus in the present Yogyakarta *kraton* one may enter through the eastern gate and, crossing a number of courts, one would (if it were permitted) arrive at the king's private quarters. The resemblance is not fortuitous, for the Kingdom of Heaven is an idealized projection of the kingdom on earth. It is, however, important to note that such compounds differ completely from the Indian conception of the Mahāmeru.[92]

As noted earlier, Panataran is devoted to Śiva as Lord of the Mountain(s), in this case especially the Kĕlud. As one of Java's most active volcanoes it was, like the Bromo, an object of veneration. It seems, indeed, as though the worship of mountains as abodes of divine power, though Austronesian in origin, became more common or explicit in the fourteenth

90 Lamb, 'Misc. Papers', 79–81.

91 For the Durgā see Stutterheim, *Cultuurgeschiedenis*, 72, fig. 10. The Prajñāpāramitā of Singosari is illustrated in all works on Indonesian art, e.g. Karl With, *Java, Brahmanische, Buddhistische und eigenlebige Architectur und Plastik auf Java*, Hagen, 1920, plates 138–9.

92 H. J. J. Winter, 'Science', in A. L. Basham, ed., *A Cultural History of India*, Oxford, 1975; P. S. Rawson, 'Early Art and Architecture', ibid., 204. 'Each temple is conceived, as the Buddhist stūpa was, as "the axis of the world", symbolically transformed into the mythical Mount Meru, around which are slung, like garlands, the heavens and the earth.' The Buddhist system of cosmology, as followed in Indonesia, it seems, is set out in detail in such texts as the *Abhidharmakośa*, book III.

and fifteenth centuries. Thus, the numerous little sanctuaries discovered on the slopes of the Penanggungan in east Java have already been mentioned, and two large sites of mainly the fifteenth century have been discovered on the slopes of the Lawu, viz. Sukuh and Cĕṭa. At Sukuh the cult of the linga of Śiva, though always characteristic of Śaivism, was more pronounced than elsewhere. It appears, however, that this cult was primarily associated not with fertility but with the liberation of the soul.

This cult was linked with that of Bhīma, one of the five Pāṇḍava heroes of the *Mahābhārata*, known for his enormous force. There are a number of Bhīma statues from Sukuh and contemporary sites, and also literary works in which Bhīma is represented as a saviour who, like Avalokiteśvara in Buddhism, even goes to hell to redeem sinners. Some late Old Javanese texts, such as the *Nawaruci*, *Dewaruci*, and *Bimasuci*, assign an important role to Bhīma. These texts have a strong mystical flavour. The Bhīma tradition, linked with speculation about death and immortality, has persisted in Bali also in the shadow theatre (*Bhimaswarga*).[93] Another late text, the *Tantu Panggĕlaran*, composed about 1500, describes numerous hermitages and communities of ascetics especially in the mountain areas.[94] When parts of the lowlands had already been Islamized, Brahmanic culture still survived in the mountainous areas of eastern Java for a considerable time.

## Buddhism

Buddhism, like Islam and Christianity, but in contrast to Austronesian beliefs, Brahmanism and Śaivism, is a world religion, which can be studied from numerous manuals. This section is therefore mainly confined to aspects which received particular emphasis in maritime Southeast Asia, but also covers the expansion of Buddhism and its place in the history and culture of the area.

The Buddhist doctrines are based on the revelation by Lord Buddha of the Four Noble Truths—the awareness that worldly existence is a form of suffering, that the causes of suffering can be determined, that therefore suffering can be eliminated, and that, finally, there is a Path leading to that end. However, the actual Buddhist doctrines reflect a rational approach. This includes a theory of causation which traces the miseries of existence back to ignorance (*pratītyasamutpāda*),[95] following which all things are linked in a web of cause-and-effect relations containing twelve categories. The suffering that forms part of life stems from ignorance of the true nature of things. Beings are condemned by ignorance to a constant round of rebirth in conditions governed by *karma(n)*—the law by which all morally qualified acts, good or evil, necessarily carry their fruits, sometimes in this life, more often in the next. This belief, closely interwoven with the theory of transmigration of the soul (or of its equivalent) pervades

93 M. Prijohoetomo, *Nawaruci*, Groningen-'Batavia', 1934, 1–139; *Bhīmasuci*, ibid., 140–213; R. Ng. Poerbatjaraka, 'Dewa-Roetji', *Djawa*, XX (1940); H. I. R. Hinzler, *The Bima Swarga in Balinese wayang* in VKI, 90, The Hague, 1981.

94 Th. G. Th. Pigeaud, *De Tantu Panggĕlaran*, The Hague, 1924.

95 This twelvefold chain of causes and effects was well-known all over the Buddhist world. In Java it has been found inscribed on a set of gold plates, together with an elaborate commentary; see de Casparis, *Prasasti Indonesia*, II (1956) no. III; Buchari, *Prasasti Koleksi Museum National*, Jakarta, 1985–6, 224–35.

all Indian thought. In the older form of Buddhism, the doctrine of the Elders (Theravāda), the supreme ideal of the pious Buddhist is to achieve a complete cessation of the circle of rebirths to attain *nirvāṇa*. This form of Buddhism is the norm in most of mainland Southeast Asia, as we have seen.

In maritime Southeast Asia, however, there is hardly any evidence of Theravāda, but another form of Buddhism called Mahāyāna (the 'Great Vehicle') emphasizes the gradual rise to the perfection of Buddha-hood through a long succession of existences as a Bodhisattva: a being, not necessarily human, striving for Buddha-hood and following a way of life which may ultimately lead to that end. Some Bodhisattvas, thought to abide on the verge of Buddha-hood, received special veneration, as did the ever-increasing number of Buddhas. Thus a new pantheon developed: it consisted of different kinds of Buddhas, in iconography distinguishable by the position of their hands; many different Bodhisattvas, each recognizable by particular emblems; and their female counterparts (Tārā). Even Hindu gods were incorporated into Mahāyāna, though at a lower stage than the Buddhist deities.

As to the influence of Buddhism in maritime Southeast Asia we have to distinguish between the western part of the area (Sumatra, western Malaysia and west Borneo) and its eastern part (Java, Nusa Tenggara and east Borneo). Whereas Buddhism prevailed in most of its western part until the coming of Islam, it flourished in the eastern zone mainly during certain periods. In Java these are the Śailendra period (c.750–850) and the Singhasari-Majapahit period (especially c.1250–1400). During the intervening period Buddhism continued to have followers, but remained somewhat in the background.

In Java Buddhism was strongly patronized by the Śailendra kings (c.775–860), as reflected in art and architecture. The archaeological sources, which include also a number of inscriptions, give us a fair idea of Buddhism as professed during that period.

The greatest of all Buddhist monuments in the region, Borobuḍur in central Java, is often described as a gigantic stupa. But, although there are numerous stupas on terraces, which recall the *maluwa* and *pesāwa* of the Sri Lankan stupas,[96] Borobuḍur is different in that the galleries and terraces predominate, whereas the main stupa functions as a kind of crown. A more satisfactory interpretation is that of a *stūpa-prāsāda*, a term occurring in the *Sang Hyang Kamahāyānikan*. The second part of the compound indicates a building consisting of several storeys or terraces. Borobuḍur has also, but less successfully, been described as a Tantric *maṇḍala*: a (magical) circle or closed sacred area within which certain rites could be carried out. Although Borobuḍur may well have been *used* as a huge *maṇḍala*, it is unlikely that this was the intention of its creator(s), for clearly Tantric features are not apparent in Borobuḍur. Others have seen the monument as a monumental encyclopaedia of Buddhism, a view based on the illustration of numerous types of buildings, including palaces and stupas, many kinds of ships, trees, animals, crowns, etc. Its reliefs depict

[96] R. Silva, *Religious Architecture in Early and Medieval Sri Lanka*, Meppel, 1987, 19–26.

basic Mahāyāna texts with the help of which a keen student could receive excellent instruction under the guidance of a teacher.[97]

On more than one occasion, a name occurring in two inscriptions of 842, Bhūmisaṃbhāra, has been identified with Borobuḍur and it has been concluded from its description as a *kamūlān*, 'place of origin', that the monument marks the 'cradle' of the dynasty of the Śailendras ('Lords of the Mountain'). In this manner the dynasty would emphasize both its piety and its authority. Such an interpretation does not rule out the likelihood that Borobuḍur was also used as an encyclopaedia of Buddhism or, a few centuries later, as a Tantric *maṇḍala*.[98]

The conception of the other two great Buddhist monuments of central Java, Caṇḍi Sewu and Plaosan,[99] is quite different. Caṇḍi Sewu ('A Thousand Temples') at Prambanan, about thirty kilometres east of Yogyakarta, is a vast complex consisting of one large temple in the middle, surrounded by four rows of small temples, about 250 in all. It reflects the conception of a vast Buddhist pantheon with Buddhas, Bodhisattvas and other superior beings, each assigned to its proper place in the sacred hierarchy. Its building may have started in or shortly before 782 and must have continued till well into the ninth century.

The northern complex of Caṇḍi Plaosan, one kilometre distant from Sewu, also comprises numerous structures, but there are important differences. At the centre there are two large, two-storey buildings separated by a wall, with a similar wall separating both from three rows of small temples and stupas. The two main buildings were built at the expense of the king and queen respectively; whereas many of the small structures carry short inscriptions, each indicating the name and title of the dignitary or official who contributed to its foundation.

Like Borobuḍur, these buildings are all inspired by Mahāyāna with strong emphasis on the worship of Bodhisattvas, Tārās, and some Hindu gods such as Kubera, Guardian of the North and associated with wealth.

97 This is not the right place to discuss the manifold problems of the interpretation of Borobuḍur—problems which are commensurate with the size and richness of the monument. Actually, most of the interpretations that have been proposed long ago are clearly out of date (though still repeated in some modern publications). The best works at present available are Soekmono, *Chandi Borobudur. A Monument of Mankind*, Amsterdam and Paris: UNESCO, 1976; Jacques Dumarçay, *Borobuḍur*, Kuala Lumpur, 1978; and Jan J. Boeles, *The secret of Borobudur*, Bangkok, 1985.

98 De Casparis, *Prasasti Indonesia*, 1950, 134–92; De Casparis 'The Dual Nature of Borobuḍur', in Luis Gomez, and Hiram W. Woodward, eds, *Borobudur, History and Significance of a Monument*, Ann Arbor, 1980. As to its interpretation as a Tantric *maṇḍala*, based partly on a passage in the *Nāgarakĕrtāgama*, where Budur (*sic*) is mentioned in a list of buildings of the Vajradhara sect (canto 77, verse 3), as well as on a passage in the *Sang Hyang Kamahāyānikan* (see the bibliographic essay for this chapter), Stutterheim was probably the first to propose the interpretation of Borobuḍur as the Tantric *maṇḍala*, i.e. primarily an object of meditation. The idea of Borobuḍur being a kind of Encyclopaedia of Buddhism was first proposed by Siwaramamurti. Although both interpretations are correct as Borobuḍur has probably been used as a maṇḍala and as an encyclopaedia providing information on many topics (not only on Buddhism), it is unlikely that either was the original purpose in the mind(s) of its creator(s).

99 Jacques Dumarçay, *Candi Sewu et l'architecture bouddhique du centre de Java*, Paris, EFEO, 1981; Indonesian edition under the title *Candi Sewu dan Arsitektur Bangunan Agama Buda di Jawa Tengah*, Pusat Penelitian Arkeologi Nasional, Depdikbud, 1986; De Casparis, 'Short Inscriptions from Tjandi Plaosan-Lor', *Berita Dinas Purabakala*, no. 4 (1958).

The Śailendras were outward-looking and in regular contact with other Buddhist kingdoms. Thus, an inscription of 782 mentions a monk from Gauḍa, present (northern) Bangladesh, who consecrated a Mañjuśrī image at or near Caṇḍi Sewu. Ten years later learned monks from Sri Lanka inaugurated a replica of the 'Abhayagiri of the Sinhalese monks', while teachers from Gurjaradeśa, modern Gujerat, took part in the consecration of the main building of Caṇḍi Plaosan. An inscription from Nālandā in Bihar (India) deals with a monastery built there by order of the Śailendra king, presumably on behalf of Indonesian students and pilgrims staying at or visiting Nālandā, one of the greatest centres of Buddhist learning at that time.

At the time of the Nālandā foundation (c. 860) the Śailendras were no longer reigning in Java but had moved to Śrīvijaya in southern Sumatra. Their successors in Java, though by no means hostile to Buddhism, did not patronize it. We have to wait till the second half of the thirteenth century before we witness a revival of Javanese Buddhism.

In Sumatra, on the other hand, Buddhism continued to flourish under the patronage of the kings of Śrīvijaya, but left few great monuments. Sumatra is not so poor in monuments as has sometimes been thought, but they bear no comparison with those of Java, either in number or in splendour. This has been attributed to the mercantile spirit of the empire, but there were probably other factors involved. As the soil of southern Sumatra is generally poor, the country did not produce the dense agricultural population with its reserve of labour necessary for the construction of great monuments. This same Śrīvijaya sponsored, however, great monuments in countries as far away as India and China. Thus, at the turn of the millennium the king of Śrīvijaya had a large monastery constructed on the east coast of South India, as well as a temple in Canton.[1]

In the thirteenth and fourteenth centuries Buddhism again flourished not only in Sumatra but also in Java. King Kĕrtanagara of Singhasari (r. 1268–92) was known, at least after his death, as Śiva-Buddha, but neither his inscriptions nor the long *Nāgarakĕrtāgama* passage dealing with his reign show unambiguous evidence of Śaivism. Both are imbued with the spirit of Tantric Buddhism, in particular Vajrayāna, a sect which attributes superhuman power to the vajra, mentioned earlier. Different rituals in which this symbol played an important part were performed in order to shorten the otherwise long road towards Buddha-hood and Nirvāṇa. The nature of these ceremonies, which are only alluded to in our texts, is difficult to determine since the most important text mentioned in this connexion, the *Subhūtitantra*, has not yet been identified. A late source, the Old Javanese *Pararaton*, attributes to Kĕrtanagara the performance of rituals involving the use of alcoholic drinks and other excesses, but there is no contemporary evidence to prove that such rituals were actually carried out.[2]

1 G. Cœdès, *The Indianized States of Southeast Asia*, ed. Walter F. Vella, trans. Susan Brown Cowing, Honolulu, 1968, 141f.

2 ibid., 198f.; but see also *Nāg*. XLIII-1 to 5 with Pigeaud's discussion of these difficult verses in *Java*, IV. 128–34. Cf. also the older interpretations proposed by J. L. Moens, 'Het Buddhisme op Java in zijn laatste bloeiperiode', TBG, 44 (1924), and P. H. Pott, *Yoga and Yantra*, The Hague, 1966, 124f. and 130f.

Buddhism remained important throughout the fourteenth century, as reflected in art and literature. Some of the most important texts composed in that period are Buddhist in character,[3] but the clearest evidence is archaeological. A number of the most important temples are Buddhist. Foremost among these is Caṇḍi Jago (or Tumpang) near present Malang, east Java. Its Buddhist character is clearly reflected not in its architecture or narrative reliefs, but in its statuary, which represents a Buddhist Tantric pantheon. These splendid images can now be studied in different museums. They are carved in a soft style and carry inscriptions in Nāgarī script of a type current in northeastern India, in particular Orissa, in this period. This may also be the strongest indication of an influx from India of new ideas and practices into Buddhism, although Buddhism in India was in serious decline at that time. This was not, however, the case with the entire subcontinent, for Mahāyāna continued to flourish in some areas, in particular coastal Orissa (Ratnagiri, Udayagiri and Lalitagiri). A possible relationship between this region and east Java has never been adequately studied, but it seems likely. From the end of the fourteenth century, however, there are very few, if any, Buddhist remains and this religion seems to have faded away even before the Islamization of Java.

In Sumatra, the kingdom of Śrīvijaya, which had patronized Buddhism for six centuries, declined in the thirteenth century but was succeeded by Malāyu, which had its centre in present Jambi but moved to the west coast by the beginning of the fourteenth century. Unlike Śrīvijaya, Malāyu maintained close relations with Java. In 1284 King Kĕrtanagara sent a curious composite statue, consisting of copies of statues of Caṇḍi Jago in east Java, to the king of Malāyu. It was escorted by a high delegation and received by the Malāyu authorities with great pomp. These details are recorded in the Old Malay inscription carved on the back of the statue.[4]

Sixty years later it changed place again, this time to west Sumatra by order of one of the most fascinating figures on the politico-religious scene of the fourteenth century: King Ādityavarman (r. c. 1347–79). Possibly of partly Javanese descent, he spent his early career in Majapahit but returned to Sumatra before 1347. There he issued a large number of inscriptions in Sanskrit and Old Malay, written in a characteristic local script, and also one in Tamil. These texts are difficult to understand owing to the use of curious ungrammatical forms of Sanskrit and of esoteric Tantric terminology, the precise meaning of which is still imperfectly known. As to the type of Tantrism followed by Ādityavarman there is a statement that the king was 'always concentrated on Hevajra', a demonic form of the Jina Akṣobhya,[5] whose worship involved bloody and erotic rituals, the latter in conjunction with female partners. Eating and drinking, presumably of palm wine, are also mentioned, but it is doubtful whether such excesses regularly took place. In any case, they did not prevent

[3] Such as the *Nāgarakĕrtāgama*, the *Sutasoma* and the *Kuñjarakarṇa*. For these texts see P. J. Zoetmulder, *Kalangwan. A Survey of Old Javanese Literature*, The Hague, 1974.

[4] N. J. Krom, 'Een Sumatraansche Inscriptie van koning Kṛtanagara', *Versl. Med. Kon. Ak. Wet.*, Afd. Lett. 5, (1916).

[5] Satyawati Suleiman, 'The Archaeology and History of West Sumatra', *Berita Pusat Penelitian Purbakala dan Peninggalan Nasional*, 12 (1977). She correctly read *hewajra* in the last line of one of the Suroaso inscriptions (p. 11).

Ādityavarman from reigning for at least thirty-two years and becoming the spiritual father of the kingdom of Minangkabau. It is curious that not a single temple built by Ādityavarman has hitherto come to light, and only very few images. One of these few is, however, the largest statue discovered in Indonesia: a huge two-armed, horrific Bhairava,[6] a demonic form of Śiva represented nude and brandishing a knife, while standing on a corpse above a pedestal decorated with human skulls.

Finally, attention is called to the important site of Padang Lawas in south Tapanuli. Ruins of at least sixteen brick temples and stupas were found in this arid plain, probably part of the ancient kingdom of Panai, with its capital situated on the river of that name. Originally a dependency of Śrīvijaya, it made itself independent in or before the thirteenth century. Apart from an important set of Buddhist bronzes, dated 1039, most other antiquities seem to belong to the thirteenth century. The brick temples are remarkable for the reliefs depicting dancing Yakṣas and other demons.[7]

Nothing more is heard of Buddhism after Ādityavarman. It is unlikely that the esoteric and demonic form of Buddhism would have appealed to the population as a whole, unlike Theravāda on the mainland which was, and is, a truly popular religion. Already half a century before Ādityavarman a Muslim kingdom had been established at Pasai on the northeast coast of Sumatra. Its first ruler Malik al-Salih died in 1297. Other Muslim kingdoms and sultanates arose in ports of eastern Sumatra during the fifteenth century.

## TWO SPECIAL PROBLEMS

Before discussing early Islam in Southeast Asia, it is proper to consider two special problems which have given rise to much discussion. They concern the generally held views that kings were regarded as gods and that there was a considerable degree of religious syncretism. Both views are open to serious doubt.

Historians of ancient India have given much thought to the problem of the kings' divinity. As kingship in Southeast Asia was strongly influenced by Indian ideas, some points have to be made.

First of all it should be emphasized that pre-partition India is a vast subcontinent with a written history that can be traced back to the second millennium BC. Generalizations are therefore often misleading.

Second, one has to be clear about the concept of divinity. In Christianity and Islam, divinity implies perfection and the absolute. Indian thought recognizes different stages or degrees of divinity, whereas the absolute—designated by terms such as *mokṣa, nirvāṇa, sac-cid-ānanda* according to various creeds—is a state far beyond the mere divine. It is true that kings were generally addressed as *deva*, usually translated as 'god', but this was

6 F. M. Schnitger, *The Archaeology of Hindoo Sumatra*, Leiden, 1937, plates XIII–XVI. The height of the statue is 4.41 m!

7 Rumbi Mulia, 'The ancient kingdom of Panai and the ruins of Padang Lawas', *Berita Pusat Penelitian Arkeologi Nasional*, 14 (1980).

a formality which would not necessarily imply a belief in the king's divinity. Although some passages in the texts are ambiguous, there is now a large measure of consensus among scholars to the effect that kings were not, as a rule, considered divine, but there were probably exceptions in particular periods or regions, or in the minds of some of the king's subjects.

Third, even if kings were considered to some extent divine, they would have shared this 'divinity' with many other creatures, including some priests and cows, or even snakes and trees.

Finally, there are many passages in texts and inscriptions in which kings are compared with deities in a manner suggesting a close relationship, if not identity, with deities. Thus, as early as the fourth century CE King Samudra Gupta is described as the equal of the Lokapālas (*Dhanada-Varuṇendrāntaka-sama*, 'the equal of Kubera, Varuna, Indra and Yama').[8] Such phrases, which are confined to court poets intent on bestowing exaggerated praise on their patrons, carry little weight as arguments in favour of the king's divinity. On balance it may therefore be concluded that kings were not considered divine in any real sense in ancient India.[9]

By and large, the same applies to Southeast Asia, but the matter is far more complicated. Not surprisingly, as far as the deification of rulers is concerned, there are considerable differences among individual areas of the region, partly due to differences in official religions. Thus, the very idea of deification of kings is contrary to the monotheism of Islam. This is not the case with Theravāda Buddhism, but there the position of the gods (*deva*) is a modest one: they lead a happy life but, although they live very long, they are not immortal. In addition, their world is quite separated from ours. This would not have encouraged kings to seek identification with gods. The same applies to Mahāyāna, but there the multitude of Buddhas and Bodhisattvas provides an opportunity for ambitious rulers to claim the status of one of those superior beings. Their superiority was, however, mainly confined to wisdom and charity rather than to superhuman power. As we shall see, however, these concepts of Mahāyāna may have significant implications for some Buddhist kings. 'Hinduism', on the other hand, in particular Śaivism, provided the kings with opportunities to receive the kind of worship reserved to gods during, or more often after, their life on earth. The survey which follows will therefore mainly be confined to Mahāyāna and Śaivism. Because of the differences among various areas it seems necessary to separate mainland and maritime Southeast Asia.

In mainland Southeast Asia, there was a major religious dimension to kingship, but it is necessary to remember that, whatever it implies for the notion of royal divinity, it did not mean that any ruler once crowned was treated by everybody with awe-filled veneration and unquestioning obedience. The fallible humanity of a king was commemorated by the

[8] D. C. Sircar, *Select Inscriptions bearing on Indian History and Civilization*, 2nd edn. Calcutta, 1965, book III, no. 2: Allahabad Pillar Inscription of Samudragupta, pp. 262–8, line 26.

[9] The supposed divinity of ancient Indian kings has long been a point of controversy among Indologists, but the *communis opinio* is perhaps best summarized by A. L. Basham, *The Wonder that was India*, London, 1954 (reprint 1961), 81–8.

constant need to fight enemies abroad, in the provinces, at court and within his own family.

The significance of the idea of divine kingship, then, is not as an instrument of enhanced power. It is, rather, a ritual statement. But this statement, though it may not have worked magic for the political fortunes of rulers, may be important enough in its own way as an expression of cosmological belief about the spiritual forces informing the operation of human society and nature. Further, we must remember that the agrarian societies with which we are dealing lacked the modern idea of an impersonal state commanding a loyalty from its citizens that transcends the claims of individuals in government. In its place, the legitimacy of a ruler required a symbolism that could be supplied by religious categories.

There are various sorts of evidence of the divine sanction for kingship. One is constituted by the Indochinese linga cult, where the lingas were given the names of kings who endowed them in combination with Śiva's title Īśvara. As we have seen, the Chams had such cults at Mi-son, with a Bhadreśvara and subsequently a Śambhubhadreśvara. In Angkor, above all, many lingas and statues of gods were endowed by kings and by members of the royal family and the great men of the land.

A special case in Angkor, which has commonly been treated as an example of the royal linga cult but needs to be considered separately, is the *devarāja* cult instituted by the founder, Jayavarman II, to sanctify the independence and unity of the Khmer kingdom. It is known from only a few inscriptions, which show that the cult was maintained by a number of subsequent kings, and that it had attached to it a specially assigned lineage of priests.

Much has been written about this cult by modern scholars. Cœdès regarded it as more or less identical to the cult of the great 'temple-mountains', the pyramidal monuments which so many rulers built.[10] More recently Kulke has argued against this, identifying the *devarāja* instead as a portable and probably bronze icon which could be installed at different places.[11] The name of the cult, as Filliozat was the first to argue, need not be translated as 'god-king' (comporting the idea of royal divinity); it could refer instead to Śiva as 'King of the Gods'. Filliozat, who argued for a South Indian provenance of the cult, has further proposed that the Śiva cult thus attested was one in which the devotees had a sophisticated theology of Śiva as the supreme deity and unique and universal sovereign. The *devarāja*, therefore, was not confused with the person of the individual king; the divine self of Śiva is eternally pure, and no earthly ruler, even if partaking of divinity to the extent that in his innermost self he comes from Śiva, can possess that purity.[12]

Other aspects of the cult have been explored. Claude Jacques has examined it through the Khmer-language terms used in the inscriptions,

10 Cœdès wrote on the subject in various places. A summary of his views is in *Angkor—an Introduction*, trans. E. F. Gardiner, Hong Kong, 1962, 22ff.

11 'Der Devarāja-Kult', *Saeculum*, 25, 1 (1974); trans. I. W. Mabbett, as *The Devarāja Cult*, Cornell University Southeast Asia Program, Data Paper no. 108, Ithaca, 1978.

12 J. Filliozat, 'Sur le Çivaïsme et le Bouddhisme du Cambodge, à propos de deux livres récents', *BEFEO*, 70 (1981).

and suggested that, instead of the Khmer expression *kamrateṅ jagat ta rāja* being a translation of the Sanskrit *devarāja*, it may be the other way round—the Sanskrit term may name no Indian god at all but refer to a purely local god of a sort that may be called upon to protect a lineage or, in this case, a royal line.[13]

This reminds us of Paul Mus' view of the evolution from prehistoric cults of earth gods, their icons often consisting of rough stones, to linga cults which took over the same religious meaning that the earth gods had possessed. In one sense, the imported linga cult melted into the local tradition, appealing to the same set of ideas as did the cult of the territorial earth spirit; in another sense, the local tradition evolved into a more sophisticated ritual inspired by the imported myth—both perspectives, in Mus' interpretation, would be legitimate. Either way, a cult such as the *devarāja* should be seen as having signified to its worshippers the king as ritual embodiment of the patron god. Filliozat argued against this identification, asserting that Śiva's transcendence and purity excluded it. Both interpretations could, however, be right—one on the level of theology, the other on that of the sociology of religion.

The idea of royal divinity, however, depends upon more than just the linga cults and divinized statues of royalty. There are, for example, the shrines dedicated to royal ancestors which have as icons statues of gods and goddesses identified with human ancestors. At Angkor, Indravarman I dedicated the Preah Koh to the former king Jayavarman II and his wife, to Indravarman's own parents, and to his maternal grandparents. One can no doubt see in such a practice elements of the tradition indigenous to the soil which, on Mus' reconstruction, saw ancestors—especially ancestors of community chiefs—as merging with community gods. Such a merging is well attested in Chinese indigenous religion, and there are traces of such thinking in Indian ideas about the afterlife entered by ancestors.

But perhaps the most conspicuous sort of evidence is the symbolism implicit in the architecture of many Southeast Asian capital cities and the great monuments which were often constructed in their centres to represent the Mahāmeru, the home of the gods and *axis mundi*. A particularly elaborate example is constituted by Angkor Thom, capital city of Jayavarman VII, and the Mahāyāna Buddhist shrine, the Bayòn, in the centre of it: the whole complex was rich in cosmological meaning, representing on one level the myth of creation by churning the ocean of milk, and the causeways that approached the city walls being assimilated to Indra's rainbow, the ascent to heaven. The king sent twenty-three statues of himself to the provinces, and in return received images of the gods of the localities which were housed in the Bayòn's galleries; thus the Bayòn, as home of the gods, embodied all the spiritual energies of the kingdom.

Vietnam, which inherited the more secular Chinese traditions, was a different case, but there were similar ideas at work: the rulers were not

[13] C. Jacques, 'The Kamraten Jagat in ancient Cambodia', in Karashima Norobu, ed., *Indus Valley to Mekong Delta: explorations in epigraphy*, Madras, 1985.

perhaps seen as gods, but they had spiritual or quasi-divine characteristics often expressed in Buddhist terms. As Keith Taylor has put it, they 'stimulated and aroused the supernatural powers dwelling in the terrain of the Vietnamese realm'.[14]

What one can infer from such evidence of royal divinization is perhaps that in order to understand it we must revise our conceptions of the nature of divinity. In the cultures of monsoon Asia, divinity was a quality of the sacred world that lies unseen and implicit in the things of the world around us, like electromagnetic radiation or gravity. It could make itself accessible and potent through ritual. Kingship was itself a kind of ritual, serving to centre the kingdom on an individual, just as a shrine could centre it on an icon; in each case, the spiritual energy of the gods in the sacred world would be manifested.

Compared with mainland Southeast Asia, we notice many differences in maritime Southeast Asia as far as the divinization of kings is concerned, although there seems to be some agreement in its principal features.

Living kings were not generally regarded as gods. Thus, one of the best-known (semi-)historical texts, the *Pararaton*, tells us how the last king of Kaḍiri in east Java, Kĕrtajaya, wished to be venerated as a deity. When the courtiers were reluctant, the king decided to teach them a lesson. After briefly leaving the audience hall he returned complete with four arms, a third eye in the middle of his forehead and other marks of Śiva. The ministers and courtiers were, however, unimpressed. Suspecting some kind of magical trick, they left the palace to join the insurgents.[15] The anecdote suggests that some kings may have tried to get themselves venerated as gods, but without success.

Of King Kĕrtanagara of Singhasari in east Java it is known that, in 1289, he had himself consecrated as the Jina Akṣobhya, as described in the Sanskrit inscription carved on the lotus cushion of a large Akṣobhya statue, which can therefore be considered an idealized representation of the king.[16] It should, however, be emphasized that Akṣobhya, though endowed with superhuman qualities, is not a god but a transcendental Buddha: a state of perfection which, at least in principle, can be attained by any living being. This did not, however, prevent Kĕrtanagara from being killed in an attack by the subordinate ruler of Kaḍiri.

There is, however, a different conception which seems to have been generally adhered to in maritime Southeast Asia, at least in some areas and periods. It implies that kings were originally divine beings who descended to earth for the benefit of mankind, but returned to heaven as soon as their task was accomplished. This return required, however, the performance by the deceased king's successor of the appropriate rituals. Such rites are

[14] 'Authority and legitimacy in eleventh century Vietnam', in Marr and Milner, 143.

[15] Harry J. Benda and John A. Larkin, *The World of Southeast Asia, Selected Historical Readings*, translated from the Dutch by Margaret W. Broekhuysen, New York, Evanston, London, 1967, 38f.

[16] This statue, probably originating from the area around Trowulan, East Java, now stands in a park near Jalan Pemuda at Surabaya. For the inscription see H. Kern, *Verspreide Geschriften*, VII, The Hague, 1917 (originally published in 1910). For important corrections see R. Ng. Poerbatjaraka, 'De inscriptie van het Mahākṣobhya-beeld te Simpang (Soerabaja)', BKI, 78 (1922).

described in Indian texts, in particular the so-called *śrāddha*, which had to be performed by the king's eldest son at regular intervals after death. Indonesian sources mention, however, only a single great *śrāddha* to be carried out twelve years after the death of a royal person. The great *śrāddha* for the benefit of the soul of the Rājapatnī in Majapahit has already been described. We saw that the queen was transformed into Prajñāpāramitā as a result of the ceremony, and was thenceforward worshipped in a temple near present Tulung Agung south of Kaḍiri.[17]

King Jayanagara, the second ruler of Majapahit (1309–21), is said to have been deified as both Viṣṇu and the Jina Amoghasiddhi, and other kings and queens were deified in a similar manner.[18] On the other hand, most kings of Kaḍiri (mainly twelfth century) are described as incarnations of Viṣṇu, or rather of mythical kings who were themselves incarnations of Viṣṇu, such as Rāma, Paraśurāma, Kriṣṇa and Vāmana. Thus, one king is described as *Madhusūdanāvatāra* (incarnation of Viṣṇu as Kriṣṇa, slayer of the demon Madhu) or as *Vamanāvatāra* (incarnation of Viṣṇu as the Dwarf who conquered the world with three steps). Being a second-degree incarnation of the god dilutes the divine element, which is even further watered down by the fact that the king is often described as being merely a partial incarnation (*aṃśavatāra*) of the god (or his incarnation). The king's 'divinity', if this is the right term, was therefore strictly limited.[19]

Whatever their status during life, kings were sometimes worshipped as gods after their death when, as the poet puts it, 'they returned home to the gods' abode' (*Nāg*. 41–4a). This suggests that the king was a deity who temporarily stayed on earth in the guise of a human being but returned 'home' when his task was accomplished. The fact that this 'return' was often brought about by human violence (only one king of the Singhasari dynasty died a natural death) does not seem to have made any difference: while abiding on earth the king naturally behaved like a human being and suffered the consequences of his acts.

As stated above with reference to the Rājapatnī, many kings after the beginning of the second millennium were venerated in the form of a statue of the deity into whom the king had 'returned' after his death on earth. It is thought that many of the extant stone statues of Śiva and Viṣṇu, especially those with unusual attributes and individual facial expression, represent deified rulers or members of the royal family.[20] This is quite likely. It has, however, also been assumed that the temples known to have been dedicated to deceased kings were actually mausoleums in which the mortal remains after a king's cremation were kept in an urn deposited in a pit below the principal cult image. Such pits occur in all Śaiva temples, but their contents have usually been disturbed by treasure-hunters. On the

17 Pigeaud, *Java*, I and III, cantos LXIII–LIX and IV, 169–211.

18 For Jayanagara's apotheosis see canto XLVIII of the same publication.

19 cf. Sanskrit *aṃśāvataraṇa*, title of sections 64–7 of the Indian *Ādiparvan*. The Old Javanese *Ādiparwa* (ed. Juynboll, The Hague, 1906, 47f.) mentions *angsāwatāra*: 'it always seems to mean that only part of the god was incarnated': Stutterheim, 'Some remarks on pre-Hinduistic burial customs on Java', *Studies in Indonesian Archaeology*, 1956 (originally published in 1939), 71 n. 18.

20 Stutterheim in the preceding article and in 'Een Oud-Javaansche Bhīma-cultus', *Djåwå*, XV (1935).

one hand, in none of the pits discovered intact have any human remains been identified; any ashes found have proved to be of vegetable or animal origin. The idea of the god arising as a Phoenix out of his ashes finds no support in Indonesian religion, in which corporeal remains were generally considered polluting (as in India), to be disposed of as completely as possible. Thus, in present-day Bali the ashes remaining after a cremation are taken to the ocean.[21]

If temples dedicated to the cult of defunct rulers were not mausoleums they could have been cenotaphs, but it is preferable to abandon the funerary association altogether and regard the temples concerned as commemorative monuments devoted to the cult of the deity with whom the essence of the deceased would have merged. With the help of the *Ñagarakĕrtāgama* and other texts, it is often possible to determine whether a certain temple is dedicated to the cult of a deified ruler or to a deity as such. Thus, the large Amoghapāśa of Caṇḍi Jago is an effigy of King Viṣṇuvardhana of Singhasari (r. 1248–68) according to the text (*Nāg.*, 41–4), while of King Anuṣapati (r. 1227–47?) it is stated (41–1) that he returned 'home to Girīndra's [Śiva's] abode . . . in the likeness of Śiva, splendid, in the eminent *dharma* [religious domain] in Kidal' (i.e. Caṇḍi Kidal near present Malang).

On the other hand, there are many east Javanese temples without any known association within a defunct ruler. Thus the greatest temple complex of the province, Caṇḍi Panataran, was a state temple devoted to Śiva as Lord of the Mountains. In many cases, however, the sources do not permit us to decide in favour of either alternative.

The second problem concerns the so-called syncretism of Śaivism and Buddhism. Here, too, the issue is more complicated than it may seem at first. Following H. C. Kern and W. H. Rassers,[22] it has long been accepted that the two main religions merged into one from the reign of Kĕrtanagara (1268–92). More recent research has, however, demonstrated that our sources do not warrant such a conclusion. Except perhaps for one or two individual cases, such as that of Kĕrtanagara, known as *sang Śiva-Buddha* after his death (if not during his life), there was no true syncretism but a more complicated and more interesting relationship between those two religions. As early as the eighth century CE the stone inscription of Kĕlurak, central Java, dated 782, writes of the Mañjuśrī image, the erection of which is the main object of the incription, that 'this is the majestic Vajrabearer (vajrabhṛt), Brahmā, Viṣṇu and Maheśvara', thus suggesting that the Bodhisattva embodies, as it were, Indra and the three main gods of Hinduism. It would, however, be wrong to regard this passage as an expression of syncretism. It is much better explained as an expression of the universality of the image, which embraces these gods but also conceals in its interior (*antargatāṅ sthitāḥ*) the Buddha, the Dharma and the *Saṅgha*.[23]

21 Soekmono, 'Candi: Fungsi dan Pengertiannya', thesis, Universitas Indonesia, 1974. An English edition of this important work is in preparation.

22 *Çiva dan Buddha. Dua karangan tentang Çiwaïsme dan Buddhisme di Indonesia*, with an introduction by Edi Sedyawati, Jakarta, 1982.

23 F. D. K. Bosch, 'De inscriptie van Keloerak', TBG, 48 (1928).

Even an 'orthodox' Mahāyāna text such as the *Daśabhūmikasūtra* equates the highest Bodhisattva stages with those of the great Hindu gods.[24]

Most modern scholars, for example J. Gonda, Hariati Soebadio and Soewito Santoso, have rightly rejected the use of the term syncretism. Gonda replaced it by 'coalition', suggesting a close link between the two religions. Soebadio devoted an important section of the introduction to her edition of the *Jñānasiddhānta*, an Old Javanese text of the Majapahit period (?), to this problem. Though accepting Gonda's term, she interpreted it as 'a striving for the same ultimate goal using different ways' and, on the basis of some verses of the probably contemporary *Sutasoma*, compared it with 'climbing a mountain. Different ways are used, but in the end the same peak is reached. Nevertheless the ways that are used are considered different.' In addition, she rightly pointed out that 'many facts plead for a longstanding peaceful coexistence of Buddhism and Śiwaism', perhaps including 'plain borrowing of a Buddhist text by Śaivites, and adapting it for the Śaivite purposes'.[25]

There remains, however, a serious problem concerning Kĕrtanagara. The statement that 'the king as the highest principle in the country quite logically would have been identified also with the highest principles of the religions in his country' is unexceptionable, but it is strange that no other king is ever described as Śiva-Buddha. The compound does not indicate a composite deity such as Hari-hara—half Viṣṇu half Śiva—for no Śiva-Buddha image is known to have existed. It is therefore more likely that the king's memory was worshipped in a temple with both a Śiva and a Buddha image. This agrees with a difficult passage in the *Nāgarakĕrtāgama* (56–2), which describes a temple (Jajawi, i.e. the present Caṇḍi Jawi) having a Śiva statue below (*i sor*) but a statue of the Buddha Akṣobhya above (*i ruhur*). This suggests a two-storey temple with a Śiva image in the lower, and a Buddha image in the upper storey. This is a good illustration of Soebadio's view that Śaivism and Buddhism, though united in one building, are also separated: truly a good example of *Bhinneka Tunggal Ika*![26]

There are also other contexts in which the term syncretism has been used, probably with better justification. This applies not only to Hari-hara, but also to the absorption of ancient Austronesian deities into the great religions. In the former case, however, the process had already taken place in India; in the latter it is preferable to use other terms, such as acculturation.

In conclusion, it is clear that the term 'syncretism' requires inverted commas, or else it should be avoided. The same applies to other uses of this term, for example, in respect of Islam in Java or of the influence of the Austronesian substratum on the great religions.

[24] See also the *Daśabhūmikasūtra*, ed. Rahder, Utrecht-Leuven, 1926, in particular the Seventh Stage. Cf. also Rahder, 'Daśabhūmika-Sūtram. Seventh Stage', *Acta Orientalia*, IV (1926). The most detailed analysis of the Śiwa-Buddha concept is that by Soewito Santoso in his edition of the *Sutasoma. A Study in Javanese Wajrayāna*, Śatapiṭaka Series, vol. 213, New Delhi, 1975, ch. IV, 40–127.

[25] Gonda, 'Śiva in Indonesien', *Wiener Zeitschrift für die Kunde Südasiens*, XIV (1970); Soebadio, *Jñāasiddhānta*, 1971.

[26] cf. also Max Nihom, *Studies in the Buddhist Tantra*, Leiden, 1982, for a different interpretation.

## THE BEGINNINGS OF ISLAM

In contrast to the predominance of Theravāda Buddhism on the mainland, Islam became the predominant religion of maritime Southeast Asia except for most of the Philippines. Islam appeared in the area, however at a late stage, more than six centuries after its foundation. The earliest Muslim kingdom arose at Pasai near present Loh Seumawe on the north coast of Aceh, just before the end of the thirteenth century. At about the same time we notice the earliest Muslim tombs in east Java (except for an isolated example in the eleventh century).[27] Islamization was slow at first, mainly owing to the presence of strong Hindu-Buddhist kingdoms. Their decline in the fifteenth century stimulated the expansion of Islam.

The conversion to Islam of the king of Melaka (Malacca), founded around 1400, was a strong incentive to further Muslim expansion, especially after the middle of the fifteenth century, when Melaka had developed into the greatest commercial centre of Southeast Asia.

From there Islam soon spread to other centres in the area, in particular to those with which Melaka had close commercial relations. Muslim kingdoms or principalities, often styled sultanates, arose in such centres and these, in turn, became secondary foci of further expansion. During the fifteenth century Muslim kingdoms emerged on the west coast of the Malay peninsula in Perak and Kedah, as well as in Pahang, Kelantan and Terengganu, where Muslim laws had already been promulgated at the end of the fourteenth century,[28] and also at Pattani in southern Thailand. Similar developments took place in the river ports on the east coast of Sumatra, for example at Siak and Kampar. This 'network' of Muslim states confirmed Melaka's hegemony in the straits until its conquest by the Portuguese in 1511.

In Java, some of the Muslim tombs at Troloyo near ancient Majapahit, about sixty-five kilometres southwest of Surabaya, may belong to the end of the thirteenth century, but the inscribed tombstones have disappeared. We still have, however, a few tombstones with dates in the latter half of the fourteenth century. Such stones, called *maesan* in Javanese, are of a peculiar shape. At Troloyo they carry a date in the Śaka era (starting from 78 CE) and in Old Javanese script on the front within a panel of rich floral decoration. On the back there often is an inscription in Arabic script: a quotation from the Koran (Qur'an) or another holy text. But, strange though it may seem, the names of the deceased are never mentioned. Nevertheless, their proximity to the royal court of Majapahit strongly suggests that the deceased were closely associated with the court. The shape of the *maesan*, their ornamentation, and especially the use of Old Javanese numerals in the Śaka era suggest that the deceased were Indo-

[27] For the inscription of Leran, East Java, see J. P. Moquette, 'De oudste Mohammedaanse Inscriptie of Java, m.n. de Grafsteen te Leran', in *Handelingen 1ste Congres voor de Taal-, Land-, en Volkenkunde van Java*, 1919, and Paul Ravaisse, 'L'inscription coufique de Léran à Java', TBG, 45 (1925).

[28] H. S. Paterson, 'An early Malay Inscription from Trĕngganu', JMBRAS, 2 (1924); C. O. Blagden, ibid., 258–63; M. B. Hooker, 'The Trĕngganu Inscription in Malayan Legal History', ibid, 49 (1976); Hooker, *Islamic Law in South-east Asia*, Singapore, 1984.

nesians rather than foreign merchants; it would follow that there were already a considerable number of Muslims among the officials and dignitaries of the court of Majapahit when the empire was still at the height of its power.[29]

A recently discovered, probably apocryphal, text, the so-called *Malay Annals* of Semarang and Cheribon,[30] assigns the main part in the Islamization of Java to Chinese Muslims. Although this text cannot be accepted as evidence, this does not necessarily exclude the possibility of Chinese influence on the progress of Islam. Actually, one of the principal assistants of the Chinese admiral Ch'eng Ho, named Ma-huan, was a Muslim who stayed in Java in 1403. His presence may have strengthened Islam in Java, but the new religion had already taken root before his arrival.

Javanese tradition, on the other hand, attributes the Islamization of the island to nine preachers (*wali-sanga*),[31] the first of whom was a clearly historical figure: Malik Ibrāhīm, whose tomb at Gresik near Surabaya is dated 1419. The tombstone (*nisān*) indicates that the deceased was a trader from Gujerat, but of Persian origin, and mentions no missionary activities. The neighbouring site of Giri, however, soon became an important Muslim centre with the establishment of a dynasty of so-called 'priest-kings'. Their influence on religious, and probably also political, developments in Java and Maluku, at least until the sixteenth century, should not be underrated.

In Javanese tradition the *wali* were associated with particular mystical doctrines. They would also have taken an important part in the construction of the oldest mosque in Java at Demak east of Semarang, at the beginning of the sixteenth century.

This mosque is a typical example of the early Javanese mosque in which pre-Muslim building traditions were adapted to the requirements of Islam. The result is a building that differs considerably from the mosque in India or in the Middle East. The Javanese mosque has a square ground-plan with a pointed roof consisting of up to five storeys. It has a verandah at the entrance and is surrounded by a low wall with a more or less elaborate gateway. It generally stands on the western side of a carefully oriented square (*alun-alun*), as found in all important towns in Java. The absence of statuary is compensated for by the richness in decoration with a profusion of geometric, floral and sometimes even animal motifs. It has been suggested that the prototype of the mosque was the traditional cock-fight arena.[32] In addition to that of Demak the mosques at Mantingan (near Jepara) and Sendang Duwur (on the north coast, north of Lamongan), though substantially rebuilt in later times, still contain sixteenth-century

[29] Louis-Charles Damais, 'Études Javanaises I. Les tombes musulmanes datées de Tràlàyà', BEFEO, 48 (1959), plates I-XXXIV.

[30] H. J. De Graaf, and Th. G. Th. Pigeaud, *Chinese Muslims in Java in the 15th and 16th century*, Monash Papers on Southeast Asia, no. 12, Melbourne, 1984.

[31] Zoetmulder in Stöhr and Zoetmulder, *Les Religions d'Indonésie*, 338–45; H. J. de Graaf and Th. G. Th. Pigeaud, 'De eerste Moslimse vorstendommen op Java', VKI, 69, The Hague, 1969.

[32] H. J. De Graaf, 'The Origin of the Javanese Mosque', SEAH, 4 (1963); G. F. Pijper, 'De Moskeeën van Java' in *Studiën over de geschiedenis van de Islam in Indonesia 1900–1950*, Leiden, 1977, 13–62.

ornamental panels sculpted according to the ancient tradition. In many respects there is no clear break with the pre-Muslim past.

As to the religion itself there is a strong tendency towards mysticism flourishing by the side of orthodox Islam. In north Sumatra (Aceh) this mysticism remains well within the grounds of orthodox Islam, but in Java the influence of pre-Islamic doctrines is undeniable. The classical Brahmanic doctrine prescribes a life of contemplation, preferably in a forest hermitage, for all Hindus of the higher social strata after they had performed their worldly duties. Such a quiet life, far from the turmoil and temptations of the world, would create the right atmosphere for the contemplation of the secrets of being and non-being, of relative and absolute truth and of unification with the universal soul. Some forest hermitages attracted pupils from far away, so that such *āśramas* developed into centres of education. This Indian tradition seems to have been widely followed in ancient Java where, as we have seen, sites such as the Dieng plateau became important educational centres for the élite. In lieu of paying fees, the pupils carried out all required services. They owed absolute obedience to the Guru and worked in fields and gardens reclaimed from the forest. The larger *āśramas* were mainly self-sufficient communities. Similar centres, called *maṇḍalas*, proliferated in the last century of Majapahit and are described in texts like the *Tantu Panggĕlaran*.[33]

After the introduction of Islam such institutions continued as *pesantren* or *pondok*, where pupils study the sacred texts under the guidance of a teacher. One of the most famous centres, Giri, has already been mentioned; it flourished till the middle of the seventeenth century, when Sultan Agung of Mataram conquered the area and made an end to the influence of the priestly 'dynasty' ruling there. About that time, however, another strong Muslim centre emerged at Kajoran, east of Yogyakarta. Little is known of the doctrines preached there, but during a critical period in the third quarter of the seventeenth century the *ulamā* of Kajoran conspired with a rebellious prince of Mataram, as well as with troops from Sulawesi and Madura, to make an end to the reign of Sultan Agung's successor, Amangkurat I (1677), who was considered unorthodox. As often happens in such cases, it is difficult to decide how far religious motives, especially resistance to court ceremonies and practices deemed contrary to strict Islamic teaching, were the principal factor involved. It should not be forgotten that the Muslim foundations, like their earlier Hindu-Buddhist counterparts, had important material interests, especially land and labour, which they enjoyed on a privileged basis in the so-called *pĕrdikan* villages. True religious conflicts have always been rare in Java, but religious factors were often involved in dynastic or agricultural conflicts.

In Java, with its glorious pre-Muslim tradition, Islam had to compromise with long-established attitudes. Already at an early stage there is evidence of speculation about the fundamental identity of the old and new religions. Thus there is a statement ascribed to one of the ancestors of the Mataram dynasty to the effect that 'there is no difference between Buddhism [which

[33] Pigeaud, *De Tantu Panggĕlaran*.

included other religions of Indian origin] and Islam: they are two in form, but only one in essence [literally: name]'.[34]

This tendency to compromise is clearly reflected in the Javanese shadow theatre (*wayang kulit*) with its plots based on the great Indian epics (*Mahābhārata* and *Rāmāyaṇa*), but adapted to Javanese tradition. The characters are represented by flat leather puppets, elaborately carved and painted, which are 'brought to life' by a puppeteer (*ḍalang*), who moves the puppets and makes them talk. The Muslim prohibition against the representation of living beings is avoided by giving the puppets a very peculiar shape. A striking feature is the part played by 'clowns' (*pånåkawan*), such as Sĕmar, a retainer of the hero Arjuna, who, despite his funny appearance, often pronounces basic truths in the form of jokes.[35] Though only superficially influenced by Islam, these *wayang* performances often give splendour to Muslim celebrations, for example circumcisions, and are introduced by some pious words.

Other Javanese ceremonies, too, show the strength of ancient tradition. Most of the important occasions, such as those connected with the 'rites de passage', are concluded with a ceremonial meal (*slamĕtan*).[36] Depending on the nature of the occasion, such as birth, circumcision, commemoration of the death of a relative and many others, the *slamĕtan* has special features. Though attended by an official of the local mosque and preceded by Muslim prayers, the *slamĕtan* has a strong traditional character, reminding one of similar ceremonial meals in the ancient period, for example those described in the inscriptions at the inauguration of a sacred foundation. Originally perhaps a purification rite, it has gradually become a means to strengthen friendship and solidarity between the participants.

Indian influence was insignificant outside Java, Sumatra and the Malay peninsula. Islam was generally established there at a late stage, either from Melaka (as in Brunei) or, more often, from Java, especially from the great Muslim centres at Giri (Gresik), Tuban, Surabaya and others. As, however, these developments took place in or after the sixteenth century, they will be considered in another chapter.

On the eve of the Portuguese conquest of Melaka (1511) Islam was firmly established in the main centres in northern Sumatra, west Malaysia, west Kalimantan and on the north coast of Java. The Portuguese and Spanish activities in maritime Southeast Asia not only failed to stem the expansion of Islam, except in the northern and central Philippines and eastern Indonesia, but may, on the contrary, even have intensified it. Islam may have been felt as a strong spiritual force capable of resisting the ruthless encroachment by Western conquerors upon major parts of maritime Southeast Asia.

[34] P. J. Zoetmulder, *Pantheisme en Monisme in de Javaansche Soeloek-litteratuur*, Nijmegen, 1935, 346f. My English version is based on the Dutch translation in Zoetmulder's work.

[35] There is much literature on these 'clowns'. See e.g. Ph. Van Akkeren, *Een gedrocht en toch de volmaakte mensch. De Suluk Gatolotjo*, The Hague, 1951; James R. Brandon, *On thrones of Gold. Three Javanese Shadow Plays*, Cambridge, Mass., 1970.

[36] Geertz, *Religion of Java*, 30–85; Zoetmulder in Stöhr and Zoetmulder, *Les Réligions*, 323–5.

# BIBLIOGRAPHIC ESSAY

## The Mainland

Sources for religion in early periods, primary and secondary alike, tend not to be distinct from sources for other aspects of history—religion pervades them all. Of general works on early history containing information about religion, chief mention must be made of the general summary of the period by a pioneering scholar, G. Cœdès' *Les États Hindouisés d'Indochine et d'Indonésie*, Paris, 1964 (*The Indianized States of Southeast Asia*, ed. Walter Vella, trans. Susan Brown Cowing, Honolulu, 1968). More up-to-date scholarship is to be found in some relatively recent collections of articles such as D. G. Marr and A. C. Milner, eds. *Southeast Asia in the 9th to 14th Centuries*, Singapore and Canberra, 1986, and R. B. Smith and W. Watson, eds. *Early South East Asia: Essays in Archaeology, History and Historical Geography*, New York, 1979. This latter is particularly important for the archaeology of the historical period. A valuable recent synthesis, with implications for our understanding of the evolution of religious cults from prehistoric times, is C. Higham's *The Archaeology of Mainland Southeast Asia*, Cambridge, 1989. Another is E. Slamet-Velsink, *Emerging Hierarchies*, Leiden, 1986.

Not many secondary sources are dedicated to religious history in the early period, though there are relevant sections in K. L. Hazra, *History of Theravada Buddhism in Southeast Asia*, Calcutta, 1982.

Most of the research results, including editions of inscriptions and other primary material, are to be found in the pages of journals. For Indochina these include most notably the *Bulletin de l'École Française d'Extrême-Orient*, Paris, which has appeared since 1901; relevant contributors include L. Finot, E. Huber, P. Dupont, G. Cœdès, and more recently J. Filliozat and C. Jacques.

Among primary sources bearing on the region in general, conspicuous are the accounts by travellers from outside, such as I Ching and Chou Ta-kuan: I Ching, *A Record of the Buddhist Religion as Practised in India and the Malay Archipelago*, trans. J. Takakusu, Oxford, 1896; Chou Ta-kuan, *Mémoires sur les coutumes de Cambodge de Tcheou Takouan*, trans. P. Pelliot (Oeuvres Posthumes de P. Pelliot, vol. 3), Paris, 1951. I Ching also wrote accounts of the travels through the region of other Buddhist pilgrims: I Ching, *Chinese Monks in India*, trans. Latika Lahiri, Delhi, 1986. For the earliest period, a useful collection of primary source material (especially Chinese accounts), analysed and discussed by Paul Wheatley from the point of view of historical geography, is *The Golden Khersonese: Studies in the Historical Geography of the Malay Peninsula before A.D. 1500*, Kuala Lumpur, 1966.

Champa is something of a Cinderella in modern research. Its inscriptions have been studied in articles by E. Huber and others in the BEFEO, and edited by R. C. Majumdar, in vol. I, *Champa*, of his series *Ancient Indian Colonies in the Far East*, Lahore, 1927, though it must be said that there is plenty of room for more work on Cham epigraphy. J. Boisselier's

*La Statuaire de Champa*, Paris, 1963, contributes to the history of religious art in the period.

Cambodia is comparatively well served. G. Cœdès' *Inscriptions du Cambodge*, Hanoi and Paris 1937–66, 8 vols, incorporates most of the known epigraphy (nearly all of which, of course, is concerned with matters of religion). More recent contributions are by J. Filliozat and C. Jacques and others, especially in the pages of the BEFEO. Important is the work of Kamaleswar Bhattacharya, notably *Les Religions Brahmaniques dans l'Ancien Cambodge*, Paris, 1961; his articles on religious history include for example 'La secte des Pāśupata dans l'ancien Cambodge,' *Journal Asiatique*, 243 (1955).

Further west, in the area of the Mon, Pyu and Burman peoples before the rise of the Thai states, the outlines of history are vague and problematic. G. Cœdès' *Le Royaume de Dvāravatī*, Bangkok, 1929, offers interpretations of Mon religious culture. G. H. Luce worked extensively on the ancient cultures of Burma, and his *Phases of Pre-Pagan Burma, Languages and History*, 2 vols, Oxford, 1985, surveys the early period.

Material available on Burmese archaeology is scant and patchy; tantalizing results of excavations of Pyu sites are reported by Aung Thaw in *Report on the Excavations at Beikthano*, Rangoon: Ministry of Union Culture, 1968, and *Historical Sites in Burma*, Rangoon: Ministry of Union Culture, 1972, with claims for the beginnings of Buddhism.

Pagan is somewhat better served, with a number of relevant inscriptions edited in the series *Epigraphia Birmanica*. Secondary sources include G. H. Luce, *Old Burma—Early Pagan*, 3 vols, New York, 1969–70; Than Tun, *History of Buddhism in Burma, A.D. 1000–1300*, Rangoon, 1978 (JBRS, 61.1,2, *separatum*); and Nihar Ranjan Ray, *Sanskrit Buddhism in Burma*, Calcutta, 1936. Many relevant articles appear in the *Journal of the Burma Research Society*.

The epigraphy of the Thai kingdoms is represented particularly in G. Cœdès, *Reçueil des Inscriptions du Siam*, 2 vols, Bangkok, 1924, and a series of studies of inscriptions by A. B. Griswold and Prasert na Nagara in the *Journal of the Siam Society*, appearing from vol. 56 (1968) to vol. 63 (1975); important is the one on the famous Ramkamhaeng inscription, 'The inscription of King Rama Gamhen of Sukhodaya (1292 A.D.)', JSS, 59, 2 (1971). A. B. Griswold has written extensively on Thai religious art (for example, 'Imported images and the nature of copying in the art of Siam,' in Ba Shin et al., eds, *Essays Offered to G. H. Luce*, Ascona: Artibus Asiae, 1966, II. 37–73). Religious art is also served by J. Boisselier's *La Sculpture en Thailande*, Paris, 1974.

Vietnamese culture is not characterized in the same way as the 'Indianized' states by inscriptions associated with temples, and literary sources are relatively more important. These are exploited for religious history by Tran Van Giap in 'Le Bouddhisme en Annam des origines au XIIIe siècle', BEFEO, 32 (1932). A standard synthesis much used in the past is Le Thanh Khoi's *Le Viet-nam, Histoire et Civilisation*, Paris, 1955, which contains comments on montagnard religious practices. A major recent summary with much on religious history is K. W. Taylor's *The Birth of Vietnam*, Berkeley, 1983.

## Maritime Southeast Asia

The sources available for the religion of early maritime Southeast Asia are, on the whole, less easily accessible than those for the mainland. Although many Old Javanese and Old Balinese inscriptions have been published (though not always according to present-day standards), relatively few have been translated, and then mostly into Dutch or Indonesian.

Almost all English translations are those by H. Bh. Sarkar, published in 1971 and 1972 in two volumes as *Corpus of the inscriptions of Java*. As has been noticed above (note 4), this is a useful, almost indispensable, work, which has, however, to be used with caution. The translations are based on old transcriptions by Brandes and Krom, about which a little more is said below; no fresh reading of the originals was possible. Although the author is the foremost Indian scholar of Old Javanese language and literature, he has little experience with the very special idiom of the Old Javanese charters and therefore often gives a wrong or incorrect impression of the purport of a considerable number of these texts. In addition, the inscriptions reproduced and translated in these volumes are only those dated before 929 CE.

The most comprehensive collection of inscriptions is that by Brandes and Krom, mentioned in note 4 above. Like the preceding work, this collection is indispensable, although it is unsatisfactory in several respects. The transcriptions by Brandes were sometimes produced in a final form, more often as provisional drafts, not meant to be published in that form. In the absence of any better transcripts, Krom rightly decided that also the latter ought to be published. Although Krom must often have made his own, more precise, transcriptions, he preferred, no doubt out of piety towards Brandes, to produce the drafts in exactly the form in which they were left by Brandes at his death. Although Krom's feelings deserve full respect, it would have been better for the progress of Old Javanese studies if he had been less conscientious.

Of the later inscriptions there are a number, mainly dated during the fourteenth century, available in English translation by Th. Pigeaud in vol. III of his monumental *Java in the 14th Century: A Study of Cultural History*. As in Sarkar's work the translations are based on existing transcriptions which are generally reliable—partly because they are all on copper plates which are still in an excellent condition. Although Pigeaud was undoubtedly one of the best Western scholars of pre-modern and modern Javanese literature and culture, his translations sometimes suffer from his conviction that Javanese civilization hardly changed during the centuries, so that the ancient texts could be interpreted with the help of his excellent knowledge of more recent forms of the language. There are obvious dangers if this conviction is applied with reference to religion. It is true that the conversion to Islam did not imply a complete break with the past (as argued above, there was some continuity in certain fields), yet Pigeaud has perhaps gone farther in this respect than is warranted by the sources. Moreover, Pigeaud wrongly assumed that ancient Javanese society was 'feudal' in character. As a consequence he translated a number of important Old Javanese terms by equivalents of English feudalism in particular.

The main Old Javanese text discussed by Pigeaud is the *Nāgarakĕrtāgama*, written by a court poet in the middle of the fourteenth century. It is the basic text for our knowledge of Old Javanese religious ideas and institutions in that period, supplemented by a few other Old Javanese texts and inscriptions. It should, however, be emphasized that the *Nāgarakĕrtāgama* belongs to the court circles and only occasionally throws some light on the religious observances of the majority of the population. But this is the case with almost all our sources for ancient Southeast Asia.

The archaeological sources may in some cases offer some materials on popular religion. Although the artisans worked under the supervision of priests and other members of the élite, they themselves belonged to lower strata of the society and it was inevitable that their own ideas were sometimes reflected in the buildings and iconography of ancient Indonesia. Thus, Borobuḍur not only shows us numerous types of buildings associated with Buddhism and, occasionally, other religions but also, especially in the reliefs, examples of the manner in which buildings (such as stupas) were worshipped. Different types of heavens and hells are represented. We also get an impression of the garments and paraphernalia of monks, ascetics and priests of different orders and of their attitudes towards other classes of the population. In this respect the reliefs of the East Javanese period (tenth to fifteenth century) are even more valuable for all the details that are provided.

Also the statuary is important for our knowledge of religion. It should be emphasized that the statues are not only icons that are worshipped for their own sake, but rather function as a means to enable the worshipper to form an idea of the shape that the deity can take. It is difficult to pay homage to a mental idea of the deity. For most of the population it was therefore important that they could have a visible shape of the deity in front of their eyes. Iconography can therefore help us to understand how the pious represented their gods.

Also, other objects used in religious worship have been found in considerable quantity, thus enabling us to visualize some aspects of actual religious rites. Among these I may mention lamps—usually offered to the deity as votive gifts—sacrificial vessels of all kinds, mirrors, sacrificial plates (*talam*), different tools, etc.

As to foreign sources, the accounts by the Chinese pilgrim I Ching have already been discussed in the section on mainland Southeast Asia. The other foreign accounts, whether Chinese or Arabic, are of only minor importance for the study of religion.

Only one of the secondary works is directly concerned with the religions of Indonesia. This is the study by W. Stöhr and J. Zoetmulder mentioned in note 8 above. The section written by Stöhr deals with the tribal beliefs and rituals in Indonesia, which are not discussed in this chapter because they have been known only since recent times. Zoetmulder's section, however, is of direct importance as a supplement to this chapter since it is mainly concerned with religious concepts (Hindu, Buddhist and Muslim), as reflected in literature.

Another important work, mentioned earlier, is Pigeaud's study on fourteenth-century Java. Especially in vol. IV there are important, but somewhat controversial, chapters on religious institutions and practices in the Majapahit empire. Pigeaud's strong conviction of continuity in Javanese religion, also after the coming of Islam, lends a particular colour to his analysis.

As religion is inextricably interwoven with social and political life in ancient maritime Southeast Asia, it is inevitable that all works on the ancient history of the area give some attention to religion. Thus, all the general works mentioned at the beginning of this bibliographical essay discuss various aspects of religious developments in the area.

In addition a few works deserve particular attention. Thus, N. J. Krom's works *Hindoe-Javaansche Geschiedenis*, 2nd edn. The Hague, 1932, *Inleiding tot de Hindoe-Javaansche Kunst*, 2nd edn, The Hague, 1923, and *Barabudur, Archaeological Description*, 2 vols, The Hague, 1927, contain invaluable data and discussions on Buddhism in ancient Java. Some of the most important contributions by W. F. Stutterheim, which often present original views on many aspects of Indonesian (in particular, Javanese) religion, are available in English translation as *Studies in Indonesian Archaeology*, The Hague, 1956. This volume contains, in particular, his study of Borobuḍur, briefly discussed in this chapter, as well as a very important study on an aspect of ancient Austronesian religion, 'Some remarks on pre-Hinduistic burial customs on Java'. In addition, there are important articles on a ninth-century copper plate with a drawing of a Mother Goddess with a long Sanskrit *mantra* (mystical or magical formula), and on the Javanese Bhima cult, also briefly discussed in this chapter. As nearly all ancient Malaysian, Indonesian and Philippine antiquities were inspired by religion, most publications on archaeology are important for our knowledge of ancient religion in the area. They can be found in e.g. the *Tijdschrift voor de Taal-, Land- en Volkenkunde*, the *Bijdragen tot de Taal- Land- en Volkenkunde*, the *Journal of the Malay Branch of the Royal Asiatic Society*, and many others. The last-mentioned journal and the *Federation Museums Journal* contain some important articles by H. G. Quaritch Wales and Alastair Lamb on the excavations in the state of Kedah.

Among the increasingly numerous and important studies published in Indonesia three Ph.D. theses of the Universitas Indonesia at Jakarta should be mentioned. The work by Soekmono, *Candi, Fungsi dan Pengertiannya*, Jakarta 1974, an English edition of which is in preparation, throws important new light on the meaning and significance of ancient temples and images. The work by Edi Sedyawati, *Pengarcaan Ganesa masa Kadiri dan Sinhasari*, Jakarta, 1985, will also soon appear in English: it deals with the iconography and religious significance of the elephant-headed god Gaṇeśa, who enjoyed much popular worship in ancient Java, Sumatra and Bali. Finally, the no less important thesis by Hariani Santiko, *Kedudukan Bhatari Durga di Java pada Abad X-XV Masehi*, Jakarta, 1987, analyses the significance of this fierce goddess, usually represented victoriously standing on the back of the buffalo demon.

Much has been written on the provenance of early Islam in Malaysia, Indonesia, Brunei, Champa and the southern Philippines (especially Mindanao and the Sulu Archipelago). J. E. Moquette's article on the Muslim tombstones of Pasai and Gresik (*Tijdschrift*, LIV 1912), which traces

Indonesian Islam back to Gujerat, has long been accepted as a convincing argument, but G. E. Marrison, 'The coming of Islam to the East Indies', JMBRAS, 24 (1951), has rightly emphasized the strong arguments in favour of South India, some of which had already been proposed by Van Ronkel, as the area from which Islam spread to Indonesia and Malaysia. The best analysis of this problem, as well as of others connected with early Islam in maritime Southeast Asia, is by S. Q. Fatimi, *Islam Comes to Malaysia*, Singapore, 1963. Unfortunately the author has not used the article by L.-C. Damais, 'Études Javanaises. I. Les Tombes Musalmanes datées de Tralaya' (Troloyo), BEFEO 48 (1956), in which the importance of Islam during the empire of Majapahit is pointed out on the basis of the dated Muslim graves in the immediate vicinity of the royal residence. The earliest dates found on these stones are about contemporary with those on the earliest tombs in the northern Sumatra (Pasai). These data, which are unexceptionable, put the problem of early Islam in Southeast Asia in a new light. Although the role of Melaka in Muslim expansion is beyond doubt, the Troloyo stones prove that Islam was already firmly established in eastern Java by the end of the thirteenth century, more than a century before the foundation of Melaka.

# INDEX

Printed in the United States
120496LV00002B/123/A

9 780521 663694